CANADIAN
ORGANIZATIONAL
BEHAVIOUR

CANADIAN
ORGANIZATIONAL
BEHAVIOUR

Steven L. McShane

Faculty of Business Administration
Simon Fraser University

IRWIN
Burr Ridge, Illinois
Boston, Massachusetts
Sydney, Australia

Cover photo: *Rich Ergenbright International Photography*

Part photos:

PART I	*Courtesy of Crown Cork and Seal Canada*
PART II	*Courtesy of Northstar Energy Corporation*
PART III	*Courtesy of Royal Bank of Canada*
PART IV	*Courtesy of MacDonald Dettwiler & Associates*
PART V	*Courtesy of Canadian National*

Senior sponsoring editor: Roderick T. Banister
Project editor: Waivah Clement
Production manager: Ann Cassady
Designer: Larry J. Cope
Art manager: Kim Meriwether
Compositor: Bi-Comp, Inc.
Typeface: 10/12 Times Roman
Printer: R. R. Donnelley & Sons Company

ISBN 0-256-11531-1

Printed in the United States of America
3 4 5 6 7 8 9 0 DOC 9 8 7 6 5 4 3

Dedicated with love and devotion to Donna,
and to our wonderful daughters,
Bryton and Madison

PREFACE

Organizational behaviour is an exciting field of study that offers a wealth of knowledge to help you understand, predict, and manage behaviour in organizational settings. *Canadian Organizational Behaviour* takes a distinctly Canadian perspective of contemporary organizational behaviour concepts and practices. It is intended to help you make sense of organizational behaviour in Canada and abroad, and to give you the tools to work more effectively within organizations.

Canadian Organizational Behaviour includes several distinguishing characteristics, including a strong Canadian orientation, theory–practice link, contemporary theory foundation, and inclusion of emerging issues. There are also several valuable learning elements within the textbook and supplementary materials for the instructor. These features and pedagogical devices will make your journey through this text both meaningful and enjoyable.

Canadian Orientation

Canadian Organizational Behaviour has been written specifically for the Canadian audience, although it may be used by students in other countries (just as American texts have been used in Canada and elsewhere for so many years). This Canadian orientation has been achieved in three ways:

- **Canadian examples.** This text introduces more than 100 real-life organizational examples to place contemporary organizational behaviour theories and concepts within the Canadian context. Each chapter begins with a vignette about the experiences of a specific Canadian organization. Several additional organizational incidents are strategically located through each chapter, either highlighted as Perspective boxes or inserted in the main text. For example, you will learn about employee motivation at The Body Shop, job redesign at Imperial Oil, perceptions of unfair pay at Jay Norris Canada, self-managing work teams at Pratt & Whitney, organizational culture at

Four Seasons Hotels, organizational change management at Labour Canada, conflict management at Cardinal River Coals, and organizational design at Bombardier.

- **Canadian cases.** One or two cases, as well as an experiential exercise, are included at the end of each chapter. Most cases are located in a Canadian rather than American setting. I have written and class-tested several of these cases (e.g., Western Agencies Ltd., Vêtements Ltée, Nupath Foods Ltd., and A Window on Life). Others are organizational behaviour classics that originate in Canada or have been suitably adapted.

- **Canadian scholarship.** While the material presented in this text is drawn from the global literature on organizational behaviour, it places somewhat more emphasis than other texts on Canadian scholarship. This is reflected both in the chapter endnotes and the relative emphasis of some topics, such as organizational loyalty, self-managing work teams, and stress management.

Although *Canadian Organizational Behaviour* emphasizes the Canadian context, it also introduces several international issues and examples. For instance, you will read about employee motivation at a department store in mainland China, a circle organizational structure in Brazil, the use of "stomach language" in Japan, and perceptual errors that occurred when doing business with Egyptians.

Theory—Practice Link

An organizational behaviour textbook should be relevant as well as interesting. Therefore, every attempt has been made to link the theories and concepts presented in *Canadian Organizational Behaviour* to actual organizational events and practices. The examples running throughout the text provide an important link between the theories and organizational realities. They make the concepts more meaningful to students and reflect the relevance and excitement of this field. I have also ended most discussions of organizational behaviour theory and concepts with their practical implications. For example, you will learn how to analyze employee performance problems, increase employee loyalty, improve decision making in crisis situations, control organizational politics, and diagnose the best organizational structure.

Contemporary Theory Foundation

Canadian Organizational Behaviour has a strong practical orientation and tends to avoid detailed summaries of specific research studies. Nevertheless, the material presented in this textbook represents a careful synthesis of contemporary writing by organizational behaviour scholars in Canada and elsewhere. Look at the endnotes for each chapter and you will find that the text material integrates dozens of articles and monographs, most of which have been published within the past few years.

Emerging Concepts and Practices

The field of organizational behaviour is in a state of rapid transition. Organizational writers are adopting new perspectives and placing more emphasis on organizational effectiveness and productivity. *Canadian Organizational Behaviour* includes discussion of many of these emerging concepts and issues, including transformational leadership, parallel learning structures, business negotiations, self-managing work teams, pay equity, employment equity, discipline without punishment, ethical decision making, organizational citizenship, cluster and circle organizational structures, procedural justice, and crisis decision making.

Learning Elements

Several learning elements have been included to make your reading of this textbook easier, more enjoyable, and ultimately more memorable.

Learning Objectives and Chapter Outline. Several learning objectives and an outline of the main topic headings are listed at the beginning of each chapter to guide you through the main points of the material that follows.

Chapter Vignette and Photo. Every chapter begins with a vignette about a Canadian organization that relates to some of the concepts presented within the chapter. Each vignette is accompanied by a photograph of the organization that adds more visual meaning to the story.

Perspective Boxes and In-Text Examples. On average, each chapter includes three or four boxed stories, called *Perspectives*, that describe specific organizational incidents in Canada and elsewhere. These anecdotes are strategically placed around the organizational behaviour concepts and practices that they portray. Each chapter also includes several in-text examples to further anchor the concepts to organizational realities.

Graphic Exhibits. To help you make sense of the conceptual material, several graphic diagrams are included in each chapter. These exhibits visualize key elements of the theory being presented or pull together different parts of the chapter.

Marginal Notes and End-of-Text Glossary.   While I have tried to minimize unnecessary jargon, the field of organizational behaviour (and virtually every other discipline) has its own language. To help you learn this language, key terms are highlighted in bold and brief definitions of them appear in the margin. These definitions are also presented in an alphabetical glossary at the end of the text.

Chapter Summary and Discussion Questions.   Each chapter closes with a summary and list of discussion questions. The chapter summary highlights important material, while the discussion questions help you to check your understanding of the main points in the chapter.

Chapter Cases and Exercises.   Every chapter includes one or two cases as well as an experiential exercise. The cases encourage you to use organizational behaviour knowledge as a tool to diagnose and resolve organizational problems. The exercises enable you to become part of a simulated organizational experience and to see how organizational behaviour theories and concepts fit reality.

Indexes.   A company index, name index, and subject index are included at the end of this textbook to help you search for relevant information and make this book a valuable resource for years to come.

Supplementary Materials

Canadian Organizational Behaviour includes a variety of supplemental materials to help instructors prepare and present the material in this textbook more effectively.

Instructor's Manual.   The instructor's manual includes a chapter summary and lecture outline for each chapter. It provides solutions to the end-of-chapter discussion questions and cases, as well as notes and supporting materials (where applicable) for the experiential exercises. The instructor's manual also includes a large set of transparency masters as well as notes for additional lecture topics.

Test Bank.   The test bank includes 20 multiple choice and 20 true/false questions for each chapter. Also included are several additional open-ended or essay-type questions, with answers.

Irwin's Computerized Testing System.   This microcomputer testing system is available for the IBM PC. It lets instructors select and edit test items from the printed test bank as well as add their own questions.

Teletest. Instructors may obtain laser-printed tests of their choice by contacting the publisher by telephone or facsimile machine and specifying the desired questions drawn from the test bank.

ACKNOWLEDGMENTS

I work at a very special place called the Faculty of Business Administration at Simon Fraser University. Don't be misled by the institutional title. There is a special chemistry here that minimizes organizational politics (unique in universities!) and maximizes the interests of students, researchers, the business community, and other stakeholders. For their continued support, guidance, and friendship, I would especially like to thank my colleagues in the organizational behaviour area: Mark Wexler, Rosalie Tung, Dean Tjosvold, Bob Rogow, Larry Pinfield, Stephen Havlovic, Barrie Gibbs, Gervase Bushe, and Stephen Blumenfeld. I also owe a special debt of gratitude to Dean Stan Shapiro for being a superb role model, and for protecting me while I wrote this book from the more onerous administrative duties that accompany a professor's job.

Several colleagues from other colleges and universities across Canada also provided valuable feedback and suggestions as reviewers of this textbook. I want to thank each of these people for sharing their ideas with me: Brenda Bear, Northern Alberta Institute of Technology; Richard Foggo, Southern Alberta Institute of Technology; Brian Harrocks, Algonquin College; Jack Ito, University of Regina; Anwar Rashid, Ryerson Polytechnical Institute; and John Redston, Red River Community College.

My students deserve special mention because they have shaped this textbook in many ways. For several years, they have educated me through the rigorous team projects that I have assigned. For the past year, several classes of BUS372 students read loose-leaf binders of the draft, provided useful feedback, and allowed me to test new cases and exercises on them. While the galleys and page proofs were being prepared, the managers and professionals in my Executive MBA course further scrutinized the book and provided an excellent testing ground for the management cases. Their enthusiasm for the project doubled my energy.

Among those who assisted directly on *Canadian Organizational Behaviour,* Lenard Reid deserves special credit. Lenard demonstrated his innovation and entrepreneurship as he searched out relevant organizational behaviour examples in Canada. He single-handedly contacted over two dozen companies for the photographs that you see in this book. It has been a privilege to work with Lenard on this project. Many thanks are also extended to Anne Courtney, Tammi Mason, Henrick Jorgennsen, and Karim Karmali for their valuable research assistance, particularly in finding relevant anecdotal material and the latest conceptual literature.

Rod Banister, senior sponsoring editor, planted the initial seed for this project and, through his uncanny diplomacy and unwavering support, saw that it became a reality. It's an honour to know Rod and to be associated with him. I also extend my appreciation to project editor Waivah Clement and to others at Richard D. Irwin and Times-Mirror Professional Publishing, Ltd., for their superb professionalism.

Finally, I save the most important gratitude to my wife and best friend, Donna McClement, and to our wonderful daughters, Bryton and Madison. They give special meaning to my life and I am forever thankful for their continued love and support. I dedicate this book to them.

Steven L. McShane

CONTENTS
IN BRIEF

CONTENTS

3   Process Theories of Motivation   **80**

4   Performance Appraisal, Rewards, and Discipline   **120**

5 Job Design and Stress Management **158**

III INDIVIDUAL AND INTERPERSONAL PROCESSES **204**

6 Interpersonal and Organizational Communication **206**

IV TEAM PROCESSES 360

10 Team Dynamics and Effectiveness 362

11 Employee Involvement and Team Decision Making 400

12 Organizational Power and Politics **442**

13 Organizational Conflict, Negotiation, and Justice **478**

16   Organizational Culture, Socialization, and Careers   **596**

17   Organizational Structure and Design   **638**

CANADIAN
ORGANIZATIONAL
BEHAVIOUR

PART

I

INTRODUCTION

CHAPTER 1

**Introduction to the Field of
Organizational Behaviour**

QUALITY IMPROVEMENT PROCESS

CUSTOMER ⇌ SUPPLIER

SALES ⬌ MANUFACTURING

MUTUAL { TRUST RESPECT BENEFIT

Crown Cork and Seal, a subsidiary of Continental Can Canada Inc., is dedicated to the quality improvement process. Through extensive training and employee involvement, the company is creating a working environment which is open to innovation and better ideas—an organizational ingredient necessary to effectively manage continual and accelerating change, and to create a competitive advantage.

1

Introduction to the Field of Organizational Behaviour

LEARNING OBJECTIVES

After reading this chapter, you should be able to:

Define
An organization.

Identify
Three reasons for studying organizational behaviour.

Diagram
An organization from an open systems perspective.

Discuss
The three fundamental perspectives of organizational effectiveness.

Compare
Organizational effectiveness with productivity.

Campbell Soup

David Clark, president of Campbell Soup Co. Ltd., was horrified to learn that the cost of making Campbell Soup products in Canada was anywhere from 25 to 40 percent more expensive than at its plants in the United States. Moreover, Campbell Soup's U.S. plants were generally less productive than most competitors, putting the Canadian operations in a more dismal light.

Clark knew that the future of his Canadian food processing plants was at stake. "My greatest fear is that I'll end up running a string of warehouses instead of a company," Clark confided. Fortunately, as part of its worldwide restructuring, Campbell's American head office allowed Clark to keep his three main Canadian plants open to produce fewer, more specialized products, but only if it could be done cost effectively. Clark was given 18 months to make the transformation.

First, Campbell Soup's managers were divided into nine 'power teams' and challenged to several 'impossible' assignments. When each team was asked to generate $100,000 for the bottom line within three months, they collectively produced $700,000 in cost savings. For example, the Toronto team was able to reduce 120,000 defective cases of soup sitting in its warehouse to only 20,000 cases by repairing the crooked labels and dented cans.

Clark's next step was to create a more productive work force by talking with production staff and showing them previously confidential information about the company's competitive position. Charts were posted in the cafeteria of each plant showing the facility's competitiveness on any given day. Employees at Campbell Soup's Listowel, Ontario, plant declared that they would become "the best frozen food plant in the world" if the company removed the bureaucracy and controls. Clark obliged by creating self-managing work teams and removing three out of five layers of management, turning the redundant managers into coordinators of the new team approach. Some of the middle managers resisted and a few left the company, but others adjusted well to their new roles. Explains one converted supervisor: "Now I coach people, get input from them and ask them to make decisions. It takes a load off me and we end up happier on both sides."

Productivity improvement at Campbell Soup's Canadian operations is already apparent. For example, it used to cost $3.87 more to produce a case of soup at the company's Toronto plant than at its North Carolina plant; this gap has been reduced to only 32¢. Rather than closing production facilities, Campbell Soup will be expanding its Canadian operations to serve the huge U.S. market. Even the hard-line cost-cutters at U.S. headquarters are admiring the productivity increases. Meanwhile, Campbell Soup's Canadian managers are continually challenged to further improve productivity and organizational effectiveness. For Clark, it's now a matter of "keeping the goals impossible enough."[1]

Campbell Soup's recent experience provides an appropriate beginning to this book about organizational behaviour. It is a story about a Canadian organization facing competition in an international context. Canadian organizations are entering a global economy and must be prepared for the challenges that lie ahead. The fact that Campbell Soup is a U.S.-owned business and its Canadian operations have been given a mandate to produce specific products for the international market (called *world product mandating*) makes this story even more representative of recent Canadian events. Throughout this book, you will read about experiences in dozens of other Canadian organizations in the private sector, public sector, and quasi-public sector, and how these events may be understood and managed through organizational behaviour theories and concepts.

This vignette is also about *productivity* and *organizational effectiveness*. You will see these terms used quite frequently in this book because organizational behaviour is interested not only in understanding organizations, but also in improving them. *Organizational effectiveness* and *productivity* are ubiquitous terms, so we will examine their meaning later in this chapter.

Finally, the Campbell Soup story highlights many topics in the exciting field of organizational behaviour. David Clark, his managers, and everyone in Campbell's food processing plants pulled together and worked smarter to accomplish organizational goals and, at the same time, fulfill their personal needs. The transformation was not easy. Conflicts occurred, some people resisted the changes, and a few (including three vice-presidents) left the company. Clark's leadership was put to the test and new management strategies—goal setting, feedback, organizational change, job design, and self-managing teams, to name a few—were needed to make the organization more effective.

This book is about people working within organizations. Its main objective is to help you to understand behaviour in organizations and to work more effectively in organizational settings. While it may seem most applicable to managers, organizational behaviour knowledge is actually useful to anyone who works in and around organizations. In this opening chapter, we introduce you to the field of organizational behaviour, outline the main reasons why you should know more about it, describe the fundamental perspectives behind the study of organizations, and shed some light on the concepts of organizational effectiveness and productivity. We conclude with an overview of the contents of this book.

THE FIELD OF ORGANIZATIONAL BEHAVIOUR

Organizational behaviour (OB) is the study of what people think, feel, and do in and around organizations. It examines the behaviours of individuals working alone or in teams as well as the thought processes and structural contexts surrounding these actions. It considers how organizational characteristics, management practices, reporting relationships, physical settings,

organizational behaviour (OB)

The study of what people think, feel, and do in and around organizations.

and other factors influence individual and team behaviour. Through systematic inquiry, OB researchers try to predict and understand what influences behaviours within organizations and how these behaviours influence organizational effectiveness.

By saying that organizational behaviour is a field of study, we mean that experts have been accumulating a distinct knowledge about behaviour within organizations—a knowledge base that becomes the foundation of this book. The fact that most OB texts discuss similar topics is evidence that OB has evolved into a reasonably well-defined field of inquiry. This is really quite remarkable considering that OB is still in its infancy. It emerged as a distinct field of inquiry in the 1930s or 1940s and continues to evolve as new perspectives and theories develop or are imported from other disciplines.

What Are Organizations?

The field of organizational behaviour may be quite recent, but organizations are as old as the human race. Archaeologists have discovered massive temples dating back to 3500 B.C. that must have been constructed through the organized actions of many people. In fact, the ability of these organizations to complete their daunting objectives suggests not only that complex organizations existed, but that they were reasonably well-managed.[2]

organizations
Social entities in which two or more people work interdependently through patterned behaviours to accomplish a set of goals.

Naturally, our definition of organizational behaviour would be incomplete without further explaining what we mean by the term organizations. Basically, **organizations** are social entities in which two or more people work interdependently through deliberately structured patterns of interaction to accomplish a set of goals. This is a rather complex definition, so let's break it down into its three basic elements.[3]

Social Entities.   Organizations are not buildings or equipment or products. They are social phenomena—groupings of human beings—and, consequently, require at least two people interacting toward some purpose. Why do people form or join organizations? Basically, they believe that their personal goals can be achieved more effectively by working in concert with others than alone. We will come back to this point in the next chapter because joining a company and attending work at scheduled times are important behaviours for the effective functioning of organizations.

Deliberately Structured Patterns of Interaction.   Organizations consist of deliberately structured patterns of interaction—repeated routines of behaviour—that presumably help the organization achieve its objectives. At the Bank of Nova Scotia, for instance, tellers might update hundreds of chequing accounts and process as many deposit or withdrawal transactions every day. They get supervisors to sign off on large withdrawals and collaborate with coworkers to complete certain assignments such as cheque processing.

These patterned interactions help the financial institution to survive and prosper by serving its clients, suppliers, shareholders, and others affected by the organization.

Organizational Goals.   **Organizational goals** are a desired state of affairs that the social entity is trying to achieve.[4] Organizations typically have several goals, some of which may be (and often are) in conflict with others. Some may be impossible to realize. Nevertheless, goals represent the main reason why organizations exist. Who establishes these goals? Certainly top management and the board of directors play an important role, but it is incorrect to say that they alone are responsible. Rather, goals are ultimately formed through a complex interplay of influence and action by the entire organizational collective as well as special interest groups outside the organization.[5]

organizational goals
A desired state of affairs that organizations try to achieve.

At this point we should make a distinction between stated goals and actual goals.[6] Most formal organizations have mission statements saying why they exist and what they hope to accomplish. Top managers also introduce new strategies and directions for the organization that seem to represent organizational goals. But these are only stated goals. They may distort, rationalize, or even conceal some essential aspects of the organization's true aims. Thus, we must distinguish stated goals from the goals that organizational members actually strive for.

Organizational goals also differ from individual goals. People help achieve organizational goals primarily because these actions are also perceived to fulfill their personal objectives. Employees may enjoy their work and identify with the organization's goals, but they ultimately seek to fulfill their personal goals. These personal goals are based on individual needs, which we will discuss in the next chapter.

WHY STUDY ORGANIZATIONAL BEHAVIOUR?

In all likelihood, you are reading this book as part of a required course in organizational behaviour. Why is this topic usually part of the required curriculum, and why should you take this course? Exhibit 1–1 outlines three main reasons for studying organizational behaviour.

Satisfying the Need to Predict and Understand

Every one of us has an inherent need to know about the world in which we live. We want to predict and understand events to satisfy our curiosity and to map out life's events more accurately. Organizations affect virtually every part of our lives, so it only makes sense that we should be interested in knowing when, how, and why organizational events occur.[7] The ability to

EXHIBIT 1–1	Reasons for Studying Organizational Behaviour

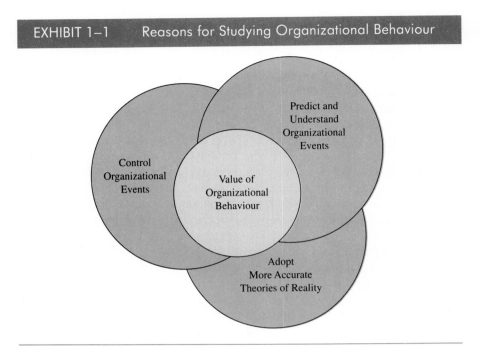

predict and understand behaviour is especially important for people working within organizations because they need to know when others will work cooperatively, complete their assigned tasks, show up for work, and so on.

The field of organizational behaviour tries to predict and understand organizational phenomena by using scientific research to discover systematic relationships among events. Human behaviour is highly complex, so it is unlikely that we will be able to predict *exactly* what people will do in a particular situation. Nevertheless, by studying organizational behaviour you will gain a better understanding of why some people are more productive than others, why employees in one organization have more "team spirit" than others, why some companies fail while others survive, and so on. This book introduces many theories to satisfy your curiosity and create more certainty about why these and other organizational phenomena occur.

Adopting More Accurate Theories of Reality

Through personal observation and listening to others' experiences, you have already formed numerous personal theories to make sense of the world. Some of these generalizations may be highly effective or, at least, predict behaviour in many situations. Even so, you will find that the theories and concepts presented in this book will further clarify or crystalize these personal views of the world.

Of course, not all of your personal theories of organizational life are accurate, even though many appear to be common sense. Consider the following popular beliefs about behaviour in organizations:

• A happy worker is a productive worker.
• People are unlikely to repeat bad decisions.
• Conflict undermines effective decision making.
• It is better to negotiate alone than as a team.

Most people would say that these statements are obviously true. After all, they make a lot of sense, don't they? Yet systematic research suggests that these statements are *incorrect* or, at best, correct under very limited circumstances. Unfortunately, people who continue to rely on these and other erroneous beliefs may eventually make disastrous decisions or act inappropriately in a particular situation. The field of organizational behaviour uses scientific research methods and applied logic to test the accuracy of personal theories in organizational settings. The knowledge gained by reading this book should help you to confirm and challenge your personal theories as well as adopt new perspectives of reality. In the long run, this knowledge will help you improve your personal effectiveness and well-being in organizational settings.

Controlling Organizational Events

Perhaps the most practical reason for learning about organizational behaviour is that the theories and concepts described in this book have direct implications for the practice of management. Through OB research, we now understand how to make better decisions, structure organizations to fit the surrounding environment, improve individual performance, build employee commitment, and help work teams operate more effectively. At a more interpersonal level, OB theories prescribe ways to persuade and negotiate, manage conflict, and communicate with others in organizational settings.

It is our opinion that everyone should master the knowledge and skills required to work more effectively with people in organizational settings. Campbell Soup president David Clark emphasizes this point when he says that Canadian managers need to do a better job of bringing the best out of people in organizations. Says Clark: "We're good at leveraging capital and technology, but we're lousy at leveraging human capital."[8]

While organizational behaviour takes a prescriptive view, it does so in the context of theory and research. OB scholars use scientific research to build strong theory that, in turn, provides the essential foundation for effective management practice (see Exhibit 1–2). Basically, we are saying that the best organizational practices are those built upon sound organizational behaviour theory and research.

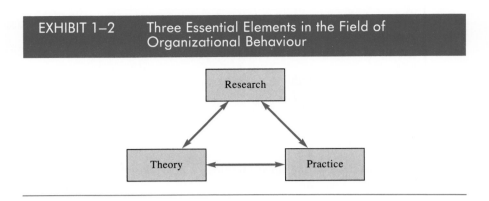

EXHIBIT 1–2   Three Essential Elements in the Field of Organizational Behaviour

Most OB scholars now agree that organizational behaviour must be prescriptive as well as descriptive. That is, organizational research should recommend ways to improve organizations rather than just describe organizational phenomena. This issue actually has a long and thorny history, because early organizational researchers were closely linked with industry and were harshly criticized for being servants of industrial power and manipulators of defenseless workers.[9] It is now generally believed that OB researchers should state the management implications of their work. Without well-founded prescriptions, the field of organizational behaviour loses respectability and society fails to benefit from potentially valuable organizational research.[10]

FUNDAMENTAL PERSPECTIVES OF ORGANIZATIONAL BEHAVIOUR

Over the years, the field of organizational behaviour has adopted several perspectives that establish fundamental beliefs and assumptions about how organizations operate and how organizational research should be conducted. These perspectives are not necessarily unique to this field—some are also found in other behavioural sciences—but you should understand them to gain a better appreciation of the material in this and other organizational behaviour texts. Let's now examine these perspectives in more detail.

OB as a Multidisciplinary Field

The study of organizational behaviour is multidisciplinary because, as Exhibit 1–3 shows, many of the theories, concepts, and methods to enhance our understanding of organizations have been adopted from other disciplines. We might even venture to say that the field is *cross-disciplinary,* because some of its topics cross several disciplines rather than just one.

EXHIBIT 1–3	Multidisciplinary Perspective of Organizational Behaviour	
Discipline	**Research Emphasis**	**Relevant Topics**
Psychology	Individual behaviour	Motivation, perception, attitudes, personality, job stress, job enrichment, performance appraisals, leadership
Sociology	Interpersonal relations and social systems	Team dynamics, work/non-work roles, organizational socialization, communication patterns, organizational power, status systems, organizational structure
Anthropology	Relationship between social units and their environments	Corporate culture, organizational rituals, cross-cultural aspects of OB, organizational adaptation
Political science	Individual and group behaviours within political systems	Intergroup conflict, coalition formation, organizational power and politics, decision making, organizational environments
Economics	Rational behaviour in the allocation of scarce resources	Decision making, negotiation, organizational power
Industrial engineering	Efficient operation of physical human behaviour	Job design, productivity, work measurement

Psychology and sociology provided much of initial foundation of organizational behaviour, but more recent contributions can be traced to anthropology, political science, economics, and industrial engineering. OB researchers continue to scan these and other disciplines for new concepts, models, and perspectives that will help them better understand and predict organizational events.

Psychology.   Psychology has probably been the greatest contributor to the field of organizational behaviour. Industrial and organizational (I/O) psychologists are specifically interested in individual behaviour in organizations, and their contributions to the field of organizational behaviour are most apparent in the areas of employee motivation, job stress, perception, job enrichment, performance appraisals, personality, leadership, and employee attitudes. Canadian I/O psychologists have applied these concepts in industry since the 1930s and a few firms, such as Ontario Hydro, hired I/O psychologists after the Second World War to test the industrial applications of psychology.[11] Today, I/O psychology is so closely linked with organizational behaviour and human resource management that many Canadian researchers in this field are located in business schools rather than psychology departments, although the number of I/O psychology scholars within psychology departments is increasing.

Sociology.   Whereas psychologists focus on the individual, sociologists are generally more interested in the organization's social system. They tend to study organizations in terms of a collection of people with different roles, statuses, and authority, operating as a social entity to accomplish a set of objectives. We will draw upon sociological concepts mainly in the areas of team dynamics, organizational socialization, work/non-work roles, communications, organizational power, leadership, and organizational structure.

Anthropology.   The field of anthropology attempts to understand the relationship between societies and their environments. Anthropologists investigate how societies develop norms, values, rituals, and practices that serve a functional purpose in the context of their surroundings. As a recent contributor to organizational behaviour, anthropology directs our attention to the fact that each organization has its own culture, complete with observable artifacts and underlying cultural values. A few Canadian organizational researchers have drawn extensively from anthropology to understand how corporate cultures develop and function.

Political Science.   Political scientists typically study individual and group behaviours within government and other political systems and institutions. Yet they share common interests with organizational behaviour scholars in the study of intergroup conflict, power within organizations, political behaviour within organizations, coalition formation, and the process of decision making.[12]

Economics.   Economic theory has contributed to organizational behaviour mainly in the areas of decision making, negotiation, and power. However, one could argue that OB has recently had as much effect on economics as vice versa. This is especially true with respect to decision theory, where organizational researchers have redefined economic assumptions about information accessibility and cost.

Industrial Engineering.   Finally, the field of industrial engineering has contributed to organizational behaviour, particularly with respect to work efficiency, productivity, and work measurement. Some of Canada's leading management consulting firms, including Woods Gordon and Stevenson Kellogg, were initially in the industrial engineering business, focussing their attention on work efficiency principles such as time and motion study (see Chapter 5).

Organizations as Open Systems

open systems
Systems that interact and are interdependent with their external environment.

Organizations do not exist in isolation from the world around them. Instead, they are **open systems,** meaning that they interact and are interdependent with their external environment. This is in contrast to closed systems which exist independently from anything beyond their boundaries. A **system** is an interdependent set of parts that functions as a whole to achieve a set of goals.[13]

Exhibit 1–4 presents a simplified perspective of organizations as open systems. Organizational systems acquire resources from their external environment, including raw materials, human resources, information, financial support, and equipment. Technology (such as equipment, work methods, and information) is used to transform these inputs into various outputs, which are then returned to the external environment for use by others in that environment. The organization receives feedback from the external environment regarding the use of these outputs and the availability of future inputs. This process of input–transformation–output–feedback is cyclical and, ideally, self-sustaining so that the organization may continue to survive and prosper.

Viewing organizations as open systems is extremely useful because it shows us that the external environment is always changing and organizations that do not adapt quickly enough may not survive. Organizational leaders must constantly be aware of new competitors, rising or falling interest rates, changing government regulations, shifting customer needs, and the

system

An interdependent set of parts that functions as a whole to achieve a set of goals.

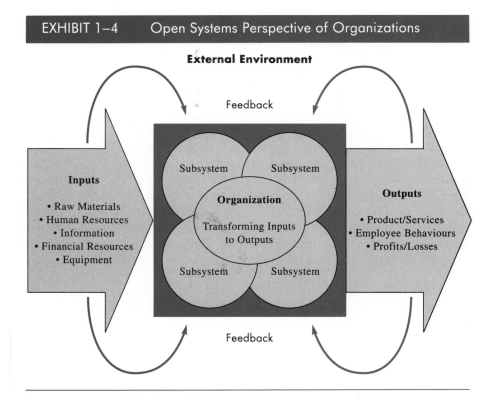

EXHIBIT 1–4   Open Systems Perspective of Organizations

External Environment

Feedback

Inputs

• Raw Materials
• Human Resources
• Information
• Financial Resources
• Equipment

Subsystem   Subsystem

Organization

Transforming Inputs to Outputs

Subsystem   Subsystem

Outputs

• Product/Services
• Employee Behaviours
• Profits/Losses

Feedback

PERSPECTIVE 1–1   Unintended Consequences of Change at Alcan Aluminum

Alcan Aluminum Ltd. places a high priority on employee motivation and satisfaction and has introduced numerous human resource innovations to improve the quality of life for its employees. However, some organizational changes have had unintended consequences and, as a result, have been less effective than expected.

One such incident occurred at Alcan's plant in Kingston, Ontario. A personnel specialist proposed that time clocks be removed from the shop floor. With only limited discussion, the personnel manager agreed that time clocks were demeaning and that approximately 1,000 hourly employees should be put on straight salary. For the first few weeks, these employees enjoyed their new freedom, but problems emerged over the next several months. A few

people began to show up late, leave early, or take extended lunch breaks. Only 5 percent of the employees were taking this unscheduled time off, but others working the required full shift found the situation unfair. The problem had to be managed.

Supervisors were asked to observe and record when the employees came or went and to confront those abusing their salaried positions. But the supervisors had no previous experience with keeping attendance and many lacked the necessary interpersonal skills to discuss the matter with subordinates. Employees resented the reprimands, and relations with supervisors deteriorated. Supervisors were also unable to effectively manage as many people because of the additional responsibilities. After just a few months, Al-

availability of input resources such as skilled employees and raw materials. They must continually search for ways to efficiently and effectively process inputs to useful outputs.

This point is illustrated in our opening vignette. Campbell Soup was forced to adapt to a changing environment where competitors were becoming more productive, free trade was replacing trade barriers, and the U.S. head office could no longer be counted on for financial support. The survival of Campbell Soup's Canadian plants depended on their ability to adapt to these environmental changes.

The systems view also points out that organizations have many parts that must coordinate effectively with each other in the process of transforming inputs to outputs. Thus, achieving organizational goals requires monitoring interdependencies in the transformation process as well as monitoring inputs and outputs. Managers must watch for dysfunctional conflict between departments, monitor employee satisfaction, and ensure that communication systems are structured in a way to facilitate rather than inhibit information flow.

Finally, the systems view reminds us that human organizations are incredibly complex. They include many components (called *subsystems*) in the form of employees with unique roles, coalitions with distinct objectives, organizational structures, technologies, and so on. Organizational members display self-awareness and process information through abstract constructs such as language and other symbols. An organization may therefore be viewed as a complex network of multiple cause–effect relationships in which

can found it necessary to reduce the supervisors' span of control.

But the problems did not end there. Under the salary system, pay was no longer docked when employees were late. Instead, punishment took the form of a letter placed in the employee's personnel file, but this required yet more time and additional skills from the supervisors. Employees did not want these letters to become a permanent record, so they filed grievances with their union. As grievances were passed up the hierarchy, both union officials and upper-level managers spent more time handling these disputes, leaving less time for other management duties.

As Alcan discovered, the simple action of remov-

ing time clocks was associated with many consequences that disrupted other parts of the organization. It influenced employee tardiness and absenteeism, the nature of supervisory duties, relations between employees and supervisors, the type of discipline used, the supervisors' span of control, the number of grievances, and the overall work climate at Alcan's Kingston plant. Even senior managers and union officials were affected by the removal of time clocks.

The final irony is that eighteen months after the time clocks were removed, a personnel specialist concluded after talking with several employees that "nobody minded punching the time clocks anyway."

Source: R. L. Daft, *Organization Theory,* 3rd ed. (St. Paul, Minn.: West, 1989), pp. 16–17.

a particular event or behaviour may have several outcomes. Management actions may have their intended consequences, but it is quite likely that some unintended consequences will also appear. This point is illustrated in Perspective 1–1, which describes an incident at Alcan Aluminum's plant in Kingston, Ontario.

Applying the Scientific Method

OB theories are rigorously tested to determine how well they predict what goes on within organizations. Those of us who make our careers in this field collect information in accordance with the **scientific method.** This is not, as it may sound, a single procedure for collecting data; rather, the scientific method is a set of principles and procedures to help us systematically understand previously unexplained phenomena.

OB researchers observe organizational events, form a theory or draw upon existing theories to explain the observations, form hypotheses to test the theory in other organizational settings, and collect data to find out whether the hypotheses accurately predict these phenomena. Throughout this book, we will present theories that have received some degree of support based on scientific research. We will not present much of this research directly, although pertinent articles will be cited at the end of each chapter. Instead, our focus will be on relevant theories supported by this research, how they help us predict and understand patterns of behaviour within organizations, and what implications they offer for better management practice.

scientific method
A set of principles and procedures to systematically understand previously unexplained phenomena.

middle-range theories
Theories that attempt to explain specific aspects of organizational behaviour, rather than everything in the field.

It would be nice to offer you one grand theory to understand and predict everything that goes on in organizations. Some early researchers tried to find an elusive metatheory of organizations, but, alas, human behaviour is too complex. Consequently, organizational theorists have concentrated on **middle-range theories,** each with a relatively narrow focus on a particular aspect of organizational behaviour. For example, some theories explain employee motivation, others explain leadership, still others explain team dynamics, and so on.[14] To make matters more complex, OB theories usually take a contingency approach, which we discuss next.

The Contingency Approach

contingency (or situational) approach
The idea that a solution may be effective in some situations but not others.

"It depends" is a phrase that OB scholars often use to answer a question about the best solution to an organizational problem. The statement frustrates students and managers to no end, yet it reflects an important perspective, called the **contingency (or situational) approach,** to understanding and predicting organizational events. Basically, the contingency approach suggests that a particular management practice may be extremely effective under some conditions but not others. No single solution is best in all circumstances. Thus, when faced with a particular problem or opportunity, managers must diagnose the situation by examining the characteristics of individuals, work teams, and organizational environment and select the most appropriate strategy *under those conditions*.[15]

Why does the field of organizational behaviour present so many contingency-oriented theories rather than universal or "one best way" models? The reason, quite simply, is that many early OB theories were universal but failed to adequately predict and explain organizational phenomena. It appears that organizational life presents too many exceptions to these universal rules. For example, early leadership researchers tried unsuccessfully to discover the best style of leader behaviour. Subsequent studies revealed that leaders should use one style (e.g., participation) for certain employees and situations and another style (e.g., direction) at other times and for other employees. Organizational concepts must reckon with different environments, individual dispositions, technologies, cultures, and other factors that can potentially moderate the relationship between an event and its consequences.

While contingency-oriented theories are necessary in most areas of organizational behaviour, we should also be wary about carrying this philosophy to an extreme.[16] Some contingencies are fundamental to understanding and predicting human behaviour; others are trivial. We need to balance our sensitivity of contingent factors with the need for the parsimony of universal theories. Given the complexity of organizational life, universal theories will never perfectly depict the truth, but complex theories that account for the marginal influences of moderating variables will also prove to be of limited value. In short, organizational theories often require a contingency perspective, but we should welcome universal theories where a contingency model offers little advantage.

Multiple Levels of Analysis

Organizational events can be studied from three levels of analysis: individual, team, and organizational (see Exhibit 1–5). The individual level includes the characteristics and behaviours of employees as well as the thought processes that are attributed to them, such as motivation, perceptions, personalities, attitudes, and decisions. This level of analysis is quite important because we actually observe the behaviour of individuals, not organizations. Nevertheless, organizational researchers recognize phenomena at these higher levels of analysis. Work teams are not simply the sum of individual behaviours—they include norms, cohesiveness, and interpersonal roles. Power, organizational politics, and leadership are also team-based topics. The organizational level of analysis mainly considers the structure of relationships among people within the firm as well as organizational values, socialization processes, and external environments.

   As you can see, most OB topics tend to emphasize one level of analysis or another. Employee attitudes are usually examined at the individual level while organizational structures are usually discussed at the organizational level. This is a convenient way to present OB knowledge, but to fully comprehend what goes on in organizations, we recommend that you examine every organizational phenomenon from all three levels of analysis. For instance, communication is ordinarily identified as a team-based process, yet it

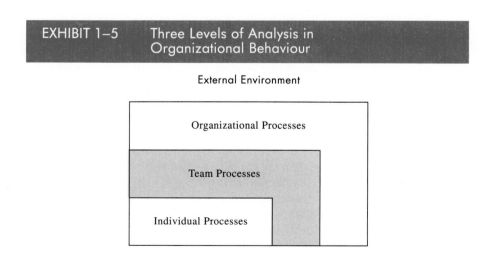

EXHIBIT 1–5   Three Levels of Analysis in Organizational Behaviour

External Environment

Organizational Processes

Team Processes

Individual Processes

PERSPECTIVE 1–2   Drexis Inc.'s Goal: Becoming the Hertz Rent-a-Car of the Computer Business

When Drew McDougall started Drexis Inc. in 1984, he had $30,000 in savings, a two-bedroom apartment he shared with his sister, and an idea. As a partner with investment dealer Gordon Capital, McDougall knew that firms often need computer systems for a few weeks or months, but the only options available at the time were to buy a system or lease one for a year or more. McDougall decided to offer a third option by purchasing several Compaq computers with his savings and renting them out.

For the first 10 months McDougall was the only Drexis employee, plugging away from his apartment, raising financing, and paying himself no salary. But the computer rental company soon began hiring staff as McDougall landed contracts with such blue-chip companies as the Bank of Montreal, Coopers & Lybrand, and Royal Trust. By the fifth year of business, Drexis employed 16 people and had outlets in Toronto, Montreal, and Ottawa. Revenues in 1989 were $2.7 million, return on equity was an impressive 21 percent, and the company's 42 other investors saw the value of their shares rise from $20 to $200. McDougall's goal is for Drexis to become a dominant force in the North American computer rental market.

includes individual thoughts and behaviours and is affected by organizational characteristics. This book places communication in the individual/ interpersonal part because it is linked with perceptions and attitudes, whereas some OB texts place it in the team or organizational processes sections. This reflects the fact that OB topics can be studied from different levels of analysis and that some writers emphasize one level more than another regarding the topic of communication.

ORGANIZATIONAL EFFECTIVENESS: DOING THE RIGHT THINGS

organizational effectiveness
A multifaceted concept in which the organization "does the right things". This includes achieving organizational goals, adapting as an open system to the external environment, and addressing stakeholder needs.

Throughout this book, we will discuss how various employee behaviours and management strategies can enhance or undermine **organizational effectiveness.** It seems rather obvious that organizations should be effective and that managerial practices should be evaluated in terms of their contribution to organizational effectiveness. But what do we mean by the phrase *organizational effectiveness*?

An extremely general answer might be that an organization is effective when it does "the right things." But this leads to another question: What *are* the right things? Alas, there is no simple answer.[17] Consider the effectiveness of Drexis Inc., described in Perspective 1–2. The company is still a long way from achieving its goal of becoming the "Hertz Rent-a-Car of the computer business." But several other indicators point to the company's success, including high productivity, employee commitment, customer satisfaction, and a healthy return on shareholder equity. Clearly, effectiveness is a broad concept with many interpretations.[18] In this section, we will review

"We intend to be the Hertz Rent-a-Car of the computer business," he says.

How has Drexis managed such rapid growth? McDougall believes there are several contributing factors. The company has a strong focus on customer satisfaction. For example, the company recently invested $60,000 in a computer system that monitors the inventory of rental equipment so staff can determine in a moment how many systems are available and for how long. McDougall measures productivity and service quality in an objective way and pays close attention to details like revenues per employee. Employee loyalty is rewarded with profit-sharing and stock option plans. McDougall emphasizes teamwork by encouraging social interaction—in 1988 he flew his entire staff and their families to Disney World—and paying sales staff salaries rather than straight commission. These actions have paid off. Only two people have left Drexis since the company started.

Source: B. McDougall, "Only the Strong Can Survive," *Small Business* 8 (January 1989), pp. 36–39.

the three dominant perspectives of organizational effectiveness. Together, these models will give you a clearer understanding of what we mean by this otherwise elusive concept.

Goal Attainment Approach

Earlier in this chapter, we learned that organizations are social entities in which two or more people work interdependently through patterned interaction to accomplish a set of goals. Given this definition, it is not surprising that the **goal attainment approach,** which measures effectiveness in terms of progress toward the organization's goals, is the oldest and most widely held perspective of an organization's effectiveness.[19] Thus, if the Four Seasons Hotel strives for customer satisfaction, it will be effective to the extent that it satisfies customers. If Drexis Inc.'s goal is to be the largest computer rental company in Canada, then effectiveness is determined by its relative position in this industry.

goal attainment approach
Measuring effectiveness in terms of progress toward organizational goals.

Limitations of the Goal Attainment Approach. The goal attainment approach is intuitively appealing and has been the dominant perspective of organizational effectiveness for the past 100 years or more, but it has a number of limitations.[20] First, many goals are abstract and therefore cannot be easily or accurately measured. Companies may strive for abstract goals but never know with sufficient certainty that they are achieving them. In this respect, the goal attainment approach often fails to fulfill our need to measure organizational effectiveness.

EXHIBIT 1–6   The 12 Most Frequently Cited Organizational Goals

Organizational Goal	Percent Mentioning Goal
Profitability	89%
Growth	82
Market share	66
Social responsibility	65
Employee welfare	62
Product quality and service	60
Research and development	54
Diversification	51
Efficiency	50
Financial responsibility	49
Resource conservation	39
Management development	35

Source: Y. K. Shetty, "A New Look at Corporate Goals," Copyright 1979 by the Regents of the University of California. Reprinted from the *California Management Review*, Vol. 21, No. 2. By permission of The Regents.

Second, organizations typically have many goals. Exhibit 1–6 lists the most frequently mentioned organizational goals in a survey of the largest firms in the United States. Some businesses in that survey cited up to 18 objectives that they strive for, with most mentioning 5 or 6. Organizations with multiple goals face the dilemma that some of their objectives are in conflict with others.

Consider Du Pont Canada Ltd., which wants to create a safe and nurturing work environment for employees, protect the environment, maintain a favourable community image, and be relatively competitive and profitable. In fact, Du Pont's profitability goal is to "rank among the top 25 percent of major Canadian companies."[21] These are noble objectives, but at some point they may work against each other. The company must spend large sums of money to reduce pollution and improve employee safety, but these expenditures cut into profits, at least in the short term.

Another limitation is that organizational goals are subjective. It would be easy for a chief executive officer to operate an effective organization according to the goal attainment model by simply setting modest objectives. For instance, suppose that Company A wants to achieve a 10 percent return on equity, while Company B strives for a 15 percent return. If both report a 12 percent return this year, can we conclude that Company A is effective because it exceeded its goal, while Company B is not because it fell short of its objective? This may be the conclusion based on the goal attainment model, whereas most of us would say that both are equally effective with respect to return on equity.

Systems Approach

The systems model, which we introduced earlier in this chapter, was first brought to organizational behaviour in the 1950s as an alternative to the goal attainment approach to organizational effectiveness.[22] By viewing organizations as open systems, effectiveness takes on a much broader meaning. While the goal attainment model emphasizes organizational outputs such as profitability and market share, the systems model also emphasizes the inputs and processes or means of reaching these objectives. In particular, it considers the extent to which the organization is able to acquire valued resources, adapt to changes in the external environment, and coordinate its subsystems efficiently in the transformation of inputs to outputs.[23]

The systems model also places more emphasis on employee well-being—job satisfaction, job stress, employee commitment, and the like—because employees represent the most important input to the organizational system. In general, the systems approach uses the concepts of survival, flexibility, and maintenance as measures of organizational effectiveness.

Limitations of the Systems Approach.   While the systems approach is a general improvement over the goal attainment approach, some of the concepts it uses to define effectiveness—including organizational health, survival, flexibility, and adaptability—are ambiguous and difficult to measure. Moreover, this approach emphasizes the need to balance inputs, outputs, and internal dynamics of the system, but it does not specify how this is achieved. Thus, the dilemma of conflicting goals exists just as much in systems theory as in the goal attainment approach. Finally, the systems approach theoretically considers inputs, transformations, and outputs, but many writers adopting this perspective tend to ignore output measures. With this bias, organizations may be judged effective because they are able to acquire resources even though their output has little societal value.[24]

Stakeholder (Multiple Constituency) Approach

According to Bill Somerville, former chief executive officer (CEO) of National Trust, the effectiveness of his company can be measured in terms of how well it serves three groups in society—shareholders for a reasonable rate of return, depositors (and other clients) for stability, and his staff for a good place to work and an opportunity for advancement.[25] Somerville's statement reflects the **stakeholder or multiple constituency model,** which assesses organizational effectiveness in terms of the preferences of its stakeholders.[26] Stakeholders are the numerous groups within and outside of the

stakeholder or multiple constituency model
Measuring effectiveness in terms of addressing the preferences of its stakeholders—groups with a vested interest in the organization.

organization that have a vested interest in the organization and its activities. Somerville believes that National Trust should emphasize the interests of shareholders, clients, and employees, but the financial institution probably pays attention to other groups as well. Exhibit 1–7 identifies several prominent stakeholders and the criteria that each typically uses to determine organizational effectiveness.

The stakeholder approach emerged in the late 1970s as organizations faced increasing pressure to become socially responsible. Today, more than ever, senior executives face vocal coalitions that attempt to redirect organizational activities toward their objectives. The stakeholder perspective of organizational effectiveness helps managers map out the organization's constituents and establish strategic objectives that consider their diverse interests.[27]

Stakeholders have conflicting interests, so organizations need to decide which will be given the highest priority.[28] The most common option is to favour stakeholders who have the greatest power over the organization. If suppliers are powerful, they should receive the organization's attention before other interests. Another strategy is to serve the needs of all constituents equally and, where inequalities exist, serve the least advantaged group until equality is restored. This idea is gaining support, but it may be risky if other stakeholders do not hold the same philosophy. A third perspective suggests that the priority of stakeholders changes over the organization's life cycle, so that one group might be most important when the business is formed whereas others gain importance as it matures.[29] Finally, some writers claim that the relative priority of stakeholders is an arbitrary decision and that organizational effectiveness can only be examined separately for each constituent.

EXHIBIT 1–7	Examples of Stakeholder Effectiveness Criteria
Stakeholder	**Effectiveness Criteria**
Owners/shareholders	Dividends, share price
Employees	Pay, interesting work, promotion opportunities
Customers	Quality, service, price
Suppliers	Timely payments, future sales potential
Government	Adherence to laws, payment of taxes, creation of employment
Charities	Reliable source of funds, seconding staff for administration
Special interest groups	Environmentally friendly, adherence to trading sanctions

Before leaving the topic of organizational effectiveness, you may have noticed that the three perspectives—goal attainment, systems, and stakeholder—are not mutually exclusive. Goal attainment emphasizes organizational outcomes, which are also represented (although not emphasized) in the systems model. Both of these models indirectly consider the interests of organizational stakeholders. For example, the frequently mentioned goal of profitability is linked to the interests of owners and shareholders. Systems theory suggests that employee interests must be recognized so that the organization's subsystems coordinate smoothly. Overall, it appears that all three perspectives must be considered when discussing the complex topic of organizational effectiveness.

PRODUCTIVITY: DOING THINGS RIGHT

Productivity refers to organizational efficiency, and is ordinarily measured in terms of the ratio of inputs to outcomes in some aspect of the productive process.[30] An organization increases its productivity when the level of output produced increases relative to the level of inputs received by the system. Campbell Soup, described at the beginning of this chapter, increased productivity by dramatically reducing the cost of production. Productivity improvement is also possible in the public sector.[31] For example, the Canadian government's Bureau of Labour Information was created in 1986 from three former branches and now processes twice as many client requests with 39 percent fewer staff members.[32] In both of these examples, productivity improved because the organizations transformed more output with relatively fewer inputs.

productivity
The organization's efficiency in transforming inputs to outputs.

Productivity is not the same as organizational effectiveness. While effectiveness considers the organization's activities regarding inputs, transformations, and outputs, productivity pays particular attention to the transformation process. If, as we stated earlier, an effective organization does the right things, then a productive organization does things right. Notice that an organization might be extremely productive, yet ineffective. For example, a Saskatchewan manufacturer might produce furniture very efficiently, yet it would be ineffective if its products did not keep pace with changing consumer tastes.

Productivity is a multidimensional concept; it cannot be measured by one variable or indicator. London Life Insurance Company in London, Ontario, recognizes this fact and has developed over 90 different variables to measure productivity. In one department, productivity might be measured as the number of health claim cheques issued per hour. In another, it might be the number of pages typed per hour.[33] Garrett Manufacturing Ltd., a Canadian electronics firm, has also devoted considerable time to identifying key productivity improvement indicators for every department and to forming an overall composite measure by prioritizing these departmental measures. Exhibit 1–8 lists the fourteen productivity indicators used by Garrett to maintain its competitive position in the world market.

| EXHIBIT 1–8 | Productivity Improvement Measures at Garrett Manufacturing Ltd. | |

Department	Productivity Indicator(s)	Weight
Accounting	$\dfrac{\text{Value added}}{\text{Total company salaries}}$	Not applicable
Contracts	$\dfrac{\text{Repeat business bookings}}{\text{Total bookings}}$	.06
Engineering	$\dfrac{\text{Customer funded engineering}}{\text{Total engineering dollars}}$	.11
	$\dfrac{\text{Forecasted engineering labour rate}}{\text{Actual engineering labour rate}}$	.06
	$\dfrac{\text{Direct time by direct engineering}}{\text{Total time by direct engineering}}$	.06
Materiel	$\dfrac{\text{Materiel costs of shipments}}{\text{Shipments}}$	.11
	$\dfrac{\text{Materiel department wages}}{\text{Materiel cost of shipments}}$	.06
Personnel	Direct labour absenteeism	.06
Customer support	$\dfrac{\text{Total warranty costs}}{\text{Total material + Direct labour dollars}}$	.06
Production	$\dfrac{\text{Direct labour wages}}{\text{Shipments}}$	.18
	$\dfrac{\text{Production direct labour headcount}}{\text{Production total labour headcount}}$	.06
Quality assurance	$\dfrac{\text{Total quality costs}}{\text{Total material + Direct labour dollars}}$	.06
	$\dfrac{\text{Total quantity of units rejected}}{\text{Total quantity of units inspected}}$	.06
Sales	$\dfrac{\text{Total sales department costs}}{\text{Total bookings}}$	.06
	Total	1.00

Source: W. C. Tate, "Measuring Our Productivity Improvements," *Business Quarterly*, Winter 1984, p. 90.

The measures used in each department at Garrett and London Life are partial productivity indicators because they compare output to only one input category, such as the cost of human resources or equipment. Total factor productivity, on the other hand, includes all input factors in the equation: raw materials, human resources, information, financial resources, and equipment. Most organizations use several partial productivity measures because total factor productivity is an incredibly complex calculation.

Productivity in the Canadian Economy

We often hear about productivity in terms of Canada's position relative to other countries. This macro level of productivity analysis is of particular interest to economists and has an important effect on our standard of living and global trade competitiveness. How productive is Canadian industry compared with other nations? Countries use a variety of concepts and measurement techniques to determine their productivity, so it is quite difficult to accurately compare Canada's competitive position. Fluctuating currencies further confound the results. However, recognizing these limitations, it appears that Canada's productivity is best described as a mixed bag.[34]

The good news is that we have the second-highest labour productivity in the world, higher than Germany or Japan but somewhat lower than the United States. There are several reasons for this.[35] A larger percentage of the population is of working age than any other industrial nation, meaning that there are more people working and fewer to support in retirement. Our work force is much younger than in Japan, Germany, and many other countries, which increases our capacity for flexibility and adaptability. A third factor is that Canada's economy is still largely resource-based. This gives us a relative advantage in the cost of energy and raw materials. Moreover, the resource sector is capital intensive, so employees are extremely productive on an output-per-person basis when they operate this expensive equipment.

The bad news is that Canada has one of the lowest levels of productivity *growth* among industrialized nations. In other words, our competitive edge is slipping away as other nations improve their efficiency faster than we improve ours. In 1988, for instance, output per person-hour in the business sector increased by 1.5 percent in Canada and 1.8 percent in the United States. The gap is much larger in the manufacturing sector, where Canada reported a 1.7 percent productivity increase in 1988 compared with 3.6 in the United States. Japan's rate of productivity growth is even higher, typically exceeding 5 or even 6 percent annually. Several explanations have been offered for Canada's relatively poor record of productivity improvement, including lack of research and development, poor investment in new equipment, and the high cost of government.

Productivity and Organizational Behaviour

So what does organizational behaviour have to do with national productivity growth? In our opinion, human behaviour in organizations is ultimately the most important factor. A country's productivity is determined by the effi-

PERSPECTIVE 1–3   Working Smarter to Improve Productivity: Three Canadian Examples

Continuous productivity improvement has become the watchword of the 1990s. But how can productive efficiency be improved? For each of these companies, the basic philosophy is that employees know where inefficiencies exist and how they can be overcome.

- At Toyota's assembly plant in Cambridge, Ontario, employees were able to cut 36 seconds off the previous four-minute time needed to turn out a four-door Corolla. This allowed the facility to bump annual production up from 50,000 to 60,000 vehicles by adding only 80 more production employees. To achieve higher production efficiency, employees completely redesigned their jobs and reassigned tasks within each work team. They also designed innovative systems to facilitate work production, including a dolly system to carry tools and parts that travel along with the moving assembly line. The dollies save time by eliminating the need to walk back and forth between the parts and assembly areas. Another innovation, built by the tire mounting team, is a pneumatic table that rises as the supply of tire rims diminishes. This saves time and fatigue of bending over further as assemblers get near the bottom of the pile.

- The original objective of Canadian General Electric's (CGE) jet engine plant in Bromont, Quebec, was to produce 500 sets of motor parts per year. The operation's 405 employees produced 426 sets in 1985, a couple of years before the productivity target was expected. By 1987, 500 employees had produced 1,041 sets and the number of hours required to complete a set of motor parts had dropped by 57 percent. CGE's strategy at the Bromont plant is to use self-managing work teams—

ciency of its organizations and, as you will recall, organizations are simply people working together to accomplish objectives. So aside from extraneous currency fluctuations and bad weather, people directly or indirectly make the difference in a country's standard of living.

Technology is quite properly credited with some productivity improvement, but we must not forget that new equipment and processes are ultimately invented by people working in organizations and that managers and other organizational members decide to adopt this technology into the production process. The important role of human behaviour in technological productivity is most apparent when the technology fails to deliver improved efficiency. For example, John Deere introduced a robotic welder at its farm machinery plant in Welland, Ontario, but soon discovered that the robot frequently missed the welding spot. The problem was that the technology was too inflexible and there was too much variance in the part being welded. The robot is appropriate for simple jobs, but someone chose the wrong technology for the wrong job.[36] The point here is that technology can only improve productivity when people make effective decisions and engage in appropriate actions. Thus, the first step to productivity improvement is to have effective employees.

This point is echoed by Gary McCullough, manager of the General Motors facility in Oshawa. "I think GM learned some hard lessons in the 1980s. There used to be a mind-set that automation was the only way to be competi-

production groups that have almost complete autonomy over the production process. This creates a more motivated work force and reduces the need for supervisors and quality control inspectors. Bromont's work force is also highly flexible, as everyone learns several tasks.

- Esso Resources Canada Ltd. of Calgary, a subsidiary of Imperial Oil Ltd., expects productivity to double by the year 2000. Most of this increased efficiency is expected to result from the company's new high involvement management (HIM) philosophy, which delegates more autonomy to work teams. Just two years after being introduced, HIM's effect on Esso's productivity is quite appar-

ent. Garry Wagner, who supervises a 25-member production team at Esso's Leduc Field Operations, recites the operation's productive gains: "Our operating costs will be down $2 million to $10 million this year and at least half of that is attributable to the increased efficiency of the team. [For instance] following a suggestion from our team, a job which previously required six employees is now done by four." Esso has eliminated entire layers of bureaucracy, resulting in fewer filters, funnels, and bottlenecks. Explains one employee: "We clearly see this as giving us a competitive advantage. It is something we feel we have to do to remain competitive on the international market."

Sources: K. Romain, "Teamwork at Toyota Raises Corolla Output," *Globe and Mail*, February 22, 1990, pp. B1, B4; "Productivity Awards Show Importance of Employee Involvement," *Worklife Report* 6, no. 5 (1989), pp. 4–5; and P. S. Taylor, "Esso Taps Its Best Resource," *Western Report* 4, no. 45 (November 27, 1989), pp. 17–18.

tive—I'll probably get my wrists slapped for saying this, but we now know that wasn't true." Instead, claims McCullough, better management, not more expensive technology, is the real key to raising productivity and ensuring higher quality.[37] The idea that productivity improvement begins with the organization's work force has been recognized for many years in Japan and other countries that are not blessed with the natural resources Canada has so readily available. Recently, Canadian industry seems to be wakening up to this basic fact and, like the organizations described in Perspective 1–3, is introducing innovative approaches to productivity improvement through employees. These and other management strategies will be discussed throughout this book.

ORGANIZATION OF THIS BOOK

This concludes our opening discussion of the organizational behaviour field. Now let's introduce you to the rest of this book. *Canadian Organizational Behaviour* is organized into five parts, including this introduction. As Exhibit 1–9 illustrates, the remaining parts basically conform to the three levels of organizational behaviour: individual, team, and organization. In keeping with our emphasis on productivity and organizational effectiveness, we start by examining the dynamics of individual behaviour and performance, and then examine other individual and interpersonal processes. The book

EXHIBIT 1–9   Organization of This Book

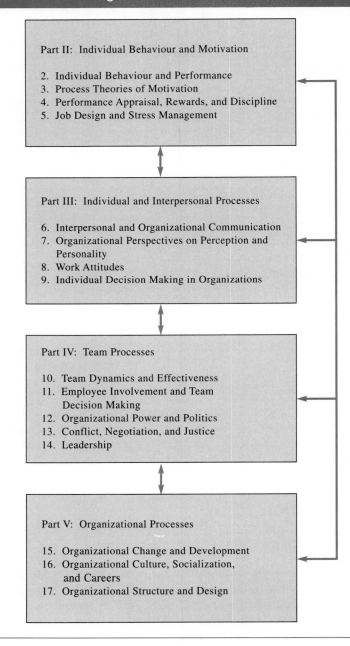

Part II: Individual Behaviour and Motivation

2. Individual Behaviour and Performance
3. Process Theories of Motivation
4. Performance Appraisal, Rewards, and Discipline
5. Job Design and Stress Management

Part III: Individual and Interpersonal Processes

6. Interpersonal and Organizational Communication
7. Organizational Perspectives on Perception and Personality
8. Work Attitudes
9. Individual Decision Making in Organizations

Part IV: Team Processes

10. Team Dynamics and Effectiveness
11. Employee Involvement and Team Decision Making
12. Organizational Power and Politics
13. Conflict, Negotiation, and Justice
14. Leadership

Part V: Organizational Processes

15. Organizational Change and Development
16. Organizational Culture, Socialization, and Careers
17. Organizational Structure and Design

then turns to team-based aspects of organizational behaviour and concludes with topics normally associated with the organizational level of analysis.

Part II begins with Chapter 2, which describes different types of performance-based behaviour, presents a general model of individual behaviour and performance, and explores the topics of goal setting and feedback. Chapter 3 introduces three theories that explain how people are motivated to choose different courses of action. Based on the concepts introduced in the previous two chapters, Chapter 4 discusses three sets of interrelated organizational practices affecting individual behaviour and performance: performance appraisal, reward systems, and employee discipline. Job design and work-related stress are the two themes of Chapter 5. Both issues affect the motivation and ability to complete job duties as well as other performance-related behaviours such as turnover and absenteeism.

Part III emphasizes other individual processes as well as those relating to interpersonal events within organizational settings. Chapter 6 is about communicating in organizations, including the dynamics of interpersonal communication, barriers to effective organizational communication, and strategies to improve both interpersonal and organizational communication. We discuss perception in Chapter 7, including the processes of attribution, self-fulfilling prophecies, perceptual errors, and ways to improve perceptual accuracy. This chapter also introduces the concept of personality and its relevance to organizational behaviour. Our discussion of work attitudes, the theme of Chapter 8, includes a basic model of work attitudes, two important work attitudes (job satisfaction and organizational commitment), the process of persuasion (attitude change), and the dynamics of prejudice and other forms of discrimination. The final chapter in Part III (Chapter 9) describes individual perspectives on organizational decision making and highlights three decision-making topics of particular importance to managers: intuition, crisis management, and ethics.

Part IV turns to the increasingly important elements of team processes. In Chapter 10, we look at the dynamics and effectiveness of work teams. Specific topics include team context and design, team development, norms, cohesiveness, and strategies to build more effective work teams. Chapter 11 examines employee involvement and team decision making and introduces two innovative forms of employee involvement: quality circles and self-managing work teams. Chapter 12 investigates the factors that influence individual power as well as the sources of and remedies for political behaviour in organizations. We learn about the dynamics of organizational conflict, negotiation, and procedural justice in Chapter 13, including the causes and consequences of conflict, factors leading to more effective negotiation with others, and the important elements of fair organizational practices. Chapter 14 presents several models of leadership, including the emerging topics of transformational leadership and the romance of leadership.

The final section of this book, Part V, focusses on organizational level phenomena. We learn about organizational change and development in Chapter 15, including strategies to reduce resistance to change and institutionalize organizational transformations. Chapter 16 introduces three organizational topics: organizational culture, socialization, and career management. In particular, we learn how to strengthen organizational values, help newcomers adapt more quickly to new organizational settings, and address the dynamics of career patterns in contemporary organizations. The final chapter of this book, Chapter 17, examines the different forms of organizational design, and the contingencies that affect the best structural configuration in a particular environment.

SUMMARY

• Organizational behaviour is a relatively young field of inquiry that studies what people think, feel, and do in and around organizations. It includes the behaviours of individuals working alone and in teams as well as the thought processes and structural contexts surrounding these actions. Organizations are social entities—groupings of human beings—in which two or more people work interdependently through deliberately structured interaction patterns to accomplish a set of goals. Organizational goals are a desired state of affairs that the social entity is trying to achieve.

• People are interested in the study of organizational behaviour for many reasons. Virtually every one of us is affected by organizational activities, so we have a natural interest in knowing when, how, and why organizational events occur. People working in organizations want to be able to predict and understand behaviour and to make sense of their organizational context. Studying organizational behaviour will help you test personal theories of human behaviour in organizations and to adopt new perspectives of reality. Finally, OB theories and concepts have direct implications for the practice of management.

• The field of organizational behaviour is multidisciplinary, that is, it has been built upon theories and concepts adopted from other disciplines. OB theories and concepts undergo rigorous testing using the scientific method. Generally, this involves observing organizational phenomena, forming a theory or drawing upon existing theories to explain the observed events, forming hypotheses to test the theory in other organizational settings, and collecting data to find out whether the hypotheses accurately predict these phenomena. The complexity of human behaviour requires several interrelated theories rather than a single grand theory.

• Organizational behaviour views organizations as open systems—an interdependent set of parts that functions as a whole to achieve a set of goals and is interdependent with its external environment. Most OB theories also take a contingency approach, that is, they suggest that a particular management practice may be extremely effective under some conditions but not others. Finally, organizational events can be studied from an individual, team, or organizational level of analysis.

• Organizational effectiveness is a ubiquitous and elusive concept that can be best understood in terms of three perspectives: goal attainment, systems theory, and stakeholders. None of these approaches alone is sufficient, so all three must be recognized when discussing the complex topic of organizational effectiveness. Productivity refers to organizational efficiency and is ordinarily measured in terms of the ratio of inputs to outcomes in some aspect of the productive process. Productivity focusses on the transformation of inputs to outputs and is a multidimensional concept. The basic view of this book is that while productivity is a function of all elements in the transformation process (equipment, information, finances, etc.), the first step to productivity improvement is to have effective employees.

DISCUSSION QUESTIONS

1. How important are goals to organizations?
2. How might non-managers use organizational behaviour knowledge?
3. "Organizational theories should follow the contingency approach." Comment on the accuracy of this statement.
4. Why are organizations considered open systems?
5. How does the goal attainment perspective differ from the systems perspective of organizational effectiveness?
6. Defend the "power" variation of the stakeholder perspective of organizational effectiveness. Provide an example of this approach in an organization.
7. How does productivity differ from organizational effectiveness?
8. How is Canada's labour productivity affected by organizational behaviour?

NOTES

1. W. Trueman, "Alternate Visions," *Canadian Business,* March 1991, pp. 28–33.

2. L. E. Greiner, "A Recent History of Organizational Behavior," In S. Kerr (ed.), *Organizational Behavior* (Columbus, Ohio: Grid, 1979), pp. 3–14.

3. D. Katz and R. L. Kahn, *The Social Psychology of Organizations* (New York: Wiley, 1966), Chapter 2.

4. A. Etzioni, *Modern Organizations* (Englewood Cliffs, N.J.: Prentice Hall, 1964), Chapter 2.

5. R. Cyert and J. G. March, *A Behavioral Theory of the Firm* (New York: Wiley, 1963); and C. Hardy, *Strategies for Retrenchment and Turnaround: The Politics of Survival* (Berlin: Walter de Gruyter, 1990), Chapter 14.

6. Katz and Kahn, *The Social Psychology of Organizations.*

7. Etzioni, *Modern Organizations,* p. 1.

8. Trueman, "Alternate Visions," p. 32.

9. P. R. Lawrence, "Historical Development of Organizational Behavior," in J. W. Lorsch (ed.), *Handbook of Organizational Behavior* (Englewood Cliffs, N.J.: Prentice Hall, 1987), pp. 1–9; and D. S. Pugh, "Modern Organizational Theory: A Psychological and Sociological Study," *Psychological Bulletin* 66 (1966), pp. 235–51.

10. L. L. Cummings, "Toward Organizational Behavior," *Academy of Management Review* 3 (1978), pp. 90–98; K. W. Thomas and W. G. Tymon, Jr., "Necessary Properties of Relevant Research: Lessons from Recent Criticisms for the Organizational Sciences," *Academy of Management Review* 7 (1982), pp. 345–52.

11. E. C. Webster, "I/O Psychology in Canada from Birth to Couchiching," *Canadian Psychology* 29 (1988), pp. 4–10; and J. P. Meyer, "Organizational Psychology in the 1980s: A Canadian Perspective," *Canadian Psychology* 29 (1988), pp. 18–29.

12. C. Hardy, "The Contribution of Political Science to Organizational Behavior," in J. W. Lorsch (ed.), *Handbook of Organizational Behavior* (Englewood Cliffs, N.J.: Prentice Hall, 1987), pp. 96–108.

13. L. von Bertalanffy, C. G. Hempel, R. E. Bass, and H. Jonas, "General Systems Theory: A New Approach to Unity of Science," *Human Biology* 23 (December 1951), pp. 302–61; and F. E. Kast and J. E. Rosenzweig, "General Systems Theory: Applications for Organization and Management," *Academy of Management Journal* (December 1972), pp. 447–65.

14. C. C. Pinder and L. F. Moore, *Middle Range Theory and the Study of Organizations* (Boston: Martinus Nijoff, 1980).

15. H. L. Tosi and J. W. Slocum, Jr., "Contingency Theory: Some Suggested Directions," *Journal of Management* 10 (1984), pp. 9–26.

16. Lawrence, "Historical Development of Organizational Behavior."

17. K. S. Cameron and D. A. Whetton, *Organizational Effectiveness: A Comparison of Multiple Models* (New York: Academic Press, 1983); R. M. Steers, *Organizational Effectiveness: A Behavioral View* (Santa Monica, Calif.: Goodyear, 1977); and P. S. Goodman and J. M. Pennings (eds.), *New Perspectives on Organizational Effectiveness* (San Francisco: Jossey-Bass, 1977).

18. J. L. Brown and R. E. Schneck, "Determinants of Organizational Effectiveness," *Canadian Journal of Administrative Sciences* 1(1984), pp. 29–49.

19. J. L. Price, "The Study of Organizational Effectiveness," *The Sociological Quarterly* 13 (1972), pp. 3–15.

20. R. H. Hall, "Effectiveness Theory and Organizational Effectiveness," *Journal of Applied Behavioral Science* 16 (1980); and W. C. Birdsall, "When Benefits Are Difficult to Measure," *Evaluation and Program Planning* 10 (1987), pp. 109–18.

21. J. M. Stewart, "Less Is More," *Canadian Business Review* 16, no. 2 (Summer 1989), pp. 46–49.

22. B. S. Georgopoulos and A. S. Tannenbaum, "A Study of Organizational Effectiveness," *American Sociological Review* 22 (1957), pp. 535–40.

23. E. Yuchtman and S. Seashore, "A System Resource Approach to Organizational Effectiveness," *American Sociological Review* 32 (1967), pp. 891–903.

24. A. G. Bedeian and R. F. Zammuto, *Organizations: Theory and Design* (Hinsdale, Ill.: Dryden, 1991), Ch. 2.

25. Tessa Wilmott, "Somerville Wears Conservatism on Sleeve," *Financial Post,* January 24, 1989, p. 19.

26. R. M. Kanter and D. Brinkerhoff, "Organizational Performance: Recent Developments in Measurement," *Annual Review of Sociology* 7 (1981), pp. 321–49; T. Connolly, E. M. Conlon, and S. J. Deutsch, "Organizational Effectiveness: A Multiple Constituency Approach," *Academy of Management Review* 5 (1980), pp. 211–18; and R. F. Zammuto, "A Comparison of Multiple Constituency Models of Organizational Effectiveness," *Academy of Management Review* 9 (1984), pp. 606–16.

27. G. T. Savage, T. W. Nix, C. J. Whitehead, and J. D. Blair, "Strategies for Assessing and Managing Organizational Stakeholders," *Academy of Management Executive* 5, no. 2 (May 1991), pp. 61–75.

28. Zammuto, "A Comparison of Multiple Constituency Models of Organizational Effectiveness"; M. Keeley, "Impartiality and Participant-Interest Theories of Organizational Effectiveness," *Administrative Science Quarterly* 29 (1984), pp. 1–20.

29. K. S. Cameron and D. A. Whetton, "Perceptions of Organizational Effectiveness over Organzational Life Cycles," *Administrative Science Quarterly* 26 (1981), pp. 525–44.

30. T. H. Mahoney, "Productivity Defined: The Relativity of Efficiency, Effectiveness, and Change," in J. P. Campbell, R. J. Campbell, and Associates (eds.), *Productivity in Organizations* (San Francisco: Jossey-Bass, 1988), pp. 13–39; and Etzioni, *Modern Organizations,* pp. 8–10.

31. J. Nollet and J. Haywood-Farmer, "A Model of Productivity in Public Services," *Canadian Journal of Administrative Sciences* 8 (1991), pp. 9–17.

32. Auditor General of Canada, *Report to the House of Commons, Fiscal Year ended 31 March, 1988* (Ottawa: Supply and Services Canada, 1990), Exhibit 4.6.

33. P. E. Larson, "Achieving Corporate Excellence," *Canadian Business Review,* Winter 1987, pp. 38–40; and J. Fleming, *Merchants of Fear: An Investigation of Canada's Insurance Industry* (Toronto: Penguin, 1986), pp. 197–98.

34. Statistics Canada, *System of National Accounts: Aggregate Productivity Measures, 1988* (Ottawa: Minister of Supply and Services Canada, 1990); and Organization for Economic Cooperation and Development, *OECD Economic Outlook* (Paris: OECD, June 1990).

35. P. Kovacs, "How Do We Stack Up?" *Small Business* 8 no. 1 (January 1989), pp. 24–29.

36. K. Benzing, "Failures on the Road to Innovation," *Financial Post,* February 22, 1989, p. 15.

37. R. Laver, "The Future of the Car," *Maclean's,* April 15, 1991, p. 45.

CHAPTER CASE

THE CITY OF CALGARY'S WATERWORKS PILOT PRODUCTIVITY PROGRAM: THE CASE OF A "NEAR RUN THING"

The City of Calgary's transmission and distribution section (TDS) employs nearly 300 people and plays a vital role in constructing and maintaining water lines throughout the city. This is a significant task in a city with over 600,000 people, where 3,000 kilometres of underground pipe carry 177 billion litres of water annually.

The engineering department, which oversees TDS and other units in the waterworks division, learned through a series of interviews that TDS employees had numerous ideas about how to improve productivity. Upon discovering this, the city engineer (the person in charge of the engineering department) eagerly supported an organized effort to document and implement these ideas. And so was born the Waterworks Pilot Productivity Program, which was intended to harness the productive energies and ideas of TDS employees and to determine whether such a scheme could be applied across the entire engineering department.

The Waterworks Program was intended to be participative and, as a first step, management resurveyed TDS employees to confirm that they had ideas about how to improve productivity in their units. Next, the city engineer and other management staff gave the program credibility and momentum by personally introducing the concept to union executives and employees. During these presentations, management emphasized that the productivity improvement process is formidable and that inevitably there would be some difficulties. These warnings were soon to become understatements of the problems that lay ahead.

The next step was to form a labour-management committee within TDS, called the Methods Research Committee, which consisted of 35 to 40 employees and managers. Several special study groups were established within this committee to address specific problem areas and recommend solutions. The initial survey of employees had identified 21 areas of concern, such as inadequate field equipment repairs, unavailability of materials, and utility location delays. When each study group had completed its analysis, it submitted a formal solution paper or report to the Methods Research Committee. This information was then forwarded to senior management for final approval and implementation.

Productivity Results

The Waterworks Pilot Productivity Program was clearly successful from a cost control perspective. Employees became more conscious of the need for productivity improvement and, together with implementation of the 21 initiatives, the section achieved dramatic savings during the first year. For example, the cost of repairing the City of Calgary's water mains declined by 25 percent, repair costs to underground service connections declined by 17 percent, expenditures for overtime dropped by 72 percent, and equipment costs were brought down by over 20 percent.

Through better control and scheduling, the number of vehicles and major equipment pieces in use was reduced to a daily average of 224, down from 292 the previous year. A new inventory delivery service to the field was introduced, which reduced the cost of local inventory by $250,000. Moreover, safety statistics improved to the point that the waterworks division won the engineering department's much-coveted safety award. Overall, in the program's first year, the City of Calgary's transmission and distribution section realized a $4 million surplus in their operating budget of $18.5 million, following five consecutive years of operating deficits. In the second year, with only a $17 million budget base, TDS realized nearly a $3 million surplus.

A Pandora's Box

These results make the Waterworks Program sound like every organization's dream come true, but the improvement process also opened a Pandora's box of problems that no one had anticipated. Soon after the program was underway, it became clear that key elements in the organization—middle management in particular—were showing a distinct reluctance to climb aboard. These managers felt that they had little to gain and a great deal to lose from the initiative. Their authority was being tampered with and they were now faced with employee issues for which they had no experience or training. For example, employees were trained to be more cost conscious and they soon put these skills to work. But this led to embarrassing or confrontational episodes with middle managers who were being shown evidence of their own frailty.

The Waterworks Program adopted the most basic definition of productivity—output over input—so that employees could release their creative energies and not be hampered by narrow indicators. Unfortunately, this resulted in the formation of several distinct interpretations of productivity when viewed by different units within the engineering department. The failure to develop a common vocabulary and set of definitions became a major stumbling block when employees from the different sections met. Disagreements set the stage for many passionate arguments among divisions and sections within the engineering department over such subtle nuances as efficiency versus effectiveness and cost savings versus cost avoidance. These unique vocabularies reinforced existing rivalries among the various sections and sometimes made it difficult to take ideas that worked in one group and successfully transplant them into another.

In their eagerness to embrace employee involvement, management failed to identify subjects and areas that were off-limits to the study groups. With such loose marching orders, it was not long before the study groups were raising eyebrows and blood pressures as they trespassed across one traditional barrier after another in search of improved productivity. Departmental boundaries, management prerogatives, line/staff relationships, and powerful vested interests all were bruised or buffeted in the search for solutions.

Finally, the Waterworks Pilot Productivity Program demonstrated the complexity of a billion-dollar corporation like the City of Calgary. As solutions were implemented, managers and employees alike could see how changes in one area sent ripples throughout the organization and caused difficulties in other areas. A productivity improvement that saved a dollar in one section may have cost the organization two dollars in another area. Unless management thought through the initiative and saw the big picture, some ideas would end up costing more instead of saving money.

Overall, the City of Calgary achieved significant productivity improvement through the Waterworks Program experiment. On the strength of this success, the city has launched an ambitious service improvement program, and the engineering department's initiative has been expanded from TDS to other sections. This experiment also taught several lessons to senior managers at the City of Calgary and opened their eyes to the complexity and risks of this level of organizational transformation. Even the most successful productivity programs are "near-run things." There are mistakes, false starts, misunderstandings, and unexpected developments. To their credit, the City of Calgary's engineering department staff realized that mistakes are a sign of effort, not a symptom of failure. They are milestones along the road to success, although at the time they may look more like headstones than milestones.

Source: Adapted from B. Sheehy, "A Near-Run Thing: An Inside Look at a Public-Sector Productivity Program," *National Productivity Review*, Spring 1985, pp. 139–45.

Discussion Questions

1. Use systems theory to explain how the City of Calgary's Waterworks Pilot Productivity Program opened a Pandora's box of problems for management.

2. Document some of the productivity measures that might be used in the transmission and distribution section.

3. Identify the organizational behaviour concepts that apply to specific aspects of this case.

EXPERIENTIAL EXERCISE

ORGANIZATIONAL EFFECTIVENESS EXERCISE

Purpose. This exercise is designed to help you understand the stakeholder perspective of organizational effectiveness, to make you more aware of the various strategic constituencies that have vested interests in different organizations, and to demonstrate the difficulty of reconciling conflicting effectiveness criteria of competing stakeholders.

Canadian Airlines International

Name of Stakeholder	Stakeholder's Primary Criterion for Determining Organizational Effectiveness	How Important Should This Stakeholder Be?
————	———————————————	————
————	———————————————	————
————	———————————————	————
————	———————————————	————
————	———————————————	————
————	———————————————	————
————	———————————————	————
————	———————————————	————
————	———————————————	————
————	———————————————	————

Instructions.   The instructor will form teams of four to five people. Two well-known Canadian organizations are named in this exercise: Canadian Airlines International and Toronto General Hospital. (Your instructor may substitute other organizations for these.) Each team will identify the different types of stakeholders that likely have a vested interest in each organization's activities. The team will then identify the main criterion that each stakeholder uses to determine the organization's effectiveness. Finally, team members will try to reach a consensus on how important each stakeholder listed *should* be to the organization: high, medium, or low. The team should be prepared to explain the criterion or perspective used to determine the relative importance of each stakeholder.

Toronto General Hospital

Name of Stakeholder	Stakeholder's Primary Criterion for Determining Organizational Effectiveness	How Important Should This Stakeholder Be?
_____	_____	_____
_____	_____	_____
_____	_____	_____
_____	_____	_____
_____	_____	_____
_____	_____	_____
_____	_____	_____
_____	_____	_____
_____	_____	_____

II

INDIVIDUAL BEHAVIOUR AND MOTIVATION

Patrick Trautman, a Northstar
Energy Corporation field operator,
checks operations at the Duhamel
gas plant in Alberta. Northstar is
actively engaged in natural gas
exploration, production, processing,
and marketing in Canada and is
known for its development of
significant gas reserves at below
average industry costs.

Individual Behaviour and Performance

LEARNING OBJECTIVES

After reading this chapter, you should be able to:

Identify
Five types of performance-related behaviours.

Explain
The four factors that affect individual behaviour and performance.

Identify
Three strategies to match employee abilities with job requirements.

Describe
Three content theories of motivation.

Discuss
The management implications of content theories of motivation.

List
The characteristics of effective goal setting and feedback.

CHAPTER OUTLINE

Types of Performance-Related Behaviour

A Model of Individual Behaviour and Performance

Ability

Role Perceptions

Situational Contingencies

Employee Motivation

Content Theories of Motivation

Goal Setting

Providing Effective Feedback

Yellowknife Mines

Giant Yellowknife Mines Ltd. (now Royal Oak Mines Inc.) had been dogged by high-cost production in its underground gold operation at Yellowknife, Northwest Territories. The company introduced technical and administrative measures to cut production expenses, but this was not enough. Mine manager Steve McAlpine determined that the only way to avoid shutting down operations was through a more productive work force.

Giant Yellowknife took several steps to increase employee performance. First, communication channels were opened so that the mine's 400 employees would have clearer and higher performance expectations and, as soon as was practical, would know how their actual performance compared with those expectations. Supervisors received training to improve their management skills in decision making, planning, and employee relations. Managers at all levels participated in a job clarification program in which participants developed a better understanding of their organizational roles. Finally, senior management involved lower-level staff in strategic and operational decision making. By delegating these tasks, supervisors and their staff would experience more challenge and esteem in their jobs.

Giant Yellowknife's strategy of increasing employee abilities, motivation, and role perceptions had a dramatic effect on productivity. In less than two years, the cost of gold production at the mine dropped by $192 per ounce (from $549 to $357 per ounce). Management discovered that employees have a huge capacity to absorb information and to translate this knowledge into higher job performance. Supervisors learned how to take new initiatives and to involve employees directly in the decision-making process. And Giant Yellowknife's staff responded to senior management's commitment by working harder—and working smarter—toward achieving individual and corporate objectives.[1]

Giant Yellowknife's experience illustrates that there are many ways to make employees more productive while also fulfilling their personal needs. In this example, supervisors improved their performance through management skills training, employees developed a better awareness of their roles in fulfilling corporate objectives, and everyone was challenged through goal setting and increased involvement.

This chapter introduces the dynamics of individual behaviour in organizations, with a particular emphasis on performance-related activities. We begin by describing different types of performance-based behaviour. Next, a general model of individual behaviour and performance is presented, followed by a more detailed overview of the four elements of this model. The final sections of this chapter explore the topics of goal setting and feedback—two important concepts and practices in the management of organizational behaviour.

TYPES OF PERFORMANCE-RELATED BEHAVIOUR

The field of organizational behaviour includes all activities occurring in and around organizations. We are particularly interested in **performance-related behaviours**—those behaviours that directly or indirectly influence the achievement of organizational objectives. The number of performance-related behaviours is limitless, but we can classify them roughly into the five groups shown in Exhibit 2–1.[2]

performance-related behaviours

Behaviours that directly or indirectly influence the achievement of organizational objectives.

Joining the Organization

Organizations need people with the required abilities, talents, and attitudes to perform the necessary roles and tasks. In this respect, it is desirable to have qualified individuals apply for a job, participate in the company's selection activities, and accept the employment offer.

A common strategy to increase the number of qualified people willing and able to become organizational members is to advertise job openings. When Red Lobster recently opened a restaurant in Chicoutimi, Quebec, it received more than 1,000 applicants for 100 openings because of its effective job

---

EXHIBIT 2–1   Types of Individual Behaviour in Organizations

Type of Behaviour	Examples
Joining the organization	• Submitting a job application. • Attending selection activities. • Accepting employment offer.
Remaining with the organization	• Not searching for work with another firm. • Not accepting work with another firm.
Maintaining work attendance	• Attending work at scheduled times. • Showing up for work on time.
Performing required job duties	• Completing tasks quickly. • Completing tasks without error.
Exhibiting organizational citizenship	• Cooperating with coworkers. • Providing valuable suggestions. • Learning beyond job requirements.

Source: Based on T. S. Bateman and C. P. Zeithaml, *Management: Function and Strategy* (Homewood, Ill.: Irwin, 1990), pp. 516–17; and D. Katz and R. L. Kahn, *The Social Psychology of Organizations* (New York: Wiley, 1966), pp. 337–40.

advertising. Rather than simply describing what the job required, the advertisements emphasized what Red Lobster could do for its employees. In fact, the company required no experience and enticed applicants with the realistic promise of flexible hours and potential job advancement. One of the restaurant chain's favourite ad slogans is "Be the Pilot of Your Own Ship."[3]

Other recruiting activities specifically motivate those with the desired qualifications to decide to accept the employment offer. Highly qualified applicants may be offered larger paycheques and other job perquisites. Some firms have special hiring bonuses for applicants who accept the job offer.[4] The important point here is that the job candidate's action of joining the firm is just as important as the organization's action of offering employment.

Remaining with the Organization

After hiring qualified employees, organizations must continue their efforts to keep them. Unfortunately, the turnover rate in some businesses is alarmingly high. For example, the annual rate of turnover in the Canadian fast-food industry is almost 300 percent; in the hospitality sector it is 111 percent.[5] Turnover can be very costly because companies have lost some of their training investment, particularly when people leave soon after receiving this training. There are also expenses in temporarily reassigning the work and recruiting, selecting, and training another employee to permanently fill the vacancy. Finally, high turnover rates can disrupt work activities of remaining staff and may affect their performance long after a replacement has been hired.

There are many causes of employee turnover.[6] Some people are motivated to join another organization where they expect better financial rewards or interesting work. Of course, employees may be motivated to quit but remain with the firm because they cannot find alternate employment. Others leave for reasons largely beyond their control, such as when their spouse is transferred to another location. One study reported that this is the main cause of turnover among female Royal Canadian Mounted Police (RCMP) officers. Even women married to other RCMP officers quit because the organization often does not accept marriage as a justification for transferring both employees.[7]

Organizations typically encourage employees to remain, but they may also want poor performers to look for employment elsewhere by withholding salary increases and promotions. If this does not work and retraining or job transfers are not feasible, poor performers leave the company involuntarily by being dismissed. Companies with very low quit rates rely on retirements to create new vacancies. This provides hiring and promotion opportunities for new people with fresh ideas and perspectives. Finally, incentives may be offered for employees to voluntarily quit during economic downturns so that management is not forced to lay people off.

Maintaining Work Attendance

Even when there is sufficient staff to perform the required tasks, organizations must ensure that people show up for work at the scheduled times. In other words, employees contribute to organizational effectiveness by minimizing absenteeism and lateness. Statistics Canada estimates that the average employee is absent from scheduled work 8.6 days per year.[8] The annual cost of absenteeism in Canada is believed to be at least *$10.5 billion*. At the Bank of Montreal, 54,000 hours of productive work time are lost *each week* to absenteeism. The company estimates that absenteeism costs $18 million per year in salaries alone.[9]

Exhibit 2–2 highlights the main reasons why employees do not fulfill their work attendance obligations. There is some evidence that absenteeism is primarily caused by the lack of motivation to attend work, whereas lateness is mainly affected by circumstances beyond the employee's control, such as a car that won't start or a subway system that is behind schedule.[10] Employees are more likely to miss scheduled work when they dislike their job and

EXHIBIT 2–2   A Model of Work Attendance

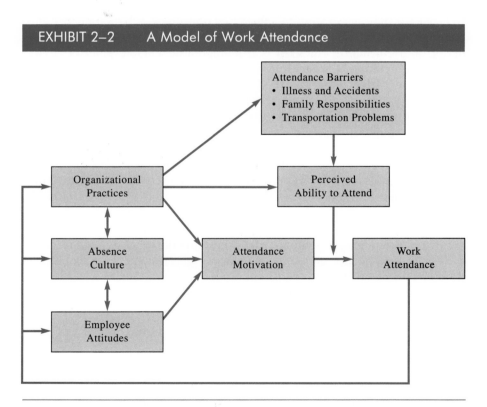

Source: Adapted from S. R. Rhodes and R. M. Steers, *Managing Employee Absenteeism* (Reading, Mass.: Addison-Wesley, 1990), p. 57.

organizational policies provide no disincentive to engage in this behaviour. For instance, generous sick leave policies significantly increase absenteeism because they reduce the financial penalty otherwise associated with this behaviour.[11] Of course, even with a strong attendance motivation, employees might be absent or late due to poor weather conditions, illness, family responsibilities, or transportation problems.[12]

Employers have implemented several strategies to maintain good work attendance. Some offer financial incentives, while others have instituted strict absence control measures to prevent employees from abusing sick leave privileges. At B. C. Sugar, where the annual absenteeism rate has exceeded 22 days per employee, a nurse personally visits the homes of some employees who call in sick, particularly if they have a history of unexplained absences. To address problems relating to the ability to attend work, a few firms provide emergency transportation during snowstorms or have introduced workplace day-care facilities.

Performing Required Job Duties

performance standard
A minimum acceptable level of job performance.

In order for the organization to achieve its objectives, job incumbents must complete the tasks assigned to them above minimum performance standards. A **performance standard** is a minimum acceptable level of performance. Completing at least 15 production units per hour is an example of a highly quantitative performance standard, whereas providing satisfactory customer service is a more subjective standard. Performance standards are thresholds against which employees may be judged. If performance falls below the standard, managers are typically required to take some sort of action, such as providing corrective training.[13]

Virtually every job has more than one performance dimension, that is, incumbents must perform more than one type of activity. As an example, foreign exchange traders at the Bank of Montreal must be able to identify profitable trades, work cooperatively with clients and coworkers in a stressful environment, assist in training new staff, and work on special telecommunications equipment without error. These job duties often require different skills and talents and may influence organizational effectiveness to different degrees. Only by considering all major dimensions can we fully understand the nature of a particular employee's job performance.

Exhibiting Organizational Citizenship

organizational citizenship behaviours
Employee behaviours that extend beyond the required job duties, such as helping others and facilitating a positive work environment.

Employees typically contribute to organizational effectiveness by working beyond the required job duties, such as helping others and facilitating a positive work environment.[14] These extra role activities, known as **organizational citizenship behaviours,** are typically overlooked by the reward system, but they are nevertheless beneficial to the organization and its stakeholders. For most of this century, management writers have commented that organi-

EXHIBIT 2–3	Types of Organizational Citizenship Behaviour	
Type of Behaviour	**Definition**	**Example**
Altruism	Helping others with their work.	Explaining a new company procedure to a coworker.
Courtesy	Providing consideration to others.	Informing a coworker that you will be using the lab tomorrow.
Sportsmanship	Gracefully tolerating the occasional impositions and nuisances of organizational life.	Saying nothing when the secretary forgets to identify you as a contributor to a report.
Civic duty	Maintaining responsible, constructive involvement in organizational developments.	Responding to your telephone messages soon after receiving them.
Conscientiousness	Complying with the spirit as well as the letter of corporate policies.	Keeping a record of company equipment borrowed with permission in case any is lost in transit.

Sources: Based on D. W. Organ and T. S. Bateman, *Organizational Behavior,* 4th edition (Irwin: Homewood, Ill., 1991), pp. 275–76; and D. W. Organ, ''The Motivational Basis of Organizational Citizenship Behavior,'' *Research in Organizational Behavior* 12 (1990), pp. 43–72.

zational citizenship is an indispensable part of organizational behaviour.[15] Recent studies on this topic have attempted to understand the types of behaviour that may be classified as good organizational citizenship. Exhibit 2–3 presents a preliminary list of such behaviours.

A MODEL OF INDIVIDUAL BEHAVIOUR AND PERFORMANCE

By now, you can see that individual behaviour is influenced by many diverse factors originating either from the person or the surrounding environment. By understanding these determinants, we can better manage employees so that they help the organization achieve its objectives.

Virtually every topic in this book is relevant to the causes of employee behaviour, but as a useful starting point, individual behaviour and performance may be viewed as functions of the four factors shown in Exhibit 2–4. These variables include:

1. *Ability*—The learned capability and natural aptitude to perform some behaviour.

2. *Role perceptions*—The beliefs about what is required to achieve the desired results.

3. *Situational contingencies*—Environmental factors beyond the employee's control (at least, in the short run) that either constrain or facilitate individual behaviour and performance.

4. *Motivation*—The internal forces that arouse, direct, and maintain a
    person's voluntary choice of behaviour.

Generally speaking, all four conditions must be present in order for employees to perform their jobs effectively. If any element weakens, employee
performance will decrease. For example, highly qualified salespeople who
understand their job duties and have sufficient resources will not perform
their jobs as well if they lack the motivation and effort to market the company's products or services. Similarly, those who are highly motivated to close
a sale are unlikely to be successful if they lack sufficient knowledge about
the product.

This model emphasizes the fact that poor performance may be due to a
variety of causes. Too often, managers assume that employees who perform
the job poorly are lazy or that the reward system does not provide enough
incentive for them to work harder. This diagnosis is sometimes true, but
other possible causes—such as the lack of proper training, inadequate resources, or unclear work objectives—are frequently ignored. Subsequently,
actions to improve employee motivation may be a waste of time if the cause
of poor performance is actually one or more of the other elements in the
model. Let's take a closer look at these four components of individual performance.

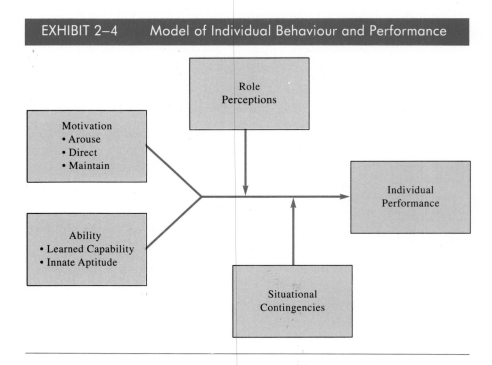

EXHIBIT 2–4   Model of Individual Behaviour and Performance

ABILITY

Ability includes both the learned capability and innate aptitude to engage in a task.[16] Learned capabilities include the necessary skills and knowledge developed from experience or practice required to complete the task. For example, an investment analyst is more likely to perform the job successfully if he or she keeps abreast of the latest stock offerings and market trends. People become productive word processing operators by practicing their typing skills and learning about different software commands and options. Matching employee abilities with job requirements has a significant effect on the quantity and quality of work output and may improve work attendance and reduce turnover.[17]

People have natural talents, called **aptitudes,** which help them learn specific tasks more quickly and perform them better. Experts have defined dozens of aptitudes pertaining to sensory capacity, motor functions, mechanical and clerical potential, intellectual abilities, creativity, and other facets of human activity. A few of these are listed in Exhibit 2–5. Specific aptitudes contribute to performance only when they are matched with corresponding job requirements. For instance, finger dexterity—the ability to handle small objects with the fingers—is probably more important for em-

ability
The learned capability and innate aptitude to engage in a task.

aptitudes
Natural talents which help people learn specific tasks more quickly and perform them better.

EXHIBIT 2–5	Selected Mental and Physical Aptitudes
Numerical aptitude	Ability to perform mathematical operations quickly and accurately.
Verbal aptitude	Ability to understand the meaning of words and to use them effectively.
Auditory acuity	Ability to distinguish the pitch and loudness of different sounds.
Colour discrimination	Ability to perceive or recognize similarities or differences in colours; to distinguish shades or other values of the same colour; to recognize harmonious or contrasting colour combinations.
Manual dexterity	Ability to move arms and hands easily and skillfully in handling fairly large objects under speeded conditions.
Finger dexterity	Ability to make skillful and controlled manipulations of small objects, involving primarily finger movements.
Spatial reasoning	Ability to mentally visualize or assemble two- or three-dimensional figures or objects.
Clerical perception	Ability to perceive details, including similarities, differences, and errors, in verbal or tabular material.

ployees working with micro-sized precision parts at Litton Systems Canada Ltd. than for warehouse workers in the same firm who typically grasp large objects.

Job Analysis

job analysis
Systematic collection of information about jobs, including required tasks, equipment and other resources used, work context characteristics, and required employee attributes.

To match employee skills, knowledge, and aptitudes with the required tasks, organizations must first conduct a job analysis. **Job analysis** involves systematically collecting the following information about jobs:[18]

- Required job duties.
- The equipment and other resources used to perform the job.
- Characteristics of the work context.
- Employee characteristics required to perform the job successfully.

job specification
A description of the aptitudes, skills, and knowledge required to perform the job as well as preferred work-related interests.

Job analysis is typically conducted by interviewing job incumbents and their supervisors, but task inventory questionnaires and observation may also be used to collect this information. The results are then written into job descriptions. The employee characteristics required to perform the job successfully are known as **job specifications** and include aptitudes, skills, and knowledge as well as information about the work-related interests. For example, a job specification for salesclerks at The Bay might include verbal fluency, basic mathematical skills, and an interest in working with people.

The Canada Employment and Immigration Commission, a department of the Canadian government, has analyzed thousands of jobs across the country and has prepared a large inventory of job descriptions called the *Canadian Classification and Dictionary of Occupations* (CCDO). CCDO job descriptions help job applicants find out more about jobs and enable vocational counsellors to connect people to jobs that match their abilities and interests.

EXHIBIT 2–6	Matching Abilities with Job Requirements
Method	**Description**
Selection	• Collect information about knowledge, skills, aptitudes, interests, and other characteristics of job applicants.
	• Match applicant characteristics with required job duties and job specifications.
Training	• Employ systematic programs to help employees acquire necessary skills and knowledge more quickly.
	• Conduct training needs assessment to determine whether training is required, where, and for whom.
Job redesign	• Identify employee's existing abilities.
	• Alter job duties to match existing abilities.

With a clear understanding of the job, employers next try to ensure that people have the qualities required for the jobs to which they are assigned. In other words, the incumbents' abilities should be the same as those stated in the job specification. Three of the most common strategies include selection, training, and job redesign (see Exhibit 2–6).

Selection

Employee selection involves collecting information about the characteristics of job applicants and evaluating this information in light of the job duties and specifications identified through job analysis. Basically, selected applicants must possess the required abilities to do the job, and the job should include tasks that are valued by job applicants.[19] Supervisors, human resource staff, and sometimes coworkers assess job candidates through application forms, employment interviews, ability tests, and a variety of other selection methods. As Exhibit 2–7 illustrates, job applicants may be evaluated several times using different selection methods before finally being accepted for employment.[20]

Current employees may go through a similar process when being considered for promotion or transfer. For example, Montreal-based Alcan Ltd. (the world's largest aluminum manufacturer), uses **assessment centres** to identify production staff who are able to assume supervisory jobs. This selection method uses team exercises, team discussions, and interviews with assessors to determine which employees possess the skills required for promotion.[21] Whether for outside applicants or current employees seeking promotion, the purpose of the selection process is the same: to identify people who are qualified for the job.

employee selection

The process of deciding which applicants would best perform the job. This involves collecting information about the characteristics of job applicants and evaluating this information in light of the job duties and specifications identified through job analysis.

assessment centres

An employee selection procedure that uses group exercises, group discussions, and interviews with assessors to decide the best job candidate(s).

Training

Training programs are designed to help employees improve job performance by learning job-related skills and knowledge. Some programs also attempt to improve employee motivation and role perceptions. Training cannot change the natural aptitudes that employees possess, but effectively designed and

---

EXHIBIT 2–7   The Employee Selection Process

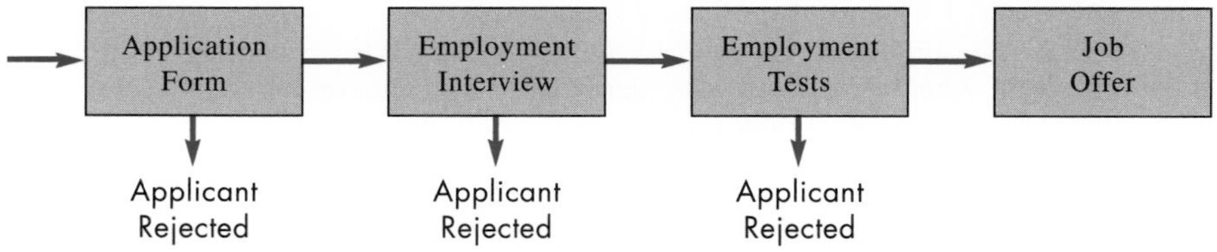

Application Form → Employment Interview → Employment Tests → Job Offer

Application Form → Applicant Rejected
Employment Interview → Applicant Rejected
Employment Tests → Applicant Rejected

implemented programs can allow people to acquire skills and knowledge more efficiently. According to one estimate, training is one of the most effective management interventions for improving employee productivity.[22]

Canadian firms collectively invest nearly $1.5 billion annually on formal employee training. This figure is somewhat misleading, because three-quarters of Canadian companies spend nothing on formal training whereas most training funds are spent by a handful of firms. Xerox Canada invests $1,600 per employee each year on training and IBM Canada spends almost twice that amount per employee annually. Stadium Corp., which operates Toronto's Skydome, has established "Skydome University" in which most full-time employees will eventually complete several customer service courses to make the entertainment centre more competitive.[23] Of course, the quality of training depends not only on the financial investment, but also on the design and implementation of these programs. Exhibit 2–8 highlights the main features of well-designed and well-implemented training programs.

Job Redesign

Rather than changing the job incumbent through selection or training, organizations may consider changing the job to match the employee's existing abilities. If an employee cannot perform a particular task in the original job

---

EXHIBIT 2–8   Maximizing Training Effectiveness

- Conduct a training needs assessment to determine whether training is required to improve individual performance, where it is required, and for whom.
- Based on the needs assessment, establish behavioural objectives of the training program.
- Ensure that trainees possess the abilities and motivation necessary to successfully complete the program.
- Present information in a manageable and logical sequence, using language and examples that increase its meaningfulness to trainees.
- Provide sufficient opportunities to practice what has been taught in an environment that is comparable to the actual work site (e.g., practice on similar equipment).
- Provide effective feedback to trainees as they practice the newly learned skills.
- Ensure that the work environment supports continued use of the skills and knowledge learned in the training program.
- Evaluate training effectiveness by investigating trainee reactions to the program, whether trainees have learned the information presented, and whether trainees are applying the learned activities on the job.

Sources: Based on I. L. Goldstein, *Training in Oganizations* (Monterey, Calif.: Brooks/Cole, 1986); and K. N. Wexley and G. P. Latham, *Developing and Training Human Resources in Organizations,* 2nd edition (Glenview, Ill.: HarperCollins, 1991).

description, it may be possible to assign this duty to someone else until the employee develops the requisite knowledge and skills. Several organizations, such as Volvo and Shell Canada Resources, have developed team-based production systems in which new staff are given a few basic tasks. As they learn new skills, employees receive more challenging assignments with a correspondingly higher rate of pay.

ROLE PERCEPTIONS

Role perception refers to a person's beliefs about what is required to achieve desired results. In terms of job performance, employees understand the specific tasks that make up the job, their relative importance, and the preferred behaviours to accomplish those tasks. Role perceptions steer the employee's effort toward a particular set of goals. If those goals are inappropriate, then performance suffers because effort and ability have been directed toward the wrong activities.[24]

People develop inaccurate role perceptions if they receive inconsistent information from different sources. For example, your supervisor may emphasize that customer service is most important, but coworkers convince you that it is more important to work on inventory controls. Personal needs, values, and previous training also affect your perception of the relative importance of different job duties.

Role perceptions may become distorted because the organization provides insufficient information about the job duties or the procedures required to accomplish those work objectives. This problem may be minimized by carefully analyzing the job and presenting the results to job incumbents. Managers should also be encouraged to regularly review the job duties of their employees, provide frequent and meaningful performance feedback, and work with employees in setting specific work-related goals for the future. We will discuss goal setting and feedback in more detail later in this chapter.

role perception
A person's beliefs about what is required to achieve the desired results, including the specific tasks that make up the job, their relative importance, and the preferred behaviours to accomplish those tasks.

SITUATIONAL CONTINGENCIES

Situational contingencies are environmental conditions surrounding the job that may constrain or facilitate employee behaviour and performance. At least in the short term, they are beyond the individual's control. Situational constraints interfere with the conversion of the individual's motivation and ability into effective work performance. In particular, a job cannot be done well if there is not enough time, people, budget, or facilities.[25]

Facilitating conditions potentially increase performance without any changes in motivation, ability, or role perceptions. For example, new technology may dramatically increase employee productivity. Redesigned workstations may reduce the amount of physical movement required to complete the job. Increased payroll budgets allow departments to hire more people to

situational contingencies
Environmental conditions surrounding the job and beyond the employee's immediate control that constrain or facilitate employee behaviour and performance.

handle the volume of work. Each of these facilitators may result in higher productivity even though employee abilities, motivation, and role perceptions are unaltered.

EMPLOYEE MOTIVATION

motivation

The internal forces that arouse, direct, and maintain a person's voluntary choice of behaviour.

Motivation is defined as the internal forces that arouse, direct, and maintain a person's voluntary choice of behaviour.[26] *Arousal* refers to the fact that motivational forces rise to a level of intensity sufficient to initiate behaviour. Motivation also has *direction* in the sense that it is aimed at achieving specific objectives or goals rather than random behaviours. Finally, motivation exists over a period of time. Employees are able to *maintain* their effort to perform the job until they decide to stop or they no longer have the capacity to carry on.

The Motivation Process: A Basic Framework

needs

Deficiencies that energize or trigger behaviours to satisfy those needs.

Exhibit 2–9 provides a useful framework to understand the elements of employee motivation. In most contemporary theories, the process of employee motivation begins with individual needs. **Needs** are deficiencies that energize or trigger behaviours to satisfy those needs. Some needs are physiological, such as the need for shelter, while others are psychological or sociological, such as the need for friendship. The important point to remember is that the stronger a person's needs, the more motivated he or she will be to satisfy those needs. Conversely, a satisfied need does not motivate.

Unfulfilled needs create a tension that triggers a search for ways to reduce or satisfy them. Specifically, employees consider relevant goals for need gratification and engage in behaviours that are believed to accomplish those goals. In some situations, goal accomplishment automatically results in the desired effect, such as the feeling of achievement when someone completes a challenging task. In other cases, the desired outcomes are contingent on the effective distribution of rewards by others. For example, you might put a lot of effort into performing your job, but this is no guarantee that you will receive the desired pay increase.

content theories of motivation

Theories that attempt to explain how people have different needs at different times.

In the final stage of the motivational process, employees reassess the extent that their needs have been satisfied. If need deficiencies persist, then the motivation process follows through another cycle as employees search for other goals and behaviours that may achieve the desired result. If a particular need becomes satisfied, employee motivation may be directed toward satisfying another need.

process theories of motivation

Theories that describe the processes through which needs are translated into behaviour.

Motivation theories can generally be placed into two categories. **Content theories of motivation** attempt to explain how people have different needs at different times. The next section presents three popular content theories of motivation: Maslow's need hierarchy, Alderfer's ERG theory, and McClelland's theory of learned needs. **Process theories of motivation** describe the

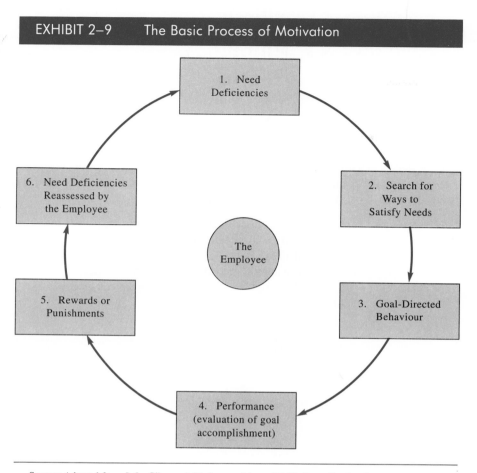

EXHIBIT 2–9   The Basic Process of Motivation

Source: Adapted from J. L. Gibson, J. M. Ivancevich, and J. H. Donnelly, Jr., *Organizations: Behavior, Structure, Processes* (Homewood, Ill.: Irwin, 1991), p. 101.

processes through which needs are translated into behaviour. These models explain how people choose goal-directed behaviours to satisfy their needs, but they do not directly explain how need deficiencies emerge. Chapter 3 describes the three prominent process models of motivation: expectancy theory, operant conditioning, and equity theory. A fourth process theory— goal setting—is described later in this chapter because it addresses both motivation and role perceptions, as previously noted.

CONTENT THEORIES OF MOTIVATION

Much of the earliest work on motivation focussed on the idea that people are motivated by the desire to satisfy unfulfilled needs. Over the years, psychologists have identified and categorized literally dozens of different needs that energize behaviour. Three of the best-known content theories are described below, including Maslow's need hierarchy theory, Alderfer's ERG theory, and McClelland's theory of learned needs.

Maslow's Need Hierarchy Theory

need hierarchy theory
Maslow's content theory of motivation, stating that people have a hierarchy of five basic needs—physiological, safety, belongingness, esteem, and self-actualization—and that as a lower need becomes gratified, individuals become motivated to fulfill the next higher need.

Abraham Maslow's **need hierarchy theory** consists of five basic human needs classified in a hierarchy of importance, as shown in Exhibit 2–10. The lowest three needs—physiological, safety, and belongingness—are known as deficiency needs because they are necessary for the person's basic comfort. Esteem and self-actualization needs are growth needs because they address the individual's personal growth and development.[27]

• *Physiological needs*—At the most basic level, people need to satisfy their biological needs such as food, air, water, and shelter. Organizations help fulfill these needs by providing comfortable working conditions and adequate wages to purchase food and shelter. Reasonable work hours and rest breaks also give employees the opportunity to satisfy their physiological needs.

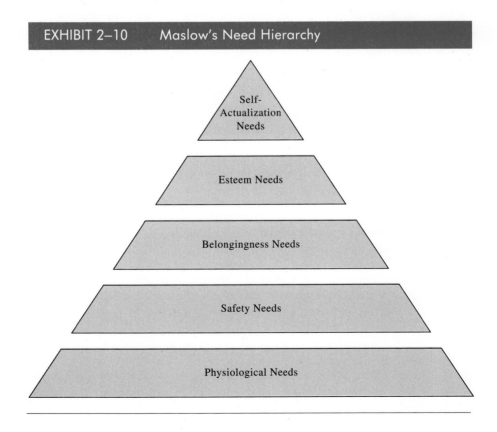

EXHIBIT 2–10   Maslow's Need Hierarchy

Self-Actualization Needs

Esteem Needs

Belongingness Needs

Safety Needs

Physiological Needs

- *Safety needs*—These include the need for a secure and stable environment and the absence of pain, threat, or illness. Employers may help satisfy safety needs by providing healthier and safer working conditions, avoiding the threat of layoffs, and providing insurance and retirement plans to protect against a sudden income loss.

- *Belongingness needs*—These needs refer to the person's need for love, affection, and interaction with other people. Organizational settings often provide opportunities to satisfy these needs as employees interact with each other throughout the workday. Office parties and sports activities also serve this important social function in the workplace.

- *Esteem needs*—The fourth level in Maslow's hierarchy refers to the need to develop self-esteem through personal achievement as well as social esteem through recognition and respect from others. Many companies, such as McDonald's, London Drugs, and Save-On Foods, motivate employees through this need by having an "Employee of the Month" whose picture is prominently displayed. Royal Bank and IBM Canada use company magazines to announce those who have won special performance awards.

- *Self-actualization needs*—The highest need level, according to Maslow, is the need for self-fulfillment—a sense that the person's potential has been realized. Several motivational strategies described in this book, including goal setting and job redesign, are based on this objective of helping employees experience self-actualization.

The basic premise of Maslow's model is that the lowest needs in the hierarchy are initially the most important and people are motivated to satisfy them first. Higher-order needs are not a significant source of motivation until the lower needs have been met. Physiological needs are initially the most important. As they become gratified, safety needs become the strongest motivator of behaviour. As safety needs are satisfied, belongingness needs become most important, and so forth. This is known as the **satisfaction-progression process** because as a need level is satisfied, the individual progresses to the next-higher level in the hierarchy. The exception to this process is self-actualization; according to Maslow, as people experience self-actualization they desire more rather than less of this need. Thus, with the exception of self-actualization, a satisfied need does not motivate.

Maslow's need hierarchy is intuitively appealing and has become one of the best-known management theories. However, research indicates that employee needs are more dynamic and unstable than Maslow's model suggests.[28] Gratification of one need level does not necessarily lead to increased motivation to satisfy the next need level. There is also evidence that people try to satisfy several need levels simultaneously rather than one at a time. Another problem is that individual needs do not cluster neatly around the

satisfaction-progression process
A basic premise in need hierarchy theory that people become increasingly motivated to fulfill a higher need as a lower need is gratified.

five categories described in the model. Overall, the need hierarchy model probably does not help us to understand the dynamics of employee motivation, but it has laid an important foundation for other need theories.

Alderfer's ERG Theory

ERG theory
Alderfer's content theory of motivation, stating that there are three broad human needs: existence, relatedness, and growth.

Clayton Alderfer has proposed a model, known as **ERG theory,** which attempts to overcome the criticisms of Maslow's need hierarchy theory. ERG theory groups human needs into three broad categories: existence, relatedness, and growth. (Notice that the theory's name is based on the first letter of each of these needs.) As Exhibit 2–11 illustrates, existence needs correspond to Maslow's physiological and physically related safety needs. Relatedness needs refer to Maslow's interpersonal safety, belongingness, and social-esteem needs. Growth needs correspond to Maslow's self-esteem and self-actualization needs.[29]

EXHIBIT 2–11	Maslow's and Alderfer's Need Theories Compared

Maslow's Need Hierarchy

Alderfer's ERG Theory

Self-Actualization Needs

(self)
– – – – Esteem Needs – – – – – – – – – – – – – – –
(social)

Belongingness Needs

(interpersonal)
– – – – Safety Needs – – – – – – – – – – – – – – – –
(physical)

Physiological Needs

Growth Needs

Relatedness Needs

Existence Needs

ERG theory also applies the satisfaction-progression process. As the lowest-level needs are satisfied, people progress to next-higher level in the ERG need hierarchy. However, Alderfer's theory differs from Maslow's by introducing a **frustration-regression process.** This process suggests that people who are unable to satisfy a higher need become frustrated and regress back to the next-lower need level. For example, if an individual's existence and relatedness needs have been satisfied, but growth need fulfillment has been blocked, he or she will become frustrated and relatedness needs will once again emerge as the dominant source of motivation.

ERG theory overcomes some of the limitations in Maslow's need hierarchy by providing a simpler and less-rigid explanation of the dynamics of employee needs. Human needs cluster more neatly around the three categories proposed by Alderfer than the five categories in Maslow's hierarchy. The combined processes of satisfaction-progression and frustration-regression also provide a more accurate explanation of why employee needs change over time. Overall, support for ERG theory is promising, but it is a fairly recent concept and more study is required.

frustration-regression process
A basic premise in ERG theory that people who are unable to satisfy a higher need become frustrated and regress back to the next lower need level.

McClelland's Theory of Learned Needs

David McClelland has devoted his career to studying three basic needs that he considers particularly important sources of motivation:[30]

- *Need for achievement*—A desire to accomplish moderately challenging performance goals, be successful in competitive situations, assume personal responsibility for work (rather than delegating it to others), and receive immediate feedback.
- *Need for power*—A desire to control one's environment, including people and material resources. Some people have a high "socialized power" need in which they seek power for altruistic purposes, whereas those with a strong "personal power" need seek power for the experience of power itself and to fulfill personal interests.
- *Need for affiliation*—A desire to seek approval from others, conform to their wishes and expectations, and avoid conflict and confrontation. People with a strong affiliation need want to form positive relationships with others, even if this results in lower job performance.

Research suggests that people with a high need for achievement make better entrepreneurs because they are able to work alone toward the challenging goal of establishing a new business. They tend to perform less well as senior executives, however, because these posts require incumbents to delegate work and seldom provide immediate feedback. The best managers are those with a moderately high need for socialized power because they use power to achieve organizational objectives. Effective managers must also

---

PERSPECTIVE 2–1   Satisfying Employee Needs through Flexible Benefits

Several Canadian firms have introduced flexible benefits systems to give employees the opportunity to participate in the composition of their individual benefit packages. These plans include a set of *core benefits* required for all employees (such as basic health insurance, unemployment insurance, and long-term disability), plus a *flexible dollar allowance* to purchase optional benefits. For example, an employee might be given $1,000 in flexible dollars with which to purchase additional vacations, a more complete dental plan, and additional life insurance.

The amount of flexible dollars allotted by the employer typically increases with the employee's base salary. However, some plans allow employees to increase the flexible dollar allowance by "selling" certain core benefits. For instance, employees at Cominco Ltd. may sell up to five holidays. They may also sell their basic medical coverage if this benefit is provided through their spouse's benefit plan.

Flexible benefit systems are expensive to implement, but they appear to be a success among employees and employers. A senior manager at Saskatchewan-based International Minerals and Chemicals Ltd. explains the main advantage of flexible benefits: "Our employees have the opportunity to choose coverage that's most suitable for them, and they can change the benefits as their needs change over time."

The work force of the 1990s is more diverse than ever before and people want benefits to fit their own personal needs rather than those of the average worker. This was quite apparent when Reichhold Ltd. introduced flexible benefits at its operations in Thunder Bay and North Bay. Virtually every employee made changes to the previous benefit package, particularly by increasing or decreasing the amount of life insurance and dental plan coverage.

Flexible benefits also allow employers to add more

---

have a fairly low need for affiliation so that their decisions and actions are influenced more by the need to accomplish organizational objectives than by a personal need for approval.[31]

Learning Needs. McClelland believes that needs are basically learned and reinforced rather than instinctive (as Maslow's and Alderfer's theories assume). He proposes, for instance, that the need for achievement is nurtured early in life through children's books, parental styles, and social norms. He has also demonstrated that adults may develop stronger needs through training and socialization.

McClelland has demonstrated that the achievement motive may be learned through a training program that he developed. Trainees are taught to act like people with a high need for achievement by recognizing and practicing imaginative stories written by high achievers. Achievement oriented behaviours are practiced in business games and trainees examine their own personal and work situations to see whether a high need for achievement is consistent with their self-image, values, and career plans. Finally, trainees complete a detailed achievement plan for the next two years and form a reference group with others in the program to maintain their new-found achievement motive style.[32]

optional benefits. At a time when benefits represent over one-third of an employee's total compensation, many companies cannot afford to add more perquisites in traditional plans. In a flexible plan, however, new benefits options can be added at almost no additional expense. For example, when National Life of Canada recently introduced a flexible benefits system, it was able to include public transit passes, day-care subsidies, and several other new options. Employees may use their flexible benefit dollars to select one or more of these benefits as well as those previously available.

In addition to these advantages, Reichhold Ltd. introduced flexible benefits because it was more consistent with the open, participative management style that emerged in their firm over the previous decade.

Rather than telling employees what they wanted, Reichhold management wished to open up the communication channels with its staff and let them decide which benefits they preferred.

Employee benefits may be the forgotten element of compensation in most firms, but flexible plans have shown that benefits can give employers the competitive edge. Managers at Cominco Ltd. observe that their system has had a positive effect on the firm's ability to attract and retain employees. For example, one employee refused to transfer to a Cominco subsidiary that did not have a flexible benefits system. The employee finally consented to the transfer when Cominco agreed to administer his benefits through their own flexible benefits plan.

Sources: S. Deller, "Flexing Your Benefits," *Benefits Canada* 10 (March 1986), pp. 31–35; B. Aarsteinsen, "Workers Can Choose Own Benefits," *Globe and Mail*, August 21, 1986, p. B16; and M. Gibb-Clark, "They've Got a Ticket to Ride," *Globe and Mail*, January 10, 1991, p. B5.

Businesspeople completing McClelland's program have shown significant improvement compared to a matched sample of nontrainees. For example, course participants in several small cities in India subsequently started more new businesses, had greater community involvement, invested more in expanding their businesses, and employed twice as many people as nonparticipants. Research on similar achievement-motive courses for small-business owners in North America reported dramatic increases in the profitability of the participants' businesses.

Managerial Implications of Content Theories

Content theories of motivation suggest that different people have different needs at different times. Therefore, to increase work motivation, organizations must look carefully at the variety of jobs and rewards that employees desire. Organizational surveys can be conducted to find out which organizational rewards are valued more than others across the work force and within occupational groups or job levels. At the departmental level, supervisors should pay more attention to the needs and reward preferences of individual employees. The type of jobs and assignments that people receive should also be more carefully matched to their dominant needs. For example, employees with strong affiliation needs may be more effective in jobs that involve working directly with clients or other people.

Another solution is to offer employees their choice of rewards.[33] Most organizations currently distribute the same reward, such as a salary increase or bonus, to all employees with good performances. In a flexible reward system, some employees who perform well might trade part of the bonus for extra time off. This idea has already been introduced in the form of flexible employee benefits. **Flexible benefits** programs allow employees to select benefits that match their particular needs. As Perspective 2–1 explains, this strategy serves the interests of both employees and the organization. The important point to remember here is that employees are not all alike; rewards that motivate some people will not work for others.

flexible benefits
Employee benefits programs that allow employees to select benefits matching their particular needs.

GOAL SETTING

Employee motivation and performance are strongly influenced by the extent to which people are directed by goals. **Goals** are the immediate or ultimate objectives that employees are trying to accomplish from their work efforts. There are many types of goals, including deadlines, performance standards, quotas, and budget requirements, as the following examples illustrate:

goals
The immediate or ultimate objectives that employees are trying to accomplish from their work efforts.

- Finish the meeting with this client by 11 A.M. (deadline goal).
- Keep product rejects below 1.5 percent (performance standard goal).
- Make 10 calls to new customers each week (quota goal).
- Keep the marketing cost of widgets under $50,000 this year (budget goal).

Goal setting is effective because it improves role perceptions by focussing employee efforts on the required task. It also enhances employee motivation by emphasizing the intrinsic reward of task accomplishment. Many Canadian organizations are dedicated to goal setting for supervising employees and directing the organization. For example, Sunquest Vacations Ltd. has 20 percent of the Canadian tour business partly because president Pat Brigham sets tough goals for his staff. This emphasis on goals is even reflected in the company's motto of "No empty seats," referring to the objective that its charter flights should be fully booked.[34]

Characteristics of Effective Goals

Goal setting may seem like a rather simple procedure, but the four conditions diagrammed in Exhibit 2–12 are necessary to maximize task effort and performance.[35]

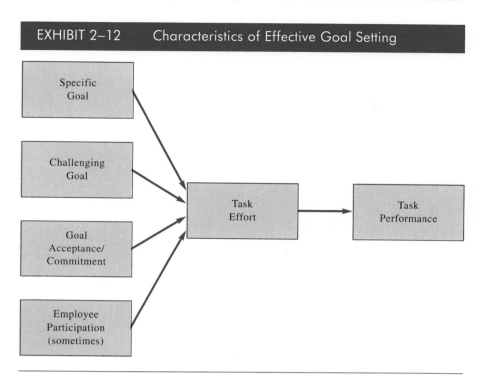

EXHIBIT 2–12   Characteristics of Effective Goal Setting

Specific Goals.   Employees put more effort into a task and tend to reach substantially higher levels of performance when they work toward specific performance goals rather than "do your best" targets. A specific goal would typically include a quantitative level of change over a specific time period, such as "Reduce scrap rate by 7 percent over the next six months." Specific goals communicate more precise performance expectations, resulting in a more efficient and reliable application of individual effort.

Challenging Goals.   Employee motivation and performance increase with the level of goal difficulty—up to a point. Generally speaking, harder goals lead to greater effort and persistence than easier goals. Also, the more challenging the goal, the greater the potential reward in terms of self-actualization.[36] Of course, employees will reject goals that appear to be too difficult. Consequently, managers need to carefully determine the level at which a goal is challenging but still acceptable, shown as point B in Exhibit 2–13.

Goal Commitment.   Goal setting will only work if the employee is committed to the goal. In other words, the goal must be accepted and hopefully embraced with enthusiasm by the person responsible for accomplishing that goal. Goal commitment is more likely to occur when employees have the

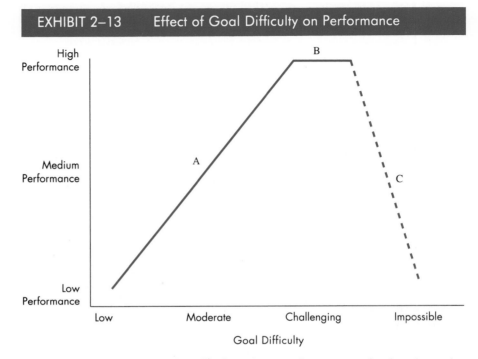

EXHIBIT 2–13   Effect of Goal Difficulty on Performance

Point A: Performance of qualified employees who are committed to the goal.
Point B: Performance of qualified employees who are committed to the goal and working at capacity.
Point C: Performance of qualified employees who lack goal commitment.

Source: E. A. Locke and G. P. Latham, *Goal Setting: A Motivational Technique That Works!* © 1984, p. 22. Reprinted by permission of Prentice Hall, Englewood Cliffs, New Jersey.

ability to accomplish the goal, believe that they can accomplish it, and have publicly shown their support for it. Goal commitment is also enhanced when coworkers support the goal and either the goal is assigned by someone respected or employees are involved in the goal-setting process.[37]

Participation in Goal Formation (Sometimes). Having employees participate in goal setting increases their performance under certain conditions.[38] First, participation tends to increase goal acceptance and commitment, so employees should help set goals when it appears that assigned goals would be rejected or receive only limited support. Second, employee participation in the goal-setting process may result in better goals. Thus, employees should be involved in the goal-setting process when their knowledge would improve goal quality.

Goal Feedback.   Feedback is another necessary condition for effective goal setting. Without feedback, employees would not know whether the goal has been achieved or even whether they are properly directing their effort toward goal accomplishment. Goal setting is most effective when feedback has certain qualities, which we discuss next.

PROVIDING EFFECTIVE FEEDBACK

Feedback is information relating to the consequences of employee behaviour. Feedback is often received from others, such as supervisors, clients, and coworkers. For example, professional sales representatives can see from a client's gestures and actions whether a particular sales approach is effective. Other sources of feedback are more impersonal, such as quarterly market share reports or daily quality control counts. The job itself can also be a source of feedback. For example, skilled tradespeople can usually see how well they have done a particular job by looking at it.[39]

Feedback is important because it helps employees *learn* whether their behaviours are having the desired effect. That is, feedback improves role perceptions. For example, by watching the dial of an instrument, a technician can tell whether the pressure valve has been opened enough or too much. By learning which actions work and which are ineffective, employees can redirect their energies to improve performance. Without feedback, learning would not be possible.[40]

Feedback may also *motivate* employees, particularly those who have a strong need for achievement.[41] When you finish a difficult task, a sense of accomplishment is felt only when you learn that your effort has been successful. Sometimes this is apparent as soon as the job is done because you can see the results. In other situations, feedback comes through others, such as praise from supervisors or customers. At the Calgary Public Library, branch supervisor Maria Vikas emphasizes quality feedback for her staff. "I show that I appreciate their work and try to praise them as frequently as I can," she says. "It's a never ending circle: the more you praise people, the better they feel and the more work they do that is worth praising."[42] Whether by improving role perceptions or motivation, feedback may significantly increase employee performance, as Perspective 2–2 illustrates.

feedback
Information relating to the consequences of employee behaviour.

Monitoring Employee Performance

One of the more contentious issues in feedback management is the use of computers and other electronic equipment to monitor employee performance. For example, a computer system at Bell Canada monitors the performance of telephone operators, including how many calls each has made, the average length of time per call, and whether this performance is better or worse than other operators on that work shift.

PERSPECTIVE 2–2   Improving Efficiency through Feedback at Westar Mining

Senior managers at Vancouver-based Westar Mining knew that its mine could be much more efficient, but they lacked the basic statistics to find out where productivity could be improved. One area of interest was the availability of the large ore-carrying dump trucks at the mine. These large vehicles are put through fairly demanding tasks and represent a large investment to the company.

Not surprisingly, ore-carrying dump trucks require occasional repair and routine maintenance, but company officers were surprised when the first data on dump truck availability began to flow into head office.

They found that over half of these trucks were in for repairs at any one time, leaving only a small proportion of the fleet available for work. This information was passed along to employees at the mine, who were also surprised to see such a low availability rate.

To resolve the problem, Westar regularly collected availability figures and widely posted this information for everyone at the mine to see. The availability of ore-carrying dump trucks began to rise noticeably and, after five years, the availability rate had increased to about 80 percent of the fleet.

Source: P. E. Larson, ''Achieving Corporate Excellence,'' *Canadian Business Review*, Winter 1987, pp. 38–40.

Critics suggest that monitoring is a repressive management control practice and an invasion of employee privacy. It can also cause supervisors to emphasize the measured elements of job performance and ignore the more subjective factors. Bell Canada stopped monitoring experienced operators for this reason. It realized that supervisors were evaluating their performance based on the number of calls and the amount of time per call, while customer service seemed to be of little importance. Now that monitoring is used only to train new staff, experienced operators believe that customer service has improved and that their supervisors seem to place more emphasis on the quality of operator service to the caller.[43]

While monitoring may have its limitations, proponents point out that this activity helps employees perform their jobs better by providing specific and timely feedback, particularly where supervisors are otherwise unable to directly observe their staff. Recent studies have concluded that most employees respond positively to monitoring when it is used to provide positive, developmental feedback.[44]

Characteristics of Effective Feedback

Organizational research has identified four basic elements of effective feedback, which may be summarized by the memorable acronym PIGS: positive, immediate, graphic, and specific (see Exhibit 2–14).[45] Job performance depends on effective feedback, so we will describe these characteristics more fully.[46]

EXHIBIT 2–14   Characteristics of Effective Feedback

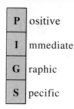

P ositive

I mmediate

G raphic

S pecific

Positive (or Neutral) Feedback.   Feedback is more useful when presented in a positive or neutral manner. People actively seek positive information about their performance and managers should go out of their way to provide this information. When the news is less favourable, feedback should be presented in a neutral form. Computer printouts, performance charts, electronic gauges, and other impersonal communication devices are very helpful in this respect because they let employees keep track of their own performance.[47] People don't like to hear bad news, of course, but they are more likely to accept this feedback from an impersonal self-generated source than from an angry division vice-president who publicly chastises employees for their sloppy work. In fact, the latter approach may cause employees to "doctor" information so that management never discovers the problem.

Immediate Feedback.   Feedback is most effective when it follows the behaviour as soon as possible because this makes the association between behaviour and consequences clearly evident. Ironically, feedback in most organizations lags by several weeks or months. In some cases, employees receive no meaningful feedback whatsoever about their personal or work unit performance even though management has this information available.

Graphic Feedback.   The saying "a picture is worth a thousand words" rings true when providing feedback in organizational settings. Many goal-setting programs introduce charts and diagrams to track changes in employee performance rather than simply telling people how they are doing. Graphic feedback helps employees visualize their progression. When prominently located in the workplace, feedback charts remind people of their goals and let them see their progress at any time.

Specific Feedback.   Just as effective goals must be specific, feedback must also be specific to the job being performed. Feedback should use objective standards such as "employee turnover has dropped to 10 percent annually" rather than "turnover has declined recently." At the same time, feedback should not become so specific that it is too complex for employees to understand.

Specific feedback also means that the information should be related to organizational goals. Without goals, feedback becomes meaningless and is often ignored.[48] Goals establish the benchmarks (i.e., what ought to be) against which feedback is judged. Thus, we come full circle to our earlier point that feedback is necessary for effective goal setting, just as goal setting is necessary for effective feedback.

SUMMARY

- Performance-related behaviours directly or indirectly influence the achievement of organizational objectives. They generally include joining the organization, remaining with the organization, maintaining work attendance, performing required job duties, and exhibiting organizational citizenship.

- Organizational citizenship behaviours contribute to organizational effectiveness by working beyond the required job duties, such as helping others and facilitating a positive work environment.

- Individual behaviour is influenced by four factors: ability (including aptitudes, skills, and knowledge), role perceptions, situational contingencies, and motivation.

- Employee ability may be matched with job requirements by conducting a job analysis, selecting people with the necessary characteristics, providing training so that employees learn job-related skills and knowledge, or changing the job to match the employee's existing abilities.

- Motivation consists of internal forces that arouse, direct, and maintain a person's voluntary choice of behaviour. The motivation process begins with need deficiencies, which cause employees to search for goals believed to satisfy them and to engage in goal-directed behaviour. Performance outcomes affect need fulfillment and the motivation process is repeated.

- Motivation theories address either the content or process of motivation. This chapter presents three content theories, which explain how people have different needs at different times.

- Maslow's need hierarchy proposes five basic needs—the lowest needs are initially most important, but higher needs become more important as the lower ones are satisfied. Alderfer's ERG theory includes three needs; in addition to Maslow's satisfaction-progression process, ERG theory states that frustrated needs cause people to fall back to the next-lower need level. McClelland studied three basic needs, which he proposed are learned rather than instinctive.

- Goal setting proposes that employee motivation and performance are strongly influenced by goals. Goals are more effective when they are specific, challenging, and accepted by the employee. Participative goal formation is important in some situations.

- Feedback is information relating to the consequences of employee behaviour. Effective feedback is positive, immediate, graphic, and specific (PIGS).

DISCUSSION QUESTIONS

1. Should organizations try to reduce employee turnover?
2. Describe five types of organizational citizenship behaviour.
3. Define aptitudes. Under what conditions are they important for employee performance?
4. Describe three ways to match employees with jobs.
5. How does McClelland's need theory differ from Maslow's need hierarchy theory and Alderfer's ERG theory?
6. Is employee participation an important element of goal setting?
7. How are goal setting and feedback related?
8. What are the advantages and disadvantages of monitoring employee performance?

NOTES

1. M. Driscoll, "Performance Test," *The Northern Miner* 5, no. 2 (February 1990), pp. 30–32.

2. T. S. Bateman and C. P. Zeithaml, *Management: Function and Strategy* (Homewood, Ill.: Irwin, 1990), pp. 516–17; and D. Katz and R. L. Kahn, *The Social Psychology of Organizations* (New York: Wiley, 1966), pp. 337–40.

3. C. Kentridge, "How to Attract and Keep Labour," *Small Business,* October 1989, pp. 43–44.

4. S. L. Rynes, "Applicant Attraction Strategies: An Organizational Perspective," *Academy of Management Review* 15 (1990), pp. 286–310.

5. "Getting and Keeping Good Employees Takes Effort," *Canadian Industrial Relations and Personnel Developments,* July 4, 1990, p. 715.

6. H. J. Arnold and D. C. Feldman, "A Multivariate Analysis of the Determinants of Job Turnover," *Journal of Applied Psychology* 67 (1982), pp. 350–60; and M. A. Abelson, "Examination of Avoidable and Unavoidable Turnover," *Journal of Applied Psychology* 72 (1987), pp. 382–86.

7. R. Linden, "Attrition Among Male and Female Members of the RCMP," *Canadian Police College Journal* 9 (1985), pp. 86–97.

8. Statistics Canada, Labour and Household Surveys Analysis Division, "Time Lost from Work for Personal Reasons," *The Labour Force,* May 1988.

9. G. Johns, "Understanding and Managing Absence from Work," in S. L. Dolan and R. S. Schuler (eds.), *Canadian Readings in Personnel and Human Resources Management* (St. Paul, Minn.: West, 1987), pp. 324–35.

10. J. Wolpin, R. J. Burke, M. Krausz, and N. Freibach, "Lateness and Absenteeism: An Examination of the Progression Hypothesis," *Canadian Journal of Administrative Sciences* 5 (September 1988), pp. 49–54; and A. Mikalachki and J. Gandz, *Managing Absenteeism* (London, Ont.: University of Western Ontario, 1982).

11. I. Ng, "The Effect of Vacation and Sick Leave Policies on Absenteeism," *Canadian Journal of Administrative Sciences* 6 (December 1989), pp. 18–27.

12. S. R. Rhodes and R. M. Steers, *Managing Employee Absenteeism* (Reading, Mass.: Addison-Wesley, 1990); N. Nicholson and G. Johns, "The Absence Culture and the Psychological Contract—Who's in Control of Absence?" *Academy of Management Review* 10 (1985), pp. 397–407;

J. K. Chadwick-Jones, *Absenteeism in the Canadian Context* (Ottawa: Labour Canada, July 1980); and D. F. Coleman and N. V. Schaefer, "Weather and Absenteeism," *Canadian Journal of Administrative Sciences* 7 no. 4 (1990), pp. 35–42.

13. R. A. Guzzo and B. A. Gannett, "The Nature of Facilitators and Inhibitors of Effective Task Performance," in F. D. Schoorman and B. Schneider (eds.), *Facilitating Work Effectiveness* (Lexington, Mass.: Lexington, 1988), pp. 21–41.

14. D. W. Organ, "The Motivational Basis of Organizational Citizenship Behavior," *Research in Organizational Behavior* 12 (1990), pp. 43–72; and R. Karambayya, "Good Organizational Citizens Do Make a Difference," in *Proceedings of the Annual ASAC Conference, Organizational Behaviour Division* 11 pt. 5 (1990), pp. 110–19.

15. C. I. Barnard, *The Functions of the Executive* (Cambridge, Mass.: Harvard University Press, 1938), pp. 83–84; and Katz and Kahn, *The Social Psychology of Organizations,* pp. 337–40.

16. C. C. Pinder, *Work Motivation* (Glenview, Ill.: Scott, Foresman, 1984), pp. 12–13.

17. J. E. Hunter and R. F. Hunter, "Validity and Utility of Alternative Predictors of Job Performance," *Psychological Bulletin* 96 (1984), pp. 72–98; and J. R. Terborg, "Validity and Extension of an Individual Differences Model of Work Performance," *Organizational Behavior and Human Performance* 18 (1977), pp. 188–216.

18. For a more detailed review of job analysis, see G. T. Milkovich, W. F. Glueck, R. T. Barth, and S. L. McShane, *Canadian Personnel/Human Resource Management: A Diagnostic Approach* (Plano, Texas: BPI, 1988), pp. 154–70.

19. L. H. Lofquist and R. V. Dawis, *Adjustment to Work* (New York: Appleton-Century-Crofts, 1969).

20. For more detail on employee selection, see R. D. Gatewood and H. S. Feild, *Human Resource Selection,* 2nd ed. (Orlando, Fla.: Dryden, 1990); and Milkovich, Glueck, Barth, and McShane, *Canadian Personnel/Human Resource Management: A Diagnostic Approach,* Chapter 9.

21. T. S. Turner and J. A. Utley, "Foreman Selection: One Company's Approach," *Personnel,* May–June 1979, pp. 47–55.

22. R. A. Guzzo, R. D. Jette, and R. A. Katzell, "The Effects of Psychologically Based Intervention Programs on Worker Productivity: A Meta-Analysis," *Personnel Psychology* 38 (1985), pp. 275–91.

23. M. Gibb-Clark, "Companies Invest More in Training," *Globe and Mail,* October 26, 1990, p. B11; and L. Goodson, "Training: Think Investment, Not Expense," *Human Resource Professional,* February 1991, pp. 18–20.

24. L. W. Porter and E. E. Lawler III, *Managerial Attitudes and Performance* (Homewood, Ill.: Irwin, 1968).

25. L. H. Peters, E. J. O'Connor, and J. R. Eulberg, "Situational Constraints: Sources, Consequences, and Future Considerations," *Research in Personnel and Human Resources Management* 3 (1985), pp. 79–115; and L. H. Peters and E. J. O'Connor, "Situational Constraints and Work: The Influences of a Frequently Overlooked Construct," *Academy of Management Review* 5 (1980), pp. 391–97.

26. Pinder, *Work Motivation,* pp. 7–10.

27. A. H. Maslow, "A Theory of Human Motivation," *Psychological Review* 50 (1943), pp. 370–96; and A. H. Maslow, *Motivation and Personality* (New York: Harper & Row, 1954).

28. M. A. Wahba and L. G. Bridwell, "Maslow Reconsidered: A Review of Research on the Need Hierarchy Theory," *Organizational Behavior and Human Performance* 15 (1976), pp. 212–40.

29. C. P. Alderfer, *Existence, Relatedness, and Growth* (New York: Free Press, 1972).

30. D. C. McClelland, *The Achieving Society* (New York: Van Nostrand Reinhold, 1961).

31. M. J. Stahl, "Achievement, Power, and Managerial Motivation: Selecting Managerial Talent with the Job Choice Exercise," *Personnel Psychology* 36 (1983), pp. 775–90; D. C. McClelland and D. H. Burnham, "Power Is the Great Motivator," *Harvard Business Review,* March–April 1976, pp. 100–10; and D. McClelland and R. Boyatzis, "Leadership Motive Pattern and Long-Term Success in Management," *Journal of Applied Psychology* 67 (1982), pp. 737–43.

32. D. C. McClelland and D. G. Winter, *Motivating Economic Achievement* (New York: Free Press, 1969); and D. Miron and D. McClelland, "The Impact of Achievement Motivation Training on Small Business," *California Management Review* 21 (1979), pp. 13–28.

33. A. Brown, "Today's Employees Choose Their Own Recognition Awards," *Personnel Administrator* 31 (1986), pp. 51–58.

34. C. Green, "Sunquest Tour Business Success No Joke," *Financial Post,* February 28, 1989, p. 16.

35. E. A. Locke and G. P. Latham, *A Theory of Goal Setting and Task Performance* (Englewood Cliffs, N.J.: Prentice Hall, 1990); A. J. Mento, R. P. Steel, and R. J. Karren, "A Meta-Analytic Study of the Effects of Goal Setting on Task Performance: 1966–1984," *Organizational Behaviour and Human Decision Processes* 39 (1987), pp. 52–83; and M. E. Tubbs, "Goal Setting: A Meta-Analytic Examination of the Empirical Evidence," *Journal of Applied Psychology* 71 (1986), pp. 474–83.

36. E. A. Locke and J. F. Bryan, "Performance Goals as Determinants of Level of Performance and Boredom," *Journal of Applied Psychology* 51 (1978), pp. 120–30.

37. E. A. Locke and G. P. Latham, *Goal Setting: A Motivational Technique That Works!* (Englewood Cliffs, N.J.: Prentice Hall, 1984), Chap. 5; Locke and Latham, *A Theory of Goal Setting and Task Performance,* Chapter 6; J. R. Hollenbeck and H. J. Klein, "Goal Commitment and the Goal-Setting Process: Problems, Prospects, and Proposals for Future Research," *Journal of Applied Psychology* 72 (1987), pp. 212–20; and E. A. Locke, G. P. Latham, and M. Erez, "The Determinants of Goal Commitment," *Academy of Management Review* 13 (1988), pp. 23–39.

38. Locke and Latham, *A Theory of Goal Setting and Task Performance,* Chapter 7.

39. M. G. Evans, "Organizational Behavior: The Central Role of Motivation," *Journal of Management* 12 (1986), pp. 203–22.

40. K. N. Wexley and G. P. Latham, *Developing and Training Human Resources in Organizations,* 2nd ed. (New York: HarperCollins, 1991), pp. 77–80; D. R. Ilgen, C. D. Fisher, and M. S. Taylor, "Consequences of Individual Feedback on Behavior in Organizations," *Journal of Applied Psychology* 64 (1979), pp. 349–71; and Locke and Latham, *A Theory of Goal Setting and Task Performance,* Chapter 8.

41. T. Matsui, A. Okada, and T. Kakuyama, "Influence of Achievement Need on Goal Setting, Performance, and Feedback Effectiveness," *Journal of Applied Psychology* 67 (1982), pp. 645–48.

42. "Profiles in Business," *Canadian Manager,* Spring 1987, pp. 11–12.

43. L. Archer, "I Saw What You Did and I Know Who You Are," *Canadian Business,* November 1985, pp. 76–83; and J. Coutts, "Bell Finds Morale Improved Since Monitoring Stopped," *Globe and Mail,* February 20, 1990, p. A14.

44. J. Chalykoff and T. A. Kochan, "Computer-Aided Monitoring: Its Influence on Employee Job Satisfaction and Turnover," *Personnel Psychology* 42 (1989), pp. 807–34.

45. F. Luthans, R. M. Hodgetts, and S. A. Rosenkrantz, *Real Managers* (Cambridge, Mass.: Ballinger, 1988), pp. 141–42.

46. T. K. Connellan, *How to Improve Human Performance: Behaviorism in Business and Industry,* (New York: Harper & Row, 1978), Chapter 8; and Locke and Latham, *A Theory of Goal Setting and Task Performance,* Chapter 8.

47. J. M. Ivancevich and J. T. McMahon, "The Effects of Goal Setting, External Feedback, and Self-Generated Feedback on Outcome Variables: A Field Experiment," *Academy of Management Journal* 25 (1982), pp. 359–72; and D. M. Herold, R. C. Linden, and M. L. Leatherwood, "Using Multiple Attributes to Assess Sources of Performance Feedback," *Academy of Management Journal* 30 (1987), pp. 826–35.

48. S. J. Ashford, "Feedback Seeking in Individual Adaptation: A Resource Perspective," *Academy of Management Journal* 29 (1986), pp. 465–87.

CHAPTER CASES

PUSHING PAPER CAN BE FUN

A large metropolitan city government was putting on a number of seminars for managers of various departments throughout the city. At one of these sessions the topic to be discussed was motivation—how we can get public servants motivated to do a good job. The plight of a police captain became the central focus of the discussion:

> I've got a real problem with my officers. They come on the force as young, inexperienced rookies, and we send them out on the street, either in cars or on a beat. They seem to like the contact they have with the public, the action involved in crime prevention, and the apprehension of criminals. They also like helping people out at fires, accidents, and other emergencies.
>
> The problem occurs when they get back to the station. They hate to do the paperwork, and because they dislike it, the job is frequently put off or done inadequately. This lack of attention hurts us later on when we get to court. We need clear, factual reports. They must be highly detailed and unambiguous. As soon as one part of a report is shown to be inadequate or incorrect, the rest of the report is suspect. Poor reporting probably causes us to lose more cases than any other factor.
>
> I just don't know how to motivate them to do a better job. We're in a budget crunch and I have absolutely no financial rewards at my disposal. In fact, we'll probably have to lay some people off in the near future. It's hard for me to make the job interesting and challenging because it isn't—it's boring, routine paperwork, and there isn't much you can do about it.
>
> Finally, I can't say to them that their promotions will hinge on the excellence of their paperwork. First of all, they know it's not true. If their performance is adequate, most are more likely to get promoted just by staying on the force a certain number of years than for some specific outstanding act. Second, they were trained to do the job they do out in the streets, not to fill out forms. All through their career it is the arrests and interventions that get noticed.
>
> Some people have suggested a number of things like using conviction records as a performance criterion. However, we know that's not fair—too many other things are involved. Bad paperwork increases the chance that you lose in court, but good paperwork doesn't necessarily mean you'll win. We tried setting up team competitions based upon the excellence of the reports, but the guys caught on to that pretty quickly. No one was getting any type of reward for winning the competition, and they figured why should they bust a gut when there was no payoff.
>
> I just don't know what to do.

Discussion Questions

1. What performance problems is the captain trying to correct?
2. Use the performance model to diagnose the possible causes of this unacceptable performance.
3. Has the captain considered all possible solutions to the problem? If not, what else might he do?

Source: T. R. Mitchell and J. R. Larson, Jr., *People in Organizations,* 3rd ed. (New York: McGraw-Hill, 1987), p. 184.

WESTERN AGENCIES LTD.

Western Agencies Ltd. is a manufacturers' agent representing Stanfields, McGregors, and several other men's fashion manufacturers in Western Canada and the Pacific Northwest of the United States. Jack Arthurs began his employment at Western as a warehouse worker in 1962. In 1965, he became a sales representative and was given responsibility for the company's business in the interior region of British Columbia. In 1973, he was transferred back to Vancouver and assigned several large accounts, including all Eaton's stores in the Lower Mainland.

Over the years, Arthurs bought shares in the company and, by 1979, held nearly one-third of the company's issued non-voting shares. He also enjoyed a special status with the company founder and president, Mr. A. B. Jackson. Arthurs was generally considered Jackson's "number 1 man" and the president frequently sought Arthurs's ideas on various company policies and practices.

In 1980, the senior Mr. Jackson retired as president of Western Agencies and his son, C. D. Jackson, became president. C. D. Jackson was seven years younger than Arthurs and had begun his career in the warehouse under Arthurs's direct supervision. Arthurs had no illusions of becoming president of Western, saying that he had neither the education nor the skills for the job. However, he did expect to continue his special position as the top salesperson in the company, although this was not directly discussed with the new president.

Until 1987, Arthurs had an unblemished performance record as a sales representative. He had built up numerous accounts and was able to service these clients effectively. But Arthurs's performance began to change for the worse when Eaton's changed its buying procedures and hired a new buyer for Western Canada. Arthurs disliked Eaton's new procedures and openly complained to the retailer's new buyer and to her superiors. The Eaton's buyer resented Arthurs's behaviour and finally asked her boss to call Western Agencies to have Arthurs replaced. The Eaton's manager advised Jackson of the problem and suggested that another salesperson should be assigned to the Eaton's account. Jackson was aware of the conflict and had advised Arthurs a few months earlier that he should be more cooperative with the Eaton's buyer. Following the formal complaint, Jackson assigned another salesperson to Eaton's and gave Arthurs the Hudson Bay account in exchange. Jackson did not mention the formal complaint from Eaton's and, in fact, Arthurs believed that the account switch was due to an internal reorganization for the benefit of other salespeople employed at Western Agencies Ltd.

At about this time, several employees noticed that Arthurs was developing a negative attitude toward his clients and Jackson. He was increasingly irritable and rude toward customers, and was making derogatory comments toward Jackson. Arthurs even advised some of the younger employees that they should leave Western Agencies Ltd. and get into a sensible business. A phenomenon known as "pulling an Arthurs" became a topic of discussion around the office, whereby Arthurs would leave the office to go home in the mid-afternoon after announcing that he had had enough. Coworkers also noticed that Arthurs was becoming increasingly forgetful. He was often unable to remember stock numbers, colour codes, product lines, packaging modes, and other information essential for serving clients efficiently and completing orders accurately. These problems were subtle in 1987, but became quite pronounced and embarrassing over the next three years.

In May 1989, Arthurs and Jackson had a conflict relating to the purchase of a new company car. According to Jackson, Arthurs presented him with a quotation for a car which, in Jackson's view, included $2,500 in unnecessary options. Jackson informed Arthurs of his concerns and instructed him to find a car worth $13,000 instead of $16,000. Jackson then left town on business and when he returned was distressed to find that Arthurs had made his proposed car purchase with almost all of the unnecessary options. Jackson issued the cheque to pay for the car, but also included a note to Arthurs saying that he had lost confidence in the sales representative. It was about this time that Jackson contemplated firing Arthurs, but decided instead to be a "nice guy" and overlook the matter.

At the end of 1989, Jackson decided to reassign the North Vancouver independent accounts from Arthurs to another Western Agencies salesperson because the existing accounts had shown minimal growth and no new accounts were being added. Arthurs acknowledged that he had no time to find new accounts, but he denied Jackson's allegation that he was inadequately servicing the existing retailers in that area. At least one retailer later stated that Arthurs serviced his account well. Moreover, the salesperson assigned this territory added only a couple new accounts over the next two years.

In early 1990, the vice-president of marketing for Fields Stores called Jackson to say that Arthurs was not providing satisfactory service and that action should be taken if Western wanted to keep the Fields account. Arthurs had handled the Fields account for four or five years and there had been no problems until a new Fields buyer arrived. The new buyer complained that Arthurs was not providing sufficient promotional advice and assistance. She also expected Arthurs to take inventory counts, a practice that Arthurs resented and did not feel was properly part of his job. This was not the only retailer who expected Arthurs to count inventory, but Arthurs let them as well as Jackson know that he was an account builder, not an inventory stock counter. Eventually, the Fields buyer did not want to deal with Arthurs at all. In March 1990, matters were brought to a head when the Fields buyer and Arthurs had a major disagreement and Arthurs was not allowed back into any Fields stores. At this point, Jackson personally took over the Fields account and sales volume doubled within a few months.

A few months later, Western Agencies suffered several embarrassments over Arthurs's mishandling of the Work Wear World account. Arthurs had landed the Work Wear account a few years earlier when it was a small retailer with only two stores, but the company had subsequently grown into a regional chain of 10 stores. Problems began when Arthurs persuaded the Work Wear buyer to purchase a new line of stock by promising a manufacturer's allowance on an older line of goods. Arthurs had no authority to do this and, when the manufacturer refused to provide the allowance, Jackson had to personally explain that the allowance promise could not be honoured.

In late 1990, Arthurs mistakenly tripled a stock order for three of Work Wear's stores. This error was discovered when the second shipment arrived and Jackson instructed Arthurs to take immediate steps to cancel the third order. Arthurs failed to do so and Work Wear wound up with three times the inventory it had ordered. Work Wear's buyer subsequently gave Jackson the distinct impression that he should remove Arthurs from the account or risk losing Work Wear's business altogether.

For Jackson, Work Wear World's complaint was the last straw. In the spring of 1991, based on the series of incidents since 1987, Arthurs was dismissed from his job at Western Agencies Ltd.

Discussion Questions

1. What evidence is there that Arthurs was not performing his job well? Relate these incidents to specific performance standards.

2. Identify the cause(s) of Arthurs's poor performance. Could any of these root causes have been avoided?

3. Comment on Jackson's management of Arthurs's performance problems? What did he do well, and what should he have done more effectively?

© 1991 Steven L. McShane. This case is based on actual events described in a Canadian court case. Only the dates and names of the main parties have been changed.

EXPERIENTIAL EXERCISE

WORK CHARACTERISTICS IMPORTANCE EXERCISE

Purpose.   This exercise is designed to help you understand the dynamics of individual needs by comparing your personal preferences for various work characteristics against the work preferences of others in the class and across Canada.

Instructions.   Working alone, rank order the work characteristics listed in the table below in terms of their personal importance to you. Mark a 1 for the most important characteristic through to 12 for the least important. When the individual rankings have been completed, the instructor will form teams of four or five people and provide rankings based on a Canada-wide survey. Members of each team will compare their rankings with each other and the Canada-wide survey. Each team will also discuss the need hierarchy category in which each job characteristic should be placed. A class discussion of the reasons for different personal needs and the management implications will follow.

Work Characteristic	Personal Importance Ranking	Canadian Importance Ranking
People are friendly	_____	_____
Work is interesting	_____	_____
Job security is good	_____	_____
Surroundings are pleasant	_____	_____
Chances for promotion are good	_____	_____
See results of work	_____	_____
Not asked to do too much work	_____	_____
Given a lot of freedom	_____	_____
Have enough authority	_____	_____
Pay is good	_____	_____
Hours are good	_____	_____
Supervisor is competent	_____	_____

3

Process Theories of Motivation

LEARNING OBJECTIVES

After reading this chapter, you should be able to:

Discuss
The management implications of expectancy theory.

Compare
OB modification with expectancy theory.

Identify
Four contingencies of behaviour reinforcement.

Describe
The steps followed when implementing OB modification.

Define
The comparison other in equity theory.

Explain
How equity theory is applied in compensation
management.

Distinguish
Pay equity legislation from equal pay legislation.

CHAPTER OUTLINE

The Body Shop

By most standards, The Body Shop is a successful organization. Without spending one cent in advertising, the environmentally conscious retailer has boasted a 40 percent increase in sales *each year* over the past five years. Employee turnover has averaged less than 5 percent per annum.

One of the main reasons for The Body Shop's success is that its work force is motivated to fulfill the company's larger vision. This vision is based on the idea that businesses should maintain ethical standards while earning profits. According to Body Shop president Margot Franssen, this means linking business enterprise with customer needs, community interests, and environmental concerns. "We believe business should be an adjunct to life. It shouldn't be the pursuit of profit, but rather, it should fulfill a vision the company has. If employees aren't motivated by money alone, why should companies [be]?"

To fulfill this vision, The Body Shop motivates employees in several ways. First, the retailer pays performance bonuses on a team basis rather than individual commissions "to avoid the cruising-shark sales approach." This provides better customer service and ensures that people entering the store aren't pressured into making purchases they don't want. To serve the larger community, The Body Shop pays employees to work on a community project of their choice. According to Franssen, employees are eager to participate in this arrangement.

Of course, money is not the only source of motivation at The Body Shop. Employees also benefit from a supportive work group and comfortable work environment. The company carefully selects people who are dedicated to customer service and environmental interests. Thus, The Body Shop's practice of having employees work on community affairs fulfills more than a financial need. Explains Franssen: "It is the obligation of employers to offer employees a chance to have meaningful, soulful jobs, to educate and create a truly global community."[1]

The Body Shop is a vanguard organization both in terms of its corporate philosophy and ability to motivate employees to achieve corporate objectives. As you can see, the company motivates its staff in many ways. The content theories presented in Chapter 2 help us understand the basic needs that motivate employees. This chapter introduces three process theories—expectancy theory, organizational behaviour modification, and equity theory—which explain how people are motivated to choose different courses of action. For the most part, these models build on need theories, but each provides a unique perspective on the dynamics of employee motivation. Managers must be able to understand and apply each of these perspectives (as well as those in Chapter 2) in order to maximize employee motivation and performance.

EXPECTANCY THEORY

Expectancy theory is based on the idea that people will direct their efforts toward those actions that are perceived to lead to desired outcomes.[2] Through past experience, people develop expectations of whether they can achieve various levels of job performance. They also develop expectations of whether job performance and other work behaviours lead to particular outcomes. Finally, people learn which outcomes directly or indirectly satisfy basic needs.

Early versions of expectancy theory emerged in the writings of Kurt Lewin and other social psychologists of the 1930s, but Victor Vroom is generally credited with clarifying the various components of this theory within the work setting.[3] The version of expectancy theory presented in Exhibit 3–1 was developed by Edward E. Lawler and is relatively easy to remember, yet very effective at explaining employee motivation.[4]

The key variable to be explained in expectancy theory is **effort**—the individual's actual exertion of energy. According to Exhibit 3–1, effort level depends on three factors: (1) effort → performance expectancy, (2) performance → outcome expectancy, and (3) outcome valences. Employee motivation is influenced by all three components of the expectancy theory model. If any component weakens, motivation weakens.

expectancy theory

A process theory of motivation based on the idea that people will direct their effort toward those actions that are perceived to lead to desired outcomes.

effort

The individual's actual exertion of energy.

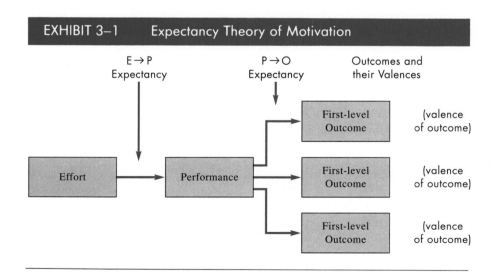

EXHIBIT 3–1   Expectancy Theory of Motivation

Effort → Performance Expectancy

**effort-to-performance
expectancy (E → P)**
An individual's perceived
probability that a particular
level of effort will result in a
particular level of
performance.

The **effort-to-performance expectancy (E → P)** is the individual's perception that his or her effort will result in a particular level of performance. Expectancy is defined as a *probability* and therefore ranges from 0.0 to 1.0. In some situations, employees may believe that they can unquestionably accomplish the task (a probability of 1.0), while in other situations they expect that even their highest level of effort will not result in the desired performance level (a probability of 0.0). In most cases, the E → P expectancy falls somewhere between these two extremes.[5]

Performance → Outcome Expectancy

**performance-to-outcome
expectancy (P → O)**
An individual's perceived
probability that a specific
behaviour or performance
level will lead to various
outcomes.

The **performance-to-outcome expectancy (P → O)** is the individual's perceived probability that a specific behaviour or performance level will lead to various outcomes. In extreme cases, employees may believe that a specific outcome will definitely occur if a particular task is accomplished (a probability of 1.0), or they may believe that this outcome definitely will not result from successful performance (a probability of 0.0). More often, the P → O expectancy falls somewhere between these two extremes. The higher the P → O expectancy, the higher the influence on employee motivation.

Outcome Valences

An infinite number of potential outcomes may result from job performance and other work behaviours, but we tend to consider P → O expectancies only for those outcomes that are of interest to us at the time. Some outcomes are basic needs, such as feelings of self-actualization. Other performance outcomes are indirectly associated with basic needs. For example, higher job performance might indirectly satisfy security needs for a newly hired employee if good performance leads to permanent job status.

valence
The anticipated satisfaction
or dissatisfaction that an
individual places on an
outcome.

Expectancy theory is less concerned with the specific outcomes believed to result from performance than with the **valences** of those outcomes to the employee. Valence refers to the anticipated satisfaction or dissatisfaction that an individual places on an outcome. Valences originate with the strength of our basic needs and range from negative to positive. Outcomes have a positive valence when they directly or indirectly satisfy the person's needs and have a negative valence when they aggravate the person's need fulfillment. Exhibit 3–2 lists the possible consequences of joining a particular company, including the valences that most people would probably assign to these outcomes. A senior manager at Toronto-based Telemedia Inc. summarizes the importance of valence in employee motivation this way: "The manager who can identify the particular needs that employees have and reward them accordingly . . . gets the most out of his people."[6]

EXHIBIT 3–2	Valences of Employment in Canada's Top Companies	

Company	Consequences of Becoming an Employee	Valence (for most of us)
Bombardier Inc.	• A work-relations committee at Valcourt enables employees to receive fair treatment.	Positive
Dupont Canada Inc.	• Better time off with pay than comparable manufacturing firms.	Positive
	• Limited promotion opportunities due to downsizing and young middle managers.	Negative
	• Employees are encouraged to take several courses to improve their knowledge.	Positive
Esso Resources Canada	• Company pays all the bills when employee is transferred.	Positive
	• Merger with Texaco has created uncertainty about future job duties and opportunities.	Negative
NovaTel Communications Ltd.	• Job applicants must complete a three-day assessment centre without pay.	Negative
	• Employees are offered far more responsibility than in other firms.	Positive

Source: Based on Eva Innes, Jim Lyon, and Jim Harris, *100 Best Companies to Work for in Canada* (Toronto: HarperCollins, 1990).

Practical Implications of Expectancy Theory

One of the appealing characteristics of expectancy theory is that it has rather explicit implications for managing employees. In order to increase employee motivation toward performance-related behaviours—or to reduce employee motivation regarding inappropriate work behaviours—managers must consider how to alter one or more components of the model.[7] Several practical applications of expectancy theory are listed in Exhibit 3–3 and described below.

Increasing the E → P Expectancy.   The expectancy that one's effort will improve job performance is influenced by actual experiences on the job and the person's general self-esteem.[8] Managers must therefore consider ways to ensure that employees are capable of reaching the desired levels of performance so that they form and maintain a strong belief that they are capable of doing the job successfully. This involves managing the other three components of the individual performance model described in Chapter 2. Specifically, employees tend to have a stronger E → P expectancy when they are provided with the necessary resources and other situational facilitators, possess the required abilities, and have clear role perceptions.

Employee aptitudes, skills, and knowledge must be matched with job requirements or the job should be changed to fit the incumbent's existing

EXHIBIT 3–3	Practical Applications of Expectancy Theory	

Expectancy Component	Managerial Objective	Management Applications
E → P expectancies	To increase the belief that employees are capable of performing the job successfully.	• Select people with the required skills and knowledge. • Provide required training and clarify job requirements. • Provide sufficient time, resources, etc. • Assign simpler or fewer tasks until employees can master them. • Show employees how their skills can accomplish the task. • Provide evidence and examples that similar employees have been successful. • Provide encouragement to employees who lack self-esteem or confidence.
P → O expectancies	To increase the belief that good performance will result in certain (valued) outcomes.	• Accurately measure job performance. • Clearly explain the outcomes that will result from future performance. • Describe how the employee's rewards have resulted from past performance. • Provide evidence and examples that good performance results in better rewards than poor performance.
Valences of outcomes	To increase the expected value of outcomes resulting from desired performance.	• Distribute rewards that employees value. • Individualize rewards. • Minimize the presence of countervalent outcomes.

abilities. For example, the Insurance Corporation of British Columbia assigns relatively simple automobile accident cases to newly hired adjusters. After a few months, when the claims centre manager sees that the adjuster feels confident with these files, more challenging cases are assigned.

Even with the requisite skills and knowledge, some employees may have a low E → P expectancy because they lack self-confidence or fail to see how their skills can help them reach the desired levels of performance. Thus, managers must use counselling and coaching skills to show how these skills and knowledge can lead to job success. Texas Instruments started using this approach after it discovered that recently hired production staff were anxious about their ability to perform the job. The company developed an orientation program in which newcomers were repeatedly informed that 99.6

EXHIBIT 3–4	Communicating the Performance–Reward Linkage at the Royal Bank

Two heads can be better than one

June Cousineau and Ann Glasford of the savings department in Calgary's Main branch proved that old adage when their idea submitted jointly to the Staff Suggestion Program got accepted.

After each had looked into separate inquiries from customers regarding service charges on statements, the pair compared notes and noticed a pattern. A number of debit memos posted to Calculator Accounts were getting through the bank's system without being assessed the appropriate service charge.

They identified the problem as a lack of something special to distinguish chargeable debit memos in the savings activity register from those that had no service charge.

Their solution was equally straightforward: Create a code to identify the chargeable debit memos. Branch operations, the referral area which evaluated the idea, accepted it and plan to put the suggestion into practice by next year.

For branch operations the cost of implementing the idea is minimal. For the bank, revenue will be realized that might otherwise be lost. And for June and Ann? Calculations are underway to determine the cash award the two women will share under the guidelines of the Staff Suggestion program.

June and Ann provide just one example of the kind of team effort that Royal bankers display every day – teamwork that pays dividends not only for the bank, but for employees themselves.

Thinking smart, working smart

Source: Royal Bank.

PERSPECTIVE 3–1   What Gets Rewarded Gets Done

Reward systems can have a powerful influence on employee motivation, but they may also motivate the wrong behaviours and inadvertently reduce other forms of performance. Here are a few examples:

- Employees at the Muskoka Canoe and Rowing Shop on Lake Muskoka, north of Toronto, received an individual cash award for each canoe sold. Canoe sales were well above expectations, but salespeople were fighting over customers and tended to ignore other duties such as refolding clothes and selling items for which there was no cash incentive. To correct these problems, the reward structure was overhauled so that salespeople received cash bonuses based on their overall performance, including sales, stock maintenance, and cooperation.
- Most companies in the Canadian mining industry have an incentive plan that has definitely increased employee productivity. Unfortunately, this reward system has also been linked with the number and severity of occupational accidents among miners. By motivating miners to complete more jobs in less time, the incentives encourage them to ignore safety procedures. Kidd Creek mine near Timmins, Ontario, is one of the few sites without special incentives and has one of the *lowest* accident records in metal mining. At least one government commission on mining safety recommended that these incentive plans be terminated in the mining industry.
- Many Canadian insurance firms pay sales agents large front-end commissions ranging from 150 to 200 percent of premiums during the year the sale was made. For example, if a customer buys a policy requiring $1,200 in first-year premium payments, the agent could immediately collect as much as $2,400 in commissions from the insurance company. Two problems result from this incentive

percent of those previously hired into the job were eventually successful. This information increased the E → P expectancy of new employees, resulting in a steeper learning curve and lower turnover.[9]

Increasing the P → O Expectancy.   The most obvious way to improve the P → O expectancy is to link rewards to performance-related behaviours. As the stories in Perspective 3–1 illustrate, this task is not as easy at it seems. Rewards may motivate undesirable behaviours with higher P → O expectancies than the intended behaviours. They may also unintentionally demotivate performance-related behaviours that are not directly rewarded.

It is also important to measure job performance accurately so that those with higher performance records must receive larger rewards. Otherwise, employees will fail to see any connection between good performance and organizational rewards. As one Montreal engineer lamented, "Ninety-nine percent of the people here are getting the same range of salary increase. Sometimes it looks like people working very hard are not getting any more appreciation or pay than someone who isn't working at all."[10] Chapter 4 examines various pay-for-performance strategies to improve the P → O expectancy.

While having a performance-based reward system is important, organizations must also communicate evidence that high-performance employees

system. First, agents become less concerned about whether the client can afford large premium payments. If the client defaults a few years later, the agent has already earned a healthy commission. Second, some unscrupulous agents engage in an illegal rebating scheme in which clients who cannot afford the premiums are offered free or discounted insurance for the first year. The agent pays for some of the first year premiums and still earns enough from the commission for a healthy income.

- Some insurance firms pay a higher commission rate to agents with higher annual sales. For exam-

ple, an agent selling policies with $50,000 in annual premiums might earn a 120 percent commission rate, whereas someone bringing in $300,000 in premiums would receive a 200 percent rate. To maximize their income, some agents group together and submit their combined sales under one person's name. The combined sales receive a much higher commission rate and the group splits a much higher income than if each worked alone. Insurance companies end up paying much higher incentives under this poorly designed incentive scheme.

Sources: Gordon Graham, "Perks that Work," *Small Business* 8 (November 1989), pp. 45–48; Ontario Ministry of Labour, *Towards Safe Production: Report of the Joint Federal–Provincial Inquiry Commission into Safety in Mines and Mining Plants in Ontario* (Burkett Commission) (Toronto: Queen's Printer, 1981); Terry Pender, "Miners' Bonus Wage System Comes under Ontario Scrutiny," *Globe and Mail*, August 22, 1986, p. A10; T. F. Cawsey and P. R. Richardson, "Employee Relations at the Kidd Creek Operations of Texasgulf Limited," in *Employee Relations Initiatives in Canadian Mining*, Proceedings No. 5 (Kingston, Ont.: Centre for Resource Studies, Queen's University, 1979), pp. 45–59; and James Fleming, *Merchants of Fear: An Investigation of Canada's Insurance Industry* (Toronto: Penguin, 1986), pp. 20, 79.

receive higher rewards. Supervisors need to carefully explain how good performance can lead to various rewards. When rewards are distributed, employees should understand how their bonus, promotion, or pay increase has been based on past performance.

Finally, employees can develop stronger P → O expectancies when they are shown past examples of the best performers receiving the highest rewards. Exhibit 3–4 shows how the Royal Bank uses advertisements in its employee magazine to let employees know that valuable ideas are rewarded. Also notice how this message attempts to increase the E → P expectancy by illustrating that average employees can make above-average contributions to the organization.

Increasing Outcome Valences. Increasing employee expectancies will have little effect on work motivation unless the performance outcomes are valued by employees. Consequently, to maximize the effectiveness of the reward system, we would ideally adapt the type of rewards offered to the needs of each individual.[11] As stated in Chapter 2, managers should pay more attention to the needs and reward preferences of individual employees. Organizations should also develop more individualized reward systems in which employees who perform well are offered a choice of rewards.

Finally, expectancy theory emphasizes the need to discover and neutralize countervalent outcomes. This refers to the situation in which some outcomes of good job performance have negative valences, thereby reducing the effectiveness of existing reward systems. For example, the motivational influence of incentive systems may be offset by team norms in which high-performance employees are chastised and labelled as "rate-busters" if they continue to exceed normal production standards. Employees who value their affiliation with coworkers will keep their performance within the levels accepted by the team even though it may mean a lower paycheque.

Does Expectancy Theory Fit Reality?

Researchers have been investigating the relevance of expectancy theory in organizational settings for the past quarter-century. Unfortunately, much of the earlier research has questionable value because of measurement and research design problems.[12] More recent studies have cleared up many of these problems, but the expectancy theory model will probably never be easy to fully test. Expectancy theory assumes that people are rational decision makers because it suggests that they tend to assess the costs and benefits of alternate courses of action and select the option with the highest payoff.[13] Consequently, the model does not perfectly represent human motivation because people are not perfectly efficient decision makers.

In spite of the conceptual and research limitations, it appears that the process of employee motivation is explained reasonably well by the expectancy theory model. All three components of the model have received some research support. There is particularly good evidence that P → O expectancies influence employee motivation.[14]

Expectancy theory addresses cognitive activities pertaining to employee motivation because it refers to employee thought processes such as expectations and feelings. In this respect, expectancy theory is quite different from the next theory we will discuss: organizational behaviour modification.

ORGANIZATIONAL BEHAVIOUR MODIFICATION

Organizational behaviour modification (OB Mod) is a theory of learning and motivation that explains organizational behaviour in terms of the events preceding and following that behaviour. This approach involves identifying and managing environmental conditions that maintain, strengthen, and weaken observable behaviour. OB Mod is an organizational variation of B. F. Skinner's theory of operant conditioning, also known as reinforcement theory, Skinnerian theory, and behaviour modification.

OB Mod is derived from two important operant conditioning concepts. First, OB Mod is a theory of **reinforcement;** it states that the likelihood that a behaviour will be repeated depends on its consequences. If a person does something that is followed by a pleasant experience, he or she will probably

reinforcement

Anything following a behaviour that increases the likelihood of the behaviour being repeated.

repeat that behaviour. On the other hand, if the behaviour is followed by an unpleasant experience or by no response at all, then it is less likely to be repeated. Notice that reinforcement explains future work experiences rather than just referring to past experiences. In this respect, OB Mod is a theory of learning as well as a theory of motivation. It explains how people learn to associate behaviours with specific outcomes. These learned responses then become the basis for future behaviour.

Second, OB Mod is a theory of **behaviourism**. It focuses entirely on behaviour and observable events, in contrast to expectancy theory, which describes beliefs and attitudes. This does not mean that OB Mod rejects the existence of human cognitions; rather, human thoughts are viewed as unimportant intermediate stages between behaviour and the environment.

behaviourism
A perspective that focusses entirely on behaviour and observable events, in contrast to thoughts and other cognitions.

A-B-Cs of OB Modification

The objective of organizational behaviour modification is to redirect behaviour by managing its antecedents and consequences. This is depicted in the A-B-C model presented in Exhibit 3–5.[15]

Antecedents.   Antecedents are environmental stimuli that provoke behaviour. They do not cause behaviour; rather, they act as *environmental cues* to inform employees that particular activities will have particular consequences. There are many types of antecedent cues: supervisors might instruct employees to follow specific procedures, buzzers might signal the end of a work shift, or a memorandum might describe a new incentive program.

Managing antecedents involves systematically introducing and removing these cues to control the likelihood of particular behaviours occurring in the future.[16] Managers must be proactive by scanning the work environment to ensure that the conditions are appropriate for productive employment. They must confirm that employees know what performance is expected, whether the standards are clear, and whether the desired behaviour can be realistically carried out.[17]

Behaviour.   *Behaviour* refers to anything that someone says or does. It may involve reducing wastage on each unit produced, reacting more quickly to specific problems, or improving attendance on scheduled workdays. Increasing the frequency or consistency of certain behaviours and reducing or eliminating undesirable behaviours are the central objectives of OB Mod programs. Thus, managers must be sure that employees are able to perform the desired behaviours and that situational contingencies such as resources and time are operating in the employee's favour.

Consequences.   Consequences are events following behaviour that influence its future occurrence. Consequences occur after the behaviour, but they are not necessarily caused by the behaviour.

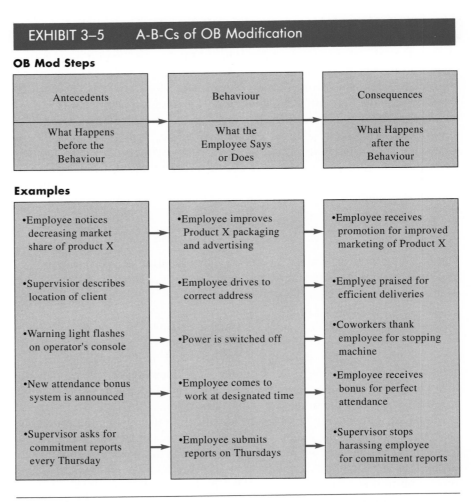

EXHIBIT 3–5   A-B-Cs of OB Modification

OB Mod Steps

Antecedents	Behaviour	Consequences
What Happens before the Behaviour	What the Employee Says or Does	What Happens after the Behaviour

Examples

•Employee notices decreasing market share of product X	•Employee improves Product X packaging and advertising	•Employee receives promotion for improved marketing of Product X
•Supervisior describes location of client	•Employee drives to correct address	•Emplyee praised for efficient deliveries
•Warning light flashes on operator's console	•Power is switched off	•Coworkers thank employee for stopping machine
•New attendance bonus system is announced	•Employee comes to work at designated time	•Employee receives bonus for perfect attendance
•Supervisor asks for commitment reports every Thursday	•Employee submits reports on Thursdays	•Supervisor stops harassing employee for commitment reports

Source: Adapted from Thomas K. Connellan, *How to Improve Human Performance* (New York: Harper & Row, 1978), p. 50.

As previously mentioned, reinforcement is one of the two dominant concepts in OB Mod, so it is only appropriate that much of our discussion of this theory is directed toward consequences. We now examine the four types of consequences—called the *contingencies of reinforcement*—and the five schedules used to administer these reinforcers.

Contingencies of Reinforcement

According to OB Mod, behaviour can be strengthened, maintained, or weakened by its consequences.[18] Four types of consequences, collectively known as the **contingencies of reinforcement,** have been identified and are summarized in Exhibit 3–6.

contingencies of reinforcement
The four types of events following a behaviour that may increase (reinforce) or decrease the likelihood that the behaviour will be repeated.

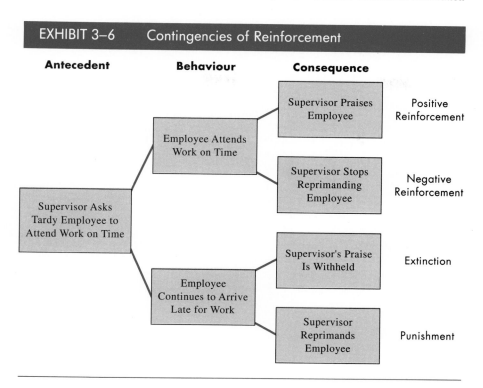

EXHIBIT 3–6   Contingencies of Reinforcement

Antecedent   **Behaviour**   **Consequence**

Supervisor Praises Employee — Positive Reinforcement

Employee Attends Work on Time

Supervisor Stops Reprimanding Employee — Negative Reinforcement

Supervisor Asks Tardy Employee to Attend Work on Time

Supervisor's Praise Is Withheld — Extinction

Employee Continues to Arrive Late for Work

Supervisor Reprimands Employee — Punishment

Positive Reinforcement.   **Positive reinforcement** occurs when the *introduction* of a desirable consequence *increases or maintains* the frequency or probability of a particular behaviour in the future. Pay-for-performance is an example of positive reinforcement because the employee's level of performance tends to increase when performance bonuses are introduced following good performance. Referring to the A-B-C model, the bonus is the consequence and job performance is the behaviour that increases when the bonus system is introduced.

Negative Reinforcement.   **Negative reinforcement** occurs when an undesirable condition is *removed or withheld* and this *increases or maintains* the frequency or probability of a particular behaviour in the future. Managers use negative reinforcement when they stop harassing employees whose substandard performance starts to improve. Withholding the harassment motivates employees to repeat those behaviours that improve their performance. Emergency alarm systems on air traffic control panels have the same effect. The irritating alarms stop only when the air traffic controller takes corrective action to avoid a mid-air collision, thus reinforcing the corrective action.

Punishment.   **Punishment** occurs when the *introduction* of an undesirable consequence *decreases* the frequency or probability of a behaviour in the future. Glenn Carpenter, president of Tabufile Atlantic Ltd. in St. John,

positive reinforcement

The introduction of a desirable consequence that increases or maintains the frequency or probability of a particular behaviour in the future.

negative reinforcement

The removal or withholding of an undesirable condition, the consequence of which is to increase or maintain the frequency or probability of a particular behaviour in the future.

punishment

The introduction of an undesirable consequence that decreases the frequency or probability of a behaviour in the future.

PERSPECTIVE 3–2   An Award for Me? No Thanks!

Poor customer service is the norm in many parts of China. One foreign visitor was so angered by service at Beijing's largest Friendship store that she fired off a letter to China's Communist Party newspaper. "[Store clerks] don't know what friendship is," she complained. "They treat customers as though they were the enemy."

Xiao Xingcai, general manager of Xian Department Store in Xian, agrees. He explains that there is plenty of recognition for good work, but guaranteed employment is the rule in China, so there it is more difficult to deal with workers who won't work. "Service in China has been bad for a long time because the state has guaranteed everything to workers."

Faced with the problem of poor service and unable to fire poor performers, the Xian retailer has tried an innovative strategy that has caught the interest of other businesses with similar problems. Amid much fanfare, the Xian retailer publicly named its "40 Worst Shop Assistants." A special plaque is hung in plain view at each transgressor's work station, complete with picture, proclaiming that he or she is a member of the "40 Worst" club. To add injury to the insult, the "winners" forfeit their monthly bonus (nearly a quarter of their paycheque) and have to write self-criticisms analyzing their shortcomings.

"It's the only system we've found to pressure workers to do better," says Bai-Shouzheng, the store's burly Communist Party secretary. "Those designated the 'worst' feel embarrassed," he reasons. "Otherwise our efforts would have no effect." Xiao Xingcai explains further: "When a seller has a plaque at her counter identifying her as the worst assistant in the store, she'll improve quickly to get it taken away."

New Brunswick, uses punishment to maintain high production standards. If employees are unable to maintain high standards, Carpenter warns them that they will lose their job if performance does not improve. According to Carpenter, this "tough love" management philosophy is usually effective enough to get employee productivity back on track, although several employees have also been fired in recent years.[19] Introducing the threat of dismissal—and actually firing those who fail to improve—are forms of punishment because they decrease the frequency of poor performance behaviours. Dismissal is an extreme and usually demeaning form of punishment in an employment setting, so employers are always looking for other strategies to redirect behaviour through punishment. One innovative approach, introduced at the Xian Department Store in Xian, China, is described in Perspective 3–2.

Negative reinforcement is often confused with punishment because both deal with undesirable consequences. However, these two contingencies are quite different. Negative reinforcement involves removing or avoiding negative consequences, whereas punishment involves introducing negative consequences. Threatening to fire an employee is an example of punishment, whereas removing the threat of dismissal is an example of negative reinforcement. Punishment and negative reinforcement also have different effects on behaviour. Punishment reduces the frequency of future behaviour, while negative reinforcement increases the frequency of future behaviour.

The big question, of course, is how to select the 40 worst clerks from among the store's staff of 800. In a spirit of democracy, Xian Department Store's management set up a ballot box at the customer service desk and urged shoppers to vote for the worst salespeople. They found an all-too-willing electorate. Then, the managers culled their personnel reports and made selections of their own. Offenses ranged from ignoring customers to throwing things at them.

Hu Ping, one of the throwers, found her name on the "40 Worst" list. She was busy chatting with colleagues at her hardware counter when a woman approached and asked about buying an electric socket. Hu ignored the customer and then pointedly served others who arrived later. When the woman persisted, the salesclerk reared back and launched a socket at her. "Here's your socket," she snapped. "Couldn't you see I was busy?" Aside from wounded pride, there were no injuries.

Xian Department Store's "40 Worst" award seems to be having the desired effect on sales staff, but the retailer is having second thoughts about introducing a similar award for the worst manager. "It's a very complicated system," the store manager nervously suggests. "It's really too difficult to decide who's the worst manager." Perhaps a ballot box in the staff lunchroom is a fitting solution?

Source: Based on A. Ignatius, "Now if Ms. Wong Insults a Customer, She Gets an Award," Reprinted by permission of *THE WALL STREET JOURNAL,* pp. A1, A17. © January 24, 1989, Dow Jones & Company, Inc. All Rights Reserved Worldwide.

Extinction. **Extinction** occurs when a desirable consequence is *removed or withheld*, which *decreases* the frequency or probability of a behaviour in the future. For example, outstanding employees might stop receiving a performance bonus if their performance slips. Removing the performance bonus is intended to decrease the behaviours that have led to poor performance. Behaviour that is no longer reinforced tends to disappear or be extinguished. In this respect, extinction is a do-nothing strategy.[20]

extinction
The removal or withholding of a desirable condition, the consequence of which is to decrease the frequency or probability of a behaviour in the future.

Comparing Reinforcement Strategies

All four reinforcement contingencies are found in organizations, but which tends to be the best? Conventional wisdom suggests that the most effective strategy is to follow desired behaviours with positive reinforcement and follow undesirable behaviours with extinction (removing or withholding the positive reinforcer). Punishment and negative reinforcement can also influence behaviour, but there are risks involved with these approaches, particularly with excessive use of punishment.[21] We will look more closely at this issue, in the context of rewarding and disciplining employees, in Chapter 4.

Schedules of Reinforcement

In addition to the contingencies of reinforcement, OB Mod emphasizes the timetable or schedule that should be followed to maximize the reinforcement effect. In fact, some research suggests that the schedule of reinforcement may have a greater effect on employee motivation than the size of the reinforcer.[22] The five schedules of reinforcement are summarized in Exhibit 3–7.

continuous reinforcement schedule
A schedule that reinforces behaviour every time it occurs.

Continuous Reinforcement.   A **continuous reinforcement schedule** occurs when employees are reinforced every time they complete the required behaviour. With frequent reinforcement, new behaviour is learned quickly; when the reinforcer is removed, the behaviour is quickly extinguished. For this reason, continuous reinforcement is most effective in learning situations. When practising new skills, trainees might be congratulated every

EXHIBIT 3–7   OB Mod Schedules of Reinforcement

Reinforcement Schedule	Description	Effect on Behaviour	Organizational Example
Continuous	Reinforcer follows every occurrence of desired behaviour.	Establishes or extinguishes new behaviour quickly.	Praise immediately after every desired behaviour.
Fixed ratio	Reinforcer occurs after a specific number of desired behaviours.	Same as continuous schedule when reinforcer follows every behaviour. Less frequent reinforcement tends to result in steady rate of behaviour; relatively quick extinction of behaviour when reinforcer removed.	Piece rate; attendance rewards.
Variable ratio	Reinforcer occurs after a variable number of desired behaviours.	Produces a high rate of steady behaviour; highly resistant to extinction when reinforcer is removed.	Praise; successful sales calls.
Fixed interval	Reinforcer occurs after a fixed time period during which desired behaviour occurs.	Inconsistent effect on frequency of behaviour; relatively quick extinction of behaviour when reinforcer is removed.	Weekly paycheque.
Variable interval	Reinforcer occurs after a variable time period during which desired behaviour occurs.	Produces a high rate of steady behaviour and a slower rate of extinction when reinforcer is removed.	Promotions; safety inspections.

Sources: Adapted from Fred Luthans and Robert Kreitner, *Organizational Behaviour Modification and Beyond* (Glenview, Ill.: Scott, Foresman, 1985), pp. 56–59; and O. Behling, C. Schriesheim, and J. Tolliver, "Present Theories and New Directions in Theories of Work Effort," *Journal of Supplement Abstract Service of the American Psychological Association,* 1974, p. 57.

time they finish the task correctly, or they might receive immediate feedback from a computer program when they provide the correct answer to each skill-testing question.

As behaviours become established, it is better to replace continuous reinforcement with an intermittent schedule (the other four types listed in Exhibit 3–7). Employee activities that have been supported by intermittent schedules of reinforcement are more resistant to extinction if the rewards are unexpectedly removed. Intermittent reinforcement is also more practical because it is usually difficult or inconvenient to reward someone every time he or she completes a task well.

Fixed Ratio.   The **fixed ratio schedule** follows the pattern of reinforcing behaviour after it has occurred a fixed number of times. Continuous reinforcement is actually a variation of this schedule, whereby behaviour is reinforced every time desired behaviour occurs. More often, however, fixed ratio reinforcement involves administering a reinforcement after every 5, 50, 500, or other number of occurrences of the behaviour. Attendance incentive systems often use a fixed ratio schedule by offering a bonus or paid day off for every 100 days of attendance. Piece rate systems sometimes follow this schedule by paying employees after a fixed number of production units have been completed.

> **fixed ratio schedule**
> A schedule that reinforces behaviour after it has occurred a fixed number of times.

Variable Ratio.   The **variable ratio schedule** is similar to a lottery because the reinforcer is applied after the desired behaviour occurs a varying number of times. Salespeople experience variable ratio reinforcement because they make a successful sale after a varying number of client calls. They might make four unsuccessful calls before receiving an order on the fifth one. This is followed by 15 unsuccessful sales calls before another sale is made. One successful sale might be made, *on average*, in every 10 calls, but this does not mean that every tenth call will be successful.

> **variable ratio schedule**
> A schedule that reinforces behaviour after it has occurred a varying number of times around some average.

The variable ratio schedule is considered most effective for motivating employees because the desired behaviour is highly resistant to extinction when the reinforcer is removed.[23] It is also cost effective because employees are rewarded infrequently using a random timetable. One problem with variable ratio schedules is that they do not easily fit into most personnel procedures and, therefore, may be difficult to implement. Some employees also resent variable ratio schedules because they resemble lotteries or gambling procedures.[24] However, lotteries have been used effectively to reinforce some employee behaviours. Volkswagen, the German automobile manufacturer, uses a lottery to increase participation in its suggestion program. Employees who make suggestions have a chance to win stereo sets, bicycles, and holidays as typical prizes. Everyone also receives a smaller prize when they submit their ideas for improved productivity.[25]

fixed interval schedule
A schedule that reinforces behaviour after it has occurred for a fixed period of time.

Fixed Interval.   The **fixed interval schedule** occurs when behaviour is reinforced after a fixed period of time. Most people are paid on a fixed interval schedule because they work throughout the pay period—whether weekly, biweekly, or monthly—and receive a paycheque at the end of that period. As long as the job is performed satisfactorily, a paycheque is received on the appointed day. For over 20 years, the Plastics Division of Canadian General Electric has had a 'Double or Nothing' safety incentive program that follows a fixed interval schedule. Each employee receives $50 after the work unit has completed 250,000 person-hours without a lost-time injury (approximately 3 months in a 500-person plant). The award is doubled if the number of accident-free hours is doubled.[26] Notice that this is a fixed interval rather than fixed ratio schedule because awards are distributed after a fixed period of time, not after a fixed number of safe work behaviours.

variable interval schedule
A schedule that reinforces behaviour after it has occurred for a variable period of time around some average.

Variable Interval.   The **variable interval schedule** involves administering the reinforcer after a varying period of time. Promotions typically follow this schedule because they occur at uneven time intervals. The first promotion might be received after two years of good performance, the next after four years, and the third after 18 months, and so on. Promotions are usually interval-based rather than behaviour-based because people are typically promoted after a period of time rather than after a desired number of behaviours.

Shaping Complex Behaviour

In OB Mod's purest form, people are reinforced only when they exhibit desired behaviour. But many activities are quite complex and employees are initially unable to perform the desired behaviour exactly as required. Without some early reinforcement, employees become frustrated as they continually fail to produce the ideal behaviour.

shaping
The strategy of initially reinforcing crude approximations of the ideal behaviour, then increasing reinforcement standards until only the ideal behaviour is rewarded.

The solution to this dilemma is to initially reinforce crude approximations of the ideal behaviour, then increase reinforcement standards until only the ideal behaviour is rewarded. This process is called **shaping.**[27] For instance, a trainee might be praised initially for backing a dump truck anywhere near the desired dump location. As the trainee improves, the supervisor would provide praise only as the truck is placed close to the dump location and eventually only when the vehicle is driven to the exact location.

OB Mod Program Implementation Steps

OB Mod concepts are routinely applied in organizational settings. However, experts recommend a programmatic approach to OB Mod by following through the steps shown in Exhibit 3–8.[28] First, the critical behaviours that need to be strengthened or weakened are identified. These behaviours must

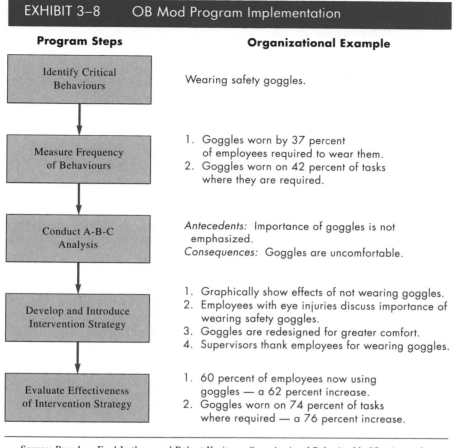

EXHIBIT 3–8   OB Mod Program Implementation

Program Steps

Organizational Example

Identify Critical
Behaviours

Wearing safety goggles.

Measure Frequency
of Behaviours

1. Goggles worn by 37 percent
   of employees required to wear them.
2. Goggles worn on 42 percent of tasks
   where they are required.

Conduct A-B-C
Analysis

Antecedents: Importance of goggles is not
   emphasized.
Consequences: Goggles are uncomfortable.

Develop and Introduce
Intervention Strategy

1. Graphically show effects of not wearing goggles.
2. Employees with eye injuries discuss importance of
   wearing safety goggles.
3. Goggles are redesigned for greater comfort.
4. Supervisors thank employees for wearing goggles.

Evaluate Effectiveness
of Intervention Strategy

1. 60 percent of employees now using
   goggles — a 62 percent increase.
2. Goggles worn on 74 percent of tasks
   where required — a 76 percent increase.

Source: Based on Fred Luthans and Robert Kreitner, *Organizational Behavior Modification and
Beyond* (Glenview, Ill.: Scott, Foresman, 1985), p. 76.

be measurable and related to the employee's job performance. In our example, we measure how often safety goggles are currently used and find out
whether wearing them is important.

Second, the critical behaviours are measured to serve as a baseline for
later evaluation of the intervention. This typically involves tallying the number of times the behaviour occurs, such as the number or percentage of
employees required to wear goggles who are actually wearing them. Third,
an A-B-C analysis is conducted to identify which antecedents and consequences are maintaining the desirable or undesirable behaviours. Experts
carefully observe and interview employees to identify the relevant environmental conditions leading up to and following the critical behaviours. They
may discover, for instance, that employees don't wear safety goggles because they are uncomfortable.

The first three stages provide the necessary background and data for the OB Mod intervention (the fourth step). The appropriate intervention must be developed and applied effectively as an antecedent and/or consequence of the target behaviour. For example, if the A-B-C analysis determines that safety goggles are uncomfortable, one intervention may be to develop more comfortable goggles. The target behaviour must also be measured throughout the intervention stage. The final stage of an OB Mod program is to evaluate the effectiveness of the intervention strategy. By examining changes in the critical behaviour before and during the intervention, we can determine the extent to which behaviour has been redirected as intended.

Practices and Problems with OB Modification

Organizational behaviour modification is widely applied in industry. Managers *informally* use OB Mod principles every day to motivate and train employees. They give people a pat on the back at random times to recognize good performance; they might provide almost continuous feedback to staff learning a new task; they apply disciplinary procedures to those with marginal performance. These actions consider both the contingencies and schedules of reinforcement and recognize—at least implicitly—the basic philosophy of OB Mod in organizational settings.

It is difficult to find any examples of *formal* OB Mod programs in Canadian business, but applications have been reported in the United States at General Electric, Michigan Bell, and Connecticut General Life Insurance. These and other field studies have demonstrated that OB Mod can effectively improve employee productivity, work attendance, safe work behaviours, and sales volume.[29] Critics point out, however, that some "successful" OB Mod programs have not actually been very cost effective. The results of several OB Mod applications have also been difficult to judge due to research design problems.[30] Other problems with the OB Mod strategy include the following.

Limited Behaviours.   Formal OB Mod programs are best suited to controlling routine, physical activities such as work attendance, sales calls, and safety procedures.[31] It is much easier to observe and reinforce these behaviours than management and professional activities.

Diminishing Reinforcer Effect.   In several OB Mod programs, the reinforcer has eventually worn off. Caterpillar of Canada Ltd. experienced this problem in its attendance incentive program a few years ago. The heavy machine manufacturer offered employees one half-hour of paid time off for every week of perfect attendance. When these half-hour credits had accumulated to eight hours, employees could take a day off with pay. Unfortunately, the novelty of the attendance bonus soon wore off and absenteeism rose from 8.3 percent to over 9 percent the following year.[32]

Failure to "Explain" Reinforcement.   Critics point out that OB Mod describes a reinforcer as any consequence that increases the probability of future behaviour, but it does not explain which consequences are reinforcing or why they increase future behaviour. When identifying pay as a positive reinforcer, for example, we are tempted to say that employees *perceive* a pay-for-performance linkage and that employees *value* pay, but these statements are unacceptable to OB Mod because the theory relies solely on behaviours. In this respect, expectancy theory and other cognitive models may provide a clearer understanding of employee motivation.

Ethical Implications.   OB Mod is viewed by some as unethical because it overtly attempts to manipulate or control employee behaviour and treats people as animals with low intelligence.[33] As a counterargument, OB Mod experts point out that everything we do to change employee behaviour is a form of manipulation. This boils down to the long-standing debate of whether human behaviour is freely determined by the individual or is fatalistically determined by the environment.[34] We will not enter this debate here, but continued concerns over the manipulative perspective of OB Mod will cast a shadow over the theory for some time to come.

EQUITY THEORY

Equity theory is a theory of **distributive justice** because it explains how people develop perceptions of fairness in the distribution and exchange of resources. It is also a theory of employee motivation by explaining what people want to do when they feel inequitably treated. Equity theory applies to any situation where people share or exchange resources, but our discussion will focus on exchanges between the organization and its employees. There are four basic elements in the equity process: outcome/input ratio, comparison other, equity evaluation, and consequences of inequity.[35]

Outcome/Input Ratio

Inputs represent employee contributions to the organization, such as skill, effort, experience, amount of time worked, and actual productivity. In other words, inputs are investments into the exchange relationship. Outcomes are the things employees receive from the organization in exchange for the inputs. Outcomes may include pay, an office with a window, better assignments, promotions, social status, and recognition.

Both inputs and outcomes are weighted by their importance to the individual, and these weights vary from one person to the next. Some people may view seniority as a valuable input that therefore deserves higher outcomes from the organization. Others may reject the value of seniority and, instead, consider job effort and performance as the most important contribu-

equity theory
A process theory of motivation that explains how people develop perceptions of fairness in the distribution and exchange of resources.

distributive justice
Perceptions of fairness in the exchange and distribution of resources, such as employee effort for financial rewards.

tions in the exchange relationship. Similarly, equity theory recognizes that people have different needs and therefore value outcomes differently. Some employees don't mind their colleagues having a nicer office because it is unimportant to them while others feel unfairly treated under these circumstances.

Comparison Other

Another important feature of equity theory is the comparison other. Equity theory states that we compare our situation with another person or group of people called a *comparison other*. However, the theory does not tell us who the comparison other is in a particular situation. Employees might compare themselves with specific people inside or outside the organization, but some research suggests that they more frequently collect information on several referents to form a generalized comparison other. There is also some evidence that managers and professionals are more likely to choose comparison others from other organizations, whereas people in less-skilled positions tend to compare themselves with coworkers within their own firm.[36] For the most part, however, the comparison other is not easily identifiable.

Equity Evaluation

According to equity theory, employees form an outcome/input ratio and compare this with the ratio of the comparison other. This evaluation is shown in Exhibit 3–9 with three different comparison situations. The first comparison illustrates the *equity condition* in which the person's outcome/input ratio is the same as the comparison other's ratio. The amount of inputs and outcomes must be proportional, but they do not have to be the same amount. For instance, equity may be felt when we are working harder than the comparison other and are receiving proportionally higher rewards as a result.

Inequity feelings emerge when the person's ratio is significantly different from the comparison other's. People tend to ignore minimal differences, but inequity occurs when the difference in ratios exceeds a threshold level. *Underreward inequity* occurs when the person's ratio is significantly lower than the comparison other's. This may occur when two people provide the same inputs to the organization but the other person receives more outcomes, as the second comparison in Exhibit 3–9 illustrates. Underreward inequity may also occur when the outcomes are the same but the comparison other's inputs are lower, or in any other situation where the person's ratio is lower than the comparison other's.

Overreward inequity occurs when the person's ratio is significantly higher than the comparison other's. The third comparison in Exhibit 3–9 illustrates one possible situation leading to overreward inequity, namely where the person receives more outcomes than the comparison other even though the

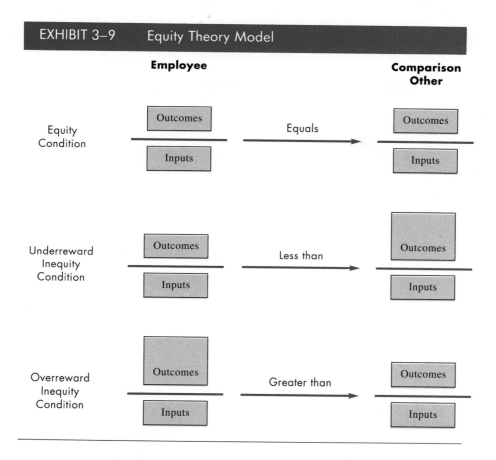

EXHIBIT 3–9   Equity Theory Model

inputs are the same. This type of inequity would also occur when the person isn't working as hard as the comparison other to receive the same outcomes, or in any other situation where the person's ratio is higher than the comparison other's.

Consequences of Inequity

Inequity creates an uncomfortable tension that is both stressful and dissatisfying. Employees are motivated to reduce or eliminate this tension by correcting the inequitable situation. Researchers have identified six possible ways to reduce feelings of inequity.[37]

Changing Inputs.   Employees who feel underrewarded tend to reduce their work effort and productivity, particularly if they are on a fixed salary where lower effort does not also reduce their outcomes. Those who feel overpaid sometimes (but not very often) increase their inputs by working harder and producing more.

Changing Outcomes.   Employees who feel underrewarded might try to increase their outcomes by asking for an increase in their own rewards. If this strategy does not work, they might become motivated to join a labour union to force these changes on management at the bargaining table.[38] Employees who feel underrewarded might also try to increase their outcomes by using company facilities and equipment for personal use.

Changing Perceptions.   Since feelings of equity are based on perceptions, it is possible for employees to distort inputs and outcomes to restore equity feelings. Research has found that this is the most frequently used strategy for overrewarded employees. It is more palatable for overrewarded employees to restore equity feelings by increasing the perceived importance of their experience or seniority than to actually work harder or ask for a pay reduction![39]

Leaving the Field.   In some cases, employees who believe they are treated unfairly will try to get away from the inequitable situation. In this respect, equity theory explains some instances of employee turnover and job transfer. This alternative also explains why absenteeism may be higher for inequitably treated employees even when they are not paid for this time off.

Acting on the Comparison Other.   Another possible way to restore equity is to change the inputs or outcomes of the comparison other. If you feel overrewarded, you might encourage the referent to work at a more leisurely pace. If you feel underrewarded, you might subtly suggest that the comparison other should be doing a larger share of the workload.

Changing the Comparison Other.   Finally, employees who feel inequitably treated might decide to replace the comparison other with someone with a more compatible outcome/input ratio. As mentioned earlier, most people tend to create a generalized comparison other rather than a specific person, so it may be fairly easy to adjust the comparison other's features in order to reduce inequity feelings.

The Equity Process: An Organizational Example

Now that the basic components have been described, let's apply equity theory to an actual business incident. Perspective 3–3 describes the experience of Jay Norris Canada Inc., a Montreal mail-order house, in which some employees felt that they were unfairly paid. Equity theory can help us examine this experience more fully.

The most important input mentioned in Perspective 3–3 appears to be employee productivity, specifically the number of orders processed per day. Employees complaining about the existing system did not accept age or seniority as acceptable inputs in the exchange process. The critical outcome

---

PERSPECTIVE 3–3   Fair Pay in a Montreal Mail-Order House

Jay Norris Canada Inc., a Montreal mail-order house with annual sales of $50 million, had been experiencing declining employee morale and motivation because many of the company's 400 staff members felt inequitably paid. Wages were based mainly on seniority, and the company's existing performance appraisal system was so subjective that some employees were evaluated as good performers even if they didn't do their job very well.

"People were complaining that their salaries weren't fair," explains René Schubert, vice-president of finance and administration at Jay Norris. "Long-timers were getting more salary, but they were sometimes poorer workers than others in the office. Someone processing 400 orders per day was maybe making less than the older guy doing 250 orders per day."

To restore feelings of equity, the company decided to pay employees more on the basis of their performance than their seniority. It also introduced a new performance appraisal system in which supervisors rate employees using objective standards. For example, "good performance" might mean that the employee typically fills 350 orders per day, whereas "excellent" might be 400 orders per day. Schubert stresses that getting supervisors to reach a consensus on the meaning of "good" or "poor" performance has been challenging, but it is important that they all see performance the same way so that salaries and pay increases are decided fairly.

Source: Cathy Hilborn, "Worker Incentives Can Backfire," *Small Business,* August 1989, pp. 7–8.

---

in this example is employee salaries, although other rewards and perquisites might also be considered. With respect to the comparison other, disgruntled employees were clearly comparing themselves to others within the organization, particularly older workers in the same job. Finally, Perspective 3–3 describes how employees who felt inequitably rewarded dealt with this tension. Specifically, they complained to management and eventually received a compensation system that more closely reflects their perceptions of fairness. According to equity theory, these employees attempted to change their outcomes and were successful in doing so.

Nothing is said about the older employees at Jay Norris, but we know that overrewarded employees tend to justify this situation by concluding that their inputs are more valuable than originally perceived. In our example, most of the older workers probably believed that age and seniority were important enough to justify their higher salaries. It would be equally interesting to examine their equity perceptions after the new reward system was introduced.

Equity Research and Implications

The Jay Norris example illustrates that equity theory can explain motivation and behaviour in the workplace. Scholarly studies also support the practical value of equity theory, but the research is far from complete.[40] For example, most of the earlier studies were based on short-term comparisons in laboratory settings and used pay as the only outcome.[41] Fortunately, some recent evidence suggests that equity theory is effective in field settings when either monetary or nonmonetary outcomes are involved.[42]

In terms of management implications, equity theory emphasizes the social comparison process and its implications for employee motivation and behaviour. The theory clearly advises us to treat people fairly in the distribution of organizational rewards. If feelings of inequity are sufficiently strong, employees may put less effort into the job, leave the organization, steal resources or time (e.g., absenteeism), or join a labour union to force management to correct inequities.

Maintaining feelings of equity is not an easy task because employees have different opinions regarding which inputs should be rewarded (e.g., seniority versus performance) and which outcomes are more valuable than others.[43] However, managers can at least establish acceptable criteria for reward allocation and clearly communicate this information so that everyone understands how organizational outcomes are distributed. They should also be sensitive to employee equity feelings and change the criteria for reward distribution when it becomes apparent that most employees feel the current system is unfair.

Equity in the Pay-Setting Process

Since equity theory has focussed mainly on monetary rewards, it is not surprising that compensation specialists have developed some rather elaborate procedures to ensure that people receive "a fair day's pay for a fair day's work." In particular, organizations consider three types of comparison other when deciding how much employees should be paid.[44] Exhibit 3–10 summarizes the three types of referents in the pay-setting process.

Employee Equity.   Employees compare themselves with coworkers in the same job. A production employee might feel inequitably treated because he or she is receiving less pay than someone else in the same job. One possible

EXHIBIT 3–10	Three Types of Equity in the Pay-Setting Process
Type of Equity	**Description**
Employee equity	Individual compares own outcome/input ratio with people in the same job within the same organization.
External equity	Individual compares own outcome/input ratio with people in other organizations, particularly in the same or similar jobs.
Internal equity	Individual compares own outcome/input ratio with people in the other jobs within the same organization.

solution is to establish a fixed pay policy whereby everyone in the job receives the same wage rate. This policy is effective if everyone contributes equally, but employee inequities may exist otherwise. An alternative solution may be to establish a range of pay for each job, with each employee's pay level within that range based on seniority or performance appraisal ratings. A third strategy would be to totally link pay levels within the job to individual contributions, such as sales volume or production output. Each of these methods is certainly better than a piecemeal compensation policy for rewarding employees, but none provides a perfect solution.

External Equity.   External equity involves comparing one's outcomes with people in other organizations. For example, an accountant with Coopers Lybrand might compare her salary and benefits with a friend working at Deloitte Touche in the same position. Organizations try to maintain external equity by annually surveying the salaries paid by other organizations and using this information to establish new pay levels for each job. Their ultimate objective is to provide competitive monetary rewards to attract new employees while preventing labour costs from escalating out of hand.

Internal Equity.   Employees also compare themselves with coworkers in different jobs within the organization. For example, nurses might feel inequity if they discover that their salary is the same as the hospital's entry-level technicians', which they believe make a lower contribution to the organization. To minimize inequities between jobs, many organizations use a process called **job evaluation.** Job evaluation involves systematically evaluating the worth of each job within the firm based on the duties performed and required employee characteristics. This rating process allows the company to develop a job hierarchy for the purpose of establishing pay differentials.[45] In general, jobs are placed in higher pay grades if they require more skill, effort, and responsibility, and involve harsher working conditions. Job evaluation is an imperfect system, but it enables firms to estimate whether nurses, for instance, should receive a higher or lower salary than entry-level technicians. By measuring these differences, internal inequities can be minimized.

job evaluation
A procedure for systematically evaluating the worth of each job within the firm based on the duties performed and required employee characteristics.

PAY EQUITY: AVOIDING DISCRIMINATION AGAINST WOMEN

Equity theory provides an important foundation for Canadian legislation governing fairness in compensating women compared with men. At one time, many employers paid women less than men for performing the same work. But society began to see the inequity of this practice and, in 1951, the Ontario government introduced **equal pay for equal work** legislation that prohibited employers from paying women less than men in the same jobs. Similar equal pay statutes were subsequently passed in other Canadian jurisdictions.[46]

equal pay for equal work
Legislation prohibiting employers from paying women less than men performing the same job content.

The goal of equal pay legislation was to ensure that women earned the same pay rates as men in jobs with the same or similar duties. For example, pay discrimination would exist in an organization that pays seamstresses (mostly women) less than tailors (mostly men) because people in both jobs perform similar tasks. Of course, men and women could still receive different paycheques based on differences in seniority, performance appraisals, and other "justifiable" factors. In some respects, equal pay is a form of employee equity because the comparison other is a male employee in the same or similar job in the same organization.

From Equal Pay to Pay Equity

It soon became apparent that equal pay legislation did not prohibit all forms of pay discrimination against women. Specifically, many employers were paying employees in "female-dominated" jobs (e.g., secretaries, nurses) less than those in "male-dominated" jobs (e.g., truck drivers, welders) even though both were of similar value to the organization. These jobs could not be compared under the original statutes because they involved different job duties.[47]

pay equity
Legislation that requires pay levels assigned to female-dominated jobs to be comparable to those assigned to male-dominated jobs of similar value within the same establishment.

To address this problem, **pay equity** legislation (also called *equal pay for work of equal value* or *comparable worth*) was introduced. Many jurisdictions in Canada currently have some form of pay equity legislation, at least for public sector employees. Private sector employees in Ontario, Quebec, and in federally regulated firms (e.g., banks, airlines, TV stations) are also covered by pay equity. Under pay equity, the pay levels assigned to female-dominated jobs should be comparable to those assigned to male-dominated jobs "of similar value" within the same company. This is basically the same as internal equity, described earlier, because employees compare themselves with coworkers in different jobs within the organization. Job evaluation procedures are used to determine whether two jobs have similar value to the organization. The gender dominance of a job is typically measured by the percentage of women or men in the job.[48]

Let's look at an actual example of pay discrimination in Canada to see how pay equity legislation works in practice. Not long ago, Canadian government librarians (mostly women) complained that they were paid less than the government's historical researchers (mostly men) even though the two jobs were believed to be of equal value to the organization. Human rights officials conducted a job evaluation that revealed that the two jobs had similar job worth ratings and, therefore, made a similar contribution to the organization. Pay discrimination had occurred because the Canadian government was paying the predominantly female librarians less than the male-dominated researchers even though both occupations had the same level of job worth. To correct this internal inequity, the librarians received immediate pay increases as well as higher back wages.[49]

Opposition to Pay Equity

While few people would dispute the moral value of pay equity, there is still much disagreement over the need for legislation and the ability to control pay discrimination.[50] One concern is that pay equity interferes with the labour market and that, if left alone, the natural forces of supply and demand will correct pay discrimination. Most experts, however, don't believe that the labour market is as efficient as these idealists purport. Others complain that pay equity is expensive and requires more paperwork and bureaucracy than it is worth. Some studies confirm that adjusting women's wages will be costly. Many employers who have recently completed pay equity analyses will confirm that the process is time-consuming and often difficult.

Finally, there is evidence that pay discrimination represents a relatively small proportion of the wage gap between men and women. Women currently earn, on average, only two-thirds of the earnings of men, but **occupational segregation** appears to be the primary culprit, not pay inequities. Occupational segregation refers to barriers against women and other identifiable groups in entering higher-paying jobs in our society.

occupational segregation
Barriers that prevent or inhibit women and other identifiable groups from entering higher paying jobs in our society.

EMPLOYEE MOTIVATION: A FINAL WORD

Throughout Chapter 2 and Chapter 3 we have introduced several theories and models of employee motivation. Maslow's need hierarchy, Alderfer's ERG, and McClelland's theory of learned needs attempt to explain how people have different needs at different times. Goal setting, expectancy theory, OB Mod, and equity theory describe the processes through which these needs are translated into behaviour.

While reading this material, at times you may well have wondered why some ingenious organizational theorist didn't try to weave these concepts into a single unifying theory. The fact is that several writers *have tried* to produce integrated models of employee motivation, but they have not been very successful. At best, these models emphasize one perspective (typically expectancy theory) and ignore others. At worst, they confuse students with a multitude of boxes and lines. While these attempts to develop an integrated model of employee motivation are noble, they simply lend further support to the idea introduced in Chapter 1 that middle-range theories, each with a relatively narrow focus, provide a better appreciation of organizational behaviour.

While we cannot present a meta-theory of employee motivation, we can alert you to the fact that the seven middle-range motivation theories presented in this book are not completely independent of one another. We have already noted, for example, how OB Mod and expectancy theory are similar in some respects. We also introduced the basic motivation process in Chapter 2 (Exhibit 2–9) that links together need and process theories as well as motivational management practices discussed in Chapters 4 and 5. By understanding each motivation theory in the context of this general framework, you can begin to see how they relate to each other.

SUMMARY

- Expectancy theory is based on the idea that people will direct their effort toward those actions that are perceived to be achievable and lead to desired outcomes.

- Based on expectancy theory, managers should increase the E → P expectancy by hiring and training people to be able to perform the job and build their self-confidence. The P → O expectancy can be increased by measuring performance accurately, rewarding only good performers, and showing employees that rewards are actually performance-based. Finally, outcome valence should be increased by finding out what employees want and using these resources as rewards.

- OB Mod is based on the concept of reinforcement, which states that the likelihood that behaviour will be repeated depends on its consequences, and on the concept of behaviourism, which urges managers to focus on behaviours rather than unobservable attitudes and perceptions.

- OB Mod attempts to redirect behaviour by managing its antecedents and consequences. Antecedents are environmental stimuli that provoke (not necessarily cause) behaviour. Consequences are events following behaviour that influence its future occurrence. Consequences act as a form of positive reinforcement, negative reinforcement, punishment, or extinction. The schedules of reinforcement also influence behaviour.

- OB Mod is used informally every day to manage employees, but it is best suited only to observable behaviours, reinforcers may have a diminishing effect, and the theory is subject to ethical and conceptual criticisms.

- Equity theory explains how people determine their perceptions of fairness using four elements: input/outcome ratio, comparison other, equity evaluation, and consequences of inequity. The theory also explains what people are motivated to do when they feel inequitably treated.

- Organizations attempt to address the equity concept in the pay-setting process by using procedures to compare earnings between employees within and between organizations.

- Most jurisdictions in Canada currently have some form of pay equity legislation (also called *equal pay for work of equal value* or *comparable worth*), at least for the public sector. Under pay equity, the pay levels assigned to female-dominated jobs should be comparable to those assigned to male-dominated jobs ''of similar value'' within the same company.

DISCUSSION QUESTIONS

1. Does expectancy theory explain what motivates employees?
2. What can managers do to increase the P → O expectancy for job performance?
3. What are the two main concepts underlying OB modification?
4. What are the A-B-Cs of OB modification?
5. Which reinforcement schedule is most effective for new employees? Which is most effective for experienced employees? Explain why.
6. What is the comparison other in equity theory?
7. Why is it difficult to maintain feelings of equity among employees?
8. What procedures have compensation specialists developed to strive for equity in the pay-setting process?
9. How does equal pay for equal work legislation differ from the more recent pay equity legislation?

NOTES

1. J. Deverall, "Keeping Workers Happy an Art, Bosses Say," *Toronto Star,* November 1, 1986, p. A8; and C. Yetman, "Profits with Principles Earns Dedicated Staff," *Human Resources Professional,* May 1991, p. 12ii.

2. D. A. Nadler and E. E. Lawler, "Motivation: A Diagnostic Approach," in J. R. Hackman, E. E. Lawler III, and L. W. Porter (eds.), *Perspectives on Behavior in Organizations,* 2nd ed. (New York: McGraw-Hill, 1983), pp. 67–78; and V. H. Vroom, *Work and Motivation* (New York: Wiley, 1964).

3. K. Lewin, "Psychology of Success and Failure," *Occupations* 14 (1936), pp. 926–30; and Vroom, *Work and Motivation.*

4. This hybrid of expectancy theory has been described in J. P. Campbell, M. D. Dunnette, E. E. Lawler, and K. E. Weick, *Managerial Behavior, Performance, and Effectiveness* (New York: McGraw-Hill, 1970), pp. 343–48; E. E. Lawler, *Motivation in Work Organizations* (Monterey, Calif.: Brooks/Cole, 1973), Chapter 3; and Nadler and Lawler, "Motivation: A Diagnostic Approach."

5. T. Janz, "Manipulating Subjective Expectancy through Feedback: A Laboratory Study of the Expectancy–Performance Relationship," *Journal of Applied Psychology* 67 (1982), pp. 480–85; and H. Garland, "Relation of Effort–Performance Expectancy to Performance in Goal-Setting Experiments," *Journal of Applied Psychology* 69 (1984), pp. 79–84.

6. D. Stoffman, "The Power of Positive Strokes," *Canadian Business,* October 1987, p. 94.

7. Nadler and Lawler, "Motivation: A Diagnostic Approach," pp. 70–73.

8. Lawler, *Motivation in Work Organizations,* pp. 53–55.

9. E. R. Gomersall and M. S. Myers, "Breakthrough in On-the-Job Training," *Harvard Business Review* 44 (July–August 1966), pp. 62–72.

10. R. Maynard, "How Do You Like Your Job?" *Report on Business Magazine,* November 1987, p. 117.

11. K. R. Brousseau and J. B. Prince, "Job–Person Dynamics: An Extension of Longitudinal Research," *Journal of Applied Psychology* 66 (1981), pp. 59–62.

12. J. P. Campbell and R. D. Pritchard, "Motivation Theory in Industrial and Organizational Psychology," in M. D. Dunnette (ed.) *Handbook of Industrial and Organizational Psychology* (Chicago: Rand McNally, 1976), pp. 63–130; T. R. Mitchell, "Expectancy Models of Job

Satisfaction, Occupational Preference, and Effort: A Theoretical, Methodological, and Empirical Appraisal,'' *Psychological Bulletin* 81 (1974), pp. 1053–77; and H. J. Arnold, ''A Test of the Validity of the Multiplicative Hypothesis of Expectancy–Valence Theories of Work Motivation,'' *Academy of Management Journal* 24 (1981), pp. 128–41.

13. Vroom, *Motivation and Work,* pp. 14–19.

14. C. C. Pinder, *Work Motivation: Theory, Issues, and Applications* (Glenview, Ill.: Scott, Foresman, 1984), pp. 144–47; and U. R. Larson, ''Supervisor's Performance Feedback to Subordinates: The Effect of Performance Valence and Outcome Dependence,'' *Organizational Behavior and Human Decision Processes* 37 (1986), pp. 391–409.

15. F. Luthans and R. Kreitner, *Organizational Behavior Modification and Beyond* (Glenview, Ill.: Scott, Foresman, 1985); and T. K. Connellan, *How to Improve Human Performance* (New York: Harper & Row, 1978).

16. Luthans and Kreitner, *Organizational Behavior Modification and Beyond,* Chapter 5.

17. Connellan, *How to Improve Human Performance,* p. 51.

18. Luthans and Kreitner, *Organizational Behavior Modification and Beyond,* pp. 49–56.

19. R. Wright, ''Motivation Magic Made Simple,'' *Small Business,* March 1990, p. 80.

20. Luthans and Kreitner, *Organizational Behavior Modification and Beyond,* pp. 53–54.

21. Luthans and Kreitner, *Organizational Behavior Modification and Beyond,* pp. 139–144; and W. R. Nord, ''Beyond the Teaching Machine: The Neglected Area of Operant Conditioning in the Theory and Practice of Management,'' *Organizational Behavior and Human Performance* 4 (1969), pp. 375–401.

22. G. Yukl, K. N. Wexley, and J. E. Seymore, ''Effectiveness of Pay Incentives under Variable Ratio and Continuous Reinforcement Schedules,'' *Journal of Applied Psychology* 56 (1972), pp. 19–23.

23. L. M. Saari and G. P. Latham, ''Employee Reactions to Continuous and Variable Ratio Reinforcement Schedules Involving a Monetary Incentive,'' *Journal of Applied Psychology* 67 (1982), pp. 506–08.

24. Yukl, Wexley, and Seymore, ''Effectiveness of Pay Incentives under Variable Ratio and Continuous Reinforcement Schedules.''

25. W. Goldsmith and D. Clutterbuck, *The Winning Streak* (London: Weidenfeld & Nicholson, 1984), p. 111.

26. A. Robert, ''Thoroughly Modern Motivation,'' *The Human Resource* vol. 6, no. 6 (April 1990), p. 22.

27. Pinder, *Work Motivation,* p. 198; and Luthans and Kreitner, *Organizational Behavior Modification and Beyond,* pp. 63–64.

28. Luthans and Kreitner, *Organizational Behavior Modification and Beyond,* pp. 75–92.

29. K. O'Hara, C. M. Johnson, and T. A. Beehr, ''Organizational Behavior Management in the Private Sector: A Review of Empirical Research and Recommendations for Further Investigation,'' *Academy of Management Review* 10 (1985), pp. 848–64; W. C. Hamner and E. P. Hamner, ''Behavior Modification on the Bottom Line,'' *Organizational Dynamics* 4 (Spring 1976), pp. 8–21; and Luthans and Kreitner, *Organizational Behavior Modification and Beyond,* pp. 173–75.

30. L. M. Schmitz and H. G. Heneman III, ''Do Positive Reinforcement Programs Reduce Employee Absenteeism?'' *Personnel Administrator* 25 (September 1980), pp. 87–93; G. A. Merwin, J. A. Thomason, and E. E. Sanford, ''A Methodological and Content Review of Organizational Behavior Management in the Private Sector: 1978–1986,'' *Journal of Organizational Behavior Management* 10 (1989), pp. 39–57; and F. Andrasik, ''Organizational Behavior Modification in Business Settings: A Methodological and Content Review,'' *Journal of Organizational Behavior Management* 2 (1979), pp. 85–102.

31. Pinder, *Work Motivation,* pp. 223–27.

32. C. Sinclair, ''Absenteeism's Plague Has no Simple Cure,'' *Financial Times,* June 11, 1990, p. 7.

33. Pinder, *Work Motivation,* pp. 230–32; T. C. Mawhinney, ''Philosophical and Ethical Aspects of Organizational Behavior Management: Some Evaluative Feedback,'' *Journal of Organizational Behavior Management* 6 (Spring 1984), pp. 5–31; and F. L. Fry, ''Operant Conditioning in Organizational Settings: Of Mice or Men?'' *Personnel* 51 (July/August 1974), pp. 17–24.

34. B. F. Skinner, *Beyond Freedom and Dignity* (New York: Knopf, 1971).

35. J. S. Adams, "Toward an Understanding of Inequity," *Journal of Abnormal and Social Psychology* 67 (1963), pp. 422–36; R. T. Mowday, "Equity Theory Predictions of Behavior in Organizations," in R. M. Steers and L. W. Porter, *Motivation and Work Behavior* (New York: McGraw-Hill, 1987), pp. 89–110; and K. S. Cook and T. L. Parcel, "Equity Theory: Directions for Future Research," *Sociological Inquiry* 47 (1977), pp. 75–88.

36. T. P. Summers and A. S. DeNisi, "In Search of Adams' Other: Reexamination of Referents Used in the Evaluation of Pay," *Human Relations* 43 (1990), pp. 497–511; and P. S. Goodman, "An Examination of the Referents Used in the Evaluation of Pay," *Organizational Behavior and Human Performance* 12 (1974), pp. 170–95.

37. J. S. Adams, "Inequity in Social Exchange," in L. Berkowitz (ed.) *Advances in Experimental Psychology* (New York: Academic Press, 1965), pp. 157–89.

38. T. A. Kochan, *Collective Bargaining and Industrial Relations* (Homewood, Ill.: Irwin, 1980), pp. 142–45.

39. E. Hatfield and S. Sprecher, "Equity Theory and Behavior in Organizations," *Research in the Sociology of Organizations* 3 (1984), pp. 95–124.

40. P. S. Goodman and A. Friedman, "An Examination of Adams' Theory of Inequity," *Administrative Science Quarterly* 16 (1971), pp. 271–88; and R. D. Pritchard, M. D. Dunnette, and D. O. Jorgenson, "Effects of Perceptions of Equity and Inequity on Worker Performance and Satisfaction," *Journal of Applied Psychology* (Monograph) 56 (1972), pp. 75–94.

41. Cook and Parcel, "Equity Theory: Directions for Future Research"; G. C. Homans, "Status among Clerical Workers," *Human Organizations* 12 (1953), pp. 5–10; M. Patchen, *The Choice of Wage Comparisons* (Englewood Cliffs, N.J.: Prentice Hall, 1961); and J. S. Adams and W. E. Rosenbaum, "The Relationship of Worker Productivity to Cognitive Dissonance about Wage Inequities," *Journal of Abnormal and Social Psychology* 46 (1962), pp. 161–64.

42. J. Greenberg and S. Ornstein, "High Status Job Title as Compensation for Underpayment: A Test of Equity Theory," *Journal of Applied Psychology* 68 (1983), pp. 285–97; G. R. Oldham and H. E. Miller, "The Effect of Significant Other's Job Complexity on Employee Reactions to Work," *Human Relations* 32 (1979), pp. 247–60; and R. Vecchio, "Predicting Worker Performance in Inequitable Settings," *Academy of Management Review* 7 (1982), pp. 103–10.

43. R. P. Vecchio and J. R. Terborg, "Salary Increment Allocation and Individual Differences," *Journal of Organizational Behaviour* 8 (1987), pp. 37–43.

44. G. T. Milkovich, W. F. Glueck, R. T. Barth, and S. L. McShane, *Canadian Personnel/Human Resource Management: A Diagnostic Approach* (Plano, Texas: BPI, 1988), Chapter 14; and R. Thériault, "Key Issues in Designing Compensation Systems," in S. L. Dolan and R. S. Schuler (eds.), *Canadian Readings in Personnel and Human Resource Management* (St. Paul, Minn.: West, 1987), pp. 226–44.

45. T. A. Mahoney, "Understanding Comparable Worth: A Societal and Political Perspective," *Research in Organizational Behavior* 9 (1987), pp. 209–45.

46. L. Niemann, *Wage Discrimination and Women Workers: The Move Towards Equal Pay for Work of Equal Value in Canada* (Ottawa: Minister of Supply and Services Canada, 1984).

47. Labour Canada, *Equal Pay for Work of Equal Value* (Ottawa: Minister of Supply and Services Canada, 1986); N. Agarwal, "Pay Discrimination: Evidence, Policies, and Issues," in H. C. Jain and P. J. Sloane, *Equal Employment Issues* (New York: Praeger, 1981), pp. 118–43; and J. G. Campbell, "Equal Pay for Work of Equal Value in the Federal Public Service of Canada," *Compensation Review*, 1983, pp. 42–51.

48. M. Gunderson and R. E. Robb, "Equal Pay for Work of Equal Value: Canada's Experience," *Advances in Industrial and Labor Relations* 5 (1991), pp. 151–68; and Steven L. McShane, "Two Tests of Direct Gender Bias in Job Evaluation Ratings," *Journal of Occupational Psychology* 63 (1990), pp. 129–40.

49. Canadian Human Rights Commission, *Equal Pay Casebook, 1978–1984* (Ottawa: Canadian Human Rights Commission, 1984), pp. 5–6.

50. J. Breckenridge, "Equal Pay's Unequal Effect," *Report on Business*, December 1985; "Reason Is Loser as Pay Equity Rolls On," *Financial Post*, September 13, 1986, p. 8; W. Watson, "Pay

Equity: Idea Whose Time Has Passed,'' *Financial Post,* April 2, 1986; and M. Gunderson, *Costing Equal Value Legislation in Ontario: A Report to the Ontario Ministry of Labour* (Toronto: Ontario Ministry of Labour, 1985).

CHAPTER CASES

STEELFAB LTD.

Jackie Ney was an enthusiastic employee when she began working in the accounting department at Steelfab Ltd. In particular, she prided herself on discovering better ways of handling invoice and requisition flows. The company had plenty of bottlenecks in the flow of paperwork throughout the organization and Jackie had made several recommendations to her boss, Mr. Johnston, which would improve the process. Mr. Johnston acknowledged these suggestions and even implemented a few, but he didn't seem to have enough time to either thank her or explain why some suggestions could not be implemented. In fact, Mr. Johnston didn't say much to any of the other employees in the department about anything they did.

At the end of the first year, Jackie received a 6 percent merit increase based on Mr. Johnston's evaluation of her performance. This increase was equal to the average merit increase among the 11 people in the accounting department and was above the inflation rate. Still, Jackie was frustrated by the fact that she didn't know how to improve her chances of a higher merit increase the next year. She was also upset by the fact that another new employee, Jim Sandu, received the highest pay increase (10 percent) even though he was not regarded by others in the finance department as a particularly outstanding performer. According to others who worked with him on some assignments, Jim lacked the skills to perform the job well enough to receive such a high reward. However, Jim Sandu had become a favoured employee to Mr. Johnston and they had even gone on a fishing trip together.

Jackie's enthusiasm toward Steelfab Ltd. fell dramatically during her second year of employment. She still enjoyed the work and made friends with some of her coworkers, but the spirit that had once carried her through the morning rush hour traffic had somehow dwindled. Eventually Jackie stopped mentioning her productivity improvement ideas. On two occasions during her second year of employment, she took a few days of sick leave to visit friends and family in New Brunswick. She had used only two sick days during her first year and these were for a legitimate illness. Even her doctor had to urge Jackie to stay at home on one occasion. But by the end of the second year, using sick days seemed to "justify" Jackie's continued employment at Steelfab Ltd. Now, as her second annual merit increase approached, Jackie started to seriously scout around for another job.

Discussion Questions

1. What symptom(s) exist in this case to suggest that something has gone wrong?
2. What are the root causes that have led to these symptoms?
3. What actions should the organization take to correct these problems?

PAMELA JONES, FORMER BANKER

Pamela Jones enjoyed banking. She had taken a battery of personal aptitude and interest tests that suggested she might like and do well in either banking or librarianship. Since the job market for librarians was poor, she applied for employment with a large chartered bank, the Bank of Winnipeg, and was quickly accepted.

Her early experiences in banking were almost always challenging and rewarding. She was enrolled in the bank's management development program because of her education (a B.A. in languages and some postgraduate training in business administration), her previous job experience, and her obvious intelligence and drive.

During her first year in the training program, Pamela attended classes on banking procedures and policies, and worked her way through a series of low-level positions in her branch. She was repeatedly told by her manager that her work was above average. Similarly, the training officer who worked out of the main office and coordinated the development of junior officers in the program frequently told Pamela that she was "among the best three" of her cohort of 20 trainees.

Although she worked hard and frequently encountered discrimination from senior bank personnel (as well as customers) because of her sex, Pamela developed a deep-seated attachment to banking in general, and to her bank and branch in particular. She was proud to be a banker and proud to be a member of the Bank of Winnipeg.

After one year in the management development program, however, Pamela found she was not learning anything new about banking or the B. of W. She was shuffled from one job to another at her own branch, cycling back over many positions several times to help meet temporary problems caused by absences, overloads, and turnover. Turnover—a rampant problem in banking—amazed Pamela. She couldn't understand, for many months, why so many people started careers "in the service" of banking, only to leave after one or two years.

After her first year, the repeated promises of moving into her own position at another branch started to sound hollow to Pamela. The training officer claimed that there were no openings suitable for her at other branches. On two occasions when openings did occur, the manager of each of the branches in question rejected Pamela, sight unseen, presumably because she hadn't been in banking long enough.

Pamela was not the only unhappy person at her branch. Her immediate supervisor, George Burns, complained that, because of the bank's economy drive, vacated customer service positions were left unfilled. As branch accountant, Burns was responsible for day-to-day customer service. As a result, he was unable to perform the duties of his own job. The manager told Burns several times that customer service was critical, but Burns would have to improve his performance on his own job. Eventually, George Burns left the bank to work for a trust company, earning 70 dollars a month more for work similar to that he had been performing at the B. of W. This left Pamela in the position of having to supervise the same tellers who had trained her only a few months earlier. Pamela was amazed at all the mistakes the tellers made, but found it difficult to do much to correct their poor work habits. All disciplinary procedures had to be administered with the approval of Head Office.

After several calls to her training officer, Pamela was finally transferred to her first "real" position in her own branch. Still keen and dedicated, Pamela was soon to lose her enthusiasm.

At her new branch, Pamela was made "assistant accountant." Her duties included the supervision of the seven tellers, some customer service, and a great deal of paperwork. The same economy drive that she had witnessed at her training branch resulted in the failure to replace customer service personnel. Pamela was expected to pick up the slack at the front desk, neglecting her own work. Her tellers seldom balanced their own cash, so Pamela stayed late almost every night to find their errors. To save on overtime, the manager sent the tellers home while Pamela stayed late, first to correct the tellers' imbalances, then to finish her own paperwork. He told Pamela that as an officer of the bank, she was expected to stay until the work of her subordinates, and her own work, were satisfactorily completed. Pamela realized that most of her counterparts in other B. of W. branches were willing to give this sort of dedication; therefore, so should she. This situation lasted six months with little sign of change in sight.

One day, Pamela learned from a phone conversation with a friend at another branch that she would be transferred to Hope, British Columbia, to fill an opening that had arisen. Pamela's husband was a professional, employed by a large corporation in Vancouver. His company did not have an office in Hope; moreover, his training was very specialized, so that he could probably find employment only in large cities anyway.

Accepting transfers was expected of junior officers who wanted to get ahead. Pamela enquired at Head Office and learned that the rumor was true. Her training officer told her, however, that Pamela could decline the transfer if she wished, but he couldn't say how soon her next promotion opportunity would come about.

Depressed, annoyed, disappointed, and frustrated, Pamela quit the bank.

Discussion Questions

1. What symptom(s) exist in this case to suggest that something has gone wrong?
2. What are the root causes that have led to these symptoms?
3. What actions should the organization take to correct these problems?

Source: C. C. Pinder, *Work Motivation* (Glenview, Ill.: Scott, Foresman, 1984), pp. 317–318.

EXPERIENTIAL EXERCISE

PREDICTING HARRY'S WORK EFFORT

Purpose: This exercise is designed to help you understand expectancy theory and how its elements affect a person's level of effort toward job performance.

Instructions: This exercise may be completed either individually or in small teams of four or five people. When the individuals (or teams) have completed the exercise, the results will be discussed and compared with others in the class.

Read the following interview case. Then, using the chart at the end of the case, determine whether Harry will engage in high or low performance effort under the conditions described. Valence scores range from -1.0 to $+1.0$. All expectancies are probabilities ranging from 0 (no chance) to 1.0 (definitely will occur). The effort level scores are calculated by multiplying each valence by the appropriate $P \rightarrow O$ expectancy, summing these results, then multiplying the sum by the $E \rightarrow P$ expectancy.

Interviewer: Hi, Harry. I have been asked to talk to you about your job. Do you mind if I ask you a few questions?

Harry: No, not at all.

Interviewer: Thanks, Harry. What are the things that you would anticipate getting satisfaction from as a result of your job?

Harry: What do you mean?

Interviewer: Well, what is important to you with regard to your job here?

Harry: I guess most important is job security. As a matter of fact, I can't think of anything that is more important to me. I think getting a raise would be nice, and a promotion would be even better.

Interviewer: Anything else that you think would be nice to get, or for that matter, that you would want to avoid?

Harry: I certainly would not want my buddies to make fun of me. We're pretty friendly, and this is really important to me.

Interviewer: Anything else?

Harry: No, not really. That seems to be it.

Interviewer: How satisfied do you think you would be with each of these?

Harry: What do you mean?

Interviewer: Well, assume that something that you would really like has a value of +1.0 and something you would really not like, that is you would want to avoid, has a value of −1.0, and something you are indifferent about has a value of 0.

Harry: OK. Getting a raise would have a value of .5; a promotion is more important, so I'd say .7; and having my buddies make fun of me, .9.

Interviewer: But, I thought you didn't want your buddies to make fun of you.

Harry: I don't.

Interviewer: But, you gave it a value of .9.

Harry: Oh, I guess it should be −.9.

Interviewer: Ok, I just want to be sure I understand what you're saying. Harry, what do you think the chances are of these things happening?

Harry: That depends.

Interviewer: On what?

Harry: On whether my performance is high or just acceptable.

Interviewer: What if it is high?

Harry: I figure I stand about a 50–50 chance of getting a raise and/or a promotion, but I also think that there is a 90 percent chance that my buddies will make fun of me.

Interviewer: What about job security?

Harry: I am certain my job is secure here, whether my performance is high or just acceptable. I can't remember the last guy, who was doing his job, and got fired. But if my performance is just acceptable, my chances of a raise or promotion are about 10 percent. However, then the guys will not make fun of me. That I am certain about.

Interviewer: What is the likelihood of your performance level being high?

Harry: That depends. If I work very hard and put out a high degree of effort, I'd say that my chance of my performance being high is about 90 percent. But if I put out a low level of effort, you know—if I just take it easy—then I figure that the chances of my doing an acceptable job is about 80 percent.

Interviewer: Well, which would you do: put out a low level or a high level of effort?

Harry: With all the questions you asked me, you should be able to tell me.

Interviewer: You may be right!

Harry: Yeah? That's nice. Hey, if you don't have any other questions, I'd like to join the guys for coffee.

Interviewer: OK, thanks for your time.

Harry: You're welcome.

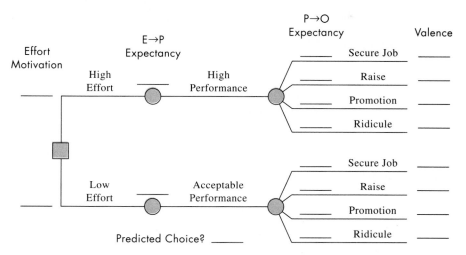

Please fill in the blanks and calculate the effort motivation for each choice.

Source: Robert J. Oppenheimer, Concordia University, Montreal. Used with permission.

4

Performance Appraisal, Rewards, and Discipline

LEARNING OBJECTIVES

After reading this chapter, you should be able to:

Evaluate
The effectiveness of a performance appraisal system.

Describe
The management by objectives process.

Indicate
The important features of an effective performance appraisal review.

List
Several types of individual and team rewards.

Explain
Why some performance-based reward systems are ineffective.

Critique
The use of punishment in organizations.

Contrast
Progressive discipline from positive discipline.

CHAPTER OUTLINE

Evaluating Employee Performance

Performance Appraisal Methods

The Performance Appraisal Review

Reward Systems

Discipline and Punishment

Canadian Hunter

Canadian Hunter Exploration Ltd. stays ahead of the competition by hiring the best people and rewarding them handsomely for their accomplishments. Pay is outstanding by the historically generous standards of the oil patch. Clerical staff earn the top 15 to 20 percent pay rates in the industry, and some professional groups receive more than the highest industry levels. Employee benefits at the Calgary-based oil and gas exploration firm seem endless: six weeks' annual vacation after just five years seniority, allowances for meals and accommodation at nearby national parks, educational assistance, a stock savings plan, office kitchens stocked with refreshments and muffins, ski trips, and more.

Exceptional effort is recognized in several ways. Department managers can provide small dinner parties or time off for their staff. Senior officials may authorize company-paid trips for an employee and spouse, or up to a month's bonus pay. High achievers among the lower-salaried employees sometimes get a leather pouch with 50 gold dollars. More significant achievements—such as the discovery of a new oil field—are rewarded by a net profit interest in the field, which could reach a value exceeding $1 million.

Profit sharing is the norm at Canadian Hunter. President John Masters and executive vice-president Jim Gray have an agreement with Noranda Inc., Hunter's parent company, to receive 12.5 percent of the net profit from oil and gas fields after exploration and development costs have been paid. This amount ranges from $10 million to $15 million annually. Half of this money is distributed to about 75 Hunter employees as a reward for the part they have played in hydrocarbon discoveries.

To keep top talent from leaving Hunter, there is a delay before employees are entitled to their profit share, and anyone leaving the company forfeits half of his or her award. Masters says that sharing the wealth of the company with many employees is an effective strategy. He also believes that employees perform at 95 percent of their potential compared with perhaps 40 percent in the big oil companies around Calgary. "I'd say we probably have more millionaires in Canadian Hunter than any other company in town," he boasts. No wonder Canadian Hunter employees smile a lot![1]

Canadian Hunter is a trendsetter in the management of formal rewards. It may seem obvious to most of us that higher-performing employees should receive higher rewards, but many Canadian companies still do not link pay to individual or team performance.[2] Notice that Canadian Hunter strategically uses a variety of incentives to motivate different employee behaviours, from joining and staying with the company to putting more effort into discovering new oil and gas fields. This reflects our discussion in Chapter 2 that there are many types of performance-related behaviours, each of which affects the organization's effectiveness.

This chapter applies many of the concepts described in the previous two chapters by presenting three interrelated organizational practices: performance appraisal, reward systems, and employee discipline. The chapter begins by examining the characteristics of effective performance appraisal systems, the different appraisal methods, who conducts performance appraisals, and what conditions should exist in the appraisal review.

Next, the important topic of organizational reward systems is presented. Specifically, the objectives of formal reward systems are discussed and several reward practices used in Canadian industry are summarized. The final part of this chapter is directed toward several issues dealing with employee discipline and punishment. This may seem like a rather sour approach to managing employee performance, but it is a very common practice and worthy of discussion. As we will see, disciplining employees may be effective, but it also carries risks.

EVALUATING EMPLOYEE PERFORMANCE

Employee behaviours and their consequences are often measured and evaluated through performance appraisal systems.[3] **Performance appraisal** is the systematic *process* of determining the extent to which employees are performing their jobs effectively, communicating this information to job incumbents, and developing strategies to improve areas of poor performance. We emphasize the word *process* because appraisals are not simply rating forms, documents, or management controls; they represent an ongoing series of activities to improve and maintain employee performance. In terms of the five types of employee behaviours described in Chapter 2, performance appraisals typically focus on required job duties and their outcomes. To a lesser extent, work attendance and organizational citizenship behaviours are also evaluated.

performance appraisal
The systematic process of measuring and communicating how well employees are performing their jobs, as well as developing strategies to improve areas of poor performance.

Purposes of Performance Evaluation

Performance appraisals serve the two purposes listed in Exhibit 4–1: judgmental and developmental. Performance ratings serve a judgmental function to the extent that they identify which employees should receive organizational rewards and sanctions. Specifically, many Canadian organizations—such as Imperial Oil, NOVA, and General Motors of Canada—are placing greater emphasis on performance appraisal results to decide salary increases and promotions. They are also relying more on appraisal ratings to identify those who should be laid off or dismissed due to marginal performance.[4]

EXHIBIT 4–1	Two Purposes of Performance Appraisal Systems

Judgmental Functions	Developmental Functions
Salary increases	Training
Promotions and demotions	Coaching and counselling
Selection for special assignments	Referral to employee assistance programs
Layoffs	Career planning
Dismissals	

Performance appraisal results also serve a developmental purpose by providing performance feedback and identifying employees who require further training. As instruments for employee development, performance appraisal systems provide valuable feedback to employees who have been trying to perform well and can help retain ambitious, capable employees instead of losing them to competitors. They also provide a formalized means of communicating and documenting dissatisfaction with unacceptable employee performance and efforts to improve it.

Performance appraisals help managers coordinate and direct all four elements of the individual performance model described in Chapter 2. First, they improve employee *motivation* by identifying which employees are performing well, thereby enabling managers to link rewards with desired behaviour. Through appraisal feedback, employees develop clearer *role perceptions* and agree with supervisors on the relative importance of future work objectives. Appraisal results help managers determine the extent to which employee *abilities* are matched with job requirements. Finally, some performance appraisal systems examine potential *situational contingencies* that facilitate or constrain the employee's opportunity to accomplish job-related goals. These functions of performance appraisals are illustrated in Perspective 4–1, which describes how Imperial Oil Ltd. improved employee performance by revamping its appraisal system.

Characteristics of Effective Performance Appraisals

In spite of their potential value to organizational effectiveness, performance appraisal systems are often criticized for their imperfections. While many articles have been written on the "do's" and "don'ts" of designing these systems, it is important to examine the fundamental characteristics underlying appraisal effectiveness. Generally speaking, performance appraisal systems are more likely to be effective if they are reliable, valid, sensitive, practical, and acceptable.[5]

PERSPECTIVE 4–1   Reviving Employee Effectiveness through Performance Appraisals

A few years ago, senior management at Imperial Oil Ltd. took a close look at the way employee performance was rewarded. They didn't like what they saw. The company recognized seniority and seemed to stifle individual achievement. In the words of Donald McIvor, Imperial Oil's CEO at the time: "I realized that this organization was as bureaucratic as the post office. There was a horrible stultifying atmosphere."

With tumbling profits and increasing turbulence in the energy industry, Imperial Oil had to place more emphasis on individual effort and performance. The company wanted to know which employees were achieving results so that they could be properly rewarded. It wanted to identify those who were ready for higher responsibilities in the organization so that they could be promoted. Imperial Oil also could no longer afford to retain poor performers, so it wanted to know who could not meet the minimum performance standards. To accomplish these objectives, the company needed a better performance appraisal system.

Imperial Oil made performance appraisal a top priority and spent 18 months making the system more accurate and acceptable. Employee participation in the process was increased, performance ratings were scrutinized more carefully, performance standards were more carefully established, and information about each individual's performance was collected more diligently. Today, Imperial Oil is more confident that the best people are identified for promotion and rewards and that performance problems are more quickly identified and corrected.

Sources: Based on J. Terry, "In Praise of Appraisals," *Canadian Business*, December 1984, pp. 81–85; and E. Innes, R. L. Perry, and J. Lyon, *The 100 Best Companies to Work for in Canada* (Toronto: HarperCollins, 1990), pp. 210–12.

Reliable.   Appraisal results should be consistent. This means that different supervisors (or other raters) should have the same results for a particular employee and that the performance ratings provided by one rater should not change within a very short period of time, such as a few hours or days.

Valid.   Performance ratings should accurately estimate the employee's true performance level during the performance period. Specifically, important performance dimensions should be included in the evaluation instrument, and these job elements must be linked with organizational objectives. At the same time, the appraisal system should ignore information that is either irrelevant or beyond the control of job incumbents. Supervisors typically examine a sample of employee behaviours and results, so it is their duty to ensure that this information is relevant and representative. Supervisors and others conducting the appraisal should also minimize perceptual errors (described in Chapter 7).

Sensitive.   The appraisal system should be able to sufficiently distinguish employees who perform their jobs well from those who do not. It should also be able to differentiate the various performance dimensions within each employee so that the aspects of job performance needing improvement are clearly identified. For example, an appraisal should be able to point out that a particular employee has good customer service behaviour but does not cooperate sufficiently with coworkers.

Practical.   The appraisal system should be cost effective. It should neither be too expensive to develop nor too cumbersome to implement. For example, supervisors should not have to spend too much of their time recording employee activities.

Acceptable.   Acceptability is perhaps one of the most important and, until recently, most overlooked characteristics of an effective performance appraisal system. *Perceived fairness* is the watchword here. The more employees believe the appraisal process is fair, the more they will view the results as credible and meaningful. Supervisors must also accept the performance appraisal system because this will affect their motivation to rate employees accurately and communicate appraisal results more fully.[6]

Employees with better performance appraisal results are certainly more likely to believe that the system is fair. Yet the following characteristics of the performance appraisal *process* also seem to affect perceived fairness:[7]

- Employees are given the opportunity to participate in the appraisal process.
- Performance outcomes are based on established and agreed-upon goals, and these objectives are discussed in the performance review.
- The employee being appraised believes that the rater is knowledgeable of the job and has had sufficient opportunity to observe the employee perform the job.
- The performance dimensions on which employees are evaluated are perceived to be relevant.
- The performance appraisal is conducted at least once a year.

PERFORMANCE APPRAISAL METHODS

Many types of performance appraisals dot the Canadian business landscape. Some emphasize employee traits; others focus on behaviours and results. Some compare performance against objective performance standards; others compare an employee's performance directly against the performance of coworkers. In many cases, organizations use two or more appraisal methods for a particular group of employees. The appraisal methods described here represent the most common varieties found in Canadian organizations.

Graphic Rating Scales

graphic rating scale
A type of performance appraisal instrument that presents raters with a list of subjective performance dimensions upon which employees are evaluated.

Graphic rating scales present supervisors (or other raters) with a list of subjective performance dimensions (such as "quality of work") upon which each employee is evaluated. Sometimes the evaluator has the option of using only dimensions that clearly apply to the individual's job. More often, all employees are evaluated on all dimensions. Graphic rating scales are popular in Canada because they provide standardized results, require relatively little time to complete, and are generally acceptable to the people being evaluated.[8]

An example of a graphic rating scale used by Air Canada is shown in Exhibit 4–2. This instrument includes seven performance dimensions and is used for administrative and technical support personnel. Supervisors rate each dimension of the employee's performance on a four-point scale, from "Unsatisfactory" to "Outstanding." Written comments on each dimension are also provided.

Although it is one of the oldest and most widely used performance appraisal techniques, the graphic rating scale has received much criticism. Since most dimensions are broadly defined, this method may provide inadequate information for developmental purposes such as employee feedback and training needs assessment. Graphic ratings are subject to a number of perceptual errors (discussed in Chapter 7) because evaluators are required to provide subjective impressions of employee performance. On the other hand, this procedure can be reasonably effective if performance dimensions and levels are clearly defined and evaluators are properly trained.[9]

Behaviourally Anchored Rating Scales

Behaviourally anchored rating scales (BARS) are graphic rating scales with the performance levels anchored by job-related behaviours.[10] These behaviours, known as **critical incidents,** represent specific examples of effective or ineffective behaviour in a specific job. A BARS scale used by a Canadian forest products company to evaluate supervisors with respect to crew training is presented in Exhibit 4–3. This is only one of several dimensions in the company's performance appraisal for supervisors.

The BARS format tends to be more reliable and valid than the graphic rating scale because performance levels are anchored by observable behaviours, thereby making the supervisor's evaluations less subjective. Behavioural anchors also increase the method's acceptability to those being rated. However, BARS can be quite time-consuming and expensive to develop, particularly when different scales must be developed for several unique job groups.

behaviourally anchored rating scale
A performance appraisal instrument similar to graphic rating scales with the performance levels anchored by job-related behaviours.

critical incidents
Specific examples of effective or ineffective behaviour in a specific job, typically used to review employee performance or develop behaviourally anchored rating scales.

Management by Objectives

Based on a disenchantment with the subjective methods described above and an increasing recognition that goal setting is a powerful motivational tool, several experts advocate **management by objectives (MBO)** as a performance appraisal strategy. MBO is widely used in Canada for evaluating the performance of managers and, to a lesser extent, technical and support staff.

management by objectives
A performance appraisal method whereby employee performance is evaluated against pre-established goals.

EXHIBIT 4–2   Graphic Rating Scale at Air Canada

PERFORMANCE REVIEW - ADMINISTRATIVE & TECHNICAL SUPPORT PERSONNEL
ÉVALUATION DU RENDEMENT - PERSONNEL DE SOUTIEN ADMINISTRATIF ET TECHNIQUE

PLEASE REFER TO GUIDELINES ON REVERSE FOR COMPLETION *POUR REMPLIR LA FICHE, VOIR DIRECTIVES AU VERSO*

Emp No. *Matricule*	Name *Nom*		Title *Fonction*		Location *Lieu*
Group *Groupe*	Service Date *Date d'entree en service*	Entry date present job *Date d'affectation au poste actuel*	Review date *Date de l'évaluation*	Last review date *Date de la dernière évaluation*	Next review date *Date de la prochaine évaluation*

Probation - First 6 months *Fin période d'essai* ☐	Six months Review *Évaluation semestrielle* ☐	Annual Review *Évaluation annuelle* ☐

OUTSTANDING *EXCEPTIONNEL*
SUPERIOR *SUPÉRIEUR*
FULLY COMPETENT *PLEINEMENT SATISFAISANT*
SOME IMPROVEMENT/DEVELOPMENT REQUIRED *À AMÉLIORER/PERFECTIONNER LÉGÈREMENT*
SUBSTANTIAL IMPROVEMENT REQUIRED *À AMÉLIORER NETTEMENT*
UNSATISFACTORY *INSATISFAISANT*

CHECK APPROPRIATE BOX
COCHER LA CASE APPROPRIÉE

COMMENTS (including development recommendations)
OBSERVATIONS (y compris les recommandations de perfectionnement)

R E S U L T A T S
RÉSULTATS

WORK ACCOMPLISHMENTS — QUALITY OF WORK
RÉALISATIONS PROFESSIONNELES — QUALITÉ DU TRAVAIL

WORK ACCOMPLISHMENTS — QUANTITY OF WORK
RÉALISATIONS PROFESSIONNELLES — QUANTITÉ DE TRAVAIL

A P T I T U D E S
APTITUDES

ATTITUDE & INTERPERSONAL SKILLS
COMPORTEMENT ET RELATIONS AVEC AUTRUI

INITIATIVE
INITIATIVE

ABILITY TO LEARN, INCLUDING SELF DEVELOPMENT ACTIVITIES
FACILITÉ D'ADAPTATION, EFFORTS DE PERFECTIONNEMENT

TECHNICAL SKILLS
QUALITÉS TECHNIQUES

ATTENDANCE, PUNCTUALITY
ASSIDUITÉ, PONCTUALITÉ

OVERALL PERFORMANCE
NOTATION GÉNÉRALE

Prepared by *Établi par* _____	Name *Nom*	Title *Fonction*	Date
Approved By *Visa* _____	Name *Nom*	Title *Fonction*	Date

Employee's comments, interests & aspirations
Observations de l'employé, intérêts & aspirations

Employee's Signature
Signature de l'employé

ACF683A(9-87)

Reproduced with permission of Air Canada.

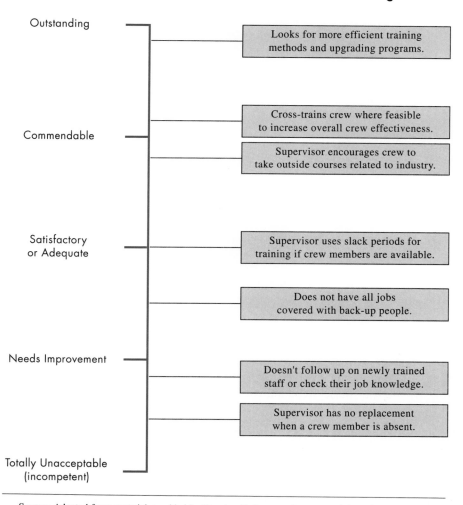

EXHIBIT 4–3   Example of a Behaviourally Anchored Rating Scale

Performance Dimension: Ensure Effective Crew Training

Outstanding

> Looks for more efficient training methods and upgrading programs.

Commendable

> Cross-trains crew where feasible to increase overall crew effectiveness.

> Supervisor encourages crew to take outside courses related to industry.

Satisfactory or Adequate

> Supervisor uses slack periods for training if crew members are available.

> Does not have all jobs covered with back-up people.

Needs Improvement

> Doesn't follow up on newly trained staff or check their job knowledge.

> Supervisor has no replacement when a crew member is absent.

Totally Unacceptable (incompetent)

Source: Adapted from material provided by Douglas H. Lawson, Lawson and Associates, North Vancouver.

In some firms, such as Black and Decker Canada Inc., MBO is a management philosophy rather than just a performance appraisal tool because goal setting is deeply embedded in management practice.

MBO was first introduced by Peter Drucker in the 1950s, based on his work at General Electric. Others, including Canadian writer Bill Reddin,

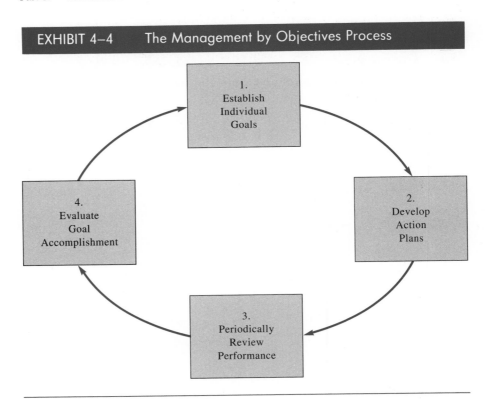

EXHIBIT 4–4   The Management by Objectives Process

have further popularized this performance appraisal technique.[11] Many forms of MBO have evolved over the years, but each variation generally follows the four basic steps shown in Exhibit 4–4.

Establish Individual Goals. The first step is for the supervisor and employee to jointly establish *specific, measurable goals* for the employee to accomplish over a *specific time period*. Individual goals are based on job duties as well as organizational and departmental objectives (see Exhibit 4–5). Organizational objectives are developed through strategic planning and include specific goals for key results areas of the organization (e.g., markets, products, social responsibility, etc.). These organizational objectives are "cascaded" down to establish departmental goals which, in turn, are cascaded down to become the foundation upon which individual goals are established.[12] Participation is an important element in MBO, so the supervisor and employee should mutually agree on all goals in the MBO process, including the relative priority of each goal.

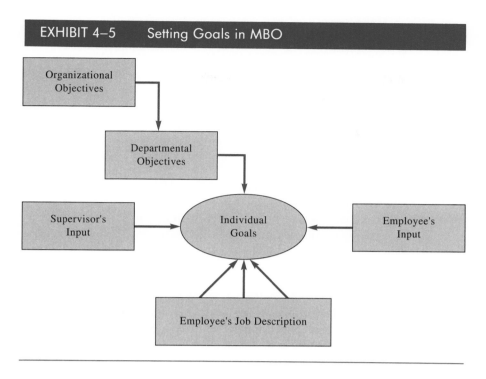

EXHIBIT 4–5   Setting Goals in MBO

Develop Action Plans.   As part of the goal-setting process, the supervisor and employee identify the means by which each goal should be achieved. At Montreal's Maimonides Hospital, for example, supervisors and employees must answer the following questions in the action planning stage:[13]

- What has to be done?
- How will it be done?
- Who will do it?
- When is it to be done?

In many MBO programs, action plans also clarify the resources required and which other employees are required to help fulfill the performance objectives. This ensures that situational contingencies facilitate rather than impede performance objectives.

Periodically Review Performance.   The MBO process encourages frequent, informal discussions throughout the performance period as well as three or four formal meetings in which the supervisor and employee review progress toward each performance goal. These interim reviews also provide the opportunity to alter goals if circumstances have changed. A&W Food Services of Canada requires supervisors to arrange quarterly reviews to ensure that employees receive ongoing feedback. A&W calls its quarterly review process a ''no surprises system'' because it ensures that employees are regularly informed of their progress.[14]

Evaluate Goal Accomplishment.   At the end of the performance period, the supervisor works with the employee to identify the extent to which goals have been met or exceeded. MBO emphasizes measurable goals, so evaluating goal accomplishment is fairly straightforward. At this time, the supervisor and employee establish new goals, and the MBO process is repeated.

MBO has been widely praised because it focusses on objective performance standards that are clearly associated with organizational objectives. Employees typically participate in the process, thereby increasing their perceptions that the system is fair. The periodic reviews provide plenty of constructive feedback. Most important, MBO is goal-oriented. It directs employees toward specific targets of future performance rather than reflecting on subjective interpretations of past accomplishments or failures.[15]

MBO also has its limitations.[16] The system is very time consuming and can degenerate into a paperwork jungle. While the evaluation stage is relatively objective, establishing performance goals is open to a number of human errors and inconsistencies. In particular, it is difficult to determine whether one manager's goals are just as difficult as another's. When used to decide organizational rewards, MBO may lead employees to direct their energy only toward the measurable goals that have been identified in the performance review; more subtle forms of performance with long-term consequences may be overlooked.

Who Conducts Performance Appraisal?

The immediate supervisor is typically responsible for conducting performance appraisals, but other people may also be involved.[17] Canadian Pacific Hotels begins the performance appraisal process by having job incumbents complete a self-appraisal. Self-appraisals tend to increase the perceived fairness of the system, although they often provide inflated results. Imperial Oil encourages employees to provide ''mini-appraisals'' on their coworkers. These peer ratings may be useful where the work is complex and supervisors cannot observe performance, but information from coworkers is sometimes biased and the activity may adversely affect team cohesiveness. Subordinates may be asked to evaluate their supervisors through organizational surveys that are presented to the supervisor in summary form for developmental purposes. Finally, Mohawk Oil and other organizations use a management committee to review the appraisals conducted by supervisors on their employees. These reviews act as a control mechanism against distorted ratings and may provide some consistency among supervisors.

While various people might conduct the appraisal, they should:

- Be in a position to observe the employee's behaviour and performance.
- Be knowledgeable about the dimensions or features of performance.
- Have an understanding of the scale format and the instrument itself.
- Be motivated to do a conscientious job of evaluating.[18]

THE PERFORMANCE APPRAISAL REVIEW

The purpose of the **performance appraisal review** is to inform employees about their performance appraisal results, explain how these results were determined, discuss future performance goals, and identify the means by which performance shortcomings may be improved. Ideally, these activities will boost employee performance and satisfaction by providing a valuable source of feedback and motivation. In practice, interviews are the weak link in the performance appraisal process. Employees are often defensive and supervisors may become authoritarian when they discuss the results. It is little wonder that the performance appraisal review is dreaded by so many supervisors and subordinates.[19] To avoid these problems, supervisors and others conducting the appraisal review need to consider the frequency and timing of the meeting, the preparation required, and the purpose and style of the interview.[20]

performance appraisal review
The process of communicating performance appraisal results to employees and discussing strategies for improving performance in the future.

Frequency and Timing

Reviews are typically held only once a year to coincide with the formal performance appraisal, but the preferred strategy is to conduct development meetings throughout the year so that performance feedback is received quickly. First City Trust and other firms recognize this by encouraging quarterly reviews as well as special appraisals and reviews at the end of a major project. This aligns the performance evaluation process more closely with natural work cycles.

Interview Preparation

Supervisors should receive training in interview and interpersonal skills. Specifically, they must know how to give useful feedback, handle the difficult task of communicating negative feedback, minimize employee (and supervisor) defensiveness when it arises, and keep the discussion on a positive and future-oriented track. Before meeting with the employee, the supervisor should carefully review the appraisal results, particularly the facts and criteria upon which the employee was evaluated.[21]

Interview Purpose and Style

Most performance appraisal reviews try to combine evaluation and development, but it is difficult to coach employees while announcing their salary increase and future promotion opportunities. As a vice-president at Toronto-based Honeywell Ltd. explains: "Sometimes an employee won't hear a word you're saying about his performance and development because he's waiting for the raise."[22] One solution is to first discuss salary and other judgmental issues, then coach employees at later meetings, preferably several times throughout the year.[23]

Employee defensiveness is a major problem in appraisal reviews, but here are several elements of an effective review to minimize this problem:[24]

- Allow enough time to conduct the review and remove any interruptions.
- Encourage employees to participate in the interview by asking open-ended questions about their behaviour and feelings about the appraisal results.
- Discuss job-related behaviour, not personalities or ambiguous criteria.
- Give the interview a future-oriented perspective by focussing on goals and performance improvement.
- Be supportive and constructive throughout the interview.

REWARD SYSTEMS

reward system
The activity of distributing money and other extrinsic benefits to motivate employees toward fulfilling organizational objectives.

An organizational **reward system** distributes money and other extrinsic benefits to motivate employees toward fulfilling organizational obligations. Many types of rewards exist and serve many specific purposes. Exhibit 4–6 lists the basic types of formal organizational rewards as well as the main objectives for which they are used.

Reward System Objectives

Attract and Retain Employees.   Organizational rewards motivate people to join and remain organizational members. The size of the paycheque and other job perquisites are strong inducements for job applicants to choose one organization over another. Some firms have special hiring bonuses for applicants who accept the job offer.[25] Reward systems also influence the extent to which employees are motivated to search for and accept employment with another firm.

Change Specific Behaviours.   Some incentives are introduced to influence specific behaviours. Attendance records can be improved by rewarding employees who show up for scheduled work. Safe work behaviours can also be improved through reward systems. Quaker Oats in Peterborough, Ontario, evaluates and rewards production managers who encourage employees to maintain safe work behaviours. Vancouver City Savings Credit Union offers special incentives to employees who lose weight or jog 1,000 miles per year.

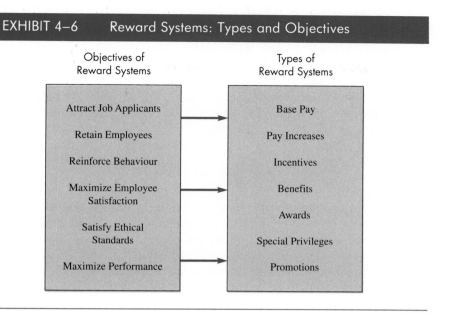

EXHIBIT 4–6   Reward Systems: Types and Objectives

Objectives of
Reward Systems

Attract Job Applicants

Retain Employees

Reinforce Behaviour

Maximize Employee
Satisfaction

Satisfy Ethical
Standards

Maximize Performance

Types of
Reward Systems

Base Pay

Pay Increases

Incentives

Benefits

Awards

Special Privileges

Promotions

The German unit of computer-maker Atari rewards nonsmoking employees with six extra vacation days a year on the basis that this is how much time others spend on smoking breaks.[26]

Maximize Employee Satisfaction.   Pay, benefits, and other extrinsic rewards represent the most obvious factors influencing employee satisfaction. Although not necessarily the most important causes of job satisfaction, reward systems must nevertheless be managed effectively to ensure that employees feel equitably treated.[27]

Satisfy Ethical Standards.   Employees receive at least some compensation and benefits to satisfy legal requirements as well as the broader ethical standards of our society. Most employers are required to pay employees at least the minimum wage as well as mandatory benefits such as paid vacations and holidays. Beyond these standards, many firms offer long-term disability insurance and pension plans to ensure that employees have adequate income protection during retirement or in the event of a non-work injury.[28]

Maximize Performance.   There is overwhelming evidence that productivity increases between 20 to 40 percent when companies switch from time-based (e.g., hourly, straight salary) to performance-based reward systems.[29] Performance-based reward systems are hardly a recent phenomenon in Canada. One hundred years ago, Timothy Eaton was awarding bonuses to clerks with the highest monthly sales. Many years before that, the Hudson's Bay Company introduced an incentive system whereby voyageurs were paid based on distance travelled rather than a daily rate. This encouraged people to accept the arduous task of crossing the Canadian wilderness for the company.[30]

Organizational reward systems may be linked to the performance of individuals, work teams, or the entire organization. Some performance indicators, such as performance appraisal results, are subjectively based. Other reward systems link employee compensation to objective measures of work output, cost savings, or profitability.

Individual Pay Increases

Most employees have come to expect annual pay increases, but the criteria on which these increases are decided have been shifting over the past decade. In the early 1980s, over three-quarters of the Canadian work force received pay increases based solely on inflation and/or seniority. Today, nearly half receive pay increases based in part on individual performance.[31] General (or across-the-board) increases are usually determined through labour union negotiation or a management decision related to the rate of inflation and the company's ability to pay. Seniority-based increases occur where the job has a pay range and employees progress through the range on the basis of their length of time in the job. Someone entering the position might receive the minimum rate and would receive the maximum rate after four or five years. Labour unions prefer seniority-based increases because they rely on objective information rather than management's more subjective estimates of employee performance.

Performance-Based Increases.   While seniority-based pay increases are still common, many employees progress through the pay range based solely on job performance. Most performance-based pay increase guidelines use performance appraisals as the indicator of performance. The largest salary increase is awarded to employees with the highest appraisal ratings, the second-highest increase is awarded to those with the second-highest ratings, and so on.[32]

One of the problems with traditional merit increase systems is that employees reach the top of the pay range for their job and continue to receive a large paycheque even if their performance is now only satisfactory. To remedy this problem, some companies have established a **re-earnable bonus** system, which typically includes a combination of salary increase and cash award.[33] At CNCP Telecommunications, employees with above-average performance ratings receive a salary increase plus a cash award calculated as a percentage of annual salary. The cash award must be re-earned the following year, which motivates employees to continue performing the job well. Satisfactory performance is awarded the salary increase without the cash award. Employees with a marginal performance rating receive less than the full salary increase.

re-earnable bonus
A reward system that typically includes a combination of salary increase and cash award for those who perform their jobs well.

Pay for Knowledge

Several Canadian companies have introduced **pay-for-knowledge** (or *skill-based pay*) systems, in which employees within a job classification receive higher pay rates with the number of skill modules they have mastered.[34] The main objective of this pay strategy is to develop a flexible, multiskilled work force by motivating employees to learn more than one skill. As a new skill is mastered, the employee's pay rate is increased. Employees typically perform only one skill area at a time, but their pay rate is based on the number of areas for which they are currently qualified.

Pay-for-knowledge plans were pioneered in the 1970s by Procter & Gamble and are applied to nonmanagement employees in team-based work units, such as at Northern Telecom, Shell Canada, Westinghouse, and Canadian General Electric. It is difficult to determine the effect of pay-for-knowledge on employee satisfaction and productivity because it is usually introduced along with some form of job redesign. However, preliminary research suggests that employees working under this type of compensation plan are more satisfied, committed, and productive than those under traditional pay systems. Due to the increased ability to move multiskilled employees to other jobs, organizations with pay-for-knowledge plans are potentially more effective. However, pay-for-knowledge results in higher payroll costs and some frustration because employees can "top out" as they finally master all of the skill modules. Training costs also increase because staff members spend more time learning new skills.[35]

pay-for-knowledge
A reward system in which employees within a job classification receive higher pay rates with the number of skill modules they have mastered.

Nonmonetary Rewards

Not all organizational rewards are found in the employee's paycheque. Employers offer a wide variety of employee benefits (see Exhibit 4–7) that cost the average company in Canada about one-third of total payroll. Many of these benefits are required by law; others are negotiated or offered voluntarily by the employer. The major benefits provided by Canadian employers are briefly described below, beginning with the most costly item:

- *Paid time off*—Compensation for time not worked is the most expensive type of employee benefit and includes vacations, holidays, coffee breaks, rest periods, and other special leaves (e.g., jury duty, parental leave, educational leave, etc.).
- *Insurance-based benefits*—Employers cover some or all of the costs or premiums for several insurance plans to protect the employee's financial well-being. These include long-term disability, medical, unemployment, worker's compensation, life, and other insurance plans.
- *Pension plans*—Employers support the employee's financial security during retirement, at least by co-contributing to the Canada/Quebec

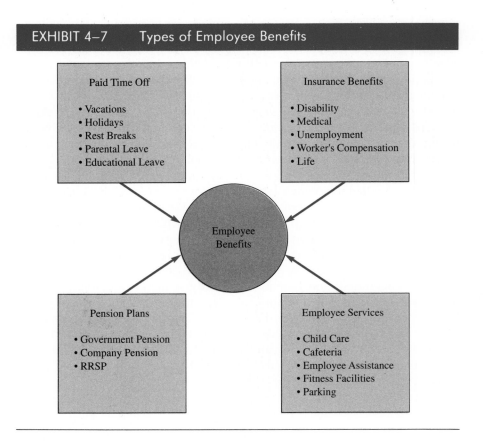

EXHIBIT 4–7   Types of Employee Benefits

Paid Time Off

• Vacations
• Holidays
• Rest Breaks
• Parental Leave
• Educational Leave

Insurance Benefits

• Disability
• Medical
• Unemployment
• Worker's Compensation
• Life

Employee Benefits

Pension Plans

• Government Pension
• Company Pension
• RRSP

Employee Services

• Child Care
• Cafeteria
• Employee Assistance
• Fitness Facilities
• Parking

Pension plan. They may also have a company-sponsored plan and contribute through stock ownership subsidies to the employee's personal Registered Retirement Savings Plan.

• *Employee services*—This is something of a catch-all category of employee benefits that include subsidized cafeterias, free parking lots, child care, employee assistance programs, in-house fitness centres, discounts on company products, counselling programs—even the frozen turkey that many employers still distribute to their employees at Christmas!

Most employee benefits are contingent upon the individual's continued membership in the organization. Seniority is often a determining factor in the length of employee vacations and the vesting of pension plans (i.e., the employee's legal ownership of the money in the pension fund). Some perquisites are based on status. For instance, senior executives at the Canadian Imperial Bank of Commerce have exclusive access to a private dining room.

PERSPECTIVE 4–2   Motivating Employees at Fifth Wheel

Fifth Wheel Truck Stops, a popular highway restaurant in Milton, Ontario, held a 12-week staff incentive called "Mother's Watching You" in which employees could earn points for improving attendance, working overtime, improving customer relations, and generally helping the company. Those with the most points at the end of the promotion won prizes ranging from accommodation for two at a nearby hotel to a "Fifth Wheel" corporate jacket. These prizes were purchased by the restaurant or donated by local merchants.

The average cost of the prizes was only $35—$400 in total—yet the incentive system's effect on employee behaviour was amazing. Recalls John Schouten, manager of the Fifth Wheel restaurant:

> Absenteeism became negligible as the staff were keen to win prize points for merchandise. Customer service significantly improved—even the customers noticed and complimented the staff and management. Employee commitment to work harder and be more friendly became more obvious to everyone. Our staff were more turned on by the prizes than they would have been by cash awards. Getting a corporate jacket which could be worn to work and in town meant more to our staff than winning a $50 cash prize.

Source: Bob McClelland, "Using Staff Incentives to Cut Down Turnover," *Canadian Hotel & Restaurant* 67 (February 1989), pp. 22, 25.

Other benefits are introduced to solve recruiting or attendance problems. Many firms have introduced subsidized day-care because this privilege reduces absenteeism and is a strong incentive for many job applicants to join these firms. However, a few employee benefits are linked to employee performance. As an example, one imaginative Canadian firm gives the best parking spot to the "employee of the month."[36]

Organizational Awards.   Many companies have discovered that plaques, gifts, pins, and other nonmonetary awards are powerful incentives, particularly in relation to their relatively low cost. These rewards sometimes seem contrived, but Laura Secord and other businesses have been able to make them work effectively. Says a Laura Secord executive: "I used to think the traditional pins and watches were rather wimpy . . . but at Laura Secord I learned you can personalize all of that and make it real and meaningful."[37] As Perspective 4–2 describes, nonmonetary prizes can have powerful effect on employee motivation when they are linked to job performance and other desired behaviours.

Promotions and special assignments represent another form of nonmonetary reward. Salary increases usually accompany promotions, but promotions alone are a form of recognition for past performance or service and a symbol of the company's confidence in the employee's future performance. Employees might also be awarded temporary assignments that are highly valued for their challenge, opportunity for travel, or other characteristics. We will discuss these and other career issues in Chapter 16.

Individual Incentives

In several occupations, employees receive lump-sum rewards either as the basis of their paycheque or as supplemental earnings. Some of the more common individual incentives are summarized below.[38]

piecework
A reward system that ties earnings to the number of units produced by the individual.

Piecework.   Piecework ties earnings to number of units produced by the individual. The employee is often guaranteed a pay rate for performing an expected minimum output, called a *standard*. For production over the standard, the employee is paid so much per piece produced.

commissions
A reward system that ties earnings to the sales volume produced by the individual.

Commissions.   Commissions are similar to piecework except that earnings are based on sales volume rather than units produced. Many realtors, brokers, automobile salespeople, and insurance agents are paid straight commission. More often, employees receive a straight salary with commissions representing between 20 to 40 percent of their annual income.

standard hour plan
A reward system that assigns a unit of time to each task and pays the employee for that time whether the job actually required more or less time to complete.

Standard Hour Plans.   A standard hour plan assigns a unit of time to each task and pays the employee for that time whether the job actually required more or less time to complete. This method is commonly used to pay automobile mechanics. Suppose a mechanic earns $15 per hour and is given an engine tune-up job with a standard time of one hour. If the mechanic is productive, the job might only require 45 minutes, but the mechanic still receives one full hour of pay for the task.

bonus
A reward system that provides a lump-sum payment to reward employees for achieving specific objectives.

Bonuses.   Bonuses are short-term, lump-sum payments typically used to reward middle and upper management for achieving specific objectives, such as sales volume or market share. Bonuses comprise an increasing proportion of management and executive compensation in Canada.

Employee Share Ownership. Several Canadian businesses offer company stock to employees at a discounted rate. At the Royal Bank, for instance, employees can have up to 6 percent of their salary deducted to purchase company stock at market rates. The company contributes an additional 50 cents for every dollar the employee invests in company stock. The idea behind share ownership is that employees feel that they share a common interest with the company which, in turn, increases their work motivation and desire to increase corporate profitability. About 64 percent of the companies listed on the Toronto Stock Exchange have share ownership plans, and their productivity is 24 percent higher than firms without these plans. Of course, employee share ownership puts employee capital at risk because company share values may decrease as well as increase in value. The employee-owned company is an extreme variation of the share ownership reward strategy. In several cases, employees or managers have bought the company when it was about to fold (e.g., Lamford Forest Products in British Columbia) or the parent firm was willing to divest the operation (e.g., Britex Ltd. in Nova Scotia).[39]

Team-Based Incentives

Some incentives are more appropriately applied to work teams rather than individual employees. Most of these plans reward teams on the basis of either productivity improvement or profits.

Productivity Improvement Plans.   **Productivity improvement** or **gainsharing plans** such as Scanlon and Improshare focus on cost reductions and increased labour efficiency. Specifically, employees devise ways to reduce the cost of labour and/or supplies, and subsequent financial gains are shared with the company using a predetermined formula. Bonuses are distributed monthly or quarterly and some of the money is withheld in case productivity falls.[40] Although increased motivation and productivity improvements are generally found in firms with these plans, only a few dozen productivity-sharing plans apparently exist in Canada.[41] One type of productivity improvement plan, at E. D. Smith and Sons, is described in Perspective 4–3.

productivity improvement (or gainsharing) plan
A reward system usually applied to work teams that pays bonuses to employees based on cost reductions and increased labour efficiency.

Profit-Sharing Plans.   **Profit sharing** is any arrangement where the employer shares a portion of corporate profits with a designated group of employees.[42] The underlying philosophy is similar to that of stock ownership, namely, that participating employees identify more closely with the company and its goal of profitability. Profit sharing increases the employee's burden of sharing the costs of economic recession, but there is evidence that it also reduces the risk of being laid off.[43]

profit sharing
A reward system where the employer shares a portion of corporate profits with a designated group of employees.

An estimated 30,000 profit-sharing plans exist in Canada. Most of these limit participation to senior executives, although an increasing number of plans include nonmanagement staff. Some nonmanagement plans distribute profit shares quarterly or annually as a cash bonus. Lincoln Electric Co. of Canada Ltd., which has had an all-cash plan since 1940, claims that this form of distribution provides a clear incentive to employees. Other firms have a deferred profit-sharing plan (DPSP) in which the employee's profit share is registered into a trust until retirement. A third option, used by Winnipeg-based Comcheq Services Limited, is to use both cash awards and deferred payments to distribute profits. These combination plans offer the advantages of immediate reward and income protection for the employee.[44]

Problems with Reward Systems

As mentioned earlier, there is considerable evidence that organizational reward systems can motivate employees to work harder, reinforce desirable behaviours (e.g., attendance), and encourage innovative ideas to improve

PERSPECTIVE 4–3   Sharing Productivity Improvements at E. D. Smith and Sons

"Prosperity Plan" is an appropriate name for the productivity improvement plan at E. D. Smith and Sons of Winona, Ontario. The food processing firm introduced the plan in 1986 to encourage employees to reduce costs and reap financial gains from their ideas. To explain the plan, employees attended a special orientation session and met with management again a few weeks later to ask any follow-up questions. Employees were immediately concerned that productivity improvements would result in layoffs, but the company emphasized that while some transfers might be required, no one would be laid off as a result of the plan.

Prosperity Plan emphasizes team involvement. All employees are invited to form "Count Me In" teams, consisting of three to eight members, which meet once each month on company time to brainstorm ideas that will help cut operating expenses. Each team must fully research its ideas and produce feasibility and cost studies, along with projected savings. A company-wide Prosperity Plan committee reviews all

ideas and decides whether to proceed with a proposal.

Concepts that result in measurable savings provide immediate financial benefits to those team members who devised the cost-saving idea as well as to other nonmanagement employees. When an idea is accepted, each member of the team that submitted the proposal immediately receives a merit award of between $50 and $150, depending on the expected amount saved. Half of the money E. D. Smith expects to save from an idea during the coming year is placed in a Prosperity Plan Fund, which is distributed every six months to all nonmanagement employees.

By all accounts, E. D. Smith's productivity improvement program has had a successful beginning. In July 1988, every employee received $1,850 from the Prosperity Plan Fund and some employees have received more than $3,500 in merit awards for their ideas. Over half of the company's 260 nonmanagement employees have joined Count Me In teams.

Sources: L. Medcalf, "Prosperity Plan," *Plant Management & Engineering* 46 (December 1987), pp. 16–17; and "E. D. Smith Introduces Innovative Employee Bonus System," *Canadian Industrial Relations and Personnel Developments*, January 25, 1989, p. 531.

productivity. Yet many firms claiming to have performance-based reward systems receive few of the benefits because they violate some of the basic motivational principles described in the previous two chapters. Experts have identified several possible reasons why organizational rewards do not motivate employees as intended.[45]

Poor Performance–Reward Linkage.   Although many firms claim to pay people based on their performance, many employees do not believe that their performance is linked to reward outcomes (i.e., a low $P \rightarrow O$ expectancy). Reward systems that defer payments also weaken the pay–performance linkage because the reward is not experienced immediately following the performance. The linkage is usually weaker for organizational reward systems because individual employees typically have little direct effect on organizational productivity and profitability. For this reason, organizational-level plans tend to be more effective in small firms where individual behaviours can influence organizational effectiveness more directly.

Highly Interdependent Jobs. Individual incentive systems are inappropriate in operations where jobs are highly interdependent because employees have less control over their own performance and individual output is difficult to measure. Individual incentive systems may also reduce worker cooperation where resources are shared. In these situations, it is better to introduce team-based incentive plans in spite of their weaker performance–reward linkage. Rather than focussing on each employee's output, the entire plant's operating results are used to calculate financial rewards. Most team plans also require good labour–management relations, stable production output, and sufficient autonomy or opportunity for employees to control production and costs.[46]

Biased Performance Appraisals. Some rewards are distributed based on performance appraisal results, but appraisals may be inaccurate or, at least, employees believe they are inaccurate. Recent evidence suggests that appraisal results and the corresponding merit increase recommendations are influenced by factors other than job performance. For example, higher increases are often given to irreplaceable employees who can easily find alternate employment. Employees with organizational connections (e.g., friendship with the president) also tend to receive higher increases.[47]

Insufficient Reward Coverage. As expectancy theory and organizational behaviour modification have predicted, incentives tend to draw effort toward those things that get rewarded and away from other job duties. The quantity of sales or output may increase, but other aspects of performance may be ignored. Piecework may increase the number of units produced per day, but the quality of the product may decrease.

Rewards Are Not Rewarding. Many so-called "rewards" have little value and may, in fact, be insulting to employees. Some merit increase plans offer "outstanding" employees only 2 or 3 percent more pay than "average" employees. Employees are quick to spot these bad deals and consequently redirect their energies toward activities with greater returns.[48] In other situations, the rewards are large but do not correspond to employee needs. As an example, one Canadian firm tried to make its sales force more competitive by offering salary bonuses of up to 40 percent. The plan failed because most salespeople were over 50 years old and didn't value pay as much as other possible rewards.[49]

DISCIPLINE AND PUNISHMENT

Punishment was defined in Chapter 3 as the *introduction* of an undesirable event that *decreases* the frequency or probability of certain behaviours recurring. The concept of **corrective discipline** is more ambiguous, but it usually refers to the act of formally punishing employees who violate an organi-

corrective discipline
The act of formally punishing employees who violate an organizational rule or procedure.

zational rule or procedure. The objective is to regulate the behaviour of employees engaging in inappropriate activities as well as to deter others from practising these behaviours.[50]

Punishment and discipline were once neglected topics in organizational behaviour, partly because early writers had too quickly concluded that punishment was ineffective or, at best, had only a temporary influence on employee behaviour. It is now evident that verbal warnings, work suspensions, and the mere introduction of well-defined disciplinary procedures may potentially reduce absenteeism, increase work output, and minimize work errors in some situations.[51]

Most organizations use some form of corrective discipline procedure to control work behaviours. Management reprimands employees if they engage in undesirable behaviour, and assigns penalties to discourage these actions from recurring. However, punishment is also an extremely complex and potentially risky strategy to suppress or eliminate unwanted behaviours.[52]

Progressive Discipline

progressive discipline

An organizational discipline procedure where the severity of punishment increases with the frequency and severity of the infraction.

Many organizations use a system of progressive discipline to discourage inappropriate behaviour.[53] Basically, **progressive discipline** involves administering more severe forms of punishment based on the frequency and severity of the infraction. As Exhibit 4–8 shows, the first violation of a company rule is typically met with a verbal reprimand by the employee's immediate supervisor. The second infraction results in a written warning placed in the employee's personnel file. The third infraction invokes a short-term suspension from work without pay. If the behaviour is repeated, the employee may receive a longer suspension and eventually permanent dismissal.

Progressive discipline begins with mildly aversive sanctions so that the employee has an opportunity to correct the undesirable behaviour before harsher penalties are applied. However, the severity of the offense also affects the type of discipline received. The first incidence of lateness may result in a reprimand, whereas theft, dishonesty, insubordination, and willful misconduct are usually considered more serious infractions and first offenses often result in a suspension or possibly immediate dismissal.[54]

EXHIBIT 4–8   The Progressive Discipline Process

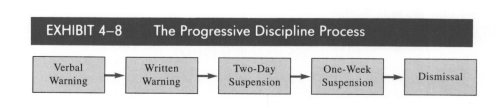

Verbal Warning → Written Warning → Two-Day Suspension → One-Week Suspension → Dismissal

Problems with Punishment

We have stated that punishment is *potentially* effective, but it may also have undesirable consequences if applied inappropriately. One potential problem is that punishment sometimes evokes an adverse emotional reaction to the supervisor and company. Interpersonal relations become strained, employees may feel more apathy toward the job or more hostility toward the organization, and the probability of sabotage may increase. For example, at a Frito-Lay plant where managers fired 58 of the 210 employees in less than one year, employees retaliated by putting obscene messages on the potato chips they packaged.[55]

Another problem is that punishment tells employees which actions are inappropriate, but it does not help them to learn appropriate behaviours. Indeed, with increased hostility and interpersonal distance from the supervisor, employees may become more resistant to adaptive learning. A third concern is that punishment tends to be effective only when the source of punishment is nearby. This follows the old adage that "when the cat's away, the mice will play." In fact, some theorists suggest that punishment treats people like children, with the result that employees will eventually act more immaturely on the job.[56]

Finally, punishment can be costly. Suspending an employee without pay forces the company to hire temporary help or increase overtime. Coworkers must sometimes be bumped into other jobs to fill the vacancy. This disrupts the work flow and increases production costs.

Using Punishment Effectively

Most of the potential problems described above are less likely to occur if certain conditions apply. One major review of the subject has identified several conditions under which punishment may be applied effectively in organizations.[57]

Apply Immediately.   Punishment should be administered as soon as the undesirable behaviour occurs. This effectively communicates that the employee's actions are unacceptable and provides a clear link between the behaviour and the organizational consequences.

Use Moderately Intense Sanctions.   Moderately intense levels of punishment should be applied in most situations. This principle is contrary to most progressive discipline procedures, in which the first offense typically calls for a mild verbal reprimand. But mild punishment might not communicate the seriousness of the problem; harsh punishment, on the other hand, could create undesirable anxiety and impede adaptive learning. Except for severe infractions, the solution is to apply moderately intense sanctions.[58]

Apply Consistently. Punishment should be consistent across time and across employees in order to maintain perceptions of equity. Consistency across time basically calls for a continuous reinforcement schedule, that is, applying punishment every time the undesirable behaviour occurs. Consistency across employees involves administering the same sanctions to different people who engage in the same infractions. To ensure that disciplinary treatment remains consistent, Dofasco Inc. in Hamilton, Ontario, has a policy interpretation group that keeps a precedent book. Each disciplinary action is recorded and can be referred to when similar situations arise.[59] Unfortunately, recent evidence suggests that most organizations tend to be quite inconsistent in their disciplinary process.[60]

Explain the Punishment Action. Employees who are punished should be given clear, unambiguous reasons for the organizational action. They should also be told about future consequences if the undesirable activities recur.

Describe Preferred Behaviour. Recall that punishment identifies undesirable behaviours, but it does not direct employees to the preferred behaviour. Thus, when disciplining employees, supervisors must specifically describe the correct behaviour and reinforce these desired behaviours (or approximations of them) when they are observed.

Punisher Characteristics. Supervisors are more likely to apply punishment effectively if they have established close relationships with and respect from employees. Experts also emphasize the need to treat the matter impersonally, that is, focus on the behaviour rather than the person.

Mixed Consequences Model

Few companies would consider using only positive reinforcement or punishment to control employee behaviour; rather, they tend to use a combination of positive and negative sanctions at appropriate times. Positive reinforcement and extinction are effective for reinforcing desired behaviours and above-average performance, but they do not address poor performance or major work violations. It seems inappropriate to simply withhold a pay increase to someone who has stolen company property, for example.

mixed consequence approach

A management practice that applies each of the four contingencies of reinforcement following various changes in employee performance.

In order to leverage the consequences of behaviour across all levels of performance, it may be more effective to use a **mixed consequence approach.**[61] This strategy uses all four reinforcement contingencies described in Chapter 3 at appropriate levels of performance, as illustrated in Exhibit 4–9.

Positive reinforcement is administered following good performance or as performance improves, and extinction is used when performance slips. Decreasing performance is also addressed by helping employees overcome deficiencies and through other supportive management practices. Persistent poor performance, however, leads to the application of penalties and even-

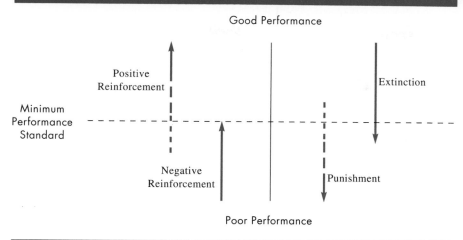

EXHIBIT 4–9   The Mixed Consequences Model of Discipline

tually to warnings of dismissal. Negative reinforcement—the removal of punishers—is administered along with positive reinforcement as marginal performance improves. For example, the supervisor would stop criticizing the marginal employee's performance and would thank him or her for improved results. An increasing number of companies have introduced mixed consequences systems to improve poor performance and control employee absenteeism. Perspective 4–4 describes how this strategy helped improve attendance at J. M. Schneider Inc.

Discipline without Punishment

Given the problems that punishment may generate, a few organizations have introduced disciplinary procedures that try to avoid the use of punishment. The concept of **discipline without punishment,** or positive discipline, was introduced at a Canadian plywood mill almost 30 years ago. It received little attention until the 1970s when an American human resource manager applied it to a Frito-Lay plant and later, as an independent consultant, to numerous other organizations. Today, positive discipline has replaced traditional disciplinary procedures at several Canadian firms, including New Brunswick's Department of Transport, MacMillan Bloedel, Prince George Pulp and Paper, and Union Carbide Canada.[62]

The basic objectives of positive discipline are to counsel employees who have violated company rules, to elicit their participation in the problem-solving process, and to gain their agreement for future behaviour or to consider future career plans elsewhere. The process typically includes four steps (see Exhibit 4–10).

discipline without punishment
A management practice that tries to avoid the use of punishment by counselling employees who have violated company rules and inviting them to participate in finding a solution to the problem.

PERSPECTIVE 4–4   Using the Mixed Consequences Approach to Reduce Absenteeism

In 1987, absenteeism at J. M. Schneider Inc. was hovering around 10 percent. This is close to the average rate in the Canadian manufacturing industry, but it was unacceptable to Schneider's management. To improve attendance on scheduled workdays, the Kitchener, Ontario, meat processing company introduced a mixed consequence attendance control program.

This multipronged strategy involves administering both rewards for good attendance and penalties for those with chronic attendance problems. Employees with perfect attendance receive a congratulatory letter, a token gift, and recognition in the company's newsletter. Those who are absent for justifiable health or personal reasons receive support through the com-

pany's help programs. Based on the principle that 20 percent of the people cause 80 percent of the problem, Schneider also targets chronic leave-takers. Those with poor attendance records are disciplined after one or two offences.

Schneider's mixed consequence strategy has paid off handsomely. By 1989, absenteeism among the company's 2,200 employees had dropped to 7.4 percent and the meat processor has saved over $1 million in lost time. The program also sent an important message to employees. "It's made a world of difference," says Wayne Short, Schneider's national employee relations manager. "The employee is made to recognize his or her importance to the company."

Source: Clayton Sinclair, "Absenteeism's Plague Has no Simple Cure," *Financial Times of Canada*, June 11, 1990, p. 7.

EXHIBIT 4–10   The Discipline without Punishment Process

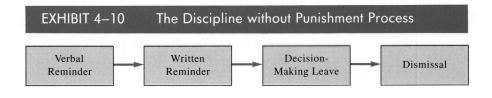

Verbal Reminder.   The first step is a *reminder* that a company rule has been violated and to gain the employee's agreement to solve the problem. This may sound euphemistic, but a reminder restates the importance of the rule or standard whereas a reprimand or warning threatens future disciplinary action.

Written Reminder.   If the offense is repeated, the supervisor again discusses the matter with the employee in a serious manner but without threats. They review reasons why the rule or standard must be observed, discuss the employee's failure to abide by the original agreement (in Step 1), and reaffirm the employee's agreement to solve the problem. Specific goals and action plans are formed (see the discussion of the goal-setting process in Chapter 2) to help the employee eliminate the gap between actual and desired performance. The supervisor summarizes their conversation in a written memorandum and places a copy in the employee's personnel file.

Decision-Making Leave.   The third step in positive discipline is known as a "decision-making leave". This is a paid, one-day leave of absence in which the employee is asked to decide whether he or she is willing to make a "total performance commitment" by changing the unwanted behaviour or to quit and find more satisfying work elsewhere. The next day, the employee announces his or her decision and, if it is to stay, then the supervisor and employee develop specific goals and an action plan for improvement. These plans are documented and placed in the personnel file.

Dismissal.   If the person decides to stay with the organization and correct the behaviour problem, the supervisor makes it clear that the next offense will result in the employee's dismissal. Employers must be certain that if dismissal is required, this action does not violate the employee's rights. Unionized employees can only be fired for "just cause," while nonunion employees can be fired for just cause or with reasonable notice (whether or not there is just cause).

But in the spirit of positive discipline, even dismissal may be reversed in some organizations. For example, Steelcase, the office furniture manufacturer, is known for its "second chance" employees. These are people who have been dismissed and subsequently hired back on the belief that they will turn around. As a fork-lift operator with the firm explains: "They might send you out the door, and a few weeks later call you up and say, 'Have you straightened out yet?' It's a chance to come back, start fresh."[63]

SUMMARY

• Performance appraisal systems measure how well employees are performing their jobs. Appraisal results help decide who should receive organizational rewards and who requires training and other developmental assistance. Performance appraisal systems are more likely to be effective if they are reliable, valid, sensitive, practical, and acceptable.

• Popular appraisal methods include graphic rating scales, behaviourally anchored rating scales, and management by objectives (MBO). Graphic rating scales are the most popular, but they also tend to be the most subjective. MBO is more objective, but may be time-consuming and overlook performance dimensions that are not easily measured.

• Performance appraisal reviews are more effective when they are held frequently and soon after the completion of natural work cycles. Supervisors should receive interview and interpersonal skills training. Separate meetings should be held for judgmental and developmental activities.

• Organizations use a wide variety of rewards to attract, retain, and motivate employees. Rewards include individual increases, pay-for-knowledge systems, individual and team incentives, and nonmonetary benefits. Many of the problems companies experience with their reward systems are addressed in the motivation theories described earlier in this book.

• Most organizations in Canada and elsewhere use some form of corrective discipline to control work behaviours. Progressive discipline is most frequently applied, although the mixed consequences and positive discipline models are being adopted in a few companies. Discipline can be an effective practice, but it also may be risky if punishment is applied inappropriately.

DISCUSSION QUESTIONS

1. How may employers create a performance appraisal system that is more acceptable to employees?

2. Compare and contrast graphic rating scales with behaviourally anchored rating scales.

3. What are some of the potential problems with management by objectives as a performance appraisal and reward management system?

4. What are the main objectives of performance appraisal reviews?

5. List the five objectives of reward systems and illustrate how each might be accomplished.

6. What is a pay-for-knowledge plan and why would companies want to implement this form of compensation?

7. How does positive discipline differ from progressive discipline?

8. What are the potential problems with using punishment in organizations, and how can these problems be minimized?

NOTES

1. E. Innes, J. Lyon, and J. Harris, *The 100 Best Companies to Work for in Canada* (Toronto: HarperCollins, 1990), pp. 34–37.

2. D. Tyson, "Pay-for-Performance Makes Sense for More Major Companies," *Financial Post,* November 12, 1983, p. 14; and M. Salter, "Pay Now Tagged More to Results," *Financial Post,* October 15, 1983, p. 24.

3. K. R. Murphy and J. N. Cleveland, *Performance Appraisal: An Organizational Perspective* (Boston: Allyn & Bacon, 1990); H. J. Bernardin and R. W. Beatty, *Performance Appraisal: Assessing Human Behavior at Work* (Boston: Kent, 1984); and S. J. Carroll and C. E. Schneier, *Performance Appraisal and Review Systems* (Glenview, Ill.: Scott, Foresman, 1982).

4. B. Gates, "Managers Look to Merit Pay to Boost Productivity," *Financial Post,* November 23, 1985, p. 18; V. Galt, "Employers Tying Pay to Performance," *Globe and Mail,* November 4, 1985, p. B1; and S. Luce, *Retrenchment and Beyond: The Acid Test of Human Resource Management* (Ottawa: Conference Board of Canada, 1983), pp. 43–45.

5. W. F. Cascio, "Scientific, Legal, and Operational Imperatives of Workable Performance Appraisal Systems," *Public Personnel Management* 11 (1982), pp. 367–75.

6. Bernardin and Beatty, *Performance Appraisal*, pp. 267–77; R. Folger and J. Greenberg, "Procedural Justice: An Interpretive Analysis of Personnel Systems," *Research in Personnel and Human Resources Management* 3 (1985), pp. 141–85; and R. J. Burke and D. S. Wilcox, "Characteristics of Effective Employee Performance Reviews and Development Interviews," *Personnel Psychology* 22 (1969), pp. 291–305.

7. R. J. Burke, W. Weitzel, and T. Weir, "Characteristics of Effective Employee Performance Review and Development Interviews: Replication and Extension," *Personnel Psychology* 31 (1978), pp. 903–19; and E. M. Evans and S. L. McShane, "Employee Perceptions of Performance Appraisal Fairness in Two Organizations," *Canadian Journal of Behavioural Science* 20 (1988), pp. 177–91.

8. T. A. DeCotiis, "An Analysis of the External Validity and Applied Relevance of Three Rating Formats," *Organizational Behavior and Human Performance* 19 (1977), pp. 247–66; and U. Wiersma and G. P. Latham, "The Practicality of Behavioral Observation Scales, Behavioral Expectation Scales, and Trait Scales," *Personnel Psychology* 39 (1986), pp. 619–28.

9. D. E. Smith, "Training Programs for Performance Appraisal: A Review," *Academy of Management Review* 11, no. 1 (1986), pp. 22–40.

10. D. P. Schwab, H. G. Heneman III, and T. A. DeCotiis, "Behaviorally Anchored Rating Scales: A Review of the Literature," *Personnel Psychology* 28 (1975), pp. 549–62; and J. Goodale and R. Burke, "BARS Need Not Be Job Specific," *Journal of Applied Psychology* 60, no. 3 (1975), pp. 389–91.

11. P. Drucker, *The Practice of Management* (New York: Harper and Brothers, 1954), Chapter 11; W. J. Reddin, *Effective Management by Objectives* (New York: McGraw-Hill, 1971); and G. Odiorne, *Management by Objectives* (New York: Pitman, 1964).

12. Carroll and Schneier, *Performance Appraisal and Review Systems*, pp. 142–43; and H. Weihrich, *Management Excellence: Productivity through MBO* (New York: McGraw-Hill, 1985), Chapters 4 and 5.

13. M. Radcliffe, "MBO: An Approach to Quality Assurance," *Dimensions*, February 1989, pp. 14–16.

14. J. Terry, "In Praise of Appraisals," *Canadian Business*, December 1984, pp. 81–85.

15. J. Carroll, Jr., and H. L. Tosi, Jr., *Management by Objectives* (New York: MacMillan, 1973); J. N. Kondrasuk, "Studies in MBO Effectiveness," *Academy of Management Review* 6 (1981), pp. 419–30; and E. A. Locke, "The Ubiquity of the Technique of Goal Setting in Theories of and Approaches to Employee Motivation," *Academy of Management Review* 3 (1978), pp. 594–601.

16. For a review of these limitations, see Carroll and Schneier, *Performance Appraisal and Review Systems*, pp. 149–52; and Bernardin and Beatty, *Performance Appraisal: Assessing Human Behavior at Work*, pp. 116–24.

17. H. H. Meyer, "Self-Appraisal of Job Performance," *Personnel Psychology* 33 (1980), pp. 291–95; Terry, "In Praise of Appraisals"; A. S. DeNisi, W. A. Randolph, and A. G. Blencoe, "Potential Problems with Peer Ratings," *Academy of Management Review* 26, no. 3 (1983), pp. 457–64; and G. W. Bush and J. W. Stinson, "A Different Use of Performance Appraisal: Evaluating the Boss," *Management Review*, November 1980, pp. 14–17.

18. K. N. Wexley and R. Klimoski, "Performance Appraisal: An Update," *Research in Personnel and Human Resources Management* 2 (1984), pp. 35–79.

19. B. Rice, "Performance Review: The Job Nobody Likes," *Psychology Today*, September 1985, pp. 30–36; and Carroll and Schneier, *Performance Appraisal and Review Systems*, pp. 161–62.

20. D. Cederblom, "The Performance Appraisal Interview: A Review, Implications, and Suggestions," *Academy of Management Review* 7, no. 3 (1983), pp. 219–27; D. R. Ilgen, C. D. Fisher, and M. S. Taylor, "Consequences of Individual Feedback on Behavior in Organizations," *Journal of Applied Psychology* 64 (1979), pp. 349–71; and Carroll and Schneier, *Performance Appraisal and Review Systems*, Chapter 7.

21. Bernardin and Beatty, *Performance Appraisal*, pp. 278–80.

22. Terry, "In Praise of Appraisals," p. 85.

23. H. H. Meyer, E. Kay, and J. R. P. French, Jr., "Split Roles in Performance Appraisal," *Harvard Business Review* 43, no. 1 (January–February 1965), pp. 123–29. For a contrary view, see B. Prince and E. E. Lawler III, "The 'Split Roles' of Performance Appraisal Revisited," *Organizational Behavior and Human Decision Processes*, June 1986.

24. R. J. Burke and D. S. Wilcox, "Characteristics of Effective Employee Performance and Development Interviews," *Personnel Psychology* 22 (1969), pp. 291–305; Cederblom, "The Performance Appraisal Interview: A Review, Implications, and Suggestions"; and Bernardin and Beatty, *Performance Appraisal.*

25. S. L. Rynes, "Applicant Attraction Strategies: An Organizational Perspective," *Academy of Management Review* 15 (1990), pp. 286–310.

26. A. Robert, "Thoroughly Modern Motivation," *Human Resource,* April 1990, p. 22; Innes, et al., *The 100 Best Companies to Work for in Canada;* and "German Firm Awards Extra Vacation Days to Non-Smokers," *Human Resource Management in Canada,* February 1990, para. 84.7.

27. E. E. Lawler, *Pay and Organization Development* (Reading, Mass.: Addison-Wesley, 1981), pp. 11–15.

28. G. Milkovich, W. Glueck, R. Barth, and S. L. McShane, *Canadian Personnel/Human Resource Management: A Diagnostic Approach* (Toronto: BPI, 1988), Chapter 16.

29. A. N. Nash and S. J. Carroll, Jr., *The Management of Compensation* (Monterey, Calif.: Brooks/Cole, 1975).

30. G. G. Nasmith, *Timothy Eaton* (Toronto: McClelland & Stewart, 1923), p. 91; and P. C. Newman, *Caesars of the Wilderness* (Toronto: Viking, 1987), p. 121.

31. K. Noble, "Study Shows Firms to Link Pay with Performance," *Globe and Mail,* October 3, 1984, p. B19.

32. D. P. Schwab and C. A. Olson, "Merit Pay Practices: Implications for Pay–Performance Relationships," *Industrial and Labor Relations Review* 43 (1990), pp. 237s–55s; and R. L. Heneman, "Merit Pay Research," *Research in Personnel and Human Resources Management* 8 (1990), pp. 203–63.

33. J. S. Overstreet, "The Case for Merit Bonuses," *Business Horizons,* May–June 1985, pp. 53–58; B. Gates, "Managers Look to Merit Pay to Boost Productivity," *Financial Post,* November 23, 1985, p. 18; and V. Galt, "Employers Tying Pay to Performance," *Globe and Mail,* November 4, 1985, p. B1.

34. E. E. Lawler, *Strategic Pay: Aligning Organizational Strategies and Pay Systems* (San Francisco: Jossey-Bass, 1990); and G. D. Jenkins and N. Gupta, "The Payoffs for Paying for Knowledge," *National Productivity Review* 4, no. 2 (1985), pp. 121–30.

35. A. Armstrong, "The Design and Implementation of Pay for Knowledge and Skill Systems: An Exploratory Investigation," *Proceedings of the Annual ASAC Conference, Personnel and Human Resources Division* 12, pt. 8 (1991), pp. 21–30; and B. Sheehy and G. Peckover, "You Get What You Pay For," *Industrial Management* 14 (September 1988), pp. 25–26.

36. S. Deller, "The Daycare Dilemma," *Benefits Canada* (April 1986), pp. 15–20; K. Mahoney, "Day Care and Equality in Canada," *Manitoba Law Journal* 14 (1985), pp. 305–34; and A. Bayless, "More Than Motherhood," *Financial Times,* June 4, 1990, pp. 4, 6.

37. T. McCallum, "Fred Van Parys: Reinventing Granada Canada," *Human Resources Professional,* July 1990, pp. 11–13.

38. Milkovich, et al., *Canadian Personnel/Human Resource Management: A Diagnostic Approach,* Chapter 15; and Conference Board of Canada, *Strategic Rewards Management: The Variable Approach to Pay* (Ottawa: Conference Board of Canada, 1990).

39. D. Nightingale and R. Long, *Gain and Equity Sharing* (Ottawa: Labour Canada, 1984); K. J. Klein, "Employee Stock Ownership and Employee Attitudes: A Test of Three Models," *Journal of Applied Psychology Monograph* 72 (1987), pp. 319–32; and R. Barstow, "Stock Plan Pays Off," *Financial Times,* November 23, 1987, p. 33.

40. Nightingale and Long, *Gain and Equity Sharing;* Bruce Gates, "Gainsharing Seen as Productivity Aid," *Financial Post,* September 27, 1986; and M. Schuster, "Gain Sharing: Do It Right the First Time," *Sloan Management Review* 28 (Winter 1987), pp. 17–25.

41. Royal Commission on the Economic Union and Development Prospects for Canada (MacDonald Commission), *Report,* vol. 2, (Ottawa: Minister of Supply and Services, 1985), pp. 714–15.

42. Nightingale and Long, *Gain and Equity Sharing.*

43. J. Chelius and R. S. Smith, "Profit Sharing and Employment Stability," *Industrial and Labor Relations Review* 43 (1990), pp. 256s–73s.

44. J. Francis, "Profit Sharing Gaining Ground," *Winnipeg Free Press,* June 8, 1984, p. 46.

45. W. Clay Hamner, "How to Ruin Motivation with Pay," *Compensation Review,* 3rd Quarter 1975, pp. 88–98.

46. Lawler, *Pay and Organization Development,* p. 144.

47. K. M. Bartol and D. C. Martin, "When Politics Pays: Factors Influencing Managerial Compensation Decisions," *Personnel Psychology* 43 (1990), pp. 599–614.

48. R. E. Kopelman, *Managing Productivity in Organizations* (New York: McGraw-Hill, 1986), pp. 45–46.

49. M. Gibb-Clark, "Cynicism of Employees Seen Growing," *Globe and Mail,* October 20, 1988, p. B8.

50. R. D. Arvey and A. P. Jones, "The Use of Discipline in Organizational Settings: A Framework for Future Research," *Research in Organizational Behavior* 7 (1985), pp. 367–408.

51. C. A. O'Reilly III and B. A. Weitz, "Managing Marginal Employees: The Use of Warnings and Dismissals," *Administrative Science Quarterly* 25 (1980), pp. 467–84; and R. D. Arvey and J. M. Ivancevich, "Punishment in Organizations: A Review, Propositions, and Research Suggestions," *Academy of Management Review* 5 (1980), pp. 123–32.

52. H. P. Sims, Jr., "Further Thoughts on Punishment in Organizations," *Academy of Management Review* 5 (1980), pp. 133–38.

53. D. E. Dimick, "Employee Control and Discipline," *Relations Industrielles* 33 (1978), pp. 23–36.

54. H. W. Arthurs, D. D. Carter, and H. J. Glasbeek, *Labour Law and Industrial Relations in Canada* (Toronto: Butterworths, 1981); and H. A. Levitt, *The Law of Dismissal in Canada* (Aurora, Ont.: Canada Law Book, 1985).

55. P. Johnson, "Discipline without Punishment," *Financial Times,* April 20, 1981, pp. H16–H17; and D. N. Campbell, R. L. Fleming, and R. C. Grote, "Discipline without Punishment—at Last," *Harvard Business Review* 63 (July–August 1985), pp. 162–74.

56. C. Argyris, *Personality and Organization* (New York: Harper & Bros, 1957).

57. Arvey and Ivancevich, "Punishment in Organizations: A Review, Propositions, and Research Suggestions."

58. J. M. Beyer and H. M. Trice, "A Field Study of the Use and Perceived Effects of Discipline in Controlling Work Performance," *Academy of Management Journal* 27 (1984), pp. 743–64.

59. P. Menyasz, "Dofasco Maintains 'Open Door' Policy with Its Employees," *Canadian HR Reporter,* April 18, 1988, p. 9.

60. B. S. Klaas and H. N. Wheeler, "Managerial Decision Making about Employee Discipline: A Policy-Capturing Approach," *Personnel Psychology* 43 (1990), pp. 117–34.

61. R. E. Kopelman and G. O. Schneller IV, "A Mixed-Consequence System for Reducing Overtime and Unscheduled Absences," *Journal of Organizational Behavior Management* 3, no. 1 (1981), pp. 17–28.

62. J. Huberman, "Discipline without Punishment," *Harvard Business Review* 42 (July–August 1964), pp. 62–68; J. Huberman, "Discipline without Punishment Lives," *Harvard Business Review* 53 (4) (1975), pp. 6–8; Johnson, "Discipline without Punishment"; Campbell, Fleming, and Grote, "Discipline without Punishment—at Last"; and M. Thompson, "New Brunswick's Paul Theriault," *Canadian HR Reporter,* April 4, 1988, p. 5.

63. R. H. Waterman, Jr., *The Renewal Factor* (New York: Bantam, 1987), pp. 251–52.

CHAPTER CASE

VÊTEMENTS LTÉE

Vêtements Ltée is a chain of men's retail clothing stores located throughout the province of Quebec. Two years ago, the company introduced new incentive systems for both store managers and sales employees. Store managers in each store receive a salary with annual merit increases based on sales above targetted goals, store appearance, store inventory management, customer complaints, and several other performance measures. Some of this information (e.g., store appearance) is gathered during visits by senior management, while other information is based on company records (e.g., sales volume).

Sales employees are paid a fixed salary plus a commission based on the percentage of sales credited to that employee over the pay period. The commission represents about 30 percent of a typical paycheque and is intended to encourage employees to actively serve customers and to increase sales volume. Since returned merchandise is discounted from commissions, sales staff are discouraged from selling products that customers do not really want.

Soon after the new incentive systems were introduced, senior management began to receive complaints from store managers regarding the performance of their sales staff. They observed that sales employees tended to stand near the store entrance waiting for customers and would occasionally argue over "ownership" of the customer. Managers were concerned that this aggressive behaviour intimidated some customers. It also tended to leave some parts of the store unattended by staff.

Many managers were also concerned about inventory duties. Previously, sales staff would share responsibility for restocking inventory and completing inventory reorder forms. Under the new compensation system, however, few employees were willing to do these essential tasks. On several occasions, stores have faced stock shortages because merchandise was not stocked or reorder forms were not completed in a timely manner. Potential sales have suffered from empty shelves when plenty of merchandise was available in the back storeroom or at the warehouse. The company's new automatic inventory system could reduce some of these problems, but employees must still stock shelves and assist in other aspects of inventory management.

Store managers have tried to correct the inventory problem by assigning employees to inventory duty, but this has created resentment among the employees selected. Other managers have threatened sales staff with dismissals if they do not do their share of inventory management. This strategy has been somewhat effective when the manager is in the store, but staff members sneak back onto the floor when the manager is away. It has also hurt staff morale, particularly relations with the store manager.

To reduce the tendency of sales staff to hoard customers at the store entrance, some managers have assigned employees to specific areas of the store. This has also created some resentment among employees stationed in areas with less traffic or lower-priced merchandise. Some staff have openly complained of lower paycheques because they have been placed in a slow area of the store or have been given more than their share of inventory duties.

Discussion Questions

1. What symptom(s) exist in this case to suggest that something has gone wrong?
2. What are the root causes that have led to these symptoms?
3. What actions should the organization take to correct these problems?

EXPERIENTIAL EXERCISE

CHOOSING THE APPROPRIATE LEVEL OF DISCIPLINE

Purpose.   Using any form of punishment in organizations is, at best, a difficult and awkward business. This exercise is designed to help you understand the difficulties of applying organizational discipline and to understand how managers differ in their diagnoses of situations where some form of discipline might be applied.

Instructions.   Each of the four incidents below involve a work infraction that has been brought to your attention. Following each incident are six possible actions that you have authority to take. Read each incident, indicate your preferred disciplinary action, and explain why this alternative has been selected over the others. When you have finished, the instructor may form small teams of 4 to 5 people to discuss each member's results, or the exercise may be discussed directly with the entire class.

Incident 1

Kelly, one of your firm's truck drivers, has apparently made insulting comments to a customer when delivering the company's product to the customer's business. The insult occurred when the customer asked for proof that Kelly worked for the company. Upon hearing about this, you confronted Kelly, but the driver denied insulting the customer. Later, after receiving irrefutable evidence that Kelly did make insulting comments, Kelly admits the misconduct and signs a written letter of apology to the customer. However, Kelly does not seem to feel any remorse about the incident. Kelly has five years of continuous, full-time service with your company and has no criminal record or record of drug or alcohol abuse. The workplace is not unionized and there is no threat of unionization.

Please indicate which of the following actions to take:

_____   *a.*   No action.

_____   *b.*   Verbal warning.

_____   *c.*   Written warning (repetition may eventually result in dismissal).

_____   *d.*   Written final warning (repetition will result in dismissal).

_____   *e.*   Dismissal with notice or severance payment.

_____   *f.*   Immediate dismissal without notice or severance payment.

Incident 2

You have learned that Kelly, a sales representative in your company, has recently given discounts to members of his/her immediate family who have purchased the firm's products. Kelly is fully aware of the company's policy that special discounts are not allowed to customers or staff. These discounts have been substantial, ranging from 10 percent to 40 percent of the price normally offered for the product to the public. Kelly has five years of continuous, full-time service with your company and has no criminal record or record of drug or alcohol abuse. The workplace is not unionized and there is no threat of unionization.

Please indicate which of the following actions to take:

_____   *a.*   No action.

_____   *b.*   Verbal warning.

_____   *c.*   Written warning (repetition may eventually result in dismissal).

_____   *d.*   Written final warning (repetition will result in dismissal).

_____   *e.*   Dismissal with notice or severance payment.

_____   *f.*   Immediate dismissal without notice or severance payment.

Incident 3

Kelly, a forklift operator with your company, has been seen "showing off" to coworkers by driving the forklift in a dangerous manner. During the observed incident, Kelly ran into a skid of the company's product, damaging several boxes and slightly denting the forklift. Total uninsured damages to the company resulting from this incident will be about $500. Kelly and other employees have recently been notified of the company's rules and safety standards regarding the operation of company vehicles. Kelly's antics are clearly in violation of these rules and standards. Kelly has five years of continuous, full-time service with your company and has no criminal record or record of drug or alcohol abuse. The workplace is not unionized and there is no threat of unionization.

Please indicate which of the following actions to take:

_____   *a.*   No action.

_____   *b.*   Verbal warning.

_____   *c.*   Written warning (repetition may eventually result in dismissal).

_____   *d.*   Written final warning (repetition will result in dismissal).
_____   *e.*   Dismissal with notice or severance payment.
_____   *f.*   Immediate dismissal without notice or severance payment.

Incident 4

Kelly, a dental technician in your company, dislikes removing containers of garbage and waste from the lab after work and has successfully used a variety of tactics to get other employees to perform this task. The job description clearly states that dental technicians remove the garbage and waste. Coworkers have complained to you about Kelly's attempts to get others to remove the containers of garbage. Kelly has admitted to you that he/she dislikes performing the task and has implied that he/she will refuse to do so if ordered. Kelly has five years of continuous, full-time service with your company and has no criminal record or record of drug or alcohol abuse. The workplace is not unionized and there is no threat of unionization.

Please indicate which of the following actions to take:

_____   *a.*   No action
_____   *b.*   Verbal warning
_____   *c.*   Written warning (repetition may eventually result in dismissal).
_____   *d.*   Written final warning (repetition will result in dismissal).
_____   *e.*   Dismissal with notice or severance payment.
_____   *f.*   Immediate dismissal without notice or severance payment.

Source: Based on an executive M.B.A. research project by Ian C. M. Leask and supervised by Steven L. McShane, Simon Fraser University.

Job Design and Stress Management

LEARNING OBJECTIVES

After reading this chapter, you should be able to:

Describe
The advantages and disadvantages of job specialization.

Diagram
The job characteristics model of job design.

Indicate
Five strategies to enrich jobs.

Explain
Why job enrichment does not always increase worker motivation.

Explain
How work and family demands may become stressors.

Identify
Five ways to manage workplace stress.

Imperial Oil Ltd.

When Imperial Oil Ltd. replaced its outdated human resources information computer system, it realized that the new technology would mean changes in jobs and work processes. To avoid the stress of uncertainty and the risk of creating demeaning jobs, Imperial Oil kept clerical staff informed of the changes and involved them in developing the new workflow pattern.

"During that time, [the clerical employees] lost any fear they may have had," says Maureen Donlevy, an automation consultant hired by Imperial Oil to implement the technology. "They began to look forward to the arrival of the computers."

Imperial Oil also took pains to redesign clerical jobs so that they would become more interesting and varied. Explains Donlevy: "We tried not to fracture jobs, so that people felt they weren't just a cog in the machinery. Workers need a sense of the significance of their work. They like to be able to feel that it has some impact."

Rather than centralizing the system, clerical workers in each branch now enter data directly and keep track of their own employee information databases. This provides added challenge and responsibility compared to the previous arrangement where clerical staff simply gathered the data and shipped it off to Toronto.

"I personally welcomed the added responsibility," explains Deborah Ford, an Imperial Oil employee who worked in the Edmonton branch when the new computer system was introduced. "You have a much greater feeling of ownership of the data you work with."[1]

Job design has a powerful influence on employee attitudes and performance, as Imperial Oil's experience illustrates. It may seem rather obvious to us today that the tasks people are assigned affect their motivation, but this fact was once overshadowed by the objective to improve worker efficiency through narrow, repetitive work. Imperial Oil's introduction of new technology was also successful because management recognized that work-related stress can have a tremendous impact on employee behaviour. Without information and involvement, employees may have had difficulty coping with the dramatic changes. This could have led to higher absenteeism, turnover, and illness, as well as reduced job performance.

Job design and work-related stress are the two themes of this chapter. Both issues affect motivation and ability to complete job duties as well as other performance-related behaviours such as turnover, absenteeism, and physical health. The chapter begins by describing early management thought in the field of job design, namely the emphasis on work efficiency through job specialization. We then introduce the job characteristics model to better understand how the tasks people perform affect their attitudes and motivation. Next, several specific job design strategies are presented and the effectiveness of recent job design interventions are discussed. The second half of this chapter looks at work-related stress, including the causes and consequences of stress and the factors that cause some people to experience stress where others do not. The final section of this chapter looks at ways to manage work-related stress from either an organizational or individual perspective.

JOB DESIGN

Job design involves assigning tasks to a job and distributing work throughout the organization.[2] Some jobs have very few tasks, each requiring limited skill or effort. Other jobs include a very complex set of tasks and can be accomplished by only a few highly trained tradespeople or professionals.

job design
The process of assigning tasks to a job and distributing work throughout the organization.

The tasks that people perform are constantly changing. Computer technology often affects job duties,[3] although management can sometimes influence the way jobs are designed, as we saw in the Imperial Oil story. Organizational restructuring also involves job redesign, such as when the Bank of Montreal dramatically changed branch manager job duties a few years ago. Finally, Ford of Canada, Gulf Canada, and hundreds of other firms have deliberately altered job duties to increase employee motivation.

Job design is important because of its influence on employee attitudes, motivation, and productivity. As we shall see, job design often produces an interesting conflict between employee motivation and ability. To understand this issue more fully, we begin by describing early job design efforts that have tried to increase work efficiency through job specialization.

JOB DESIGN AND WORK EFFICIENCY

A fundamental concept in early management theory is that work efficiency increases with the **division of labour**—the subdivision of work into separate jobs assigned to different people. Subdivided work leads to **job specialization** because each job now includes a narrow subset of the tasks necessary to complete the product or service. Job specialization increases work efficiency in several ways:[4]

division of labour
The subdivision of work into separate jobs assigned to different people.

job specialization
The result of division of labour where each job now includes a narrow subset of the tasks required to complete the product or service.

• Jobs can be mastered quickly because work cycles are short and tasks are therefore repeated more frequently. For example, assembly workers would typically have less than one minute to complete their task on a product before starting it again on the next product.

- With fewer tasks to juggle, employees spend less time changing activities or being distracted from their work.
- Training costs are reduced because employees require fewer physical and mental skills to accomplish the assigned work.
- Employees with specific aptitudes or skills can be matched more precisely to the jobs for which they are best suited.

Job specialization has been applied for centuries, but its economic benefits were popularized over 200 years ago by Adam Smith in his famous example of pin manufacturing.[5] According to Smith, there are several distinct operations in pin manufacturing, such as drawing out the wire, straightening it, cutting it, sharpening one end, grinding the other end, putting on the head, whitening the head, and so forth. In one factory where these tasks were divided among 10 people, Smith reported that the work team could produce almost 4,800 pins per day. But if the same 10 people made their own pins separately and independently, they would produce only 100 to 200 pins per day!

Adam Smith was mainly writing about horizontal job specialization, in which the basic "doing" tasks required to provide a product or service are divided into different jobs, as shown in Exhibit 5–1. Vertical job specialization, on the other hand, refers to the division of physical tasks from the administration of these tasks (planning, organizing, scheduling, etc.). In other words, vertical job specialization divorces the "thinking" job functions from the "doing" functions.

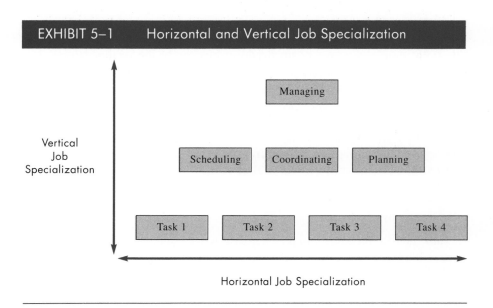

EXHIBIT 5–1   Horizontal and Vertical Job Specialization

Scientific Management

One of the strongest advocates of vertical and horizontal job specialization was Frederick Winslow Taylor, an industrial engineer from Pennsylvania, who introduced the principles of **scientific management** during the early 1900s.[6] Taylor described scientific management as a revolutionary way for management and workers to view their respective roles. In practice, it involves systematically determining how work should be partitioned into its smallest possible elements and how the process of completing each task should be standardized to achieve maximum efficiency.

Taylor advocated vertical job specialization so that detailed procedures and work practices are developed by engineers, enforced by supervisors, and executed by employees. In Taylor's words: "All possible brain work should be removed from the shop floor and centred in the planning and laying out department."[7] Taylor paid just as much attention to horizontal job specialization. His "functional foreman" strategy, for instance, represents a form of horizontal job specialization of management tasks. Taylor recommended that one supervisor should manage the speed of the operation, another should manage inspection, another should be the disciplinarian, and so forth.

Several practices, many of which are described elsewhere in this book, grew out of scientific management. Taylor is perhaps most responsible for emphasizing the need for goal setting, employee training, and incentive systems to increase worker productivity. Frank and Lillian Gilbreth were enthusiastic followers of the scientific management philosophy and are largely credited with developing procedures known as **time and motion study.** Time and motion study involves systematically observing, measuring, and timing the smallest physical movements to identify more efficient work behaviours. The idea is that there is one best way to lay bricks, staple papers together, or engage in any other observable behaviour.[8] Time and motion study is still applied in industry by industrial engineers.

There is ample evidence that scientific management has improved efficiency in many work settings. One of Taylor's earliest interventions was at a ball bearing factory where 120 women each worked almost 55 hours per week. Through job specialization and work efficiency analysis, Taylor was able to increase production by two-thirds using a work force of only 35 women working fewer than 45 hours per week. Taylor was also able to virtually double the employees' previous wages. No doubt, some of the increased productivity can be credited to improved training, goal setting, and work incentives, but job specialization has also contributed to the success of scientific management.

Scientific management has been just as successful in Canada. In 1927, an American industrial engineer was hired by Toronto's York Knitting Mills to increase productivity through time and motion study and wage incentives. The results were so dramatic that Douglas Woods (York's owner) and two

scientific management

The process of systematically determining how work should be partitioned into its smallest possible elements and how the process of completing each task should be standardized to achieve maximum efficiency.

time and motion study

The process of systematically observing, measuring, and timing the smallest physical movements to identify more efficient work behaviours.

colleagues formed their own consulting firm to practise a variation of scientific management known as the "York Plan." The firm eventually expanded into other management consulting services and eventually became Woods Gordon, one of Canada's largest consulting firms.[9]

Problems with Job Specialization

Job specialization may be the most efficient way to design the workplace, but this strategy can actually lead to lower productivity because it ignores the effects of job content on the employee.[10] Some of the negative consequences of job specialization are described below.

Worker Alienation.   To most employees, repetitive work is tedious, boring, trivial, and socially isolating. People who work in these jobs every day tend to experience **worker alienation,** in which they feel powerlessness and meaninglessness in their work lives, increasing removal from social norms, and a psychological separation of oneself from the activities being performed. Worker alienation is manifested in many ways, including increased absenteeism and tardiness, lower productivity, increased sabotage, and some physical ailments.[11]

worker alienation
A psychological state whereby employees feel powerlessness and meaninglessness in their work lives, increasing removal from social norms, and a psychological separation of oneself from the activities being performed.

Product Quality.   Employees in simplified jobs are less likely to care about product or service quality because they are unable to identify with the results of their work. This is apparent in traditional assembly line operations where employees performing a small task tend to let mistakes pass further up the line rather than correcting them. One General Motors employee recalls life on the line before recent improvements were introduced: "The product was going down the line with no one paying any attention to it. 'Ship it! Ship it!' they said."[12]

Market Wages.   Rather than reducing the cost of labour, job specialization has often forced companies to pay higher wages—some call it discontentment pay—to compensate for the repetitive and boring characteristics of narrowly defined work.[13] Labour unions have also been very effective at organizing and negotiating higher wages for employees in repetitive jobs. Even though many people are qualified to perform simplified work, few are motivated to apply for the job unless extrinsic rewards are offered to compensate for the poor job content.

Turnover and Absenteeism.   Most employees try to escape the effects of tedious work through turnover and absenteeism. Turnover rates in some assembly line operations exceed 100 percent. This increases the costs of recruitment and training, often exceeding the financial gains of higher productivity through job specialization. Absenteeism is also higher among employees who are dissatisfied with the content of their jobs, particularly where they can make use of paid sick leave to compensate for the time off work.[14]

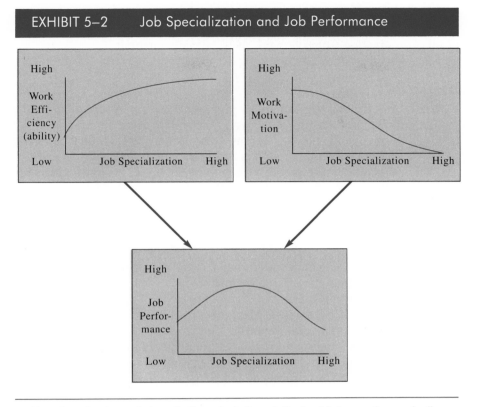

EXHIBIT 5–2   Job Specialization and Job Performance

Note: Assuming that extrinsic motivation, role clarity, and situational factors are the same in all cases, job performance is the result of work efficiency multiplied by work motivation.

Work Motivation.   Perhaps the most important reason why scientific management has not been as successful as expected is that job content is a source of motivation. As we learned in Chapter 2, ability and motivation are two central ingredients in job performance, so job specialization may have a curvilinear effect on job performance, as shown in Exhibit 5–2. As jobs become specialized, more people have the requisite skills and knowledge but the work becomes less motivating. As jobs become more complex, work motivation tends to increase but the ability to perform the job decreases. Maximum job performance occurs somewhere between these two extremes, where most people can eventually perform the job tasks efficiently, yet the work is interesting.

JOB DESIGN AND WORK MOTIVATION

Industrial engineers may have overlooked the motivational effects of job characteristics, but it is now the central focus of most job design interventions. While the problems with monotonous work had been raised by critics in the 1920s and earlier, it was not until Frederick Herzberg introduced his motivator-hygiene theory of work motivation in the 1950s that the full importance of motivation from the work itself became apparent.[15]

Motivator–Hygiene Theory

motivator-hygiene theory
A theory developed by Herzberg based on the idea that employees are motivated by characteristics of the work itself (called motivators) rather than the work context (called hygienes).

Herzberg's **motivator–hygiene theory** proposes that employees are primarily motivated by characteristics of the work itself, such as recognition, responsibility, advancement, achievement, and personal growth. These factors are called motivators because employees experience job satisfaction when they are received and are therefore motivated to obtain them. In contrast, factors extrinsic to the work, called hygienes, affect the extent to which employees feel job dissatisfaction. Hygienes include job security, working conditions, company policies, coworker relations, and supervisor relations. Improving hygienes will reduce job dissatisfaction, but they will have almost no effect on job satisfaction or employee motivation. Notice that motivator–hygiene theory views job satisfaction and dissatisfaction as independent rather than opposite to each other. Improving motivators increases job satisfaction, but it does not decrease job dissatisfaction. Improving hygienes reduces job dissatisfaction but it does not increase job satisfaction.

Herzberg's work made an important contribution to the field job design because it cast a spotlight on job content as a source of employee motivation. When motivator–hygiene theory was first introduced, many researchers were preoccupied with physical and social conditions of the workplace and industrial engineers were focussed on job content from an efficiency (i.e., ability) standpoint. Few writers had addressed the idea that employees can be motivated by the work itself. Motivator–hygiene theory has since led to considerable study into the motivational potential of jobs.[16]

Ironically, the validity of motivator–hygiene theory has fallen into doubt and some writers have suggested that the theory should be laid to rest.[17] The problem is that researchers have been unable to distinguish job satisfaction from job dissatisfaction. In other words, it appears that both hygienes and motivators can affect employee motivation. The basic elements of motivator–hygiene theory may be questioned, but there is no doubt of its impact on the direction of job design research and practice.

THE JOB CHARACTERISTICS MODEL

job characteristics model
A job design model that relates five motivational properties of jobs to the individual's psychological states and several personal and organizational consequences.

One of the most important breakthroughs in job design following Herzberg's motivator–hygiene theory has been Hackman and Oldham's **job characteristics model,** shown in Exhibit 5–3.[18] Developed in the 1970s, this model provides a detailed presentation of the motivational properties of jobs as well as specific personal and organizational consequences of these properties. The job characteristics model identifies five core job dimensions that lead to three psychological states. Employees who experience these psychological

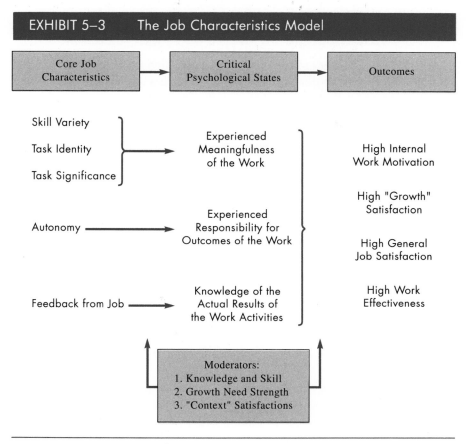

EXHIBIT 5–3   The Job Characteristics Model

Source: J. R. Hackman and G. Oldham, *Work Redesign* (Reading, Mass.: Addison-Wesley, 1980), p. 90.

states tend to have higher levels of intrinsic work motivation (motivation from the work itself), job satisfaction (particularly satisfaction with the work itself), and work effectiveness.

Core Job Characteristics

Hackman and Oldham's model identifies five core job characteristics: skill variety, task identity, task significance, autonomy, and job feedback. Desirable work outcomes increase when jobs are redesigned such that they include more of these characteristics.

Skill Variety.   **Skill variety** refers to the extent that a job requires employees to use different skills and talents to complete a variety of work activities. For example, sales clerks who normally only serve customers might be assigned

skill variety
The extent that a job requires employees to use different skills and talents to complete a variety of work activities.

the additional duties of stocking inventory and occasionally changing store-front displays.

task identity
The degree to which a job requires completion of a "whole" or identifiable piece of work.

Task Identity.   **Task identity** is the degree to which a job requires completion of a whole or identifiable piece of work, such as doing something from beginning to end rather than just part of it. An employee who assembles an entire television converter rather than just solders in the power supply would develop a stronger sense of ownership or identity with the final product. Task identity is also enhanced when there is a visible outcome of the work.

task significance
The degree to which the job has a substantial impact on the organization and/or larger society.

Task Significance.   **Task significance** is the degree to which the job has a substantial impact on the organization and/or larger society. Jobs that have a noticeable effect on the health, safety, and happiness of others tend to have higher levels of task significance. For instance, Canadian coast guard radio operators would feel a high sense of task significance because the quality of their work affects the safety of others.

autonomy
The degree to which a job gives employees the freedom, independence, and discretion to schedule their work and determine the procedures to be used to complete the work.

Autonomy.   Jobs with high levels of **autonomy** provide employees with freedom, independence, and discretion in scheduling the work and determining the procedures to be used to complete the work. Autonomous jobs require employees to make their own decisions rather than rely on detailed instructions from supervisors or procedure manuals.

job feedback
The degree to which carrying out the required work activities provides employees with direct and clear information about their job performance.

Job Feedback.   **Job feedback** is the degree to which carrying out the required work activities provides employees with direct and clear information about their job performance. In other words, people can tell how well they are doing based on information from the job itself. Clarence Towndrow, a heavy equipment operator in Edmonton, has a high degree of job feedback because he can see how the containment dikes he built have nice straight lines of earth and how the flat areas have been smoothly rolled.[19] Many jobs do not offer this type of feedback either because the tasks are so simplified that job performance cannot be easily observed or because there is no naturally occurring source of feedback available.

Critical Psychological States

The five core job characteristics affect employee motivation and satisfaction through three critical psychological states, namely, experienced meaningfulness, experienced responsibility, and knowledge of results.

Experienced Meaningfulness.   Work outcomes improve when employees believe that their work is worthwhile or important, according to their own value system. Three core job characteristics—skill variety, task identity, and task significance—directly contribute to the job's meaningfulness. If the job has high levels of all three characteristics, employees are likely to feel that their job is highly meaningful. Meaningfulness drops as the job loses one or more of these characteristics.

Experienced Responsibility.   Work motivation and satisfaction require employees to feel that they are personally accountable for the outcomes of their efforts. They must control their level of job performance and therefore be responsible for their successes and failures. Only one job characteristic— autonomy—directly contributes to the level of experienced responsibility.

Knowledge of Results.   Employees must be able to receive information on a fairly regular basis about the results of their work behaviours. Knowledge of results can originate from coworkers, supervisors, or clients, but these feedback sources do not come from the job itself. The job characteristics model identifies job feedback as the only job characteristic that contributes to knowledge of results.

Individual Differences

Increasing one or more of the five core job characteristics does not always have the desired effect on employee motivation. Rather, several contingency factors must be considered, including the job incumbent's knowledge and skill, satisfaction with the work context, and growth need strength.

Knowledge and Skill.   One contingency factor is the extent to which employees have the ability to perform jobs with higher meaningfulness and responsibility. They must possess the required skills for the additional job duties and be able to make decisions if they are given more autonomy. Without these prerequisites, job redesign is more likely to reduce productivity and increase worker stress.

Satisfaction with the Work Context.   Job design is less likely to result in positive work outcomes when employees are dissatisfied with their working conditions, job security, salaries, and other aspects of the work context. Until the organization attends to these basic needs, changes to the work itself will have less than acceptable results.

Growth Need Strength.   Increasing the motivational value of jobs will improve motivation and satisfaction only for employees with strong growth needs.[20] Not everyone wants interesting or challenging work. Some try to complete the job with minimal work effort and direct their energies to non-work activities; others may find interest in relatively repetitive tasks and perhaps feel threatened if the job is enriched. For example, a pioneer job design researcher wrote many years ago about a woman whose job consisted of packing electric light bulbs in tissue—approximately 13,000 bulbs every day for a total of over 50,000,000 bulbs over the 12 years that she had held the job. The woman assured the researcher that her work was very interesting. Sometimes she grabbed the bulb in a different way and sometimes the packing did not run smoothly. And she always found something interesting to observe or think about. What is to many people a boring task was sufficiently interesting to this person.[21]

JOB DESIGN STRATEGIES TO INCREASE WORK MOTIVATION

In this section, we introduce several job design strategies that have been used to reverse job specialization and thereby increase employee motivation and satisfaction.

Job Rotation

job rotation
The practice of moving employees from one job to another for the purposes of reducing monotony and increasing skill variety.

Job rotation is the practice of having employees move from one job to another, as shown in Exhibit 5–4. Some job rotation programs are formally scheduled and range from a few hours to several weeks in each job, while other programs are based on informal arrangements among several employees and the supervisor. Job rotation is commonly used in self-managing work teams (see Chapter 11) so that team members become multiskilled.

EXHIBIT 5–4   Job Rotation and Job Enlargement

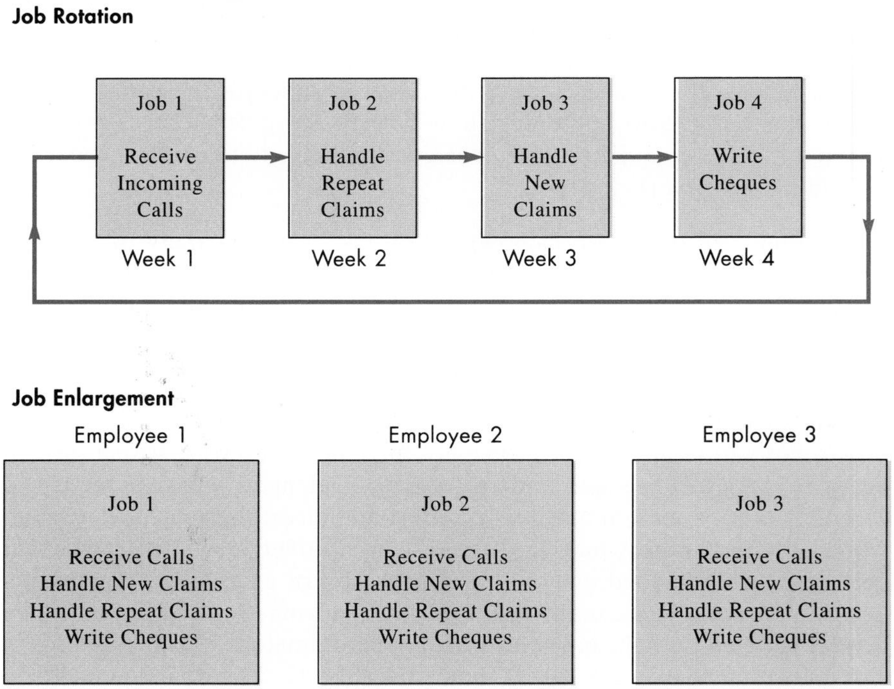

Job Rotation

Job 1	Job 2	Job 3	Job 4
Receive Incoming Calls	Handle Repeat Claims	Handle New Claims	Write Cheques
Week 1	Week 2	Week 3	Week 4

Job Enlargement

Employee 1	Employee 2	Employee 3
Job 1	**Job 2**	**Job 3**
Receive Calls	Receive Calls	Receive Calls
Handle New Claims	Handle New Claims	Handle New Claims
Handle Repeat Claims	Handle Repeat Claims	Handle Repeat Claims
Write Cheques	Write Cheques	Write Cheques

To reduce fatigue and increase productivity, Domtar introduced a job rotation program among production staff at its corrugated container plant in Toronto. Employees move to different jobs and machines two or three times daily. The program is mainly controlled by employees, and some elect not to participate. According to the plant manager, productivity has increased, workers are less fatigued, and the work force is more flexible in job assignments as a result of the job rotation program.[22]

Job rotation is not a true job design strategy because neither the job nor the employee has been changed. Some critics have charged that job rotation barely influences intrinsic motivation because employees simply work at several boring jobs rather than just one. However, as the Domtar experience indicates, job rotation does reduce monotony and increase the variety of skills used.

Job Enlargement

Job enlargement involves increasing the number of tasks employees perform *within* a job (see Exhibit 5–4). An assembly line worker might be given seven or eight tasks to perform rather than only two or three. This lengthens the work cycle so that tasks are repeated less frequently. Job enlargement is sometimes called horizontal job loading because it reverses the results of horizontal job specialization.

There is evidence that job enlargement increases job satisfaction, intrinsic motivation, and possibly productivity. For example, National Cash Register in Waterloo and GTE Canada in Lethbridge introduced job enlargement programs in their assembly line operations and found that this technique increased the quality of work produced as well as employee satisfaction. Similar results have been reported at IBM and Maytag in the United States.[23]

Some writers, including Herzberg, are critical of job enlargement because it merely involves employees doing more tasks rather than more meaningful work.[24] Instead, these critics suggest that the only way to improve work motivation is through job enrichment.

job enlargement
A job design strategy to increase skill variety by broadening the range of tasks employees perform within their job.

Job Enrichment

Job enrichment is based on Herzberg's motivator–hygiene theory that employee motivation is enhanced when the job provides opportunities for recognition, responsibility, advancement, achievement, and personal growth. The responsibility for scheduling, coordinating, and planning work is assigned to the employees who actually make the product or provide the service. Job enrichment is sometimes called vertical job loading because it reverses the process of vertical job specialization.

Hackman and his colleagues recommend five techniques to improve the motivational potential of jobs.[25] As Exhibit 5–5 illustrates, these "implementing principles" pinpoint which of the five core job characteristics will

job enrichment
A job design strategy that assigns responsibility for scheduling, coordinating, and planning work to employees who actually make the product or provide the service.

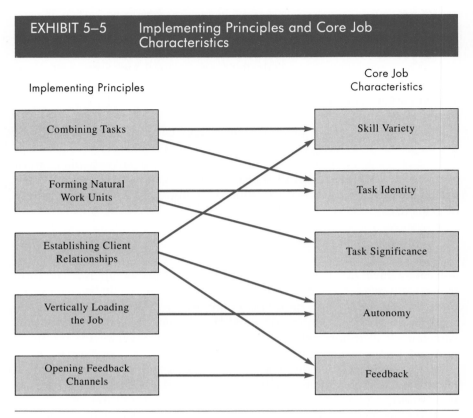

EXHIBIT 5–5   Implementing Principles and Core Job Characteristics

Implementing Principles

Core Job Characteristics

Combining Tasks

Forming Natural Work Units

Establishing Client Relationships

Vertically Loading the Job

Opening Feedback Channels

Skill Variety

Task Identity

Task Significance

Autonomy

Feedback

Source: J. R. Hackman and G. Oldham, *Work Redesign* (Reading, Mass.: Addison-Wesley, 1980), p. 135.

be affected. This is important because the best job design technique will depend on which core job characteristics are lacking in that particular situation.

Combining Tasks.   Whenever possible, fractionalized tasks should be combined to form new, larger modules of work. For instance, Philips Electronics production employees in Toronto were given several dozen components to solder on a printed circuit board, a job requiring up to 10 minutes to complete, rather than just soldering a few components in less than 1 minute.[26] This form of job redesign increases skill variety as well as task identity, particularly when the additional job duties are related to the same product or service.

Forming Natural Work Units.   Forming natural work units refers to the notion of combining tasks in a logical or complete grouping. A natural grouping might refer to completing an entire task, such as assembling an entire toaster rather than just some parts of it. Or it might involve completing assignments required for a specific client group, such as providing typing services to specific managers rather than receiving random work in a typing pool. By forming natural work units, jobholders develop a sense of responsibility for an identifiable body of work. They feel a sense of ownership and therefore tend to increase job quality. In terms of core job characteristics, forming natural work units increases task identity and task significance because employees perform a complete product or service and can more readily see how their work affects others.

Establishing Client Relationships.   As mentioned, some natural work units involve assigning an employee to a specific client group, such as serving people or other organizations in a specific region. Establishing client relationships takes this one step further by putting employees in *direct contact* with the client group rather than using the supervisor as a go-between. The key factor is direct communication between the employee and the client. The client submits work and provides feedback directly to the employee rather than through a supervisor. This technique was introduced in the personnel services group of Miracle Food Mart, a subsidiary of Steinberg's Limited, as described in Perspective 5–1. Establishing client relationships increases skill variety, autonomy, and feedback.

Vertical Loading.   We have already described vertical loading as the most essential element in job enrichment, namely, giving employees control over scheduling, coordinating, and planning their work. In practice, vertical loading involves letting jobholders decide work methods, check quality, establish work schedules, decide how to solve problems, and even have knowledge of and control over financial budgets. In each case, employees are given more autonomy over the work process.

Opening Feedback Channels.   Employees usually receive some feedback from their supervisors, but job design experts are interested in ways to generate meaningful feedback through the job itself, neutral feedback devices, or clients. Direct feedback can be increased by having employees manage their own quality control, sending them computerized performance reports, installing self-monitoring equipment, or having them receive feedback directly from clients. In short, opening feedback channels involves removing barriers to existing information sources as well as establishing new mechanisms so that jobholders can check their job performance without the supervisor's assistance.

JOB DESIGN PROSPECTS AND PROBLEMS

Job enrichment, job enlargement, and, to a lesser extent, job rotation, have been tremendously popular in recent years. These job redesign strategies existed in only 2 percent of Canadian firms before 1960, compared with

PERSPECTIVE 5–1   Job Enrichment at Miracle Food Mart

Miracle Food Mart's Personnel Services Group in Toronto consisted of seven clerical employees who compiled and maintained the files of approximately 5,000 employees in the Ontario region and provided store managers and insurance firms with information from those files on request. In the early 1970s, the work was organized in such a way that each employee kept records on one or two specific topics. For example, one clerk kept all employee records on hospital insurance and would be the only person to answer questions on that topic. If the person was on vacation or absent, the work would pile up or the Personnel Services manager would step in temporarily.

The Personnel Services manager was concerned about the performance and morale of her staff. Turnover and absenteeism were very high and the manager noticed that job pressure and monotony were taking their toll on staff morale. Meanwhile, store managers and other "clients" were complaining that they had to call several personnel clerks to get answers to different questions. It took them "hours, even days" to resolve relatively minor problems because it was difficult to pin down the person responsible for a particular matter.

To correct this situation, the manager conceived the idea of rearranging the work in such a way that each employee would learn to handle all aspects of the group's function (about 20 to 30 tasks) for a specific set of clients rather than specialize in narrow areas for all clients. It was thought that if each clerk could handle all enquiries, the work would be more interesting and clients would be saved considerable time and inconvenience.

The proposed job redesign was presented at a staff meeting and it was eventually agreed that the employees would train each other in their various specialties. Retraining was expected to take approximately 12 months and two temporary employees were hired to help with work overload during the transition phase. During the retraining phase, employees developed a set of procedures to explain the various tasks. They also standardized desks so that they could fill in for one another in case of illness or other absence. Thus, backlogs would not build up and service would not be interrupted.

Most clients required the same type of personnel services, so between 12 and 14 stores were assigned to each employee. The clerks were now responsible for handling all data and enquiries from these stores.

almost 30 percent today. Most programs have been introduced within the past decade. Job redesign interventions also have a high survival rate; over 90 percent of them are still in existence, a much higher success rate than most management interventions.[27]

But to what extent does job enrichment improve employee effectiveness? There is clear evidence that employees in enriched jobs experience higher job satisfaction, particularly those with high growth need strength. Absenteeism and turnover are also significantly lower when the core job characteristics are improved. Job redesign has a weaker influence on work performance. However, productivity gains are noticeable when task identity and job feedback are improved and when employees have a high growth need strength.[28]

One aspect of performance that most clearly improves with job enrichment is the quality of work. Error rates, number of defects, and other quality indicators tend to improve because job enrichment increases the jobholder's

Each clerk became familiar with the managers, bookkeepers, and others concerned and soon referred to them as her "people." As a natural evolution, clerks added typing duties to their job and the departmental stenographer position was closed when it became vacant. All clerks now wrote and signed their own correspondence to their clients, a task previously completed by the Personnel Services manager. Clerks also added the task of coordinating the computer payroll data input done by each store. This task had been a rather awkward responsibility for the Accounting Department before the Personnel Services clerks accepted this role.

The results of job enrichment in Miracle Mart's Personnel Services group have been dramatic. The workload increased substantially during the next three years, yet the seven clerks were able to handle this growth along with the additional typing and payroll coordinating duties. In fact, service became more efficient; store managers particularly noted how personnel clerks now developed a responsible personal relationship with the store and problems got resolved quickly and reliably. The increase in productivity, together with added competence and skills, made it possible to increase pay rates. Absenteeism decreased noticeably and, by all reports, morale improved. Turnover declined, and while only three of the original seven clerks remained after three years, most of those who left did so for reasons of pregnancy, not dissatisfaction.

Based on this experience, job enrichment was eventually introduced in other areas of Miracle Mart and its parent firm, Steinberg's. For example, job enrichment in Steinberg's shipping department resulted in a 25 percent decrease in absenteeism and a productivity increase from 125 units shipped per person-hour before the intervention to 171 units afterwards. These improvements have remained for at least five years.

Sources: I. S. G. Meadows, "Innovative Work Arrangements: A Case Study in Job Enrichment—Miracle Food Mart (Subsidiary of Steinberg's Limited) Personnel Services," Report #14, Research Branch, Ontario Ministry of Labour, June 1975; and M. Witten, "Punching in 'Quality' on the Old Shop Floor," *Maclean's*, April 2, 1979, pp. 36a–36b.

felt responsibility and sense of ownership over the product or service. Quality improvements are particularly noticed when the job enrichment intervention involves completing a natural work unit or establishing client relationships.[29]

Obstacles in Job Design

One of the nagging difficulties with job design research and practice is that Hackman and Oldham's job characteristics model, as well as existing job characteristics measures, are far from perfect.[30] One problem is that they seem to ignore task interdependence and possibly other relevant job characteristics, while some elements of the model have questionable links to the work itself.[31] For instance, a recent study in Hong Kong concluded that task significance refers to the relationship of a job to others rather than to actual job duties.[32] There is also an ongoing debate on the extent to which employee perceptions of the job differ from objective job duties. Employees may perceive their jobs based more upon what coworkers say than the objective job characteristics.

Redesigning jobs is a form of organizational change and, as such, is likely to face resistance by many people affected. Some Air Canada employees had misgivings about the airline's attempt to increase their autonomy because they had been accustomed to authoritarian structures. Similarly, a few highly skilled employees at Alcan's smelter in Arvida, Quebec, did not want to continue the company's job enrichment program because they feared a loss of status and authority as previously less-skilled employees learned more aspects of the work process.[33]

Most job enrichment interventions alter the role of supervisors, particularly where employees assume many of the scheduling and control functions previously assigned to management. At some worksites, this has caused supervisors to resist job design changes even when their future employment is secure. Introducing job enrichment must therefore be accompanied by effective change management strategies, including retraining to help supervisors adjust to their new roles.[34]

Labour union leaders have been bitter foes of job specialization and scientific management, yet few have been enthusiastic about job enrichment programs. Many union leaders complain that job enrichment programs try to get more work out of employees for less money. At best, critics view job enrichment as a rationalized work arrangement introduced where job specialization is unprofitable. In other words, they conclude that job enrichment exists because it strengthens management's control, not because of a true interest in the employee's mental health.[35]

Throughout this chapter, we have mainly emphasized redesigning individual jobs. Yet many organizations have found it difficult to introduce individual-level job enrichment programs because the technology is fixed or the work cycle is too complex for one person to handle alone. For example, it would not be reasonable to have one employee make an entire automobile or operate an entire petrochemical process. Consequently, there is a distinct trend toward self-managing work teams and related team-based interventions.[36] These practices will be discussed in Chapter 11 after we have introduced team dynamics and decision-making concepts.

Finally, we must remember that job design usually involves trade-offs. On the one hand, job specialization may improve work efficiency by reducing job requirements, but job performance may decline as employee motivation falls. On the other hand, job enrichment may increase employee satisfaction, attendance, and work motivation, but productivity may fall if jobs become too challenging. As jobs become over-enriched, the organization must increase recruiting and training costs to find people capable of performing the work. To the extent that job worth is based on the complexity of work (see Chapter 3), compensation costs may rise as enriched jobs receive higher job evaluation scores than simplified jobs.[37] Furthermore, while job enrichment is known to improve product quality, error rates may actually increase and employees may begin to experience work-related stress when tasks become too challenging.[38] Work-related stress can lead to numerous other undesirable outcomes, as we will learn later in this chapter. Overall, managers must find an appropriate balance between job enrichment and job specialization to maximize employee effectiveness.

WORK-RELATED STRESS

Barry Hall was ambitious and hard-working in a competitive and highly responsible job. But as the administrative director of Manulife Financial's Canadian marketing division, Hall also realized that he was over-stressed. His brow often rained sweat, his face flushed with higher-than-normal blood pressure, and he looked weary from lack of sleep. A computerized health questionnaire determined that Hall's chances of heart attack or stroke over the next 10 years were higher than normal for someone his age. Manulife Financial was concerned about the effects of stress on its employees, so it placed Hall and several other managers into a stress management program. Hall spent three days in a southern Ontario retreat learning better nutritional habits, tension-releasing exercises, and basic relaxation techniques.[39]

Many businesses are discovering that stress is costly to both the individual and the organization. Some sources estimate that stress costs tens of billions of dollars each year in Canada due to lower productivity and higher absenteeism, turnover, alcoholism, and medical attention.[40] Work-related stress can also cost employers in arbitration awards, court decisions, and possibly occupational health and safety premiums.[41] However, stress is not always bad. In fact, low levels of stress are a necessary part of life. In this section, we look at the dynamics of work-related stress, its impact on organizational behaviour, and ways to deal with excessive levels of stress.

What Is Stress?

Stress is an adaptive response to a situation that is perceived as challenging or threatening to the person's well-being.[42] Stress has both psychological and physiological dimensions. Psychologically, people perceive a situation and interpret it as challenging or threatening. This cognitive appraisal leads to a set of physiological responses, such as higher blood pressure, sweaty hands, and a faster heartbeat.

We often hear about stress as a negative consequence of modern living. People are stressed from overwork, job insecurity, competition, and the increasing pace of life. This describes distress, where people experience stress beyond their capacity to resist the stressful conditions. There is also a positive side of stress, called eustress, which is a necessary part of of life. Eustress refers to relatively low levels of stress over a short time period. Eustress is necessary to activate and motivate people to achieve goals,

stress
An individual's adaptive response to a situation that is perceived as challenging or threatening to the person's well-being.

change their environments, and succeed in life's challenges. However, research has generally found more evidence of distress than eustress in organizational settings.[43] Employees frequently experience enough stress to undermine their job performance and increase their risk of mental and physical health problems. Consequently, most of our discussion will focus on distress rather than eustress.

General Adaptation Syndrome

general adaptation syndrome
A model of the stress process consisting of three stages: alarm reaction, resistance, and exhaustion.

The stress experience has been described as a process called the **general adaptation syndrome.** Dr. Hans Selye, a pioneer in stress research in Montreal, has discovered that people adapt to stressful situations in three stages: alarm reaction, resistance, and exhaustion, as shown in Exhibit 5–6.[44]

Alarm Reaction.   In the alarm reaction stage, the perception of a threatening or challenging situation causes the brain to send a biochemical message to various parts of the body, resulting in increased respiration rate, blood pressure, heartbeat, muscle tension, and other physiological responses. Initial exposure to the stressor reduces the person's survival capabilities and in extreme circumstances may cause death due to shock. In most situations, the alarm reaction alerts the person to the environmental condition and prepares the body for the resistance stage.

Resistance.   The resistance stage involves introducing various biochemical, psychological, and behavioural mechanisms to deal with the stressor. For example, adrenalin increases and the individual may try to overcome or

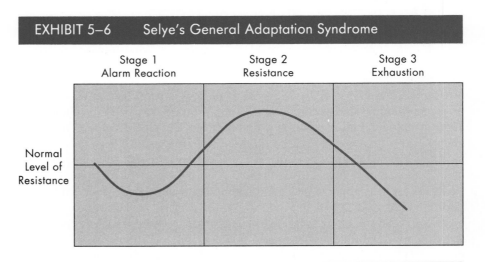

EXHIBIT 5–6   Selye's General Adaptation Syndrome

| | Stage 1
Alarm Reaction | Stage 2
Resistance | Stage 3
Exhaustion |

Normal Level of Resistance

Source: J. L. Gibson, J. M. Ivancevich, and J. H. Donnelly, *Organizations: Behavior, Structure, Processes,* 7th ed. (Homewood, Ill.: Irwin, 1991), p. 225.

remove the stressor. However, this resistance is directed only to one or two stressors, so that the person becomes more vulnerable to other stressors. This explains why employees are more likely to catch a cold or other illness when they have been working under pressure.

Exhaustion. People have a limited resistance capacity and, if the stressor persists, will eventually move into the exhaustion stage as this capacity diminishes. In most work situations, the general adaptation syndrome process ends long before total exhaustion. Employees resolve tense situations before the destructive consequences of stress become manifest, or they withdraw from the stressful situation, rebuild their survival capabilities, and later return to the stressful environment with renewed energy. However, people who frequently experience the general adaptation syndrome, particularly the exhaustion stage, have increased risk of long-term physiological and psychological damage. While it is possible to rebuild short-term energy, people have only a limited lifetime reserve of energy to resist extremely stressful situations.

The general adaptation syndrome describes the stress experience, but this is only part of the picture. In order to effectively manage work-related stress, we must understand the causes and consequences of stress as well as individual differences in the extent to which people experience stress in a particular situation.

STRESSORS: THE CAUSES OF STRESS

Stressors, the causes of stress, include any environmental conditions that place a physical or emotional demand on the person.[45] There are numerous stressors in organizational settings in addition to those found in other life activities. Exhibit 5–7 lists four types of work-related stressors: physical environment, role-related, interpersonal, and organizational stressors.

stressor
Any environmental condition that places a physical or emotional demand on the person.

Physical Environment Stressors

Some stressors are found in the physical work environment, such as excessive noise, poor lighting, and safety hazards. Construction workers and loggers often experience stress because they must regularly face unpleasant weather and hazardous working conditions. Office staff may also experience stress from poor lighting, stale air, and the perpetual drone of central air circulation systems (called "white noise" or "acoustic mist").[46]

Role-Related Stressors

Role-related stressors include conditions where employees have difficulty understanding, reconciling, or performing the various roles in their lives. Four particularly important role-related stressors are described here.[47]

EXHIBIT 5–7   Causes and Consequences of Stress

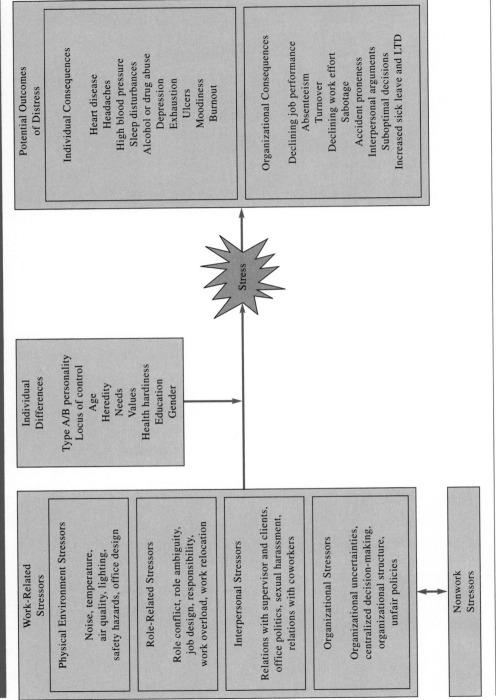

Sources: Based on J. M. Ivancevich and M. T. Matteson. "Worksite Stress Management Interventions." *American Psychologist* 45 (1990). pp. 252–61; and J. C. Quick and J. D. Quick. *Organizational Stress and Prevention Management* (New York: McGraw-Hill. 1984). Chapters 2. 3. and 4.

Role Conflict.   People experience **role conflict** when they face competing demands. There are two different forms of role conflict, each of which is a potential stressor. **Person-role conflict** occurs when obligations of the job are incompatible with personal values, such as when a manager who believes in maintaining full employment is assigned the task of closing a plant and laying off the work force. **Intra-role conflict** occurs when the individual receives contradictory messages from different people, as when one coworker recommends that you smile at customers more often while another tells you that being nice to customers is a waste of time. Both forms of role conflict are common when people enter and leave the organization or are transferred to another department, because these events require adjustments in other life activities and personal values.[48]

Role Ambiguity.   **Role ambiguity** exists when employees are uncertain about their job duties, performance expectations, level of authority, and other job conditions. Most employees experience role ambiguity when entering a new job, but this role stressor is also commonly felt at other times.

Work Overload/Underload.   **Work overload** occurs when employees cannot keep up with deadlines or are given work that is beyond their skills or abilities. **Work underload** refers to situations where employees receive too little work or are given tasks that do not make sufficient use of their skills or abilities.

Task Characteristics.   Task characteristics may be stressors, particularly if they include decision making, monitoring equipment, or exchanging information with others.[49] Some jobs, such as farming, are particularly stressful because jobholders lack control over events affecting them.[50]

Interpersonal Stressors

These include any conflicts the person may have with others. Insurance adjusters, bill collectors, and unemployment insurance agents often experience stress because they must work with clients in sensitive and difficult situations, as Perspective 5–2 describes. Ineffective supervision and leadership, office politics, and sexual harassment are also interpersonal stressors.[51] In extreme cases, Canadian firms may be sued by employees who can demonstrate that management's actions have caused them mental distress.[52]

Organizational Stressors

Various organizational actions may lead to distress. One of the most powerful of these is the threat or experience of job loss. Involuntary terminations, factory closings, and the experience of unemployment all contribute to individual stress.[53] Mergers and acquisitions can be another powerful stressor

role conflict
Any situation where individuals face competing demands, such as where obligations of the job are incompatible with the individual's personal values (person-role conflict) or where the individual receives contradictory messages from different people (intra-role conflict).

role ambiguity
Any situation where employees are uncertain about their job duties, performance expectations, level of authority, and other job conditions.

work overload
Any situation where employees cannot keep up with deadlines or are given work that is beyond their skills or abilities.

work underload
Any situation where employees receive too little work or are given tasks that do not make sufficient use of their skills or abilities.

PERSPECTIVE 5–2   Interpersonal Stressors at Canada Employment Centres

Employees at Canada Employment Centres face the threat of physical violence and daily verbal abuse from frustrated unemployed workers and job seekers, particularly as staff shortages cause long delays in processing unemployment insurance claims.

Says Jim Chorostecki, senior Ontario representative of the Public Service Alliance of Canada, "Clients throw telephones around, they throw staplers around . . . verbal abuse is an everyday occurrence."

Physical assaults are rare, but they have also occurred. A male receptionist at a Vancouver unemployment insurance office was stabbed in the shoulder and chest with a paring knife by a hostile man who was having trouble with his unemployment insurance report cards. Another angry client drove her car through the brick wall of a Canada Employment Centre in Windsor, Ontario.

The federal government is concerned about the stressful situation that its employees face. "We are aware of the load, we are aware that the staff is under pressure, and we're trying to adapt," says a senior government official. Unfortunately, the Canada Employment Centre work force has actually decreased in recent years, resulting in work overload and increased interpersonal stressors as members of the public take their frustrations out on civil servants.

Source: C. McLaren, "Tempers Flare at Centres for Jobless," *Globe and Mail*, November 2, 1990, pp. A1, A4.

because they lead to organizational uncertainties and interpersonal conflicts. For example, when Amoco Canada acquired Calgary-based Dome Petroleum, over 2,500 employees signed up for the company-sponsored stress management seminars to help them cope with this takeover.[54]

Work–Family Stressors

Although our discussion has been directed toward work-related factors, Exhibit 5–7 acknowledges that there is a substantial interaction between work and nonwork roles. The death of a spouse, divorce, jail detention, or financial worries can all affect the employee's ability to fulfill work obligations, but work activities tend to have an even stronger influence on nonwork activities, particularly family life.[55] Work-related stressors figure into the work–family relationship in several ways.

Time-Based Conflict. Employees often experience stress due to insufficient time to adequately satisfy the demands of both work and family. Naturally, stress tends to increase with the number of hours of paid employment because this leaves fewer hours available to fulfill family obligations. Longer commuting time and extensive business travel also tend to increase stress in family relations.[56]

The problem of balancing one's time between work and family is particularly acute for women, because they tend to do most of the household chores even while holding down a full-time job.[57] As Perspective 5–3 describes,

PERSPECTIVE 5–3   "Having It All": Supermoms of the 1990s

Sherry Cooper might be called one of the supermoms of the 1990s. In addition to being the mother of a 10-year-old son, Cooper is director of bond and money market sales at Burns Fry Ltd., a macho job in the male-dominated securities industry. In spite of the tough challenges of working in an organization unfamiliar with women at the top, Cooper is able to manage both family needs and the demands of her job.

"Having it all" describes the ideal situation for women entering the upper echelons of industry and still having the benefits of family life. But at least one critic wonders whether the supermom of the 1990s is simply a prescription for superstress. While women are accepting increasing responsibility in business, their male counterparts are not embracing the role of homemaker quite as readily. Research indicates that when women enter the work force, they tend to keep most of their home responsibilities as well. Corporations are sometimes slow to respond to the changing family demands on its professionals and executives. Adding traditional men's work to traditional women's work inevitably results in the traditional nervous breakdown.

Many supermoms admit that it is not easy to be everything to everyone. Kathleen Christie, of Deloitte & Touche management consultants, was able to have two children and develop her career until she was made partner in charge of the Toronto consulting practice. However, her children demanded more of her time when they reached the ages of 4 and 7 years old. "It just got to the point where the hours and the demands of the job were greater than I was prepared to give, and I give a lot." Fortunately, the firm agreed to give Christie a six-month sabbatical to catch up on family life.

Even when women can manage their time, juggling work and family responsibilities is complicated, particularly when they call for completely different roles and behaviour. "One minute you're going to a board meeting and the next you're going to a Beaver meeting," says Gail Cook-Bennett, another Toronto-based management consultant. A vice-president with Mary Kay Cosmetics Ltd. in Mississauga adds her concerns: "Sometimes I feel that I'm not doing either job marvelously. But I'm hard on myself. Nobody puts that guilt on me but me."

Until men increase their contribution to homemaking and business learns to accommodate the new social order, many supermoms will experience frustration and stress. As comedian Lily Tomlin puts it: "If I knew what it would have been like to have it all, I would have settled for less."

Sources: B. Dalglish, "Having It All," *Maclean's,* September 3, 1990, pp. 32–35; and A. Kingston, "Beyond the Fantasy of the Supermom," *Financial Times,* September 10, 1990, p. 13.

some writers glorify the 1990s role of the "supermom," while others suggest that women are actually super stressed by the impossible time-based conflicts that society expects them to overcome.

Work Schedules.   An inflexible work schedule creates a special form of time-based conflict that can take a heavy toll on family life because it prevents employees from effectively juggling work and family duties. Shiftwork is another time-based stressor in family life; rotating shifts can disrupt routine family activities while night shifts tend to increase the spouse's concern for the other's safety.[58]

Role Behaviour Conflicts. Another source of stress is the incompatible characteristics of some work and family roles. Managers often emphasize impersonal and logical behaviour at work, yet they must display compassion and emotion at home.[59]

Work Stress Spillover. Many of the negative consequences of work-related stress spill over into the employee's family role. Employees with work-related tensions often find it difficult to enjoy family activities. The stress of work often becomes the foundation of stressful relations at home.

Stress and Occupations

Different types of stressors are found in different occupations. Among Canadian air traffic controllers, for instance, the most prominent stressors include poor equipment, the fear of causing an accident (called collisionitis), and

EXHIBIT 5–8	Stressors Contributing to Job Stress among Canadian Air Traffic Controllers	

Rank Order	Stressor	Perceived Effect on Stress*
1.	Poor equipment	2.02
2.	Fear of causing an accident	1.70
3.	Peak traffic situations	1.68
4.	Poor relationship with management	1.58
5.	Bilingualism issue	1.56
6.	Bad weather	1.27
7.	General work environment	1.22
8.	Having to report a coworker's error	1.17
9.	Fear of failing annual medical	1.13
10.	Comparison of pilot's status and salary	1.08
11.	Fear of slowing down as a controller	1.08
12.	Uncertainty regarding legal liability	1.04
13.	Shiftwork	0.98
14.	Boredom	0.98
15.	Conflict with aircrews	0.75
16.	Having to work so closely with coworkers	0.66
17.	Adjusting to procedure changes	0.66
18.	Too much scheduled overtime	0.39

*Controllers were asked to indicate on a 4-point scale (0–3) the degree to which these factors contributed to job stress.
Source: A. McBride, "'High Stress' Occupations: The Importance of Job Components versus Job Categories," in R. J. Burke (ed.), *Current Issues in Occupational Stress: Research and Intervention* (Toronto: Faculty of Administrative Studies, York University, 1984), p. 10.

work overload during peak traffic situations (see Exhibit 5–8).[60] As a Winnipeg controller concluded: "That's the sheer terror, because you're working a lot of airplanes through a small area. . . . There's a lot of stress, and eventually it just wears you down."[61]

   Air traffic controllers, waiters/waitresses, managers, and other jobs are often labelled as high-stress occupations, but an important point to remember is that a major stressor to one person is insignificant to another. The next section discusses individual differences in stress.

INDIVIDUAL DIFFERENCES IN STRESS

Individual differences represent another element in the relationship between stressors, stress, and stress consequences. Individual characteristics moderate the extent to which different people experience stress or exhibit a specific stress outcome in a given situation. Two people may be exposed to the same stressor, such as the threat of job loss, yet they experience different levels of stress or different stress symptoms.

   Individual factors affect the stress experience in at least three ways. First, different levels of stress may be experienced because people perceive the situation differently. For example, those with low self-esteem might see job loss as a threat while those with higher self-esteem might not.[62] Second, people may have different threshold levels of resistance to a stressor. Younger employees generally experience fewer and less severe stress symptoms because they have a larger store of energy to cope with high stress levels than older employees do. Finally, people may experience the same level of stress and yet exhibit different stress outcomes because they use different strategies to cope with the stress. For example, there is some evidence that women are more likely to seek emotional support from others in stressful situations, whereas men try to change the stressor or use less-effective coping mechanisms.[63]

Type A/Type B Personality

Perhaps the most important individual difference among those listed in Exhibit 5–7 is the Type A/Type B personality. In the 1950s, two cardiologists noticed that patients with premature coronary heart disease exhibited common behaviours that were collectively labelled a **Type A behaviour pattern.** Like Barry Hall described earlier, people with Type A personalities are hard-driving, competitive individuals with a strong sense of time urgency. They are also more likely to be impatient, lose their temper, talk rapidly, and interrupt others during conversations. In contrast to Type A's, people with a **Type B behaviour pattern** are less competitive and less concerned about time limitations. Type B's may be just as ambitious as Type A's where the situation is challenging, but they generally approach life more casually and sys-

type A behaviour pattern

A behaviour pattern associated with people having premature coronary heart disease; Type As tend to be impatient, lose their temper, talk rapidly, and interrupt others.

type B behaviour pattern

A behaviour pattern of people with low risk of coronary heart disease; Type B's tend to work steadily, take a relaxed approach to life, and are even-tempered.

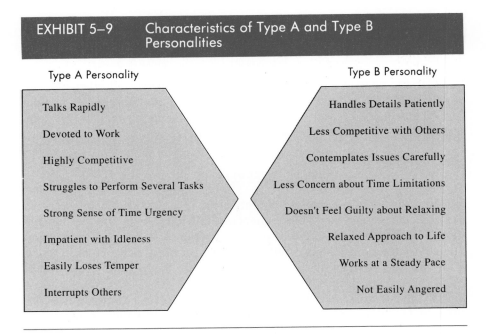

EXHIBIT 5–9   Characteristics of Type A and Type B Personalities

Type A Personality

- Talks Rapidly
- Devoted to Work
- Highly Competitive
- Struggles to Perform Several Tasks
- Strong Sense of Time Urgency
- Impatient with Idleness
- Easily Loses Temper
- Interrupts Others

Type B Personality

- Handles Details Patiently
- Less Competitive with Others
- Contemplates Issues Carefully
- Less Concern about Time Limitations
- Doesn't Feel Guilty about Relaxing
- Relaxed Approach to Life
- Works at a Steady Pace
- Not Easily Angered

tematically (see Exhibit 5–9).[64] The important point, however, is that Type A's are more likely than Type B's to experience distress and its physiological symptoms (such as heart disease) when exposed to a stressor.

In terms of job performance, Type A's tend to work faster than Type B's, choose more challenging tasks, have higher self-motivation, and are more effective in jobs involving time pressure. On the other hand, Type A's are less productive than Type B's in jobs requiring patience, cooperation, and thoughtful judgment.[65] Since Type A's tend to be irritable and aggressive, they generally have poorer interpersonal skills. Studies report that middle managers tend to have Type A personalities, while top level executives tend to have Type B personalities.[66] This may suggest that Type B's receive more promotions due to their superior human relations skills.

CONSEQUENCES OF DISTRESS

As mentioned earlier, low levels of stress, called *eustress,* are important in everyday life. Eustress activates people so that they can meet the challenges of everyday life. But high degrees of stress or prolonged stress diminishes the individual's resistance, resulting in detrimental consequences for both the employee and the organization. This often creates a vicious circle whereby stress leads to a dysfunctional consequence (such as alcoholism) which, in turn, becomes a stressor leading to further dysfunctional consequences. Some of the more common outcomes of distress in organizations were listed earlier in Exhibit 5–7.

Individual Consequences

High levels of stress may affect employees both emotionally and physically. Emotionally, distressed employees may feel fatigued, depressed, and moody. Physiologically, they may experience such symptoms as high blood pressure, ulcers, sexual dysfunctions, headaches, and coronary heart disease.

Approximately 10 percent of the Canadian work force has ulcers and other digestive system diseases. These ailments are caused by excessive secretion of gastric juices, often resulting from anxiety and worry. Coronary heart disease is one of the most disturbing effects of stress in modern society. This disease, including strokes and heart attacks, was virtually unknown a century ago but is now the leading cause of death among Canadian adults.[67] Hypertension refers to high blood pressure and is one of the major factors leading to heart disease. It is estimated that between 15 and 33 percent of Canadians have some level of hypertension. Once again, stress is often identified as the primary cause.[68]

Job Burnout.   Job burnout has become a well-known term even though it was coined only 20 years ago. **Burnout** refers to the process of exhaustion, depersonalization, and reduced personal accomplishment resulting from prolonged exposure to stress.[69] It is most common among employees in helping occupations (e.g., nurses, teachers, police officers). In the early stages of job burnout, people experience declining work performance, increased exhaustion and sleeplessness, and more frequent moodiness. Later stages are apparent by increased alcohol consumption, less flexible thinking, and lowered self-confidence.[70]

burnout
The process of exhaustion, depersonalization, and reduced personal accomplishment resulting from prolonged exposure to stress.

Organizational Consequences

Work-related distress produces numerous organizational consequences, including lower productivity, higher absenteeism, poorer decision making, and increased probability of accidents. The physical symptoms of stress are felt by the organization in the form of increased absenteeism and long-term disability leave.[71] The increased moodiness of high-stress employees can result in more interpersonal conflicts. Stress has a distinctly negative impact on job performance, both in terms of the quality and quantity of work produced and in the ability to serve clients. Employees under stress also make suboptimal decisions and are more likely to cause or be involved in workplace accidents.[72]

MANAGING WORK-RELATED STRESS

Equipped with a better understanding of the causes and consequences of stress, we can now identify several ways to effectively manage workplace stress (see Exhibit 5–10). One strategy is to directly remove unnecessary stressors or at least minimize the employee's exposure to them. Another is

EXHIBIT 5–10   Stress Management Interventions

Removing the Stressor
- Management practices
- Organizational communication
- Job design
- Physical environment

Withdrawing from the Stressor
- Work breaks
- Sabbaticals
- Stabilization zones
- Person–job fit

Changing Stress Perceptions
- Self-esteem
- Type A personality

Controlling the Consequences of Stress
- Relaxation and meditation
- Fitness and lifestyle programs
- Employee counselling

Social Support
- Social activities

to temporarily remove employees from the stressful environment. A third stress management approach involves helping employees alter their interpretation of the environment so that it is not viewed as a serious stressor. Fourth, organizations can encourage employees to build better physical defenses against stress experiences. Finally, stress is often effectively managed through social support. These stress management interventions are described in more detail below.

Removing the Stressor

Much work-related stress is a result of unnecessary problems in the working environment. Therefore, an effective strategy is to remove unnecessary stressors, reduce the employee's exposure to them, or develop a better fit between the individual and the environment.

Management Practices.   According to one study, Canadian managers place poor management at the top of the list of work-related stressors.[73] This suggests that employee distress can be reduced by introducing the management practices recommended in this book.

Organizational Communication.   Role ambiguity and uncertainty over work activities are common stressors that can be reduced by improving organizational communications. Senior managers should keep employees informed about events affecting the organization and employees should communicate with other people to coordinate their work more effectively. Thus, the concepts and ideas presented in the next chapter on individual and organizational communication (Chapter 6) would help eliminate some organizational stressors.

Job Design.   Another way to reduce stress is by redesigning jobs so that they provide a more reasonable level of workload and time pressure, and give employees more autonomy over decisions affecting them.[74]

Physical Environment.   Physical changes to the work environment can reduce the risk of employee distress. For example, several firms have introduced improved overhead lighting diffusers to improve productivity by easing worker stress.[75] Introducing safer working conditions has the double benefit of improving the firm's occupational health and safety record and reducing the level of employee stress.

Withdrawing from the Stressor

If the stressor cannot be removed, perhaps employees can remove themselves from the stressor for short periods of time. Daily work breaks can reduce stress, particularly when employees are able to find quiet areas to relax without interruption. Many organizations, including the City of Toronto and the Toronto Sun Publishing Company, have introduced sabbaticals to help long-term employees restore their capacity to cope with stressful work experiences. As one *Toronto Sun* employee confirms: "Taking [a sabbatical leave] is so therapeutic, it's unbelievable. When I came back, if there was a deadline on something, I didn't let it give me anxiety attacks!"[76]

Stabilization Zones.   Many expatriates use stabilization zones—environments providing conditions similar to the home country—to help them temporarily break away from the stress of working in a foreign culture.[77] Stabilization zone activities might include attending a "Canadian night" at a club in the foreign country, taking a weekend vacation at a nearby hotel that provides home country amenities, or watching video-recorded movies and television from the home country.

Person–Job Fit.   Stress management also includes permanently removing employees from stressful jobs. Person–job fit refers to the idea that organizations should carefully place the right people into the right jobs based on their skills, knowledge, basic needs, personal values, career orientations, and ability to cope with the job environment.[78] Employee skills should be matched with job requirements because the inability to perform the job can cause stress through role overload. Employees with poor interpersonal skills should be transferred to jobs with less task interdependence before they experience job burnout. Those with high self-esteem may be more appropriate for jobs with infrequent positive reinforcement (e.g., sales jobs).

Changing Stress Perceptions

People often experience different levels of stress in the same situation because they interpret it differently. Consequently, stress can be minimized by changing the individual's perception of the situation. For example, improving self-esteem enables employees to feel more confident that they can overcome major work challenges.

People with Type A personalities are more likely to experience stress because of their fundamental interpretation of the work environment. But through therapy and reinforcement, Type A's may be able to reduce their sense of time urgency, have fewer meetings, and reduce the number of simultaneous work activities.[79]

Controlling the Consequences of Stress

Some stress management interventions help employees cope with the physiological and/or psychological consequences of stress.

Relaxation and Meditation. Relaxation and meditation programs help employees adjust their physiological response to the stressor and stress perception. In relaxation training, employees practice muscle relaxation, breathing exercises, and visualization. The objective is to achieve a relaxation response in which heart rate, blood pressure, muscle tension, and breathing rate decrease. Relaxation is best achieved in a quiet location, sitting in a comfortable chair, with the eyes closed, using a repetitive mental device (e.g., a simple sound or chant). Some employees in Tokyo relax at therapeutic centres where headphones emit soothing music while special goggles emit repetitive pulses of light.[80] Meditation is a variation of relaxation involving a specific sitting position and special repetitive chant. In general, relaxation and meditation programs have been effective, particularly in reducing blood pressure levels and muscle tension.[81]

Fitness and Lifestyle Programs. Corporate fitness programs have probably received more financial resources from Canadian business than any other strategy to combat work-related stress. Physical exercise helps employees lower their respiration, muscle tension, heartbeat, and stomach acidity, thereby reducing the physiological consequences of stress.[82] Lifestyle programs train employees and reinforce their behaviour in better nutrition and fitness, regular sleep, and other good health habits.

Although research is limited, it appears that fitness and lifestyle programs may help employees control the dysfunctional consequences of stress. A study at Canada Life Assurance Co. concluded that its exercise and lifestyle program reduced employee absenteeism, stress anxiety, and the risk of cardiovascular disease. Employees also reduced their smoking habits and developed better health attitudes. According to one estimate, corporate fitness and lifestyle programs save Canadian firms an average of $513 per employee (in 1986 dollars) in terms of increased productivity and decreased turnover, injuries, and absenteeism.[83]

Employee Counselling. Many organizations have introduced counselling services, called **employee assistance programs (EAPs),** to help employees cope with stressful life experiences and overcome ineffective coping mecha-

employee assistance programs (EAPs)
Special counselling services to help employees cope with stressful life experiences and overcome ineffective coping mechanisms such as alcoholism.

nisms such as alcoholism. Canadian EAPs typically started as alcoholism treatment programs, but most are now "broad-brush" programs, counselling employees on most work or personal problems. Family problems often represent the largest percentage of EAP referrals, although this varies with industry and location. For instance, the Bank of Montreal introduced an EAP in the 1970s to help staff cope with the trauma of bank robberies. Post-crime trauma counselling is still important, but the bank's program now covers other personal and work-related problems.[84]

Social Support

Social support from coworkers, supervisors, family, friends, and others is recognized as one of the more effective stress management practices. Social support refers to the person's interpersonal transaction with others and involves providing either emotional or informational support to buffer the stress experience.[85] Organizations can increase the level of social support by providing opportunities for social interaction among employees as well as their families.

Social support may reduce stress by altering the person's self-esteem, resulting in a less threatening interpretation of the stressor (e.g., "I can handle this crisis because my colleagues have confidence in me"). Second, social support may provide information or other resources so that the employee can remove the stressor (e.g., a new employee learns from coworkers how to handle a difficult customer). Finally, social support can help buffer the stress experience directly when the employee perceives that he or she is not facing the stressor alone. This last point is basically the idea that "misery loves company." People seek emotional support from others when they face threatening situations.[86]

SUMMARY

• Job design involves assigning tasks to a job and distributing work throughout the organization. Job characteristics affect employee performance by altering work efficiency (e.g., competency requirements) and worker motivation.

• Job specialization involves reducing the number of tasks assigned to a job. This increases work efficiency because employees master the tasks more quickly, spend less time changing tasks, require less training, and can be matched more closely with the jobs best suited to their skills. Scientific management represents a systematic analysis to determine how work should be partitioned into its smallest possible elements and how the process of completing each task should be standardized to achieve maximum efficiency.

• Job specialization can reduce job performance if work efficiency is offset by lower work motivation, worker alienation, higher turnover and absenteeism, and higher salaries to compensate for boring work.

• Modern job design strategies reverse job specialization through job rotation, job enlargement, and job enrichment. Herzberg's motivator–hygiene theory is largely responsible for emphasizing the motivational benefits of the work itself. Hackman and Oldham's job characteristics model is the most popular foundation for recent job redesign interventions because it specifies job elements, psychological states, and individual differences.

• As a form of organizational change, job enrichment is not always easy to implement, but there is evidence that morale improves and both turnover and absenteeism decrease. Work motivation increases and there is some beneficial effect on work productivity, particularly in the quality of work output.

• Stress is an adaptive response to a situation that is perceived as challenging or threatening to the person's well-being. Distress represents high stress levels that have negative consequences, whereas eustress represents the moderately low stress levels needed to activate people. The stress experience, called the *general adaptation syndrome,* involves moving through three stages: alarm, resistance, and exhaustion.

• Stressors are the causes of stress and include any environmental conditions that place a physical or emotional demand on the person. Stressors are found in the physical work environment, the employee's various life roles, interpersonal relations, and organizational activities and conditions. Conflicts between work and family obligations represent a frequent source of employee stress.

• People have different stress reactions to stressors. Those with Type A personalities are particularly known to have higher levels of distress in a particular situation.

• High levels of stress may affect employees both emotionally (as distressed employees may feel fatigued, depressed, and moody) and physiologically (they may experience such symptoms as high blood pressure, ulcers, sexual dysfunctions, headaches, and coronary heart disease). Job burnout is another personal consequence of too much stress. Work-related stress can result in lower productivity, higher absenteeism, poorer decision making, and increased probability of accidents.

• Many interventions are available to manage work-related stress. Some directly remove unnecessary stressors or temporarily remove employees from the stressful environment. Others help employees alter their interpretation of the environment so that it is not viewed as a serious stressor. Fitness and lifestyle programs have also been introduced to encourage employees to build better physical defenses against stress experiences.

DISCUSSION QUESTIONS

1. Under what conditions would job specialization be most appropriate?
2. Comment on the following statement: "Job specialization increases employee performance."
3. Why doesn't job enrichment always increase employee motivation?
4. Compare and contrast job rotation with job enlargement.
5. Describe two common work–family stressors.
6. Explain why two people in the same situation do not necessarily experience the same level of stress.
7. Do people with Type A personalities make better managers? Why or why not?
8. How might fitness programs help employees working in stressful situations?

NOTES

1. G. Blackwell, "Before Going Online, Imperial Oil Got Its Staff Onside," *Canadian Business* 61 (August 1988), p. 74.

2. L. E. Davis, "Job Design and Productivity: A New Approach," *Personnel,* March 1957, pp. 418–30.

3. R. J. Long, *New Office Information Technology: Human and Managerial Implications* (London: Crom Helm, 1987); and J. W. Medcof, "The Effect of Extent of Use and Job of the User upon Task Characteristics," *Human Relations* 42 (1989), pp. 23–41.

4. H. Fayol, *General and Industrial Management,* translated by C. Storrs (London: Pitman, 1949); E. E. Lawler III, *Motivation in Work Organizations* (Monterey, Calif.: Brooks/Cole, 1973), Chapter 7; and M. A. Campion, "Ability Requirement Implications of Job Design: An Interdisciplinary Perspective," *Personnel Psychology* 42 (1989), pp. 1–24.

5. A. Smith, *The Wealth of Nations* (London: Dent, 1910).

6. F. W. Taylor, *The Principles of Scientific Management* (New York: Harper & Row, 1911); and D. A. Wren, *The Evolution of Management Thought* (New York: Ronald Press, 1972).

7. Cited in H. Mintzberg, *The Structuring of Organizations* (Englewood Cliffs, N.J.: Prentice Hall, 1979), p. 74.

8. W. J. Duncan, *Great Ideas in Management* (San Francisco: Jossey-Bass, 1989), Chapter 4.

9. R. Fulford, "Firm Management," *Saturday Night,* September 1983, pp. 42–48, 52.

10. E. E. Lawler III, *High-Involvement Management* (San Francisco: Jossey-Bass, 1986); and C. R. Walker and R. H. Guest, *The Man on the Assembly Line* (Cambridge, Mass.: Harvard University Press, 1952).

11. R. Kanungo, *Work Alienation: An Integrative Approach* (New York: Praeger, 1982); M. Seeman, "On the Meaning of Alienation," *American Sociological Review* 24 (1959), pp. 783–91; and R. Blauner, *Alienation and Freedom: The Factory Worker and His Industry* (Chicago: University of Chicago Press, 1964).

12. M. Michaels, "Hands Across the Workplace," *Time,* December 26, 1988, pp. 12–17.

13. Lawler, *Motivation in Work Organizations,* p. 150.

14. D. Farrell and C. L. Stamm, "Meta-Analysis of the Correlates of Employee Absence," *Human Relations* 41 (1988), pp. 211–27.

15. F. Herzberg, B. Mausner, and B. B. Snyderman, *The Motivation to Work* (New York: Wiley, 1959).

16. R. M. Steers and L. W. Porter, *Motivation and Work Behavior,* 4th ed. (New York: McGraw-Hill, 1987), p. 462.

17. A. K. Korman, *Industrial and Organizational Psychology* (Englewood Cliffs, N.J.: Prentice Hall, 1971), p. 149; and N. King, "Clarification and Evaluation of the Two Factor Theory of Job Satisfaction," *Psychological Bulletin* 74 (1970), pp. 18–31.

18. J. R. Hackman and G. Oldham, *Work Redesign* (Reading, Mass.: Addison-Wesley, 1980).

19. R. Maynard, "How Do You Like Your Job?" *Report on Business Magazine,* November 1987, pp. 112–25.

20. P. E. Spector, "Higher-Order Need Strength as a Moderator of the Job Scope–Employee Outcome Relationship: A Meta-Analysis," *Journal of Occupational Psychology* 58 (1985), pp. 119–27.

21. A. C. MacKinney, P. F. Wernimont, and W. O. Galitz, "Has Specialization Reduced Job Satisfaction?" *Personnel* 39 (1962), pp. 8–17.

22. J. Mansell, *An Inventory of Innovative Work Arrangement in Ontario* (Toronto: Ontario Ministry of Labour, 1978), pp. 23–24.

23. Mansell, *An Inventory of Innovative Work Arrangements in Ontario,* pp. 66–68; M. N. Kiggundu, "Structuring and Scheduling of Work," in K. M. Srinivas (ed.), *Human Resource Management: Contemporary Perspectives in Canada* (Toronto: McGraw-Hill Ryerson, 1984), p. 321; P. P. Schoderbek and W. E. Reif, *Job Enlargement: Key to Improved Performance* (Ann Arbor, Mich.: University of Michigan, 1969); and M. D. Kilbridge, "Reduced Costs through Job Enlargement: A Case Study," *The Journal of Business,* October 1960, pp. 357–62.

24. F. Herzberg, "One More Time: How Do You Motivate Employees?" *Harvard Business Review* 46, no. 1 (January–February 1968), pp. 53–62.

25. J. R. Hackman, G. Oldham, R. Janson, and K. Purdy, "A New Strategy for Job Enrichment," *California Management Review* 17, no. 4 (1975), pp. 57–71.

26. I. S. G. Meadows, "Innovative Work Arrangements—A Case Study in Job Enrichment: Philips Electronics Limited, Leaside, Ontario," unpublished paper, Ontario Ministry of Labour, Research Branch, July 1976.

27. R. J. Long, "Patterns of Workplace Innovation," *Relations Industrielles* 44 (1989), pp. 805–26.

28. Y. Fried and G. R. Ferris, "The Validity of the Job Characteristics Model: A Review and Meta-Analysis," *Personnel Psychology* 40 (1987), pp. 287–322; and B. T. Loher, R. A. Noe, N. L. Moeller, and M. P. Fitzgerald, "A Meta-Analysis of the Relation of Job Characteristics to Job Satisfaction," *Journal of Applied Psychology* 70 (1985), pp. 280–89.

29. R. E. Kopelman, "Job Design and Productivity: A Review of the Evidence," *National Productivity Review* 4, no. 3 (1985), pp. 237–55.

30. R. W. Griffin, "Toward an Integrated Theory of Task Design," *Research in Organizational Behavior* 9 (1987), pp. 79–120; and G. Johns, J. L. Xie, and Y. Q. Fang, "Mediating Effects of Psychological States in Job Design," *Proceedings of the Annual ASAC Conference, Organizational Behaviour Division* 12, pt. 7 (1991), pp. 11–20.

31. M. N. Kiggundu, "Task Interdependence and the Theory of Job Design," *Academy of Management Review* 6 (1981), pp. 499–508.

32. P. H. Birnbaum, J. L. Farh, and G. Y. Y. Wong, "The Job Characteristics Model in Hong Kong," *Journal of Applied Psychology* 71 (1986), pp. 598–605.

33. S. Wright and S. Lareau, "An Analysis of Work Improvement in Air Canada," in B. Cunningham and T. White (eds.), *Quality of Working Life: Contemporary Cases* (Ottawa: Labour Canada, 1984), pp. 145–71; and J. T. Archer, "Achieving Joint Organizational, Technical, and Personal Needs: The Case of the Sheltered Experiment of Aluminum Casting Team," in L. E. David, A. B. Cherns, and Associates (eds.), *The Quality of Working Life, Vol. 2* (New York: Free Press, 1975), pp. 253–68.

34. W. Westley, *Quality of Working Life: The Role of the Supervisor* (Ottawa: Labour Canada, 1981); and E. E. Lawler III, J. R. Hackman, and S. Kaufman, "Effects of Job Redesign: A Field Experiment," *Journal of Applied Social Psychology* 3 (1973), pp. 49–62.

35. C. Pinder, *Work Motivation* (Glenview, Ill.: Scott, Foresman, 1984), pp. 257–58; and J. Rinehart,

"Improving the Quality of Working Life through Job Redesign: Work Humanization or Work Rationalization?" *Canadian Review of Sociology and Anthropology* 23 (1986), pp. 507–30.

36. J. B. Cunningham, "A Look at Four Approaches to Work Design," *Optimum* 20, no. 1 (1989/90), pp. 39–55.

37. Campion, "Ability Requirement Implications of Job Design: An Interdisciplinary Perspective"; and R. B. Dunham, "Relationships of Perceived Job Design Characteristics to Job Ability Requirements and Job Value," *Journal of Applied Psychology* 62 (1977), pp. 760–63.

38. R. Martin and T. D. Wall, "Attentional Demand and Cost Responsibility as Stressors in Shopfloor Jobs," *Academy of Management Journal* 32 (1989), pp. 69–86.

39. V. Ross, "Stress: The Business of Coping," *Maclean's,* May 5, 1980, pp. 46–52.

40. M. Dewey, "Stress on the Job Is a $13 Billion Problem for Industry," *Globe & Mail,* November 9, 1981, p. B3; and Dr. Earle, personal communication, November 1990.

41. M. Strauss, "Burnout Compensable as Work-Related Injury, N.S. Arbitrator Rules," *Globe and Mail,* June 4, 1985, p. M3; and M. T. Matteson and J. M. Ivancevich, *Controlling Work Stress* (San Francisco: Jossey-Bass, 1987).

42. R. J. Burke and T. Weir, "Coping with the Stress of Managerial Occupations," in C. L. Cooper and R. Payne (eds.), *Current Concerns in Occupational Stress* (London: John Wiley & Sons, 1980), pp. 299–335; M. T. Matteson and J. M. Ivancevich, *Managing Job Stress and Health* (New York: Free Press, 1982); and J. C. Quick and J. D. Quick, *Organizational Stress and Prevention Management* (New York: McGraw-Hill, 1984).

43. M. Jamal, "Job Stress and Job Performance Controversy: An Empirical Assessment," *Organizational Behavior and Human Performance* 33 (1984), pp. 1–21.

44. H. Selye, *Stress without Distress* (Philadelphia, Pa.: J.B. Lippincott, 1974).

45. Quick and Quick, *Organizational Stress and Prevention Management,* p. 3.

46. S. Rauchman, "What You Can't See Can Hurt You," *Canadian Occupational Safety,* 27 (March–April, 1989), pp. 20–21; E. Rockett, "White Noise: Will the Hissing Have to Stop?" *Maclean's,* December 11, 1978, p. 52b.

47. E. R. Kemery, A. G. Bedeian, K. W. Mossholder, and J. Touliatos, "Outcomes of Role Stress: A Multisample Constructive Replication," *Academy of Management Journal* 28 (1985), pp. 363–75; and R. L. Kahn, D. M. Wolfe, R. P. Quinn, J. D. Snoek, and R. A. Rosenthal, *Organizational Stress: Studies in Role Conflict and Ambiguity* (New York: Wiley, 1964).

48. D. L. Nelson, "Organizational Socialization: A Stress Perspective," *Journal of Occupational Behaviour* 8 (1987), pp. 311–24; and C. C. Pinder and G. A. Walter, "Personnel Transfers and Employee Development," *Research in Personnel and Human Resources Management* 2 (1984), pp. 187–218.

49. J. B. Shaw and J. H. Riskind, "Predicting Job Stress Using Data from the Position Analysis Questionnaire," *Journal of Applied Psychology* 68 (1983), pp. 253–61.

50. G. S. Lowe and H. C. Northcott, *Under Pressure: A Study of Job Stress* (Toronto: Garamond Press, 1986); and R. Karasek and T. Theorell, *Healthy Work: Stress, Productivity, and the Reconstruction of Working Life* (New York: Basic Books, 1990).

51. J. Seltzer and R. E. Numerof, "Supervisory Leadership and Subordinate Burnout," *Academy of Management Journal* 31 (1988), pp. 439–46; and H. C. Jain and P. Andiappan, "Sexual Harassment in Employment in Canada," *Relations Industrielles* 41 (1986), pp. 758–76.

52. For example, see *Colasurdo* v. *CTG Inc. et al.* (1988), 18 CCEL 264; and *Pilato* v. *Hamilton Place Convention Centre Inc.* (1984) 45 OR (2d) 652.

53. R. J. Burke, "The Closing at Canadian Admiral: Correlates of Individual Well-Being 16 Months after Shutdown," *Psychological Reports* 55 (1984), pp. 91–98; J. P. Grayson, "The Closure of a Factory and Its Impact on Health," *International Journal of Health Services* 15 (1985), pp. 69–93; and C. R. Leana and D. C. Feldman, "Individual Responses to Job Loss: Perceptions, Reactions, and Coping Behaviors," *Journal of Management* 14 (1988), pp. 375–89.

54. R. J. Burke, "Managing the Human Side of Mergers and Acquisitions," *Business Quarterly,* Winter, 1987, pp. 18–23; and T. Carlisle, "Amoco Hit by Culture Shock as Dome's Spirit Lives On," *Financial Post,* March 25–27, 1989, pp. 1–2.

55. R. J. Burke and C. A. McKeen, "Work and Family: What We Know and What We Need to Know," *Canadian Journal of Administrative Sciences* 5 (December 1988), pp. 30–40; R. J. Burke and P. Bradshaw, "Occupational and Life Stress and the Family," *Small Group Behavior* 12 (1981), pp. 329–75; and B. Sass, "The Centrality of Work," *Work & Stress* 2 (1988), pp. 255–60.

56. R. J. Burke, T. Weir, and R. E. Duwors, "Work Demands on Administrators and Spouse Well-Being," *Human Relations* 33 (1980), pp. 253–78.

57. M. D. Lee, "Intentional Life Space Design: A Strategy for Dual Earner and Single Parent Families," *Canadian Journal of Administrative Sciences* 5 (December 1988), pp. 41–50.

58. G. L. Staines and J. H. Pleck, "Work Schedule Flexibility and Family Life," *Journal of Occupational Behaviour* 7 (1986), pp. 147–53; and M. Jamal, "Shift Work Related to Job Attitudes, Social Participation and Withdrawal Behavior: A Study of Nurses and Industrial Workers," *Personnel Psychology* 34 (1981), pp. 535–47.

59. J. H. Greenhaus and N. J. Beutall, "Sources of Conflict between Work and Family Roles," *Academy of Management Review* 10 (1985), pp. 76–88.

60. A. McBride, "'High Stress' Occupations: The Importance of Job Components versus Job Categories," in R. J. Burke (ed.), *Current Issues in Occupational Stress: Research and Intervention* (Toronto: Faculty of Administrative Studies, York University, 1984), pp. 1–24; G. Shouksmith and S. Burrough, "Job Stress Factors for New Zealand and Canadian Air Traffic Controllers," *Applied Psychology: An International Review* 37 (1988), pp. 263–70; and Matteson and Ivancevich, *Managing Job Stress and Health,* p. 90.

61. B. Bird, "Jobs and Stress," *Winnipeg Free Press,* October 29, 1985, p. 27.

62. R. S. Lazarus, *Psychological Stress and the Coping Process* (New York: McGraw-Hill, 1966).

63. E. R. Greenglass, R. J. Burke, and M. Ondrack, "A Gender-Role Perspective of Coping and Burnout," *Applied Psychology: An International Review* 39 (1990), pp. 5–27; and T. D. Jick and L. F. Mitz, "Sex Differences in Work Stress," *Academy of Management Review* 10 (1985), pp. 408–20.

64. M. Friedman and R. Rosenman, *Type A Behavior and Your Heart* (New York: Knopf, 1974); and J. H. Howard, D. A. Cunningham, and P. A. Rechnitzer, "Health Patterns Associated with Type A Behavior: A Managerial Population," *Journal of Human Stress* 2, no. 1 (1976), pp. 24–31.

65. M. Jamal, "Type A Behavior and Job Performance: Some Suggestive Findings," *Journal of Human Stress* 11, no. 2 (Summer 1985), pp. 60–68; and C. Lee, P. C. Earley, and L. A. Hanson, "Are Type A's Better Performers?" *Journal of Organizational Behavior* 9 (1988), pp. 263–69.

66. E. Greenglass, "Type A Behaviour and Occupational Demands in Managerial Women," *Canadian Journal of Administrative Sciences* 4 (1987), pp. 157–68; and R. A. Baron and J. Greenberg, *Behavior in Organizations,* 3rd ed. (Boston: Allyn & Bacon, 1990), p. 194.

67. C. Nair, F. Colburn, D. McLean, and A. Petrasovits, "Cardiovascular Disease in Canada," *Statistics Canada Health Reports* 1, no. 1 (1989), pp. 1–22.

68. J. A. Lischeron, "Occupational Health: Psychosocial Aspects," *Human Resource Management: Contemporary Perspectives in Canada,* pp. 425–55.

69. R. J. Burke, "Toward a Phase Model of Burnout: Some Conceptual and Methodological Concerns," *Group and Organization Studies* 14 (1989), pp. 23–32; R. J. Burke and G. Deszca, "Correlates of Psychological Burnout Phases among Police Officers," *Human Relations* 39 (1986), pp. 487–502; and C. Maslach, *Burnout: The Cost of Caring* (Englewood Cliffs, N.J.: Prentice Hall, 1982).

70. L. Moss, *Management Stress* (Reading, Mass.: Addison-Wesley, 1981).

71. A. Arsenault and S. Dolan, "The Role of Personality, Occupation, and Organization in Understanding the Relationship between Job Stress, Performance, and Absenteeism," *Journal of Occupational Psychology* 56 (1983), pp. 227–40; and V. V. Baba and M. J. Harris, "Stress and Absence: A Cross-Cultural Perspective," *Research in Personnel and Human Resources Management, Supplement 1* (1989), pp. 317–37.

72. Jamal, "Job Stress and Job Performance Controversy: An Empirical Assessment"; S. J. Motowidlo, J. S. Packard, and M. R. Manning, "Occupational Stress: Its Causes and Consequences for Job Performance," *Journal of Applied Psychology* 71 (1986), pp. 618–29; and G. Keinan, "Decision Making under Stress: Scanning of Alternatives under Controllable and Uncontrollable Threats," *Journal of Personality and Social Psychology* 52 (1987), pp. 638–44.

73. J. H. Howard, "Stress and the Manager: Perspectives," in A. S. Sethi and R. S. Schuler, *Handbook of Organizational Stress Coping Strategies* (Cambridge, Mass.: Ballinger, 1984), pp. 233–49.

74. R. A. Karasek, Jr., "Job Demands, Job Decision Latitude, and Mental Strain: Implications for Job Redesign," *Administrative Science Quarterly* 24 (1979), pp. 285–308.

75. L. G. Stulberg, "Bad Air Can Smother Productivity," *Financial Post,* August 8, 1990, p. 13.

76. C. Cornell, "Loving It and Leaving It," *Human Resources Professional,* April 1991, pp. 19–22.

77. N. J. Adler, *International Dimensions of Organizational Behavior* (Boston, Mass.: Kent, 1986), p. 195.

78. R. J. Burke and G. Deszca, "Career Orientations, Satisfaction and Health among Police Officers: Some Consequences of Person–Job Fit," *Psychological Reports* 62 (1988), pp. 639–49; and C. Cherniss, *Professional Burnout in Human Service Organizations* (New York: Praeger, 1980).

79. N. S. Bruning and D. R. Frew, "Can Stress Intervention Strategies Improve Self-Esteem, Manifest Anxiety, and Job Satisfaction? A Longitudinal Field Experiment," *Journal of Health and Human Resources Administration* 9 (1986), pp. 110–24; E. Roskies, *Stress Management for the Healthy Type A* (New York: Guilford Press, 1987); and J. C. Levenkron and L. G. Moore, "The Type A Behavior Pattern: Issues for Intervention Research," *Annals of Behavioral Medicine,* 1988, pp. 78–83.

80. M. Alpert, "How Japan's Workers Relax," *Fortune,* April 23, 1990, p. 17.

81. A. S. Sethi, "Meditation for Coping with Organizational Stress," in Sethi and Schuler, *Handbook of Organizational Stress Coping Strategies,* pp. 145–65; K. R. McLeroy, L. W. Green, K. D. Mullen, and V. Foshee, "Assessing the Effects of Health Promotion in Worksites: A Review of Stress Program Evaluations," *Health Education Quarterly* 11 (1984), pp. 379–401; and L. R. Murphy, "Occupational Stress Management: A Review and Appraisal," *Journal of Occupational Psychology* 57 (1984), pp. 1–15.

82. L. E. Falkenberg, "Employee Fitness Programs: Their Impact on the Employee and the Organization," *Academy of Management Review* 12 (1987), pp. 511–22; R. J. Shephard, M. Cox, and P. Corey, "Fitness Program Participation: Its Effect on Workers' Performance," *Journal of Occupational Medicine* 23 (1981), pp. 359–63; and J. H. Howard, P. A. Rechnitzer, and D. A. Cunningham, "Coping with Job Tension—Effective and Ineffective Methods," *Public Personnel Management* 4 (1975), pp. 317–26.

83. P. Stulberg, "Business Finds Working Out Pays Dividends," *Financial Post,* January 26, 1990, pp. 11–13; and K. LaPointe, "Company and Workers Benefit from Fitness Plan, Studies Show," *Winnipeg Free Press,* September 4, 1986, p. 35.

84. A. Morantz, "Helping Employees Cope with Personal Problems," *Worklife* 3, no. 1 (1983), pp. 10–12; M. Roy-Brisebois, "Victim Assistance: An Example of Meeting the Work-Related Needs of Employees," in R. Thomlison (ed.), *Perspectives on Industrial Social Work Practice* (Ottawa: Family Service Canada, 1983); and P. Conlon, "Show You Care," *Canadian Business,* April 1987, pp. 64, 66, 108, 109.

85. J. S. House, *Work Stress and Social Support* (Reading, Mass.: Addison-Wesley, 1981); and S. Cohen and T. A. Wills, "Stress, Social Support, and the Buffering Hypothesis," *Psychological Bulletin* 98 (1985), pp. 310–57.

86. S. Schachter, *The Psychology of Affiliation* (Stanford, Calif.: Stanford University Press, 1959).

CHAPTER CASES

SOLCOM ENGINEERING LTD.

Solcom Ltd. is a large engineering firm that employs over 1,500 people in its operations throughout Canada. The company is headquartered in Winnipeg and has been in operation since 1962.

The Personnel Records office at Solcom consists of five clerical employees who compile and maintain the necessary record keeping on personnel files and answer questions about personnel-related issues. Each clerk keeps records and answers enquiries in a different functional area within personnel records. One person is responsible for handling employee pensions, another takes care of insurance plans, a third is responsible for vacation entitlements, and so on. For example, when someone becomes a Solcom employee, the Personnel Records office clerk responsible for pensions receives the new employee's file and prepares information within her area of responsibility. The file is then passed on to the other clerks to input information on their functional area.

Solcom's operations have been expanding quickly and several problems with the Personnel Records office are emerging. Line managers complain that it is difficult to determine who in Personnel Records is responsible for each particular personnel function. They also note that the clerks seemed to "care" more about their particular personnel area (e.g., vacations, pensions) than about the overall quality of the personnel records and employee needs. Furthermore, personnel records are sometimes incomplete because one or more clerks do not receive the file from other clerks for updating.

The Personnel Records clerks are also showing signs of frustration as it becomes more difficult to coordinate the workload with other staff in the Personnel Records office. This is creating some tension among the clerks. The job is somewhat monotonous after employees spend more than one year responsible for the same personnel records area. These factors are resulting in serious morale problems, high turnover, and decreasing productivity within the Personnel Records office. The manager of Personnel Records and the director of Human Resources realize that changes are needed, but it is not clear to them how to improve the situation.

Discussion Questions

1. List the symptoms that suggest there is something wrong in this department.
2. Which of the five job characteristics seem to have low values in the Personnel Records office clerical jobs?
3. Which implementing principles should be used to redesign these jobs? Identify the job characteristics that would improve if these implementing principles are used. What effect would these actions have on the symptoms listed in Question 1?
4. What would happen if the company introduced a job rotation program for these clerical staff?

JIM BLACK: SALES REPRESENTATIVE

Jim Black impatiently drummed the steering wheel and puffed a cigarette as his car moved slowly northbound along the Don Valley Parkway. Traffic congestion was normal in the late afternoon, but it seemed much heavier today. In any event, it was another irritation that was going to make him late for his next appointment.

As a sales representative at Noram Canada Ltd., Jim could not afford to keep clients waiting. Sales of compressed oxygen and other gases were slower during this prolonged recession. Other compressed gas suppliers were eager to grab new accounts and it was becoming more common for clients to switch from one supplier to another. Jim pressed his half-finished cigarette against the ash tray and accelerated the car into another lane.

Buyers of compressed gases knew that the market was in their favour and many were demanding price discounts and shorter delivery times. Earlier in the week, for example, one of Jim's more demanding customers telephoned for another shipment of liquid oxygen to be delivered the next morning. To meet the deadline, Jim had to complete an expedited delivery form and then personally convince the shipping group to make the delivery in the morning rather than later in the day. Jim disliked making expedited delivery requests, even though this was becoming increasingly common among the reps, because it often delayed shipment of Noram's product to other clients. Discounts were even more troublesome because they reduced his commission and, except for very large orders, were frowned upon by Noram management.

Meanwhile, at Noram Canada's headquarters in nearby Brampton, senior managers were putting more pressure on sales reps to produce. They complained that the reps weren't aggressive enough and area supervisors were told to monitor each sales rep's monthly numbers more closely. Jim fumbled for another cigarette as the traffic stopped momentarily.

Two months ago, the area sales supervisor had "a little chat" (as he called it) with Jim about the stagnant sales in his district and loss of a client to the competition. It wasn't exactly a threat of being fired—other reps also received these chats—but Jim felt nervous about his work and began having sleepless nights. He began making more calls to potential clients, but was only able to find this time by completing administrative paperwork in the evenings. The evening work wasn't helping relations with his family.

To make matters worse, Noram's parent company in New York announced that it planned to sell the Canadian operations. Jim had heard rumours that a competitor was going to purchase the firm, mainly to expand its operations through Noram's Western Canadian sales force and production facilities. The competitor was well established in Ontario and probably wouldn't need a larger sales force here, so Jim's job would be in jeopardy if the acquisition took place. Jim felt another headache coming on as he stared at the endless line of red tail-lights slithering along the highway ahead.

Even if Jim kept his job, any promotion into management would be a long way off if the competitor acquired Noram Canada. Jim had no particular desire to become a manager, but his wife was eager for him to receive a promotion because it would involve less travel and provide a more stable salary (less dependent on monthly sales). Business travel was a nuisance, particularly for out-of-town appointments, but Jim felt less comfortable with the idea of sitting behind a desk all day.

The loud honk of another car startled Jim as he swerved into the exit lane at Eglington Avenue. A few minutes later, he arrived at the client's parking lot. Jim rummaged through his brief case for some aspirin to relieve the headache. He heaved a deep sigh as he glanced at his watch. Jim was fifteen minutes late for the appointment.

Discussion Questions

1. What stress symptoms is Jim experiencing?
2. What stressors can you identify in this case?
3. What should Jim do to minimize his stress?

© 1991 Steven L. McShane.

EXPERIENTIAL EXERCISE

BEHAVIOUR ACTIVITY PROFILE—THE TYPE A SCALE

Purpose.   This exercise is designed to help you estimate the extent to which you follow a Type A behaviour pattern. It also shows you specific elements of Type A patterns in various life events.

Instructions.   This is a self-diagnostic exercise to be completed alone. Each of us displays certain kinds of behaviours, thought patterns of personal characteristics. For each of the 21 sets of descriptions below, circle the number that you feel best describes where you are between each pair. The best answer for each set of descriptions is the response that most nearly describes the way you feel, behave, or think. Answer these in terms of your regular or typical behaviour, thoughts, or characteristics.

1. I'm always on time for appointments.	7 6 5 4 3 2 1	I'm never quite on time.
2. When someone is talking to me, chances are I'll anticipate what they are going to say, by nodding, interrupting, or finishing sentences for them.	7 6 5 4 3 2 1	I listen quietly without showing any impatience.

3. I frequently try to do several things at once.   7 6 5 4 3 2 1   I tend to take things one at a time.

4. When it comes to waiting in line (at banks, theatres, etc.), I really get impatient and frustrated.   7 6 5 4 3 2 1   It simply doesn't bother me.

5. I always feel rushed.   7 6 5 4 3 2 1   I never feel rushed.

6. When it comes to my temper, I find it hard to control at times.   7 6 5 4 3 2 1   I just don't seem to have one.

7. I tend to do most things like eating, walking, and talking rapidly.   7 6 5 4 3 2 1   Slowly.

Total Score 1–7 _____ = S

8. Quite honestly, the things I enjoy most are job-related activities.   7 6 5 4 3 2 1   Leisure-time activities.

9. At the end of a typical workday, I usually feel like I needed to get more done than I did.   7 6 5 4 3 2 1   I accomplished everything I needed to.

10. Someone who knows me very well would say that I would rather work than play.   7 6 5 4 3 2 1   I'd rather play than work.

11. When it comes to getting ahead at work nothing is more important.   7 6 5 4 3 2 1   Many things are more important.

12. My primary source of satisfaction comes from my job.   7 6 5 4 3 2 1   I regularly find satisfaction in nonjob pursuits, such as hobbies, friends, and family.

13. Most of my friends and social acquaintances are people I know from work.   7 6 5 4 3 2 1   Not connected with my work.

14. I'd rather stay at work than take a vacation.   7 6 5 4 3 2 1   Nothing at work is important enough to interfere with my vacation.

Total Score 8–14 _____ = J

15. People who know me well would describe me as hard driving and competitive.   7 6 5 4 3 2 1   Relaxed and easygoing.

16. In general, my behaviour is governed by a desire for recognition and achievement.   7 6 5 4 3 2 1   What I want to do—not by trying to satisfy others.

17. In trying to complete a project or solve a problem I tend to wear myself out before I'll give up on it.   7 6 5 4 3 2 1   I tend to take a break or quit if I'm feeling fatigued.

18. When I play a game (tennis, cards, etc.) my enjoyment comes from winning.   7 6 5 4 3 2 1   The social interaction.

19. I like to associate with people who are dedicated to getting ahead.   7 6 5 4 3 2 1   Easygoing and take life as it comes.

20. I'm not happy unless I'm always doing something.   7 6 5 4 3 2 1   Frequently, "doing nothing" can be quite enjoyable.

21. What I enjoy doing most are competitive activities.   7 6 5 4 3 2 1   Noncompetitive pursuits.

Total Score 15–21 _____ = H

Impatience (S)	Job Involvement (J)	Hard Driving and Competitive (H)	Total Score (A) = S + J + H

The Behaviour Activity Profile attempts to assess the three Type A coronary-prone behaviour patterns, as well as provide a total score. The three a priori types of Type A coronary-prone behaviour patterns are shown:

Items	Behaviour Pattern		Characteristics
1–7	Impatience	(S)	Anxious to interrupt. Fails to listen attentively. Frustrated by waiting (e.g., in line, for others to complete a job).
8–14	Job involvement	(J)	Focal point of attention is the job. Lives for the job. Relishes being on the job. Immersed by job activities.
15–21	Hard driving/ competitive	(H)	Hardworking, highly competitive. Competitive in most aspects of life, sports, work, etc. Racing against the clock.
1–21	Total score	(A)	Total of S + J + H represents your global Type A behaviour.

Score ranges for total score are:

Score	Behaviour Type
122 and above	Hard-core Type A
99–121	Moderate Type A
90–98	Low Type A
80–89	Type X
70–79	Low Type B
50–69	Moderate Type B
40 and below	Hard-core Type B

Percentile Scores

Now you can compare your score to a
sample of over 1,200 respondents

Percentile Score	Raw Score	
Percentage of Individuals Scoring Lower	**Males**	**Females**
99%	_____ 140	_____ 132
95	_____ 135	_____ 126
90	_____ 130	_____ 120
85	_____ 124	_____ 112
80	_____ 118	_____ 106
75	_____ 113	_____ 101
70	_____ 108	_____ 95
65	_____ 102	_____ 90
60	_____ 97	_____ 85
55	_____ 92	_____ 80
50	_____ 87	_____ 74
45	_____ 81	_____ 69
40	_____ 75	_____ 63
35	_____ 70	_____ 58
30	_____ 63	_____ 53
25	_____ 58	_____ 48
20	_____ 51	_____ 42
15	_____ 45	_____ 36
10	_____ 38	_____ 31
5	_____ 29	_____ 26
1	_____ 21	_____ 21

The Royal Bank of Canada is the country's largest financial institution and the fifth largest bank in North America. Royal Bank's foreign exchange and money market traders are among the best in the world and transact over $12 billion each day. At the main Toronto dealing room, Karen Luprypa and Dan Taylor take a moment to discuss late-breaking market developments.

6

Interpersonal and Organizational Communication

LEARNING OBJECTIVES
After reading this chapter, you should be able to:

Explain
Why communication is important in organizational settings.

Diagram
The communication model.

Discuss
The advantages of the different communication channels.

Outline
The main features of grapevine communication.

Discuss
The advantages and disadvantages of ambiguity in communication.

Describe
The different ways that people tend to cope with information overload.

List
The main features of effective listening.

B.C. Tel

British Columbia Telephone Company (B.C. Tel) is one of Canada's best employers and was recently selected for the Canadian government's prestigious Business Excellence award as a tribute to its impressive product and service quality. Yet just 10 years ago, the company was an autocratic monopoly with poor employee relations and a reputation for poor service. A six-week strike in 1981 dramatized the gulf that existed between management and employees.

How has B.C. Tel managed such a revolutionary transformation in employee relations and service quality? The company made many improvements, but perhaps the most important was communications between management and employees. Frequent departmental meetings are now held to share information with employees and listen to their ideas. Annual employee surveys help senior managers understand general opinions, emerging trends, and potential problems. The People's Choice Award is an unusual communication program in which employees nominate managers who deserve recognition. The company's Speak Out program lets employees voice their concerns, make suggestions, or ask questions in confidence to people further up the organizational ladder. Quality circles and a suggestion system serve as conduits for creative ideas from employees to make the telephone company more productive.

B.C. Tel takes downward communications just as seriously. *Perspectives,* the company's monthly news magazine, communicates recent developments to all 19,000 current staff and retirees. A quarterly video program features company news and conversations with senior executives. An electronic bulletin board has been set up on the company's computer system so that employees can learn the latest news before it becomes public. According to a recent survey, most B.C. Tel employees learn about corporate news from company sources instead of through the grapevine or outside media.[1]

This chapter is about communicating in organizations—from interpersonal exchanges between two people to structured, organizationwide communication programs. As the dramatic turnaround at B.C. Tel illustrates, communication is important for organizational effectiveness. We begin this chapter by looking more closely at the importance of organizational communication. Next, we describe a model of interpersonal communication, the different channels and directions of communicating, and the various barriers to effective communication in organizations. Several strategies to improve both interpersonal and organizational communication are outlined in the final sections of this chapter.

THE IMPORTANCE OF COMMUNICATION

Communication refers to the process by which information is transmitted and understood between two or more people. Effective communication occurs when the sender's thoughts are transmitted to and *understood by* the intended receiver. Notice the emphasis on the word *understood*. Ensuring that the sender's message is correctly understood by the receiver is the key to good communication.

Communicating with superiors, subordinates, peers, and people outside of the organization consumes between 50 and 80 percent of a typical manager's workday.[2] This activity is perhaps most important as a means of coordinating individual activities toward organizational goals.[3] In terms of the performance model described in Chapter 2, communication clarifies role perceptions and assists in motivating employees. Through communication, employees learn about their tasks, performance standards, and coworker expectations. Coordination also occurs more subtly when employees communicate corporate cultural values and assumptions so they have a shared interpretation of the workplace and the external environment.[4] Without communication, organizations would consist of a collection of people working independently toward their own goals.

Communication is essential for effective decision making. Without communication, decision makers would have difficulty understanding organizational problems or opportunities, and would have limited knowledge of decision alternatives and outcomes.

Finally, communication serves an emotional function. People need to communicate with each other to fulfill their social interaction needs and to establish or clarify their self-image in the work group. Socially directed communication maintains the employee's relations with others for purposes of influence and future information exchange. To some extent, all communication has an emotional or social function because the way we interact with others indicates how we feel about them.

Communication errors can be costly. Consider the following incidents, which can be traced to communication problems:[5]

- A warehouse employee in Toronto shipped a large piece of equipment at great expense to a customer's offices in London, England. The order form indicated "London" and did not specify that the intended destination was the customer's offices in nearby London, Ontario.
- Four Royal Air Force jets were speeding across England when the rear pilot saw one of the other three catch fire. He quickly radioed, "You

communication
The process by which information is transmitted and understood between two or more people.

PERSPECTIVE 6-1   Tuning in to Employee Involvement

Buckman Labs is a highly successful American firm that manufactures and markets specialty chemicals in several countries. The manufacturing manager of its plant in Belgium attempted to improve communications among departments by issuing specially designed walkie-talkies to 18 employees. The system would allow warehouse workers to contact the shipping department or the lab supervisor to call the production line, for instance, without interfering with other employees using the walkie-talkies.

But the walkie-talkies of two employees didn't work properly. Rather than receiving only each other's signals, they picked up conversations from every walkie-talkie in the plant. Consequently, these two employees had a much better knowledge of what was happening throughout the operation. They didn't tell anyone about the flawed equipment, but the manufacturing manager discovered the problem when he noticed that these two employees were becoming much more involved in staff meetings. Compared to those with the restricted walkie-talkies, the two employees were asking lots of questions and offering solutions to problems in other departments.

When informed that the walkie-talkies didn't work as intended, the manufacturing manager didn't try to get them fixed. Instead, he traded in the other walkie-talkies for less expensive sets that would allow employees to listen in on all other conversations.

Source: *Thriving on Chaos* (pp. 287–88) by Tom Peters. Copyright © 1987 by Excel, a California Limited Partnership. Reprinted by permission of Alfred A. Knopf, Inc.

are on fire—eject!'' The pilot in the burning plane bailed out and parachuted to safety. Unfortunately, the pilot of another plane that was not on fire also bailed out in response to the rear pilot's command. Both jets crashed, costing the British government one million dollars each.

- Managers in a northern Ontario lumber camp were perplexed when the accident rate increased after safety posters were put up around the camp. They soon discovered that many workers could not read very well and were therefore imitating the illustrations on the safety posters. The workers were unable to read the printed message telling them *not* to do the things shown.

Beyond these colourful anecdotes, scientific research indicates that communication has an impact on organizational effectiveness.[6] Opening up communication channels throughout the organization increases production efficiency and reduces both absenteeism and production costs. The quality of the manager's communication behaviour significantly influences employee performance which, in turn, influences organizational performance.

Effective communication is believed to increase organizational innovation because information and ideas flow more freely. It increases job satisfaction and reduces turnover because communication serves a social function that bonds people closer to the organization. Improving the flow of organizational information satisfies a basic need to understand the surrounding environment. Better communications between superiors and subordinates also tends to improve the employee's sense of self-worth because the exchange symbolizes the employee's value to the organization. Employees who are kept informed about organizational activities also tend to have a stronger sense of identity with the company and are more willing to become involved.[7] This point is illustrated in the experience of a Belgian firm, as described in Perspective 6–1.

A MODEL OF COMMUNICATION

To understand the complex processes of communicating between people within organizations, you should first learn about the basic features of all communication transactions. A model of interpersonal communication provides a useful starting point. Six basic steps are involved in this process, as Exhibit 6–1 illustrates.[8]

Forming the Intended Message

The first step is for the sender to have a concept, attitude, or fact that is believed to have some value to others. As previously indicated, effective communication occurs when these thoughts are received and understood by the intended receiver.

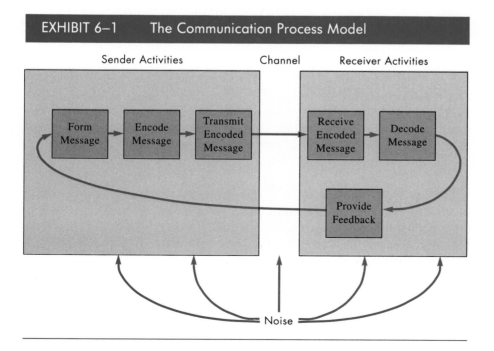

EXHIBIT 6–1   The Communication Process Model

Encoding the Intended Message

We cannot put our thoughts directly into the heads of others; rather, we must translate them into symbols that are transmitted to the receiver. The sender attempts to find words, gestures, voice intonations, and other symbols or signs to which the receiver hopefully attaches the same meaning. The difficulty is in finding symbols or signs with a common meaning between sender and receiver. Certain words or gestures may have different interpretations because the sender and receiver have unique past experiences.

Transmitting the Encoded Message

Next, the sender transmits the encoded message through one or more media to the intended receiver. Symbols and signs may be sent by several means, such as a face-to-face conversation, a letter, a telephone call, electronic mail, facial expressions, or pictures. Communication effectiveness depends on which medium is used because some are more appropriate than others for certain messages and situations.[9]

Receiving the Encoded Message

For effective communication, the receiver must be both motivated and able to tune in to the sender's message. Problems may occur, however, either in the receiver's ability to read, listen to, or observe the message, or in the media through which the message has been sent. Sometimes messages are sent through organizational channels that never reach the intended receiver.

Decoding the Received Message

The receiver decodes the message by assigning meaning to the symbols. Decoding symbols with the same meaning as the sender intended is the essence of good communication. Decoding creates the difference between understanding the message and merely receiving it.

Providing Feedback

In most organizational situations, the sender looks for evidence that the other person or group has received and understood the message. This feedback may come in the form of a formal acknowledgement, such as a "Yes, I know what you mean" from the receiver, or more indirectly from the receiver's subsequent actions. Even the receiver's failure to respond to the sender's message provides feedback, although silence is often an ambiguous form of communication. Also notice that feedback repeats the communication process. Intended feedback is encoded, transmitted, received, and decoded from the receiver to the sender of the original message.

This model of communication should not be viewed as a free-flowing conduit through which information is exchanged.[10] Rather, the transmission of meaning from one person to another is hampered by psychological, social, and structural barriers that distort and obscure the sender's intended message. These barriers are often called *noise* in the communication process. It is also useful to remember that employees communicate in many ways and at different levels of consciousness. The next section describes the various channels of communicating within organizations.

CHANNELS OF COMMUNICATION

Three basic channels of communication are available in organizations: written, verbal, and nonverbal. Within each channel are several methods of communicating, each with unique characteristics and advantages.

Written communication may take the form of a casual note asking a coworker to lunch, an electronic mail message informing department staff of an upcoming meeting, or a detailed report proposing a revision to the accounting system. Effective written communication depends on selecting the appropriate format, because the type of document used can transmit different meanings to the receiver.[11] For example, preparing a formal memorandum to ask a coworker to lunch is more inefficient than a handwritten note and may inaccurately convey a sense of formality to the occasion.

Electronic mail systems and facsimile machines are beginning to revolutionize written communication in organizations. One study of an electronic mail system at Bell Canada discovered that communication initially flowed vertically between employees and their immediate superiors, but the pattern later changed to the situation where everyone was sending electronic messages to everyone else.[12] One potential problem with this trend, according to other research, is that the number of messages transmitted increases to the point that managers are overloaded with electronic memos.[13]

Verbal communication ranges from a casual conversation between two employees standing by the coffee machine to a recorded speech by the president of General Motors of Canada shown on the company's TV monitors. Most verbal communication enables the sender to receive immediate feedback, thereby speeding up the process of exchanging information. In addition, the meaning of verbal communication messages are typically influenced by nonverbal communication symbols, as we will discuss next.

Nonverbal Communication

Nonverbal communication includes actions, gestures, facial expressions, the sender's appearance, the timing of the message, the context of the message—almost anything that is not verbal or written. It is perhaps the most important communication method because the largest amount of information in face-to-face meetings is expressed through nonverbal symbols.[14] More-

nonverbal communication
The transmission of meaning through any means other than words, such as actions, gestures, facial expressions, the sender's appearance, the timing of the message, and the context of the message.

over, nonverbal cues tend to influence the meaning assigned by the receiver to verbal information. Many years ago, for example, middle managers at General Electric engaged in price fixing even after being advised by senior executives not to do so. The managers ignored the verbal message because superiors typically winked their eye while giving the warning. Whether the winks were telling managers to ignore the verbal warnings or were simply a ritualistic symbol of friendship (as some GE executives claimed) is still a matter of debate.

Nonverbal communication is often necessary in production areas where physical distance or machine noise prevents effective verbal exchanges and the need for immediate feedback precludes written communication. In a fascinating study of workers in several Canadian sawmills and logging operations, Meissner observed over 100 signals used to communicate task information and maintain social relations.[15] As the distance between two workers increased, the percent of nonverbal communication increased substantially. An example of nonverbal communication in a sawmill is shown in Exhibit 6–2.

Canadian managers on international assignments must pay close attention to nonverbal messages because these symbols often have different meanings in other cultures. For example, Canadian managers shake their head from side to side to say "No," but this means "Yes" to many Yugoslavians. Filipinos raise their eyebrows to give an affirmative answer, yet Arabs interpret this expression (along with clicking one's tongue) as a negative response.[16] Misinterpreting these cues in a business setting can mean the difference between reaching agreement on a commercial venture and returning home empty-handed.

EXHIBIT 6–2	Nonverbal Communication in a Canadian Sawmill

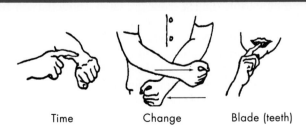

Time   Change   Blade (teeth)

"It's time to change the saw blade!"

Source: M. Meissner, "The Language of Work," in R. Dubin, *Handbook of Work, Organization, and Society* (Chicago: Rand McNally, 1976), p. 262.

In some cultures, nonverbal communication is the primary method of transmitting the sender's true meaning. For example, to avoid offending or embarrassing an associate, Japanese managers will often say what the other person wants to hear (called *tatemae*) but send more subtle nonverbal cues indicating the sender's true feelings (called *honne*). It is for this reason that focussing on nonverbal communication is so important to people working in multicultural organizations. This point is illustrated in Perspective 6–2.

Choosing the Best Communication Medium

As with so many aspects of organizational behaviour, the best communication channel depends on the situation. Verbal communication tends to be most effective when the sender wants to persuade or motivate the receiver. This may be due to the more personal nature of this channel as well as the benefit of immediate feedback so the sender can find out whether the receiver has accepted (as opposed to merely received and understood) the information.

Written communication is a more effective means of recording and presenting technical details, as long as the language is compatible with the receiver's knowledge of the subject. Employees receiving written information tend to have a higher comprehension of the material than when it is received verbally.[17] However, written methods usually take longer to prepare, transmit, and receive feedback from than verbal communication.

Nonverbal communication is useful when noise or distance interferes with other methods in information exchange. It also amplifies or redirects the meaning of verbal communication. However, nonverbal messages can be extremely ambiguous. For example, one Canadian researcher describes a plant superintendent in a concrete block plant who picked up a piece of broken brick while talking with the supervisor. This action had no particular meaning to the superintendent—just something to toy with during the conversation. Yet as soon as the senior manager had left, the supervisor ordered a half-hour of overtime for the entire crew to clean up the plant. He had mistakenly thought the superintendent was signalling him that the plant was messy.[18]

Media Richness.   Daft and his associates suggest that communication methods can be organized into a hierarchy of media richness, as shown in Exhibit 6–3.[19] **Media richness** refers to the capacity of a communication method to transmit information. This information capacity depends on the method's ability to handle multiple information symbols simultaneously, facilitate rapid feedback, and tailor the message to personal circumstances.

media richness
The capacity of a communication medium to transmit information.

Face-to-face interaction is at the top of the scale because the sender can simultaneously transmit information verbally and nonverbally, the receiver can provide immediate feedback, and the information exchange can be cus-

PERSPECTIVE 6–2   Understanding True Intentions through "Stomach Language"

Sterling Drugs was beginning to penetrate the Japanese market for over-the-counter pharmaceuticals, but the venture was not profitable enough to support the expensive advertising and sales force needed to maintain these sales. As head of Sterling's Japanese operations, Mark Zimmerman decided the answer was to approach a large Japanese pharmaceutical firm to act as Sterling's distributor outside the main cities and to supplement Sterling's sales force in Tokyo, Osaka, and other large centres.

Although Sterling Drugs had a long-established relationship with the Japanese firm, Zimmerman felt it would be best to approach top management only after an informal consensus had been obtained at the lower levels of the Japanese company. After initial enquiries, middle managers stated their willingness to discuss the distribution proposal. Several working-level meetings took place between middle managers of the two companies with much discussion and presentations exchanged on the distribution proposal. As discussions progressed, Sterling Drugs also set up its own task force to conduct extensive market research on the idea.

Finally, Zimmerman decided that it was time to take the proposal to top management of the Japanese company. He was confident from the middle management meetings that there would be no surprise or disagreement from top management about the distribution proposal. But when Zimmerman began to explain the idea, the president of the Japanese company pretended that this was the first time he had heard about the proposal and said that he could not

EXHIBIT 6–3   A Hierarchy of Media Richness

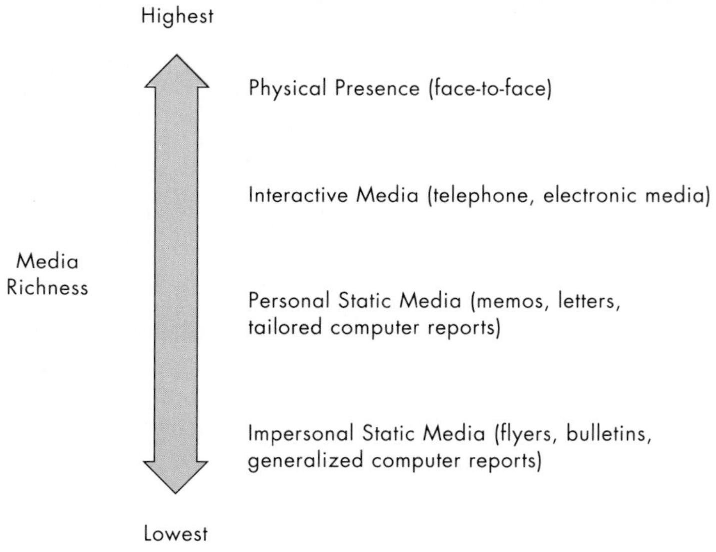

Highest

Physical Presence (face-to-face)

Interactive Media (telephone, electronic media)

Media Richness

Personal Static Media (memos, letters, tailored computer reports)

Impersonal Static Media (flyers, bulletins, generalized computer reports)

Lowest

Source: R. Lengel and R. Daft, "The Selection of Communication Media as an Executive Skill," *Academy of Management Executive* 2, no. 3 (August 1988), p. 226.

comment on anything so major until his subordinates had every opportunity to discuss the proposal among themselves! After several unsuccessful attempts to get the proposal again elevated to top management of the Japanese firm, Sterling Drugs gave up on the distribution proposal.

Months later, a trusted friend in the Japanese pharmaceutical firm advised Zimmerman that senior management had told others to verbally be supportive of Sterling Drug's proposal (*tatemae*) in order not to offend Zimmerman and his colleagues, but to leave more subtle, nonverbal cues that the Japanese firm was not really interested (*honne*). In hindsight, Zimmerman realized that he had pressed for the meeting with top management when middle managers of the Japanese firm would have taken that initiative if there was true interest in the project. Some of Sterling Drug's own staff had noticed other nonverbal messages indicating the Japanese firm's disinterest, but did not want to embarrass Zimmerman with this information because he had already informed Sterling Drug's head office in New York that the other firm was favourable to the distribution plan.

Source: Based on M. Zimmerman, *How to Do Business with the Japanese: A Strategy for Success* (New York: Random House, 1985), pp. 59–60.

tomized to suit the situation. Some electronic media are almost as rich as face-to-face interactions, but they do not allow the sender to use nonverbal cues as effectively. Next down the list are personalized written methods such as memos and letters. Impersonal documents represent one of the ''leanest'' communication methods.

The preferred communication method depends on whether the message is routine or nonroutine. Nonroutine messages are communicated in novel situations where the sender and receiver have little common experience. For instance, richer media should be used in unexpected emergencies because there is a high risk of misunderstanding and confusion. It would be quite inappropriate to prepare a memorandum at such times. In routine situations, on the other hand, less rich methods can be used because the sender and receiver have a common understanding and expectations.

So far, we have seen that effective communication depends on your awareness of the communication process and your selection of the appropriate communication channel for the situation. In the next section, we discuss another important consideration—the direction of communication within the organization.

COMMUNICATION IN ORGANIZATIONAL HIERARCHIES

Organizational communication flows in three directions: upward, downward, or horizontally, as depicted in Exhibit 6–4. Each of these information flows serves different functions to organizational effectiveness.

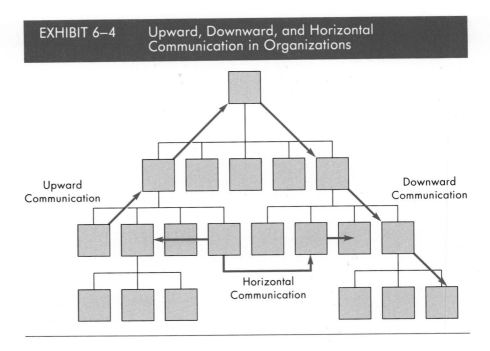

EXHIBIT 6–4   Upward, Downward, and Horizontal Communication in Organizations

Upward Communication

Downward Communication

Horizontal Communication

Downward Communication

Downward communication flows from upper to lower levels in the organizational hierarchy, such as from supervisors to their subordinates. Downward messages coordinate activities by communicating expected standards of performance, providing job-related information and feedback, and instilling common organizational values and beliefs.[20]

Some organizations suffer from too much downward communication in the form of memos, directives, and procedures. These excessive controls can thwart individual initiative and undermine job satisfaction. Downward communication is often insufficient, however, on matters of importance to employees. One major survey has identified the type of information that Canadian and American employees are most interested in receiving from their immediate supervisors and senior managers. This information is listed in order of importance in Exhibit 6–5.

The survey also reports that top executives were ranked as the third most *preferred* source of organizational information (after immediate supervisor and small group meetings), whereas their *current* ranking was only eleventh out of fifteen sources. This is consistent with early research reporting that subordinates receive much less organizational information than their superiors believe.[21] In other words, employees want managers to communicate with them more often.

EXHIBIT 6–5	Organizational Information of Interest to Employees

Rank	Subject	Percentage "Very Interested" or "Interested"
1	Organizational plans for the future	95.3%
2	Productivity improvement	90.3
3	Personnel policies and practises	89.8
4	Job-related information	89.2
5	Job advancement opportunities	87.9
6	Effect of external events on my job	87.8
7	How my job fits into the organization	85.4
8	Operations outside of my department or division	85.1
9	How we're doing versus the competition	83.0
10	Personnel changes and promotions	81.4
11	Organizational community involvement	81.3
12	Organizational stand on current issues	79.5
13	How the organization uses its profits	78.4
14	Advertising/promotional plans	77.2
15	Financial results	76.4
16	Human interest stories about other employees	70.4
17	Personal news (birthdays, anniversaries, etc.)	57.0

Source: R. Foltz, "Communication in Contemporary Organizations," in Carol Reuss and Donn Silvis (eds.), *Inside Organizational Communication* (New York: Longman, 1985), pp. 8–9. Reprinted with permission.

Upward Communication

Upward communication flows up the organizational hierarchy (see Exhibit 6–4) and serves four major functions:

* Provides management with feedback on its initiatives.
* Provides management with information for decision making.
* Initiates management action on issues of concern to lower-level employees.
* Builds commitment through employee participation.

Although upward communication has received much attention by management consultants and writers,[22] this type of interaction is still largely underdeveloped in most firms. Supervisors generally feel that they understand their employees' concerns, but subordinates claim that their supervisors do not have a good comprehension of their problems.[23]

upward communication
The movement of information from lower to upper levels in the organizational hierarchy.

Horizontal Communication

horizontal communication
The exchange of information among people at the same level in the organizational hierarchy.

Horizontal communication involves the interaction of people at the same level in the organization and includes communication between coworkers in the same work group or in different departments or divisions of the company. Horizontal communication is important because it allows employees to coordinate their work and solve mutual problems or conflicts. It also provides mutual support and cohesiveness to the work team.

Communicating through the Grapevine

Whether the direction is upward, downward, or horizontal, some communication activities are sanctioned by the organization while others are not. Formal communication follows the organization's chain of command and is usually prescribed in job descriptions. For example, Ian Sinclair maintained a strict formal communication pattern when he was the CEO of Canadian Pacific by regularly seeing only those people who directly reported to him.[24]

grapevine
The organization's informal communication network that is formed and maintained by social relationships rather than the formal chain of command.

The **grapevine,** on the other hand, is the organization's main network of informal communication. The grapevine is based on social relationships rather than organizational charts or job descriptions, but it is nevertheless a vital activity.

Grapevine activity tends to increase when employees lack information about a situation of interest to them and when they are insecure about organizational events. These informal exchanges provide employees with needed social interaction and convey important task information that has not been considered in the formal organizational structure.[25] The grapevine is an important means through which employees fulfill their need to know about the organization. For example, new employees generally receive more information about the organization informally from coworkers than from the supervisor, orientation programs, or other formal interactions.[26]

The grapevine is one of the least understood phenomena in organizational behaviour. Research has identified several interesting features of grapevines, some of which are contrary to popular beliefs.[27]

Accuracy.   Most grapevine information is surprisingly accurate. Experts estimate that over 75 percent of grapevine information is relatively undistorted. This is largely because "media rich" channels, such as face-to-face interactions, are typically used and both sender and receiver are motivated to communicate the details accurately.

Relevance.   Up to 80 percent of grapevine information pertains to organizational activities, rather than personal gossip.

Selectivity.   Grapevine information is not passed indiscriminately among the work force; rather, people tend to contact only coworkers they know and believe would value the information. Some employees rarely receive grapevine information because they are not integrated in the social network of the organization.

Speed.   Grapevines transmit information to a large number of people very rapidly. In many cases, people receive news from the grapevine before they hear about it through formal channels. For example, a study of Canadian government engineers reported that 32 percent of those who had been transferred first heard about their transfer through the grapevine.[28]

Transmission Pattern.   Grapevine information is not passed from one person to the next in a sequence. Rather, a small number of employees are senders to a large number of receivers. Only a small percentage of people receiving grapevine information send the information on to others. This "cluster chain," as it is called, is illustrated in Exhibit 6-6.

The grapevine may be fast and relatively accurate, but even this form of organizational communication cannot completely escape the various barriers to communication. Some of the more powerful barriers are discussed in the next section.

EXHIBIT 6–6   Transmission Pattern of Grapevine Communication

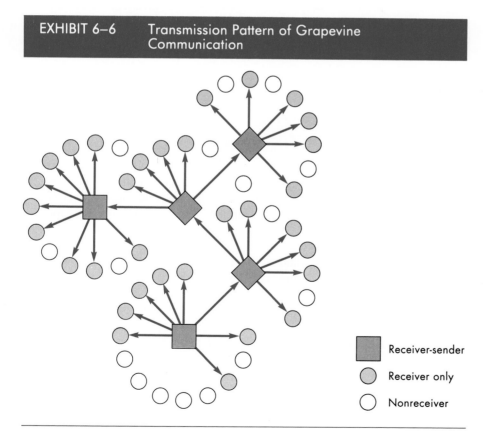

☐ Receiver-sender

○ Receiver only

○ Nonreceiver

BARRIERS TO EFFECTIVE COMMUNICATION

In spite of the best efforts of sender and receiver to communicate, several factors inhibit the effective exchange of information. Six of the most troublesome barriers are language, filtering, physical settings, perceptual errors, information overload, and cultural differences.

Language

People must assign meaning to words, gestures, and written symbols because they carry no inherent meaning with them. Unfortunately, a symbol does not always have the same meaning to the sender and receiver. Language becomes a barrier when the sender uses jargon or ambiguous language.

jargon
Technical language understood by members of a particular occupational group or recognized words with specialized meaning in specific organizations or social groups.

Jargon. **Jargon** can be technical language of a particular occupational group (such as medical or legal terms) or recognized words with specialized meanings in specific organizations or social groups. Jargon can be an efficient means of communicating meaning when both sender and receiver understand this specialized language. It also establishes group membership and social status by identifying outsiders or novices based on their lack of knowledge of the group's specialized language. Jargon is part of the process of developing shared beliefs and meaning among team members; it is one of the basic elements for transmitting and sustaining corporate culture.[29]

In spite of these functions, jargon is a barrier when used to communicate important information to outsiders. Senders accustomed to jargon often have difficulty translating meaning to nonexperts, resulting in misunderstanding.

Ambiguity.   Language can also act as a barrier when a particular word or symbol has several meanings. The sender uses a word with the assumption that the receiver will assign a particular meaning to it, but the receiver could interpret the term differently. An example of this occurred when a supervisor asked one of his employees to ''go out back and pull a stack of buckets apart.'' Separating the stacked buckets should have taken 20 minutes, but the employee had not returned after two hours. The supervisor went to investigate, only to find the employee literally ripping the buckets apart. The supervisor and the employee had no difficulty assigning meaning to the phrase ''pull apart''; unfortunately, they used different meanings for this ambiguous phrase.[30]

Some messages have a common *factual* meaning between sender and receiver but have a different *emotional* meaning. As an example, in the early days of commercial aviation, passengers often heard flight attendants make the following announcement: ''We're flying through a *storm*. You had better fasten your *safety* belts; it will be less *dangerous*.'' Factually, the passengers understood what they should do and why they should do it. But at an

---

PERSPECTIVE 6–3   Hazing the Shareholder: A Primer on Reading Annual Reports

Annual reports are supposed to be the primary medium through which the company's health is communicated to its shareholders, but journalist Harry Bruce doubts that the message is getting across. His review of several Canadian annual reports points out the tendency of public relations staff to distort reality through ambiguous prose and hyped up forecasts of the future. Says Bruce: "Billion-dollar corporations that reward competence in other disciplines somehow can't produce annual reports that demonstrate competence in writing."

Annual report writers use a variety of euphemisms that serve to either hide unmentionable news or make rather humdrum events sound important. For example, they mention "increased competitive activities" to refer to the competition, things are "acquired" rather than simply bought, and the company has "facilities" rather than just offices and factories. Instead of strikes, annual report writers prefer to speak of "costly industrial work stoppages."

Bruce cites an annual report from Provigo Inc.—Canada's second-largest food distributor and majority shareholder of Sports Experts—that refers to sportsgear as "leisure articles." Provigo's report also boasts "an operating entity [to establish] home improvement centres"; most of us would recognize these as hardware stores. In addition, the company announced that it had introduced a new "customer reception philosophy." According to Bruce, this probably means that salesclerks who are rude to customers will get the axe.

Bruce states that the word "enhanced" has been mashed into meaninglessness by annual report writers. For example, an annual report by Canada Development Corporation applauded itself for *enhancing* its reputation for being able to add value to its holdings, *enhancing* its reputation for being at the forefront of technology, and *enhancing* its financial flexibility. Reports by other companies described their plans to enhance employees, images, asset bases, and production flexibilities.

To show that annual reports can be kept short, simple, and infinitely more readable, Bruce quotes the text of a U.S. bank holding company's annual report, which has only this to say: "Your company had a very good year. Some of it was due to luck; some of it was due to good planning and management. We hope you enjoy the numbers and pictures." Now that's a message most of us can understand!

Source: H. Bruce, "Perfectly Unclear," *Canadian Business* 60, no. 3 (March 1987), pp. 84–85, 114. Reprinted by arrangement with Bella Pomer Agency, Inc.

---

emotional level, the message evoked an unintended reaction by making some passengers feel that the plane was about to crash. To give passengers a better sense of security, the message was eventually changed as follows: "We're flying through some *turbulence* now. Please fasten your *seat* belts; you will be more *comfortable*."[31]

Ambiguous language is deliberately used to either obscure bad news or make unimportant events sound impressive. Politicians are often accused of sending ambiguous messages for these reasons, but organizational examples also exist. Perspective 6–3 describes how ambiguity is used in some Canadian annual reports to shareholders.

Rather than undermining communication effectiveness, ambiguous language may actually be an important instrument in some situations. During times of turbulence and change, such as when a new set of organizational values are evolving or a new strategic direction is being negotiated, managers are wise to apply ambiguous symbols to reflect the "unified diversity" of the moment.[32] For instance, it would be inappropriate to quantify a new set of organizational objectives before the various organizational coalitions have accepted a general theme. Consequently, effective leaders often use vague terms, such as "laying pipe" or "wild geese" to reflect these general themes.

Ambiguous language, in the form of organizational stories and similes, is commonly used to describe the company's stated beliefs so that they are interpreted broadly enough to apply to diverse organizational events. Similarly, management writers have recognized the value of metaphors as a form of abstract communications to represent ways of thinking about complex organizational events.[33] Metaphors are relatively simple on the surface, yet they convey a wealth of rich meaning without becoming so precise that they fail to represent the event. For example, saying that organizations are "machines" or "organisms" sends a complex and imprecise message, yet this ambiguity reflects the level of complexity of the situation that the sender is trying to communicate.

Filtering

Messages may be filtered, simplified, or stopped altogether on their way up or down the organizational hierarchy. A few studies have discovered that between 30 and 80 percent of formal downward communication from top management never reaches the lowest-level employees.[34]

Information transmitted up the organizational hierarchy is often filtered in order to place employees in the best light to their superiors. This is particularly true when the information is not favourable and the sender has strong career mobility aspirations or security needs. The extent that organizational values promote open communication is another influence on the amount of filtering in upward communication.[35]

Finally, status differences may cause filtering up the organizational hierarchy because employees hesitate to communicate with senior executives. This problem exists even in companies where open communication is emphasized. Says the CEO of Steelcase, an office furniture manufacturer: "For an employee to come to the president or chairman of the company, he's got to feel he's got a problem. It probably took him three days to get the nerve to do it."[36]

Physical Settings

The physical arrangements of the workplace, including the distance between people and the characteristics of offices, can either facilitate or inhibit communication among work teams and organizational levels.

Physical Distance. A rather obvious fact, although frequently forgotten, is that we tend to interact more with people who are located near us than with those further away. Managers have many spontaneous meetings involving people they run into. Engineers frequently get ideas through face-to-face interactions and are reluctant to travel far from their desks.

Physical proximity has a particularly strong influence on the frequency of communication between subordinates and their bosses.[37] Since corporate head offices are often located in different buildings or geographic areas from production operations, communications between senior management and the work force are often quite limited. Consequently, many firms are moving their executives closer to the action. At National Life Assurance Co. in Toronto, for instance, most top managers were moved out of their executive suites (called ''Mahogany Row'' for their rich brown mahogany walls) into more pedestrian offices where their employees are located. Canada Packers took more drastic action by completely shutting down its Toronto headquarters and transferring 70 people out to the company's plants. ''We want to shorten the lines of communication and make managers more involved,'' explains Canada Packers president David Newton. ''We want them back 'living over the shop.' ''[38]

Office Arrangement. Office arrangements act as a barrier to communication between managers and their subordinates in two ways. First, office symbols such as office size, furniture quality, and location in the building convey nonverbal messages regarding the incumbent's status. As previously noted, status differences may discourage effective information exchange between sender and receiver.

Second, seating arrangements and desk location during the communication episode affect the degree that employees feel comfortable and welcome in the manager's office.[39] Two office arrangements with different effects on the receiver are illustrated in Exhibit 6–7. In the closed arrangement, the manager's desk faces the door and separates the employee from the manager. In effect, the desk is both a physical and communication barrier between the sender and receiver. In the open arrangement, the desk faces a side wall and the employee sits to one side of the manager so that the desk is not between them. This setting facilitates open communication because the manager is seen as a helper or equal to the employee.

Perceptual Errors

In the process of receiving messages, we normally select and highlight certain symbols and screen out others. Some parts of the message are screened out because they have no meaning to us, whereas other parts are remembered because they are consistent with our current beliefs or are important to us.

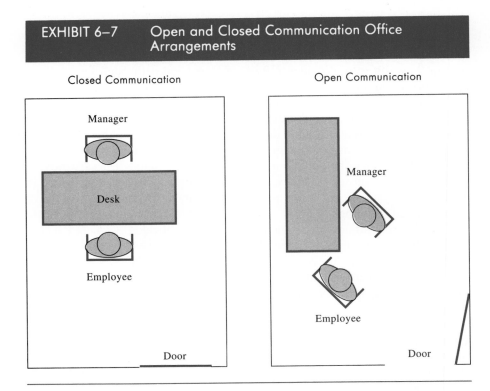

EXHIBIT 6–7   Open and Closed Communication Office Arrangements

Selecting and screening out information is part of our perceptual process, which will be discussed in more detail in Chapter 7. At this point, we should point out that perceptual differences between the sender and receiver represent another barrier to effective communication. The sender and receiver have different backgrounds—a different set of idiosyncratic goggles, as Marshall McLuhan once said—that cause them to emphasize different parts of the message episode. These differences result in a less-than-perfect transmission of meaning.

Information Overload

information overload

A condition where messages are transmitted faster or in greater quantity than the employee can process effectively.

One of the most frequently mentioned communication problems in organizations is **information overload.** This refers to the condition where messages are being transmitted faster or in greater quantity than the employee can process effectively. Information overload is particularly common in senior management jobs where large volumes of information are received in the form of telephone calls, postal mail, computer printouts, and meetings.

Communication researchers have identified several coping mechanisms to deal with information overload.[40] They are effective in some situations but may result in valuable information loss in others.

Omitting.   People subconsciously deal with information overload by simply ignoring messages. However, deciding which messages to receive and which to ignore is an almost random process that can cause valuable information to be lost. A more conscious form of omitting is practised at Federal Express, through a program called Operation Namedropper. Twice each year, managers can call in to headquarters to get their names deleted from distribution lists for specific memos and computer printouts that pile up on their desks but are never read.

Buffering.   Another solution to overload may be to have subordinates serve as information buffers. That is, they screen all messages and only those considered important are forwarded to the manager.

Summarizing.   Rather than reading all information, managers may assign subordinates the task of reviewing and reorganizing it into summary form. Project reports often have an "executive summary," which busy managers read instead of the full document. Some firms cater to the demand for summarized information by publishing brief summaries of popular management books.

Specializing.   Managers often have enough job flexibility to delegate some tasks to their employees. This enables managers to reduce information overload by diverting information relating to those tasks to the subordinates assigned the delegated work.

Prioritizing.   If information overload is temporary, managers may prioritize messages and develop a waiting queue. The most important documents or meetings will be handled first and the least important ones last. In other cases, the queue is prioritized on a first in/first out basis.

Cultural Differences

Canada's work force is growing more culturally diverse. Historically, French and English cultures have co-existed, but Canada's multicultural heritage has since expanded to include many other ethnic groups. Similarly, women now represent a large proportion of the labour force. In fact, by the year 2000, the traditional white male will represent only about 20 percent of the persons entering the work force; most new recruits will consist of ethnic and racial minorities and women.

Ebco Industries is a typical example of the trend toward a multicultural work force. The 900 people employed by the Richmond, British Columbia, manufacturer represent 50 different national, linguistic, and cultural groups. Recognizing this diversity, the company has a multicultural committee that schedules holidays around the employees' different religious beliefs and organizes multicultural food festivals and picnics. Says Helmut Eppich, Ebco's founder and CEO: "I myself was an immigrant so I feel a lot of empathy for immigrants and minorities."[41]

Canada's multicultural work force offers many potential advantages.[42] For example, in Chapter 10 we will describe how heterogeneous work teams tend to be more innovative because they are able to see organizational problems and opportunities from several perspectives. However, cultural differences can also create a significant communications barrier. In a multicultural organization, senders and receivers must overcome different languages, accents, nonverbal cues, and behavioural norms. People from one ethnic group may be less willing to communicate with those from another group because employees do not feel as comfortable interacting with co-workers from different backgrounds. Unfortunately, this distance also leads to less understanding of the other person, so that perceptual errors are more likely to occur when communication is between culturally different employees.

Barriers to communication are deeply embedded in interpersonal exchanges and organizational practices. Nevertheless, several strategies are available to combat these problems. Some of the more effective ways of improving interpersonal and organizational communication are described next.

IMPROVING INTERPERSONAL COMMUNICATION

It is only fitting that the final sections of this chapter should examine strategies to avoid or overcome the problems of communicating in an organizational setting. We begin by looking at interpersonal communication strategies to get your message across and to listen effectively (see Exhibit 6–8).

EXHIBIT 6–8	Improving Interpersonal Communication

Getting Your Message Across	Effective Listening
• Empathize.	• Don't talk.
• Repeat the message.	• Empathize.
• Use timing effectively.	• Be interested.
• Be descriptive.	• Show interest.
	• Provide feedback.
	• Resist distractions.
	• Capitalize on listening speed.
	• Delay evaluation.

Getting Your Message Across

Communicating effectively with another person requires not only that you know what message to send, but also that you understand the receiver and the communication situation. This involves empathizing with the receiver, repeating the message, choosing an appropriate time for the conversation, and being descriptive rather than evaluative.

Empathize.   Selecting appropriate words and symbols can be best accomplished by imagining yourself as the other person and thinking about how that person will decode the message. Which words might trigger the wrong emotional response? Which words are ambiguous? Which words or symbols may be meaningless to the other person? By considering the receiver's background and current situation, these potential barriers will be recognized and avoided.

Repeat the Message.   Since people do not hear or understand every part of the message the first time, it is useful to add some redundancy into the conversation. This is done by repeating the message in a different way and explaining some points more fully. Technical issues should be rephrased three or four times to facilitate the learning process. The old saw "Tell them what you're going to tell them; tell them; then tell them what you've told them" reflects this need for redundancy.

Use Timing Effectively.   The message you send to another person competes simultaneously with other messages and noise also directed toward that person. Therefore, to increase the chance that your message will be heard and understood, find a time when the receiver is not as busy or is less likely to be distracted by other matters.

Be Descriptive.   Supervisors can minimize employee defensiveness when discussing poor performance or other sensitive issues by being descriptive rather than evaluative.[43] Basically, the key element is focussing on the problem, not on the person. First, describe the events factually rather than label the employee. It is better to say "This is what happened" than to say "You're a so-and-so because you. . . ." Next, describe your reaction to the event rather than accuse the employee. For example, it's better to say "I was disappointed with last month's sales figures in your district" than to say "You did a miserable sales job last month." Finally, rather than pointing to the employee as the problem, suggest things the employee can *do* to improve. This places the supervisor in a helping role and allows the employee to acknowledge the problem without threatening self-esteem.

Effective Listening

Listening is at least as important as talking. As one sage wisely wrote: "Nature gave people two ears but only one tongue, which is a gentle hint that they should listen more than they talk."[44] Supervisors need to be good listeners to receive useful information and to encourage their employees to communicate in the future. Here are the main elements of effective listening.[45]

Don't Talk. It is often tempting to interrupt the speaker to add an important point or redirect the conversation toward something of immediate interest to you. Don't! Give the speaker an opportunity to complete the message and allow a brief pause before responding. When it is your turn to speak, be sure that your message links up with the speaker's previous message.

Empathize. Recall that our interpretation of the message may be different than the sender's intended meaning. By attempting to see the message from the other person's point of view, misunderstanding is less likely to occur.

Be Interested. Too often, we close our minds soon after a conversation begins because the subject is boring. Walking away or interrupting is rude and may jeopardize future communication opportunities. It's better to take the view—probably an accurate one—that there is always something of value in a conversation; it's just a matter of actively looking for it.

Show Interest. Effective listening also involves *showing* the speaker that you are interested in the conversation. Nonverbal cues, such as making eye contact, tell the speaker that you are paying attention and value the person's time. During comfortable breaks in the conversation, it is also helpful to use verbal acknowledgments, such as "Yes, I understand."

Provide Feedback. In addition to being attentive, listeners can capture the correct meaning by rephrasing the speaker's ideas at appropriate breaks ("So you're saying that . . . ?"). This provides the speaker with feedback to check whether meaning has been transmitted effectively. It also shows the speaker that you are listening and interested in the conversation.

Resist Distractions. Listeners must work at this. Make a serious effort to pay attention to what the speaker is saying and tune out noise, surrounding activities, and so on. You should also work at ignoring irrelevant nonverbal cues, such as the speaker's voice quality and bad speaking habits.

Capitalize on Listening Speed. Our speed of thought is three times faster than the average rate of speech (450 words/minute versus 125 words/minute). Rather than being impatient and distracted during this extra time, review the conversation and organize it into key points.

Delay Evaluation.   It is natural to want to label a message as right/wrong or bad/good, but early evaluation may cause the listener to screen out important points later in the conversation. Therefore, postpone your evaluation of the message until the speaker has finished.

Communication can be significantly improved if organizational members develop their interpersonal communication skills. But more formalized practices are also needed to overcome barriers built into the organization's design. These practises are discussed next.

IMPROVING ORGANIZATIONAL COMMUNICATION

This chapter has focussed not only on communication between people, but communication that takes place within organizations. Increasingly, companies are paying more attention to how they formally communicate with employees. Some firms conduct communication audits to identify the extent to which current levels of upward, downward, and horizontal communication meet both employee and organizational needs.[46] As part of its employee involvement philosophy, Fraser Inc., a New Brunswick pulp and paper manufacturer, carefully reviewed the means of formal communication with employees. Exhibit 6–9 lists the eight ways that Fraser found to exchange meaningful information with its staff. Several effective strategies to improve communication across organizational levels are described in this section.

EXHIBIT 6–9   Fraser Inc.'s Communication Program

1. Quarterly and annual report literature is mailed directly to the homes of all employees.
2. Crew meetings are scheduled, where production crews review safety items, production figures, targets, employee issues, etc.
3. Quarterly operating reviews and status updates are provided for key staff and the union executive.
4. There are special communication sessions that deal with important issues of the day.
5. Biweekly newsletters for each company operation are distributed to all employees in that unit.
6. A quarterly publication is mailed to all employees.
7. There are quarterly review meetings, where sales/marketing staff and production management meet with machine crews to review problems and success areas.
8. Annual reviews are conducted by uppermost management for all employees.

Source: Based on C. Despres, "Employee Participation: One Company's Approach," *Canadian Forest Industries,* August 1983, pp. 34–38.

Employee Newsletters and Reports

Fraser Inc., B.C. Tel, and numerous other organizations use various print media—including newsletters, magazines, paycheque flyers, employee annual reports, and posters—to inform employees about activities throughout the company.[47] Videotaped messages from senior management to employees are also becoming popular because they represent a more information-rich medium than printed documents. Quarterly magazines are a popular print medium, and include the latest marketing developments, new production facilities, human resource management program activities, and news about individual employees. As stated in the opening vignette, B.C. Tel sends each of its 19,000 employees and retirees a copy of *Perspectives,* shown in Exhibit 6–10.

Some companies provide employee annual reports that present a simplified version of corporate financial statements found in shareholder annual

---

EXHIBIT 6–10   Communicating through Employee Magazines at B.C. Tel

Source: B.C. Telephone Company. Used with permission.

reports.[48] These reports also include commentary from senior management on corporate objectives and policies; the impact of the economy on employment within the firm; and the effectiveness of the company in marketing, production, and other areas. Employee annual reports have gained considerable popularity in Great Britain, where companies are required by law to provide employees with the same information provided to shareholders.

Visible Management

Management experts recommend that managers get out of their offices more often and talk (or better yet, listen) face-to-face with employees several levels down the organizational hierarchy. This practise is popularly known as **management by wandering around (MBWA),** a phrase coined at Hewlett-Packard and popularized by Ouchi and Peters and Waterman.[49] The idea is that by communicating directly with employees, managers will be better informed about employee concerns and organizational activities.[50]

Samuel Bronfman, founder of the world's largest distiller, Seagram Co., practiced MBWA many years ago by asking questions to anyone in his employ. As Peter C. Newman recounts, "[Sam Bronfman] was continually on the telephone directly to the people who did things. . . . He never wrote memos and never dictated letters, preferring to root about for himself among the various Seagram hierarchies, getting everybody's advice. . . ."[51]

Hayes-Dana, an automobile parts manufacturer with 51 plants and offices across Canada, places a strong emphasis on visible management. The company deliberately keeps each unit to a maximum of 200 people to facilitate direct contact between management and employees. "That's about the capacity of a plant manager to know everyone," says Hayes-Dana CEO John Doddridge. "If you know the people in your plant on a first-name basis, then you have no problem expressing your concerns and ideas."[52]

management by wandering around
A management practise of having frequent face-to-face communication with employees so that managers are better informed about employee concerns and organizational activities.

Suggestion Plans

Suggestion plans are designed to encourage employees to submit ideas for improving product quality and work efficiency. Ideally, this becomes an efficient conduit for top management to hear about productivity improvement ideas. By providing a financial reward to those who submit implemented ideas, suggestion plans also motivate employees to think creatively about how to make the organization more effective.

Suggestion plans can be very effective.[53] For example, Royal Bank of Canada paid its employees approximately $400,000 in 1988 for suggestions that are expected to save the bank almost $14 million over the next three years. The Canadian Federal Government's suggestion plan has been operated by the Treasury Board since 1952. Between 1986 and 1988 over 2,200 suggestions were approved, with an estimated savings over $200 million. Northern Telecom reported savings of $2.7 million in 1985 from the 3,900

suggestion plan
A reward system that encourages employees to submit ideas for improving product quality and work efficiency.

suggestions implemented during the previous year. Canadian Pacific Ltd., which has been rewarding employee suggestions since 1934, saved an estimated $2.3 million in 1984.

In order to be successful, suggestion plans should be introduced in a climate of trust between management and employees. They should be communicated clearly, and winning suggestions should be celebrated to facilitate role modelling. For example, the success of Northern Telecom's suggestion plan is partially attributed to its annual suggestion system awards dinner. Most of all, the system must be fair. The reasons for rejecting an idea must be carefully explained.

Organizational Surveys

Employees are occasionally asked to communicate their opinions or attitudes toward a variety of issues through organizational surveys. The reasons for conducting organizational surveys are quite varied. In larger firms, such as Royal Bank and IBM Canada, surveys are conducted regularly to gauge changes in employee morale. Some of these attitudes, including job satisfaction and organizational commitment, will be discussed in Chapter 8 on employee attitudes. It is increasingly common for new chief executives to request employee surveys to help them make sense of the organization. For example, soon after becoming president of Montreal's public transit system, Louise Roy surveyed the company's 8,000 employees to get a sense of how they perceived the organization. This information helped her reorganize the firm and work toward building a better labour relations climate.[54] Other questionnaires focus on specific policy issues. Both Chevron Canada and the Insurance Corporation of British Columbia, for instance, have surveyed employees to provide input on corporate policies.[55]

Organizational surveys provide upward communication from employees to top management, but the process should also involve downward communication by having managers discuss the results with groups of employees to help solve problem areas. In this regard, survey feedback can be a powerful instrument for organizational change.

SUMMARY

• Communication consists of forming, encoding, and transmitting the intended message to a receiver, who then decodes the message and provides feedback (including silence) that the sender uses to determine whether the message was received and understood. Effective communication occurs when the sender's thoughts are transmitted to and understood by the intended receiver.

• Communication channels include written, verbal, and nonverbal, each of which has several methods of transmitting information. The best communication method depends on the situation.

• Communication flows upward, downward, and horizontally in organizations. Some communication activities are formally prescribed by job descriptions and organizational charts, but informal communication such as the grapevine is also pervasive in organizations.

• Managers need to be aware of numerous barriers to effective communication, including jargon, ambiguous language, filtering, physical distance, office arrangements, perceptual errors, information overload, and cultural differences.

• Some communication problems can be minimized by applying several principles of effective interpersonal skills, described in this chapter.

• Several organizational activities, including newsletters, suggestion plans, and employee surveys, also improve communication across organizational levels.

DISCUSSION QUESTIONS

1. What is "noise" in the communication process?
2. Electronic mail has become an increasingly popular means of communication in organizations. What are the advantages and disadvantages of this communications medium?
3. Under what conditions is nonverbal communication useful in organizations?
4. Many people believe that the organizational grapevine randomly communicates misleading and nonrelevant information among employees. Is this generally true? Should managers try to eliminate the organizational grapevine?
5. Under what conditions is ambiguity good and bad in the communications process?
6. How do physical settings influence the communications process?
7. What communication problems tend to occur in workplaces where employees are culturally diverse? How might organizations overcome many of these problems?
8. What is visible management? What are the benefits of this communications practice?

NOTES

1. D. W. Champion, "Quality—A Way of Life at B.C. Tel," *Canadian Business Review,* Spring 1990, pp. 32–34; J. Friesen and S. Mitchell, "Newsletters: The Silent Salesmen," *B.C. Business,* February 1988, pp. 32–39; *British Columbia Telephone Company Annual Reports* (1983–1988); and *Perspectives* (B.C. Tel news magazine), (various issues).

2. H. Mintzberg, *The Nature of Managerial Work* (New York: Harper & Row, 1973); R. Stewart, *Contrasts in Management* (Maidenhead, England: McGraw-Hill, 1976); and E. T. Klemmer and

F. W. Snyder, "Measurement of Time Spent Communicating," *Journal of Communication* 22 (June 1972), pp. 142–58.

3. W. Scott and T. Mitchell, *Organizational Theory: A Structural and Behavioral Analysis* (Homewood, Ill.: Irwin, 1976), Chapter 9.

4. T. Deal and A. Kennedy, *Corporate Cultures: The Rites and Rituals of Corporate Life* (Reading, Mass.: Addison-Wesley, 1982), Chapter 5; and J. S. Ott, *The Organizational Culture Perspective* (Pacific Grove, Calif.: Brooks/Cole, 1989), pp. 26–35.

5. G. Milkovich, W. Glueck, R. Barth, and S. McShane, *Canadian Personnel/Human Resource Management: A Diagnostic Approach* (Plano, Texas: Business Publications, 1988), p. 194; W. Haney, *Communication and Interpersonal Relations*, 4th ed. (Homewood, Ill.: Irwin, 1979), p. 318; and M. Ritts, "What if Johnny Still Can't Read," *Canadian Business*, May 1986, p. 54.

6. H. C. Jain, "Supervisory Communication and Performance in Urban Hospitals," *Journal of Communication* 23 (1973), pp. 103–17; C. Downs, P. Clampitt, and A. L. Pfeiffer, "Communication and Organizational Outcomes," in G. Goldhaber and G. Barnett (eds.), *Handbook of Organizational Communication* (Norwood, N.J.: Ablex, 1988), pp. 171–211; and P. Muchinsky, "Organizational Communication: Relationships to Organizational Climate and Job Satisfaction," *Academy of Management Journal* 20 (1977), pp. 592–607.

7. R. J. Burke and D. S. Wilcox, "Effects of Different Patterns and Degrees of Openness in Superior–Subordinate Communication on Subordinate Satisfaction," *Academy of Management Journal* 12 (1969), pp. 319–26; R. M. Kanter, *The Change Masters* (New York: Simon & Schuster, 1983); and R. T. Mowday, L. W. Porter, and R. M. Steers, *Employee–Organization Linkages* (New York: Academic Press, 1982).

8. K. J. Krone, F. M. Jablin, and L. L. Putnam, "Communication Theory and Organizational Communication: Multiple Perspectives," in F. M. Jablin, L. L. Putnam, K. H. Roberts, and L. W. Porter (eds.), *Handbook of Organizational Communication: An Interdisciplinary Perspective* (Newbury Park, Calif.: Sage, 1987), pp. 18–40; and B. Hawkins and P. Preston, *Managerial Communication* (Santa Monica, Calif.: Goodyear, 1981).

9. R. Daft and R. Lengel, "Information Richness: A New Approach to Managerial Behavior and Organization Design," *Research in Organizational Behavior* 6 (1984), pp. 191–233.

10. S. Axley, "Managerial and Organizational Communication in Terms of the Conduit Metaphor," *Academy of Management Review* 9, no. 3 (1984), pp. 428–37.

11. S. Long, "The Manager's Role in Communicating for Results," *Business Quarterly*, Spring 1988, pp. 67–71.

12. N. F. Leduc, "Communicating through Computers: Impact on a Small Business Group," *Telecommunications Policy* 4 (1979), pp. 235–44.

13. M. Culnan and M. L. Markus, "Information Technologies," in Jablin et al. (eds.), *Handbook of Organizational Communication: An Interdisciplinary Perspective*, pp. 420–43.

14. M. Hayes, "Nonverbal Communication: Expression without Words," in R. Huseman, C. Logue, and D. Freshley (eds.), *Readings in Interpersonal and Organizational Communication*, 3rd ed. (Boston: Holbrook, 1977), pp. 55–68; and A. Mehrabian, *Silent Messages*, 2nd ed. (Belmont, Calif.: Wadsworth, 1981).

15. M. Meissner, "The Language of Work," in Robert Dubin (ed.), *Handbook of Work, Organization, and Society* (Chicago: Rand McNally, 1976), pp. 205–79.

16. P. Harris and R. Moran, *Managing Cultural Differences* (Houston: Gulf, 1987); and P. Ekman, W. V. Friesen, and J. Bear, "The International Language of Gestures," *Psychology Today*, May 1984, pp. 64–69.

17. L. Porter and K. Roberts, "Communication in Organizations," in M. Dunnette (ed.), *Handbook of Industrial and Organizational Psychology* (Chicago: Rand McNally, 1976), pp. 1553–89.

18. Meissner, "The Language of Work," p. 244.

19. Daft and Lengel, "Information Richness: A New Approach to Managerial Behavior and Organization Design"; R. Lengel and R. Daft, "The Selection of Communication Media as an Executive Skill," *Academy of Management Executive* 2 (August 1988), pp. 225–32; and G. Huber and R. Daft, "The Information Environments of Organizations," in Jablin et al. (eds.), *Handbook of Organizational Communication: An Interdisciplinary Perspective*, pp. 130–64.

```

20. G. Kreps, *Organizational Communication* (White Plains, N.Y.: Longman, 1986), p. 197.

21. R. A. Weber, "Perceptions of Interactions between Superiors and Subordinates," *Human Relations* 23 (1970), pp. 235–48.

22. I. S. Shapiro, "Managerial Communication: The View from the Inside," *California Management Review,* Fall 1984, pp. 157–72.

23. R. Likert, *New Patterns of Management* (New York: McGraw-Hill, 1961), p. 52.

24. P. C. Newman, *The Canadian Establishment* (Toronto: McClelland and Stewart, 1979), p. 184.

25. H. Mintzberg, *The Structuring of Organizations* (Englewood Cliffs, N.J.: Prentice Hall, 1979), pp. 46–53.

26. W. M. Evan, "Peer-Group Interaction and Organizational Socialization: A Study of Employee Turnover," *American Sociological Review* 28 (1963), pp. 436–40; and C. Fisher, "Organizational Socialization: An Integrative Review," *Research in Personnel and Human Resources Management* 4 (1986), pp. 101–46.

27. K. Davis and J. Newstrom, *Human Behavior at Work: Organizational Behavior,* 7th ed. (New York: McGraw-Hill, 1985), pp. 314–20; K. Davis, "Management Communication and the Grapevine," *Harvard Business Review* 31 (September–October 1953), pp. 43–49; Kreps, *Organizational Communication,* pp. 202–06; and T. Caplow, "Rumors in War," *Social Forces* 25 (1947), pp. 298–302.

28. R. J. Burke, "Quality of Organizational Life: The Effects of Personnel Job Transfers," in V. Mitchell (ed.), *Proceedings of the Academy of Management* (Vancouver: Academy of Management, 1973), p. 242.

29. The relevance of jargon in corporate culture is described throughout several chapters in L. R. Pondy, P. J. Frost, G. Morgan, and T. C. Dandridge (eds.), *Organizational Symbolism* (Greenwich, Conn.: JAI Press, 1983).

30. J. T. Miller, "Communication . . . or Getting Ideas Across," *S.A.M. Advanced Management Journal,* Summer 1980, p. 34.

31. W. Haney, *Communication and Organizational Behavior* (Homewood, Ill.: Irwin, 1973), p. 443; also see C. H. Weaver, "The Quantification of the Frame of Reference in Labor Management Communication," *Journal of Applied Psychology* 42 (1958), pp. 1–9.

32. E. M. Eisenberg, "Ambiguity as a Strategy in Organizational Communication," *Communication Monographs* 51 (1984), pp. 227–42; and R. Daft and J. Wiginton, "Language and Organization," *Academy of Management Review* 4 (1979), pp. 179–91.

33. G. Morgan, *Images of Organizations* (Beverly Hills, Calif.: Sage, 1986).

34. The problems with downward communication are summarized in D. Fisher, *Communication in Organizations* (St. Paul, Minn.: West, 1981).

35. M. J. Glauser, "Upward Information Flow in Organizations: Review and Conceptual Analysis," *Human Relations* 37 (1984), pp. 613–43.

36. R. Waterman, Jr., *The Renewal Factor* (New York: Bantam, 1987), p. 175.

37. T. Davis, "The Influence of the Physical Environment in Offices," *Academy of Management Review* 9, no. 2 (1984), pp. 271–83; and S. B. Bacharach and M. Aitken, "Communications in Administrative Bureaucracies," *Academy of Management Journal* 20 (1977), pp. 365–77.

38. J. Fleming, *Merchants of Fear: An Investigation of Canada's Insurance Industry* (Markham, Ont.: Penguin, 1986), pp. 281–85; and O. Bertin, "130 Jobs Cut at Canada Packers," *Globe & Mail,* August 22, 1990, p. B7.

39. D. E. Campbell, "Interior Office Design and Visitor Response," *Journal of Applied Psychology* 64 (1979), pp. 648–53; and P. C. Morrow and J. C. McElroy, "Interior Office Design and Visitor Response: A Constructive Replication," *Journal of Applied Psychology* 66 (1981), pp. 646–50.

40. C. Stohl and W. C. Redding, "Messages and Message Exchange Processes," in Jablin et al. (eds.), *Handbook of Organizational Communication: An Interdisciplinary Perspective,* pp. 451–502.

41. D. Broome, "Crossing the Cultural Divide," *Business in Vancouver,* October 30, 1990, pp. 19–21.

42. For a review of the main issues on cultural diversity in Canadian organizations, see the series of articles edited by R. J. Burke, "Managing an Increasingly Diverse Work Force," *Canadian Journal of Administrative Sciences* 8 (1991).
```

43. D. Whetton and K. Cameron, *Developing Managerial Skills* (Glenview, Ill.: Scott, Foresman, 1984), pp. 204–06.

44. Cited in Davis and Newstrom, *Human Behavior at Work: Organizational Behavior,* p. 438.

45. R. Nichols, "Listening Is a 10-Part Skill," *Nation's Business* 45 (July 1957), pp. 56–60; J. Brownell, *Building Active Learning Skills* (Englewood Cliffs, N.J.: Prentice Hall, 1986); and A. Mikalachki, "Does Anyone Listen to the Boss?" *Business Horizons,* March–April 1982, pp. 34–39.

46. R. Kanungo, *Biculturalism and Management* (Toronto: Butterworths, 1980), Chapter 8; and H. C. Jain, "Organizational Communication: A Case Study of a Large Urban Hospital," *Relations Industrielles* 31 (1977), pp. 588–608.

47. C. Emig, "Matching Media with Audience and Message," in C. Reuss and D. Silvis (eds.), *Inside Organizational Communication* (New York: Longman, 1985), pp. 115–28; and Peter C. Jackson, *Corporate Communications for Managers* (London: Pitman, 1987).

48. J. C. C. Macintosh, "Reporting to Employees: Identifying the Areas of Interest to Employees," *Accounting and Finance* 27, no. 2 (November 1987), pp. 41–52; and N. R. Lewis, L. D. Parker, and P. Sutcliffe, "Financial Reporting to Employees: The Pattern of Development 1919 to 1979," *Accounting, Organizations and Society* 9 (1984), pp. 275–89.

49. W. Ouchi, *Theory Z* (New York: Avon Books, 1981), pp. 176–77; and T. Peters and R. Waterman, *In Search of Excellence* (New York: Harper and Row, 1982), p. 122.

50. R. D'Aprix, "The Oldest (and Best) Way to Communicate with Employees," *Harvard Business Review,* September–October 1982, pp. 30, 32; and T. Peters, *Thriving on Chaos* (New York: Knopf, 1987), Chapter L-4.

51. P. C. Newman, *Bronfman Dynasty* (Toronto: McClelland and Stewart, 1978), pp. 36–37.

52. D. Silburt, "Top Secrets of Management," *Canadian Business,* July 1987, p. 28, 30.

53. Royal Bank of Canada, *Annual Report, 1988* (Montreal: Royal Bank of Canada, 1989); Auditor General of Canada, *Report of the Auditor General to the House of Commons, Fiscal Year Ended 31 March 1989* (Ottawa: Minister of Supply and Services, 1989), p. 184; and "Northern Telecom Canada Limited's Employee Suggestions Program Record," *Canadian Industrial Relations and Personnel Developments,* June 12, 1985, p. 685.

54. K. Dougherty, "Transit Chief Champions Montreal's Uneasy Riders," *Financial Post,* September 1, 1989, p. 11.

55. Information about some of these firms is based on interviews by BUS 481 students Linda Olsen, Doris Deiter, Tracy Herndier, and Garth Jesperson. Also see L. Gutri, "No Stone Unturned," *Canadian HR Reporter,* September 5, 1988, p. 8.

CHAPTER CASE

GET THE JOB DONE

Jack Forrester, 35, is a bloodstock agent in the thoroughbred horse industry. As bloodstock agent, he locates and brings together buyers and sellers of thoroughbred horses and breeding rights. He has achieved tremendous success through his hard work and his knowledge of thoroughbred bloodlines. He started his business five years ago, and he now employs eight other agents, three secretaries, an office manager, and me. Jack hired me four months ago and told me that I was the "assistant office manager." I thought that was (and is) a grand job title, even though no one ever told me what I was supposed to do. But the pay is great for a part-time job (I am a third-year college student), and I am learning a lot about an interesting industry. I am also learning a lot about people.

I stood by the door of Forrester's office. Forrester was on the phone, and before I could knock, he motioned for me to come in and sit down. His desk was covered by numerous reports, memos, horse sale catalogs, telephone messages, and racing results. Other reminders on bits of paper were taped to the wall, and a "to do" list with at least 10 entries was taped to the base of the telephone. Evidently these were things that he had "to do" immediately. While talking on the phone, he added another item to this list.

As he continued the phone conversation, he was shaking his head and signing letters at the same time. Finally, he put his hand over the phone and said to me, "This is Robinson in Florida on that two-year-old filly deal. All the tests on her are not in yet, but he insists on giving me every detail on the entire test procedure. The guy is going to drive me nuts."

Turning his attention back to the phone, Forrester removed his hand and resumed talking. "Right, Robbie, OK. . . . Great. . . . OK. . . . Sure. . . . Call me back on that. . . . Terrific. . . . Bye."

Forrester hung up the phone with a sigh of relief and looked at me. "Do you know what I like about you, Tinsley?" I didn't have time to answer, nor did he, because the phone range again. "Yeah. . . . Fine. . . . Terrific. . . . Count me in. . . . Bye." At this point, his secretary looked in and said, "John Towne of Winthrop Farms is on hold. It sounds urgent."

Forrester shook his head again and went back to the telephone. After a few minutes of conversation, he put his hand over the receiver and called to his secretary. "Get Johnson and Burke in here, fast." Johnson was the office manager, and Burke was an agent. They arrived as he hung up the phone.

"Burke," he said, "you know that deal you put together for the syndication of that three-year-old, Ol' Blue? Well, they don't like it. Put this information into it and tell me what effect the changes will have on us. When you get it finished, bring it to me so I can call Towne back." Burke left.

"Johnson, I want all of the training fees, jockey expenses, and all other expenses on that horse. Don't give them to me by the month like you did last time. I need totals in all categories, and for crying out loud, this time break out the 'other' category a little better. I looked real bad last week when Towne asked me what the $6,300 in *other expenses* was for. I want all the information at my fingertips in case we've got to go to war with these people." Johnson left.

"Now Tinsley, what did you need me for?"

"Just sign this bill of sale," I said. "No reason to spend a lot of time on it. It's for the sale of that yearling you asked me to take care of."

"That's what I like about you, Tinsley," he said as he leaned back in his chair and signed the bill of sale. "When I give you a job, you listen, and then you do it right the first time, and then you tell me when it's done. You don't tell me how you did it, the problems you're having doing it, who you met while doing it, and every other Mickey Mouse detail. If the rest of the people around here had that ability, I might be able to get some work done. I think I got more work done five years ago when I had nobody working for me."

As I left his office, I didn't have time to thank him because the phone began ringing.

Discussion Questions

1. Identify the communication barriers apparent in this case.
2. How well does Forrester manage the flow of communications through his office? What can he do to improve the situation?
3. What are some of the potential negative consequences of the way that Forrester communicates with others?

Source: J. M. Ivancevich, J. H. Donnelly, Jr., J. L. Gibson, J. R. Collins, and N. A. Neilsen, *Canadian Management: Principles and Functions* (Homewood, Ill.: Irwin, 1991), pp. 358–59.

EXPERIENTIAL EXERCISE

EFFECTIVE INTERPERSONAL COMMUNICATIONS

Purpose.   This exercise is designed to help you develop more effective interpersonal communication skills, particularly in terms of helping others communicate more openly with you.

Instructions.   Read the four incidents below. The first three incidents represent situations where someone is telling you about his or her work-related problem. Following each incident are five possible ways that you might reply. Rank these responses in terms of how you would reply, with 1 indicating your most preferred reply and 5 indicating your least preferred reply. Identify the strengths and weaknesses with each reply. For the fourth incident, you are asked to indicate which of the two statements is more appropriate in the context described.

This exercise may be completed either individually or in small teams of four or five people. When the individuals (or teams) have completed the exercise, each of the incidents will be discussed and the results compared with others in the class.

INCIDENT 1

I don't understand it. The executive committee knows how hard pressed we are to get these designs out over the next year, yet our team doesn't receive any money in next year's budget for new hires to ease off the workload. Surely the company has enough money for another person in our department. Don't they think we provide a valuable service?

Rank

_____ a. I can understand why you're upset, but I'm sure that we can find some sort of solution if you'll be patient just a while longer.

_____ b. I'm sorry, but your budget proposal for a new hire looked pretty weak to the executive committee. You're going to have to live with this one.

_____ c. Sure, your group is suffering. We're all suffering through this belt tightening. I can point you to other project teams who are just as mad as you are about this situation.

_____ d. You sound really upset about this. Do you really feel that the executive committee doubts the value your group provides to the company?

_____ e. Do you really need another person to do the work? Can't you just reschedule people or have them put in some overtime until the workload eases?

INCIDENT 2

I'm fed up with the way my boss runs this department. She doesn't seem to have any idea of the problems we face with clients every day or with the lack of support from the company to secure new orders. I've tried to tell her that the salespeople can't do their jobs without new samples and telemarketing support, but she just seems to smile and ignore my requests.

Rank

_____ a. I know what you mean. The boss I worked for a few years ago in an accounting department was just waiting for retirement and wouldn't do anything to help his people. I think he was afraid that demanding more resources would jeopardize his pension.

_____ b. You're really having trouble getting your work done effectively with this supervisor, aren't you?

_____ c. I suggest that you go directly to your boss's superior and let him know about your concerns. This isn't going to get resolved unless you take action now.

_____ d. Gee, that must be frustrating. But, you know, it's just as likely that your boss is trying but isn't getting any support from above. Have you thought of that?

_____ e. Why don't you think your boss is doing anything to help you?

INCIDENT 3

I worked really hard this past year and all you give me is an "above average" performance rating. You know I've been in this job longer than anyone else and I know it better than anyone else. There's an "excellent" rating, but I don't see you giving it to anybody. Do I have to walk on water before you give me the top merit increase?

Rank

_____   *a.*   You really don't know what I look at to decide merit increases, do you?

_____   *b.*   Don't be upset. It's true that very few people get "excellent" ratings, but company policy dictates that only 5 percent of the employees receive the highest increases.

_____   *c.*   Tell me how you think you deserved the highest merit increase. Maybe I overlooked something, or perhaps we just need to understand the performance criteria more clearly.

_____   *d.*   What are you complaining about? Most people in this department would kill for an "above average" rating and you come to me as if it's a sign of failure.

_____   *e.*   You seem to be saying that you deserve an "excellent" rating with the highest merit increase rather than the "above average" rating your actually received, right?

INCIDENT 4

Jim Shanti is a 54-year-old sales supervisor whose performance has recently been declining. In particular, he has acted rudely to his own staff by criticizing them in public. He has not been very helpful to sales supervisors in other regions when they call for information. A few recent incidents have been noted where Jim has received telephone messages from clients and has made no apparent attempt to return their calls. As Jim's supervisor, you are holding a private meeting with him to discuss his recent performance. Which statement in each pair would you use to create a more effective dialogue?

1. [ ] *a.* Jim, your recent actions are quite wrong, you know.
    [ ] *b.* Jim, I have been quite concerned about the fact that you aren't getting back to clients who call.

2. [ ] *a.* I understand that you spoke harshly to Sandra the other day in front of her coworkers.
    [ ] *b.* You're a real goof for speaking harshly the other day to Sandra in front of her coworkers.

3. [ ] *a.* I don't think you're motivated enough to do this job anymore, Jim.
    [ ] *b.* One possible solution is to set a goal of returning all your calls within 24 hours. Does this sound reasonable to you?

Organizational Perspectives on Perception and Personality

LEARNING OBJECTIVES

After reading this chapter, you should be able to:

Describe
The perceptual process.

Explain
How people manage their self-presentation to others.

Discuss
How self-fulfilling prophecy influences employee
performance.

Define
The halo effect.

Explain
How the Johari Window can help improve our perceptual
accuracy.

Discuss
The implications of personality for organizational
behaviour.

Dome Petroleum

Dome Petroleum was once a dazzling star in Alberta's oil patch, serving as a role model of Canadian initiative in oil exploration. In the early 1980s, chairman Jack Gallagher and president Bill Richards wanted to expand their operations by purchasing another Canadian oil exploration company, Hudson's Bay Oil and Gas (HBOG), from its American owner, Conoco Inc. However, a direct purchase of HBOG stock in Canada would have had unfavourable tax implications, so Gallagher and Richards planned to buy Conoco stock in New York and later swap it for HBOG stock.

Before buying Conoco shares on the New York Stock Exchange, Gallagher and Richards wanted to talk with Conoco chairman Ralph Bailey to be sure that the American company did not view Dome's actions as a hostile takeover. In April 1981, Dome's chairman and president met with Bailey to discuss the complicated acquisition strategy. Conoco was previously unaware of Dome's plans and, as the meeting began, Bailey warned that he was there merely to listen. Gallagher and Richards were certain that Conoco wanted to sell HBOG because Canada's energy legislation at the time made HBOG a poor investment for the American firm. They perceived Bailey's silence as an implied agreement to proceed with their offer and thought the Conoco chairman was trying to be discreet on this sensitive issue. However, Bailey later claimed that he was unimpressed with Dome's plan and was trying to give the Calgary oilmen the cold shoulder.

In May 1981, based on their perceptions of that meeting, Gallagher and Richards launched the largest takeover that the world had ever seen by offering to purchase Conoco shares on the New York Stock Exchange. Conoco's chairman was surprised and outraged by this move and tried to block Dome's takeover plans. Dome was ultimately successful, but the heavy debt incurred from the hostile purchase (nearly $2 billion), together with rising interest rates and falling oil prices, nearly bankrupted the Calgary firm. Gallagher and Richards were eventually forced out of Dome Petroleum and the firm was sold to Amoco Petroleum, an American oil firm, in 1987.[1]

perception
The process of selecting, organizing, and interpreting information in order to make sense of the world around us.

The April 1981 meeting with Gallagher, Richards, and Bailey dramatically illustrates the importance of perceptions in organizational behaviour. Whether you are evaluating an employee's performance or interpreting a CEO's silence, perceptions are a necessary and often troublesome part of managing people and organizations. **Perception** is the process of receiving information about and making sense of the world around us. It involves deciding which information to notice, how to categorize this information, and how to interpret it within the framework of our existing knowledge.

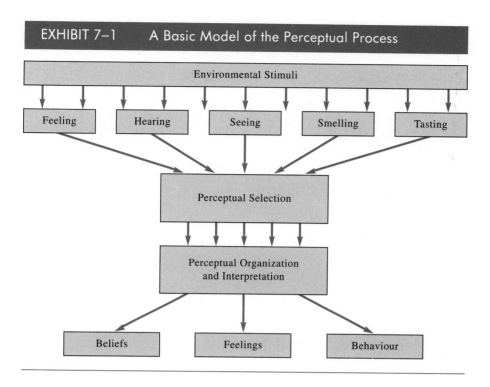

EXHIBIT 7–1   A Basic Model of the Perceptual Process

The model in Exhibit 7–1 shows that the perceptual process begins when environmental stimuli are received through our senses. Only some of this information passes through the perceptual selection phase and is organized and interpreted. The perceptual process is obviously very important because it determines our perspective of reality and thereby influences our attitudes and behaviour toward clients, coworkers, and superiors.[2] Within organizations, our perception of others is a major part of organizational behaviour because it heavily influences employee activities.

This chapter begins by examining the factors that influence our selection, organization, and interpretation of information in organizations. Next, we discuss how perceptions are ''managed'' by the people being observed and explain how our perceptions of others can influence reality through a phenomenon called *self-fulfilling prophecy*. Several common perceptual errors in organizations are then described and ways to improve perceptual accuracy are proposed. Finally, this chapter introduces the concept of personality and its relevance to organizational behaviour.

PERCEPTUAL SELECTION

We are constantly bombarded with information received through the five senses: feeling, hearing, seeing, smelling, and tasting. It would be impossible to attend to each of these stimuli—there are simply too many to notice all at

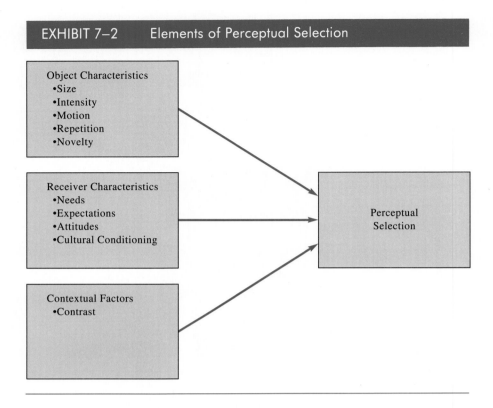

EXHIBIT 7–2   Elements of Perceptual Selection

Object Characteristics
•Size
•Intensity
•Motion
•Repetition
•Novelty

Receiver Characteristics
•Needs
•Expectations
•Attitudes
•Cultural Conditioning

Contextual Factors
•Contrast

Perceptual
Selection

once. To avoid chaos, only information believed to be important is recognized or selected, while the rest is screened out. A sawmill operator working on a piece of electronic equipment might ignore the smell of freshly cut logs or the sound of coworkers talking nearby. Yet a small flashing red light on the console is immediately noticed because it signals that the saw blade is overheating.

The process of filtering information received by our senses is called **perceptual selection.** Whether we select or screen out information depends on the characteristics of the object, perceiver, and situation (see Exhibit 7–2).

perceptual selection
The process of filtering (selecting and screening out) information received by our senses.

Characteristics of the Object

The extent to which objects are noticed depends on their size, intensity, motion, repetition, and novelty. The red light on the sawmill operator's console receives attention because it is bright (intensity), flashing (motion), and a rare event (novelty). It also has symbolic importance to the operator. The safety poster shown in Exhibit 7–3 has a higher probability of being noticed by employees if it is large (size), has high contrast (intensity), and is placed throughout the office or factory (repetition).

EXHIBIT 7–3   Large, High Contrast Safety Posters
                Attract Attention

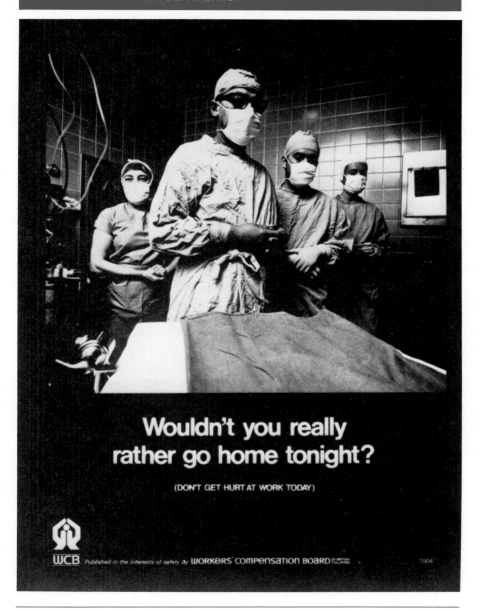

Source: Workers Compensation Board of British Columbia. Used with permission.

Size, intensity, motion, repetition, and novelty apply to the perception of people as well as to inanimate objects. We are more likely to notice people by what they wear, the way they behave, and the way they talk. An argument in the hallway may stand out because it is loud (intensity) and is an unusual event (novelty). Organizational status also affects whether certain people and their actions are noticed. We are more likely to concentrate on the statements and actions of top management than of peers and subordinates. Some research suggests that we might even distort our perception of a person's height based on his or her status.[3]

Characteristics of the Perceiver

Several features of the perceiver affect perceptual selection, including prepotent needs, expectations, attitudes, and cultural conditioning.

Needs.   We are more likely to recognize objects and events that help us satisfy prepotent needs. While reviewing the morning paper, an Air Canada executive would probably notice a headline about a new marketing strategy at Canadian Airlines because the manager has a strong need to know about the company's competitors.

Expectations.   Perceptual selection is also influenced by what we expect to find in a particular situation. We develop beliefs about numerous situations in our lives through socialization, past experience, occupational training, and learning from others. These beliefs condition us to be ready to expect certain events, while information falling outside those expectations is typically ignored.

We can see the effect of expectations on perceptual selection when comparing how people in different departments or occupational specialties perceive a problem or opportunity. In a well-known study, 23 executives employed in different departments of a large manufacturing firm were asked to read a lengthy and detailed case about a steel company and then write a brief statement on what they considered the most important problem in the case.[4] As Exhibit 7–4 reveals, the problem definition was influenced by the managers' departmental affiliations and occupational backgrounds, which had conditioned them to select different information to understand the case.

Attitudes.   Our attitudes and values provide another basis on which we screen out or select information. Information is more likely to be noticed if we have strong positive or negative feelings toward it or if it is consistent with our attitudes. For example, research on employment interviews suggests that many interviewers who develop positive feelings toward the job applicant early in the interview tend to subsequently screen out negative information and remember positive information.[5]

EXHIBIT 7–4	Effect of Departmental Affiliation on Selective Perception

		Type of Problem Mentioned		
Department	Total Number of Executives	Sales	"Clarify Organization"	Human Relations
Sales	6	5	1	0
Production	5	1	4	0
Accounting	4	3	0	0
Miscellaneous*	8	1	3	3
Totals	23	10	8	3

* Includes two managers in legal department, two in research and development, and one each in public relations, industrial relations, medical, and purchasing. Solutions provided by two of the 23 managers were not classified.

Source: D. C. Dearborn and H. A. Simon, "Selective Perception: A Note on the Departmental Identification of Executives," *Sociometry* 21 (1958), pp. 140–44.

Cultural Conditioning. Cultural conditioning influences whether information is recognized or ignored by establishing the norms and patterns against which behaviour is judged.[6] In a conversation between a Canadian and a Brazilian, the Canadian may notice and even feel uncomfortable by the close physical distance between them, whereas the Brazilian, who is accustomed to smaller personal space in social interactions, does not notice the physical distance. Only when the Canadian steps back to a more comfortable distance might the Brazilian suddenly feel that the two are too far apart.

Characteristics of the Situation

The extent to which we notice an event or person also depends on the context in which it is sensed. In particular, things that *contrast* against the background have a higher probability of being noticed. You might notice that a client has an Australian accent if the meeting takes place in Fredericton, but not if it takes place in Melbourne, Australia, particularly if you have been living there for some time. On the contrary, it would be your Canadian accent that stands out!

PERCEPTUAL ORGANIZATION AND INTERPRETATION

Even after many stimuli are screened out, we still need to organize and interpret the selected information in order to make sense of our environment. To organize and interpret incoming information, we look at its context and identify it with the patterns and categories we have developed over the years.

Figure/Ground Organization

figure/ground principle
A principle of organizing information whereby our perceptions of objects (figures) depend on the contexts (ground) in which they are perceived.

Earlier we mentioned that the context in which an object is found affects whether or not it is selected. The context also influences our organization and interpretation of that information based on the **figure/ground principle.** This principle refers to the idea that our perceptions of objects (figures) depend on the contexts (ground) in which they are perceived. Figure/ground principle has many applications in organizations. For instance, it explains why we quickly conclude that a person working near a filing cabinet is a secretary or filing clerk and that someone filling a duffel bag with paper is a mailroom clerk. In each case, contextual cues help us to quickly interpret the behaviour and identities of the people being observed.

The figure/ground principle is apparent in performance evaluation because employee performance is often judged against the performance of others in the department or occupation. Average performers become marginal when others provide superior work, but in a group of new employees with marginal performance, average performance looks more favourable. In short, our evaluation of an employee's performance tends to vary with the context in which it is observed.[7]

Perceptual Grouping Principles

Perceptual organization and interpretation also involves grouping information into recognizable and manageable patterns or categories. If we initially perceive someone as aggressive, subsequent information about the person is usually interpreted in terms of the initial impression. We have a category called "aggressiveness" and are quick to place the coworker in this category based on the first information received. People use several principles to group information, including proximity, continuity, closure, and similarity.

- *Proximity*—Physical proximity is often used to group objects together. For instance, we tend to group people together based on their departmental affiliation. If the group is perceived to be inefficient, each member of that group is typically viewed the same way.
- *Continuity*—We tend to organize seemingly random events into continuous patterns. Managers frequently see trends in market share information only to learn later that this trend did not exist.
- *Closure*—When a picture is incomplete, we try to fill in the missing pieces based on past experience. While walking by a coworker's office, you hear her talking and assume she is meeting with someone. In fact, she may be in the room alone thinking out loud or practising an upcoming speech.

PERSPECTIVE 7–1   Cultural Misinterpretations Can Be Costly

After entertaining his Canadian guest, an Egyptian executive offered joint partnership in a business venture. Delighted with the offer, the Canadian suggested that they meet again the next morning with their respective lawyers to fill in the details.

The Egyptians never arrived. Was the problem that Egyptians are not punctual? That they expect counteroffers? That lawyers are not available in Cairo? None of these explanations was true, although the Canadian executive considered them all.

At issue was the perceived meaning of inviting lawyers. The Canadian saw the lawyers' presence as facilitating the successful completion of the negotiation. The Egyptian interpreted it as signalling the Canadian's mistrust of his verbal commitment. Canadians often use the impersonal formality of a lawyer's services to finalize an agreement, whereas Egyptians more often depend on a personal relationship developed between bargaining partners for the same purposes.

Source: N. Adler, *International Dimensions of Organizational Behavior* (Belmont, Calif.: Wadsworth, 1986), p. 92. Used with permission.

- *Similarity*—We group objects together if they have similar characteristics. Using this principle, several Canadian firms try to create the perception of a more homogeneous work force by establishing specific dress codes. At Honda of Canada's manufacturing plant in Alliston, Ontario, for example, all associates (i.e., employees) wear the same uniform—a white coat, white trousers, and white and green baseball caps. This symbolizes the team concept that everyone is working for the same corporate objectives.[8]

Perceptual organization helps us to make sense of the workplace, but it might also inhibit creativity and open-mindedness. For instance, the continuity principle may prevent managers from noticing new market opportunities because they either ignore discrepant information or interpret it in a manner consistent with past trends. The similarity principle might cause us to assume incorrect information about a job applicant whose physical appearance (e.g., long hair, leather jacket, etc.) is similar to someone who was recently dismissed from the organization.

Perceptual organization and interpretation are also dependent on cultural conditioning. Even if we notice the same things as a business partner from another country, the information may be interpreted differently, resulting in costly misunderstandings. Perspective 7–1 presents such an example of cultural differences in perceptual organization and interpretation.

Attribution Theory

An important aspect of perceptual organization and interpretation involves explaining why events occur. This is known as the **attribution process**—making inferences about the causes of behaviour.[9] Managers have a strong

attribution process

A perceptual process whereby we interpret the causes of behaviour in terms of the person (internal attributions) or the situation (external attributions).

need to understand why a particular event or behaviour occurs so that they can feel more confident about how to correct or reinforce it in the future. The attribution process is particularly important when we are asked to explain someone's behaviour or when our expectations are disconfirmed.[10]

Attributing someone's behaviour involves deciding whether it is largely due to factors beyond the individual's control (*external attributions*), such as luck and the availability of resources, or to personal characteristics, such as ability and motivation (*internal attributions*). These inferences are based on whether the behaviour is:

* Similar to the person's past behaviour in that situation (consistency).
* Similar to the behaviour of others in that situation (consensus).
* Similar to the person's behaviour in other situations (distinctiveness).

Supervisors who see an employee perform a task poorly would make an external attribution if the employee usually performs this task well (low consistency), other employees also perform this task poorly (high consensus), and the employee performs other tasks well (high distinctiveness). An internal attribution, on the other hand, would be made under conditions of high consistency, low consensus, and low distinctiveness.[11]

Attributing behaviour to internal versus external factors affects our reaction to that event.[12] Let us say that an employee completes an excellent assignment but the supervisor believes this performance is due more to the assistance of coworkers than to the individual's own skill and motivation. This external attribution may result in a lower performance rating because the supervisor believes that credit should go to the coworkers, not to the employee.[13]

Attributing our own behaviour to internal or external causes also has implications for organizational behaviour. If we perform a task well but attribute it to luck or favourable conditions, the external attribution generates a low effort-to-performance expectancy and motivation remains low, even if good performance is rewarded. Making an internal or external attribution also affects whether our job satisfaction increases when we perform a task well. We feel a sense of accomplishment (a type of job satisfaction) when we complete a task successfully, but only if we believe that this success is due to internal causes.[14]

IMPRESSION MANAGEMENT

Rather than being passive objects in the perceptual process, people actively "manage" their public images. When making a sales call, we dress appropriately and behave in a way that will encourage the client to do business. In labour negotiations, our appearance and actions show others that we will bargain fairly but firmly. When meeting senior managers, we try to convey an image of ourselves that will advance our career in the organization.

The idea that people manage the identities that others assign to them is called **impression management**.[15] People routinely manage their self-presentation by following social norms and customs without really considering their impact. Other impression management activities, such as ingratiation, are often quite deliberate.

impression management

The process of attempting to manage the identities that others assign to us.

Ingratiation

Ingratiation is a specific type of deliberate impression management by which individuals try to create a more favourable impression of themselves to others.[16] Three specific strategies have been identified to achieve this goal.[17] Self-presentation strategies involve directly managing your appearance and behaviour to create a favourable impression (see Exhibit 7–5). For example, you might read *Dress for Success* to learn how to portray a more professional image.[18]

Target-directed strategies focus on making others feel good about themselves, which is often reflected back on the person who created the feeling.

ingratiation

An impression management strategy whereby individuals deliberately try to create a more favourable impression of themselves to others.

| EXHIBIT 7–5 | Impression Management: Letting Others See What We Want Them to See |

Source: The Far Side by Gary Larson is reprinted by permission of Chronicle Features, San Francisco, Calif.

PERSPECTIVE 7–2   Victorious Ingratiation

In 1922, after centuries of bitter antagonism, the Turks determined to drive the Greeks forever from Turkish territory.

Mustapha Kemal, leader of the Turkish forces, made a Napoleonic speech to his soldiers, saying, "Your goal is the Mediterranean," and one of the bitterest wars in modern history was on. The Turks won the conflict. When two Greek generals, Tricoupis and Dionis, made their way to Kemal's headquarters to surrender, the Turkish people called down the curses of heaven upon their vanquished foes.

But Kemal's attitude was free from triumph.

"Sit down, gentlemen," he said, grasping their hands. "You must be tired." Then, after discussing the campaign in detail, he softened the blow of their defeat. "War," he said, as one soldier to another, "is a game in which the best men are sometimes worsted."

Even in the full flush of victory, Kemal remembered this important rule: *let the other person save face.*

Source: D. Carnegie, "Let the Other Man Save His Face," in *How to Win Friends and Influence People* (New York: Simon & Schuster, 1936).

Direct flattery is a target-directed strategy because it makes others feel good and tends to make them see you in a more favourable light. Agreeing with or conforming to the opinions of others also tends to increase their approval of you. Target-directed strategies are particularly effective—and morally correct—when the ingratiator flatters or sympathizes with a defeated competitor. This may occur when one manager is promoted instead of a colleague, or when one sales representative wins a large contract over another. Perspective 7–2 presents another example of target-directed ingratiation in a seemingly unlikely setting.

Finally, ingratiation may take the form of third-person directed strategies. Here, you say something nice about someone to a third person, who hopefully will relay this conversation back to the person being praised. For example, an employee who wants to present a positive image to her supervisor might compliment the supervisor's leadership to a coworker. The coworker mentions this conversation to the supervisor, who then has a more favourable impression of the employee who provided the original compliment.

Ingratiation affects others' perceptions of you in some situations but not in others. For example, people will react negatively to flattery if they suspect the ingratiator's motives. Status differences may also determine the effectiveness of ingratiation.[19]

Impression management is an important concept in organizational behaviour because it recognizes the significance of self-presentation activities. Business researchers and practitioners have come to realize that the company's image is often as important to customers as the tangible product or service being provided.[20] Organizational effectiveness can increase by training employees to more carefully manage their self-presentation to the public. For example, during the economic recession of the early 1980s, the Canadian Broadcasting Corporation asked its journalists to stop wearing fur coats, to offset the growing impression that the CBC journalists were over-paid and rather elitist. John Owen, executive producer of *The National,* explained that wearing expensive coats "is a message to our viewers that seems to say that we're rich and you're not." Changing their attire did not necessarily improve the reporters' journalistic skills, but it did improve CBC's public image. Says Owen: "Perception is a reality in this business."[21]

SELF-FULFILLING PROPHECY

Self-fulfilling prophecy occurs when one person inaccurately perceives a second person and the resulting expectations cause the second person to act in ways consistent with the original perception.[22] In other words, our percep-tions can influence reality. If a new employee is hired and the supervisor forms an initial impression that the recruit will be a poor performer, this expectation affects the way the supervisor acts toward the employee. With-out realizing it, the supervisor's behaviour may cause the employee to per-form the job poorly. Consequently, the supervisor's perception of the new hire, even if originally incorrect, is confirmed.

Exhibit 7–6 outlines the four basic steps in self-fulfilling prophecy.[23] The model is described in terms of a supervisor–subordinate relationship, but the phenomenon exists in a variety of situations. For instance, some of the earliest work in this field studied the influence of teacher expectancies on the subsequent behaviour and performance of elementary school children.[24]

Expectations Formed.   First, the supervisor forms an impression of the employee and, from this perception, develops expectations about the em-ployee's future behaviour. These expectations are sometimes inaccurate because people tend to form first impressions from limited information.

Behaviour toward Employee.   The supervisor's perceptions and expectan-cies affect the way he or she treats employees.[25] Specifically, high-expec-tancy employees (those who are expected to do well) receive:

- More emotional support through nonverbal cues (e.g., more smiling and eye contact).
- More frequent and valuable feedback and reinforcement.
- More challenging goals and better training.
- More opportunities to demonstrate their performance.

Effect on Employee.   Employees react to the supervisor's actions in two ways. First, high-expectancy employees learn more skills and knowledge to do the job than low-expectancy employees because they receive higher-quality training and more opportunities to practice their skills. Second,

self-fulfilling prophecy
A phenomenon whereby an observer's perception of someone causes the other person to actually behave in a manner consistent with the observer's expectation.

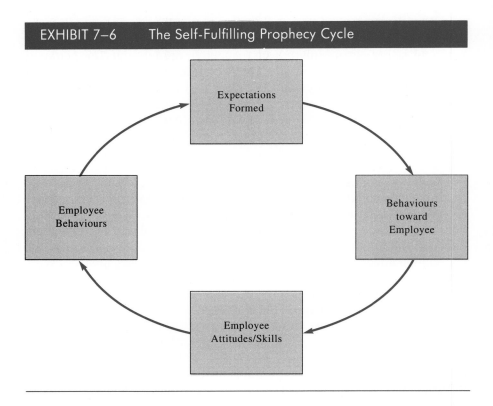

EXHIBIT 7–6   The Self-Fulfilling Prophecy Cycle

based on the supervisor's subtle cues, employees tend to adjust their self-esteem in line with the supervisor's expectations. High-expectancy employees become more motivated because they develop a higher effort-to-performance expectancy and set a higher level of achievement for themselves.

Employee Behaviours.   With better skills and higher motivation, high-expectancy employees demonstrate better performance. This is observed by the supervisor and reinforces the original perception that the employee performs the job well.

Self-Fulfilling Prophecy in Practice

Although self-fulfilling prophecy has mainly been studied in school settings, there is increasing evidence of this effect in organizations. In one study, four Israeli Defence Force combat command course instructors were told that one-third of the incoming trainees had high command potential, one-third had normal potential, and the rest had unknown potential. The trainees had been randomly placed into these categories by the researchers, but the instructors were led to believe that this was accurate information. At the end of the course, high-expectancy soldiers did indeed perform significantly better than trainees who had been assigned to the other groups. They also had more favourable attitudes toward the course and the instructor's leadership effectiveness.[26] Similar effects of self-fulfilling prophecy have been reported in studies on hard-core unemployed trainees and poor-performance sailors in the U.S. Navy.[27]

Self-fulfilling prophecy is a potentially valuable tool with which to improve employee performance and the organization's effectiveness, yet it can also undermine an employee's aspirations and self-esteem when the supervisor has concluded that the employee has limited potential. Too often, the supervisor's perceptions leading to self-fulfilling prophecy are based on inaccurate information and perceptual errors that distort the information that is received. We turn next to a discussion of several perceptual errors in organizational settings.

PERCEPTUAL ERRORS

It is quite clear that selecting, organizing, and interpreting information is at best an imperfect process. Some of the more troublesome errors that distort our ability to perceive organizational events are described below.

The Halo Effect

Halo effect occurs when our general impression of a person, usually based on one prominent characteristic, colours our perception of other characteristics of that person.[28] If we meet a client who speaks in a friendly manner, we tend to infer a host of other favourable qualities about him or her. If a colleague doesn't complete tasks on time, we tend to view his or her other traits unfavourably. In each case, one trait important to the perceiver forms a general impression, and this impression becomes the basis for judgments about other traits.

Halo effect is most prevalent when concrete information about several characteristics of the person or object being perceived is missing.[29] The perceiver fills in the missing information with general impressions. Halo effect also occurs when the perceiver is not motivated to carefully observe the perceived object or person or is unaware that halo can occur.

There is much concern about the effect of halo in performance appraisal ratings.[30] Consider two employees who actually have the same level of performance with respect to quality of work, quantity of work, and customer relations, but one tends to be late for work. Tardiness might not be an important factor in work performance, but the supervisor has a negative impression of employees who are late for work. Halo effect would cause the supervisor to rate the tardy employee lower on *all* performance dimensions because the tardiness has created a negative general impression of that employee. The punctual employee would tend to receive higher ratings on *all*

halo effect
A perceptual error whereby our general impression of a person, usually based on one prominent characteristic, biases our perception of other characteristics of that person.

performance dimensions even though his or her performance level is actually the same as that of the tardy employee. Consequently, halo effect distorts our judgments and can result in poor decision making.

Primacy and Recency Effects

primacy effect
The tendency to quickly form an opinion of people or evaluate them based on the first information we receive about them.

The **primacy effect** is the tendency to quickly form an opinion of people based on the first information we receive about them. First impressions provide a convenient anchor to integrate subsequent information about people, but they are typically formed quickly with little information because people have a strong need to "make sense" of others. Less weight is given to later information about the person, particularly if it is inconsistent with the initial impression.[31]

The primacy effect is a common perceptual bias in employment interviews because interviewers tend to quickly form impressions of job applicants. These impressions take shape within the first few minutes of the interview or even prior to the interview from information in the application form.[32] Once an impression is formed, interviewers pay less attention to new information.

The statement "first impressions are lasting impressions" is true in most situations, but there are circumstances in which the most recent information has a greater influence on our evaluation of others. This is known as the **recency effect**.[33] The recency effect dominates when there is a long delay between when the first impression is formed and when the person is evaluated. In other words, the most recent information dominates our impression of someone when the first impression has worn off with the passage of time.[34] This is known to occur in performance appraisals where supervisors must recall every employee's performance over the previous year. Recent performance information dominates the evaluation because it is the most easily recalled. Some employees are well aware of the recency effect and use it to their advantage by getting their best work on the manager's desk just before the performance appraisal is conducted.

recency effect
The tendency to give more weight to recent information when evaluating someone.

Attribution Errors

Attribution was earlier described as the process of inferring the causes of behaviour. While this is a normal process in perceptual organization and interpretation, people make attribution errors that can lead to inaccurate perceptions of the situation.[35] Two systematic attribution errors are the actor-observer error and self-serving bias.

actor-observer error
A perceptual error whereby people tend to attribute their own actions more to external factors and the behaviour of others more to internal factors.

Actor-observer error is the tendency for people to attribute their own actions to external factors and the behaviour of others to internal factors. When employees arrive late for work, we are more likely to think that they are not motivated, whereas we see our own lateness resulting from a road construction delay or a car that won't start. Since the situational factors influencing the behaviour of others are not easily seen, we tend to conclude that the behaviour is due to the person's own effort or ability. In contrast, we are more sensitive to external causes of our own behaviour, and tend to recognize these in the attribution of our own actions. In organizational settings, this can lead to conflict between supervisors and employees over the degree to which employees should be held responsible for their poor performance or excessive absenteeism.[36]

Self-serving bias is the tendency for people to attribute their own success to internal factors and to attribute their failures to external factors.[37] Simply put, we take credit for our successes and blame others or the situation for our mistakes. Regrettably, self-serving bias can cause supervisors to discount the good performance of subordinates and inflate their responsibility for poor performance. When an employee performs the job well, the supervisor may take more credit than is deserved for this success, leaving the employee with less credit. When the subordinate performs poorly, self-serving bias may cause the supervisor to attribute most of the folly to the subordinate's lack of motivation or ability rather to external causes (such as the supervisor's own leadership).

The existence of self-serving bias in corporate life has been well-documented. In a unique study of corporate annual reports, researchers discovered that organizational successes were typically explained by internal attributions such as management strategy, work force qualities, and research/development efforts. When discussing the organization's poor performance, on the other hand, external attributions dominated, including the level of competition, inflationary pressures, and other environmental factors.[38]

self-serving bias
A perceptual error whereby people tend to attribute their own success to internal factors and to attribute their failures to external factors.

Projection

Projection is the tendency to ascribe one's own characteristics to others.[39] If we are eager to be promoted, we might think that others are similarly motivated. Projection is typically invoked as a defense mechanism to protect our self-concept. If we do something dishonest, we are likely to downplay the importance of the work rule infraction by claiming that "everyone does it." We feel more comfortable with the thought that others possess our negative traits, so we are quick to see these traits in others even though they actually do not possess them.

projection
A perceptual error whereby people tend to ascribe their own characteristics to other people.

Stereotyping

Recall that perceptual organization involves grouping information about people into manageable categories. Creating a unique perceptual category for everyone would be too complex, so people are assigned to social categories developed from the perceiver's past experience and learning. **Stereotyp-**

stereotyping
The process of using a few observable characteristics to assign someone to a preconceived social category and then assuming that the person also possesses other (usually less observable) characteristics of the group.

PERSPECTIVE 7–3   Breaking the Traditional Stereotype

In the early days, the ghost of Florence Nightingale hovered over Canadian nurses, urging them to sacrifice their identities for medical service. This is reflected in the motto of the first Canadian school of nursing: "I see and am silent." Says Vera Chernecki, president of the Manitoba Organization of Nurses' Associations, "At one time we were the handmaidens to the doctors, the bedpan handlers."

But times have changed. Nursing schools teach the complexities of power relationships and conflict management. At conventions, nurses attend workshops on lobbying and political action. And in hospital corridors, they challenge the authority of doctors and administrators. Bolstered by a favourable public image and enlightened by lessons of the women's movement, nurses have become a major force in the politics of Canadian health care.

Leaders of the nursing unions have worked hard to overturn yesterday's passive stereotypes of the profession. They have spoken out on contentious issues involving health care administration and government action. Judith Hibberd, a professor of nursing at the University of Alberta, describes the new relationship with hospital administration: "Union representatives are monitoring every decision that hospital management is making. They're quite willing to challenge ordinary management decisions."

Nurses have also tested their political powers at various levels of government. For example, nursing associations across the country launched a massive lobbying campaign in support of the federal government's 1984 Canada Health Act revisions, which penalized provinces allowing doctors to extra-bill patients. The legislation was strongly opposed by the

---

ing is the process of assigning people to preconceived social categories and then attributing the group's characteristics to members of that social category.[40] There are three steps in this process:

1. Through experience and learning, we develop categories of people (e.g., dentist, female, New Democrat, Asian) and to each category are assigned numerous characteristics (e.g., conservatism, intelligence, hobbies, communication skills).

2. People are assigned to one or more social categories, based on easily identifiable characteristics.

3. The cluster of traits belonging to a particular social category are attributed to people identified as members of that group.

Stereotyping can be a useful process to the extent that it helps us to make sense of the world more efficiently. We can see observable characteristics of a person and quickly infer other information, including unobserved attitudes and personality characteristics. But stereotyping frequently causes incorrect perceptions and expectations.

First, it is unlikely that most of the traits assigned to a particular social category will actually be found in every person identified with that group. For example, while it may be true that some accountants avoid risk, many accountants are not risk averse. Second, many widely held stereotypes clus-

powerful medical lobby, but the nurses' campaign flooded Ottawa with enough petitions, letters, and telephone calls to carry the changes through Parliament.

The changing image of nurses comes at a time when the traditional stereotype is no longer satisfactory to people entering the work force. "Nursing is a job ghetto," explains Greg Patterson, a registered nurse in Winnipeg. "Some people associate nursing with women and therefore it is devalued." To combat the increasing workload and passive hospital role, nurses' unions across Canada have become more militant. The nurses' union in Alberta, for instance, is now the standard-bearer for the labour movement in that province. Other unions wait to see what the nurses do before deciding their own actions.

Lobbying governments, questioning other medical authorities, and watching the actions of hospital administrators are dramatic changes for members of an occupation that once viewed its members as doctors' handmaidens. "As a group, we were always scared to hurt the nursing image," says Irene Gouin, a nurse at Edmonton General Hospital. "But we've learned to become self-assertive as a profession."

Sources: G. York "Nursing a Cause," *Globe and Mail*, February 27, 1988, pp. D1, D8; and D. Roberts, "Nurses' Wages Not Sole Issue on Picket Line," *Globe and Mail*, January 10, 1991, p. A4.

ter traits together that, in reality, are not associated. For example, a common stereotype is that athletes have lower intelligence, but there is actually no such relationship.

Finally, we sometimes assign people to the wrong social category because of an imperfect association of traits. For instance, if we see a man and woman in white uniforms standing beside a patient's bed, we tend to classify the man as a medical doctor and the woman as a nurse. In this incident, assigning these people to their respective occupations is based on an observable trait (gender) and the context of the observation (hospital). But if the woman is actually a medical doctor, we would incorrectly attribute nurse characteristics to her and make erroneous expectations about her behaviour. We would likely act differently toward her until we learned that she is actually a medical doctor.

As a form of perceptual organization, stereotyping influences our interpretation of events and the actions taken in response to them. Look at the first column of Exhibit 7–7 and see whether you would interpret these situations differently if the person being observed was male or female.

Stereotyping people in organizations leads not only to incorrect assumptions about them, but also to prejudice and employment discrimination. These important topics will be discussed in Chapter 8. Various occupational groups diligently work to either maintain or change their image to gain self-esteem for their members or strengthen the standards they want to portray.

EXHIBIT 7–7   Gender-Based Stereotypes of Office Behaviour

| | Interpretations | |
Incident	Male Manager	Female Manager
A family picture is prominently placed on the employee's desk.	Ah . . . *he* is a solid, responsible family man.	Mm . . . *she* places her family before her career.
The employee is talking with coworkers.	*He* must be discussing the latest deal.	*She* must be gossiping.
The employee is out of the office today.	*He* must be meeting customers.	*She* must be out shopping.
The employee is having lunch with a company vice-president.	*He* is on his way up.	*She* may be having an affair with him.
The employee has a cluttered desk.	*He* is obviously a hard worker and a busy man.	*She* is obviously a disorganized scatterbrain.
The employee is getting married.	*He* will become more settled and mature.	*She* will get pregnant and leave.

Source: Adapted from: N. Josefowitz, *Paths to Power* (Reading, Mass.: Addison-Wesley, 1980), p. 60.

For example, auditors and accountants continually work to preserve their credibility as responsible and impartial evaluators of financial statements.[41] Other groups, such as nurses, have worked equally hard to alter their traditional stereotype, as Perspective 7–3 describes.

IMPROVING PERCEPTUAL ACCURACY

The Greek philosopher Plato wrote long ago that we see reality only as shadows reflecting against the rough wall of a cave.[42] In other words, reality is filtered through an imperfect perceptual process. We may not be able to bypass the perceptual process, but we can try to minimize our distortion of reality. This section describes ways to improve perceptual accuracy.

Be Aware of Perceptual Errors

You can increase perceptual accuracy by understanding the perceptual errors described in this chapter as well as the general limitations of selecting, organizing, and interpreting information. Research on performance appraisal training has found that becoming aware of some perceptual errors can minimize rating bias.[43] No doubt awareness would also reduce errors in other situations.

Postpone Impression Formation

We have learned that first impressions are usually lasting impressions and that people tend to quickly draw conclusions in order to make sense of things. Yet these sensemaking practices more often than not lead to inaccurate perceptions. It is much better to postpone forming impressions and avoid making stereotyped inferences or other perceptual grouping techniques until more information is received. For example, managers should consciously avoid forming an impression of job candidates until the interview is over, references have been checked, and other selection data have been reviewed.[44] Some errors can also be reduced by ensuring that sufficient objective information is received. By documenting objective evidence of employee performance, for example, supervisors tend to rely less on general impressions (stereotypes and halo) and make fewer attribution errors.[45]

While postponing first impressions, supervisors should put the self-fulfilling prophecy phenomenon to work by developing and communicating positive expectations to all employees and work teams. Management's role is to develop, monitor, and reinforce an environment in which employees are given the opportunity to stretch their abilities in a culture of trust and support. Organizational change efforts can be more successful when change agents exhibit contagious enthusiasm for their projects.[46]

Empathize with Others

Empathy refers to a person's ability to understand the feelings, thoughts, and situation of others.[47] The ability to empathize with others helps to minimize certain perceptual biases, particularly actor-observer attribution errors. By understanding the environment within which employees work, supervisors are more likely to correctly recognize external causes of performance and behaviour.[48]

There are several ways to increase our empathy with others. Direct communication and interaction is perhaps one of the easiest methods, particularly in work teams and related situations where people must listen and learn from each other.[49] For example, to develop the interpersonal skills of its managers, Federal Express created a day-long program in which managers teamed up with blind people to complete a series of tasks. At the end of the day, the blind participants discussed how they were treated by the Federal Express managers in terms of the managers' consultation and patience with their partners.[50]

Another strategy is to literally place yourself in the other person's shoes. One hospital in Vancouver follows this strategy by having new employees tour the premises in a wheelchair (as most patients travel) and drink coffee from a straw (as most patients must do) during the orientation program. Similarly, supervisors who have worked in the jobs now held by their subordinates are also better able to empathize with the problem and limitations they face. The manager of a large General Motors plant in Michigan tries to keep in touch with production staff by donning overalls once a month to help build cars. This experience helps the manager to appreciate any changes offered by employees.[51]

Compare Perceptions with Others

Another useful approach, particularly when the situation is inherently subjective and additional information is not available, is to compare your perceptions with others. This often helps to understand the issue from different points of view. If your colleagues have different backgrounds but generally the same perceptions of the situation, then there is reason to be more confident in your interpretation. Of course, there is no way to know for sure that your perceptions are correct, but they are less likely to be wrong if people with different backgrounds have the same general interpretation of the situation.

Know Yourself: Applying the Johari Window

Fewer perceptual errors are made when we are aware of and sensitive to our own values, beliefs, and prejudices. By understanding ourselves, a particular perception can be scrutinized to ensure that it is based on the information received and not distorted by personal traits.[52] Similarly, our colleagues are less likely to misunderstand our statements or actions when they know about our attitudes and past experiences.

Johari Window

A model of personal and interpersonal understanding that encourages disclosure and feedback to increase the open area and reduce the blind, hidden, and unknown areas of oneself.

The idea that mutual understanding improves perceptual accuracy and communication is represented in a useful model called the **Johari Window.**[53] Developed by Joseph Luft and Harry Ingram (hence the name *Johari*), this model divides information about yourself into four "windows"—open, blind, hidden, and unknown—based on whether your own values, beliefs, and experiences are known to you and to others.

As we see in Exhibit 7–8, the *open area* includes information about you that is known to you as well as others. For example, both you and your coworkers may be aware that you don't like to be near people who smoke cigarettes. The *blind area* refers to information that is known to others but not to yourself. For example, your colleagues might notice that you are embarrassed and awkward when meeting someone confined to a wheelchair, but you are unaware of this fact. Information known to yourself but unknown to others is found in the *hidden area*. We all have personal secrets about our likes, dislikes, and past experiences. Finally, the *unknown area* includes your values, beliefs, and experiences that are known to neither you nor others.

The Johari Window prescribes more open interpersonal relations because people understand each other better and tend to work together more effectively as the amount of information in the open area increases. Suppose that

EXHIBIT 7–8   Johari Window

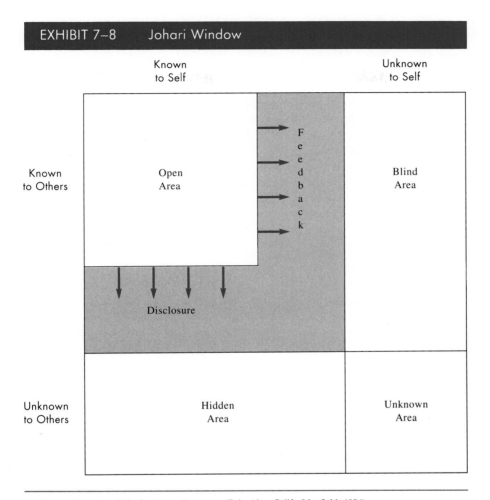

Source: Based on J. Luft, *Group Processes* (Palo Alto, Calif.: Mayfield, 1984).

both you and your coworkers are aware that you do not like a particular client that treated you poorly a few years ago. If the client meets with you to reestablish the relationship, you might be more open-minded about this business opportunity if you are conscious of your negative feelings. If you act harshly to the client, your colleagues are likely to understand the reason for your behaviour and draw this to your attention. Recognizing and acknowledging your weaknesses to others also reduces your likelihood of projecting those traits onto others.[54]

According to the Johari Window, you can increase the open area through disclosure and feedback. *Disclosure* involves informing others of your beliefs, feelings, and experiences that may influence the working relationship. This does not mean that you divulge everything about yourself to others, but only traits that can significantly affect your perceptions and actions in the work environment. Disclosure can be a risk to the impression that others have of you, but the process should be reciprocal. Fortunately, recent studies have found that self-disclosure by one person tends to cause others to make a self-disclosure.[55] Ultimately, this increases the open area of everyone in the work group by reducing their hidden area.

Feedback from others is required to increase the open area by reducing the blind area. For example, if you acted harshly toward a client, your coworkers would provide valuable feedback by confiding their observations of your behaviour. Thus, you and your coworkers must work together to reduce perceptual biases and improve interpersonal communication.

PERSONALITY

Garrett Herman may not be a household name, but the CEO of brokerage firm Loewen Ondaatje is a personality to be reckoned with in Canada's investment industry. Herman has been called a "robobroker" with a strong internal locus of control, an overpowering need for achievement, and a single-minded determination to get the job done. In the early 1970s, as a young investment sales representative in Montreal, Herman aggressively built up his client list by following Rolls-Royces home to get the owner's address and telephone number. Herman's distinctive personality also prevails outside the office, where he races his Porsche at a training track near Belleville, Ontario, and occasionally zips down to challenge other Porsche enthusiasts at Daytona Beach. Herman is not always popular with employees, but he is quick to say that he would rather work with someone who doesn't like him than someone who can't do the job right. Says a long-time friend: "Garrett is the ultimate bull terrier—he's very tenacious, very competitive."[56]

It is difficult to describe Garrett Herman—or anyone else—without referring to the concept of personality. Although it is rather difficult to define, personality is a handy vehicle with which to organize our perceptions of people and their behavioural tendencies. Generally speaking, **personality** refers to the relatively stable and consistent attributes of people that help to explain their behaviour.[57] There are four components of the personality concept worth noting.

personality
A set of relatively stable and consistent characteristics that help to explain a person's behaviour and distinguish him or her from other people.

Internal States.   Personality refers to the built-in characteristics of a person. We do not see Garrett Herman's aggressiveness or determination, only indirect evidence of these traits from his behaviour.

Behaviourally Based.   Personality traits are reflected in the way people act in various situations. Herman's acquaintances describe him as "aggressive" and "determined" because they have observed how he drives cars, deals with clients, waits for elevators, and so on.

Stable.   Studies have reported that people have relatively stable personality traits over several years.[58] Herman's aggressive practises as a salesperson in the early 1970s are still reflected in his personality in the 1990s. Personality changes can occur over long periods of time, however. For instance, we often hear about cocky business school graduates who have mellowed over the years or about quiet bookworms who have come out of their shells.

Consistent.   Personality traits represent *relatively* consistent patterns of behaviour over time. The word *relatively* is emphasized because people do not behave exactly the same way in different situations. For example, a talkative person would not chatter in a meeting where everyone is explicitly told to be quiet while the CEO makes an announcement. But this person may be the first to talk when the opportunity permits. Thus, we must recognize that personality mainly affects behaviour in "weak" situations, that is, situations that do not constrain the person's natural dispositions and tendencies. In "strong" situations—where behaviour is constrained by social norms or reward systems—people with different personalities would act very much the same. In the business meeting example, both talkative and quiet employees would tend to be quiet while the CEO speaks.[59]

How Do Personalities Form?

An individual's personality originates from many sources. An extreme school of thought suggests that personality is mainly inherited genetically from our parents. If this is true, then our temperament is ascribed at conception and cannot be altered by life experiences. A more common view is that our personality is shaped by both heredity and environment. Personality is developed and changed by a variety of social experiences, such as early interactions with our parents, long-term friendships and affiliations, and traumatic events. Garrett Herman's aggressiveness, for instance, may have been formed by the way his parents rewarded him as a child or by his relations with school friends years ago.

The culture within which we are raised also affects personality traits, particularly those referring to deeply embedded values.[60] This is evident in a worldwide study that revealed that the values of people employed by a large multinational corporation vary with their country of origin. Exhibit 7–9 indicates that American, Australian, and, to a lesser extent, Canadian employees of the multinational corporation are highly individualistic. That is, they believe that behaviour should be based on their own beliefs more than social norms. In contrast, employees from South American countries (Colombia, Venezuela, Chile, Peru) and some Asian countries (Taiwan, Thailand, Singapore) have a strong sense of collectivism. They identify more with the groups to which they belong and believe that group norms should determine individual behaviour. People also differ across nations in their power distance, that is, their acceptance of inequality among those in an organization or society.[61]

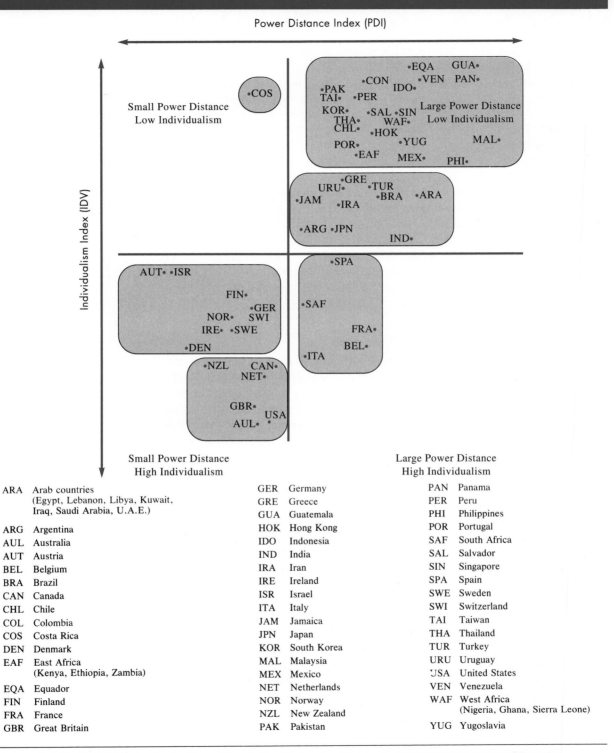

EXHIBIT 7–9   Individualism and Power Distance across Cultures

Power Distance Index (PDI)

Individualism Index (IDV)

Small Power Distance
Low Individualism

•COS

•EQA   GUA•
•CON IDO• •VEN PAN•
•PAK   •PER
TAI•
KOR•   •SAL •SIN   Large Power Distance
THA•   WAF•   Low Individualism
CHL• •HOK
POR•   •YUG   MAL•
•EAF   MEX•   PHI•

•GRE
URU• •TUR
•JAM   •IRA •BRA •ARA
•ARG •JPN
IND•

Small Power Distance
High Individualism

AUT• •ISR

FIN•
•GER
NOR• SWI
IRE• •SWE
•DEN

•NZL   CAN•
NET•

GBR•
AUL• USA•

•SPA

•SAF

FRA•
BEL•
•ITA

Large Power Distance
High Individualism

ARA   Arab countries
      (Egypt, Lebanon, Libya, Kuwait,
      Iraq, Saudi Arabia, U.A.E.)

ARG   Argentina
AUL   Australia
AUT   Austria
BEL   Belgium
BRA   Brazil
CAN   Canada
CHL   Chile
COL   Colombia
COS   Costa Rica
DEN   Denmark
EAF   East Africa
      (Kenya, Ethiopia, Zambia)

EQA   Equador
FIN   Finland
FRA   France
GBR   Great Britain

GER   Germany
GRE   Greece
GUA   Guatemala
HOK   Hong Kong
IDO   Indonesia
IND   India
IRA   Iran
IRE   Ireland
ISR   Israel
ITA   Italy
JAM   Jamaica
JPN   Japan
KOR   South Korea
MAL   Malaysia
MEX   Mexico
NET   Netherlands
NOR   Norway
NZL   New Zealand
PAK   Pakistan

PAN   Panama
PER   Peru
PHI   Philippines
POR   Portugal
SAF   South Africa
SAL   Salvador
SIN   Singapore
SPA   Spain
SWE   Sweden
SWI   Switzerland
TAI   Taiwan
THA   Thailand
TUR   Turkey
URU   Uruguay
USA   United States
VEN   Venezuela
WAF   West Africa
      (Nigeria, Ghana, Sierra Leone)
YUG   Yugoslavia

Source: G. Hofstede, ''Motivation, Leadership, and Organization: Do American Theories Apply Abroad?'' *Organizational Dynamics*, Summer 1980, pp. 42–63.

Personality and Organizational Behaviour

Personality is a practical concept in organizational behaviour because it helps us to make sense of other people, anticipate their future behaviour, and possibly increase their satisfaction and performance through better person–job matching. For instance, the effectiveness of some job design strategies and leadership styles are contingent on employee personalities.[62] Personality traits also affect the types of jobs in which people are interested. In fact, some vocational interest tools are based on personality concepts.[63]

It is still unclear how strongly personality traits are related to employee performance. Several detailed studies have concluded that personality variables are relatively poor predictors of job performance, partly because it is difficult to measure these traits accurately.[64] Recent evidence suggests that personality does have an effect on job performance but the relationship is more complex than previously thought. There is also evidence that professional interviewers often compare the applicant's personality with job requirements when deciding who should be hired.[65] Finally, a few personality theories explicitly state that people with specific problem-solving traits will perform better in certain jobs.[66] For instance, a technical job requiring analysis of detailed objective data would not be a good fit for an intuitive-type manager who is impatient with details and prefers new challenges.

Until we can measure personality more accurately and discover which traits are relevant to which tasks, selection methods other than personality measures should be used to choose job applicants. In any management activity, we must be careful neither to draw conclusions about a person's personality too quickly, nor to forget that an individual's personality may change over time. Too often, managers see problems as personality conflicts rather than diagnosing the situation to discover the underlying causes. Nobel prize-winning scholar Herbert Simon warns us that the concept of personality is unfortunately abused as "a magical slogan to charm away the problems that our intellectual tools don't handle."[67]

SELECTED PERSONALITY DIMENSIONS

There are probably as many personality traits as there are personality theories, but a few traits stand out as important influences on organizational behaviour. In Chapter 2, we described three deeply embedded motive-based personality traits, including the need for achievement (nAch), need for affiliation (nAff), and need for power (nPow). Type A and Type B personalities were also previously discussed in the context of work-related stress (Chapter 5). Let us briefly review a few other commonly mentioned personality traits.

Authoritarianism and Dogmatism

authoritarianism
A personality trait referring to the belief that leaders have a right to expect blind acceptance and respect from subordinates by virtue of their position in the hierarchy.

Authoritarianism is defined as a blind acceptance of authority. Leaders with high authoritarian personalities demand respect from subordinates and try to suppress their independence. As followers, authoritarians are more likely to obey orders and support the power held by those in higher positions.[68]

dogmatism
A personality trait referring to the extent that the person is open- or closed-minded about information contrary to his or her beliefs, and will tolerate others who deviate from organizational authority.

The concept of **dogmatism** emerged from earlier research on authoritarianism and refers to the extent to which people believe in absolute authority and are open- or closed-minded. Highly dogmatic managers are closed-minded about information that is contrary to their beliefs and are intolerant of those who do not abide by organizational authority. They also tend to make decisions quickly and are confident in their choices.[69] As you can imagine, people who are either dogmatic or authoritarian have difficulty encouraging employee involvement in organizational decisions.

Locus of Control

locus of control
A personality trait referring to the extent that people believe what happens to them is within their control; those who feel in control of their destiny have an internal locus whereas those who believe that life events are due mainly to fate or luck have an external locus of control.

Locus of control is the extent to which people believe that what happens to them is within their control. Individuals who feel that they are very much in charge of their own destiny have an internal locus of control personality, while those who think that their life events are due mainly to fate or luck have an external locus of control. Of course, externals believe that they control many specific events in their lives—such as opening a door or serving a customer—but they have a general tendency to believe that outside forces guide their fate. This is particularly apparent in novel situations where the person's control over events has not yet been experienced.

In most employment situations, people with a moderately internal locus of control perform better and are more satisfied than those with an external locus of control. Internals are particularly well-suited to jobs requiring initiative, independent action, complex thinking, and high motivation. They cope better in stressful situations and are better motivated by performance-based reward systems. Not surprisingly, internals tend to be more successful in their careers and earn more money than their external counterparts.[70] The impact of locus of control on managerial behaviour is nicely demonstrated in two fascinating studies.

- A study of senior executives in several Canadian firms found that firms led by internals pursued more innovative strategies than firms led by executives with a more external locus of control. The internals invested more in research and development, introduced new products more quickly than the competition, and made more drastic product line changes. They also pursued more aggressive strategies and planned further into the future.[71]
- A research investigation was conducted before and after flooding from Hurricane Agnes disrupted the lives of small-business owners in Pennsylvania. Owners with an external locus of control were bitter and

had difficulty coping with the disaster. Meanwhile, the internals quickly set about securing loans and other resources to rebuild their homes and businesses.[72]

Self-Monitoring

Self-monitoring refers to the extent that people are sensitive to situational cues, such as the behaviour of others, and can readily adapt their own behaviour appropriately. High self-monitors can adjust their behaviour quite easily and therefore show little stability in other underlying personality traits. In contrast, the social behaviour of low self-monitors is dominated by personal characteristics, so it is relatively easy to predict their behaviour from one situation to the next.[73]

The self-monitoring personality trait has been identified as a significant factor in many organizational activities. Employees who are high self-monitors tend to be better conversationalists, are better at impression management, and are better in boundary-spanning positions (where incumbents work with people in different departments or organizations). One study of Canadian business students also reported that high self-monitors experienced better job interview success and higher starting salary levels.[74]

self-monitoring
A personality trait referring to the extent that people are sensitive to situational cues and can readily adapt their own behaviour appropriately.

SUMMARY

- Perception is the process of selecting, organizing, and interpreting information to make sense of the world around us.

- Perceptual selection depends on the characteristics of the perceiver, the object being perceived, and the situation. To organize and interpret selected information, we look at its context and identify it with the patterns and categories we have developed over the years.

- Perceptual organization and interpretation involve making sense of the selected information by placing it in categories, filling in the missing pieces, and attributing actions to the person or situation.

- People actively manage the perceptions that others have of them by adjusting their behaviour to fit the situation. Ingratiation is a specific form of impression management whereby the employee deliberately tries to appear favourable to others through flattery, conformity, or attractive appearance.

- Self-fulfilling prophecy is another perceptual phenomenon in which one person inaccurately perceives a second person and the resulting expectations cause the second person to act in ways consistent with the original perception.

- Many perceptual errors occur in organizations, including halo effect, primacy and recency effects, attribution errors, projection, and stereotyping.

- To minimize perceptual errors, organizational members should become more aware of them; postpone their impression of others; try to empathize with others; compare their perceptions with colleagues; and become more aware of their own values, beliefs, and prejudices that may influence the perceptual process.
- Personality refers to the relatively stable and consistent attributes of people that help to explain their behaviour. Personality is shaped by both heredity and environmental factors.
- Personality traits influence the effectiveness of some job design activities and leadership styles. They also affect the types of jobs in which people are interested. The extent to which personality traits affect job performance is still unclear.
- In addition to personal motives and Type A/B personalities described in earlier chapters, some commonly mentioned traits include authoritarianism, dogmatism, locus of control, and self-monitoring.

DISCUSSION QUESTIONS

1. What characteristics of an object affect whether you will notice it?
2. What effect do attributions have on our perception of others? What are the consequences of making attribution errors?
3. Comment on the following statement: "Impression management is a devious tactic to get one's way."
4. Explain how self-fulfilling prophecies affect employee performance.
5. How can the Johari Window help us to perceive things more accurately?
6. Is an individual's personality formed genetically or through socialization? Explain your response.
7. Why might high self-monitors be better at impression management?
8. What's wrong with stereotyping people in organizational settings?

NOTES

1. J. Lyon, *Dome: The Rise and Fall of the House that Jack Built* (Toronto: Macmillan of Canada, 1983).
2. S. F. Cronshaw, and R. G. Lord, "Effects of Categorization, Attribution, and Encoding Processes on Leadership Perceptions," *Journal of Applied Psychology* 72 (1987), pp. 97–106.
3. P. R. Wilson, "Perceptual Distortion of Height as a Function of Ascribed Academic Status," *Journal of Social Psychology* 74 (1968), pp. 97–102.
4. D. C. Dearborn and H. A. Simon, "Selective Perception: A Note on the Departmental Identification of Executives," *Sociometry* 21 (1958), pp. 140–44.
5. S. J. Motowidlo, "Information Processing in Personnel Decisions," *Research in Personnel and Human Resources Management* 4 (1986), pp. 1–44.

6. E. T. Hall, *The Hidden Dimension* (Garden City, N.Y.: Doubleday, 1966).

7. J. M. Ivancevich, "Contrast Effects in Performance Evaluation and Reward Practices," *Academy of Management Journal* 26, no. 3 (1983), pp. 465–76.

8. B. English, "Orientation," *Canadian Business,* March 1988, pp. 58–72.

9. H. H. Kelley, *Attribution in Social Interaction* (Morristown, N.J.: General Learning Press, 1971).

10. T. A. Pyszczynski and J. Greenberg, "Role of Disconfirmed Expectations in the Instigation of Attributional Processing," *Journal of Personality and Social Psychology* 40 (1981), pp. 31–38.

11. H. H. Kelley, "The Processes of Causal Attribution," *American Psychologist* 28 (1973), pp. 107–28; J. M. Feldman, "Beyond Attribution Theory: Cognitive Processes in Performance Appraisal," *Journal of Applied Psychology* 66 (1981), pp. 127–48; and D. Tjosvold, "The Effects of Attribution and Social Context on Superiors' Influence and Interaction with Low-Performing Subordinates," *Personnel Psychology* 38 (Summer 1985), pp. 361–76.

12. J. D. Ford, "The Effects of Causal Attributions on Decision Makers' Responses to Performance Downturns," *Academy of Management Review* 10 (1985), pp. 770–86; and M. J. Martinko and W. L. Gardner, "The Leader/Member Attribution Process," *Academy of Management Review* 12 (1987), pp. 235–49.

13. M. G. Evans and L. T. Brown, "The Role of Attributions in the Performance Evaluation Process," *Proceedings of the Annual ASAC Conference, Organizational Behaviour Division* 10, pt. 7 (1989), pp. 31–38; T. R. Mitchell and R. E. Wood, "Supervisors' Responses to Subordinate Poor Performance: A Test of an Attribution Model," *Organizational Behavior and Human Performance* 25 (1980), pp. 123–38; A. de Carufel and J. Jabes, "Intuitive Prediction and Judgment on a Personnel Task by Naive and Experienced Judges," *Canadian Journal of Administrative Sciences* 1 (June 1984), pp. 78–94; and W. A. Knowlton and T. Mitchell, "Effects of Causal Attributions on a Supervisor's Evaluation of Subordinate Performance," *Journal of Applied Psychology* 65 (1980), pp. 459–66.

14. K. A. Brown, "Explaining Group Poor Performance: An Attributional Analysis," *Academy of Management Review* 9 (1984), pp. 54–63; and D. R. Norris and R. E. Niebuhr, "Attributional Influences on the Job Performance–Job Satisfaction Relationship," *Academy of Management Journal* 27 (1984), pp. 424–31.

15. R. A. Giacalone and P. Rosenfeld (eds.), *Impression Management in the Organization* (Hillsdale, N.J.: Lawrence Erlbaum Associates, 1989); William L. Gardner and M. J. Martinko, "Impression Management in Organizations," *Journal of Management* 14 (1988), pp. 321–38; E. Goffman, *The Presentation of Self in Everyday Life* (Garden City, N.Y.: Doubleday, 1959); and J. T. Tedeschi (ed.), *Impression Management Theory and Social Psychological Research* (New York: Academic Press, 1981).

16. E. E. Jones, *Ingratiation: A Social Psychological Analysis* (New York: Appleton-Century-Crofts, 1964); J. T. Tedeschi and V. Melburg, "Impression Management and Influence in the Organization," *Research in the Sociology of Organizations* 3 (1984), pp. 31–58; and A. MacGillivary, S. Ascroft, and M. Stebbins, "Meritless Ingratiation," *Proceedings of the Annual ASAC Conference, Organizational Behaviour Division* 7, pt. 7 (1986), pp. 127–35.

17. R. C. Liden and T. R. Mitchell, "Ingratiatory Behaviors in Organizational Settings," *Academy of Management Review* 13 (1988), pp. 572–87.

18. J. T. Molloy, *Dress for Success* (New York: Warner, 1975).

19. M. A. Iverson, "Attraction toward Flatterers of Different Statuses," *Journal of Social Psychology* 74 (1968), pp. 181–87.

20. J. A. Czepiel, M. R. Solomon, and C. F. Surprenant, *The Service Encounter* (Lexington, Mass.: Lexington Books, 1985); and D. E. Bowen, C. Siehl, and B. Schneider, "A Framework for Analyzing Customer Service Orientations in Manufacturing," *Academy of Management Review* 14 (1989), pp. 75–95.

21. M. Strauss, "Fur Flies at CBC," *Globe and Mail,* August, 9, 1983, pp. 1–2.

22. R. H. G. Field, "The Self-Fulfilling Prophecy Leader: Achieving the Metherme Effect," *Journal of Management Studies* 26 (March 1989), pp. 151–75; D. Eden, *Pygmalion in Management* (Lexington, Mass.: Lexington, 1990); and L. Jussim, "Self-Fulfilling Prophecies: A Theoretical and Integrative Review," *Psychological Review* 93 (1986), pp. 429–45.

23. Similar models are presented in R. H. G. Field and D. A. Van Seters, "Management by Expectations (MBE): The Power of Positive Prophecy," *Journal of General Management* 14 (Winter 1988), pp. 19–33; D. Eden, "Self-Fulfilling Prophecy as a Management Tool: Harnessing Pygmalion," *Academy of Management Review* 9 (1984), pp. 64–73; and R. L. Dipboye, "Self-Fulfilling Prophecies in the Selection-Recruitment Interview," *Academy of Management Review* 7 (1982), pp. 579–86.

24. R. Rosenthal and L. Jacobson, *Pygmalion in the Classroom: Teacher Expectation and Student Intellectual Development* (New York: Holt, Rinehart, & Winston, 1968); and J. B. Dusek (ed.), *Teacher Expectancies* (Hillsdale, N.J.: Erlbaum, 1985).

25. M. J. Harris and R. Rosenthal, "Mediation of Interpersonal Expectancy Effects: 31 Meta-Analyses," *Psychological Bulletin* 97 (1985), pp. 363–86.

26. D. Eden and A. B. Shani, "Pygmalion Goes to Boot Camp: Expectancy, Leadership, and Trainee Performance," *Journal of Applied Psychology* 67 (1982), pp. 194–99.

27. A. S. King, "Self-Fulfilling Prophecies in Training the Hard-Core: Supervisors' Expectations and the Underprivileged Workers' Performance," *Social Science Quarterly* 52 (1971), pp. 369–78; and K. S. Crawford, E. D. Thomas, and J. J. Fink, "Pygmalion at Sea: Improving the Work Effectiveness of Low Performers," *Journal of Applied Behavioral Science* 16 (1980), pp. 482–505.

28. W. H. Cooper, "Ubiquitous Halo," *Psychological Bulletin* 90 (1981), pp. 218–44; and R. Jacobs and S. Kozlowski," A Closer Look at Halo Error in Performance Ratings," *Academy of Management Journal* 28 (1985), pp. 201–12.

29. S. Kozlowski, M. Kirsch, and G. Chao, "Job Knowledge, Ratee Familiarity, Conceptual Similarity, and Halo Error: An Exploration," *Journal of Applied Psychology* 71 (1986), pp. 45–49; and H. C. Min, "Country Image: Halo or Summary Construct?" *Journal of Marketing Research* 26 (1989), pp. 222–29.

30. H. J. Bernardin and R. W. Beatty, *Performance Appraisal: Assessing Human Behavior at Work* (Boston: Kent, 1984).

31. C. L. Kleinke, *First Impressions: The Psychology of Encountering Others* (Englewood Cliffs, N.J.: Prentice Hall, 1975); and N. Anderson, "Information Integration Theory: A Brief Survey," in David H. Krantz (ed.), *Contemporary Developments in Mathematical Psychology* (San Fransisco: W. H. Freeman, 1974), pp. 236–305.

32. B. M. Springbett, "Factors Affecting the Final Decision in the Employment Interview," *Canadian Journal of Psychology* 12 (1958), pp. 13–22; and R. D. Arvey and J. E. Campion, "The Employment Interview: A Summary and Review of Recent Research," *Personnel Psychology* 35 (1982), pp. 281–322.

33. D. D. Steiner and J. S. Rain, "Immediate and Delayed Primacy and Recency Effects in Performance Evaluation," *Journal of Applied Psychology* 74 (1989), pp. 136–42; R. L. Heneman and K. N. Wexley, "The Effects of Time Delay in Rating and Amount of Information Observed in Performance Rating Accuracy," *Academy of Management Journal* 26 (1983), pp. 677–86; and H. J. Bernardin and R. L. Cardy, "Appraisal Accuracy: The Ability and Motivation to Remember the Past," *Public Personnel Management* 11 (1982), pp. 352–57.

34. D. G. Linz and S. Penrod, "Increasing Attorney Persuasiveness in the Courtroom," *Law and Psychology Review* 8 (1984), pp. 1–47.

35. E. E. Jones and R. E. Nisbett, *The Actor and Observer: Perceptions of the Causes of Behavior* (New York: General Learning Press, 1971); and D. R. Ilgen and J. M. Feldman, "Performance Appraisal: A Process Focus," *Research in Organizational Behavior* 5 (1983), pp. 141–97.

36. S. G. Green and T. R. Mitchell, "Attributional Processes of Leader–Member Interactions," *Organizational Behavior and Human Performance* 23 (1979) pp. 429–58; and H. J. Bernardin and P. Villanova, "Performance Appraisal," in E. A. Locke (ed.), *Generalizing from Laboratory to Field Settings* (Lexington, Mass.: Lexington Books, 1986), pp. 43–62.

37. D. T. Miller and M. Ross, "Self-Serving Biases in the Attribution of Causality: Fact or Fiction?" *Psychological Bulletin* 82(1975) pp. 213–25.

38. J. R. Bettman and B. A. Weitz, "Attributions in the Board Room: Causal Reasoning in Corporate Annual Reports," *Administrative Science Quarterly* 28 (1983), pp. 165–83.

39. T. W. Costello and S. S. Zalkind, *Psychology in Administration: A Research Orientation* (Englewood Cliffs, N.J.: Prentice Hall, 1963), pp. 36–37; and G. G. Sherwood, "Self-Serving Biases in Person Perception: A Re-examination of Projection as a Mechanism of Defense," *Psychological Bulletin* 90 (1981), pp. 445–59.

40. L. Falkenberg, "Improving the Accuracy of Stereotypes within the Workplace," *Journal of Management* 16 (1990), pp. 107–18; and M. E. Heilman, "Sex Bias in Work Settings: The Lack of Fit Model," *Research in Organizational Behavior* 5 (1983), pp. 269–98.

41. S. M. Beck and P. G. Cherry, "How the Regulators See Us," *CA Magazine,* October 1987, pp. 40–44; and J. C. Gaa, "Accountants and Society," *CGA Magazine,* October 1988, pp. 19–26.

42. Plato, *The Republic* (translation by D. Lee) (Harmondsworth, England: Penguin, 1955), Part VII, Section 7.

43. D. E. Smith, "Training Programs for Performance Appraisal: A Review," *Academy of Management Review* 11, no. 1 (1986), pp. 22–40.

44. Costello and Zalkind, *Psychology in Administration: A Research Orientation,* p. 24.

45. Martinko and Gardner, "The Leader/Member Attribution Process," p. 245.

46. Field and Van Seters, "Management by Expectations (MBE): The Power of Positive Prophecy"; Eden, "Self-Fulfilling Prophecy as a Management Tool: Harnessing Pygmalion"; and D. Eden, "OD and Self-Fulfilling Prophecy: Boosting Productivity by Raising Expectations," *Journal of Applied Behavioral Science* 22 (1986), pp. 1–13.

47. G. Egan, *The Skilled Helper: A Model for Systematic Helping and Interpersonal Relating* (Belmont, Calif.: Brooks/Cole, 1975).

48. D. B. Fedor and K. M. Rowland, "Investigating Supervisor Attributions of Subordinate Performance," *Journal of Management* 15 (1989), pp. 405–16; and T. R. Mitchell and L. S. Kalb, "Effects of Outcome Knowledge and Outcome Valence on Supervisors' Evaluations," *Journal of Applied Psychology* 66 (1981), pp. 604–12.

49. Falkenberg, "Improving the Accuracy of Stereotypes within the Workplace."

50. M. M. Starcevich, S. J. Stowell, and R. S. Yamahiro, "An Unusual Day of Development," *Training and Development Journal* 40 (March 1986), pp. 45–48.

51. J. Holushi, "New Team Spirit Starting to Pay Off in U.S. Auto Industry," *Globe and Mail,* December 30, 1987.

52. Costello and Zalkind, *Psychology in Administration: A Research Orientation,* pp. 45–46.

53. J. Luft, *Group Processes* (Palo Alto, Calif.: Mayfield Publishing, 1984). For a variation of this model, see J. Hall, "Communication Revisited," *California Management Review* 15 (Spring 1973), pp. 56–67.

54. Costello and Zalkind *Psychology in Administration: A Research Orientation,* p. 36.

55. L. C. Miller and D. A. Kenny, "Reciprocity of Self-Disclosure at the Individual and Dyadic Levels: A Social Relations Analysis," *Journal of Personality and Social Psychology* 50 (1986), pp. 713–19.

56. A. Kingston, "Trading Up," *Financial Times of Canada,* February 26, 1990, pp. 8–10; and D. McMurdy, "A Pushy Powerhouse at Merrill Lynch," *Financial Post,* March 8, 1989, p. 16.

57. W. Mischell, *Introduction to Personality* (New York: Holt, Rinehart, & Winston, 1971); and S. R. Maddi, *Personality Theories: A Comparative Analysis* (Homewood, Ill.: Dorsey Press, 1980).

58. S. Epstein, "The Stability of Behavior: I. On Predicting Most of the People Much of the Time," *Journal of Personality and Social Psychology* 37 (1979), 1097–1126.

59. H. M. Weiss and S. Adler, "Personality and Organizational Behavior," *Research in Organizational Behavior* 6 (1984), pp. 1–50.

60. S. D. Saleh, "Relational Orientation and Organizational Functioning: A Cross-Cultural Perspective," *Canadian Journal of Administrative Sciences* 4 (September 1987), pp. 276–93.

61. G. Hofstede, "Motivation, Leadership, and Organization: Do American Theories Apply Abroad?" *Organizational Dynamics,* Summer 1980, pp. 42–63. For a similar comparison of English Canadian students with their counterparts from France, see S. A. Ahmed and J. Jabes, "A Comparative Study of Job Values of Business Students in France and English Canada," *Canadian Journal of Administrative Sciences* 5 (June 1988), pp. 51–59.

62. B. M. Bass, *Stogdill's Handbook of Leadership* (New York: Free Press, 1981).

63. J. L. Holland, *Making Vocation Choices: A Theory of Careers* (Englewood Cliffs, N.J.: Prentice Hall, 1973); and J. T. Barnowe and P. J. Frost, "Person–Thing Specialization, University Experiences, and Students' Choice of Business Specialty," *Canadian Journal of Administrative Sciences* 4 (December 1987), pp. 469–78.

64. R. M. Guion and R. F. Gottier, "Validity of Personality Measures in Personnel Selection," *Personnel Psychology* 18 (1965), pp. 135–64; and N. Schmitt, R. Z. Gooding, R. A. Noe, and M. Kirsch, "Meta-Analyses of Validity Studies Published between 1964 and 1982 and the Investigation of Study Characteristics," *Personnel Psychology* 37 (1984), pp. 407–22.

65. D. V. Day and S. B. Silverman, "Personality and Job Performance: Evidence of Incremental Validity," *Personnel Psychology* 42 (1989), pp. 25–35; D. N. Jackson, A. C. Peacock, and J. P. Smith, "Impressions of Personality in the Employment Interview," *Journal of Personality and Social Psychology* 39 (1980), pp. 294–307; and D. N. Jackson, A. C. Peacock, and R. R. Holden, "Professional Interviewers' Trait Inferential Structures for Diverse Occupational Groups," *Organizational Behavior and Human Performance* 29 (1982), pp. 1–20.

66. C. Jung, *Collected Works,* H. Read, M. Fordham, and G. Adler (eds.) (Princeton, N.J.: Princeton University Press, 1953).

67. H. A. Simon, *Administrative Behavior* (New York: Free Press, 1957), p. xv.

68. T. W. Adorno, E. Frenkle-Brunswik, D. J. Levinson, and R. N. Sanford, *The Authoritarian Personality* (New York: Harper & Row, 1950).

69. M. Rokeach, *The Open and Closed Mind* (New York: Basic Books, 1960); and R. N. Taylor and M. D. Dunnette, "Influence of Dogmatism, Risk-Taking Propensity, and Intelligence on Decision-Making Strategies for a Sample of Industrial Managers," *Journal of Applied Psychology* 59 (1974), pp. 420–23.

70. P. E. Spector, "Behavior in Organizations as a Function of Employees' Locus of Control," *Psychological Bulletin* 91 (1982), pp. 482–97; and P. J. Andrisani and C. Nestel, "Internal–External Control as a Contributor to and Outcome of Work Experience," *Journal of Applied Psychology* 61 (1976), pp. 156–65.

71. D. Miller, M. F. R. Ket de Vries, and J. M. Toulouse, "Top Executive Locus of Control and Its Relationship to Strategy Making, Structure, and Environment," *Academy of Management Journal* 25 (1982), pp. 237–53.

72. C. R. Anderson, D. Hellriegel, and J. W. Slocum, Jr., "Managerial Response to Environmentally Induced Stress," *Academy of Management Journal* 20 (1977), pp. 260–72.

73. R. S. Adamson, R. J. Ellis, G. Deszca, and T. F. Cawsey, "Self-Monitoring and Leadership Emergence," *Proceedings of the Annual ASAC Conference, Organizational Behaviour Division* 5, pt. 5 (1984), pp. 9–15; and M. Snyder, "Persons, Situations, and the Control of Social Behavior," *Journal of Personality and Social Psychology* 32 (1975), pp. 637–44.

74. T. F. Cawsey, G. Deszca, R. J. Ellis, and R. S. Adamson, "Self-Monitoring and Interview Success," *Proceedings of the Annual ASAC Conference, Organizational Behaviour Division* 7, pt. 5 (1986), pp. 29–37.

CHAPTER CASE

NUPATH FOODS LTD.

James Ornath read the latest sales figures with a great deal of satisfaction. The vice-president of marketing at Nupath Foods Ltd. was pleased to see that the marketing campaign to improve sagging sales of Prowess cat food was working. Sales volume of the product had increased 20 percent in the past quarter compared with the previous year, and market share was up.

The improved sales of Prowess could be credited to Denise Roberge, the brand manager responsible for cat foods at Nupath. Roberge had joined Nupath less than two years ago as an assistant brand manager after leaving a similar job at a consumer products firm. She was one of the few women in marketing management at Nupath and had a promising career with the company. Ornath was pleased with Roberge's work and tried to let her know this in the annual performance reviews. He now had an excellent opportunity to reward her by offering the recently vacated position of market research coordinator. Although technically only a lateral transfer with a modest salary increase, the marketing research coordinator job would give Roberge broader experience in some high-profile work, which would enhance her career with Nupath. Few people were aware that Ornath's own career had been boosted by working as marketing research coordinator at Nupath several years before.

Denise Roberge had also seen the latest sales figures on Prowess cat food and was expecting Ornath's call to meet with her that morning. Ornath began the conversation by briefly mentioning the favourable sales figures, and then explained that he wanted Roberge to take the marketing research coordinator job. Roberge was shocked by the news. She enjoyed brand management and particularly the challenge involved with controlling a product that directly affected the company's profitability. Marketing research coordinator was a technical support position—a ''backroom'' job—far removed from the company's bottom-line activities. Marketing research was not the route to top management in most organizations, Roberge thought. She had been sidelined.

After a long silence, Roberge managed a weak ''Thank you, Mr. Ornath.'' She was too bewildered to protest. She wanted to collect her thoughts and reflect on what she had done wrong. Also, she did not know her boss well enough to be openly critical. Ornath recognized Roberge's surprise, which he naturally assumed was her positive response to hearing of this wonderful career opportunity. He, too, had been delighted several years earlier about his temporary transfer to marketing research to round out his marketing experience. ''This move will be good for both you and Nupath,'' said Ornath as he escorted Roberge from his office.

Roberge had several tasks to complete that afternoon, but was able to consider the day's events that evening. She was one of the top women in brand management at Nupath and feared that she was being sidelined because the company didn't want women in top management. Her previous employer had made it quite clear that women ''couldn't take the heat'' in marketing management and tended to place women in technical support positions after a brief term in lower brand management jobs. Obviously Nupath was following the same game plan. Ornath's comments that the coordinator job would be good for her was just a nice way of saying that Roberge couldn't go any further in brand management at Nupath. Roberge was now faced with the difficult decision of confronting Ornath and trying to change Nupath's sexist practises or submitting her resignation.

Discussion Questions

1. What symptom(s) exist in this case to suggest that something has gone wrong?
2. What are the root causes that have led to these symptoms?
3. What actions should the organization take to correct these problems?

© 1989 Steven L. McShane.

EXPERIENTIAL EXERCISE

MEASURING YOUR LOCUS OF CONTROL

Purpose: This exercise is designed to help you understand how some personality traits are measured and to give you a rough estimate of your level of internal or external locus of control.

Instructions: This questionnaire has 13 items, and each item has two statements. Read both statements carefully, then *select the one that you personally believe is more accurate.* For some items, you might believe that both are true or false, but you will tend to believe in one more than in the other. This is a measure of your personal beliefs, so there are no right or wrong answers.

When you have marked the preferred statement for all 13 items, turn to the scoring key at the end of this exercise and tally your score.

Question 1

a. Promotions are earned through hard work and persistence.
b. Getting promoted is really a matter of being a little luckier than the next person.

Question 2

a. Succeeding in your chosen occupation is mainly a matter of social contacts—knowing the right people.
b. Succeeding in your chosen occupation is mainly a matter of personal competence—how much you know.

Question 3

a. Achieving a successful marriage depends on the devotion and commitment of both partners to each other.
b. The most important element in a happy marriage is being lucky enough to marry the right person.

Question 4

a. It is silly to think that you can really change another person's basic attitudes.

b. When I am right, I can convince others.

Question 5

a. In our society, your future earning power depends on your ability.

b. Making a lot of money is largely a matter of getting the right breaks.

Question 6

a. I have little influence over the way other people behave.

b. If you know how to deal with people, you can lead them and get them to do what you want.

Question 7

a. In my case, the grades I receive are the result of my own efforts; luck has little or nothing to do with it.

b. Sometimes I feel that I have little control over the grades that I get.

Question 8

a. Marriage is largely a gamble that can end in divorce no matter how hard the partners try.

b. Most divorces could be avoided if both partners were determined to make their marriage work.

Question 9

a. Success in an occupation is mainly a matter of how much effort you put into it.

b. Success in an occupation is mainly a matter of luck—being in the right place at the right time.

Question 10

a. Often, the way teachers assign grades seems haphazard to me.

b. In my experience, I have noticed that there is usually a direct connection between how hard I study and the grades I get.

Question 11

a. People like me can change the course of world affairs if we make ourselves heard.

b. It is only wishful thinking to believe that you can really influence what happens in society at large.

Question 12

a. A great deal that happens to me is probably a matter of chance.

b. I control my fate.

Question 13

a. Getting along with people is a skill that must be practised.
b. It is almost impossible to figure out how to please some people.

Source: Adapted from J. B. Rotter, ''Internal Control–External Control: A Sampler,'' *Psychology Today*, June 1971, p. 42. Reprinted with permission from Psychology Today Magazine. Copyright © 1971 (P. T. Partners, L.P.).

Scoring: For each of the 13 items, one statement reflects an internal response and the other reflects an external response. For the odd-numbered items, the internal response is statement *a*. For the even-numbered items, the internal response is item *b*. Count up the total number of internal statements you selected to arrive at your locus of control score. Extreme internals would score between 10 and 13, whereas extreme externals would score between 0 and 3.

8

Work Attitudes

After reading this chapter, you should be able to:

Explain
Why managers should understand work attitudes.

Discuss
How beliefs and behavioural intentions relate to attitudes.

Describe
The relationship between job satisfaction and
job performance.

Explain
Why organizations should build a loyal work force.

Distinguish
Attitudinal commitment from continuance commitment.

List
The factors that enhance persuasive communication.

Describe
Two forms of employment discrimination.

Mark O'Neill/Financial Post

Philip Orsino loves doors. "I'm an evangelist of the door industry. I live and breathe doors." Fortunately, Orsino is also the president and chief executive officer of Toronto-based Premdor, the world's largest door manufacturer. Says Orsino, "I consider myself a very lucky person that I love to come to work every day."[1]

Jacqueline Koerner has had a less satisfactory work experience. Koerner joined a major Canadian bank in its commercial training program after completing a master's degree in trade and finance and garnering several years' experience assembling financial packages for small companies. She expected to enter a challenging position with enough autonomy to provide some creative solutions for her employer, but it didn't work out that way. "I got exceedingly frustrated," she says. "I had to go and ask before I could make a decision about even the smallest thing." Koerner quit the banking job after only one year.[2]

Work attitudes are an everyday part of organizational life. A supervisor complains about completing the monthly payroll forms; a coworker comments favourably about recent pay increases; a client tells an employee that she enjoys doing business with this organization. These statements reflect people's attitudes toward a variety of objects or events.

This chapter looks at work attitudes—how they are formed, how they can be changed, and how they relate to organizational behaviour. The chapter begins with a brief discussion of the definition and importance of studying work attitudes. Next, a basic model of work attitudes is introduced, which helps to explain how attitudes are typically formed and how they relate to behaviour. We then look at two work attitudes—job satisfaction and organizational commitment—with particular emphasis on their implications for organizational behaviour. Next, we turn to the important topic of persuasion as a means of changing work attitudes. The final section of this chapter introduces the important topic of employment discrimination, including the issues of prejudicial attitudes and systemic discrimination.

WHAT ARE ATTITUDES?

attitudes
An individual's feelings toward a person, group, event, idea or any other attitude object.

Attitudes are emotional predispositions to respond consistently toward an attitude object.[3] (An attitude object is an object, person, group, event, idea or anything else about which we might have an attitude.) In other words, attitudes represent pleasant or unpleasant feelings toward the attitude object. They are judgments about where things fall along a good–bad or positive–negative continuum. Your attitude toward coworkers is reflected in the extent to which you like or dislike them. You may have a positive attitude toward clients because you have positive feelings toward them, whereas you may have a negative emotional response to your supervisor.

A few writers suggest that attitudes are mainly influenced by personality and, consequently, are relatively stable across situations.[4] However, the generally accepted view is that our attitudes tend to change as the situation changes. Personality characteristics may have some influence on attitudes, but the situation has a more powerful effect.[5]

Attitudes motivate us to act in a certain way toward the attitude object. Consider the engineer who receives poor service from a technical instrument manufacturer and vows "I'll never buy from that supplier again!" The engineer not only has a negative attitude toward the manufacturer, but also has a predisposition to avoid buying its products. Generally, attitudes lead to behaviour. However, the attitude–behaviour link is complex, as we will discuss more fully later in the chapter.

WHY STUDY WORK ATTITUDES?

There is little doubt that work attitudes are an important part of organizational behaviour and, in particular, the effective management of employees. Experts have presented numerous reasons why managers should understand the dynamics of work attitudes.[6] We will mention a few of them here (see Exhibit 8–1).

Attitudes and Behaviour.   As we have stated, attitudes influence behaviour. In fact, certain negative work attitudes are important indicators of potentially costly behaviours such as turnover, absenteeism, sabotage, and lower

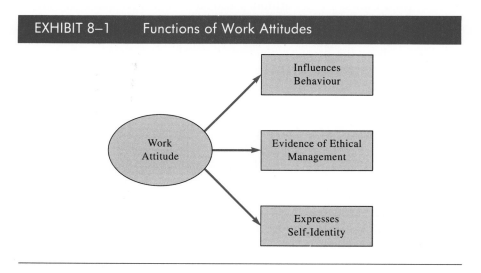

EXHIBIT 8–1   Functions of Work Attitudes

Work Attitude → Influences Behaviour

Work Attitude → Evidence of Ethical Management

Work Attitude → Expresses Self-Identity

PERSPECTIVE 8-1   Hiding Low Morale in the Canadian Public Service

In 1986, David Zussman and Jak Jabes published a study for the Treasury Board that the Canadian government did not want to hear. The University of Ottawa professors discovered that 26 percent of senior federal bureaucrats believed there was a serious morale problem in their organizations. Privy Council Clerk Paul Tellier (Canada's top civil servant) rushed to diffuse the situation by instructing his deputy ministers to communicate a good news message: THERE IS NO MORALE PROBLEM!

In spite of the deputy ministers' best attempts to deny the problem, discussion of morale problems in Canada's public service continued. The Ottawa branch of an international management association proposed a conference in 1988 to discuss the matter, but a federal election was looming and the government was not pleased with the idea of a conference further publicizing morale problems in the federal bureaucracy. So the association agreed to postpone the conference until the spring of 1989, several months after the election.

At the 1989 conference a second Zussman–Jabes study was presented, in which the authors reported that fully 40 percent of the government's senior executives now believed that there was a serious morale problem. A few months earlier, they had published other findings showing that managers in the federal public service were significantly less satisfied with most aspects of their jobs than were their counterparts in the private sector. This time no one could deny that morale problems existed among federal government employees.

Sources: S. Cameron, "Low Morale May Not Be the Worst of It for the Federal Public Service," *Globe and Mail*, May 18, 1989, p. A2; J. Jabes and D. Zussman, "Motivation, Rewards, and Satisfaction in the Canadian Public Service," *Canadian Public Administration* 31 (1988), pp. 204–25; and C. Kent, "How Low Can It Go?" *Ottawa Business Life*, April 1989, pp. 22–26, 40.

productivity. Monitoring work attitudes and taking corrective action can significantly improve the organization's financial status.[7] Attitudes are early warning signals for future behaviour problems.

Attitudes and Ethics.   Work attitudes also have ethical implications.[8] Many work attitudes, such as job satisfaction, are often viewed as proxies for the degree to which the company has maintained individual rights, provided the greatest good for the greatest number of people, and distributed rewards equitably. Management is rightfully proud when employee morale is strong because that demonstrates the high quality of management and its humanitarianism. Conversely, corporate leaders may be quick to hide or deny evidence of negative employee work attitudes, as was the case in the Canadian public service described in Perspective 8–1.

Attitudes and Self-Identity.   Finally, work attitudes shape and express an individual's self-identity.[9] People tend to express their attitudes not only to influence others, but also to let coworkers know more about themselves. Expressing our attitudes helps others understand the values we hold strongly. For example, by giving the impression that you dislike loafers on the job, you are telling others that you value the work ethic. This self-expression clarifies and communicates your self-identity to others and provides significant others with characteristics that make you unique.

FORMING WORK ATTITUDES

How are attitudes formed? This is an important question because by understanding this process we can begin to see how to change attitudes and possibly prevent people from forming inappropriate ones. Attitude formation is also the first part of a model of work attitudes that ultimately leads to work behaviours. To explain how attitudes are formed, we must first examine the beliefs that are associated with the attitude object.

Characteristics of Beliefs

Beliefs refer to our perceptions of reality and, more specifically, to the features we associate with attitude objects. The statement, "My supervisor intimidates new employees," is a belief because it describes a characteristic of a supervisor (the attitude object in this example). Notice that the statement does not evaluate the supervisor; it does not explicitly say that the supervisor is good or bad, but simply states a perceived attribute of the supervisor.

beliefs
An individual's perceptions of an attitude object's characteristics.

Beliefs may be formed from past experiences, information from others, or logical deduction.[10] We might believe that the supervisor intimidates new employees because, as a newcomer, we were intimidated by that supervisor. Alternatively, we may have heard about this characteristic from coworkers even though we have not directly observed the supervisor acting this way. Finally, we might have observed the supervisor act abruptly to people in other situations and inferred that he or she would also act this way to new staff.

Social Construction of Beliefs

Beliefs are perceptions of reality, so they are often inaccurate and subject to the perceptual errors described in the previous chapter. According to some writers, a major influence on our beliefs is the social context in which we exist.[11] In other words, our construction of reality may be based more on what others tell us than on objective experience.[12]

This influence is particularly strong as we enter new work roles. This is demonstrated in a classic study of nonmanagement employees before and after becoming either union stewards or supervisors. Those who became supervisors had developed more pro-management and anti-union attitudes, whereas those who had become union stewards had become significantly more pro-union. Two years later some supervisors were sent back to the nonmanagement ranks due to economic recession. Before long, they had returned to the more pro-union sentiments previously experienced as nonmanagement employees. Meanwhile, those who were still supervisors continued to be strongly pro-management and anti-union. These results show that our attitudes can change with the roles we enter and the people with whom we interact.[13]

Forming Attitudes from Beliefs

Whether or not beliefs are accurate, they do form the basis of new attitudes. In most situations, an attitude toward something is a result of a person's beliefs about the characteristics of that object as well as existing attitudes about those characteristics. Attitudes are basically the weighted sum of our feelings toward the attributes of the attitude object. As you develop beliefs about an attitude object, you simultaneously form an attitude toward it. The direction (i.e., positive or negative) and strength of that attitude depend on how you feel about the things you associate with the object.

The example in Exhibit 8–2 helps to illustrate this important point. Let us suppose that the hypothetical person in our example holds the following three beliefs about labour unions:

* Labour unions improve fair employment practices.
* Labour unions reduce management autonomy.
* Labour unions increase wages.

These statements describe three perceived characteristics or attributes of labour unions. The individual already has clear attitudes about these attributes. Specifically, as Exhibit 8–2 shows, this person strongly approves of fair employment practices (+ +), dislikes the infringement of management autonomy (−), and favours higher wages (+).

We can now see how our hypothetical coworker's attitude toward labour unions has been formed. The attitude is quite favourable (+ +) because

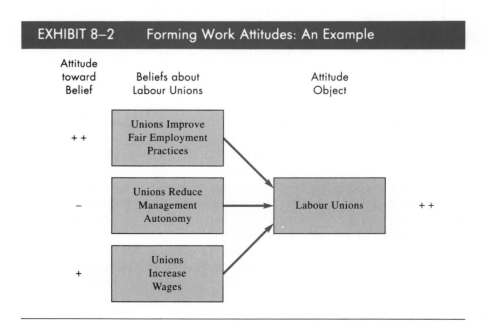

EXHIBIT 8–2   Forming Work Attitudes: An Example

Attitude toward Belief

Beliefs about Labour Unions

Attitude Object

+ +   Unions Improve Fair Employment Practices

−   Unions Reduce Management Autonomy   →   Labour Unions   + +

+   Unions Increase Wages

labour unions are associated with fair employment practices and higher wages and the individual has positive feelings toward both of these attributes. The negative sentiment toward reducing management autonomy somewhat reduces the individual's favourable attitude toward labour unions, but not enough to offset the positive characteristics of this attitude object.

The process of forming attitudes is much more complex than this, but we will mention just one more point. The example in Exhibit 8–2 shows a solid line between the three attributes and the attitude object. This suggests complete certainty that the attitude object possesses these features. In reality, of course, people are not perfectly certain about some of their beliefs. In our example, the person might believe that unions *likely* (rather than *definitely*) increase wages. Under these conditions, the attitude toward higher wages would have less influence on the person's attitude toward labour unions because of this uncertainty. This is why we say that an attitude is the *weighted* sum of our feelings toward the attributes of the attitude object. Attitudes toward higher wages and other attributes are weighted by the perceived certainty that they are characteristics of the attitude object.

WORK ATTITUDES AND BEHAVIOUR

The definition presented earlier says that attitudes are predispositions to respond to an attitude object. This means that feelings toward something motivate us to behave in certain ways toward that attitude object. The problem is that our predisposition to do something is not always translated into actual behaviour or, at least, not the behaviour we assume will result from the attitude.

Behavioural Intentions

To understand how attitudes lead to behaviour, we first need to look at an intermediate step in the process, called **behavioural intentions.** Behavioural intentions represent a motivation to perform a particular behaviour. You might hear people say that they want to wear their safety glasses. Others are unwilling to work with certain employees. Still others say that they will try to serve clients more efficiently. These are all examples of behavioural intentions. In each case, the person intends to behave in a certain way.

Attitudes influence behaviour through the behavioural intentions to engage in that behaviour. Specifically, attitudes lead to behavioural intentions which, in turn, influence actual behaviour.[14] Consider the model of work attitudes and behaviour shown in Exhibit 8–3, in which an employee is dissatisfied with the level of pay and pay practices. These attitudes are formed by the four beliefs shown in the diagram. In this example, pay dissatisfaction leads to three behavioural intentions: asking for a raise, looking for a better-paying job, wanting a labour union. Each behaviourai intention reflects the person's willingness to do something with respect to the attitude

behavioural intentions
An individual's intention (i.e., motivation) to perform a particular behaviour.

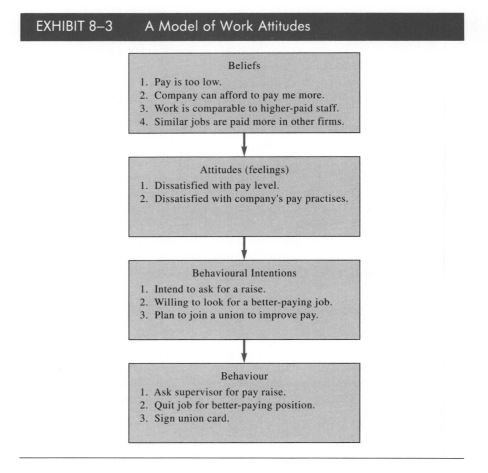

EXHIBIT 8–3   A Model of Work Attitudes

Beliefs
1. Pay is too low.
2. Company can afford to pay me more.
3. Work is comparable to higher-paid staff.
4. Similar jobs are paid more in other firms.

Attitudes (feelings)
1. Dissatisfied with pay level.
2. Dissatisfied with company's pay practises.

Behavioural Intentions
1. Intend to ask for a raise.
2. Willing to look for a better-paying job.
3. Plan to join a union to improve pay.

Behaviour
1. Ask supervisor for pay raise.
2. Quit job for better-paying position.
3. Sign union card.

objects (i.e., pay level and pay practises). Also notice that these intentions are relatively consistent with each other and with the underlying attitude. They all deal with behaviour to improve the person's level of pay and pay practises, and they all reflect the person's dissatisfaction with them.

Linking Work Attitudes to Behaviour

Behavioural intentions are better than attitudes at predicting behaviour. We can be much more certain that employees will ask their supervisor for a pay raise if we know that they intend to do so than if we only know that they are dissatisfied with their pay. The reason for this is that people with the same work attitudes develop different behavioural intentions. Some employees who are dissatisfied with their pay are quick to complain about this situation, whereas others would rather quit than approach their supervisor. People form different behavioural intentions because they have different perceptions of behavioural outcomes and hold different attitudes toward those outcomes.[15] For instance, some people prefer to change jobs rather than ask for a pay raise because they may have experienced little success in the past when asking for a raise.

But even strong behavioural intentions do not guarantee that employees will actually engage in that behaviour because *situational contingencies* weaken the attitude-behaviour relationship. In the context of work attitudes, these contingencies intervene between a behavioural intention and its associated behaviour. You may intend to have no absenteeism during the next month, but illness or something beyond your control prevents that intention from coming true. Similarly, dissatisfied employees may want to find another job but fail to do so because few alternatives exist during an economic recession. This also suggests that specific behavioural intentions are better than general behavioural intentions at predicting specific behaviours because they take contingencies into account.[16]

Cognitive Dissonance

Our model of work attitudes presents the idea that beliefs and attitudes lead to behaviours. Yet there are situations in which behaviours lead to beliefs and attitudes. People experience an uncomfortable tension, called **cognitive dissonance,** when their beliefs, attitudes, behavioural intentions, and behaviours are inconsistent with one another. To reduce this dissonance, people tend to change their attitudes so that they are more closely aligned with past behaviours.[17] Cognitive dissonance is most common when the dissonant behaviour is:

cognitive dissonance
A state of anxiety that occurs when an individual's beliefs, attitudes, behavioural intentions, and behaviours are inconsistent with one another.

- *Public*—Other people have good evidence that you engaged in the behaviour; for example, coworkers saw you shake hands with a rival employee.

- *Explicit*—You can't deny the nature of your action; for example, it is clear to others that you shook hands with a rival rather than took some other action.

- *Irreversible*—You can't undo the behaviour; a handshake is forever recorded in history.

- *Volitional*—It is apparent that you engaged in the act without coercion; for example, you cannot claim that your boss made you shake hands with the rival.

Cognitive dissonance is best described through an example. Suppose you reluctantly volunteer to take a foreign assignment on the assumption that foreign postings are necessary prerequisites to promotions into senior management. During the assignment, however, you learn that your assumption is incorrect: many people become senior managers in this firm without spending any time on foreign assignments. Research has found that people in this situation tend to change their beliefs and attitudes so that they are more consistent with the behaviour.[18] You might convince yourself that the foreign posting is not so bad after all because it will develop your management skills, or you might downplay the features that made the foreign posting undesirable in the first place. Eventually, your negative attitude toward foreign assignments changes to a more favourable one.

JOB SATISFACTION

job satisfaction
An individual's attitude toward the job and work context.

Job satisfaction represents a person's emotional reaction toward various aspects of work. It is one of the most important and widely studied work attitudes, partly because work is the place where most people expect to receive much of their life satisfaction.[19] In this respect, job satisfaction is closely associated with life satisfaction and self-identity. Employee **morale** is similar to job satisfaction in the sense that it typically refers to an emotional reaction to work, but morale usually applies to attitudes of the work team rather than the individual and may also refer to team cohesiveness and commitment.

morale
The collective attitude of members of a work team toward the job, team, and organization.

Although we often speak about job satisfaction as a single attitude, it is actually a collection of attitudes pertaining to specific aspects of the job, called **job satisfaction facets**.[20] There are many facets of job satisfaction, a sample of which is listed in Exhibit 8–4.

job satisfaction facets
Attitudes regarding specific aspects (i.e., facets) of the job and work context.

People can be satisfied with some facets of the job while simultaneously dissatisfied with others. Different types of satisfaction/dissatisfaction will lead to different intentions and behaviour. For example, you might complain to your supervisor if your pay is too low but not if you dislike your coworkers. Instead, dissatisfaction with coworkers might motivate you to ask for a transfer to another department or work team. The important point to remember is that there are many facets of job satisfaction that are associated with different aspects of the job and have different effects on employee behaviour.

EXHIBIT 8–4   Some Facets of Job Satisfaction

Competence of coworkers	Pay practises
Control over pace of work	Promotion decisions
Employee benefits	Promotional opportunities
Friendliness of coworkers	Quality of work materials
Helpfulness of coworkers	Recognition of accomplishments
Hours of work	Supervisor's emotional support
Layout of work area	Supervisor's technical support
Opportunity to practise skills	Variety of work tasks
Participation in decisions	Ventilation of work area
Pay level	Workload

While there are many aspects of job satisfaction, we can also refer to an employee's overall or global job satisfaction. **Global job satisfaction** is a composite attitude representing a unique combination of the person's feelings toward the different job satisfaction facets. Satisfaction with the work itself is usually an important component of overall satisfaction, but this varies among employees and across time. Some people emphasize pay satisfaction when they talk about their overall job satisfaction, while others may be thinking mostly about their physical working conditions.

global job satisfaction

A composite attitude representing a unique combination of a person's feelings toward the different job satisfaction facets.

A Model of Job Satisfaction

What determines the degree to which employees are satisfied or dissatisfied with their jobs? To date, the best explanation is provided by two concepts: *discrepancy theory* and *equity theory*.[21] Both concepts are adopted in the model of job satisfaction shown in Exhibit 8–5.

Discrepancy theory states that the level of job satisfaction is determined by the discrepancy between what people expect to receive and what they actually experience (i.e., actual perceptions of the job). Employees form expectations about different aspects of the job and compare them with their perceptions of reality. As Exhibit 8–5 illustrates, job satisfaction or dissatisfaction results from this comparison. Job dissatisfaction occurs when the received condition is noticeably less or worse than the expected condition. Job satisfaction improves as the person's expectations are met or exceeded (up to a point).

discrepancy theory

A theory that partly explains job satisfaction and dissatisfaction in terms of the gap between what people expect to receive and what they actually receive.

EXHIBIT 8–5	A Model of Job Satisfaction

Source: Adapted from E. E. Lawler III, *Motivation in Work Organizations* (Monterey, Calif.: Brooks/Cole, 1973), p. 75.

Equity theory is also built into Exhibit 8–5. Recall from Chapter 3 that people compare their inputs and outcomes with referent others. Equity occurs when the person and comparison other have similar input/outcome ratios. Equity theory applies to the satisfaction model in two ways. First, notice that expectations are partly formed by comparing outcomes and inputs with others. For instance, the level of pay you expect to receive depends not only on what you offer to the job (i.e., your job inputs) and how much you earned previously, but also on a comparison of the inputs and outcomes with comparison others. If you believe that your work effort, skill, and other relevant inputs are higher than those of most coworkers, you will likely have higher expectations regarding certain rewards.

Second, equity theory explains why job satisfaction does not always continue to increase as the received condition exceeds expectations. As people receive much better outcomes than they expect, they typically develop feelings of guilt and a belief that management practises are unfair to others. At first, employees adjust their expectations upward when they are overrewarded. However, in extreme circumstances where the overreward cannot be justified, feelings of inequity persist and dissatisfaction with management practises may result.

In summary, discrepancy and equity theories predict that as reality meets and exceeds expectations, job satisfaction will increase. However, when the perceived job situation is so much better than expected that the overreward creates a feeling of guilt or unfairness, job satisfaction begins to decrease.

Job Satisfaction in Canada

How satisfied are Canadians with their jobs? According to a recent Environics study, 89 percent of Canadians claim to be very or somewhat satisfied with their jobs. This observation is consistent with similar surveys conducted by Environics over the previous decade.[22] It is also almost identical to the results of a 1974 survey of Canadian work attitudes conducted by the federal government, and is comparable to other national attitude surveys.[23]

But is worker morale in Canada really this positive? It is unlikely that most Canadians are actually unhappy with their jobs, but these findings may be somewhat inflated because national attitude surveys typically rely on the single direct question "How satisfied are you with your job?" Dissatisfied employees may be reluctant to reveal their feelings in a direct question because this is tantamount to admitting that they made a poor job choice and are not enjoying life. The threat to self-esteem is so great that many downplay the negative aspects of work or consciously report higher job satisfaction than they actually feel.[24]

The biasing effect of a single direct question becomes apparent when the same employees are asked whether they would choose the same kind of work if they could start all over again. The Environics survey found that while most Canadians say they are reasonably happy with their jobs, almost half of them would choose another type of work if given the chance.[25] This contradiction further supports the idea that job satisfaction isn't quite as high as direct questions indicate.

Finally, surveys reporting that Canadians are *generally* satisfied with their jobs also indicate that people are less satisfied with *specific facets* of their jobs. Consider, for example, the results presented in Exhibit 8–6. While 89 percent of Canadian employees claim to be happy with their jobs overall, only 56 percent are satisfied with promotional opportunities and 65 percent are happy with their level of participation in organizational decisions.

Job Satisfaction and Work Behaviours

Job satisfaction is an important work attitude not only because it indicates how well the company treats its employees, but also because it has been associated with a variety of important work behaviours. Some of the more prominent effects of job satisfaction are described below.

Turnover.   Employees with higher levels of job satisfaction are consistently less likely to quit their jobs.[26] Researchers have explained, however, that turnover is affected only to the extent that job satisfaction leads to related behavioural intentions, such as the intention to search for another job. The satisfaction–turnover relationship is also influenced by the level of unemployment and the employee's perceived opportunity to find other employment. Specifically, dissatisfied employees tend to quit their jobs when several job opportunities exist.[27]

Absenteeism.   Job dissatisfaction, particularly with the work itself, tends to be related to higher levels of absenteeism.[28] Of course, some absenteeism is due mainly to factors beyond the employee's control, such as an injury or a

EXHIBIT 8–6	Job Satisfaction in Canada					
		Specific Facets of Job Satisfaction				
Level of Job Satisfaction	**General Job Satisfaction**	**Pay**	**Security**	**Benefits**	**Promotion**	**Participation**
Very satisfied	51	30	41	34	24	35
Somewhat satisfied	38	43	32	27	32	30
Somewhat dissatisfied	8	18	13	14	18	17
Very dissatisfied	2	8	10	13	15	13
Don't know/not applicable	1	1	4	12	11	5
Total	100	100	100	100	100	100

Source: R. Maynard, "How Do You Like Your Job?" *Report on Business Magazine*, November 1987, p. 115.

PERSPECTIVE 8–2   No Payoff for Job Dissatisfaction

Kim Bertram resented the way he was treated by his employer, Canada Trust. As a hard-driving loans officer and second in command at the Don Mills branch, Bertram felt that the company neither appreciated his efforts nor provided just rewards for them. In 1983, he received termination pay and moved to the Canada Permanent Trust Company as a result of some mishap at the main Toronto branch in which he believes he was scapegoated. A merger between the Permanent and Canada Trust caused Bertram to be once again employed by his former employer in 1986, but his relations with Canada Trust were still strained.

Bertram was a workaholic who received an achievement award for bringing in over $1 million in new business to the once-sleepy Don Mills branch. He trained new staff on his own time and came in weekends to complete transactions, but the branch couldn't keep up with the paperwork because it simply wasn't staffed to handle the volume of loans he

was generating. In December 1987, Bertram received a letter from management saying that he would be fired if the operation didn't shape up. Moreover, his earlier-promised pay raise was delayed as a result of the reprimand. Bertram also wasn't getting along with the branch manager at Don Mills and he believed that he deserved to manage a branch of his own.

Many people might be justifiably dissatisfied with their jobs in this situation. Some might even harbour fantasies of vengeance. But Bertram took it one step further by planning an elaborate scheme in which he and Ken Wood (a former Canada Trust employee, also disgruntled) would embezzle Canada Trust funds to the tune of $4.5 million.

The trust company had recently introduced Powerline, a personal credit product that Bertram had actually warned colleagues was vulnerable to fraud. By setting up a fictitious company and bypassing Canada Trust's security system, Bertram and Wood

blinding snowstorm.[29] Yet even in these extreme events, dedicated employees have been known to battle the elements or literally leave their hospital beds to attend work. Others would be absent at the slight hint of rain or an oncoming head cold.[30]

Physical and Mental Health.   Employees who are dissatisfied with their jobs are more likely to suffer mental and physical health problems.[31] For example, those with negative attitudes toward some aspects of their jobs may experience a loss of appetite, ulcers, difficulty in sleeping, or even an emotional breakdown.

Deviant Behaviours.   A variety of illegal or marginal activities have been linked to job dissatisfaction, although they are relatively uncommon. Assembly line workers have been known to deliberately sabotage the production line or final product either to "get back" at management or to relieve job boredom.[32] Alcoholism and drug abuse have been associated with job dissatisfaction. Once again, monotonous work is often identified as the culprit. Finally, dissatisfied employees have been known to steal from their employers, particularly to correct feelings of inequity.[33] Perspective 8–2 provides an extreme, but very real, example of this. If management had been more sensitive to employee attitudes in this situation, the costly outcomes and embarrassing publicity may have been avoided.

created Powerline accounts using fraudulent names and started writing cheques against those accounts. To cover their tracks, addresses of the imaginary clients were changed soon after the accounts were activated and most of the embezzled money was wired to a bank in Switzerland.

The scam lasted fewer than four months. At one point Bertram and Wood were writing cheques totalling as much as $600,000 a day on phony Powerline accounts. The fraud generated such an impressive business record for the Don Mills branch that the branch manager gave Bertram and his loans department a half-day holiday in early May 1988. Ironically, Bertram's promised pay increase finally came through, just as he and Wood were about to flee to Europe.

In late May, one of Bertram's assistants noticed problems with paperwork on some of the Powerline accounts. Bertram and Wood quickly activated one of their escape plans by flying to Switzerland on the Victoria holiday weekend and removing their funds in cash from the Union Bank of Switzerland before Canadian authorities could trace the money. The two travelled throughout Europe that summer on false American passports, but they quickly grew weary of being fugitives from justice. On August 22, 1988, they were arrested in London where they had registered under their own names in a four-star hotel. Bertram and Wood waived their rights to the funds and did not contest extradition back to Canada. The two disgruntled Canada Trust employees are expecting jail sentences ranging from five to ten years.

Source: Based on S. Fife and J. Castrinos, "The Powerline Swindle," *Financial Times of Canada,* April 10, 1989, pp. 22–24.

Job Performance.   Contrary to the popular cliché that "a happy worker is a productive worker," the relationship between satisfaction and performance is relatively weak and there is no evidence that satisfaction directly *causes* performance.[34] On the contrary, according to various motivation theories (see Chapters 2 and 3), satisfied employees will produce less when their needs have been fulfilled.

An alternative explanation of the job satisfaction–performance relationship, depicted in Exhibit 8–7, is that job performance leads to job satisfaction when performance is linked to extrinsic rewards such as pay increases and promotions. Higher performers receive more rewards and, consequently, are more satisfied than low-performing employees, who receive fewer rewards. Not all organizations have a good pay-for-performance system so the performance–satisfaction relationship may be weakened. (This is illustrated in Exhibit 8–7 by the dotted line between performance and extrinsic rewards.) Even with a weak link between performance and organizational rewards, however, high-performing employees are more likely to be satisfied than low performers because they are more likely to experience intrinsic rewards such as a sense of achievement when the task is accomplished.[35]

It is reasonable to conclude from our discussion that job satisfaction is a laudable organizational objective. A satisfied work force benefits not only the organization, but also the individual, and, ultimately, society. Of course,

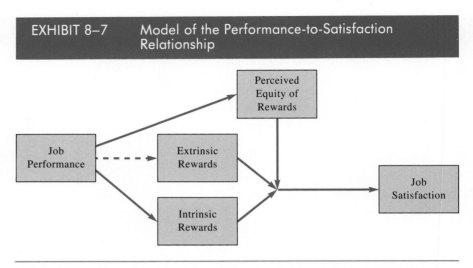

EXHIBIT 8–7   Model of the Performance-to-Satisfaction Relationship

Source: E. E. Lawler III and L. W. Porter, "The Effect of Performance on Job Satisfaction," *Industrial Relations* 7 (1967), pp. 20–28.

there are situations in which the objective of maximizing job satisfaction is in conflict with the objective of maximizing productivity. Managers must learn to find an appropriate balance.

ORGANIZATIONAL COMMITMENT

During the mid-1800s, Samuel Cunard founded the greatest steamship line ever to cover the Atlantic Ocean (Cunard Lines). The energetic Nova Scotian was able to make ship transportation dependable and safe, long before it was thought possible, by having the best ships, officers, and crew. He insisted on safety before profits and, by listening to his technical experts, was able to introduce the latest innovations. Above all, Cunard had the quaint notion that if you picked people well, paid them well, and treated them well, they would return the favour with loyalty and pride.[36]

Nearly 150 years later, business leaders still believe that **organizational commitment** plays an important role in maintaining an effective organization. Organizational commitment is typically defined as the strength of an individual's identification with and involvement in a particular organization.[37] This involves a strong belief in and acceptance of organizational goals and values, a willingness to exert considerable effort on behalf of the organization, and a strong desire to remain a member of the organization. Commitment develops more slowly and is more stable than job satisfaction and many other work attitudes.[38] Although some researchers make a subtle distinction between organizational commitment and **employee loyalty,** we will use these terms interchangeably.

organizational commitment
A complex attitude pertaining to the strength of an individual's identification with and involvement in a particular organization; includes a strong acceptance of organizational goals, as well as a motivation to work for and remain with the organization.

employee loyalty
A term commonly used to refer to organizational commitment.

Several recent articles suggest that employees are not as dedicated to their organizations as they once were. Layoffs, mergers, poor management practises, and increasing employee expectations have combined to make loyalty a luxury rather than the norm in some employment relationships.[39] Even more disappointing, according to one recent survey, is that Canadians seem to have a much lower level of pride in their organizations than their American counterparts.[40] If corporate leaders in the United States are worried about declining organizational commitment, then Canadian leaders should perhaps be even more concerned!

Is Employee Loyalty Good for the Organization?

Should managers work to build organizational commitment? Should they be concerned about the apparent decline in employee loyalty? Numerous studies on this issue conclude that organizational commitment does increase organizational effectiveness in a variety of ways. Only in cases of extreme loyalty are negative consequences expected.

Turnover and Absenteeism.   Employees who are highly committed to the organization are less likely to quit their jobs, be absent from work, or show up late for work.[41] In this respect, declining commitment may result in higher human resources costs as productive employees leave the firm or make unwarranted use of sick leave.

Work Effort and Job Performance.   Dedicated employees are more motivated to work for the organization. Whether this increased effort translates into higher performance depends on ability, role clarity, and situational contingencies. However, a recent study of managers in a Canadian food service firm did indeed find that attitudinal commitment is positively related to job performance.[42]

Organizational Citizenship.   An interesting perspective of the loyalty–performance relationship is that organizational commitment may cause employees to engage in more organizational citizenship behaviours. Recall from Chapter 2 that organizational citizenship represents employee activities that improve organizational effectiveness by helping others and facilitating a positive work environment.[43] Consequently, whether or not loyalty increases the employee's own performance, it is likely to increase organizational effectiveness through subtle organizational citizenship behaviours.

Negative Consequences.   While the benefits of organizational commitment have been widely studied, there may also be negative consequences.[44] One potential problem is that high levels of commitment may reduce turnover to such a level that the organization stagnates. Another concern is that extreme commitment is believed to reduce the individual's ability to accommodate non-work roles, such as family obligations.[45] Finally, highly dedicated individuals might engage in activities that benefit the organization but are illegal to society. For example, the president of a Montreal dredging company destroyed documents connected with a case that the RCMP were investigating. When asked why he had done this illegal act, the president replied: "For 22 years I put the company ahead of myself. I came second."[46]

Building Organizational Commitment

How do organizational leaders build and maintain a dedicated work force? The simple answer is that they practise better day-to-day management of employees. Most of the concepts and suggestions discussed in this book—from reward systems to managing team dynamics—likely influence organizational commitment in some way. Nevertheless, some practices seem to have a somewhat stronger effect on employee loyalty than others and are briefly mentioned below.

Job Security.   One of the major underpinnings of organizational commitment is the employee's perception of an ongoing employment relationship. Consequently, layoff threats are frequently identified as one of the greatest blows to employee loyalty, even among those whose jobs are not immediately at risk.[47] The value of job security is well known at IBM Canada, which (until recently) tried to retrain and transfer rather than lay off employees. Explains one senior executive: "This provides a sense of identity, a sense of security, that results in a high level of commitment."[48]

Employee Respect and Contribution.   Managers need to let employees know that they are a central part of the organization and to actually give employees a greater role in organizational activities. Careful selection and socialization practises clearly let new employees know that their employment is important. Treating employment from a career perspective—employees are joining the organization, not just accepting a job—also communicates the sense of a long-term employee–organization attachment. Making better use of employee talents requires redesigning jobs and increasing employee autonomy.[49] Creating a more egalitarian work environment—abolishing unnecessary status symbols—gives employees a greater sense of homogeneity and mutual respect.

organizational comprehension
The extent to which employees understand the organization's physical, social, and cultural dimensions.

Organizational Comprehension.   Commitment is stronger among employees with greater **organizational comprehension,** that is, a better understanding of the firm's physical, social, and cultural dimensions. By communicating organizational activities, maintaining direct contact with senior management, and having more opportunities to work directly with the firm's clients and customers, employees can make sense of their organization and develop a stronger identity with it.

Social Bonding.   Employees tend to be more strongly attached to organizations when they form positive relationships with coworkers, particularly when work team norms are consistent with organizational goals. In other words, people who identify themselves with others in the organization are more likely to feel loyal to the organization.[50] Social bonding can be facilitated by creating more team-based work activities and reward systems. Keeping work units small also increases the employee's ability to identify with the entire team.

Other Forms of Commitment

Our discussion of employee loyalty has really addressed only one form of organizational commitment, sometimes called *attitudinal commitment*. Attitudinal commitment is mentioned most often in the literature,[51] but two other forms of organizational commitment should also be briefly described.

Continuance Commitment.   You may have met people who do not particularly enjoy working for their employer but feel bound to remain with the organization because it would be too costly to quit.[52] This is known as **continuance commitment** because these employees have an instrumental reason for continuing the employment relationship. Whereas attitudinal commitment causes employees to remain because they want to, continuance commitment causes them to remain because of the threat of economic loss if they quit.

> **continuance commitment**
> An individual's willingness to remain with an organization for purely instrumental (e.g., financial) rather than emotional reasons.

Many organizations rely on continuance commitment to minimize turnover. For example, some firms use "golden handcuffs" such as low interest loans for bank employees because they financially strap people to the organization.[53] However, a recent study suggests that employees with high levels of continuance commitment actually have *lower* performance ratings![54] It seems clear that organizations need to win the hearts of employees (attitudinal commitment) and not just their pocketbooks (continuance commitment) in order to build an effective work force.

Behavioural Commitment.   **Behavioural commitment** is a form of cognitive dissonance whereby a person performs certain activities that subsequently increase attitudinal commitment. Specifically, employees initially do things that imply that they identify with the organization and believe in its goals. These behaviours are performed voluntarily (i.e., not overtly forced by the employer), are known to others, and clearly suggest that the employee is committed to the organization. Subsequently, the employee develops an attitudinal commitment that is consistent with these behaviours.[55]

> **behavioural commitment**
> A process of developing organizational commitment through cognitive dissonance.

There are many instances of behavioural commitment in organizations. A line manager might agree to visit several universities and colleges to tell students about the organization's virtues. The manager's attitudinal commitment to the organization may not be strong initially, but repeatedly promoting the organization eventually increases the manager's own attitudinal commitment. Organizations might also practise behavioural commitment by publicizing employees in the media. This visibility leads many people to increase their feelings of attachment to the organizations with which they are now so publicly connected.[56]

CHANGING ATTITUDES THROUGH PERSUASION

We are interested not only in how attitudes are formed and how they lead to behaviour, but also how to change attitudes in order to bring about more desired behaviour. One way to change attitudes is to directly communicate new information in a way that will increase the listener's probability of accepting what you are saying. This attitude change strategy is known as **persuasion.** It attempts to redirect the behaviour of others by altering their existing beliefs which, in turn, changes their attitudes. Persuasive communication is a complex topic, but the most important conditions, shown in Exhibit 8–8, deal with the characteristics of the *communicator,* the *message content,* the *communication medium,* and the people being persuaded (i.e., the *audience*).[57]

persuasion
A method of changing attitudes by directly communicating new information in a way that will increase the listener's probability of accepting what you are saying.

Communicator Characteristics

What makes one person more persuasive than another even though they utter the same words under the same conditions? The answer lies in the communicator's expertise, trustworthiness, and attractiveness to the audience.

Expertise.   Expertise is inferred in a variety of ways. One of the main factors is the speaker's background. We are more likely to accept advice on long-term debentures from a financial analyst than from the waiter at our favourite restaurant. Another feature is the language or jargon used. People who use technical language sometimes appear to be experts if there is no information to suggest otherwise. Finally, expertise tends to be inferred from the communicator's style of speech. Communicators are more likely to be seen as experts if they talk quickly and confidently than if their speech is slow and methodical. Their perceived expertise is also higher when they avoid pauses (umm, uh) and hedges (you know, I guess).[58]

Trustworthiness.   Communicators are less effective if they personally benefit from the persuasion attempt. However, trustworthiness increases when they argue against their own self-interest, as when a salesperson acknowledges a few positive features of a competitor's product. People holding respected positions are considered more trustworthy and therefore tend to be more persuasive. For example, we are more likely to be convinced by the company president than by our immediate supervisor.

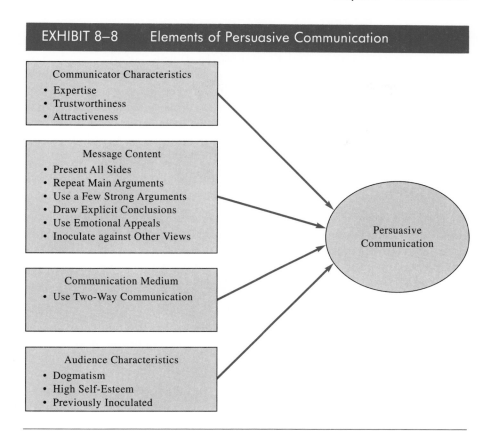

EXHIBIT 8–8   Elements of Persuasive Communication

Communicator Characteristics
• Expertise
• Trustworthiness
• Attractiveness

Message Content
• Present All Sides
• Repeat Main Arguments
• Use a Few Strong Arguments
• Draw Explicit Conclusions
• Use Emotional Appeals
• Inoculate against Other Views

Communication Medium
• Use Two-Way Communication

Audience Characteristics
• Dogmatism
• High Self-Esteem
• Previously Inoculated

Persuasive Communication

Attractiveness.   While expertise and trustworthiness are the most important factors, physically attractive people are also more persuasive than others.[59] This occurs because we tend to infer a variety of positive characteristics to those who are well-groomed and physically attractive (although not strikingly so) which, in turn, makes them appear more trustworthy and knowledgeable. We are also more persuaded by those who are similar to ourselves and with whom we identify.

Message Content

The communicator's expertise, trustworthiness, and attractiveness are most effective when the listener is not highly involved in the issue, that is, when the issue is not viewed as extremely important. When the issue *is* important, however, the message content becomes the critical feature of persuasive communication. Let us look at the characteristics of a persuasive message.

Present All Sides of the Issue.   The best strategy is to present all sides of the argument. Begin by talking about facts sympathetic to the audience's viewpoint, then shift into the theme of your position. Discussing only one point of view reduces the speaker's trustworthiness and creates a condition known as **psychological reactance.** Psychological reactance occurs when listeners feel pressured into accepting a particular point of view because they are not given the opportunity to consider other perspectives. To protect their freedom, listeners will reject the communicator's point of view without really considering its merits. Thus, presenting information on opposing positions reduces psychological reactance and increases the audience's willingness to consider the communicator's position.[60]

psychological reactance
An emotional condition that forms when people feel pressured into accepting a particular point of view because they are not given the opportunity to consider other perspectives.

Repeat Main Arguments.   Repeating the main arguments of your position two or three times increases message persuasiveness because the listener is more likely to remember these points.[61] However, you should avoid too much repetition because this may invoke psychological reactance—listeners begin to feel that the arguments are being hammered into them.

Number of Arguments.   When persuading others to change a corporate policy, the communicator should limit the discussion to only a few strong arguments because the discussion becomes too confusing beyond that point.[62]

Draw Explicit Conclusions.   It is better to draw conclusions for listeners than to let them discover the implications for themselves. While audiences tend to be more strongly persuaded when they draw their own conclusions, there is a risk that they may be wrong, particularly when the issue is complex or the audience is not motivated to analyze the information.

Use Emotional Appeals and Recommendations.   There has been a lot of debate on whether to use logic or emotion when persuading people to change their ways. The more effective strategy, it seems, is to use emotional appeals along with specific recommendations to overcome the threat. In a safety campaign, employees are more persuaded by graphic pictures of accident victims than by a lecture on recent accident statistics. People are more willing to recognize the danger and change their attitudes (and behaviour) if they are given explicit steps to avoid the danger.[63]

inoculation effect
A persuasion strategy of warning listeners that others will try to influence them in the future and that they should be wary about the opponent's arguments.

Inoculate against Other Persuasion Attempts.   Persuasive communicators use the **inoculation effect** to ensure that listeners are not influenced by other points of view.[64] This involves warning listeners that others will try to influence them in the future and that they should be wary about the opponent's arguments. This inoculation causes listeners to generate counterarguments to the anticipated persuasion attempts. For instance, a coalition that wants the company to purchase new production equipment might warn senior management that the finance department will try to convince them otherwise using specific arguments. This tends to make the finance department's subsequent persuasion attempts less convincing.

Communication Medium

Recall from Chapter 6 that two-way verbal communication tends to be most effective when the communicator wants to persuade or motivate the listener. The personal nature of this medium seems to increase the credibility of the information and it is easier for the sender to determine whether the persuasive message is having the desired effect. Two-way communication also increases the receiver's active participation in the process. As long as this participation does not involve presenting defensive statements, the receiver is more likely to be involved in the conversation and internalize some of the information presented.

Persuasion may require written documentation, however, when dealing with technical issues. Whenever written communication is necessary for this purpose, it should be combined with direct discussions for the greatest persuasive effect. The verbal exchange could repeat highlights of the report and provide graphic images for the listener, thereby adding emotional appeal to an otherwise logical message.

Audience Characteristics

Not everyone is equally persuaded by the strategies and conditions we have described. For example, it is by definition more difficult to change the opinions of people who are dogmatic.[65] People with high self-esteem also tend to be less influenced than those with low self-esteem.[66] Finally, recall that it is very difficult to persuade people who have earlier been warned of your persuasive intent.

EMPLOYMENT DISCRIMINATION

"It was a scary place to work," says Jim Spanks of his former employer, Majestic Electronics. Spanks and three other Majestic executives quit their jobs soon after being told they would be fired if they did not dismiss an employee of East Indian descent. "As far as Mr. Ramsauer [Majestic's president] was concerned, it was my responsibility to keep minorities out of here. It was something I wouldn't do, so I was always in hot water." Spanks adds that he literally had to sneak people in under Ramsauer's nose if they weren't male and white. Ramsauer denied making racist comments, although he admitted that a few may have been uttered in jest. However, the Ontario Human Rights Commission treated the matter more seriously. Concluding that Ramsauer had "made bigoted and racist remarks," the commission ordered the electronics retailer to pay the five former employees nearly $300,000 in damages.[67]

prejudice
Negative attitudes, based on unfounded or blatantly incorrect beliefs, that are directed toward people belonging to an identifiable group.

The experience at Majestic Electronics illustrates that some Canadians have negative attitudes that may adversely affect the work experiences of some labour force members. **Prejudice** refers to negative attitudes toward people belonging to a particular demographic group based on unfounded or blatantly incorrect beliefs. According to the Ontario Human Rights Commission, Majestic's president had a negative attitude toward people of other races and this resulted in an unfair barrier for them to obtain employment in that firm.

The Majestic case is not an isolated incident. Canadians view themselves as fairly tolerant people living in a multicultural society, but prejudice does exist in this country. These discriminatory attitudes are occasionally blatant, as in the Majestic incident. In many instances, however, prejudice is subtle and difficult to detect. This is apparent in an Ontario study of race discrimination described in Perspective 8–3.

Two Forms of Employment Discrimination

employment discrimination
A situation where people with equal qualifications have unequal employment opportunities due to their demographic characteristics.

The Majestic story illustrates how prejudice can lead to employment discrimination. **Employment discrimination** exists when the occupational attainment of people with similar qualifications depends on their demographic (including disability) characteristics. In other words, members of certain demographic groups have less opportunity than others to receive jobs, promotions, and other desirable employment outcomes even when they are equally qualified. In the Majestic case, the woman of East Indian descent was highly qualified (Spanks stated that she "was perfect for the job"), but she was denied an equal opportunity for employment in that firm.

systemic discrimination
A type of employment discrimination whereby seemingly neutral corporate practises have a negative effect on the employment opportunities of qualified people in certain demographic groups.

Employment discrimination due to prejudice is based on the idea of *adverse intent* because the person with the negative attitude consciously intends to limit employment opportunities of people in certain demographic groups. Another form of employment discrimination, called **systemic discrimination,** is based on the principle of *adverse effect*. Systemic discrimination occurs when seemingly neutral corporate practises have a negative effect on the employment opportunities of qualified people in certain demographic groups. For example, an employer who insists that male employees be clean-shaven may be systemically discriminating against Sikhs because they traditionally wear beards for religious reasons. Even though the employer does not have a consciously biased attitude against Sikhs, the employment practise has an unfair discriminatory effect on these people.[68]

Correcting Employment Discrimination in Canada

There is plenty of evidence that employment discrimination exists in Canada.[69] Women are occupationally segregated or *ghettoized* into low-paying jobs.[70] Native people have limited training opportunities, resulting in high unemployment. Some visible minorities face racial prejudice, as in the Ma-

---

PERSPECTIVE 8–3   No Discrimination in Canada, Eh?

Canada doesn't have many racial riots or other overt forms of racial tension, but this is hardly evidence that racial prejudice does not exist in this country. Working with the Urban Alliance on Race Relations and the Social Planning Council of Metropolitan Toronto, two York University researchers examined the extent to which visible minorities experience prejudice when seeking employment in Toronto. The results were both dramatic and disturbing.

One phase of the research matched four pairs of white and black subjects with respect to age, sex, educational, and employment histories. Each pair was instructed to appear individually as applicants in job interviews around Toronto. Of the 201 in-person job applications, a total of 36 job offers were received. White applicants received 27 of these offers, whereas black applicants received only 9 offers. Moreover, black applicants were treated discourteously or rudely in nearly 20 percent of the job postings, whereas the white applicants were invariably treated well. A few particularly blatant examples of

racial prejudice occurred in several situations where the white applicant was given an application form, an interview, or was immediately offered a position even though the black applicant had been told earlier the same day that the job was filled.

Similar results were found in the second phase of the study involving telephone enquiries. The researchers asked four types of people to call for an interview: a white majority Canadian, a black West Indian, an Indo-Pakistani, and a white immigrant with an Italian or Slavic accent. Out of the 237 jobs for which telephone enquiries were made, employers told 44 percent of the Indo-Pakistanis and 36 percent of the Black West Indians that the jobs were closed or no longer available. Thirty-one percent of the white immigrants with Italian or Slavic accents were given the same reply. When majority Canadians made the telephone calls, however, in only 13 percent of the cases did the employer say that the job was closed or no longer available.

Source: F. Henry and E. Ginzberg, *Who Gets the Work? A Test of Racial Discrimination in Employment* (Toronto: Social Planning Council of Metropolitan Toronto and Urban Alliance on Race Relations, 1985).

---

jestic case described earlier.[71] Disabled people are categorized by their disability rather than being considered for their individual potential.[72] Correcting employment discrimination is not an easy task. Organizational leaders must use every technique available—including persuasion and behavioural commitment—to root out prejudice in the workplace. They must also carefully examine the adverse effects of employment practises on the job opportunities of women, minorities, and the disabled.

Legislation protecting Canadians against discrimination in the workplace exists in every province and territory as well as in the federal government sector (e.g., banks, telephone companies, airlines). Here is a brief summary of the four types of relevant laws.[73]

Human Rights Legislation.   Human rights legislation protects people from unfair discrimination on the basis of race, colour, marital status, sex, and several other inappropriate criteria. This protection is extended to everyone (for example, men as well as women) in the workplace as well as housing and other issues outside of employment.

employment equity programs
A set of comprehensive practices introduced to eliminate systemic discrimination.

Employment Equity Legislation. **Employment equity programs** (sometimes called *affirmative action programs*) are comprehensive planning processes for eliminating systemic discrimination.[74] Employers must determine whether designated groups—women, visible minorities, natives, and the disabled—are underrepresented in their organizations compared to the relevant labour market. They must carefully ensure that their employment practises do not have an adverse effect on these groups. If designated groups are underrepresented, the organization must develop strategies to facilitate and encourage their employment.

Equal Pay/Pay Equity Legislation. As we mentioned in Chapter 3, women are protected from pay discrimination through equal pay and pay equity legislation. Equal pay statutes ensure that women receive the same pay level as men performing similar job duties in the same organization. Pay equity statutes require that men and women in jobs of similar value (as determined by job evaluation) receive similar levels of pay.

Canadian Charter of Rights and Freedoms. As part of the Canadian Constitution, the Charter of Rights and Freedoms protects every individual's right to equality and prohibits several forms of discrimination. Individual equality rights are not absolute, however. Rather, the charter places "reasonable limits" on individual rights to the extent that they unduly affect societal needs.

SUMMARY

- Attitudes are emotional predispositions to respond consistently toward an attitude object. It is important to understand the dynamics of work attitudes because they affect individual behaviour, manifest self-identities, and reflect the organization's respect for its employees. Attitudes are formed from our beliefs about the attitude object and lead to behaviour by creating desirable behavioural intentions, although this link depends on situational contingencies.

- Cognitive dissonance is a special condition in which people change their beliefs and attitudes to be more consistent with past behaviours.

- Job satisfaction refers to a set of attitudes toward various aspects of work. People tend to feel satisfied when their work expectations are realized but are not excessive. This work attitude is associated with several behaviours, including turnover, absenteeism, physical/mental health, and sabotage. High-performing employees will tend to be more satisfied than poor performers in organizations with pay-for-performance reward systems.

- Attitudinal commitment is most commonly identified with employee loyalty and refers to the strength of an individual's identification with and involvement in a particular organization. Attitudinal loyalty tends to reduce turnover and absenteeism and improve job performance.

- Continuance commitment refers to an individual's commitment to remain with an organization for purely instrumental (e.g., economic) reasons. It is a strategic rather than an emotional form of commitment and can actually reduce job performance.

- Behavioural commitment is a form of cognitive dissonance where certain behaviours cause the employee to subsequently form a strong sense of attitudinal commitment to the organization.

- Persuasion is a complex activity in which people try to redirect the behaviour of others by altering their existing beliefs which, in turn, changes their attitudes. The most important conditions in persuasion deal with the characteristics of the communicator, the message content, the communication medium, and the people being persuaded.

- Prejudice is a negative attitude toward certain people based on their demographic characteristics, and can lead to employment discrimination. Systemic barriers to equal employment opportunities represent another source of unfair discrimination.

- Numerous legal provisions exist in Canada to protect citizens from unfair discrimination. Employment equity programs, for example, explicitly correct systemic discrimination. However, organizational leaders must provide their strongest commitment to root out prejudice and other undesirable attitudes from the workplace.

DISCUSSION QUESTIONS

1. Why should managers understand work attitudes?
2. How are work attitudes formed?
3. Describe the connection between work attitudes and employee behaviour.
4. Under what conditions do employees experience cognitive dissonance? How are attitudes affected by cognitive dissonance?
5. Explain what is wrong with this statement: "Pay satisfaction increases with the size of the employee's paycheque."
6. How is continuance commitment different from attitudinal commitment?
7. What type of people are generally more persuasive communicators? Under what conditions do these communicator features have little persuasive effect?
8. Describe the two forms of employment discrimination.

NOTES

1. D. Hogarth, "Premdor CEO Lives and Breathes Doors," *Financial Post,* June 14, 1990, p. 13.

2. B. McDougall, "What's a Manager to Do with the Last of the Baby Boomers?" *Financial Times,* March 13, 1989, pp. 5–6.

3. P. Zimbardo and E. B. Ebbeson, *Influencing Attitudes and Changing Behavior* (Reading, Mass.: Addison-Wesley, 1969), p. 6; M. Fishbein and I. Ajzen, *Belief, Attitude, Intention, and Behavior* (Reading, Mass.: Addison-Wesley, 1975), p. 131; and C. C. Pinder, *Work Motivation: Theory, Issues, and Applications* (Glenview, Ill.: Scott, Foresman, 1984), p. 82.

4. B. M. Staw and J. Ross, "Stability in the Midst of Change: A Dispositional Approach to Job Attitudes," *Journal of Applied Psychology* 70 (1985), pp. 469–80.

5. U. E. Gattiker and T. W. Nelligan, "Computerized Offices in Canada and the United States: Investigating Dispositional Similarities and Differences," *Journal of Organizational Behavior* 9 (1988), pp. 77–96; and B. Gerhart, "How Important Are Dispositional Factors as Determinants of Job Satisfaction? Implications for Job Design and Other Personnel Programs," *Journal of Applied Psychology* 72 (1987), pp. 366–73.

6. D. Katz, "The Functional Approach to the Study of Attitudes," *Public Opinion Quarterly* 24 (1960), pp. 163–76; and P. C. Smith, L. M. Kendall, and C. L. Hulin, *The Measurement of Satisfaction in Work and Retirement* (Chicago: Rand McNally, 1969).

7. P. H. Mirvis and E. E. Lawler III, "Measuring the Financial Impact of Employee Attitudes," *Journal of Applied Psychology* 62 (1977), pp. 1–8; and E. E. Lawler III, *Motivation in Work Organizations* (Belmont, Calif.: Wadsworth, 1973).

8. Lawler, *Motivation in Work Organizations.*

9. Katz, "The Functional Approach to the Study of Attitudes."

10. Fishbein and Ajzen, *Belief, Attitude, Intention, and Behavior.*

11. G. Salancik and J. Pfeffer, "A Social Information Processing Approach to Job Attitudes and Task Design," *Administrative Science Quarterly* 23 (1978), pp. 224–53.

12. S. E. White and T. R. Mitchell, "Job Enrichment versus Social Cues: A Comparison and Competitive Test," *Journal of Applied Psychology* 64 (1979), pp. 1–9.

13. S. Lieberman, "The Effects of Changes in Roles on the Attitudes of Role Occupants," *Human Relations* 9 (1956), pp. 385–402.

14. P. H. Prestholdt, I. M. Lane, and R. C. Mathews, "Nurse Turnover as Reasoned Action: Development of a Process Model," *Journal of Applied Psychology* 72 (1987), pp. 221–27.

15. Fishbein and Ajzen, *Belief, Attitude, Intention, and Behavior.*

16. Pinder, *Work Motivation: Theory, Issues, and Applications,* pp. 88–89; and C. D. Fisher, "On the Dubious Wisdom of Expecting Job Satisfaction to Correlate with Performance," *Academy of Management Review* 5 (1980), pp. 607–12.

17. L. Festinger, *A Theory of Cognitive Dissonance* (Evanston, Ill.: Row, Peterson, 1957); G. R. Salancik, "Commitment and the Control of Organizational Behavior and Belief," in B. M. Staw and G. R. Salancik (eds.), *New Directions in Organizational Behavior* (Chicago: St. Clair, 1977), pp. 1–54.

18. B. M. Staw, "Attitudinal and Behavioral Consequences of Changing a Major Organizational Reward: A Natural Field Experiment," *Journal of Personality and Social Psychology* 9 (1974), pp. 742–51.

19. W. H. Schmidt and Barry Z. Posner, *Managerial Values in Perspective* (New York: American Management Association, 1983).

20. E. A. Locke, "The Nature and Causes of Job Satisfaction," in M. Dunnette (ed.), *Handbook of Industrial and Organizational Psychology* (Chicago: Rand McNally, 1976), pp. 1297–1350.

21. Lawler, *Motivation in Work Organizations,* pp. 66–69, 74–77.

22. R. Maynard, "How Do You Like Your Job?" *Report on Business Magazine,* November 1987, pp. 112–25.

23. M. Burstein, N. Tienhaara, P. Hewson, and B. Warrander, *Canadian Work Values* (Ottawa: Department of Manpower and Immigration, 1975); and T. Atkinson, "Changing Attitudes toward Work in Canada," *Canadian Business Review* 10 (Spring 1983), pp. 39–44.

24. R. L. Kahn, "The Meaning of Work: Interpretations and Proposals for Measurement," in A. A. Campbell and P. E. Converse (eds.), *The Human Meaning of Social Change* (New York: Basic Books, 1972).

25. Maynard, "How Do You Like Your Job?" p. 115. For similar results in the United States, see United States Special Task Force to the Secretary of Health, Education, and Welfare, *Work in America* (Cambridge, Mass.: MIT Press, 1973).

26. H. J. Arnold and D. C. Feldman, "A Multivariate Analysis of the Determinants of Job Turnover," *Journal of Applied Psychology* 67 (1982), pp. 350–60; and W. H. Mobley, *Employee Turnover: Causes, Consequences, and Control* (Reading, Mass.: Addison-Wesley, 1982).

27. J. N. Carsten and P. E. Spector, "Unemployment, Job Satisfaction, and Employee Turnover: A Meta-Analytic Test of the Muchinsky Model," *Journal of Applied Psychology* 72 (1987), pp. 374–81; and S. L. McShane, "Perceived Employment Opportunities as a Moderator in the Turnover Decision Process: A Conceptual and Empirical Re-assessment," *Proceedings of the Annual ASAC Conference, Organizational Behaviour Division* 7, pt. 5 (1986), pp. 136–47.

28. R. D. Hackett, "Work Attitudes and Employee Absenteeism: A Synthesis of the Literature," *Journal of Occupational Psychology* 62 (1989), pp. 235–48; and S. L. McShane, "Job Satisfaction and Absenteeism: A Meta-Analytic Re-examination," *Canadian Journal of Administrative Sciences* 1 (1984), pp. 61–77.

29. D. F. Coleman and N. V. Schaefer, "An Exploratory Investigation of the Relationship between Weather and Short-Term Absenteeism," *Proceedings of the Annual ASAC Conference, Organizational Behaviour Division* 9, pt. 5 (1988), pp. 11–20; and J. K. Chadwick-Jones, *Absenteeism in the Canadian Context* (Ottawa: Minister of Supply and Services, 1980).

30. G. Johns and N. Nicholson, "The Meanings of Absence: New Strategies for Theory and Research," in L. L. Cummings and B. M. Staw (eds.), *Research in Organizational Behavior* vol. 4 (Greenwich, Conn.: JAI Press, 1982), pp. 127–72; and R. R. Haccoun and S. Dupont, "Absence Research: A Critique of Previous Approaches and an Example for a New Direction," *Canadian Journal of Administrative Sciences* 4 (1987), pp. 143–56.

31. R. J. Burke, "Occupational and Life Strains, Satisfaction, and Mental Health," *Journal of Business Administration* 1 (1969), pp. 35–41; M. Jamal and V. F. Mitchell, "Work, Nonwork, and Mental Health: A Model and a Test," *Industrial Relations* 18 (1980), pp. 88–93; and M. J. Kavanagh, M. W. Hurst, and R. Rose, "The Relationship between Job Satisfaction and Psychiatric Health Symptoms for Air Traffic Controllers," *Personnel Psychology* 34 (1981), pp. 691–707.

32. H. L. Sheppard and N. Q. Herrick, *Where Have All the Robots Gone?* (New York: Free Press, 1972).

33. R. C. Hollinger and J. P. Clark, *Theft by Employees* (Lexington, Mass.: D.C. Heath, 1983).

34. M. M. Petty, G. W. McGee, and J. W. Cavender, "A Meta-Analysis of the Relationship between Individual Job Satisfaction and Individual Performance," *Academy of Management Review* 9 (1984), pp. 712–21; M. T. Iaffaldano and P. M. Muchinsky, "Job Satisfaction and Job Performance: A Meta-Analysis," *Psychological Bulletin* 97 (1985), pp. 251–73; and D. P. Schwab and L. L. Cummings, "Theories of Performance and Satisfaction: A Review," *Industrial Relations* 9 (1970), pp. 408–30.

35. E. E. Lawler III and L. W. Porter, "The Effect of Performance on Job Satisfaction," *Industrial Relations* 7 (1967), pp. 20–28.

36. S. Franklin, *The Heroes: A Saga of Canadian Inspiration* (Toronto: McClelland & Stewart, 1967), pp. 53–59.

37. R. T. Mowday, L. W. Porter, and R. M. Steers, *Employee Organization Linkages: The Psychology of Commitment, Absenteeism, and Turnover* (New York: Academic Press, 1982).

38. L. W. Porter, R. M. Steers, R. T. Mowday, and R. V. Boulain, "Organizational Commitment, Job Satisfaction, and Turnovers among Psychiatric Technicians," *Journal of Applied Psychology* 59 (1974), pp. 603–09.

39. S. J. Modic, "Is Anyone Loyal Anymore?" *Industry Week,* September 7, 1987, pp. 75–82; and T. F. O'Boyle, "Loyalty Ebbs at Many Companies as Employees Grow Disillusioned," *The Wall Street Journal,* July 11, 1987, p. 27.

40. R. J. Grey and G. C. Johnson, "Differences between Canadian and American Workers," *Canadian Business Review* 15 (Winter 1988), pp. 24–27.

41. Mowday, Porter, and Steers, *Employee Organization Linkages: The Psychology of Commitment, Absenteeism, and Turnover.*

42. J. P. Meyer, S. V. Paunonen, I. R. Gellatly, R. D. Goffin, and D. N. Jackson, "Organizational Commitment and Job Performance: It's the Nature of the Commitment That Counts," *Journal of Applied Psychology* 74 (1989), pp. 152–56.

43. R. Karambayya, "Good Organizational Citizens Do Make a Difference," *Proceedings of the Annual ASAC Conference, Organizational Behaviour Division* 11, pt. 5 (1990), pp. 110–19.

44. Pinder, *Work Motivation: Theory, Issues, and Applications,* pp. 105–07.

45. D. M. Randall, "Commitment and the Organization: The Organization Man Revisited," *Academy of Management Review* 12 (1987), pp. 460–71. For a contrary view, see B. S. Romzek, "Personal Consequences of Employee Commitment," *Academy of Management Journal* 32 (1989), pp. 649–61.

46. P. C. Newman, *The Canadian Establishment* (Toronto: McClelland & Stewart, 1975), p. 183.

47. S. Ashford, C. Lee, and P. Bobko, "Content, Causes, and Consequences of Job Insecurity: A Theory-Based Measure and Substantive Test," *Academy of Management Journal* 32 (1989), pp. 803–29.

48. E. Innes, R. L. Perry, and J. Lyon, *100 Best Companies to Work for in Canada* (Toronto: Collins, 1986), p. 175.

49. V. V. Baba and R. Knoop, "Organizational Commitment and Independence among Canadian Managers," *Relations Industrielles* 42 (1987), pp. 325–44; and W. L. Weber, J. J. Marshall, and G. H. Haines, "Modelling Commitment and Its Antecedents: An Empirical Study," *Canadian Journal of Administrative Sciences* 6 (1989), pp. 12–23.

50. B. Ashforth and F. Mael, "Social Identity Theory and the Organization," *Academy of Management Review* 14 (1989), pp. 20–39.

51. P. Morrow, "Concept Redundancy in Organizational Research: The Case of Work Commitment," *Academy of Management Review* 8 (1983), pp. 486–500.

52. J. P. Meyer and N. J. Allen, "Testing the 'Side-Bet Theory' of Organizational Commitment: Some Methodological Considerations," *Journal of Applied Psychology* 69 (1984), pp. 372–78; G. W. McGee and R. C. Ford, "Two (Or More?) Dimensions of Organizational Commitment: Reexamination of the Affective and Continuance Commitment Scales," *Journal of Applied Psychology* 72 (1987), pp. 638–42; and M. Withey, "Antecedents of Value-Based and Economic Organizational Commitment," *Proceedings of the Annual ASAC Conference, Organizational Behaviour Division* 9, pt. 5 (1988), pp. 124–33.

53. M. Dewey, "Perks: Golden Handcuffs for Executives," *Globe and Mail,* August 4, 1979, p. B1; and R. McQueen, *The Money-Spinners* (Toronto: Totem, 1983), p. 11.

54. Meyer et al., "Organizational Commitment and Job Performance: It's the Nature of the Commitment That Counts."

55. G. R. Salancik, "Commitment and the Control of Organizational Behavior and Belief"; R. P. Abelson, "Beliefs Are Like Possessions," *Journal for the Theory of Social Behavior* 16 (1986), pp. 223–50.

56. Baba and Knoop, "Organizational Commitment and Independence among Canadian Managers."

57. W. J. McGuire, "The Nature of Attitudes and Attitude Change," in G. Lindzey and E. Aronson (eds.), *Handbook of Social Psychology* Vol. 3 (Reading, Mass.: Addison-Wesley, 1969), pp. 136–14; D. G. Linz and S. Penrod, "Increasing Attorney Persuasiveness in the Courtroom," *Law and Psychology Review* 8 (1984), pp. 1–47; and Zimbardo and Ebbeson, *Influencing Attitudes and Changing Behavior.*

58. E. Aronson, *The Social Animal* (San Francisco: W. H. Freeman, 1976); N. MacLachlan, "What People Really Think about Fast Talkers," *Psychology Today* 113 (November 1979), pp. 112–17; N.

Miller, G. Maruyama, R. J. Beaber, and K. Valone, "Speed of Speech and Persuasion," *Journal of Personality and Social Psychology* 34 (1976), pp. 615–24.

59. M. Snyder and M. Rothbart, "Communicator Attractiveness and Opinion Change," *Canadian Journal of Behavioural Science* 3 (1971), pp. 377–87.

60. Aronson, *The Social Animal,* pp. 67–68; R. A. Jones and J. W. Brehm, "Persuasiveness of One- and Two-Sided Communications as a Function of Awareness That There Are Two Sides," *Journal of Experimental Social Psychology* 6 (1970), pp. 47–56.

61. R. B. Zajonc, "Attitudinal Effects of Mere Exposure," *Journal of Personality and Social Psychology Monograph* 9 (1968), pp. 1–27; and R. Petty and J. Cacioppo, *Attitudes and Persuasion: Classic and Contemporary Approaches* (Dubuque, Iowa: W. C. Brown, 1981).

62. Linz and Penrod, "Increasing Attorney Persuasiveness in the Courtroom," pp. 28–29.

63. Zimbardo and Ebbeson, *Influencing Attitudes and Changing Behavior.*

64. Zimbardo and Ebbeson, *Influencing Attitudes and Changing Behavior.*

65. Milton Rokeach, *The Open and Closed Mind* (New York: Basic Books, 1960).

66. M. Zellner, "Self-Esteem, Reception, and Influenceability," *Journal of Personality and Social Psychology* 15 (1970), pp. 87–93.

67. J. Lakey, "'Scary Place to Work,' Executive Says," *Toronto Star,* January 7, 1989, p. A8; and D. Wilson, "Hiring Policy 'Racist,' Firm to Pay $300,000," *Globe and Mail,* January 7, 1989, pp. A1–A2.

68. *Singh* v. *Security and Investigation Services Ltd.,* Ontario Board of Inquiry, unreported, May 31, 1977; H. C. Jain, "Recruitment of Racial Minorities in Canadian Police Forces," *Relations Industrielles* 42 (1987), pp. 790–805; and W. Black, "From Intent to Effect: New Standards in Human Rights," *Canadian Human Rights Reporter* 1 (February 1980), pp. C2–C3.

69. G. T. Milkovich, W. F. Glueck, R. T. Barth, and S. L. McShane, *Canadian Personnel/Human Resource Management: A Diagnostic Approach* (Plano, Texas: Business Publications Inc., 1988), Chapter 7.

70. P. Armstrong and H. Armstrong, *The Double Ghetto: Canadian Women and their Segregated Work* (Toronto: McClelland and Stewart, 1979); and P. Armstrong and H. Armstrong, *A Working Majority: What Women Must Do for Pay* (Ottawa: Information Canada, 1983).

71. Special Committee on Visible Minorities in Canadian Society (Daudlin Committee), *Equality Now* (Ottawa: Supply and Services Canada, 1984); and Royal Commission on Equality in Employment (Abella Commission), *Equality in Employment* (Ottawa: Minister of Supply and Services Canada, 1984), pp. 33–38, 46–51.

72. Special Committee on the Disabled and the Handicapped, *Obstacles* (Ottawa: Minister of Supply and Services Canada, 1981); M. H. Rioux, "Labelled Disabled and Wanting to Work," in *Research Studies of the Royal Commission on Equality in Employment* (Ottawa: Minister of Supply and Services Canada, 1985), pp. 613–39.

73. This material is summarized from Milkovich et al., *Canadian Personnel/Human Resource Management: A Diagnostic Approach.*

74. Abella, *Equality in Employment,* p. 193; and H. C. Jain, "Racial Minorities and Affirmative Action/Employment Equity Legislation in Canada," *Relations Industrielles* 44 (1989), pp. 593–614.

CHAPTER CASES

SEA PINES

In the spring of 1977, the coastal town of Sea Pines, Nova Scotia, retained a Toronto consulting engineer to study the effect of greatly expanding the town's sewage system and discharging the treated waste into the harbour.

At that time, fishermen in the town were experiencing massive lobster kills in the harbour and were concerned that the kills were caused by the effluent from the present Sea Pines sewage treatment plant. They were convinced that any expansion of the plant would further aggravate the problem. The fishermen invited Tom Stone, the engineer, to the monthly meeting of the local fishermen's organization to discuss their concerns. On the night of the meeting, the Legion Hall was filled with men in blue jeans and work jackets, many of whom were drinking beer. An account of this meeting follows, with Fred Mitchell, a local fisherman, speaking first.

Mitchell: Well, as you all know, Mr. Stone has been kind enough to meet with us tonight to explain his recommendations concerning the town's sewage disposal problem. We're all concerned about the lobster kills, like the one last summer, and I for one don't want to see any more sewage dumped into that harbour. [Murmurs of assent are heard throughout the hall.]
So, Mr. Stone, we'd like to hear from you on what it is you want to do.

Stone: Thank you. I'm glad to get this opportunity to hear your concerns on the lobster situation. Let me say from the outset that we are still studying the problem closely and expect to make our formal recommendation to the town about a month from now. I am not prepared to discuss specific conclusions of our study, but I am prepared to incorporate any relevant comments into our study. As most of you are probably aware, we are attempting to model mathematically, or simulate, conditions in the harbour to help us predict the effects of sewage effluent in the harbour. We . . .

Mitchell: Now wait a minute. I don't know anything about models except the kind I used to make as a kid. (Laughter.) I can tell you that we never had lobster kills like we have now until they started dumping that sewage into the harbour a few years back. I don't need any model to tell me that. It seems to me that common sense tells you that if we've got troubles now in the summer with the lobster, that increasing the amount of sewage by 10 times the present amount is going to cause 10 times the problem.

A Fisherman: Yeah, you don't need to be an engineer to see that.

Stone: While it's true that we're proposing to extend the sewage system in town, and that the resulting sewage flow will be about 10 times the present flow, the area of the sewage discharge will be moved to a larger area of the harbour, where it will be diluted with much more sea water than is the present area. In addition, if the harbour is selected for the new discharge, we will design a special diffuser to mix the treated sewage effluent quickly with ocean water. As I indicated, we are attempting to use data on currents and water quality that we collected in the harbour and combine it with some mathematical equations in our computer to help us predict what the quality in the harbour will be.

Mitchell: I don't understand what you need a computer to tell you that for. I've been fishing in this area for over 35 years now, and I don't need any computer to tell me that my lobsters are going to die if that sewage goes into the harbour.

Stone: Let me say before this goes too far that we're not talking about discharging raw sewage into the harbour. The sewage is treated and disinfected before it is discharged.

Mitchell: Isn't the sewage that's being dumped into the harbour right now being treated and disinfected, Mr. Stone?

Stone: Yes, it is, but . . .

Mitchell: The lobster still die, so it's clear to me that "treated and disinfected" doesn't solve the problem.

Stone: Our model will predict whether the treatment provided will be sufficient to maintain the water quality in the harbour at the province's standard for the harbour.

Mitchell: I don't give a damn about any provincial standard. I just care about my lobsters and how I'm going to put bread on the table for my kids! You engineers from Toronto can come out here spouting all kinds of things about models, data, standards, and your concern for lobsters, but what it really comes down to is that it's just another job. You can collect your fees for your study, go back to your office, and leave us holding the bag.

Stone: Now wait a minute, Mr. Mitchell. My firm is well-established in Canada, and we didn't get that way by giving our clients that fast shuffle and making a quick exit out of town. We have no intention of leaving you with an unworkable solution to your sewage problems. We also will not solve your sewage problem and leave you with a lobster kill problem. Perhaps I have given you the wrong impression about this modelling. We regard this as one method of analysis that may be helpful in predicting future harbour conditions, but not the only method. We have over 40 years' experience in these harbour studies, and we fully intend to use this experience, *in addition to* whatever the model tells us, to come up with a reasonable solution.

Mitchell: Well, that's all well and good, but I can tell you, and I think I speak for all the lobstermen here, that if you recommend dumping that sewage into the harbour, we'll fight you all the way down the line! (Shouts of agreement.) Why can't you pipe the sewage out to the ocean if you're so concerned about dilution? I'm sure that your model will tell you there's enough dilution out there.

Stone: I agree that the ocean will certainly provide sufficient dilution, but the whole purpose of this study is to see if we can avoid a deep ocean outfall.

Mitchell: Why?

Stone: Because the cost of constructing a deep ocean outfall in this area is very expensive—say about $500 per metre. Now, if the length of the outfall is 2,000 metres, don't you think that it makes good sense to spend a few thousand dollars studying the harbour area if we can save you millions?

Mitchell: All that money that you're going to save the town doesn't do much for the lobstermen who'll be put out of business if that sewage goes into the harbour.

Stone: As I said, we wouldn't recommend that if we thought, based on our modelling and our experience in this area, that the quality of water in the harbour would kill any lobster or any other aquatic life.

Mitchell: Well, I'm telling you again, if you try to put that stuff in our harbour, we'll fight you all the way. I think we've made our position clear on this thing, so if there are no further comments, I vote that we adjourn the meeting. (Seconded.)

When the meeting ended, the fishermen filed out, talking heatedly among themselves, leaving Mr. Stone standing on the platform.

Discussion Questions

1. What symptom(s) exist in this case to suggest that something has gone wrong?
2. What are the root causes that have led to these symptoms?
3. What actions should Stone and his firm take to correct these problems?

Source: This case was written by Terence P. Driscoll.

MICHELE FONTAINE

At age 25, Michele Fontaine was ready for corporate life. She had travelled the world, learned four languages, and completed an MBA degree at McGill with grades in the top third of her class. With an interest in a career with a financial institution, Fontaine interviewed with four of Canada's top five banks. Interviewers at two of the banks asked Fontaine the classic question put to female applicants—"Can you type?"—but she accepted a career position with the Royal Bank, partly because that organization's representative seemed more enlightened.

Fontaine was feeling confident about her decision to join the Royal Bank until she discovered that her salary was 20 percent lower than comparable MBA graduates. A few months later, Fontaine's job became redundant and she was offered a clerical position at the same rate of pay but much lower status in the corporate structure. She protested, but was assured that this was a temporary assignment. Fontaine was asked to meet with a vice-president of the bank, who rather patronizingly asked what she was so upset about and why she had complained to the personnel department about her new position.

In addition to being in a clerical position, Fontaine found herself in a sexist environment where male colleagues frequently used locker-room jargon. When one male coworker suggested Fontaine would be lousy in bed, her boss simply replied that "boys will be boys." With a job far below her qualifications and coworkers she didn't respect, Fontaine began thinking about leaving the Royal Bank. Before leaving, she contacted an employment equity officer in Montreal who was shocked to hear about Fontaine's experience. A meeting was arranged with a head office personnel officer about the prospects of joining the Royal Bank's international management program, but the officer stated that there were no openings at the moment. That statement was the final signal to quit because Fontaine knew that the bank was currently recruiting graduates into that program.

With fewer than two years of employment at the Royal Bank, Fontaine began looking for another job. As word spread about her job search, the bank offered Fontaine a promotion with the contingency that there would be no salary increase and that the promotion would be kept quiet. She resigned soon after and accepted an account management trainee position at the Toronto offices of a major U.S. bank. The salary was much higher and, says Fontaine, "I'm being treated as a person, not a male or female." Reflecting on her experience at the Royal Bank, Fontaine adds: "I'd never work for another Canadian institution. No way."

Discussion Questions

1. What evidence is provided in this case to suggest that Michele Fontaine has been subject to prejudicial attitudes?

2. Were her concerns about discrimination realistic, or could she have simply interpreted events differently than they really were?

3. Assuming that these events are accurate, what should the Royal Bank do to reduce discrimination in the workplace?

Source: Adapted from Rod McQueen, *The Moneyspinners* (Toronto: Totem, 1984), pp. 221–24. The woman's name has been changed to protect her identity. Company names are the same.

EXPERIENTIAL EXERCISE

GENERAL UNION ATTITUDE EXERCISE

Purpose: This exercise is designed to help you understand the dynamics of employee attitudes toward a specific attitude object and to practise strategies of persuasion and attitude change regarding that attitude object.

Instructions: As a first step, individuals will complete the General Union Attitude Scale presented below by circling their preferred response to each item and calculating a total score.

Next, the instructor will divide the class into two parts based on whether participants fall above or below a certain point on the scale. Each part is then divided into teams of three people. Teams with members having high scores will speak in favour of labour unions and teams with members having low scores will argue against labour unions. Students scoring in the middle of the scale will serve as observers.

Each team will be matched with a team from the other half of the class and try to convince members of the other team to change their opinion regarding labour unions. Each team first meets alone for 5 minutes to develop strategy. One observer is assigned to each team to record the process. Next, the pairs of teams (one for and one against labour unions) meet for the length of time indicated by the instructor. The objective is to convince members of the opposing team that labour unions in Canada are good or bad, depending on your team's assigned position on the issue. The two observers in each debate watch the action and share notes at the end of the meeting.

At the end of the debates, the instructor draws the class together and the observers from each debate present their findings. Discussion from other participants follows the observers' presentations.

General Union Attitude Scale

		Strongly Disagree		Neutral			Strongly Agree	
1.	Unions are a positive force in this country.	1	2	3	4	5	6	7
2.	If I had to choose, I probably would not be a member of a labour union.	7	6	5	4	3	2	1
3.	I am glad that labour unions exist.	1	2	3	4	5	6	7
4.	People would be just as well-off if there were no labour unions in this country.	7	6	5	4	3	2	1
5.	Unions are an embarrassment to our society.	7	6	5	4	3	2	1
6.	I am proud of the labour movement in this country.	1	2	3	4	5	6	7
7.	Most people are better off without labour unions.	7	6	5	4	3	2	1
8.	Employees are considerably better off when they belong to a labour union.	1	2	3	4	5	6	7

© 1991 Steven L. McShane. The General Union Attitude Scale appears in Steven L. McShane, "General Union Attitude: A Construct Validation," *Journal of Labor Research* 7 (1986), pp. 403–17.

Scoring: Add up the score for all eight items. The instructor will determine the part of the class and discussion team to which you will be assigned.

9

Individual Decision
Making in Organizations

LEARNING OBJECTIVES

After reading this chapter, you should be able to:

Diagram
The basic process of decision making.

Explain
Why people have difficulty identifying problems.

Contrast
The rational economic and bounded rationality
perspectives.

Outline
The causes of escalation of commitment to a poor decision.

Explain
Why intuitive decision making requires experience.

List
Four strategies to minimize problems in crisis decision
making.

Identify
Three basic perspectives of ethical decision making.

Canadian Tire

Canadian Tire's position as Canada's leading hardware and automotive retailer and one of the most profitable chains in the retail industry is largely due to its distinctive merchandising formula and effective franchise strategy. But Dean Muncaster, Canadian Tire's president until a few years ago, realized the firm had almost saturated the Canadian market and that something had to be done to maintain its success.

Muncaster's management team decided to expand into the U.S. market and, after comparing several possibilities, purchased White Stores Inc. of Texas in late 1981. Some losses were initially expected, but Muncaster was confident that exporting Canadian Tire's merchandising and franchising systems would make White Stores Inc. profitable by 1984. Echoing the enthusiasm of the Canadian financial community, one analyst concluded: "[The company] has entered a virtually limitless market where it faces little direct competition."

As it turned out, purchasing White Stores Inc. may have been one of the worst decisions in Canadian Tire's history. Recession hit the U.S. sunbelt with a vengeance, the strength of existing competitors was underestimated, and U.S. clones of Canadian Tire began moving into the Texas market. Canadian Tire management also overlooked the fact that White's run-down retail outlets would require expensive renovations. Rather than turning a profit, losses ballooned to over $55 million by 1984. With the benefit of hindsight, Muncaster acknowledged the difficulties of entering the U.S. market, saying "Clearly, there have been some errors in projections, but then we were starting out with little basis on which to judge."

As losses mounted, the Billes family—Canadian Tire's controlling shareholders—began to assert their influence to get rid of the Texan white elephant. In June 1985, minutes before the annual shareholders' meeting, Billes unceremoniously fired Muncaster as president of Canadian Tire. By December, Canadian Tire had a tentative agreement to sell White Stores to a U.S. firm, but the deal fell through and the retail chain was eventually abandoned. It is estimated that Canadian Tire lost nearly $300 million in the White Stores fiasco.[1]

In every Canadian organization, including Canadian Tire, decision making is a fundamental component of a manager's job, involving a degree of risk with uncertain outcomes.[2] It is a complex process of recognizing a problem or opportunity, looking for alternative ways to deal with the situation, and ensuring that the selected choice is implemented and fulfills the requirements. Managers must be aware of the problems of rationalizing their decisions and becoming committed to a course of action that may not be in the organization's best interest. Organizational decisions also affect many stakeholders. Canadian Tire's decision to first enter and then abandon the U.S. market significantly affected the lives of shareholders, franchisees, employees, suppliers, White Stores' customers, and many others.

This chapter describes various perspectives on organizational decision making, with a particular emphasis on the process and practises of individual decisions. (Chapter 11 looks more carefully at employee involvement and team decision making.) We begin this chapter by introducing a general model of decision making. We then look at each stage of the model in detail, including the problems managers face and potential solutions to these problems. The latter part of this chapter highlights three decision-making topics of particular importance to managers: intuition, crisis management, and ethics.

A GENERAL MODEL OF DECISION MAKING

Decision making may be defined as a conscious process of making choices among one or more alternatives with the intention of moving toward some desired state of affairs.[3] According to this definition, decision making is a process that travels from problem identification to evaluation of the selected alternative. Decision making involves comparing alternative directions for the organization and allocating resources toward one of those choices. In this respect, decisions represent part of the process of organizational change, and decision makers must contemplate potential resistance to this change when making a choice. Finally, decisions are made to achieve objectives, presumably in the organization's best interest. However, this is by no means an orderly process because organizational goals are often ill-defined and not fully agreed upon by others in the organization.

A general model of the decision-making process is presented in Exhibit 9–1.[4] *Problem identification* marks the first stage in the process whereby the individual becomes aware of a problem or opportunity (problem recognition) and tries to understand why it exists (problem diagnosis). This is followed by the *predecision* stage where the appropriate way to handle the problem is decided. At this stage, the decision maker considers the best decision style—whether to involve others or make the decision alone, whether to treat the issue as routine or unique, and so on.

In the *alternative development stage,* potential solutions to the problem are generated. This involves searching for existing solutions to the problem and possibly designing a custom-made solution. In the *alternative selection* stage, the decision maker compares the various strategies against a set of criteria (alternative evaluation) and then makes a choice based on this evaluation (alternative choice). *Implementation* and *feedback* represent the final

decision making
A conscious process of making choices among one or more alternatives with the intention of moving toward some desired state of affairs.

EXHIBIT 9–1   A General Model of Decision Making

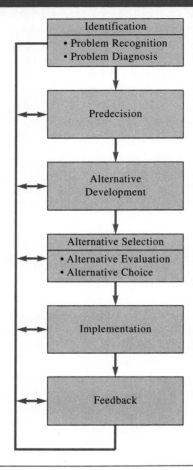

stages in the decision-making process. They involve putting the chosen alternative into practise and determining the extent to which the solution has corrected the problem or realized the opportunity.

Notice that decision makers may loop back at any time to an earlier stage in the model. For example, while developing a list of alternatives, it may become apparent that you have identified the problem incorrectly. You would then loop back to problem identification and proceed through the later stages again. As the problems become more complex, decision makers might loop back several times through various stages in the model.

The general model of decision making provides a useful framework with which to present this topic, but do not be misled by its simplicity. In reality, decision making is a complex activity and there are many problems that render it virtually impossible to make the perfect decision. This will become apparent as we look at the decision-making process in more detail.

PROBLEM IDENTIFICATION

The decision-making process begins with the recognition that a problem or opportunity exists. A *problem* is a deviation between the current and desired situations.[5] In the opening story, Canadian Tire's senior management perceived that a problem existed when they saw a gap between the firm's historical and future expansion rate within Canada. An *opportunity* is also recognized by a deviation between two conditions, but the current situation is generally satisfactory and the potentially better situation is neither planned nor expected. Opportunities may arise through new conditions in the marketplace, such as the emergence of a new client group, or through the creative process, such as discovering better ways to reduce inventory costs.

Problems and opportunities do not usually announce themselves; rather, they are defined by managers or others interested in how the organization allocates resources. Managers must actively scan through the streams of discrete and often ambiguous information to determine if something is wrong or if an opportunity exists. The perceptual process plays an important role, as do the manager's past experience and perspectives, in deciding whether certain information points to a problem that must be addressed. Employees, suppliers, clients, public interest groups, and other organizational stakeholders also attempt to shape the decision maker's perception that a problem or opportunity exists. Thus, decision making is frequently marked by politics and negotiation as vested interests try to influence decision makers in the identification and definition of the problem, as well as in the choice of alternatives.[6]

Symptoms and Causes

Deviations between current and desired organizational conditions are typically **symptoms** of more fundamental *root causes* in the organization. Through problem diagnosis, decision makers try to understand the link between the symptoms and their causes. The decision process is then directed toward changing the root causes so that the symptoms are reduced or eliminated.[7] High employee turnover, for instance, may be a symptom of (i.e., is caused by) an inequitable reward system. Rather than directly tackling high turnover, managers would diagnose its root cause(s) and then reduce or eliminate the symptom by changing the root cause(s) (in this case, by making the reward system more equitable). The distinction between symptoms and root causes is critical in effective business case analyses.

symptom
A deviation between "what is" and "what ought to be," typically signaling the existence of an underlying problem or opportunity that should be dealt with to correct the symptom.

Barriers to Problem Identification

The identification stage of decision making may seem straightforward, but managers face barriers in their attempts to effectively recognize and diagnose problems and opportunities. Several barriers to problem identification are shown in Exhibit 9–2 and are discussed below.

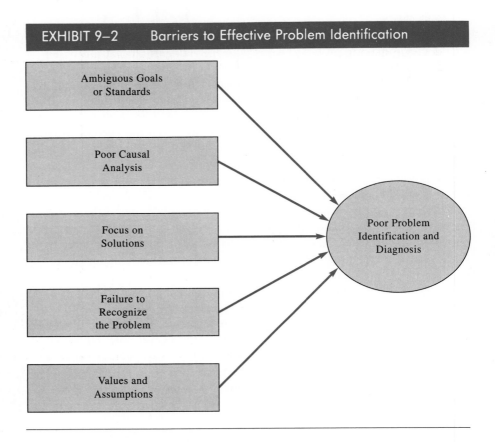

EXHIBIT 9–2   Barriers to Effective Problem Identification

Ambiguous Goals or Standards.   Problems are often difficult to define because organizational goals may be ambiguous, in conflict with each other, or not completely supported by other organizational members. Without clear goals, problems are difficult to recognize and alternatives cannot be easily selected. In some situations, problems are recognized only after drawn out discussions with various organizational stakeholders.[8] This point underlines the prevalence of organizational conflict and the importance of communication and attitude change in organizational settings (see Chapters 6 and 8).

Poor Causal Analysis.   Managers occasionally fail to identify the true cause(s) of the symptoms. This is more likely to happen when the situation is extremely complex, the setting is emotionally charged, the decision maker faces extreme time constraints, or perceptual errors distort the situation. Pressures from vested interests may cause the wrong problem to be identified, particularly when those groups have some degree of power over the decision maker.[9] Unfortunately, finding and solving the wrong problem can be quite costly, as the bed frame manufacturer described in Perspective 9–1 discovered.

PERSPECTIVE 9–1   Wrong Problem, Wrong Solution!

A British manufacturer hired a consultant to find out why sales of its iron bed frames were declining, particularly in Scotland and Wales. The consultant was known for his detailed technical analysis of statistical evidence and came highly recommended. After collecting a large amount of information on the sales force, the consultant recommended that the company's salespeople in Scotland and Wales should be replaced because, according to his analysis, they were less effective than those in England.

At great expense, the company followed the consultant's advice, but the new sales representatives fared no better than their predecessors and sales continued to decline. The company eventually learned (perhaps too late!) that the declining sales had nothing to do with the quality of the sales force. Rather, iron bedsteads were going out of fashion.

Source: J. Adair, *Management Decision Making* (Hants, England: Gower, 1985), p. 34.

Focus on Solutions.   Another common error is the tendency to define problems in terms of their solutions. You may hear someone say: ''The problem is that we need more control over our suppliers.'' The manager is basically suggesting a solution before investigating the root causes of the apparent symptoms. The tendency to focus on solutions is based on our need to reduce uncertainty, yet it can short circuit the problem diagnosis stage of decision making. Indeed, some experts believe that organizations are basically a collection of solutions looking for problems in the right settings. This ''garbage can model'' suggests that a decision occurs when the solution, problem, and setting coexist and a decision maker is there to put the pieces together! The garbage can model may be a rather extreme view of organizations as anarchies, but it does show how decisions may be driven by solutions more than problem definitions.[10]

Failure to Recognize the Problem.   Managers sometimes overlook problems because the symptoms have not been communicated to them. Negative information may be filtered or distorted as it flows up the organizational hierarchy, as we mentioned in Chapter 6.[11] Alternatively, some problems are so threatening that we ignore them or interpret them in a way that is more acceptable. This phenomenon, known as **perceptual defense,** can be a useful coping device, but it may also cause us to avoid important decisions until the situation becomes critical.[12]

perceptual defense
A phenomenon whereby individuals perceptually ignore or misinterpret information so that it is less threatening and more acceptable to them.

Values and Assumptions.   Values and assumptions pervade the decision-making process. In the problem identification stage, they establish the relative priority of competing goals. What may be viewed as a problem or opportunity to one manager is of no consequence to another because of their differing values. Consider the famous missed opportunities described in Per-

PERSPECTIVE 9–2   Famous Missed Opportunities

- Thomas Bata Sr., then CEO of Toronto-based Bata Ltd., the world's largest footwear company, was approached in the 1970s by a visitor who asked Bata for credit to finance his fledgling running shoe company. Bata was skeptical about extending credit to a stranger, and decided to reject the invitation. The visitor was the founder of Reebok International Ltd., which today is one of the leading names of athletic footwear. Meanwhile, Bata Ltd. is still struggling to secure a niche in this highly profitable sector of the footwear business.

- In 1962, Brian Epstein approached Decca Records with a demo of a new rock group he was managing. The Decca executive refused to sign the group, saying, "Groups with guitars are on their way out." Epstein also unsuccessfully peddled the demo to three other record companies before EMI Records agreed to sign the group, known as The Beatles. The rest is history!

- In 1972, the script for a low-budget movie called *American Graffiti* to be produced by a young film director, George Lucas, was rejected by several Hollywood studios on the grounds that it was "commercially unacceptable." Universal Studios initially rejected the project, but later changed its mind. *American Graffiti* became one of the highest-grossing movies of all time. In spite of Lucas's first success, Universal and other studios rejected the director's next project, a sci-fi movie. Twentieth-Century Fox reluctantly provided some development money, but Lucas was left to raise most of the funds himself. The project left Lucas financially broke and dispirited by the lack of interest from the major studios, but he still owned the picture and rights to sequels. His film, *Star Wars,* was a monumental success, as were its two sequels.

Sources: L. J. Peter, *Why Things Go Wrong* (New York: Bantam, 1984), pp. 147, 148, 150; D. Frost and M. Deakin, *I Could Have Kicked Myself* (London: André Deutsch, 1982), pp. 98, 123; and R. Collison, "How Bata Rules Its World," *Canadian Business,* September 1990, p. 28.

spective 9–2. In each case, the decision was based on false assumptions and beliefs about the future and the decision maker was unwilling (or unable) to perceive alternative scenarios.

Improving Problem Identification

Barriers to effective problem identification affect everyone, but we can minimize their effects by being aware of these limitations, discussing the situation with others, clarifying organizational goals, and practising diagnostic skills.

Be Aware of Limitations.   The first step is to be more aware of our perceptual biases and the problems that occur when identifying problems or opportunities. In this respect, the Johari Window procedure described in Chapter 7 is useful.

Discuss the Issue with Others.   Since problems and opportunities are defined as such by people, it is useful to discover whether your colleagues would also define the situation similarly, particularly when they are equally knowledgeable and experienced. If they also see the same problem and identify similar causes, you can be more confident in your judgment.

Clarify Organizational Goals.   Since ambiguous and conflicting goals tend to make problem identification difficult, this process can be improved by carefully examining organizational goals with others in the organization. Strategic planning and team building sessions are often beneficial because they force managers to better understand and agree upon organizational objectives and priorities.

Practise Diagnostic Skills.   An essential part of successful problem identification is correctly diagnosing the situation to identify the problem's root causes. Improving your diagnostic skills requires practise and experience. This book helps by presenting well-tested theories to link symptoms to root causes. Business cases provide valuable diagnostic skills training because students are required to use relevant theories to discover the causes of the apparent symptoms in the case.

PREDECISION

Once the problem or opportunity has been recognized and diagnosed, managers must decide how to proceed with the latter parts of the decision process. The selection of a particular process is called the **predecision** of decision making. Approaching the problem incorrectly can result in lost time, frustration, and possibly an incorrect answer.[13] Exhibit 9–3 lists some of the predecisions that managers should consider before actually solving the problem. Some of these predecision issues are addressed later in the chapter. (Deciding whether to involve others and what form this participation should take will be discussed in Chapter 11.) Another important predecision is whether to use a programmed or nonprogrammed procedure.

predecision
Selecting a particular decision process, such as whether to involve others and how to collect information, after a problem or opportunity has been identified.

Programmed versus Nonprogrammed Decisions

Problems can be distinguished on the basis of whether a programmed or nonprogrammed decision process can be applied to them. Repetitive and structured problems with well-defined goals can be approached using a **programmed decision** procedure because specific decision rules can be formulated to correct these discrepancies. These decision rules point to a specific solution to the problem so that the alternative development and selection stages are largely by-passed by the decision maker. Operations research professionals have an important organizational role in developing programmed decision routines for technical problems such as optimizing production schedules or product pricing for high- and low-volume customers.[14]

Nonprogrammed decisions are applied to unique, complex, or ill-defined situations requiring the manager's special attention. The full decision-making process is followed and judgment, intuition, and creativity are used

programmed decision
The decision process of relying on specific procedures to select the preferred solution without the need to identify or evaluate alternative choices.

nonprogrammed decision
The decision process applied to unique, complex, or ill-defined situations whereby the full decision-making process is followed and judgment, intuition, and creativity are used.

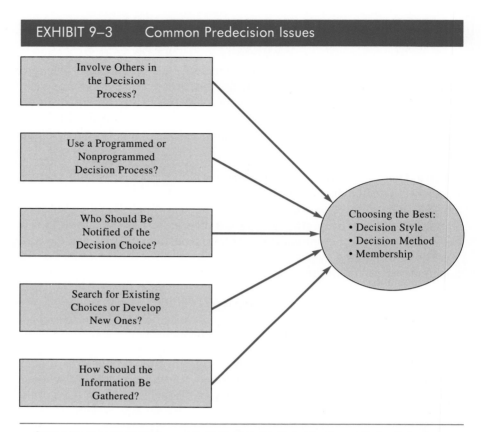

EXHIBIT 9–3   Common Predecision Issues

Involve Others in
the Decision
Process?

Use a Programmed or
Nonprogrammed
Decision Process?

Who Should Be
Notified of the
Decision Choice?

Search for Existing
Choices or Develop
New Ones?

How Should the
Information Be
Gathered?

Choosing the Best:
• Decision Style
• Decision Method
• Membership

Source: Based on W. C. Wedley and R. H. G. Field, "A Predecision Support System," *Academy of Management Review* 9 (1984), pp. 696–703.

because standard operating procedures do not exist.[15] As problems reappear, attempts are made to develop programmed decision routines. In this respect, programmed decisions drive out nonprogrammed decisions because people strive for predictable, routine situations. Canadian Tire's problem of limited growth in Canada is an example of nonprogrammed decision making because there was no ready-made procedure or policy to direct management to the best solution. Muncaster's comment that he had little basis on which to make the decision reflects the fact that there was no systematic decision formula to follow.

Generally speaking, middle- and upper-level managers are responsible for nonprogrammed decisions, whereas programmed decisions are made by supervisory and nonmanagement staff. This is consistent with the traditional rule of "management by exception," in which unique problems are passed up the organizational hierarchy. Increasingly, however, employees throughout the organization are asked to be responsible for nonprogrammed decision situations at their own level rather than referring them to superiors. For instance, in some of the Canadian operations of Pratt & Whitney and Westinghouse, self-managing work teams are responsible for making most decisions in the plant, including many of the nonprogrammed decisions previously assigned to the plant manager.[16]

Expert Systems

Some problems that appear to be of the nonprogrammed variety can be solved through computer programs called **expert systems**.[17] Typically, the user is asked many questions about the problem situation, and this information is then processed through a series of built-in decision rules until the computer program arrives at the preferred solution. These rules are usually developed by computer programmers who interview experts in the area where the system is intended to work. American Express developed an expert system that identifies bad credit risks among the firm's millions of cardholders. The computer program is appropriately called "Laurel's Brain" because its decision rules were based on the expertise of Laurel Miller, one of Amex's credit authorization managers. Laurel's Brain has substantially increased productivity and reduced financial losses and, according to Laurel Miller, makes decisions as good as his.[18]

expert systems
Computer programs that process complex decisions by adopting a series of decision rules used by human experts.

ALTERNATIVE DEVELOPMENT

The next stage in the decision-making process, particularly for nonprogrammed decisions, is to develop a list of possible solutions to the problem. There are actually two ways to develop alternatives: search and design.[19] Search involves looking around for ready-made solutions. Decision makers may try to recall solutions that have served the organization well in the past, they may passively wait for unsolicited alternatives to appear or actively invite others (such as potential suppliers) to propose solutions, or they may actively look around for solutions applied to similar problems elsewhere.

While many decisions include some form of a search for existing solutions, a few require the decision maker to design a custom-made solution or modify existing ones. Designing a solution can be costly, so this process is usually triggered only when search has been unsuccessful. The authors of one study of strategic decisions in Canadian organizations summarized the design process in this way: "Thus a solution crystallizes, as the designers grope along, building their solution brick by brick, without really knowing what it will look like until it is completed."[20] Designing a custom-made solution is a fuzzy process (at least for strategic decisions) with several loopbacks to earlier steps in the design. Invariably only one solution emerges, due to the cost and complexity of the design.

ALTERNATIVE SELECTION

The alternative selection stage involves evaluating and choosing from the courses of action available to the decision maker. One view of organizational decision making, called the **rational economic model,** suggests that managers consider all possible alternatives as well as all consequences to these alternatives, and that the decision choice represents the highest possible payoff among the many options.

rational economic decision model

A model of decision making that assumes managers consider all possible alternatives as well as all consequences to these alternatives and that the decision choice represents the highest possible payoff among the many options.

The rational economic model makes four important assumptions. Specifically, it assumes that decision makers (1) base their choice on well articulated and agreed-upon organizational goals, (2) have perfect information about cause-effect relationships and the value of outcomes, (3) are able to efficiently and simultaneously process information about all alternatives, and (4) are perfectly logical in choosing the outcome with the highest payoff. As you can imagine, the rational economic model is not very representative of actual decision-making behaviour. Let's look at these four assumptions more carefully.

Problems with Goals

The rational economic model assumes that decision makers base their choice on well articulated and agreed-upon organizational goals. Yet we have already learned that many organizational goals are ambiguous, in conflict with each other, or not completely supported by other organizational members. Goal ambiguity makes it difficult to decide the value of decision outcomes. Organizational members often disagree over the relative importance of various goals. This lack of goal consensus can lead to overt conflict among managers and can become a catalyst for organizational politics. There is also some doubt that managerial decisions are always based on organizational objectives. These concerns not only make it difficult to decide whether a problem exists, but also act as barriers to selecting the best option.

Problems with Information Search and Processing

bounded rationality decision model

A model of decision making that assumes decision makers have limited information processing capabilities and do not necessarily select the best possible alternative. It also recognizes that decisions will be based on incomplete knowledge and unclear problem definitions.

Even for reasonably simple and narrow issues, rarely is it possible to acquire all of the information relevant to each alternative or evaluate each option as completely and carefully as one might desire. We simply cannot process all of this information simultaneously. Moreover, as we discussed in Chapter 7, we frequently distort information based on our biases and perspectives.[21]

In recognition of this fact, Herbert Simon and his colleagues have proposed a theory of **bounded rationality**, which more accurately reflects the evaluation and selection of alternatives in the decision process (see Exhibit 9–4).[22] Bounded rationality describes decision makers in their true form—as people with limited information-processing capabilities who engage in a limited search for alternatives. It recognizes that decisions will be based on incomplete knowledge with only a partial comprehension of the true nature

EXHIBIT 9–4	Comparing Rational Economic and Bounded Rationality Assumptions	

Assumption	Rational Economic	Bounded Rationality
Time and cost of acquiring information	No time or cost restrictions	Requires time and cost
Quality of information	Perfect information	Imperfect information
Number of alternatives considered	All alternatives are considered	Only alternatives locally available are considered
Method of evaluating alternatives	Alternatives are evaluated simultaneously	Alternatives are evaluated sequentially
Decision standards	Fixed standard	Standard varies with quality of alternatives
Decision target	Maximizing	Satisficing

of the problem. The model acknowledges that the human capacity for formulating and solving complex problems is insufficient for objective rationality. Thus, it is better to acknowledge human limitations and prescribe a decision-making program within these parameters.

Problems with Maximization

According to the rational economic perspective, purely rational managers would maximize—that is, search for and ultimately select the best alternative available. But Simon's bounded rationality model more accurately depicts the idea that managers tend to **satisfice**—that is, look for and select the course of action that is satisfactory or good enough. What constitutes a good enough solution depends on the availability of satisfactory alternatives. Standards rise when satisfactory alternatives are easily found and fall when few are available.[23] Rationality involves first developing a complete list of alternatives so that these options may all be evaluated simultaneously. Satisficing, on the other hand, involves a sequential search for and evaluation of alternatives until the acceptable (good enough) alternative is found.

Bounded rationality suggests not only that managers are imperfect decision makers, but also that they must recognize and deal with these limits to rationality. It is a perpetual balancing act between the idealism of rationality and the realism of bounded rationality.[24]

Risk and Uncertainty in Decision Making

Risk taking is both an essential and exciting part of the managerial role, as the Northern Telecom experience described in Perspective 9–3 illustrates. **Risk** is traditionally defined as the probability that a particular choice will

satisficing
The process of looking for and selecting the course of action that is satisfactory or "good enough" rather than optimal or "the best."

decision risk
The probability that a particular choice will lead to particular outcomes; sometimes also considers the potential cost of a bad decision.

Northern Telecom (Nortel), Canada's leading tele-communications manufacturer, took a gamble in the early 1970s by being the first manufacturer of telephone networks to launch into the world of digital communication systems. Digital technology was well-known at the time, but few firms dared to apply it to the telecommunications industry. By all estimates, telephone companies did not want to replace their older, analogue switching systems with the new technology in the near future. Indeed, when Nortel launched its new digital line in 1976, representatives from American Telephone and Telegraph, the world's largest telephone company, said, "We don't see the

need right now for digital. We can see a continued expansion of our existing facilities on an analogue basis."

But Nortel researchers and executives sensed that digital would replace the more costly analogue equipment sooner than many believed. As expected, the new technology spread throughout the industry in just a few years, with Nortel riding the wave as the leading manufacturer. The risky decisions required to allocate resources to digital technology transformed Northern Telecom from a relatively unknown subsidiary of Bell Canada in the 1970s to one of the three largest telecommunications manufacturers in the

lead to specific outcomes. However, managers tend to consider risk in terms of the possibility of loss. In other words, they consider both the probability of something going wrong and the amount of resources lost if the decision fails. According to studies of Canadian, American, and Israeli managers, risk produces anxiety, fear, stimulation, and joy and is linked to the pleasure of success. As one executive explained: "Satisfaction from success is directly related to the degree of risk taken."[25]

decision uncertainty
The inability to predict future events with complete accuracy, specifically, the degree of inaccuracy of risk probabilities.

Organizational decisions also involve a degree of **uncertainty** because decision makers are unable to predict future events with complete accuracy. Decision uncertainty may be due to the uniqueness of the situation, the manager's unfamiliarity with the situation, or simply the lack of adequate information gathering. Unfortunately, uncertainty can have devastating effects. For example, Performance Sailcraft Inc. of Dorval, Quebec had a runaway success with the Laser sailboat until management made a major purchasing decision error. When the company set up its European operations in 1978, it decided to use a new glue which, as it turned out, was water soluble. Thousands of irate European owners demanded new boats while other craft using the faulty paste remained unsold. The huge losses from this fiasco were the main cause of the company's eventual failure.[26]

To reduce uncertainty, decision makers try to search out more information, but time is usually limited and collecting data can be costly. Thus, it is not uncommon for decision makers to fill in the missing information haphazardly. As described in Chapter 7, people often see trends or relationships in their environment even when these events are actually random. For example, if market share increases soon after a new sales training program is introduced, the sales manager might incorrectly believe that the training caused the market share increase. The increase may have had nothing to do

world. Today, Nortel is the world leader in digital switches with annual sales of over $6 billion.

Northern Telecom hasn't rested on its successful decisions of the past. Instead, company executives recently decided to "get the jump" on the global telecommunications market of the 1990s by launching a new line of products based on fibre-optic technology. Fibre optics is an information transmission system that sends pulses of light along hair-sized strands of glass.

Industry analysts agree that Nortel's decision is the right course of action to maintain its leadership into the next century. Large chunks of the company's resources are being allocated to develop fibre-optic systems. But Northern Telecom's decision makers know that getting the jump on the competition means making important—and usually risky—decisions long before others think the idea is feasible.

Sources: R. Siklos, "Northern's Fibre-Optic Leap into the Future," *Financial Times of Canada*, October 16, 1989, p. 26; G. Blackwell, "Northern Lights," *Canadian Business*, March 1990, pp. 40–44; J. Steed, "Canada's Giant among Giants," *Globe & Mail*, February 19, 1983, p. 10; R. Steklasa, "A Growing Fish in High-Tech Pond," *Financial Post*, October 24, 1981, pp. 21–22; and D. Walker, "Five-Year Target: $3 Billion in Sales," *Executive*, May 1977, pp. 61–70.

with sales training, but the manager's quick conclusion about the cause-effect relationship could influence his or her decision to increase the sales training budget next year.

Uncertainty Absorption.   As information flows away from its source, it loses some of the uncertainty on which it is based and develops an aura of precision.[27] This is known as **uncertainty absorption**. A satirical comment made over 80 years ago sums up the pervasiveness of uncertainty absorption and its consequences for organizational decisions:

> The government are very keen on amassing statistics. They collect them, add them, raise them to the nth power, take the cube root and prepare wonderful diagrams. But you must never forget that every one of these figures comes in the first instance from the village watchman, who just puts down what he damn pleases.[28]

A contemporary example of uncertainty absorption exists in large firms where professionals forecast consumer demand or bond market trends. Most forecasts are at least partly based on rather imprecise information, but decision makers are further removed from this uncertainty and tend to view these forecasts as objective and unbiased information. The fuzzy estimate of competitor strength generated by the forecaster becomes a near-certain fact to the senior executive.

Decision Heuristics

Decision makers use rules of thumb, called **heuristics,** to help them evaluate alternatives under conditions of uncertainty.[29] Heuristics may be well-tested standards ("only buy equipment with injection-molded components"), or

uncertainty absorption

A perceptual phenomenon whereby information loses some of the uncertainty on which it is based and develops an aura of precision as it moves away from its source.

heuristic

A "rule of thumb" (decision rule) used repeatedly by people to help them evaluate alternatives under conditions of uncertainty.

PERSPECTIVE 9—4   Ted Rogers' Winning Heuristic

Ted Rogers, founder and CEO of Rogers Communications Inc., describes his favourite heuristic: "I believe in getting in on new technology in the formative stages . . . to ride the wave of growth. Even if you make a lot of mistakes, growth covers them up. If you survive, you can do extraordinarily well."

Using this rule of thumb of staying technologically ahead of the crowd, Rogers has cultivated an impressive business empire:

- As a 26-year-old law student in 1960, Rogers bought a Toronto FM radio station (CHFI-FM) when only 5 percent of Canadians had FM receivers. FM radio is now an immensely popular broadcast medium and threatens the historical superiority of AM radio.

- In the 1960s and 1970s, Rogers entered the cable television industry when few people knew what "cable TV" meant. Today, Rogers owns Canada's largest cable firm, with 25 percent of the market.

- In the early 1980s Rogers entered the cellular telephone market by forming Cantel Inc. Senior executives at Rogers Communications advised against this move, but Rogers followed his successful decision heuristic of leading the technological edge. Cantel has since become one of the most successful firms in the Rogers family of companies, representing half of the Canadian market in this high-growth industry.

- Now Ted Rogers is eyeing the lucrative long-distance telephone market. Again relying on his rule of thumb, Rogers plans to stay ahead of the competition by using the latest technology to compete against Bell Canada and other giants in the telephone industry.

Sources: R. Fisher, "Ted's Team," *Canadian Business* 62 (August 1989), pp. 28–34; and M. Levin, "Mr. Rogers' Neighbourhood," *Financial Times,* February 26, 1990, p. 29.

they may represent superstitions with little basis in fact ("never visit new customers on the 13th of the month"). Heuristics simplify the decision-making process by focussing on only one or two important factors. Some highly respected business and political leaders rely on their heuristics to make important decisions. Perspective 9–4 describes how one Canadian business leader has prospered from his particular rule of thumb.

Improving Alternative Selection

Rather than applying quantitative methods with specific economic criteria to every problem or opportunity, the bounded rationality model suggests that we should first try to recognize our information gathering and processing limitations and then find predecision strategies that will enable us to evaluate alternatives within these limitations. For example, several qualified people should be involved where problems are complex because it is unlikely that one person possesses enough information to understand the available options.

Decision makers can also organize their evaluation process more systematically without adding too much time or cost. They should explicitly write out the criteria or heuristics used to make the decision and then compare the known alternatives on each factor. Information errors or perceptual biases can be reduced by comparing your notes with others involved in the decision process. The final decision may still be based on judgment, but summarizing the information in this way forces the decision maker to look at each alternative more carefully. Many expert systems follow this procedure and are considered quite beneficial in forcing managers to think through the evaluation and selection of alternatives more carefully.

IMPLEMENTATION

Decision making is only a mental exercise if the preferred alternative is not properly implemented. Implementation begins a new phase whereby the decision maker must rally other people and mobilize sufficient resources to translate the decision into action. The potential problems of implementation should be carefully figured into the evaluation of alternatives, but it is often difficult to anticipate resistance and resource shortages before action is taken. Implementation involves employee behaviours, so effective implementation depends on the four factors influencing individual behaviour (see Chapter 2).

Ability.   Many decisions fail because the people responsible for implementing them lack the skills or aptitude required to complete the action satisfactorily. In extraordinary circumstances, the selected course of action may be impossible for anyone to implement. In a rather extreme example, the village council in Lakefield, Ontario, passed noise abatement by-laws permitting birds to sing for 30 minutes during the day and 15 minutes at night. The village council clerk, who was flooded with calls asking how he could get the birds to stop singing, admitted that he didn't think through the implications of this decision when he wrote the legislation.[30]

Motivation.   Even if the decision can be implemented, people might not be sufficiently motivated to do so. Organizational members or other stakeholders may resist changes resulting from the decision. (We will look more closely at resistance to organizational change in Chapter 15.)

Role Perceptions.   Those implementing the decision must understand the decision and be able to see what the final product should look like. This calls for effective communication between the decision maker and those responsible for implementation. The problem of role clarity is particularly critical when the decision involves multiple goals with different priorities. For example, those responsible for implementing a new product line must understand the relative importance of product quality and quantity.

Situational Contingencies.   When evaluating alternatives, the decision maker must be sure that sufficient resources are available and that potential impediments have been checked. Many new businesses have failed because the decision makers lacked sufficient financial or other resources. Developing an action plan often helps to anticipate these obstacles to decision implementation.

FEEDBACK

After the preferred choice has been implemented, the decision maker generally looks for feedback indicating whether or not the gap between what is and what ought to be has narrowed. The success of some decisions is easily recognized because the decision criteria are objectively based. For example, a fairly clear indicator of a new product's success is its market share after a certain period of time and the level of repeat purchases. The success of other decisions may be more difficult to comprehend, however. The decision to invest resources in new equipment or organizational development training for senior managers may have long-term benefits that are difficult to separate from other events.

Postdecisional Justification

postdecisional justification

A perceptual phenomenon whereby the preferred or selected option is made to appear more attractive and the discarded options less attractive.

After making an important decision, people tend to engage in a process of **postdecisional justification** whereby the preferred or selected option is made to appear more attractive and the discarded options less attractive. In other words, we try to justify our decision, often subconsciously, to avoid feelings of cognitive dissonance.[31] For example, if you have several good job offers and have selected one of them, it is quite likely that you will try to rationalize that decision. Three postdecisional justification strategies tend to occur:[32]

1. *Look for more information*—You might listen more attentively to news about your new employer or actively review material already received about the other offers to confirm your decision.
2. *Change the importance of decision criteria*—You might subconsciously reduce the importance of the negative attributes and exaggerate the importance of the highlights of the job you have decided to take.
3. *Selectively distort information*—You might forget about negative aspects of the chosen job as well as positive features of the discarded jobs, or you might challenge the credibility of sources critical of your new employer.

Postdecisional justification reduces cognitive dissonance only until clear feedback either confirms the decision or suggests that an error has been made. Our expectations are typically inflated by this distortion and, consequently, reality may come as a painful shock when objective feedback is received. However, unequivocal negative feedback about a decision does not always lead decision makers to abandon their choice.

Escalation of Commitment

When feedback suggests that the decision was incorrect, the objective and rational decision maker would terminate the action and reconsider the problem. Yet there is plenty of evidence that people do not react to negative feedback quite so dispassionately. Particularly when implementation is expensive, those responsible for the decision often continue on the existing course of action and may even allocate more resources to the failing project. This phenomenon of investing more resources into bad decisions is known as **escalation of commitment**.[33]

escalation of commitment
The act of repeating an apparently bad decision or allocating more resources to a failing course of action.

Vancouver's Expo 86: An Escalation Example

An example of escalation of commitment occurred in the planning of Expo 86, the world's fair held in Vancouver.[34] The government of British Columbia decided during the late 1970s to host a transportation exhibition with a budget of only $78 million and revenues from concessions and gate receipts almost matching expenses. These plans soon ballooned to a much larger fair, but projected revenues increased proportionately until, by 1984, it became apparent to everyone that projected attendance and revenue figures were overly-optimistic. The project also faced labour troubles and was far behind schedule just two years before its opening in May 1986.

In April 1984, Jim Pattison (the fair's newly appointed chairman) recommended that Expo 86 be cancelled, with an estimated shutdown cost of $80 million. However, it was rumoured that the federal government would sue to get its investment back and several groups had collected petitions with thousands of signatures demanding that Expo 86 be continued. A few days later, the Premier of British Columbia announced that the fair would go on. Any deficits would be covered by lotteries and the unions would be controlled through special legislation. Even with large budget cuts in 1985, Expo 86 eventually became a $1.5 billion project with a deficit of over $300 million.

Causes of Escalation of Commitment

The Expo 86 story illustrates several factors that lead decision makers deeper into a questionable course of action. These factors are shown in Exhibit 9–5 and described below.

Perceptual Defense.   Earlier in this chapter we noted that some problems are not immediately recognized or are actively denied because the decision maker ignores or neutralizes negative information about the decision. During the infancy of Expo 86, staff reports warned of project escalations, but they were either ignored or downplayed by the government of British Columbia. The overly optimistic revenue expectations represent another perceptual defense because criticisms of these estimates were lightly dismissed.

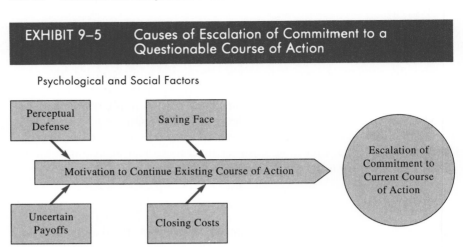

EXHIBIT 9–5   Causes of Escalation of Commitment to a Questionable Course of Action

Psychological and Social Factors

Perceptual Defense

Saving Face

Escalation of Commitment to Current Course of Action

Motivation to Continue Existing Course of Action

Uncertain Payoffs

Closing Costs

Economic and Political Factors

Saving Face.   Decision makers who are personally identified with the decision outcomes tend to persist in their course of action because it demonstrates confidence in their decision-making ability. Cancelling Expo 86 would have suggested that the Premier of British Columbia (who originally proposed the fair) made a bad decision, whereas continuing the fair would be a vote of confidence towards his leadership ability. The Premier also may have continued the project because he had repeatedly emphasized the value of the project and to reverse this position would convey an image of inconsistent leadership. Finally, the Premier's decision was face-saving for the entire province because cancellation would jeopardize British Columbia's image as a place where challenges are accomplished rather than abandoned.

Uncertain Payoffs.   In many decision situations, it is not clear whether the wrong course of action has been taken. This leaves decision makers with the possible risk of abandoning a project that may actually be correct. In the Expo 86 example, no one could prove that the fair would fail to provide long-term economic benefits to British Columbia.

Closing Costs.   Decision makers often prefer to continue on the existing course of action because of the high or unknown costs of stopping. Jim Pattison estimated the price of cancelling Expo 86 at $80 million, but his figures did not include the social and political costs of this action. The public had high expectations and were very supportive of the project. Alternative courses of action (e.g., a different public project) were unfamiliar with unknown risks.

Reducing Escalation and Postdecisional Justification

Once again, the first step to better decision making is to be aware of the human limitations that interfere with the process. By recognizing the possibility of postdecisional justification and escalation of commitment, managers will be more sensitive to their perceptions and behaviour following decision implementation. By openly discussing the decision and relevant feedback with others, you can see different perspectives more clearly. At the same time, other people can help you become aware of your perceptual biases regarding the preferred and discarded options.

Escalation of commitment can be minimized by establishing a preset level at which the decision is abandoned or reevaluated. This is similar to a "stop-loss" order in the stock market, whereby the stock is sold if it falls below a certain price. Another strategy is to separate decision choosers from decision implementers. This would minimize the problem of saving face because the person responsible for implementation and feedback would not be as personally threatened if the project were cancelled. Finally, organizational leaders can develop a culture supportive of reasonable failures.[35] Mistakes are less likely to be hidden or perpetuated when the organization rewards (or, at least, doesn't punish) those who make good tries that don't work. As an engineering analyst at John Deere Ltd. in Welland, Ontario, explains: "You have to have the courage to admit you were wrong, otherwise you just send good money after bad."[36]

INTUITIVE DECISION MAKING

The general model of decision making takes a rather systematic perspective of the subject. Yet any seasoned manager will tell you that many decisions are based more on a sixth sense or gut feeling rather than a conscious identification of problems and evaluation of alternative solutions. This is nicely phrased by the chief executive officer of Cummins Engine Company:

> When the hair on the back of my neck has just given me an unpleasant sensation, either because of a recommendation or a set of facts in front of me, I know that something is wrong. We are trying to teach our managers that when you have a sixth sense that says something is screwy, pay attention to it."[37]

Knowing when a problem or opportunity exists and selecting the best course of action without the apparent use of reasoning or logic is called **intuition**.[38] Intuition has been romanticized by some writers as the stuff inherent in great leaders and by others as the mystical outcome of right-brain or left-brain thinking. The extent to which these beliefs are true is still unclear. However, recent studies suggest that intuition is actually systematic decision making burned into our subconscious by habit. Intuitive managers see a situation and begin to sense that a problem or opportunity exists,

intuition

The phenomenon of knowing when a problem or opportunity exists and selecting the best course of action without the apparent use of reasoning or logic.

or that a particular course of action is not quite right. This sense is based on years of training and experience during which the decision maker has learned thousands of environmental patterns.[39]

This perspective of intuitive decision making is illustrated in studies of chess masters when they play several opponents at the same time. Grand masters look at the chess board, make their move without time to systematically consider the consequences, and proceed on to another board. They are able to make the right choice (most of the time) because they have learned patterns of chess arrangements and are able to quickly see when something is out of place and when an opportunity is present. In this respect, intuition involves recognizing whether the perceived situation 'fits' a previously learned pattern and, if not, knowing how to correct the situation or take advantage of the windfall.

Intuitive managers have this same skill. They recognize, almost subconsciously, when something is wrong or an opportunity may be available to benefit the organization because the situation does or does not fit the learned pattern. Some people may have a better aptitude for making decisions intuitively, but one of the most important factors is previous experience and intimate knowledge of the business environment. Intuition requires a large dictionary of patterns with which to scan the environment and make decisions more effectively. It is not surprising, then, that several writers and practitioners have concluded that seasoned managers with many years of experience in a particular industry are usually best equipped to make effective decisions.[40] As one Canadian CEO concluded: "To run a company properly you have to understand the business very well. Otherwise you might make a decision without understanding its implications."[41]

CRISIS DECISION MAKING

It was an ordinary Monday morning for Melvyn Stein, president of AHA Manufacturing, until the fax machine began producing unusual letters with impressive letterheads from Washington, D.C., law firms. The Brampton, Ontario, manufacturer of stretch limousines knew that competitors in the United States might file lawsuits against Canadian businesses for dumping their products in the U.S. market, but Stein didn't seriously believe that someone would involve AHA on this matter. Even when he realized from the faxed letters that he was being sued, Stein didn't realize at first that he was about to face a major crisis that could jeopardize the firm's survival.[42]

crisis

Any unexpected situation that seriously threatens high priority goals and requires a quick nonprogrammed decision response.

As Melvyn Stein's dilemma illustrates, a **crisis** is an unexpected situation that seriously threatens high-priority goals and requires a quick nonprogrammed decision response.[43] From this definition, we can see four components to a crisis situation. First, crises pose a serious *threat* to important goals. As in Melvyn Stein's case, events that threaten the organization's survival are most likely to be identified as a crisis. Second, crises involve *time restrictions* for a decision and effective response. Too much delay may increase the risk of failure or further loss. Third, crises represent rapidly changing circumstances that *surprise* the decision maker. There may be early signs of a crisis, but decision makers are unaware of them or do not recognize the implications for their own organization. Finally, crises are *unique situations* requiring a nonprogrammed response. They do not involve simply recognizing the problem and providing an automatic action.[44]

These four conditions—threat, time restriction, surprise, and uniqueness—potentially undermine the decision-making process. Since crises are unique, decision alternatives are typically vague and their relative merits are unclear. Time constraints make information search incomplete and haphazard. High stress levels typically result from the threat and surprise characteristics of crises, resulting in less-efficient information processing. Managers are less willing to accept the risk of custom-made solutions under crisis conditions, preferring instead to rely on solutions that have been effective in other situations. Decision making also tends to become centralized in the hands of top management, which further reduces the amount of relevant information known to those responsible for resolving the problem.[45]

Increasingly, managers are required to make important decisions under crisis conditions. The situation facing AHA Manufacturing is only one of many crises that face managers in this increasingly complex world. Exhibit 9–6 lists different types of corporate crises based on whether they originate within or outside of the firm and whether they are predicated by technical/economic or people/social/organizational factors.

Effective Crisis Management

Crises are unexpected, but specialists in crisis management advocate several strategies to improve decision making and organizational actions under crisis conditions.[46]

Interpret Early Warning Systems.   Most crises are preceded by information warning of the impending threat. For example, months before NASA's Space Shuttle *Challenger* explosion in which seven astronauts were killed, several engineers tried to inform decision makers of the potential catastrophe. One memo warning NASA officials of the almost guaranteed disaster began with the futile cry "Help!" Effective crisis management involves learning to recognize these early warning signals. In many cases, better systems must be implemented for monitoring equipment and receiving information about suppliers, customers, employees, and other stakeholders.

Develop Programmed Decision Rules.   Crises are unique, but many have occurred in other organizations. Thus, programmed decision rules for specific crisis situations can be developed by learning from the misfortunes of others. Emergency procedures are developed in this way. By learning from similar events elsewhere, organizations can compare alternate courses of

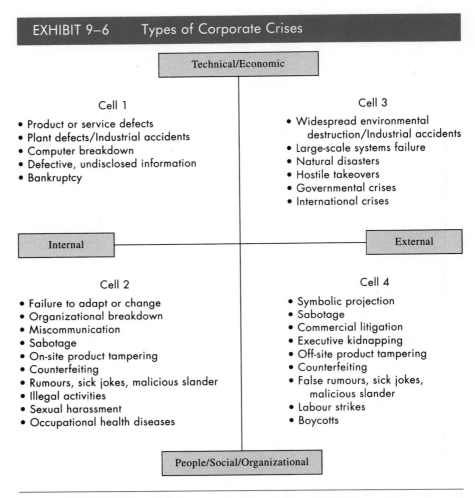

EXHIBIT 9–6 Types of Corporate Crises

Technical/Economic

Cell 1
- Product or service defects
- Plant defects/Industrial accidents
- Computer breakdown
- Defective, undisclosed information
- Bankruptcy

Cell 3
- Widespread environmental destruction/Industrial accidents
- Large-scale systems failure
- Natural disasters
- Hostile takeovers
- Governmental crises
- International crises

Internal | External

Cell 2
- Failure to adapt or change
- Organizational breakdown
- Miscommunication
- Sabotage
- On-site product tampering
- Counterfeiting
- Rumours, sick jokes, malicious slander
- Illegal activities
- Sexual harassment
- Occupational health diseases

Cell 4
- Symbolic projection
- Sabotage
- Commercial litigation
- Executive kidnapping
- Off-site product tampering
- Counterfeiting
- False rumours, sick jokes, malicious slander
- Labour strikes
- Boycotts

People/Social/Organizational

Source: I. Mitroff, P. Shivastava, and F. E. Udwadia, "Effective Crisis Management," *Academy of Management Executive* 1 (1987), p. 287.

action and develop systematic contingency plans. Those responsible for implementing these procedures can then be thoroughly trained to act quickly and effectively when the crisis occurs.

Simulate Crisis Situations. Organizations can be prepared for some crises by challenging managers to resolve hypothetical problems. H. R. MacMillan, one of the founders of Vancouver-based MacMillan Bloedel Ltd., was known for testing managers with simulated crises. For example, he wrote to a plywood plant manager on Vancouver Island: "Please tell me in not more than a page and a half what you would do if the Panama Canal were shut down tomorrow." The manager's contingency plan was expected within the week. Similar strategies are applied today by Shell Oil and other proactive firms.[47]

Develop Crisis Management Teams.   Several organizations have established special units known as *crisis management teams* to prepare for and handle special emerging situations. In the largest organizations, members of these teams have full-time responsibility in crisis prevention and preparation.[48]

Crises present a strong test of management's ability to make effective decisions under difficult circumstances. Another test, which is receiving increasing public scrutiny, is the extent to which organizational decisions are based on accepted moral principles. In the next section, we look at this important topic of ethical decision making.

ETHICAL DECISION MAKING

Managers are continually confronted with the need to make choices that affect the allocation of organizational resources. To varying degrees, these decisions have moral implications for the organization and the society in which it operates. Business ethics refers to the moral character of organizational actions, that is, the extent to which these actions represent "good" or "bad" conduct. Ethical decision making involves making choices based not only on narrow problem-relevant criteria (e.g., Is there a market for this product idea?), but also on a broader set of principles used by society to judge the morality of conduct.

Canadians tend to think that they live in a society with relatively high moral standards, but it is not difficult to find unethical business practices in this country. For example, the Economic Council of Canada reports that no fewer than 28 Canadian financial institutions failed or suffered severe difficulties during the 1980s because of "fraud and self-dealing by the owners."[49] Fortunately, several Canadian corporations have also led the business world toward higher standards of ethical conduct. Timothy Eaton, founder of Eaton's department stores, launched his enterprise in 1869 with a stern warning that his clerks should not deceive customers or sell them goods they did not need. Eaton also led North American industry in ethical conduct toward employees by working toward a more reasonable work week and providing financial, medical, and other assistance to employees.[50]

Most of us would agree that Timothy Eaton's actions are morally right while fraud and self-dealing are morally wrong, but it is very difficult to agree on the rules of ethical conduct. Three basic principles—utilitarianism, individual rights, and distributive justice—provide some guidance, but their relative priority is unclear and ethical reasoning will always be a tricky business.[51]

Utilitarianism

The best-known and perhaps the oldest moral criterion is to seek the greatest good for the greatest number of people. The moral correctness of a decision, therefore, is measured in terms of the degree of satisfaction it provides to those affected by the decision outcomes. This dictum basically requires a cost-benefit analysis of each decision alternative. But as we have emphasized throughout this chapter, it is difficult to evaluate choices accurately because of uncertainty (the lack of information) and imperfect information processing. The task is made even more difficult by the fact that it is not always clear what is good for people and, in any event, it is exceedingly difficult to measure this abstract concept.

It is also possible to think of situations in which a business decision could cause incredible danger or hardship to a few people while benefitting many others. For example, the utilitarian argument might condone a decision whereby employees would face high exposure to cancer-causing agents in the workplace in order to benefit many customers. Many people would argue that this situation is unethical, so the utilitarian perspective is insufficient.

Individual Rights

The morality of business decisions can also be judged by the extent that they uphold or violate individual rights. Individual rights are standards that provide protection to people in our society. Many individual rights are entrenched in legal statutes and common law. For example, consumers receive some protection against misleading advertising and employees receive legal protection against unsafe working conditions. However, individual rights refer to moral rights, not just those entrenched in law. Legislation helps to protect individual rights, but the morality of business decisions is not confined to legal standards.

Business decision makers must consider individual rights when choosing alternative courses of action, but this can be a rather difficult process. In some cases, individual rights accepted by most citizens have not yet received protection in law. Where statutes exist, their implications for a particular decision may be ambiguous. There is also the problem that different rights are often in conflict. The shareholders' right to be informed about corporate activities may ultimately conflict with a senior manager's right to privacy. This trade-off leads us to the third moral principle of ethical conduct, distributive justice.

Distributive Justice

The distributive justice principle requires the decision maker to distribute costs and benefits equitably. This principle is based on the equity theory described in Chapter 3. Generally speaking, distributive justice requires decision outcomes to be consistently shared proportional to the individual's contribution. The problem, of course, is that there is no agreement on what is considered an acceptable contribution. To some people, performance is the main factor, while others emphasize seniority, status, or need.

Maintaining Ethical Standards in Organizational Decisions

Organizations are facing increasing pressure to ensure that their decisions are consistent with society's moral standards. While this mandate will never be easily fulfilled, several safeguards can be introduced to ensure that decisions include ethical considerations.[52]

Distribute a Written Corporate Code of Ethics.   With the involvement of senior management and representatives from other areas of the organization, a corporate code of ethical conduct should be developed and distributed to all employees. Everyone who works at Imperial Oil is required to read the 20-page corporate code of ethics and sign a statement "to demonstrate your understanding of and compliance with policies contained in the booklet."[53] Gulf Canada's written ethical code of conduct regarding accepting gifts or entertainment is described in Exhibit 9–7.

Conduct Ethics Training Seminars.   In addition to a corporate ethical code, organizations should provide decision makers with basic training on ethical conduct. These seminars help employees work through ethical dilemmas by applying the corporate code of ethical conduct. The long-term objective is to help participants internalize these standards so that ethical considerations are addressed almost intuitively.

Link Ethical Behaviour to the Reward System.   Codes of ethical conduct should be linked to the organization's reward system. This practice is found at the Royal Bank where the company's ethical code of conduct is reviewed and discussed with employees during their performance appraisal reviews.[54] Organizational sanctions should also be linked to conscious violations of the company's moral standards. Finally, ethics should be an important factor when selecting and promoting people. This ensures that senior executives serve as exemplary role models for others to follow.[55]

Develop an Ethics Committee.   A few organizations, such as Provigo Inc. and John Labatt Ltd., have established a corporate ethics committee to resolve or give advice regarding significant moral dilemmas facing the organization and to address changing ethical standards in society. The ethics committee is usually a subcommittee of the Board of Directors that meets about six to eight times each year. While it is true that everyone should think ethically, the committee's purpose is also to remind employees of the firm's ethical code of conduct.

EXHIBIT 9–7   Gulf Canada's Ethical Conduct Guidelines Regarding Gifts and Entertainment

In the conduct of the company's business you may have to decide whether or not to offer or accept gifts or entertainment.

On some occasions giving or accepting gifts or entertainment is an appropriate business courtesy. On other occasions, however, such practises might compromise your ability to remain objective in making business decisions on behalf of the company, or might be perceived as using undue influence to seek business opportunities on our behalf.

The difficulty lies in defining the point where giving or receiving gifts or entertainment becomes unacceptable either in value or frequency. In extreme situations, gifts can be considered secret commissions, and are unlawful for both the giver and the receiver.

The following guidelines will help you decide the appropriateness of giving or accepting gifts or entertainment:

- You may accept advertising novelties of trivial value, which are widely distributed either by customers or venders.
- You may both give and receive customary business amenities such as meals, provided the expenses involved are kept to a reasonable level. You should report your entertainment expenses clearly on your expense account indicating the people you entertained and the companies they represent.

Some basic principles to consider when giving or receiving gifts or entertainment are:

- The amounts and types of gifts and entertainment you receive should meet the reciprocity test; that is, you should not accept anything that you could not give within Gulf's policy guidelines.
- They should be infrequent.
- They should serve a legitimate business purpose.
- They should be appropriate to your business responsibilities.

When you have doubts about the appropriateness of your actions, consult your supervisor.

Source: Gulf Canada Resources, *A Statement of Corporate Values and Ethics,* 1987, pp. 9–12. Reprinted by permission.

SUMMARY

- Decision making is a conscious process of making choices among one or more alternatives with the intention of moving toward some desired state of affairs. This process includes six basic steps: problem identification, predecision, alternative development, alternative selection (including evaluation and choice), implementation, and feedback.

- A variety of perceptual, structural, and informational barriers enter the decision-making process to make it virtually impossible to reach the optimal solution. Decision makers fail to recognize problems or opportunities, they are unable to get reliable information on all possible alternatives, and they may even decide to continue on a course of action that is not working as expected.

* Some decision-making problems can be minimized by being more aware of human biases in decision making, practising diagnostic skills, clarifying organizational goals, involving others in the decision-making process, identifying decision criteria more explicitly, preparing a workable action plan, and separating decision choosers from those responsible for decision implementation.

* The general model of decision making implies a systematic approach to organizational problems, but seasoned managers often rely on intuition to identify a problem or choose a workable solution. Intuition is systematic decision making burned into our subconscious by habit. Through experience, we learn to recognize when something is out of place or when an available solution fits the problem. One management writer has succinctly summed up the role of systematic and intuitive decision making by recommending that managers "get the facts, analyze them, and then do what *feels* right."[56]

* Crises are unique situations allowing limited time for a solution. They place the decision maker under stressful conditions because of the surprise and level of threat involved. Early warning signals can help managers avoid many potential crises and programmed decision rules can be developed from other crises. Crisis simulations and the development of crisis management teams can also minimize the organization's risk of a crisis.

* Virtually every decision has moral implications because it affects the well-being of others, from shareholders and suppliers to employees and the public. Three basic principles—utilitarianism, individual rights, and distributive justice—provide some guidance for decision makers when identifying problems and evaluating alternatives. To ensure that organizational decisions include ethical considerations, a corporate code of ethical conduct should be written and employees should be trained to think through problems from an ethical standpoint. Ethical decision making should be rewarded, and an ethics committee can be formed to address ethical dilemmas and evolving societal standards.

DISCUSSION QUESTIONS

1. How do problems or opportunities originate?
2. What is a predecision and how does it fit into the decision-making process?
3. What's wrong with the rational economic model of decision making in terms of selecting decision alternatives?

4. Distinguish between uncertainty and risk in decision making. What effects do each have in selecting alternatives?

5. How does postdecisional justification affect the evaluation of decision outcomes?

6. Explain how managers develop intuitive decision making.

7. What are the four conditions that result in crisis decision making? What problems do these conditions create in the decision-making process?

8. What are the three basic principles of ethical decision making?

NOTES

1. P. Cook, "Canadian Tire Expansion Concentrated on U.S. Market," *Globe and Mail,* August 10, 1981, p. B7; G. Davies, "Good Times in Bad Times," *Executive,* February 1982, pp. 26–28; F. Phillips, "Canadian Tire Finds Texas Trail a Bit Bumpy," *Financial Post,* March 26, 1983, p. 18; H. Enchin, "Canadian Tire Unit in Do-or-Die Bid to Reposition in U.S. Parts Market," *Globe and Mail,* March 30, 1985, p. B4; M. Salter, "Firing a Canadian Legend," *Maclean's,* June 17, 1985, p. 34; and K. Kidd, "Canadian Tire Agrees to Sell White Stores," *Toronto Star,* December 12, 1985, p. E1.

2. H. A. Simon, *Administrative Behavior* (New York: Free Press, 1957), pp. 1–2.

3. F. A. Shull, Jr., A. L. Delbecq, and L. L. Cummings, *Organizational Decision Making* (New York: McGraw-Hill, 1970), p. 31.

4. This model is adapted from several sources, including H. Mintzberg, D. Raisinghani, and A. Théorét, "The Structure of 'Unstructured' Decision Processes," *Administrative Science Quarterly* 21 (1976), pp. 246–75; H. A. Simon, *The New Science of Management Decisions* (New York: Harper & Row, 1960); C. Kepner and B. Tregoe, *The Rational Manager* (New York: McGraw-Hill, 1965); and W. C. Wedley and R. H. G. Field, "A Predecision Support System" *Academy of Management Review* 9 (1984), pp. 696–703.

5. B. M. Bass, *Organizational Decision Making* (Homewood, Ill.: Irwin, 1983), Chapter 3; Kepner and Tregoe, *The Rational Manager;* and W. F. Pounds, "The Process of Problem Finding," *Industrial Management Review* 11 (Fall 1969), pp. 1–19.

6. M. Lyles and H. Thomas, "Strategic Problem Formulation: Biases and Assumptions Embedded in Alternative Decision-Making Models," *Journal of Management Studies* 25 (1988), pp. 131–45; M. W. McCall, Jr., and R. E. Kaplan, *Whatever It Takes: Decision Makers at Work* (Englewood Cliffs, N.J.: Prentice Hall, 1985), Chapter 2; and D. A. Cowan, "Developing a Process Model of Problem Recognition," *Academy of Management Review* 11 (1986), pp. 763–76.

7. P. F. Drucker, *The Practice of Management* (New York: Harper & Brothers, 1954), pp. 353–57.

8. L. T. Pinfield, "A Field Evaluation of Perspectives on Organizational Decision Making," *Administrative Science Quarterly* 31 (1986), pp. 365–88; R. M. Cyert and J. G. March, *A Behavioral Theory of the Firm* (Englewood Cliffs, N.J.: Prentice Hall, 1963); and J. D. Thompson and A. Tuden, "Strategies, Structures, and Processes of Organizational Decision," in J. D. Thompson, P. B. Hammond, R. W. Hawkes, B. H. Junker, and A. Tuden (eds.), *Comparative Studies in Administration* (Pittsburgh, Penn.: University of Pittsburgh Press, 1959).

9. I. I. Mitroff, "On Systematic Problem Solving and the Error of the Third Kind," *Behavioral Science* 9 (1974), pp. 383–93; and D. Hellriegal, J. W. Slocum, Jr., and R. W. Woodman, *Organizational Behavior,* 5th ed. (St. Paul, Minn.: West, 1989), pp. 393–94.

10. M. D. Cohen, J. G. March, and J. P. Olsen, "A Garbage Can Model of Organizational Choice," *Administrative Science Quarterly* 17 (1972), pp. 1–25.

11. C. Fornell and R. Westbrook, "The Vicious Circle of Consumer Complaints," *Journal of Marketing* 48 (Summer 1984), pp. 68–78. Also see A. Tesser and S. Rosen, "The Reluctance to Transmit Bad News," *Advances in Experimental Social Psychology* 8 (1975), pp. 193–232.

12. M. Haire and W. F. Grunes, "Perceptual Defenses: Processes Protecting an Organized Perception of Another Personality," *Human Relations* 3 (1950), pp. 403–12; and Lyles and Thomas, "Strategic Problem Formulation: Biases and Assumptions Embedded in Alternative Decision-Making Models," p. 136.

13. Wedley and Field, "A Predecision Support System," p. 696; Drucker, *The Practice of Management,* p. 357; and L. R. Beach and T. R. Mitchell, "A Contingency Model for the Selection of Decision Strategies," *Academy of Management Review* 3 (1978), pp. 439–49.

14. For example, see P. K. Banerjee and B. Viswanathan, "On Optimal Rationing Policies," *Canadian Journal of Administrative Sciences* 6 (December 1989), pp. 1–6; and S. K. Goyal, "A Heuristic Scheduling Procedure for the Two Product, Single Machine Lot Size Problem," *Canadian Journal of Administrative Sciences* 1 (1984), pp. 399–407.

15. Simon, *The New Science of Management Decisions,* pp. 5–6.

16. B. McDougall, "What's a Manager to Do with the Last of the Baby Boomers?" *Financial Times,* March 13, 1989, p. 5; and L. Gutri, "Pratt & Whitney Employees Don't Want to Be Managed: Teams Demand Leadership," *Canadian HR Reporter,* May 2, 1988, p. 8.

17. C. Gower-Rees, "Automatic Pilot," *Canadian Business* 61, no. 10 (October 1988), pp. 183–85.

18. F. V. Guterl, "Computers Think for Business," *Dun's Business Month,* October 1986, p. 32.

19. Mintzberg, Raisinghani, and Théorét, "The Structure of 'Unstructured' Decision Processes," pp. 255–56.

20. Ibid., p. 256.

21. D. S. Gouran, *Making Decisions in Groups: Choices and Consequences* (Glenview, Ill.: Scott, Foresman, 1982).

22. Simon, *Administrative Behavior,* pp. xxv, 80–84; J. G. March and H. A. Simon, *Organizations* (New York: Wiley, 1958), pp. 140–41.

23. H. A. Simon, *Models of Man: Social and Rational* (New York: John Wiley & Sons, 1957), p. 253.

24. Cyert and March, *A Behavioral Theory of the Firm,* pp. 52–53.

25. J. G. March and Z. Shapira, "Managerial Perspectives on Risk and Risk Taking," *Management Science* 33 (1987), pp. 1404–418.

26. I. Anderson, "Raising the Laser: Ian Bruce Struggles to Launch the World's Most Popular Sailboat," *Canadian Business* 56 (November 1983), pp. 20, 23, 26.

27. R. N. Taylor, *Behavioral Decision Making* (Glenview, Ill.: Scott Foresman, 1984), p. 17; and March and Simon, *Organizations,* p. 165.

28. Statement made by J. Stamp, cited in D. A. Whetton and K. S. Cameron, *Developing Management Skills* (Glenview, Ill.: Scott, Foresman, 1984), p. 201.

29. Taylor, *Behavioral Decision Making,* pp. 37–39; and N. M. Agnew and J. L. Brown, "Executive Judgment: The Intuitive/Rational Ratio," *Personnel* 62, no. 12 (December 1985), pp. 48–54.

30. L. J. Peter, *Why Things Go Wrong* (New York: W. Morrow, 1985) pp. 35–36.

31. L. Festinger, *A Theory of Cognitive Dissonance* (New York: Harper & Row, 1957).

32. Taylor, *Behavioral Decision Making,* pp. 163–66.

33. B. M. Staw and J. Ross, "Behavior in Escalation Situations," *Research in Organizational Behavior* 9 (1987), pp. 39–78; and G. Whyte, "Escalation Commitment to a Course of Action: A Reinterpretation," *Academy of Management Review* 11 (1986), pp. 311–21.

34. J. Ross and B. M. Staw, "Expo 86: An Escalation Prototype," *Administrative Science Quarterly* 31 (1986), pp. 274–97.

35. J. M. Kouzes and B. Z. Posner, *The Leadership Challenge* (San Francisco: Jossey-Bass, 1987); and T. Peters, *Thriving on Chaos* (New York: Knopf, 1987), pp. 259–66.

36. K. Benzing, "Failures on the Road to Innovation," *Financial Post,* February 22, 1989, p. 15.

37. R. H. Waterman, Jr., *The Renewal Factor* (New York: Bantam, 1987), pp. 47–48.

38. P. C. Nutt, *Making Tough Decisions* (San Francisco: Jossey-Bass, 1989), p. 54; and W. H. Agor, "The Logic of Intuition," *Organizational Dynamics,* Winter 1986, pp. 5–18.

39. H. A. Simon, "Making Management Decisions: The Role of Intuition and Emotion," *Academy of Management Executive,* February 1987, pp. 57–64; and W. R. Hartston and P. C. Wason, *The Psychology of Chess* (New York: Facts on File, 1984).

40. J. P. Kotter, *The General Managers* (New York: Free Press, 1982).

41. A. R. Aird, P. Nowack, and J. W. Westcott, *Road to the Top* (Toronto: Doubleday Canada, 1988), p. 88.

42. R. Fulford, "The Final Stretch," *Vista* 2, no. 8 (November 1989), pp. 28–31.

43. D. Tjosvold, "Effects of Crisis Orientation on Managers' Approach to Controversy in Decision Making," *Academy of Management Journal* 27 (1984) pp. 130–38; C. Smart and I. Vertinsky, "Designs for Crisis Decision Units," *Administrative Science Quarterly* 22 (1977), pp. 640–58; and R. S. Billings, T. W. Milburn, and M. L. Schaalman, "A Model of Crisis Perception: A Theoretical and Empirical Analysis," *Administrative Science Quarterly* 25 (1980), pp. 300–16.

44. C. Hermann (ed.), *International Crises* (New York: Free Press, 1972); I. Devine and G. Bushe, "Integrating Research and Organizational Crisis: Antecedents, Adaptation, and Effects on Employees," *Proceedings of the Annual ASAC Conference, Organizational Behaviour Division* 5, pt. 5 (1984), pp. 61–70; S. L. Fink, J. Beak, and K. Taddeo, "Organizational Crisis and Change," *Journal of Applied Behavioral Science* 7, 1 (1971), pp. 15–37; and Gouran, *Making Decisions in Groups: Choices and Consequences,* Chapter 8.

45. I. L. Janis and L. Mann, *Decision Making: A Psychological Analysis of Conflict, Choice, and Commitment* (New York: Free Press, 1977); H. Mintzberg, *The Structuring of Organizations* (Englewood Cliffs, N.J.: Prentice Hall, 1979), pp. 308–09; and I. L. Janis, *Crucial Decisions: Leadership in Policymaking and Crisis Management* (New York: Free Press, 1989), pp. 77–84.

46. I. Mitroff, P. Shivastava, and F. E. Udwadia, "Effective Crisis Management," *Academy of Management Executive* 1 (1987), pp. 283–92; I. I. Mitroff, *Break-Away Thinking* (New York: Wiley, 1988), pp. 91–114; J. Ramèe, "Managing in a Crisis," *Management Solutions,* February 1987, pp. 25–29; and Gouran, *Making Decisions in Groups: Choices and Consequences,* Chapter 8.

47. D. MacKay, *Empire of Wood: The MacMillan Bloedel Story* (Vancouver: Douglas & McIntyre, 1982), pp. 231–32; and A. P. DeGeus, "Planning as Learning," *Harvard Business Review,* March–April 1988, pp. 70–74.

48. Mitroff et al, "Effective Crisis Management."

49. P. Mathias, "Outstanding Ethical Issues Pose Problems for All Business People," *Financial Post,* July 24, 1989, p. 22.

50. M. E. MacPherson, *Shopkeepers to a Nation: The Eatons* (Toronto: McClelland & Stewart, 1963); and G. G. Nasmith, *Timothy Eaton* (Toronto: McClelland & Stewart, 1923).

51. G. F. Cavanaugh, D. J. Moberg, and M. Velasquez, "The Ethics of Organizational Politics," *Academy of Management Review* 6 (1981), pp. 363–74; and J. R. DesJardins and J. J. McCall, *Contemporary Issues in Business Ethics* (Belmont, Calif.: Wadsworth, 1985).

52. D. Olive, *Just Rewards: The Case for Ethical Reform in Business* (Toronto: Key Porter, 1987); and J. A. Raelin, "The Professional as the Executive's Ethical Aide-de-Camp," *Academy of Management Executive* 1 (1987), pp. 171–82.

53. Olive, *Just Rewards: The Case for Ethical Reform in Business,* p. 125. For a survey of corporate codes of conduct, see R. Chatov, "What Corporate Ethics Statements Say," *California Management Review* 22, no. 4 (1980), pp. 20–29.

54. Olive, *Just Rewards: The Case for Ethical Reform in Business,* p. 125.

55. D. R. Cressey and C. A. Moore, "Managerial Values and Corporate Codes of Ethics," *California Management Review* 25, no. 4 (1983), pp. 53–57.

56. Waterman, *The Renewal Factor,* p. 75.

CHAPTER CASES

SHOOTING DOWN THE AVRO ARROW

The Canadian government decided in 1953 to develop an all-Canadian fighter jet as an enemy aircraft interceptor. Avro Aircraft Ltd. and Orenda Engines Ltd. of Malton, Ontario (both subsidiaries of A.V. Roe Canada Ltd.), were given the contract to design and build the Avro Arrow fighter jet and Iroquois engine. The Avro development team took the Arrow from first drawings to roll out of the prototype in only 28 months and, by March 1958, had completed the first test flight. Over the next year, test pilots took the Arrow close to record-breaking speeds even though engines on the test machines had lower power than the new Iroquois turbines. Experts later stated that the Avro Arrow was one of the most advanced fighter aircraft in the skies and would have remained so for another 20 years. Canada had become a mecca for aviation engineers and was at the forefront of aircraft technology. (A few years earlier, Avro engineers had also developed and flew the first commercial jetliner in North America!)

On February 20, 1959, the Right Honourable John Diefenbaker, Prime Minister of Canada, announced to a hushed audience in Parliament that the Arrow aircraft and Iroquois engine projects would be immediately cancelled. Several weeks later, the government ordered the destruction of all documentation and the six Arrow prototypes. (Fortunately, the front section of one Arrow was hidden for several years and is now on display in Ottawa.)

Why did Diefenbaker terminate the Arrow and Iroquois projects? Several writers have concluded that Diefenbaker disliked the arrogance of the Avro executives and the fact that the project was originated by the previous Liberal government. Indeed, a year before its final decision, the government was looking for evidence that the Arrow program should be scrapped. The government incorrectly concluded that fighter jets would lose their significance as nuclear missile technology developed. Ironically, the ill-fated nuclear missile program replacing the Arrow was partly responsible for the defeat of Diefenbaker's government in the following election.

The Arrow had a respectable flying range between refueling, but government officials were critical because they had mistakenly confused range with radius (which is one-half the distance). They were also concerned with the plane's flying time; again, the Arrow had a very good flying time, but the officials did not understand the new technology of using afterburners during combat.

The government was sincerely concerned about cost overruns at Avro, but Diefenbaker inflated the figures by including development and spare parts costs. He claimed that each aircraft would cost between $8 and $12 million when, in fact, Avro had announced a fixed price of $3.75 million per copy for the first 100 and $2.6 million for the next 100 just a few months before the cancellation.

Nearly 30,000 people lost their jobs as a result of the decision to terminate the Arrow and Iroquois projects. Hundreds of leading-edge engineers left Canada to participate in new challenges elsewhere. Several dozen joined NASA in the United States and played major roles in the Gemini and Apollo programs. Others joined Boeing or other aircraft firms to help develop new aircraft technology. Said one journalist: "The brutal termination of the Arrow was a devastating blow to our technological potential." Another wrote: "The cancellation of the Arrow project . . . put the kiss of death to one of the most advanced aeronautical research and development organizations in the world. In one fell swoop, a national asset . . . came to an abrupt end.''

Discussion Questions

1. What flaws, if any, do you see in Diefenbaker's decision process?
2. Did escalation of commitment occur here? Why or why not?

Sources: G. Stewart, *Shutting Down the National Dream: A. V. Roe and the Tragedy of the Avro Arrow* (Toronto: McGraw-Hill Ryerson, 1988); M. Peden, *Fall of an Arrow* (Toronto: Stoddart, 1978); The Arrowheads, *Avro Arrow* (Erin, Ontario: Boston Mills Press, 1980); and J. Floyd, *The Avro Canada C102 Jetliner* (Erin, Ontario: Boston Mills Press, 1986).

CROSS-BORDER SHOPPING

Jack Tremblay was delighted to receive a job offer from the Canadian subsidiary of TGZ Technologies Inc., a California-based manufacturer of minicomputers. Tremblay was hired as a systems engineer in the Montreal office to install the company's product and serve as a troubleshooter for clients who experienced problems.

During his first two weeks of work, Jack accompanied experienced systems engineers from the Montreal office to see how TGZ's products were installed. Jack had been a systems engineer in a related business for five years, so he could understand many of the steps the experienced engineers went through to install the equipment. However, every client has unique requests, so Jack could not install these systems until he received formal training from the company's head office in California.

At the end of two weeks, Jack was sent for an intensive one-week training program in California where he learned how to install different types of TGZ computers in a variety of situations. Jack met other recently hired systems engineers from across North America, including four other Canadians. It was a high-spirited gathering where the learning was intense and close friendships were formed. Jack returned to the Montreal office even more dedicated to the company than before and highly motivated to work with clients to install and service TGZ's products.

After three months of work, Jack returned to TGZ's head office in California for another four days of training. The participants included many of the same people he had met in the previous program. On the third day of training, Jack was approached by a production manager at TGZ's California plant. He asked Jack to take a small package back with him to Montreal, then handed over a small box containing several small components and circuits for a TGZ minicomputer that was about to be installed for a Montreal client. Although these pieces would fit into a large shaving kit, they were worth several thousand dollars in the retail market. Jack asked whether these items should be declared at Canada Customs, but the manager quickly said ''No. Uh, we will handle that. You just keep them in your luggage so that there's no confusion with the customs papers we have sent already.''

Upon his arrival in the Montreal office, Jack gave the package to the regional manager who was expecting it. "You had no trouble with Canada Customs, of course?" asked the manager. Jack explained that he said nothing about the box and was not given any special inspection. He then asked why there was so much concern about getting across the border with the parts if the customs papers had aleady been processed.

The regional manager laughed as he replied: "Is that what Choy (the production manager) told you? I bring these things across all the time. Besides, the duty is almost $500 on these parts. If we claimed everything we imported, we would probably have to raise prices by 5 or 10 percent or transfer service work to our offices in New York. And that would put you out of work! Now don't you worry about a thing."

Jack was stunned, but left without showing any emotion. He now realized that his action had violated Canadian customs law and that he may be asked to do so again. Jack decided to call the systems engineer from TGZ's Calgary office with whom he had become friends at the California training sessions. The systems engineer from Calgary said that she did not have any such experience, but her regional manager had just been hired and might not know about the practice. She suggested that Jack shouldn't worry about the incident. She was sure that import duties would be eliminated from these components over the next few years. Jack thanked his colleague for the advice and then sat in his office to decide how to handle this situation.

Discussion Questions

1. What should Jack do here? Explain your answer.
2. Would your decision be different if:
   a. Most other computer manufacturers also imported a fraction of their components without paying customs duty?
   b. The amount of duty owing in Jack's shipment was only $50 rather than $500?
   c. This practice is widespread throughout TGZ's Canadian offices and is accepted by senior management in California?

© 1991 Steven L. McShane. This case was adapted slightly from actual events reported confidentially to the author. Names, locations, and industry have been changed.

EXPERIENTIAL EXERCISE

BONUS DECISION-MAKING EXERCISE

Purpose: This exercise is designed to help you understand the impact of individual values on decision criteria and outcomes.

Instructions: Descriptions of four branch managers in the Atlantic region of a large national insurance company are described below. The regional director of the company has given your consulting team the task of allocating $60,000 in bonus money to these four managers. It is entirely up to your team to decide how to divide the money among these people. The only requirements are that all of the money must be distributed and that no two branch managers can receive the same amount. The names and information are presented in no particular order.

This exercise should first be completed individually. The instructor may then have students form small teams of four or five people. Members of each team will compare their results, identify discrepancies, and attempt to resolve these differences. The entire class will then discuss their team discussions and unresolved issues.

Bob B.

Bob has been in the insurance business for over 27 years and has spent the past 21 years with this company. A few years ago, Bob's branch typically made the largest contribution to regional profits. More recently, however, it has brought in few new accounts and is now well below average in terms of its contribution to the company. Turnover in the branch has been high and Bob doesn't have the same enthusiasm for the job as he once did. Bob is 56 years old and is married with five children. Three children are still living at home. Bob has a high school diploma as well as a certificate from a special course in insurance management.

Lee L.

Lee has been with this organization for seven years. The first two years were spent as a sales representative in the office that she now manages. According to the regional director, Lee rates about average as a branch manager. She earned an undergraduate degree in geography from Dalhousie University and worked in Nova Scotia as a sales representative for four years with another insurance company before joining this organization. Lee is divorced with two children (who are living with their father) and is 40 years old. She is a very ambitious person but sometimes has problems working with her staff and other branch managers.

Edward E.

In the regional director's opinion, Edward is on his way to becoming the best branch manager in the region and perhaps the best in the entire organization. In the two years that Edward has been a branch manager, his unit has brought in several major accounts. Edward is well-respected by his employees. At 29, he is the youngest manager in the region and one of the youngest in the country. The regional director initially doubted the wisdom of giving Edward the position of branch manager because of his relatively young age and lack of experience in the insurance industry. Edward received an undergraduate business degree from Wilfred Laurier University and worked for five years as a sales representative in Kitchener, Ontario, before joining this company. Edward is single and has no children.

Sandy S.

Sandy is 47 years old and has been a branch manager with this company for 17 years. Seven years ago, her branch made the lowest contribution to the region's profits, but this has steadily improved and is now slightly above average. Sandy seems to have a mediocre attitude toward her job but is well liked by her staff and other branch managers. Her experience in the insurance industry has been entirely with this organization and it is not clear how she became a branch manager without previous sales experience of any kind. Sandy is married and has three school-aged children. Several years ago, Sandy earned a diploma in business from a nearby community college by taking evening courses.

TEAM PROCESSES

Vancouver-based MacDonald Dettwiler is a team-based high-technology company that solves human problems through the creative integration of computer science with related technologies. One of the company's many breakthroughs is in the area of resource management systems using Landsat-5 satellite data. Here, a team of government experts uses a MacDonald Dettwiler resource management system to determine forest inventories after a forest fire in British Columbia.

10

Team Dynamics and Effectiveness

LEARNING OBJECTIVES

After reading this chapter, you should be able to:

Distinguish
Command unit teams from task forces.

Explain
Why people join teams.

Discuss
The effects of team size on team effectiveness.

Trace
The five stages of team development.

Identify
Four factors that shape team norms.

Explain
How team cohesiveness and norms relate to team
performance.

Identify
Four team-building strategies.

Oshawa Group

The Quebec City branch of Hudon et Deaudelin Ltée (H&D) is not your typical wholesale food distributor.[1] Serving independent grocers east of Trois Rivieres in the province of Quebec, H&D's recently built warehouse has no supervisors and is operated fairly independently from its parent company, the Oshawa Group. Yet the 150 people who work at H&D's Quebec City warehouse have achieved impressive standards of efficiency and inventory turnover in a competitive market.

How has H&D accomplished this enviable record? One factor is the operation's advanced computer technology to monitor inventory, orders, and productivity. But management also believes that much of the success is due to the emphasis on teams rather than individuals to get the work done. Three teams are assigned to the day shift taking care of stock replenishment, and another five teams work the night shift picking orders. Each team has five to seven members, and employee bonuses are based on the work team's results.

Each team leader is elected from the group for a two-month period, so that most members have an opportunity to hold this position at least once each year. Leaders arrive early at the warehouse to plan and organize the day's workload, such as deciding the number of checkers and lifters required. The company employs six coordinators who provide advice to the work teams and help coordinate resources between teams if problems arise.

The Quebec City food distributor also uses task forces to investigate specific problems or opportunities. For instance, a seven-person team was set up to find out how to reduce picking errors (selecting the wrong product for the customer). The team developed a cause–effect diagram that charts the number of picking errors in a four-week period. These data helped the task force decide how to best reduce the number of picking errors from the current level of 755 per month.

Hudon et Deaudelin Ltée's focus on teamwork rather than individual effort reflects a trend that is sweeping across Canada.[2] Teams are replacing individuals as the basic building block of organizations. For example, First City Trust has established "First action teams" to explore new projects and try out new ideas. When the federal government decided to transfer social housing programs to provincial authorities, Canada Mortgage and Housing Corporation established a special task force, comprised of members from all affected areas of the corporation, to manage the negotiations. Vancouver City Savings, Levi-Strauss, and many other businesses have formed employee committees to do everything from choosing compensation surveys to distributing charity funds.[3]

This chapter looks at the dynamics and effectiveness of formal work teams as well as informal groups in organizations. We begin by introducing the different types of teams that may be found in organizational settings and discuss the reasons why people want to belong to teams. A basic model of team dynamics and effectiveness is then outlined. Most of the chapter examines each part of this model, including team context and design, team development, norms, and cohesiveness. The chapter concludes with an overview of strategies to build more effective work teams.

WHAT ARE TEAMS?

Teams consist of two or more people who interact and mutually influence each other for the purpose of achieving common goals.[4] We will be using the word *team* throughout this chapter to refer to either a formal work unit or an informal group. While there may be a subtle distinction between a team and a group, the word *team* is replacing *group* in the business literature, so we use both terms interchangeably.

teams
Two or more people who interact and mutually influence each other for the purpose of achieving common goals.

Let's look more closely at the four central concepts in our definition of a team. First, a team consists of *at least two people*. There is probably an upper limit because at some point there may be so many members that they are unable to meaningfully interact with and influence each other. Second, teams exist to fulfill some *purpose*. Members of formal work teams might share the common goal of assembling a product or making a strategic decision. An informal group might develop so that its members can enjoy each other's company. Notice that members are dependent on each other because the team's goals usually cannot be accomplished alone.

Third, a team exists only when people *interact* with each other. Interaction is basically any form of communication, and may occur whether people are physically near each other or located on opposite sides of the country. Employees waiting in a cafeteria line usually do not constitute a team because they are not all conversing with each other. On the other hand, seven managers scattered across Canada who hold a teleconference meeting would represent a work team because they are interacting with each other. Finally, a team exists only when people *influence* each other. Influence may include persuasion (described in Chapter 8) or the use of power (described in Chapter 12). Also notice that influence is mutual, that is, every member is influencing and being influenced by others within the team.

TYPES OF TEAMS IN ORGANIZATIONS

Many types of teams operate within organizations. The paint crew on the morning shift, the company's health and safety committee, and employees who meet once each week to play baseball are all examples of different types

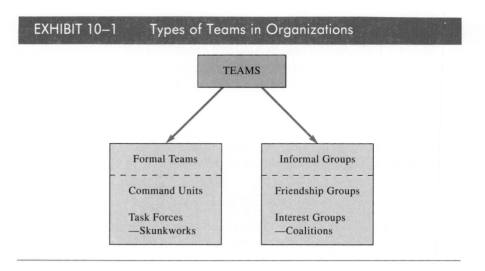

EXHIBIT 10–1   Types of Teams in Organizations

TEAMS

Formal Teams

Command Units

Task Forces
—Skunkworks

Informal Groups

Friendship Groups

Interest Groups
—Coalitions

of teams. Generally, we can distinguish formal work teams from informal groups and identify different types of teams within each of these categories (see Exhibit 10–1).

Formal Work Teams

Formal work teams are explicitly formed to accomplish a specific set of tasks for the benefit of the organization. There are basically two types of formal teams: command units and task forces.

command unit
A relatively permanent team consisting of a manager and his or her subordinates.

Command Units.   A **command unit** is a relatively permanent entity consisting of a manager and his or her subordinates. It typically represents an organizational department and corresponds to direct lines of authority on the organizational chart. As depicted in Exhibit 10–2, a production supervisor and his or her crew on a particular work shift would be called a command unit. Supervisors and the plant manager might represent another command unit. In this example, the supervisor serves as a "linking pin" between command units. This establishes a conduit for communication and maintains some degree of integration among teams.[5]

task force (or project team)
A team of people assigned to a short-term task or project.

Task Forces.   **Task forces** (also called **project teams**) consist of people assigned to a specific task or project. Members are often drawn from several departments so that different areas of expertise are represented. Task forces are usually short lived, as they disband when the task is completed. They have become the preferred strategy in many companies for resolving unique problems or opportunities. In our opening story, Hudon et Deaudelin Ltée introduced a task force to find ways of reducing picking orders. More dramatic applications can be found in the petroleum industry, where hundreds

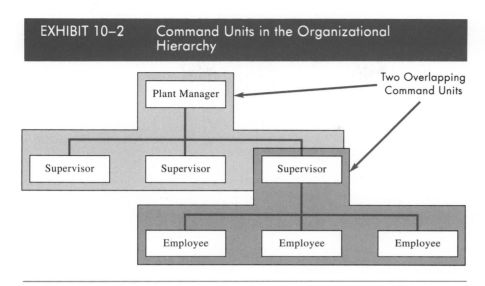

EXHIBIT 10–2   Command Units in the Organizational Hierarchy

of task forces were formed when Amoco acquired Dome Petroleum to discuss how operations of the two companies should be integrated. This team-based merger process was repeated in Imperial Oil's acquisition of Texaco Canada.[6]

Skunkworks.   Chaparral Steel, Data General, Bell Canada Enterprises, and many other firms have learned that product development is often done more effectively through special task forces called **skunkworks**.[7] Skunkworks are action-oriented teams of 5 to 25 employees drawn from several functional areas of the organization (engineering, marketing, production, etc.) who develop new products, services, or procedures. They frequently develop when an innovative employee (a *champion*) identifies an opportunity and is able to borrow people and resources (called *bootlegging*) from various places in the organization. Skunkworks are typically isolated from the rest of the organization and have a high degree of freedom, such as the ability to purchase resources and ignore the more bureaucratic rules governing other organizational units.

The term *skunkworks* was coined by Kelly Johnson in the 1940s as the name of the small band of employees he organized to design and build aircraft for Lockheed Corporation. As with other task forces, most skunkworks are temporary, disbanding when the project is finished. However, Johnson's team existed for over four decades, delivering working prototypes and sometimes production models of over 40 aircraft.[8] Skunkworks are believed to be responsible for nearly two-thirds of all product and service innovations. For example, Ford's popular Mustang was designed in the 1960s by a team of people that Lee Iacocca pulled together from design,

skunkwork
A team of employees 'borrowed' from several functional areas of the organization who develop new products, services, or procedures, usually in isolation from the organization and without the normal restrictions.

PERSPECTIVE 10–1　　Festive Occasions: The Glue That Binds Employees Together

The staff of Markham, Ontario, consulting engineers Cosburn Petterson Wardman Ltd. (CPW) don't require much motivating, but they do work under tight deadlines and can lose some of the team spirit that is essential to maintain effective relations. To ensure that everyone in the 38-employee firm works together as an effective team, Mac Cosburn and the other partners have introduced several sports activities, such as mixed baseball teams, a hockey team, and ad hoc nighttime volleyball tournaments at a neighbourhood high school.

But CPW relies on more than team sports activities to build a sense of togetherness. The company has regular "spirit-building" parties, such as bowling-and-barbeque nights, beer-and-wing nights, and an annual sailing excursion. Explains Cosburn, "If there's no excuse [to bring staff together] . . . we create an excuse every couple of months."

Revett Eldred, president of Minerva Technology Inc., also knows that festive occasions can provide the glue that binds employees into a well-integrated team. These social interaction opportunities are particularly valuable for the Calgary-based computer programming company because most of its 80 software engineers work under contract at customer sites.

"It's important to constantly bring them back for lunches and parties to keep them in touch with other employees," says Eldred. "Group activities encourage them to identify with Minerva rather than the customer site where they spend most of their time."

Sources: J. Southerst, "The Winning Way," *Profit,* November 1990, pp. 29–33; and J. Zeidenberg, "For Fun and Profit," *Profit,* November 1990, pp. 37–40.

---

marketing, and public relations. The group, called the Fairlane Committee, met regularly at a hotel of the same name rather than at Ford headquarters so that it could operate without corporate interference.[9]

Informal Groups

Informal groups are born without any direct management influence and exist primarily for the benefit of their members. Two types of informal groups within organizations are friendship and interest groups.

friendship group
An informal group bound together by common interests and the desire to affiliate with others having similar opinions.

Friendship Groups. **Friendship groups** are bound together by common interests and the desire to affiliate with people having similar opinions. Employees with common backgrounds who interact after work to enjoy each other's company may be considered friendship groups. Friendship groups engage in various activities, but their primary purpose is to interact with each other.

interest group
An informal group formed to accomplish an activity requiring some form of interaction.

Interest Groups. **Interest groups** are formed to accomplish an activity requiring some form of interaction. Here, members are motivated to join more because of their desire to accomplish a personal goal than to interact with others. Employees may become members of several interest groups based on their interest in sports, car pooling, or some other activity.

It is sometimes difficult to distinguish friendship and interest groups from formal work teams because employees working together on a project may also gather after work for social events or merely to share conversation. As Perspective 10–1 describes, many firms are discovering that social gatherings can build more effective work teams.

Coalitions.   A **coalition** is a special kind of interest group in which people form an alliance around a specific issue to influence people outside the team with respect to that issue. By banding together, coalition members reinforce and further mobilize support for their position.[10] They also hope to increase their power over individuals outside the coalition by demonstrating their strength in numbers. Coalitions typically form around issues involving perceived inequities or the allocation of resources, such as the company's selection of a particular supplier. They are relatively short-lived alliances (as are most organizational interest groups), disbanding when the issue is resolved or lost.

coalition

A special interest group in which people form an alliance around a specific issue to influence people outside the team with respect to that issue.

WHY DO PEOPLE JOIN TEAMS?

Why are people willing to join and maintain their membership in teams? In the case of formal work teams, employees usually must join or lose their job! But the issue is more complex than this because people assigned to a formal team may still leave or be frequently absent. A more fundamental explanation is that people join teams because they believe this will fulfill their personal needs better than working alone. From this perspective, we can identify three factors that attract people to teams: goal accomplishment, affiliation and status, and emotional support.

Goal Accomplishment

People often join and remain members of teams to achieve goals that cannot be accomplished individually. As we learned in our discussion of job design (Chapter 5), individuals performing specialized jobs within a team often achieve higher productivity than if each person performs all of the tasks alone. For example, individual hockey players cannot win games alone, so they join forces, divide the work, assign roles, and learn to coordinate their actions. Some members play forward, others defense, and someone serves as goaltender. As individuals learn that working together increases the probability of achieving goals, it becomes easier to attract new members who value the team's objectives, such as completing a project or winning the Stanley Cup.

Affiliation and Status

Whether or not the team's overt goals are valued by its members, individuals frequently join groups to fulfill their need for friendship and social interaction. As described in Chapter 2, most people desire friendship and approval from others. Individuals with a very high need for affiliation are particularly motivated to become team members because they want to seek approval from others, conform to those people's wishes and expectations, and avoid conflict and confrontation.[11]

In addition to receiving approval from other members, individuals may receive approval and respect from nonmembers if the team is highly regarded. A particular task force or organizational unit may be viewed as a high-status group by outsiders. This status is then ascribed to all members of the team.[12]

Emotional Support

The old saying "Misery loves company" has some merit. Under threatening circumstances, we are comforted by the physical presence of other people and are motivated to be near others, including strangers.[13] This phenomenon has been observed among soldiers under enemy fire. During the stressful conditions of battle, many soldiers tend to huddle together because it makes them feel more secure. The problem is most common among replacement soldiers—those who have recently been added to the unit—because they have not established social relations with veteran members and feel particularly insecure about battle conditions. Unfortunately, huddling together is a dangerous practice when soldiers face enemy fire. Yet even after being told repeatedly to disperse under fire, many soldiers still tend to huddle together because of the emotional support the group provides.[14]

A MODEL OF TEAM DYNAMICS AND EFFECTIVENESS

Why do some groups have a strong team spirit while others barely survive? What are the characteristics of effective teams? These questions have interested organizational theorists for some time and, as you might expect, numerous models of team effectiveness have been proposed over the years.[15]

team effectiveness

A multifaceted concept in which the team survives, successfully completes its objectives, and provides its members with satisfaction, well-being, and commitment.

Team effectiveness refers to consequences for both the group and its members. At the group level, effectiveness includes the ability to survive and perform the team's objectives successfully. At the individual level, team effectiveness includes the satisfaction, well-being, and commitment of its members. Employees who belong to effective teams are also less likely to quit their jobs, leave the team, or be absent from work and team activities.[16]

Exhibit 10–3 presents the major influences on team effectiveness that will be discussed throughout this chapter. The organization's internal and external environments can have a profound effect on what the team does, whether it has the resources to accomplish its goals, and whether members believe their membership in the team is valuable. The task that the team wants to accomplish is another important contextual factor. Team size and composition are the two most important design features of team dynamics.

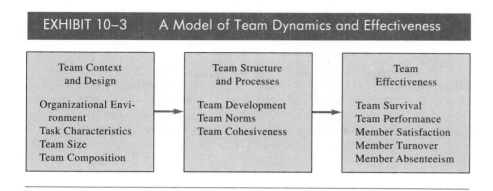

EXHIBIT 10–3   A Model of Team Dynamics and Effectiveness

Team Context and Design	Team Structure and Processes	Team Effectiveness
Organizational Environment Task Characteristics Team Size Team Composition	Team Development Team Norms Team Cohesiveness	Team Survival Team Performance Member Satisfaction Member Turnover Member Absenteeism

The ability of work teams to accomplish their objectives is affected by the number of team members and the skills, knowledge, motives, attitudes, and experiences they bring to the group.[17]

Team effectiveness is also influenced by the group's stage of development, as well as its norms and level of cohesiveness. Team members must share some common identity and be committed to the group's objectives. This involves an often lengthy process of development through stages into a mature, efficiently interacting unit. Teams must also possess enough power over individuals to ensure that they maintain their membership and contribute to the accomplishment of the team's objectives. Finally, teams must develop rules to coordinate member behaviour and maintain solidarity. These are central issues in most models of team effectiveness and we will be examining them and their consequences throughout this chapter.

TEAM CONTEXT AND DESIGN

Our discussion of team dynamics and effectiveness logically begins with the contextual factors that influence group structure and processes. These inputs include the organizational environments, task characteristics, team size, and team composition.

Organizational Environments

The organization's internal and external environments have a pervasive influence on the characteristics and experiences of work teams as well as every other aspect of organizations. The team's ability to develop into an efficiently operating unit depends on management's commitment to the team and the resources made available to it. Technology and external competition may influence the team's cohesiveness. The physical layout of the workplace affects the amount of member interaction and, consequently, may facilitate or hinder the team's development. Organizational values may shape the team's norms. Reward systems influence the team's power over its members as well as the team's objectives.

The powerful effect of physical environment on team effectiveness is illustrated in a study of wood harvesting crews in northwestern Ontario. These crews were assigned different wood lots to cut and their performance (the amount of wood cut) clearly depended on the mix of trees in the designated harvest area. Operators could harvest more efficiently where the trees were not too large or small and the area consisted mainly of a single species.[18]

Task Characteristics

The tasks required to accomplish the team's goals can affect its structure, process, and effectiveness.[19] It may also determine how the team should be designed. Two important features are task structure and the effect of individual performance on team performance.

Task Structure.   Teams are influenced by how easily the work is structured. Simple tasks can be easily routinized, so team members learn their roles fairly quickly and require minimal coordination or interaction. In contrast, teams engaged in ill-defined tasks require more time to agree on the best division of labour and the correct way to accomplish the goal. These are typically more complex tasks requiring diverse skills and backgrounds, which further strain the team's ability to develop and form a cohesive unit.[20]

Individual Performance Effect.   Employees must work interdependently on most team tasks, but the effect of each person's performance on total team performance may vary. Individual performance may influence team effectiveness in three ways: additive, disjunctive, and conjunctive (see Exhibit 10–4).[21] *Additive tasks* are those in which the team's potential performance is the sum of the performance of each member. In other words, the team's potential output would be the combination of the work accomplished by each person. With *disjunctive tasks,* the team's potential performance depends on the best performing member because the team's success ultimately depends on the one person who solves the problem or completes the activity first. Finally, *conjunctive tasks* are those in which the team's effectiveness is determined by the worst-performing member. Every team member's performance may be affected by the slowest worker (as in an assembly line) or the overall product or service may pass or fail due to one poor performer.

Whether task performance is additive, disjunctive, or conjunctive affects how the team operates and the importance of team dynamics. Conjunctive tasks require highly developed teams that can facilitate each other's work activities and resolve conflicts smoothly. Consequently, these tasks are best

EXHIBIT 10–4	How Individual Performance Affects Team Performance

Type of Interdependence	Example
Additive tasks	Several machine operators produce the same metal stamps for a customer. Each operator's output is pooled to fill the order, so the team's effectiveness depends on *every* person's performance.
Disjunctive tasks	A team of engineers must identify the main cause of a client's problem. Every team member looks for the cause, but the team's effectiveness ultimately depends on the *one* team member who discovers it and is able to convince the other team members that this is the cause.
Conjunctive tasks	A team of production employees assembles aircraft engines. How quickly the engine is assembled depends on the speed of the slowest assembler. Similarly, whether the engine passes the quality inspection depends on the quality of the poorest performer in the group.

accomplished by the smallest possible work unit. Team members assigned additive and disjunctive tasks usually work fairly independently and team performance usually increases with the number of participants. For instance, seven machine operators can finish the work faster than three, and ten engineers are more likely to identify a problem before three people would. However, there is a risk in disjunctive and additive tasks that individual members might not work as hard as when they work alone. We will return to this phenomenon, called *social loafing,* later in the chapter.

Team Size

A team must have at least two members, but the upper limit is less precise because teamwork depends on the opportunity for members to interact and influence each other. It would be extremely difficult for BASF, the German-based multinational corporation with operations on five continents, to instill a common bond or team spirit among its 18,000 employees.[22] However, Magna International and Hayes-Dana, two major automobile parts manufacturers in Canada, have attempted to develop a sense of teamwork by building mini-plants employing fewer than 200 people. Bata Footwear has taken a similar approach by shifting from large manufacturing operations that produce several different product lines to much smaller plants in which fewer employees work on a single product line. According to Bata's management, teamwork is easier to develop in mini-plants because a smaller number of employees are assigned to a particular product line work in the same area and can see the production from start to finish.[23]

Mini-plants with 100 to 200 employees may engender a stronger sense of team spirit than traditional factories and offices, but the most effective teams usually have between 5 and 10 and rarely more than 20 members. These groups have enough people with diverse skills to accomplish their objectives, yet are small enough for members to know each other, exchange ideas, and reach agreement on team goals. Larger teams are typically less effective because members consume more time and effort coordinating their roles and resolving differences.[24] Individuals have less opportunity to participate and formalized rules must be developed to divide the work and coordinate member behaviour. Members have more diverse backgrounds in larger work units, leading to the formation of subgroups around common interests and work activities. Consequently, individuals begin to form stronger commitments to subgroups than to the larger unit.

Team Composition

Team effectiveness depends on individual members with the necessary abilities, motivation, and role perceptions to accomplish the team's objectives.[25] There are a few differences between the determinants of individual and team performance, however. Individuals working alone must possess all the required skills and knowledge to accomplish the task, whereas each team member needs to bring only some of these qualifications. Everyone involved in a team-based activity should have social interaction skills, whereas this might not be an important factor in individual performance. Both teams and individuals working alone must be motivated to accomplish the assigned goal, but team members must also reach agreement on the goal, be motivated to work together rather than alone, and abide by the team's rules of conduct.

Another aspect of team composition that may affect team effectiveness is whether members are homogeneous or heterogeneous.[26] A homogeneous team may include individuals with common technical expertise, experiences, or attitudes. For example, nurses in a hospital ward would make up a relatively homogeneous work group because of their common technical background. Team members experience higher satisfaction, less conflict, and better interpersonal relations when coworkers have similar backgrounds.[27] Consequently, homogeneous teams tend to be more effective on simple tasks where a high degree of cooperation and coordination are required, such as emergency response teams.

Heterogeneous teams have members with diverse personal characteristics and backgrounds. These teams take longer to develop, experience more interpersonal conflict, and have more difficulty reaching agreement regarding group norms and goals. Nevertheless, they are generally more effective than homogeneous teams on complex projects and problem-solving tasks.[28] Skunkworks and other project groups or task forces should have a heterogeneous membership because their tasks require people from different areas of the organization with unique opinions and technical knowledge.[29]

STAGES OF TEAM DEVELOPMENT

A team must resolve several issues and pass through several stages of development before emerging as an effective unit. They must get to know each other, understand their respective roles, discover appropriate and inappropriate behaviours, and learn how to coordinate their work or social activities. This is an ongoing process because teams change as new members join and old members leave. Tuckman's five-stage model of team development, shown in Exhibit 10–5, provides a general representation of how teams evolve by forming, storming, norming, performing, and eventually adjourning.[30]

Forming

The first stage of team development is a period of testing and orientation in which members learn about each other and evaluate the benefits and costs of continued membership. People tend to be polite during this stage and will defer to the existing authority of a formal or informal leader who must provide an initial set of rules and structures for interaction. Members experience a form of socialization (described in Chapter 16) as they try to find out what is expected of them and how they will fit into the team.

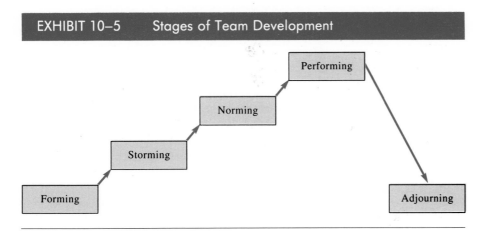

EXHIBIT 10–5   Stages of Team Development

Source: Based on B. W. Tuckman and M. A. C. Jensen, "Stages of Small-Group Development Revisited," *Group and Organization Studies* 2 (1977), pp. 419–42.

Storming

During the second stage, individual members become more proactive by taking on specific roles and task responsibilities. This process is marked by interpersonal conflict as members compete for leadership and other positions in the team. Coalitions may form to influence the team's goals and means of goal attainment. Members try to establish norms of appropriate behaviour and performance standards. This is a tenuous stage in the team's development, particularly when the leader is autocratic and lacks the necessary conflict-management skills.

Norming

During the norming stage, the team develops its first real sense of cohesion as roles are established and a consensus forms around group objectives. By now, members have developed a set of expectations and rules to help them interact more efficiently in the process of goal accomplishment. Through self-disclosure and feedback, members are also better able to understand and accept each other (see the Johari Window described in Chapter 7).

Performing

The team becomes more task-oriented as it shifts from establishing and maintaining relations to accomplishing its objectives. Team members have learned to coordinate their actions and to resolve conflicts more efficiently. Further coordination improvements must occasionally be addressed, but the greater emphasis is on task accomplishment. In high-performance teams, members are highly cooperative, have a high level of trust in each other, are committed to group objectives, and identify with the team.[31]

Adjourning

Most teams eventually come to an end. Task forces and committees terminate when they have completed the required assignment. Informal work groups may reach this stage when several members leave the organization or are reassigned to different areas of the organization. Some teams adjourn as a result of layoffs or plant shutdowns. Whatever the cause of team adjournment, members shift their attention away from task orientation to a socioemotional focus as they realize that their relationship is coming to an end.

While this model helps us to understand the dynamics of team development, it is not a perfect representation. It does not reflect the fact that team development is a continuous process. As membership changes and new conditions emerge, the team may cycle back to earlier stages in the developmental process.[32] Some groups remain in a particular stage longer than others and two stages of development may overlap.[33]

TEAM NORMS

Norms are the informal rules and standards that a team establishes to regulate and guide the behaviours of its members. They provide structure to team processes by dictating behaviours that should be enacted or avoided. Norms apply only to behaviour, not to private thoughts or feelings. They do not exist for every behaviour, however; only to those perceived to be important to the team.[34]

Specific norms may guide the way that team members should deal with clients, how they share resources with other team members, and whether they should work longer hours for the organization. Some norms improve team effectiveness by ensuring that members learn their roles and abide by them. This improves coordination and interaction as members know what is expected. Other norms might conflict with organizational objectives. For example, at the American Cyanamid plant in Niagara Falls, Ontario, supervisors who were handpicked by higher management to increase employee participation soon returned to more autocratic ways when colleagues attacked them as having been brainwashed by the company.[35] The organization wanted more democracy in the workplace but this conflicted with the supervisors' norm, which called for a less participative management style.

Conformity to Team Norms

Norms are enforced by the power that the team has over its members.[36] This power causes team members to *conform* to team norms, that is, to change their behaviour to be more in line with those norms.[37] Conformity may occur through direct pressure from other members or through the individual's natural identification with the team and its values. Every one of us has experienced direct pressure at one time or another. Coworkers may grimace or comment sarcastically to those who are late for an important meeting or don't have a task completed on time. These actions threaten the individual's affiliation need and are therefore inherently punishing. In more extreme situations, the team may temporarily ostracize deviant members or threaten to terminate their membership.

Norms are also directly reinforced through praise from high-status members, more access to valued resources, or other rewards available to the team.[38] But team members often conform to prevailing norms without direct pressure. Members of high-cohesive teams, for instance, conform to norms without direct sanctions or rewards. New members are usually motivated to conform more than veterans because they are uncertain of their status and try to become integrated into the work team.

The extent to which people conform to team norms is illustrated in the classic story of an employee who was assigned to work with a small group of pressers in a pajama factory.[39] The group had informally established a norm

norms
The informal rules and standards that a team establishes to regulate and guide the behaviours of its members.

that 50 units per hour was the upper limit of acceptable performance and, as illustrated in Exhibit 10–6, the newcomer was producing at this level soon after joining the team. However, her performance began to exceed the norm and, by Day 12, she began to be scapegoated by coworkers. The employee's performance subsequently dropped to a level acceptable to the team. On Day 20, the team had to be broken up. All team members were transferred to other jobs except the scapegoated employee, who was asked to work alone at the same pressing-room task. With the others gone, the team norm was no longer operative and, as the chart shows, the employee's performance nearly doubled in a few days. For the next 20 days, she maintained a performance level of 92 units per hour compared with 45 units in the presence of coworkers.

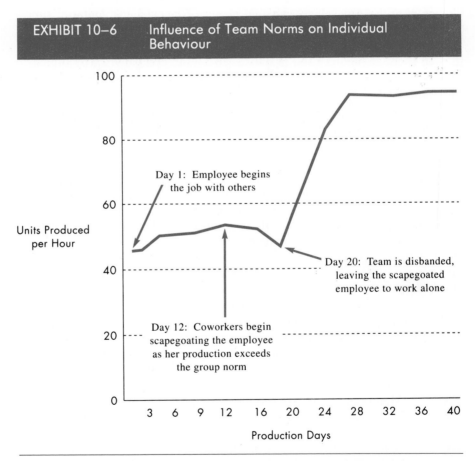

EXHIBIT 10–6   Influence of Team Norms on Individual Behaviour

Day 1: Employee begins the job with others

Day 20: Team is disbanded, leaving the scapegoated employee to work alone

Day 12: Coworkers begin scapegoating the employee as her production exceeds the group norm

Units Produced per Hour

Production Days

Source: Based on data from L. Coch and J. R. P. French, Jr., "Overcoming Resistance to Change," *Human Relations* 1 (1948), pp. 512–32.

How Team Norms Develop

Norms develop as team members learn that certain behaviours help them function more effectively. For the most part, norms develop for one or more of the reasons listed in Exhibit 10–7.[40]

Some norms are formed when team members or outsiders make *explicit statements* that are thought to aid the team's success or survival. For example, the team leader might frequently express the importance of treating customers with respect and courtesy. *Critical events* in the team's history, such as a serious injury, can trigger the development of a new norm to avoid problems in the future.

The *primacy effect,* which we defined in Chapter 7 as the tendency to quickly form opinions based on our initial experiences, may play a central role in developing team norms. The primacy effect causes initial team experiences to set the tone for future behaviours. Thus, the team's first meeting might establish norms about where people sit in the room or whether they address coworkers by their last names or nicknames. Finally, norms develop from the *expectations members bring to the team.* Some are based on prior experiences, such as the way a secretary is expected to address senior

---

EXHIBIT 10–7   How Team Norms Develop

Reason for Norm Development	Example
Explicit statements	Supervisor warns the team that drinking on the job will not be tolerated.
Critical events in the team's history	A norm of keeping the work area clean develops after a coworker injures herself from scraps left on the floor.
Primacy effect	The team's first meeting is casual and open, establishing the norm of informality and openness in future meetings.
Individual experiences from previous teams	Several members of a new medical team maintain professional distance from patients based on their experiences before the team was formed; this norm is carried over to the new medical team.

Source: Based on D. E. Feldman, ''The Development and Enforcement of Group Norms,'' *Academy of Management Review* 9 (1984), pp. 47–53.

managers. Others are embedded in the surrounding culture. The norm of reciprocity—that you are obliged to help someone who has once helped you—is found in virtually every team because this expectation is embedded in Canadian culture.[41]

Changing Team Norms

Several strategies may be applied to form positive team norms and change those which undermine organizational effectiveness. For new teams, managers should introduce performance-oriented norms at the outset and select members on the basis of the norms they bring to the group. For example, if the organization wants team norms to emphasize safety, team members should be selected who already value this standard. Selecting people with positive norms may be effective in new teams, but this strategy is less effective when adding new members to existing teams with counterproductive norms.

To change counterproductive norms in existing teams, the problem should be explicitly discussed with team members using persuasive communication tactics (see Chapter 8).[42] This strategy was effectively applied by the manager of Ikea's Vancouver store when he noticed that customer complaints were rising and employees were writing sarcastic replies on the customer comment cards. The manager made it clear to everyone that the company must have excellent customer service. The followng week, Ikea's "Moose Comment Box" yielded no customer service complaints and the company has since experienced a dramatic improvement in service standards.[43]

Team-based reward systems can sometimes shift norms away from counterproductive behaviours. A production bonus might cause the team to accept or even encourage individual members to strive for higher product quality. Unfortunately, this strategy may be ineffective when the pressure to conform to the counterproductive norm is stronger than the financial incentive. For instance, employees working in the pajama factory described earlier were paid under a piece-rate system. Most individuals in the group were able to process more units and thereby earn more money, but they all chose to abide by the group norm of 50 units per hour.

Finally, a dysfunctional norm may be so deeply ingrained that the best strategy is to disband the group and replace it with people having more favourable norms. Once again, managers should seize the opportunity to introduce performance-oriented norms when the new team is formed and select members who will bring these values to the group.

TEAM COHESIVENESS

cohesiveness
The extent to which people are attracted to the team and are motivated to remain members.

An important characteristic of any work team is its level of cohesiveness. **Cohesiveness** refers to the extent to which people are attracted to the team and are motivated to remain members.[44] It is the glue or esprit de corps that holds the group together and ensures that its members fulfill their obligations. Let's begin our discussion of this subject by examining the causes of team cohesiveness.

Causes of Team Cohesiveness

Team cohesiveness largely depends on the factors listed in Exhibit 10–8. Generally, these factors influence a person's identity with the group and the group's usefulness in fulfilling the individual's basic needs.[45] You will notice that several determinants of team cohesiveness are related to our earlier discussion on the attractiveness and development of teams. Basically, teams become more cohesive as they reach higher stages of development and are more attractive to potential members.

Member Similarity.   It is easier to develop cohesiveness in a homogeneous team than a heterogeneous team. People are motivated to interact with others having similar opinions because it confirms their perspective of reality and makes them feel more comfortable with themselves.[46] It is also easier to agree upon group objectives, the means to fulfill those objectives, and the rules applied to maintain group behaviour when members hold similar views. This, in turn, leads to less conflict within the group—another desirable quality for its members.

Member Interaction.   Team cohesiveness increases with the amount of interaction among its members.[47] Thus, cohesiveness increases when team tasks require a high level of interdependence rather than more independent

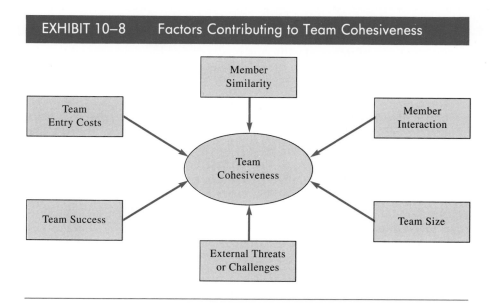

EXHIBIT 10–8   Factors Contributing to Team Cohesiveness

PERSPECTIVE 10–2   Building Cohesiveness at National Research Council

It was the worst possible news for Prince Edward Island (PEI) mussel harvesters. In early December 1987, several people had fallen ill after eating PEI mussels and the federal government banned further sales of the Island's shellfish. The government's action was swift, but the poison eventually killed three people and made 124 others ill.

The National Research Council's Atlantic Research Laboratory in Halifax was called on to help solve the mystery of the poisonous PEI mussels. Two factors pulled the Halifax team together into a cohesive unit. First, they had to isolate the poison quickly to help the recovery of those who fell ill. The longer the investigation took, the higher the chances that someone would die from the poison and the longer it would take the PEI mussel industry to get back into business. Second, staff members learned that other teams, including the world-famous toxin laboratory of Yuzuru Shimizi at the University of Rhode Island, were also trying to solve the mystery first. This formed a healthy competition that made the Halifax unit even more determined to perform well as a team. As Roger Foxall, Director of the Halifax lab, explains: "You think we didn't want to beat him [Shimizi]? He was the world's expert."

The Halifax team went into high gear on Friday, December 10th, when the news broke that a Montreal man had died from the PEI mussels. Project leader Jeff Wright collaborated with Foxall to increase the num-

activities. Teams are also more cohesive when their members are located in close physical proximity and in work spaces that allow them to interact more frequently. Wall partitions and other architectural barriers should be removed or placed in such a way that they do not reduce contact among team members. At the same time, cohesiveness may be diminished by the amount of interaction members have with employees in other groups.[48] Thus, physical space should maximize interaction among members within the group and avoid too much interaction with people in other groups. For example, to increase informal interaction and communication among its engineers, Corning Glass constructed an office building that has optimum visibility of every area with plenty of informal gathering places.[49] The building separates engineering from other organizational units but maximizes visible contact among the engineers.

External Threats and Challenges.   Cohesiveness increases when the team experiences competition or faces a challenging, yet valued, objective. The effects of competition and challenge on cohesiveness were dramatically experienced by the Halifax group that solved Prince Edward Island's toxic mussel scare a few years ago, as depicted in Perspective 10–2. Faced with the formidable challenge of identifying the toxin within a very short time and recognizing that other research groups were competing to solve the riddle first, the Halifax team became cohesive very quickly.

There are at least two reasons why challenging objectives and threats of external competition increase cohesiveness. First, teams serve an important socioemotional function, which is particularly valuable during times of trouble. As we previously learned, the physical presence of others in the same situation reduces the stress associated with the threatening situation. Sec-

ber of people committed to the project and quickly secure additional resources. For example, the Halifax lab normally sent samples to Ottawa for testing, but this was usually awkward and time-consuming, so Ottawa's facilities and technicians were sent to Halifax to work directly with the team.

On Sunday (two days after the first death), the Halifax team conducted a "mussel party," shucking mussels for the intensive work to follow. By Tuesday, they had isolated the toxin and the next day had identified its specific type. A Health and Welfare labora-

tory spent Thursday confirming the NRC Halifax team's results, while Foxall and Wright flew to Ottawa to brief other scientists late into the night. The discovery was announced in the Canadian Parliament on Friday.

The long hours of isolating a new toxin and the excitement of being the first to solve the mystery created a strong bond that was felt by the Halifax lab for some time afterwards. This team spirit also rippled across the entire National Research Council as other scientists felt a new pride in their organization.

Source: S. Strauss, "Finding Mussel Toxin Shot in Arm for NRC," *Globe and Mail*, December 29, 1987, p. D8.

ond, people are more likely to dedicate themselves to the team as the importance of the team's objective increases and the need for team rather than individual effort becomes apparent. In the toxic mussel story, individual researchers pulled together because the problem could be resolved more effectively by working as a team. Of course, cohesiveness only increases when members believe that working together is the best alternative under the circumstances. Teams may quickly fall apart otherwise.

Team Entry Costs.   Teams tend to be more cohesive when becoming a member is difficult or requires a high investment. There are at least three reasons for this. First, teams with high entry costs are more prestigious, and this status is often valued for its own sake. Second, high entry costs trigger the cognitive dissonance phenomenon described in Chapter 8. Specifically, employees are more likely to convince themselves that the resulting membership is valuable after they have sunk so much time and effort into becoming a team member. This is apparent in some fraternities and sororities where difficult initiation rites lead to greater cohesiveness. Finally, when entry costs are high, existing team members are usually more willing to welcome and support new members after they have "passed the test," possibly because they have shared a common experience.[50]

Team Success.   As a general rule, cohesiveness increases with the team's level of success.[51] Successful teams are more attractive to current and potential members because people like to be identified with success and they are more likely to believe that the group will achieve future goals that benefit its members.

Team Size.   Smaller teams tend to be more cohesive than larger teams because it is easier for a few people to agree upon goals. It is also easier for members of small teams to interact and coordinate their work activities. This does not mean that the smallest teams are the most cohesive, however. Having too few members may prevent the team from accomplishing its objectives. Continued failure may undermine the cohesiveness as members begin to question the team's ability to satisfy their needs.

Team cohesiveness may be difficult to influence, but the above discussion suggests that it is possible. Based on these factors, Exhibit 10–9 lists several actions available to team or organizational leaders to increase team cohesiveness. In situations where lower cohesiveness is desirable, the opposite recommendations may be applied.

Consequences of Team Cohesiveness

For the most part, cohesiveness is an important ingredient in the survival and success of work teams.[52] Every team must have some minimal level of cohesiveness to maintain its existence. As cohesiveness increases, members are more motivated to maintain their membership and to help the team work effectively. Members of high-cohesive teams spend more time together and share information more frequently than members of low-cohesive teams. They are generally more sensitive to each other's needs and develop better interpersonal relationships, thereby reducing potential conflict. When dysfunctional conflict does arise, members of high-cohesive teams seem to be better motivated and able to resolve these differences swiftly and effectively.[53]

EXHIBIT 10–9   Increasing Team Cohesiveness

- Select members with similar goals, attitudes, and experiences.
- Maintain high entrance standards when selecting team members. For example, potential members should pass through several interviews and possibly complete a rigorous training schedule.
- Assign team members to the same physical area, such as a separate building or floor.
- Use open office designs within the group; use walls and partitions between groups.
- Keep the team small without jeopardizing its ability to accomplish the task.
- Set challenging objectives that are valued by the team.
- Make the team aware of external threats, such as competition from other organizations.
- Facilitate and celebrate team successes. Provide sufficient resources for the team to complete its tasks. Personally recognize and publicize team accomplishments.

Members of high-cohesive units are more satisfied with other team members because they experience less stress in a cooperative work environment with like-minded colleagues. Members like each other because they share common goals, opinions, and values. Consequently, members are more reluctant to be absent from work (unless this is a team norm) or to leave the group. Since the group offers social support in stressful situations, cohesiveness and social interaction may increase the ability to tolerate dissatisfying aspects of work.[54]

Cohesiveness and Task Performance

You might think that high-cohesive teams perform their tasks more effectively than low-cohesive teams, but the relationship between cohesiveness and performance is actually more complex than this.[55] It is certainly true that members of a high-cohesive team work very well together, thereby increasing the team's ability to reach its objectives. As we have just stated, members cooperate with each other and resolve conflicts quickly. A high-cohesive team also has greater control over member behaviour because these individuals are more motivated to maintain their membership. Thus, we can expect members of high-cohesive teams to deviate from team norms less frequently and to a smaller degree.[56]

A high-cohesive team may function more effectively, but whether this translates into higher task performance depends on whether the team's norms are consistent with organizational objectives. Cohesiveness reflects the level of effort that members will allocate to the team's goals, whereas

EXHIBIT 10–10	Effect of Team Cohesiveness on Task Performance

Team Norms Compatible with Organizational Objectives	Moderately High Task Performance	High Task Performance
Team Norms Conflict with Organizational Objectives	Moderately Low Task Performance	Low Task Performance
	Low High
	Team Cohesiveness

team norms identify the ways to channel that effort.[57] This relationship is depicted in Exhibit 10–10. A high-cohesive team will achieve higher task performance *if* its norms are consistent with organizational objectives. But if norms conflict with organizational objectives, the high-cohesive team will likely have lower task performance than less-cohesive units.

OTHER TEAM EFFECTS ON INDIVIDUAL BEHAVIOUR

So far, we have discussed how people conform their behaviour to team norms. This is certainly the most important influence of teams on individual behaviour, but two other influences have also been observed: social facilitation and social loafing.

Social Facilitation

Over one hundred years ago, Norman Triplett, a social scientist, discovered that competitive cyclists raced faster in the presence of other cyclists than when they raced alone. It was initially thought that interpersonal competition caused individual performance to increase, but other studies reported the same results when the individual performed in front of a passive audience. This phenomenon, known as the **social facilitation** effect, causes individuals to perform faster, although not more accurately, on relatively simple and well-learned tasks. However, subsequent research discovered that individual performance is actually impaired rather than facilitated by the presence of others when the task is complex and requires attention to detail. This negative effect is not pronounced, but it does exist in this type of task.[58]

social facilitation
A social phenomenon whereby people develop a heightened awareness or arousal in the presence of others which causes them to perform previously learned behaviours faster than when working in isolation.

These contradictory effects confounded researchers until the mid-1960s, when Robert Zajonc proposed an elegantly simple explanation.[59] Zajonc suggested that people develop a heightened awareness or arousal in the presence of others that causes them to perform previously learned behaviours better. Basically, the presence of others increases our level of task awareness and motivation to perform well because we believe that others are evaluating our performance. Performance decreases when the task is complex and novel because the presence of others, combined with a challenging and unlearned task, overactivates us and distracts our concentration.

Social Loafing

social loafing
A social phenomenon whereby team members have lower work effort when their individual contribution to the team's performance is not easily distinguished.

Many team activities allow individuals to "slack off" or take a "free ride" on the performance of others. This phenomenon is called **social loafing** and, as mentioned earlier in this chapter, is most likely to occur in additive and disjunctive tasks where individual output is not easily distinguished. Social loafing is also more prevalent in larger teams where the actions (or inactions!) of individual team members are less noticeable and the members are less likely to feel that the group's success depends on them. Students assigned team projects are all too familiar with the social loafing concept as at least one member of the team tends to engage in this activity.[60]

Social loafing is less likely to occur when the task is interesting because individuals have a higher intrinsic motivation to perform their duties. It is less common when the group's objective is important, possibly because individuals experience more pressure from other team members to perform well. Finally, social loafing is less likely to occur in societies where individuals value team goals over individual interests. There is some evidence, for example, that this phenomenon is more common among North American than Chinese managers because the latter hold more collectivist views.[61]

TEAM BUILDING

Team building is any formal intervention directed toward improving the development and functioning of a work team.[62] It is the most common form of organizational development and, consequently, includes some of the activities that we will be discussing in Chapter 15. Team building typically uses a consultant to help the team diagnose its functional and dysfunctional attributes and to design courses of action to overcome these limitations.[63] This process may be used to accelerate the development of newly established teams, but it more often applies to existing teams that have regressed for a variety of reasons (e.g., membership turnover).

team building
Any formal intervention directed toward improving the development and functioning of a work team.

Types of Team Building

There are at least four types of team building, including role definition, interpersonal process, goal setting, and problem solving. Interpersonal process is the most common approach, but team-building efforts ordinarily include at least two of these strategies.[64]

Role Definition. The role definition perspective examines role expectations among team members and clarifies each member's future role obligations to the team. It determines whether individuals have the same role expectations that others assume of them and resolves these differences through negotiation. Roles are closely linked with team norms, so this form of team building usually influences future team norms.

Interpersonal Process. Interpersonal process interventions attempt to build trust and open communications among team members by resolving hidden agendas and misperceptions. This usually involves collecting survey information from individual team members regarding conflicts and relationship problems, followed by candid discussion of these dysfunctions. More recently, Outward Bound and other organizations have developed corporate

PERSPECTIVE 10–3   Outward Bound: Team Building in the Woods

C. David Clark, chief executive officer of Campbell Soup Co. Ltd., gathered a half-dozen vice-presidents for an eight-day experience in team building that they would never forget. The group flew to Thunder Bay, then were driven by van on increasingly rutted roads to Sturgeon Lake, 200 kilometres north. By 11 P.M., the weary Toronto executives arrived at their destination where they were met by two strapping, cheerful instructors who fitted them with camping gear and led them by canoe into the wilderness.

Clark has a vivid recollection of the experience. "We expected to find tents pitched for us, but no: there were six canoes and 12 backpacks on the side of this river. We paddled for a while—I'd never been in a canoe before—and got to sleep about 4 A.M., only to be woken up two hours later."

Campbell Soup's management team is just one of many that have experienced team building in the woods. Dozens of firms, including Apple Canada, Time Canada, Northern Telecom, and Lloyd's Bank

Canada have sent their employees on Outward Bound and other wilderness excursion programs designed to build team spirit, trust, risk taking, problem solving, and other virtues among corporate groups. The idea is that team members will forge a new awareness of each other's qualities and limitations by being placed in a challenging and unfamiliar environment. The team becomes more cohesive—or breaks apart completely—as it faces seemingly life-threatening obstacles that require collaborative effort.

Robert Ramsay, president of Remarkable Communications Ltd. in Toronto, signed up his entire office staff and a few clients for an Outward Bound experience that taught them valuable lessons in team dynamics and decision making. One day, after a six-hour paddle on Lake Nipigon, the group approached a large bog where a portage to another lake awaited them. With dry humour, the instructors told Ramsay's employees to find the portage themselves. A few strong-willed types headed off in search of the elusive

programs in which teams are placed in wilderness settings to face special challenges and threats. As Perspective 10–3 describes, this forces team members to reevaluate their relations and resolve long-standing conflicts. These experiences may also alter role definitions, as team members forge new perceptions and expectations of themselves and others in the group.

Goal Setting. This strategy involves clarifying the team's performance goals, increasing the team's motivation to accomplish these goals, and establishing a mechanism for systematic feedback on the team's goal performance. This is very similar to individual goal setting described in Chapter 2, except that the goals are applied to teams and, consequently, team dynamics must be addressed (such as goal consensus and the allocation of tasks among members).

Problem Solving. This type of team building examines the team's task-related decision-making process and identifies ways to make it more effective.[65] Each decision-making stage is examined, such as how the team identifies problems, searches for alternatives, and so on (see Chapter 9). Problem solving is a fairly recent team-building approach, but will probably become more popular as organizations make increasing use of problem-solving teams such as quality circles (described in the next chapter).

trail. One person went another way, only to return with mud up to his thighs and the message that the terrain was impassable. A third party found a drier route, but this was reported by a junior employee, so the others paid little attention. After more slogging through the muck, Ramsay's team eventually realized that the junior employee's information was valuable and should have been heeded.

James Fleming, a business writer and participant on Ramsay's expedition, observed that the bog and other experiences in the wilderness program changed the team and its members. "After four days the group had formed unbreakable bonds. . . . Underlings in the office had come to the fore and superiors had learned the wisdom of listening to new ideas, whatever their source."

Is team building in the wilderness effective? There isn't much empirical evidence yet, but anecdotal comments such as Fleming's are common. Campbell Soup's CEO believes that the program's team-building objective was "accomplished in spades." "We came to call it team bonding, since there was a real emotional linkage in the wilderness," says Clark.

"We all came back changed people, with an increased respect for each other's abilities—and weaknesses—and a real love for each other. I recall that last morning, as we stood on the side of the lake; there wasn't a dry eye in the house, as we thought back on how we had helped each other, laughed, cried, shivered and conquered mosquitoes and spiders."

Sources: A. Gould, "Sentimental Journeys," *Financial Times*, October 3, 1988, p. A6; and J. Fleming, "Roughing It in the Bush," *Canadian Business*, September 1987, pp. 49–53.

The Team-Building Cycle

No matter which approach is used, team building ordinarily follows the cycle shown in Exhibit 10–11.[66] The process begins when the team perceives that a problem exists. A consultant respected by the group is selected to coordinate and facilitate the team-building process. Next, data are collected by the consultant and the team to help determine the root causes of the symptoms or problems. This may involve in-depth, private interviews between the consultant and each team member, open data-sharing sessions where team members publicly disclose their views to others, or possibly structured questionnaires. During the diagnosis phase, these data are summarized and fed back to members for further discussion to elaborate the underlying causes of the team's problems.

The planning stage involves finding solutions to the underlying problems. The full participation of team members is particularly important here because everyone should be fully committed to the resulting objectives. In some situations, this stage establishes new norms to help the team operate more effectively. In the implementation phase, the team puts the newly prescribed behaviours into practice and avoids the old ways of operating. Subsequent team-building sessions are held to evaluate the team's progress toward its objectives and to determine whether additional problems exist. The cycle may be repeated if further problems are identified.

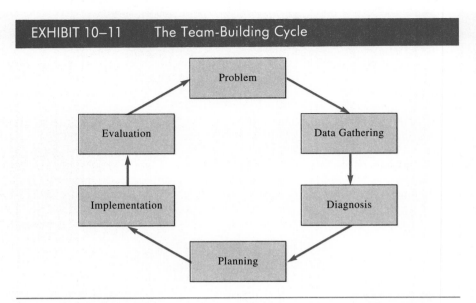

EXHIBIT 10–11   The Team-Building Cycle

Source: W. G. Dyer, *Team Building: Issues and Alternatives* (Reading, Mass.: Addison-Wesley, 1977), pp. 41–50.

Is Team Building Effective?

Team building can be costly and time-consuming, so it is important to know whether the time and money are well-spent. The answer so far is an equivocal "maybe." Most of the early research findings were favourable, but they were based mainly on anecdotal accounts. More recent empirical studies suggest that some team-building interventions are successful, but just as many fail to improve team effectiveness.[67] One problem is that we don't yet know which of the four team-building strategies is the most effective. This is because multiple approaches are typically used, and each approach may be accomplished through different methods. For example, we don't yet know whether the interpersonal process is more or less effective using the Outward Bound method or the more traditional open data-sharing session approach.

Another concern is that the success of team building (as with most other organizational change activities) depends on specific conditions. Team building is more likely to succeed when members understand, are committed to, and fully participate in the process. The intervention must also be consistent with the existing organizational system, including rewards and corporate culture. Some experts suggest that team-building interventions have failed because the team was not involved in interdependent tasks that would facilitate team dynamics.

Finally, there is the potential problem that team building is too effective. The intervention may create such a high level of cohesiveness and an insular perspective that members may become more loyal to the team than to the larger organization.[68] However, few team-building efforts seem to have had this effect. Overall, we can say that there will be an increasing need for action-oriented strategies to improve team effectiveness, but we aren't yet certain that the team-building interventions currently available provide the answer.

SUMMARY

• Teams consist of two or more people who interact and mutually influence each other for the purpose of achieving common goals. Formal teams, including command units, task forces, and skunkworks are explicitly formed to accomplish a specific set of tasks for the benefit of the organization. Informal groups, including friendship groups, interest groups, and coalitions, are formed to serve largely personal needs, such as playing hockey or satisfying the need to affiliate.

• People belong to formal or informal teams to fulfill their personal needs. Teams can often accomplish goals that cannot be achieved individually. They help fulfill an individual's need for friendship, social interaction, and status. The presence of other people also provides emotional support under threatening conditions.

• Team effectiveness includes the group's ability to survive and perform its objectives successfully as well as to maintain the satisfaction, well-being, and commitment of individual members.

• Team dynamics and effectiveness depend on various contextual factors, such as management philosophy, technology, physical layout, task characteristics, and reward systems. The size and composition of the team must also be considered. The smallest teams are typically the most effective as long as members possess the necessary skills and resources to accomplish the task. Homogeneous teams experience more cohesiveness and less conflict, but heterogeneous teams are usually more effective on complex projects and problem-solving tasks.

• Teams develop through the stages of forming, storming, norming, performing, and eventually adjourning. They begin by learning about each other and evaluating the benefits and costs of continued membership. Members then take on specific roles and try to establish norms of appropriate behaviour. A consensus eventually forms around team objectives and the unit becomes more task-oriented. Teams may cycle back through earlier stages as membership changes and new conditions emerge. As the team's existence comes to an end, members redirect their attention away from task orientation to a socioemotional focus.

• Norms are the team's informal rules and standards and exist to regulate and guide the behaviours of its members. Individual members conform to team norms through direct or indirect pressure. Norms may be influenced by critical events, explicit statements, initial experiences, and members' pre-group experiences. Leaders can sometimes shape team norms by carefully selecting members, explicitly discussing performance-oriented norms when the team is formed, and introducing rewards that support the desired norms.

• Cohesiveness refers to the extent that people are attracted to the team and are motivated to remain members. Several characteristics of the team and its surrounding environment affect cohesiveness. Cohesiveness is an important ingredient in the survival and success of work teams, but high-cohesive units have higher task performance only when their norms do not conflict with organizational objectives.

• Team building is any formal intervention directed toward improving the development and functioning of a work team. Four team-building strategies are used in industry, including role definition, interpersonal process, goal setting, and problem solving. Some team-building interventions succeed, but just as many fail to accelerate team development or improve team effectiveness.

DISCUSSION QUESTIONS

1. Describe the five stages of team development. When might a team have to cycle back through earlier stages of development?

2. Explain the relationship between team cohesiveness and task performance. How can organizational leaders make work teams more cohesive?

3. Why are skunkworks usually so successful?

4. If you were randomly assigned with four other students to complete a group project, what team-related problems might be encountered? Describe the positive characteristics of student teams in this situation.

5. Why might Outward Bound and other wilderness programs increase team cohesiveness?

6. Identify five features of the organizational environment that might hinder team development and effectiveness.

7. How do team norms develop? What might a manager do to change a counterproductive norm to one that is more consistent with organizational objectives?

8. Describe the team-building process.

NOTES

1. R. Rix, "Enlightened Program a Winner at Food Centre," *Materials Management and Distribution* 35, no. 5 (May 1990), pp. 15–16.

2. R. Anderson, "Team Approach Can Rally Workers to Perform Better," *Globe and Mail,* October 31, 1986, p. B4.

3. W. Annett, "Up with the Individual," *B.C. Business,* May 1987, pp. 54, 57; Auditor General of Canada, *Report of the Auditor General to the House of Commons, Fiscal Year Ended 31 March 1988* (Ottawa: Supply and Services Canada, 1989), Exhibit 4.8; and J. White, "Tailoring a New Workplace," *Perception* 14, no. 1 (Winter 1990), pp. 25, 44.

4. D. Cartwright and A. Zander (eds.), *Group Dynamics: Research and Theory,* 3rd ed. (New York: Harper & Row, 1968); and M. E. Shaw, *Group Dynamics,* 3rd ed. (New York: McGraw-Hill, 1981), p. 8.

5. R. Likert, *The Human Organization: Its Management and Value* (New York: McGraw-Hill, 1967).

6. J. Lanthier, "People Are the Crucial Aspect of Mergers," *Financial Post,* July 24, 1989, p. 21; and P. McLaughlin, "Merger Doctors," *Vista* 2, no. 5 (July 1989), pp. 58–61.

7. T. Peters, *Thriving on Chaos* (New York: Knopf, 1987), pp. 211–18; T. Kidder, *Soul of a New Machine* (Boston: Little, Brown, 1981); and T. Peters and N. Austin, *A Passion for Excellence* (New York: Random House, 1985), Chapters 9 and 10.

8. Peters, *Thriving on Chaos,* p. 35; Peters and Austin, *A Passion for Excellence,* pp. 164–66.

9. L. Iacocca and W. Novak, *Iacocca* (New York: Bantam, 1984), Chapter 6.

10. W. B. Stevenson, J. L. Pearce, and L. W. Porter, "The Concept of 'Coalition' in Organization Theory and Research," *Academy of Management Review* 10 (1985), pp. 256–68.

11. D. C. McClelland, *The Achieving Society* (New York: Van Nostrand Reinhold, 1961).

12. L. N. Jewell and H. J. Reitz, *Group Effectiveness in Organizations* (Glenview, Ill.: Scott, Foresman, 1981).

13. S. Schachter, *The Psychology of Affiliation* (Stanford, Calif.: Stanford University Press, 1959), pp. 12–19.

14. A. S. Tannenbaum, *Social Psychology of the Work Organization* (Belmont, Calif.: Wadsworth, 1966), p. 62.

15. For a summary of recent models, see P. S. Goodman, E. Ravlin, and M. Schminke, "Understanding Groups in Organizations," *Research in Organizational Behavior* 9 (1987), pp. 121–73.

16. D. Gladstein, "Groups in Context: A Model of Organizational Effectiveness," *Administrative Science Quarterly* 29 (1984), pp. 499–517; and G. P. Shea and R. A. Guzzo, "Group Effectiveness: What Really Matters?" *Sloan Management Review* 27 (1987), pp. 33–46.

17. A. P. Hare, *Handbook of Small Group Research,* 2nd ed. (New York: Free Press, 1976), pp. 12–15.

18. H. F. Kolodny and M. N. Kiggundu, "Toward the Development of a Sociotechnical Systems Model in Woodlands Mechanical Harvesting," *Human Relations* 33 (1980), pp. 623–45.

19. E. Sundstrom, K. P. De Meuse, and D. Futrell, "Work Teams: Applications and Effectiveness," *American Psychologist* 45 (February 1990), pp. 120–33.

20. Hare, *Handbook of Small Group Research;* and J. Kelly and J. McGrath, "Effects of Time Limits and Task Types on Task Performance and Interaction of Four Person Groups," *Journal of Personality and Social Psychology* 49 (1985), pp. 395–407.

21. I. D. Steiner, *Group Processes and Productivity* (New York: Academic Press, 1972).

22. I. H. Fazey, "Multinationals Persuading Workers to 'Wear the Shirt,'" *Financial Post,* October 10, 1989, p. 15.

23. "Quick Moves Keep Bata Competitive," *Industrial Management* 10 (November 1986), p. 6; and D. Silbert, "Top Secrets of Management," *Canadian Business,* July 1987, pp. 28–34.

24. Steiner, *Group Processes and Productivity.*

25. A. Tziner and D. Eden, "Effects of Crew Composition on Crew Performance: Does the Whole Equal the Sum of the Parts?" *Journal of Applied Psychology* 70 (1985), pp. 85–93.

26. B. M. Bass and E. C. Ryterband, *Organizational Psychology,* 2nd ed. (Boston: Allyn & Bacon, 1979).

27. J. Seltzer and R. H. Kilman, "Effect of Group Composition on Group Process: Homogeneity vs. Heterogeneity on Task and People Dimensions," *Psychological Reports* 41 (1977), pp. 1195–1200.

28. C. Kirchmeyer and J. McLellan, "Managing Ethnic Diversity: Utilizing the Creative Potential of a Diverse Workforce to Meet the Challenges of the Future," *Proceedings of the Annual ASAC Conference, Organizational Behaviour Division* 11 pt. 5 (1990), pp. 120–29.

29. Shaw, *Group Dynamics,* pp. 238–61.

30. B. W. Tuckman, "Developmental Sequences in Small Groups," *Psychological Bulletin* 63 (1965), pp. 384–99; and B. W. Tuckman and M. A. C. Jensen, "Stages of Small-Group Development Revisited," *Group and Organization Studies* 2 (1977), pp. 419–42.

31. C. Argyris, *Interpersonal Competence and Organizational Effectiveness* (Homewood, Ill.: Irwin, 1962).

32. S. J. Liebowitz and K. P. De Meuse, "The Application to Team Building," *Human Relations* 35 (1982), pp. 1–18.

33. C. J. G. Gersick, "Time and Transition in Work Teams: Toward a New Model of Group Development," *Academy of Management Journal* 31 (1988), pp. 9–41.

34. L. W. Porter, E. E. Lawler, and J. R. Hackman, *Behavior in Organizations* (New York: McGraw-Hill, 1975), pp. 391–94; and D. E. Feldman, "The Development and Enforcement of Group Norms," *Academy of Management Review* 9 (1984), pp. 47–53.

35. "Employee Involvement and the Supervisor," *Worklife Report* 7, no. 1 (1989), pp. 6–7.

36. J. W. Thibaut and H. H. Kelley, *Social Psychology of Groups* (New York: John Wiley & Sons, 1959).

37. C. A. Kiesler and S. B. Kiesler, *Conformity* (Reading, Mass.: Addison-Wesley, 1970); and B. Latané, "The Psychology of Social Impact," *American Psychologist* 36 (1981), pp. 343–56.

38. Porter, Lawler, and Hackman, *Behavior in Organizations,* pp. 399–401.

39. L. Coch and J. R. P. French, Jr., "Overcoming Resistance to Change," *Human Relations* 1 (1948), pp. 512–32.

40. Feldman, "The Development and Enforcement of Group Norms," pp. 50–52.

41. A. Gouldner, "The Norm of Reciprocity," *American Sociological Review* 25 (1960), pp. 161–78.

42. R. S. Spich and K. Keleman, "Explicit Norm Structuring Process: A Strategy for Increasing Task–Group Effectiveness," *Group & Organization Studies* 10 (March 1985), pp. 37–59; and D. C. Feldman and H. J. Arnold, *Managing Individual and Group Behavior in Organizations* (New York: McGraw-Hill, 1983), pp. 450–51.

43. B. Power, "The Driving Force," *B. C. Business,* April 1990, pp. 83–88.

44. Shaw, *Group Dynamics,* pp. 213–26; and Goodman et al., "Understanding Groups in Organizations," pp. 144–46.

45. A. Lott and B. Lott, "Group Cohesiveness as Interpersonal Attraction: A Review of Relationships with Antecedent and Consequent Variables," *Psychological Bulletin* 64 (1965), pp. 259–309.

46. L. Festinger, "Informal Social Communication," *Psychological Review* 57 (1950), pp. 271–82; J. Virk, P. Aggarwal, and R. N. Bhan, "Similarity versus Complementarity in Clique Formation," *Journal of Social Psychology* 120 (1983), pp. 27–34; and S. Seashore, *Group Cohesiveness in the Industrial Workgroup* (Ann Arbor, Mich.: Institute for Social Research, 1954).

47. A. Mikalachki, *Group Cohesion Reconsidered* (London, Ont.: School of Business Administration, University of Western Ontario, 1969); and W. Piper, M. Marrache, R. Lacroix, A. Richardson, and B. Jones, "Cohesion as a Basic Bond in Groups," *Human Relations* 36 (1983), pp. 93–108.

48. C. P. Alderfer, "An Intergroup Perspective on Group Dynamics," in J. Lorsch (ed.), *Handbook of Organizational Behavior* (Englewood Cliffs, N.J.: Prentice Hall, 1987), pp. 190–222.

49. F. Steele, *Making and Managing High-Quality Workplaces* (New York: Teachers College Press, 1986), pp. 92–94.

50. E. Aronson and J. Mills, "The Effects of Severity of Initiation on Liking for a Group," *Journal of Abnormal and Social Psychology* 59 (1959), pp. 177–81.

51. Shaw, *Group Dynamics,* p. 215.

52. Piper et al., "Cohesion as a Basic Bond in Groups," pp. 93–108; and R. D. O'Keefe, J. A. Kernaghan, and A. H. Rubenstein, "Group Cohesiveness: A Factor in the Adoption of Innovations among Scientific Work Groups," *Small Group Behavior* 6 (1975), pp. 282–92.

53. Shaw, *Group Dynamics,* p. 222.

54. C. A. O'Reilly III, D. F. Caldwell, and W. P. Barnett, "Work Group Demography, Social Integration, and Turnover," *Administrative Science Quarterly* 34 (1989), pp. 21–37.

55. C. N. Greene, "Cohesion and Productivity in Work Groups," *Small Group Behavior* 20 (February 1989), pp. 70–86; and Lott and Lott, "Group Cohesiveness as Interpersonal Attraction: Antecedents of Linking," pp. 259–302.

56. Goodman et al., "Understanding Groups in Organizations," p. 146.

57. Goodman et al., "Understanding Groups in Organizations," p. 151.

58. C. F. Bond, Jr., and L. J. Titus, "Social Facilitation: A Meta-Analysis of 241 Studies," *Psychological Bulletin* 94 (1983), pp. 265–92.

59. R. B. Zajonc, "Social Facilitation," *Science* 149 (1965), pp. 269–74.

60. R. Albanese and D. D. Van Fleet, "Rational Behavior in Groups: The Free-Riding Tendency," *Academy of Management Review* 10 (1985), pp. 244–55.

61. P. C. Earley, "Social Loafing and Collectivism: A Comparison of the U.S. and the People's Republic of China," *Administrative Science Quarterly* 34 (1989), pp. 565–81.

62. W. G. Dyer, *Team Building: Issues and Alternatives* (Reading, Mass.: Addison-Wesley, 1977), p. 41.

63. Liebowitz and De Meuse, "The Application of Team Building," pp. 1–18.

64. Sundstrom et al., "Work Teams: Applications and Effectiveness," p. 128; and M. Beer, *Organizational Change and Development: A Systems View* (Santa Monica, Calif.: Goodyear, 1980).

65. P. F. Buller and C. H. Bell, Jr., "Effects of Team Building and Goal Setting on Productivity: A Field Experiment," *Academy of Management Journal* 29 (1986), pp. 305–28.

66. Dyer, *Team Building: Issues and Alternatives,* pp. 41–50.

67. R. W. Woodman and J. J. Sherwood, "The Role of Team Development in Organizational Effectiveness: A Critical Review," *Psychological Bulletin* 88 (1980), pp. 166–86; M. E. Gist, E. A. Locke, and M. S. Taylor, "Organizational Behavior: Group Stucture, Process, and Effectiveness," *Journal of Management* 13 (1987), pp. 237–57; and Sundstrom et al., "Work Teams: Applications and Effectiveness," p. 128.

68. R. W. Boss and H. L. McConkie, "The Destructive Impact of a Positive Team-Building Intervention," *Group and Organization Studies* 6 (1981), pp. 45–56.

CHAPTER CASES

GORDON FOUNDRY CO.

Right after I graduated from the Provincial Technical Institute I accepted a position with the Gordon Foundry, a medium-sized firm located in a small town in one of the Eastern Provinces. It was a good position, because I was the assistant to Mr. Smith, who was general manager and president of the family owned company. I was anxious to learn the foundry business and since I was living alone it was not long before I literally lived in the foundry. We had many technical problems, the work was intensely interesting, and my boss was a very fine person.

The foundry workers were a closely knit group and were primarily older men. Several had spent a lifetime in the foundry. Many of them were related. They felt that they knew the foundry business from A to Z and they were inclined to "pooh-pooh" the value of a technical education. The president had mentioned to me when we discussed the duties and responsibilities of the position that no graduate of a technical institute had ever been employed in the Gordon Foundry. He added, "You will find that the workers stick pretty well together. Most of them have been working together for more than

10 years, which is rather unusual in a foundry, so it may take you some time to get accepted. But, on the whole, you will find them a fine group of workers.''

At first the workers eyed me coldly as I went around and got acquainted. Also, I noticed that they would clam up as I approached. A bit later I became aware of cat-calls when I walked down the main aisle of the foundry. I chose to ignore these evidences of hostility because I considered them silly and childish. I believed that if I continued to ignore these antics the workers would eventually stop, come to their senses, and see the ridiculousness of their behaviour.

One Saturday, about a month after I had started, I was down in the Enamel Shop. As I entered it I observed a worker who was busy cleaning the floor with a hose emitting water at pretty strong pressure. It was customary to hose down the Enamel Shop every so often. I was busy near one of the dipping tanks when, all of a sudden, I was nearly knocked down by the force of a stream of water. The worker had deliberately turned the hose on me. I knew that he had intended to hit me by the casual way in which he swung around as though he had never seen what he had done.

Discussion Questions

1. Why was the new engineer not accepted by the foundry workers?
2. Was the foundry workers' behaviour ''silly and childish,'' or was there a more significant meaning behind these actions?
3. Should the new engineer or Smith have acted any differently than they did? If so, how?

Source: © 1956 University of Alberta. Used with permission of the author, Professor W. Preshing.

THE "NO MARTINI" LUNCH

Jim Lyons had just completed his second month as manager of an important office of a nationwide sales organization. He believed that he had made the right choice in leaving his old company. This new position offered a great challenge, excellent pay and benefits, and tremendous opportunity for advancement. In addition, his family seemed to be adjusting well to the new community. However, in Jim's mind there was one very serious problem that he believed must be confronted immediately or it could threaten his satisfaction in the long run.

Since taking the job, Jim had found out that the man he replaced had made an institution of the hard-drinking business lunch. He and a group of other key executives had virtually a standing appointment at various local restaurants. Even when clients were not present, they would have several drinks before ordering their lunches. When they returned it was usually well into the afternoon and they were in no condition to make the decisions or take the actions that were often the pretext of the lunch in the first place.

This practice had also spread to the subordinates of the various executives and it was not uncommon to see various groups of salespersons doing the same thing a few days each week. Jim decided that he wanted to end the practice, at least for himself and members of his group.

Jim knew this was not going to be an easy problem to solve. The drinking had become institutionalized with a great deal of psychological pressure from a central figure—in this case, the man he replaced. He decided to plan the approach he would take and then discuss the problem and his approach for solving it with his superior, Norm Landy.

The following week Jim made an appointment with Norm to discuss the situation. Norm listened intently as Jim explained the drinking problem but did not show any surprise at learning about it. Jim then explained what he planned to do.

"Norm, I'm making two assumptions on the front end. First, I don't believe it would do any good to state strong new policies about drinking at lunch, or lecturing my people about the evils of the liquid lunch. About all I'd accomplish there would be to raise a lot of latent guilt that would only result in resentment and resistance. Second, I am assuming that the boss is often a role model for his subordinates. Unfortunately, the man I replaced made a practice of the drinking lunch. The subordinates close to him then conform to his drinking habits and exert pressure on other members of the group. Before you know it everyone is a drinking buddy and the practice becomes institutionalized even when one member is no longer there.

"Here is what I intend to do about it. First, when I go to lunch with the other managers, I will do no drinking. More importantly, however, for the members of my group I am going to establish a new role model. For example, at least once a week we have a legitimate reason to work through lunch. In the past everyone has gone out anyway. I intend to hold a business lunch and have sandwiches and soft drinks sent in. In addition, I intend to make it a regular practice to take different groups of my people to lunch at a no-alcohol coffee shop.

"My goal, Norm, is simply to let my subordinates know that alcohol is not a necessary part of the workday, and that drinking will not win my approval. By not drinking with the other managers, I figure that sooner or later they too will get the point. As you can see, I intend to get the message across by my behaviour. There will be no words of censure. What do you think, Norm?"

Norm Landy pushed himself away from his desk and came around and seated himself beside Jim. He then looked at Jim and whispered, "Are you crazy? I guarantee you, Jim, that you are going to accomplish nothing but cause a lot of trouble. Trouble between your group and other groups if you succeed, trouble between you and your group, and trouble between you and the other managers. Believe me, Jim, I see the problem, and I agree with you that it is a problem. But the cure might kill the patient. Will all that conflict and trouble be worth it?"

Jim thought for a moment and said "I think it will be good for the organization in the long run."

Discussion Questions

1. What is Jim Lyons fundamentally trying to do in this case?
2. Do you agree with Norm Landy or Jim Lyons? Why?
3. What other strategies, if any, might achieve Jim's goals?

Source: J. L. Gibson, J. M. Ivancevich, and J. H. Donnelly, Jr., *Organizations: Behavior, Structure, Processes* (Homewood, Ill.: Irwin, 1991), pp. 289–90.

EXPERIENTIAL EXERCISE

TEAM-BUILDING DIAGNOSTIC EXERCISE

Purpose: This exercise is designed to help you understand team-building concepts and to diagnose the functioning of a class project team of which you are a member.

Instructions: As a first step, individuals will complete the team-building checklist in terms of a class project team of which they are members.

When individuals have completed the checklist, members of each class project team will meet to share their results. The team should focus on areas where most members agree the team is not functioning well. Members should also discuss items where one member's diagnosis differs significantly from others'. Team members will identify three areas of team functioning that require the most improvement and will discuss what should be done to improve team effectiveness in these areas.

In some courses, members of a project team are scattered throughout different tutorials or class sections. In these circumstances, the instructor may form discussion teams of four or five students from different class project teams who compare their checklist results. The checklists will refer to different project teams, but the discussion groups can look for similarities and unique problems across project teams.

Team-Building Diagnostic Checklist

To what extent is there evidence of the following problems in your work team? Please circle the number that best represents the situation of your class project team.

	Disagree			**Agree**	
1. The project is being completed too slowly.	1	2	3	4	5
2. Members lack imagination or initiative to complete their tasks well.	1	2	3	4	5
3. Members do not encourage others to work together in better team effort.	1	2	3	4	5
4. Team members do not trust each other.	1	2	3	4	5
5. Team members do not value or reward each other's work efforts.	1	2	3	4	5
6. Team meetings are run poorly.	1	2	3	4	5
7. Team members are confused about their task assignments.	1	2	3	4	5
8. Conflicts and hostility exist among team members.	1	2	3	4	5
9. Decisions are made that some team members do not understand or agree with.	1	2	3	4	5
10. Team members are not committed to the project or their specific tasks.	1	2	3	4	5
11. Team members are afraid to speak up, don't listen, or are not talking enough to each other.	1	2	3	4	5
12. Team members complain about other members behind their backs.	1	2	3	4	5

Scoring: Add up the score for all 12 items. If your score is between 12 and 24, there is little evidence that your team needs team building. If your score is between 25 and 36, there is some evidence, but no immediate pressure, unless two or three items receive scores of 5. If your score is between 37 and 48, your team should seriously consider engaging in some form of team-building activity. If your score is over 48, team building should be a top priority to help your team complete its project more effectively.

This checklist was prepared by Steven L. McShane and is based on W. G. Dyer, *Team Building: Issues and Alternatives* (Reading, Mass.: Addison-Wesley, 1977), pp. 36–37.

11

Employee Involvement and Team Decision Making

LEARNING OBJECTIVES

After reading this chapter, you should be able to:

Describe
The different forms and levels of employee involvement.

Discuss
The potential benefits of employee involvement.

Summarize
The key elements of the Vroom–Yetton–Jago model.

Identify
The conditions under which groupthink is most likely to occur.

Explain
How team leaders can increase constructive controversy.

Discuss
The advantages and disadvantages of nominal group technique.

Describe
The main features of self-managing work teams.

CHAPTER OUTLINE

Oak Run Bakery

John Voortman, president of Oak Run Farm Bakery Ltd. near Ancaster, Ontario, swings through the front door of the company and strolls across to the production area, where he starts conversing with two bakers. Voortman enthusiastically reviews sales projections with the employees and listens intently as they discuss whether Oak Run's next product line should be waffle cones or bran muffins. Voortman scrawls notes on his morning newspaper as the employees suggest ways to adapt the company's ovens to the new products.

Voortman will take the ideas to the next meeting of the company's profit-sharing committee. The six members of this committee—one representative from each of the bakery's six departments—meet every month to evaluate employee suggestions and debate the company's short- and long-range strategy. As a private company, Oak Run has no obligation to reveal its financial conditions, but committee members have access to all corporate information, including sales and profits. The bakery's 129 staff members all get a chance to serve on the committee.

Oak Run's emphasis on employee involvement has had a tremendous impact. Morale is high and employees have developed an entrepreneurial spark that did not exist before the company developed its more participative philosophy. Voortman also believes that employee involvement, together with the company's profit-sharing plan, are responsible for improving the quality of the company's products and tripling sales to more than $20 million in the past three years. Employees are continuously trying to improve product quality by watching out for failing equipment and discovering new production methods that may not have occurred to management. Explains Voortman, "Most bakeries that have grown to our size have quality-control departments—we don't need one. There's not a person working here who would let an inferior product leave the building."[1]

John Voortman and other Canadian managers are discovering that employee involvement can improve organizational effectiveness and employee well-being. It's difficult to imagine that less than a generation ago participation was viewed by most managers as an interesting academic theory that probably had little value in practice.[2] Today, it is considered an essential component of effective management. For example, at its assembly plant in Oakville, Ontario, Ford Motor Company showed employees a prototype of the Tempo and Topaz cars two years before production and invited them to suggest improvements—something the company would not have done in the past. Employees submitted over 200 ideas on the design and assembly of the cars, and Ford took action on over 80 percent of them.[3]

This chapter continues our discussion of team dynamics from Chapter 10 by examining employee involvement and team decision making. We begin by describing the concept of employee involvement and outlining the potential benefits of having employees participate in organizational decisions. A model is then introduced that helps managers identify the optimal level of employee involvement in a particular situation. Next, we discuss the potential problems with team decision making and review several strategies to avoid these difficulties. The final sections of this chapter introduce two innovative forms of employee involvement: quality circles and self-managing work teams.

WHAT IS EMPLOYEE INVOLVEMENT?

Employee involvement (also called *employee participation*) occurs when employees take an active role in the process of making decisions that were not previously within their mandate. This includes seeking information, receiving information, and influencing others regarding a particular issue. In general, the amount of influence employees have had in a particular decision increases with their amount of involvement.[4] Notice that participation is not the same as delegating autonomy to employees. One can imagine individuals who have a high degree of autonomy over their own jobs but are unable to participate in organizational decisions. However, many high-involvement management practices, such as self-managing work teams (described later in this chapter), introduce both employee involvement and autonomy, usually within a team-based work setting.

employee involvement
The active participation of employees in decision-making processes that were not previously within their mandate.

Forms and Levels of Employee Involvement

You can see from the opening story that participation exists in different forms. Voortman involves employees through informal discussions on the shop floor, a formal suggestion plan, and an employee–management committee that reviews company information and recommends future strategies. Other companies have introduced quality circles, health and safety committees, employee attitude surveys, confidential complaint systems, self-managing work teams, and numerous other approaches to increase employee involvement in the organization.

As Exhibit 11–1 shows, employee involvement varies in terms of its formality, directness, and legal mandate.[5] Formal practices, such as Oak Run's employee–management committee, exist as a codified policy and institutionalized practice. Informal participation, on the other hand, occurs purely at the discretion of management. Some forms of employee involvement are direct in the sense that employees personally influence the decision process rather than doing so through a representative.

Finally, while most forms of employee involvement have been introduced voluntarily, some are legally mandated by government statute. For example, most health and safety committees in Canada exist because management is legally compelled to regularly meet with employees regarding these matters. Many countries have passed laws institutionalizing other forms of participative decision making.[6] Legislation in Sweden, the Netherlands, and Germany, for example, gives employees the right to consult with management through works councils. German employees also indirectly participate through representation on supervisory and management boards.

There are also different levels of employee involvement.[7] Relatively little participation is involved when a manager asks an employee for specific information without mentioning the problem for which the information will be used. More involvement occurs when employees are consulted about the problem but the final decision still rests with the manager. At the highest level of participation, employees have complete decision-making power, from problem identification to solution implementation.[8] Later in this chapter we will introduce a model that outlines five levels of employee involvement. First, let's consider the potential benefits of employee involvement for organizational effectiveness and employee well-being.

EXHIBIT 11–1	Forms of Employee Involvement
Form of Involvement	**Description**
Formality	
Formal	Institutionalized meetings or procedures such as quality circles and employee complaint systems.
Informal	Casual and undocumented activities at management's discretion, such as a shop floor chat with employees.
Directness	
Direct	Employees directly communicate with management, such as when employees propose ideas directly to management.
Indirect	Employees communicate indirectly through a representative, such as employee representation on the board of directors.
Legal mandate	
Statutory	Government-legislated activities, such as a joint health and safety committee.
Voluntary	Activity initiated by management without any force of law, such as an employee suggestion plan.

POTENTIAL BENEFITS OF EMPLOYEE INVOLVEMENT

For over 50 years, management scholars have advised that employee participation may be good for both employees and the company.[9] Four potential benefits of employee involvement have been highlighted: decision quality, decision commitment, employee satisfaction and empowerment, and employee development (see Exhibit 11–2).

Decision Quality

Decision quality refers to the extent that the decision solves the problem and is consistent with organizational objectives.[10] Many organizational decisions are complex and require information and perspectives from employees affected by the decision.[11] These employees know their jobs and work environment better than anyone else, so it only makes sense that their advice should be sought. Employee involvement may improve decision quality in at least three stages of the decision-making process (see Chapter 9).

1. *Problem identification*—Participation may lead to a more accurate definition of the problem because employees introduce more perspectives and knowledge to understand the symptoms.

2. *Alternative development*—The number of alternate solutions generated typically increases with the number of people involved. In a

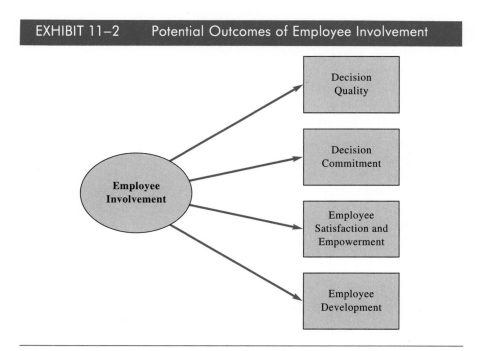

EXHIBIT 11–2   Potential Outcomes of Employee Involvement

Employee Involvement → Decision Quality

Employee Involvement → Decision Commitment

Employee Involvement → Employee Satisfaction and Empowerment

Employee Involvement → Employee Development

PERSPECTIVE 11–1   The Saga of MacMillan Bloedel's Team 100

About a century ago, fire had ravaged a plot of land on Vancouver Island called Yellow Creek 100, leaving a silvacultural wasteland. Some prime old Douglas firs remained, but the trees were scattered about and blocked by scrub brush and rough terrain. MacMillan Bloedel Ltd. had cutting rights to the Yellow Creek 100 site and wanted to replant it for a future harvest, but clearing the area would cost nearly $500,000 with little if any savings from harvestable wood.

To reduce the cost of preparing the Yellow Creek 100 site, MacMillan Bloedel's district managers decided to form a small task force, Team 100. Two riggers, two fallers, one forester, one engineer, a woods supervisor, a mechanic, a quality-control person, and an employee-relations coordinator were summoned

into a room where one of the district managers described the task in five minutes and then walked out. After the initial shock had worn off, Team 100's newly appointed members agreed that not only would they log this mess that everyone had avoided for several decades, but they were going to make money at it!

To achieve such a daunting objective, the team had to be creative and break traditions. Normally, a forester would visit the site alone, but Team 100 decided that a more accurate analysis of the situation would result if everyone involved visited at the same time. The result of this unique action was that several areas originally considered impractical for logging were included in the cutting plan. As one team member recalls: "At first people thought we were nuts.

---

well-managed meeting, team members create *synergy* by pooling their knowledge to form new alternatives that no one would have designed alone. In other words, several people working together and building on each other's strengths can potentially generate more and better solutions than if these people worked alone.

3. *Alternative selection*—With more diverse perspectives and a better representation of values, teams are more likely than the typical individual to select the best alternative. There is less chance that a grossly inaccurate solution will be selected when knowledgeable people are involved.

Involving employees in the decision-making process usually results in more informed decisions. In the 1940s, Robert Dubin explained how "expert consultation" by the employees in a Lever Brothers plant in Toronto improved production efficiency.[12] This point is also dramatically illustrated in Perspective 11–1, which describes how Team 100, a special task force of MacMillan Bloedel employees, achieved the impossible goal of profitably harvesting a silvacultural wasteland on Vancouver Island.

Decision Commitment

Canadian employees increasingly want to be involved in decisions that affect them, and often resist authoritarian dictums from senior management.[13] Employee involvement tends to minimize this resistance and increase employee motivation to implement decisions.[14] Employees are more likely to identify

Here we were going up to the site to check it out, or think of a new way to tackle a problem, and that was after our regular shift. But we were all having a great time."

Another innovation was to break the traditional—almost sacred—rule of having fallers on site first to cut up the virgin wood before other occupations venture in. Forestry crews, who are much lower on the status ladder, are normally brought in at the end of the job to clean up the site for replanting. Team 100's fallers suggested reversing the traditional order because the forestry crews could clear a path to allow the high-priced fallers speedier access to the harvestable wood. The idea improved work efficiency and, at one point, both fallers and forestry crews were working side by side, swapping information.

Beyond everyone else's expectations, Team 100 achieved its objective. Rather than costing several hundred thousand dollars, the project netted a $30,000 profit and the Yellow Creek 100 site is now returning to a picturesque Douglas fir setting.

Sources: G. Bartosh, "A Tale of a Team," *MB Journal* 10, no. 6 (June 1990), p. 8; and J. Sorenson, "MB Logging Team Kicks Convention," *Logging and Sawmilling Journal* 22, no. 1 (January 1991), pp. 11, 15.

with the decision and feel that it is part of their solution, rather than just management's directive. This is one of the reasons why Petrosar, a petrochemical plant in Sarnia, Ontario, lets employees make decisions involving millions of dollars. Says Petrosar manager John Petrie: "We feel that when you have the right people who are the most qualified with the information to make a decision, and they are responsible for making them, feelings of responsibility are enhanced and a higher level of commitment results."[15]

Employee Satisfaction and Empowerment

Job satisfaction is usually higher in organizations where employees are involved in organizational decisions.[16] One of the main reasons for this is that people feel empowered when given the opportunity to participate in decisions that affect their work lives. **Empowerment** has several meanings in the management literature, but we shall define it as a feeling of control and self-confidence that emerges when people are given power in a previously powerless situation.[17] Empowerment increases job satisfaction because employees feel less stress when they have some control over life's events. Empowerment is also a motivational experience because employees develop a strong sense of confidence in themselves.

Employee involvement is less likely to increase satisfaction or empowerment when this management practice is conducted superficially or when coworkers criticize those who become involved.[18] Even when management is serious about involving staff and coworkers support these efforts, some employees may dislike the experience because their needs and personalities

empowerment
A feeling of control and self-confidence that emerges when people are given power in a previously powerless situation.

are incompatible with a participative environment. For example, employees with a high level of authoritarianism or a low need for self-actualization would be less satisfied with high-involvement practices.[19]

Finally, we should note that the effect of employee involvement on satisfaction varies from one culture to the next. There is some evidence that employees in India prefer more autocratic managers, whereas most Swedish employees expect to be involved in organizational decisions about day-to-day operations. In Puerto Rico, one company's attempt at participative management failed because employees expected managers to exert their authority and viewed employee involvement activities as signs of weak leadership.[20]

Employee Development

Many participative management activities are a training ground where employees can develop better decision-making skills. Team decision making may offer the additional benefits of fostering teamwork and collegiality as coworkers learn more about each other and come to appreciate each other's talents.[21]

VROOM–YETTON–JAGO MODEL

Vroom–Yetton–Jago model
A model designed to help managers choose the optimal level of employee involvement in a particular situation.

Victor Vroom, along with Philip Yetton and more recently Arthur Jago, have introduced the **Vroom–Yetton–Jago model** to help managers decide how much employee involvement should occur under various conditions. This model is essentially a form of predecision (see Chapter 9) because it involves choosing the most appropriate decision process in that particular situation. Vroom and his colleagues define overall effectiveness of the decision process in terms of the four conditions described above as well as a fifth factor: time constraint.

The model considers five levels of employee participation, described in Exhibit 11–3, ranging from purely autocratic to team consensus. This includes two levels of autocratic decision making (AI and AII), two levels of consultative decision making (CI and CII), and one level of team consensus (GII). A more extreme level of participation may exist when the team makes decisions without the presence of management, but Vroom and his colleagues suggest that this may be considered a variant of GII.

Decision Tree

The Vroom–Yetton–Jago model consists of four decision trees that guide managers through the characteristics of a problem (called *problem attributes*) to determine the most appropriate level of employee involvement for that problem. Two decision trees pertain to decisions affecting a team of

| EXHIBIT 11–3 | Levels of Employee Involvement in the Vroom–Yetton–Jago Model |

Level of Employee Involvement	Description
AI	You solve the problem or make the decision yourself using information available to you at the time.
AII	You obtain any necessary information from subordinates. Subordinates provide specific information that you request, but they do not generate or evaluate solutions and might not be made aware of the problem.
CI	You share the problem with relevant subordinates individually, getting their ideas and suggestions. Subordinates do not meet together to discuss the problem. Then you make the final decision which may or may not reflect your subordinates' influence.
CII	You share the problem with subordinates in a team meeting where you receive their ideas and suggestions. Then you make the final decision which may or may not reflect your subordinates' influence.
GII	You share the problem with subordinates in a team meeting where the team collectively generates alternatives, evaluates solutions, and attempts to reach a consensus on a solution. You serve as chairperson, coordinating the discussion, keeping it focussed on the problem, and making sure that the critical issues are discussed. You do not attempt to influence subordinates to adopt your preferred solution. You are willing to accept and implement any solution that has the support of the entire team.

employees, while the other two focus on individual problems. Within each pair, one emphasizes time efficiency while the other emphasizes employee development. We will focus only on the time-driven decision tree for team issues because it is perhaps the one most frequently used by managers. This tree, shown in Exhibit 11–4, consists of eight problem attributes that distinguish the characteristics of each decision situation. Each problem attribute is phrased as a question and the appropriate answer directs the manager along a different path in the decision tree.

The decision maker begins at the left side of the decision tree and must first decide whether the problem has a high- or low-quality dimension. Most managerial decisions have a quality requirement because some alternatives are more likely than others to achieve organizational objectives. But where all of the alternatives are equally good (or bad), the manager would select the low-importance route in the decision tree. He or she would then be asked

EXHIBIT 11–4   Time-Driven Decision Tree

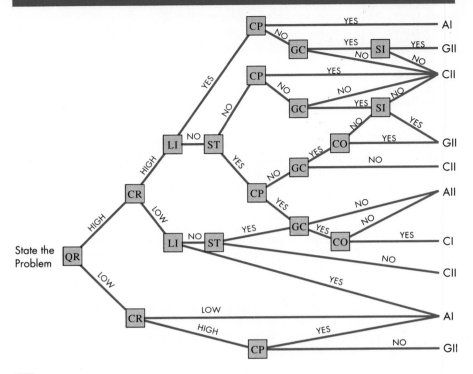

QR	Quality requirement:	How important is the technical quality of this decision?
CR	Commitment requirement:	How important is subordinate commitment to the decision?
LI	Leader's information:	Do you have sufficient information to make a high-quality decision?
ST	Problem structure:	Is the problem well structured?
CP	Commitment probability:	If you were to make the decision by yourself, is it reasonably certain that your subordinate(s) would be committed to the decision?
GC	Goal congruence:	Do subordinates share the organizational goals to be attained in solving this problem?
CO	Subordinate conflict:	Is conflict among subordinates over preferred solutions likely?
SI	Subordinate information:	Do subordinates have sufficient information to make a high-quality decision?

Source: V. H. Vroom and A. G. Jago, *The New Leadership: Managing Participation in Organizations* (Englewood Cliffs, N.J.: Prentice Hall, 1988), p. 184. © 1987 V. H. Vroom and A. G. Jago. Used with permission of the authors.

whether subordinate commitment is important to the decision. This process continues until the path leads to the recommended participation level, ranging from AI to GII. Vroom and Jago have also developed a computer software package that prompts the user with these questions and displays the appropriate participation level at the end of this process.

Does the Vroom–Yetton–Jago Model Work?

There is little doubt that the Vroom–Yetton–Jago model is a useful approach to recognizing the contingencies affecting employee involvement. The revised model presented here was published only a few years ago and, other than preliminary work by Vroom and Jago, has not been tested. But its predecessor, the Vroom–Yetton model, has received considerable empirical support based on research in Canada, the United States, and elsewhere.[22] Since Vroom and Jago introduced the revised version to improve the earlier model, it is likely that it, too, will receive strong research support.

One disadvantage with this model is that it is quite complex; it is unlikely that managers will consult their decision trees before proceeding with a course of action. Nevertheless, through case studies (such as those presented at the end of this chapter), people may learn to routinely consider the relevant problem attributes and accurately decide the best level of employee involvement in a particular situation.

TEAM DECISION MAKING

Organizational researchers have paid quite a lot of attention to team decision making—denoted by GII in the Vroom–Yetton–Jago model—because most strategic decisions are made by management teams. This form of participation has gained even more interest recently because many companies have been introducing quality circles, self-managing work teams, employee–management committees, and other participative management practises involving team-based decisions.[23]

The advantages of employee involvement described earlier apply to team decision making. When members possess the requisite skills and knowledge, the team can potentially define problems more accurately, produce a longer list of better alternatives, and select the best alternative. Decision quality is also improved as members identify and correct false assumptions or biases that some members hold regarding the issue. By participating in the team, employees are more committed to the decision, more satisfied with their jobs, and have more opportunity to improve their decision-making skills.

Problems with Team Decision Making

While team decision making is often beneficial for employees and the organization, a number of potential problems may also emerge. Team decisions usually consume more time because members must first become familiar

PERSPECTIVE 11–2   Consequences of Conformity in Team Decision Making

As part of its strategic planning process, a Canadian credit union wanted to estimate the impact of a new manufacturing plant on branch requirements. With an estimated work force of 3,500 persons, the manufacturing facility was expected to increase the demand for financial services in the community, so the credit union's board of directors and senior management agreed that another branch should be opened. The dilemma was whether to open a branch near the manufacturing plant or near the new residential development where most employees would probably locate.

Considerable disagreement arose among board members over the preferred branch location. Those preferring the residential location noted that the other site was not within walking distance of the manufacturing plant and had poor access to the main highway. However, the credit union's general manager was a dominant individual and finally swayed the decision to select the site located near the new plant.

After the manufacturing facility opened demand for financial services in the community increased as expected, but the credit union did not receive much of the new business. Subsequent analysis determined that the key reasons for the new branch's lack of success were that it was not within walking distance of the plant and was difficult to access from the main highway—the same concerns raised by opponents of the location chosen by the general manager.

Source: W. Peasgood, "Delphi Process: A Non-Confrontational Approach," *Credit Union Way* 40, no. 6 (June 1987), pp. 14–16.

---

with each other and move toward some level of team development before proceeding with the task. Heterogeneous teams tend to make better decisions, but as we learned in the previous chapter, they have more difficulty reaching agreement and tend to produce more dysfunctional conflict. Finally, teams may be ineffective where members face pressure toward conformity. Conformity is an important social control that helps teams operate more efficiently, but it may prevent members with valuable information or ideas from participating openly in the decision process.[24] This problem is reflected in the costly experience of a Canadian credit union, described in Perspective 11–2.

Groupthink

groupthink

A situation in extremely cohesive teams where members are so motivated to maintain harmony and conform to majority opinion that they withhold their dissenting opinions.

We explained in Chapter 10 that cohesiveness is usually a desirable trait in teams, but it may also lead to ineffective decisions under certain conditions. Top management and other highly cohesive teams run the risk of developing a "groupthink" perspective, which ultimately leads to ineffective and sometimes disastrous results. **Groupthink** results from social pressures on individual members to maintain harmony by avoiding conflict and disagreement.[25] Team members suppress their doubts about decision alternatives preferred by the group leader or majority of members. They become so preoccupied with demonstrating their support for the team that they try to achieve consensus at the cost of better decision making. Team members

EXHIBIT 11–5	Symptoms of Groupthink

Groupthink Symptom	Description
Illusion of invulnerability	The team feels comfortable with risky decisions because possible weaknesses are suppressed or glossed over.
Assumption of morality	There is such an unquestioned belief in the inherent morality of the team's objectives that members do not feel the need to debate whether their actions are ethical.
Rationalization	Underlying assumptions, new information, and previous actions that seem inconsistent with the team's decision are discounted or explained away.
Stereotyping outgroups	The team stereotypes or oversimplifies the external threats upon which the decision is based; enemies are viewed as purely evil or moronic.
Self-censorship	Team members suppress their doubts in order to maintain harmony.
Illusion of unanimity	Self-censorship results in harmonious behaviour, so individual members believe that they alone have doubts; silence is automatically perceived as evidence of consensus.
Mindguarding	Some members become self-appointed guardians to prevent negative or inconsistent information from reaching the team.
Pressuring dissenters	Members who happen to raise their concerns about the decision are pressured to fall into line and be more loyal to the team.

Source: Based on I. L. Janis, *Groupthink: Psychological Studies of Policy Decisions and Fiascoes,* 2nd ed. (Boston: Houghton Mifflin, 1982), p. 174–75, 256–59.

want to maintain this harmony because their self-esteem is enhanced by membership in a powerful decision-making body that speaks with one voice. Team harmony also helps members cope with the stress of making crucial top-level decisions.

Several symptoms of groupthink have been identified and are summarized in Exhibit 11–5. In general, teams overestimate their invulnerability and morality, become closed-minded to outside and dissenting information, and experience several pressures toward consensus. This is particularly true in nonprogrammed decisions where the team lacks clear guidance from corporate policies or procedures. Groupthink seems to be more prevalent under the following conditions:

- High team cohesiveness.
- The team is isolated from outsiders.
- The team leader is not impartial.

- Problems are nonprogrammed, so they cannot be resolved methodically.
- The team is homogeneous.
- The team is under stress due to an external threat.
- The team has experienced recent failures or other decision-making problems.

Groupthink has mainly been studied by analyzing policy decisions that have turned into fiascoes.[26] One example is the Bay of Pigs incident, in which John F. Kennedy's presidential advisory group supported the ill-fated 1961 attempt by Cuban exiles to overthrow Fidel Castro. Available information suggested that this action would be unsuccessful and damage the United States's relations with other countries. Yet Kennedy proceeded with the CIA-planned invasion because members of his advisory group were uncritical of the plan and dissonant information was withheld or discredited. Groupthink also explains several other ill-fated decisions, including the Watergate scandal and the fatal launching of NASA's space shuttle *Challenger*.

The groupthink concept holds much promise for understanding how top-level policy teams can make defective choices. However, a few writers have suggested that other factors also account for ineffective policy decision making.[27] One such phenomenon is group polarization, which we discuss next.

Group Polarization

The board of directors and senior management of Dofasco Inc. were recently faced with the difficult choice of writing off the company's $700 million acquisition of Algoma Steel in Sault Ste. Marie or putting more money into the plant in the hope that it would be profitable in the long run. Dofasco chose to write off its loss, but there is increasing evidence that most teams would choose the riskier option of pouring more money into Algoma Steel. Similarly, if team members initially prefer a risk-averse option, the team amplifies this tendency by selecting an even more extreme choice in this direction. The tendency for teams to make more extreme decisions than individuals working alone is known as **group polarization**.[28]

group polarization
The tendency for teams to make more extreme choices (either more risky or more risk-averse) than the average team member would if making the decision alone.

Exhibit 11–6 shows how the group polarization process operates. Individuals form initial preferences when given several alternatives. Some of these choices are riskier than others, and the average member's opinion leans one way or the other. Through open discussion, members become comfortable with more extreme positions when they realize that their views are also held by others. Persuasive arguments favouring the dominant position convince doubtful members and help form a consensus around the extreme option. Finally, since the final decision is made by the team, no individual feels personally responsible, so there is less concern about agreeing to a more extreme solution.

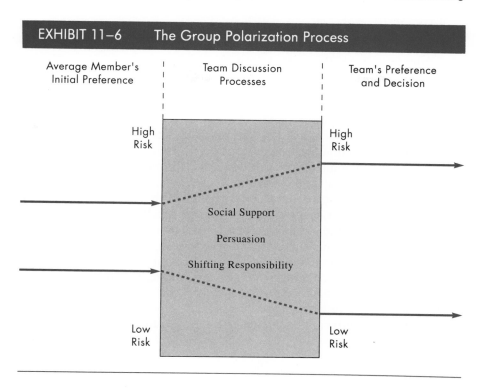

EXHIBIT 11–6   The Group Polarization Process

Group polarization explains why groups make more *extreme* decisions than the average individual, but why do teams more often make *riskier* decisions? The answer to this question lies in the perceptual distortions that influence an individual member's initial preferences. When given the choice between a certain and a risky alternative, individuals tend to initially prefer the risky option even when the probability of success is extremely low because the certain loss is viewed as more unpleasant than a more severe but less certain loss. Individuals also tend to inflate the likelihood that they will beat the odds in a risky situation (e.g., "This strategy might be unsuccessful 80 percent of the time, but it will work for me!"). Thus, when discussing their initial preferences, team members are more likely to favour the risky option.[29]

An extreme choice—whether risky or risk averse—is sometimes the correct solution to a problem or opportunity, but group polarization may account for a number of poor decisions made by organizational teams. Companies may gamble assets and develop overoptimistic forecasts of success. Under some conditions, senior executives might support a "bet your company" solution in which a large proportion of available assets is allocated to an opportunity with a relatively low probability of success. At the other extreme, teams whose members generally favour risk-averse solutions will suffer from inaction and stagnation. They will continually miss windfall opportunities and be ill-prepared for environmental changes.

IMPROVING TEAM DECISION MAKING

Considering the potential benefits of team decision making, it stands to reason that companies should try to minimize the difficulties described above. One general practice is to ensure that neither the team leader nor any other participant dominates the process. This helps minimize peer pressure and lets other team members generate more ideas. Another practice is to maintain an optimal team size—large enough that members possess the collective knowledge to resolve the problem, yet small enough that the team doesn't consume too much time or restrict individual input.[30]

Where feasible, teams should try to reach a consensus. In other words, participants should come to a unanimous or general agreement on the best alternative. Seeking a consensus requires more time, but members tend to develop a stronger commitment to the final decision and its implementation. Using majority rule or voting tends to evoke somewhat less commitment to the selected alternative, although the effect is still stronger than nonparticipation.[31]

Constructive Controversy

constructive controversy

Any situation where team members hold different opinions and assumptions and debate the issues through an open, healthy dialogue.

Teams should encourage **constructive controversy** when discussing the problem and its possible solutions.[32] Constructive controversy occurs when team members hold different opinions and assumptions and debate the issues through an open, healthy dialogue. Debate is useful, if not absolutely necessary, because members are more likely to reexamine their basic assumptions and consider other perspectives.

Constructive controversy occurs naturally when the team is comprised of heterogeneous members. This strategy has been applied successfully at Federal Industries in Winnipeg, where president John Fraser deliberately chose three vice-presidents with different backgrounds and perspectives. "A lot of people tend to hire in their own image," explains Fraser. "There's nothing worse. They all go off the cliff together because there's no counterbalance."[33]

devil's advocacy

A form of structured debate to encourage constructive controversy whereby one-half of the team looks for faulty logic, questionable assumptions, and other problems with the team's preferred choice.

Aside from selecting heterogeneous members, team leaders can encourage constructive controversy through structured debate. One such approach, called **devil's advocacy,** involves dividing the team into two subgroups. One subgroup prepares a formal statement supporting the team's preferred alternative. The other subgroup critiques this alternative by looking for faulty logic, questionable assumptions, and misinterpreted information. Teams tend to select better alternatives using devil's advocacy, but several people should represent each side and the team leader must keep the discussion constructive by focussing on the issues rather than people.[34]

So far, we have been referring to traditional team decision making, known as the *interacting* approach, whereby members meet face-to-face to suggest solutions and debate alternatives. Discussion is usually unstructured, ideas are generated and evaluated simultaneously, and there is a tendency to search for solutions before the problem is clearly understood. Consequently this process is particularly vulnerable to the concerns with team decision making described earlier. To minimize these problems, three alternative techniques have been proposed, including brainstorming, nominal group technique, and the Delphi technique.

Brainstorming

Brainstorming was developed by Alex Osborn, an advertising executive who wanted to introduce a more effective way to generate creative ideas in teams.[35] He concluded that the best way to do this is to separate the idea-generation stage of decision making from the idea-evaluation stage.

Brainstorming mainly consists of a freewheeling session in which every member generates as many alternative solutions to the problem as possible. Even crazy or seemingly impossible ideas are encouraged so that participants do not self-censor their thoughts. Members are also encouraged to combine or build upon already-presented suggestions. All ideas are recorded, usually on a flip chart, so that everyone can view them for later discussion. The most important rule in brainstorming is that no one is allowed to evaluate or criticize these ideas during the idea-generation stage. This rule creates a situation in which team members are less inhibited about presenting unusual solutions.

Brainstorming mainly focusses on the generation of creative ideas instead of the evaluation and ultimate selection of alternatives. However, after enough possible solutions have been generated, the team can use different methods to evaluate alternatives and make the final decision. For example, Hostess Foods, described in Perspective 11–3, uses brainstorming to generate alternative solutions and applies the consensus approach to arrive at the best solution.

While brainstorming seems to work well at Hostess Foods, recent evidence suggests that brainstorming rules are usually not enough to neutralize the powerful effect of team conformity.[36] People seem to censor their ideas and defer to more powerful members simply because of their mere presence in the same room. In fact, one study reported that four individuals working alone produce twice as many potential solutions to a problem than a four-person group using the brainstorming method. On a more positive note, brainstorming rules seem to minimize dysfunctional conflict among members and improve the team's focus on the required task. Brainstorming participants also interact and participate directly, thereby enhancing decision acceptance and team cohesiveness.

brainstorming
A free-wheeling face-to-face meeting in which team members generate as many alternative solutions to the problem as possible and no one is allowed to evaluate them until all ideas have been presented.

PERSPECTIVE 11–3   Consensus Brainstorming at Hostess Foods

Hostess Foods, Canada's leading potato chip manufacturer, has discovered that team decision making provides an ideal opportunity to generate action and spark new ideas, particularly in the areas of warehousing and shipping. For example, Hostess trucks can handle a 10-foot-high load of potato chip boxes, but the cardboard packaging can withstand stacks only to 7 feet. Adding an extra 3 feet to each stack would allow trucks to carry more on each load and would dramatically reduce the amount of required warehouse space. An employee involvement team eventually discovered and perfected a solution to the problem after people from many parts of the company were consulted.

Hostess Foods attributes much of its successful team decision making to a formal problem-solving strategy that emphasizes a consensus form of brainstorming. First, everyone is assigned a role, such as taking minutes, writing on the flip chart, keeping time, leading the discussion, and facilitating the discussion. Another role is that of gatekeeper, with the responsibility of drawing people into the discussion.

Next, team members suggest solutions to the issue, all of which are written down on the flip chart. Ideas are presented without argument and criticism is forbidden so that people feel comfortable about making suggestions, no matter how crazy they may seem.

When the team is satisfied with the number of ideas generated, it debates each one until a consensus is reached. Doug Hughes, a Hostess Foods team leader, explains that this decision-making stage can be a powerful catalyst for effective solutions and team development. "Any group of people can generate ideas that *might* have value, but it's going through the process of convincing other team members to agree with you that often leads to the real discoveries—and helps build that essential team commitment."

Hughes has seen the results of consensus-based brainstorming and is convinced of its effectiveness. "If you let them have it out, groups will tend to come up with a better solution than any of those people would individually. It's incredible when that kind of synergy happens. It may take more effort initially, but it makes believers out of all of them and that pays dividends again and again."

Source: "Consensus Approach Gets Results," *Industrial Management* 11, no. 8 (October 1987), p. 7.

Nominal Group Technique

nominal group technique
A structured team decision-making technique whereby members independently write down ideas, present them in turn, clarify them, and then independently rank or vote on them.

Nominal group technique involves bringing people face-to-face without allowing them to fully interact as a team. The method is called *nominal* because participants form a group *in name only*. They are not allowed to communicate with each other during either the idea-generation or decision stages in the hope that this would further reduce team pressures on individual members. The nominal group method typically includes the six steps shown in Exhibit 11–7.[37]

In the idea generation stage, team members silently and independently write down as many solutions as they can to the problem. Each member then describes one of his or her solutions to the other team members, and this cycle is repeated until all of the solutions have been described (i.e., a round-robin format). The proposed solutions are posted on a flip chart or blackboard and each one is openly discussed and clarified. Participants then silently and independently rank order or vote on each proposed solution. The

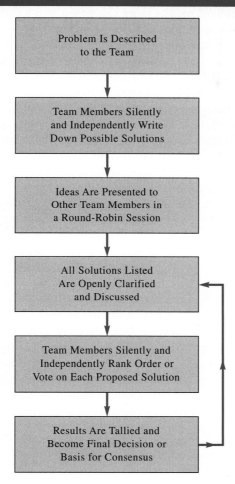

EXHIBIT 11–7   Basic Steps in the Nominal Group Technique

Problem Is Described
to the Team

↓

Team Members Silently
and Independently Write
Down Possible Solutions

↓

Ideas Are Presented to
Other Team Members in
a Round-Robin Session

↓

All Solutions Listed
Are Openly Clarified
and Discussed

↓

Team Members Silently and
Independently Rank Order or
Vote on Each Proposed Solution

↓

Results Are Tallied and
Become Final Decision or
Basis for Consensus

results are tallied and the team either forms a consensus from these results or the decision is determined by the pooled results of the vote. If a clear choice does not emerge, the team may repeat the discussion and voting stages until a consensus or clear preference emerges.

Nominal group technique was introduced in the 1970s and has been used by several Canadian firms. For example, Garrett Manufacturing Ltd., the Toronto-based high-technology and aerospace firm, used this method to develop the composite measure of companywide productivity that we described in Chapter 1 (see Exhibit 1–8). Indicators had already been developed by each department, but Garrett's central productivity committee had to determine the relative importance of these departmental indicators to arrive at a composite score for the entire firm. Committee members individually rated the departmental indicators in terms of their influence on company productivity. The tallied results were discussed and a composite scale was agreed upon by consensus in a single session.[38]

The nominal group technique appears to be a promising way to improve team decision making. Teams using the nominal technique tend to produce more and better-quality ideas than in the traditional interacting style, although some people working independently still might generate more solutions.[39] There is some weak support for the notion that nominal teams make better choices than traditional interacting groups. As a structured decision process, nominal group technique produces a high task orientation and relatively low potential for conflict within the team. However, team cohesiveness is generally lower in nominal decisions even though members still meet face-to-face. Acceptance of the final decision also tends to be lower than in interacting or brainstorming procedures, particularly when the nominal process uses a single round of voting rather than seeking consensus.[40]

Delphi Technique

Delphi technique

A structured team decision-making method that pools the collective knowledge of experts without face-to-face interaction, organizes and feeds the input back to the experts for further input, and repeats this cycle until a consensus or dissensus is reached.

The **Delphi technique** systematically pools the collective knowledge of experts on a particular subject to make decisions, predict the future, or identify opposing views (called *dissensus*). A unique feature of Delphi groups is that they do not meet face-to-face; in fact, they are often located in different parts of the world and may not know each other's identity. Another feature is that participants do not know who submits ideas other than their own. This high degree of anonymity is believed to facilitate open dialogue, particularly when panel members are employed in the same organization. The Delphi method typically includes the following steps:[41]

1. A central convenor enlists the involvement of experts on the subject.
2. The problem or challenge (e.g., predicting future events) is clearly described to each panel member.
3. Each panel member independently and anonymously submits possible solutions or comments to the central convenor.
4. The convenor records the information received from the panel and returns the compiled results to them.
5. Each member independently and anonymously submits comments on the compiled results and adds further suggestions, thoughts, and explanations on the issue.
6. Steps 4 and 5 are repeated until some form of consensus or dissensus is reached.

The Delphi technique was first introduced by the Rand Corporation in the United States during the 1950s for strategic military forecasting, such as deciding the optimal number of atomic bombs and target sites. This method has subsequently been adopted by industry and government as a procedure for forecasting future societal and technological trends. For example, British Petroleum recently used the Delphi approach to determine which environmental issues would be most relevant to the oil and gas industry in the year 2000.[42]

One advantage of the Delphi approach is that it minimizes the effects of group conformity and status. The high degree of process structure and lack of interaction also ensure that participants remain focussed on the task and have minimal potential for conflict (although conflict may still emerge in written form). A limitation of the Delphi technique is that it is very time consuming, sometimes requiring several months to complete. Recent panels have used electronic mail to speed up the process, but Delphi remains the slowest approach to reaching a solution. A second concern is that Delphi panel members tend to have less identification with the final decision because of their "remote" participation in the process. Finally, the Achilles heel of the Delphi method is that it depends on the quality of the panel, yet panel selection is ultimately a subjective decision and can easily be biased by personal preferences of the convenor.[43]

The relative effectiveness of the interacting, brainstorming, nominal, and Delphi approaches to team decision making are summarized in Exhibit 11–8. The nominal group and Delphi techniques are generally superior, although brainstorming groups may be preferred where group cohesiveness is important. Traditional interacting groups may produce high commitment to the final decision, but this can also be accomplished through brainstorming ses-

---

EXHIBIT 11–8   Effectiveness of Team Decision-Making Techniques

Effectiveness Criteria	Team Decision-Making Approach			
	Interacting	**Brainstorming**	**Nominal**	**Delphi**
Number of ideas generated	Low	Moderate	High	High
Quality of ideas generated	Low	Moderate	High	High
Social pressure	High	Low	Moderate	Low
Costs in time and money	Moderate	Low	Low	High
Degree of task orientation	Low	High	High	High
Potential conflict within the team	High	Low	Moderate	Low
Feelings of accomplishment	Varies	High	High	Moderate
Members' commitment to solution	High	Varies	Moderate	Low
Building team cohesiveness	High	High	Moderate	Low

Source: Adapted from J. K. Murnighan, "Group Decision Making: What Strategies Should You Use?" *Management Review,* February 1981, p. 61. Reprinted by permission of the publisher. © 1981, American Management Association, New York. All rights reserved.

sions where a consensus approach is used to select the preferred alternative. As you can see, unstructured interaction groups are more likely to produce conflict and consume valuable time than arrive at an optimal decision.

QUALITY CIRCLES

quality circle (QC)
A small team of employees who meet on a regular basis to identify quality control and productivity problems, propose solutions to management, and monitor the implementation and consequences of these solutions in their work area.

A **quality circle (QC)** is a small team of employees who meet on a regular basis—typically one or two hours each week—to identify quality control and productivity problems, propose solutions to management, and monitor the implementation and consequences of these solutions in their work area. Notice that these teams ordinarily recommend solutions to management; they rarely have the authority to implement changes unilaterally.[44]

QC members are typically volunteers from a particular work unit. For example, Toronto Dominion Bank's QCs consist of employees within a particular branch who have volunteered to participate in the program. The basic logic behind QCs is that properly trained shop-floor and office employees are in the best position to discover unrecognized quality problems. QC team members often receive training in data collection and statistical analysis to help them identify problems and monitor solutions. Many are also taught team problem-solving and team-building skills to help the meetings operate more smoothly.

Quality circles first appeared in Japan after World War II, where they were introduced by William Deming and other American quality-control experts. QCs later spread to North America by Lockheed and other companies who saw how successful they were in Japan. It is estimated that between 300 and 1,000 Canadian businesses have quality circles. Most are

makes people reflect on how to do their own jobs and make changes themselves. It makes their job easier and makes them more productive."

- Camco Ltd., the Montreal-based manufacturer of household appliances, was experiencing a serious and stubborn quality-control problem with nearly 40 percent of the products failing final inspection. Adding more inspectors and warning employees about the problem had little effect, so manage-

ment finally decided to introduce quality circles as a possible way to improve quality. The circles soon pinpointed several main problem areas and were the key to mobilizing a major plantwide reorganization. Product rejection rates plummeted to less than 10 percent, the number of people assigned to quality inspection has fallen from 55 to 10, and productivity per employee has increased 30 percent.

Sources: B. King, "Quality Circles Have Achieved Acceptance," *Financial Post*, January 18, 1986, p. 15; D. Rooke, "Running Around in Quality Circles," *Small Business*, February 1988, p. 68; and P. E. Larson, "Winning Strategies," *Canadian Business Review*, Summer 1989, pp. 40–42.

found in manufacturing firms, such as Canadian Gypsum, Northern Telecom, TRW Canada, and Sico Inc. However, QCs have also been introduced in several white-collar organizations, including B.C. Telephone, Maritime Telegraph and Telephone, Great-West Life Assurance Co., and Culinar Inc.[45]

Are Quality Circles Effective?

Most companies with quality circles claim that these teams are very successful. The testimonials in Perspective 11–4 and elsewhere suggest that QCs improve product or service quality, reduce production costs, reduce labour–management conflict, and improve employee motivation.[46]

These glowing tales may be accurate, but empirical studies suggest that QCs are just as likely to wither away within two or three years and barely return the cost of implementation.[47] QCs tend to be more successful in organizations that maintain a participative management philosophy and where management is willing to implement the recommended changes. The company must establish realistic employee expectations regarding the program at the outset. QCs must be seen as think tanks for quality improvement, not as conduits for personal gripes or long-standing labour–management feuds. Finally, many quality circles languish because members eventually cannot find any other issues to resolve.[48] In many cases, this problem can be avoided by training QC members to identify areas for improvement and by providing examples of improvements elsewhere.

A few writers have suggested that quality circles are basically team-based suggestion systems and only represent a starting point for employee involve-

---

PERSPECTIVE 11–5   *Self-Managing Work Teams at Pratt & Whitney*

The unique geometric shape of Pratt and Whitney's Plant #41 stands out against the wilderness near the Halifax airport. The plant, which assembles over 100 varieties of expensive light-alloy casings for aircraft engines, also stands out because it is operated almost entirely by employees. There are no middle managers, no supervisors, no executive washrooms, no executive parking spaces, and no fancy job titles. Instead, a team of five managers sets overall plant objectives, and three self-managing work teams of approximately 20 plant employees each decide how best to meet them. The plant also has a support team consisting of computer experts.

Pratt and Whitney is one of many Canadian firms leading the way toward the self-managing work team concept. The Halifax plant has a horizontal structure, in which decisions are made by the work team rather than passed down from level to level. This keeps employees involved and motivated. As senior vice-president Gilles Ouimet explains: "Today's employees are better equipped to think for themselves and they don't want to defer to authority." He adds that employees who are qualified to assume highly technical jobs "just can't be expected to shove their brains into their locker with their lunchbox before they go to work."

Employees are completely responsible for their area, from programming their machines to scheduling work shifts. Plant rules and the employee benefits package are decided by a general assembly of em-

---

ment.[49] To fully maximize employee potential and organizational effectiveness, companies should consider more advanced participative activities, such as self-managing work teams.

SELF-MANAGING WORK TEAMS

self-managing work team
A team of employees that completes a whole piece of work requiring several interdependent tasks and has substantial autonomy over the execution of these tasks.

A **self-managing work team (SMWT),** also known as an *autonomous* (or *semi-autonomous*) *work team*, is a group of employees assigned almost total responsibility for managing a specific work process.[50] The team completes a whole piece of work requiring several interdependent tasks, such as building an engine or processing chemicals, and has substantial autonomy over the execution of these tasks. The team's job is both horizontally and vertically loaded (see Chapter 5), because it includes all of the tasks required to make an entire product or service (horizontal loading) as well as most of the responsibility for scheduling, coordinating, and planning these tasks (vertical loading).

SMWTs differ from traditional work units in two ways.[51] First, they control and decide their own work activities as well as the pace of work, whereas most decisions affecting traditional teams are made by a supervisor or other management personnel. In fact, the position of supervisor is replaced by a "facilitator" or "coordinator" who provides advice and other support to team members. Second, SMWTs are responsible for most support tasks—quality control, maintenance, and inventory management—as well as the core production activities (manufacturing a product, serving a client). They order supplies, maintain equipment, and check quality standards with-

ployees. Employees even do their own hiring by working together in committees to evaluate applicants.

The self-managing work team approach, together with advanced computer-aided manufacturing systems, allow the plant to operate more flexibly. Retooling can sometimes be completed within a matter of hours rather than days. Employee morale is higher as employees have more control over their work. Absenteeism is extremely low (less than 1 percent).

Introducing self-managing work teams has required a period of adjustment, particularly for those accustomed to more traditional work arrangements. Says one Pratt & Whitney veteran of 35 years: "I knew about this idea and the way this plant would be set up before I came to Halifax, but it still took some time for me to get used to it." There is also the potential dilemma of employee career development in a structure without titles or visible steps on the corporate ladder. Still, senior management is certain that Pratt & Whitney is going the right way. "Any company that doesn't take these steps," says Ouimet, "will be struggling down the line."

Sources: J. Todd, "Firm Fashions Workplace for High-Tech Era," *Montreal Gazette*, December 12, 1987, p. B4; and L. Gutri, "Pratt & Whitney Employees Don't Want to Be Managed; Teams Demand Leadership," *Canadian HR Reporter*, May 2, 1988, p. 8.

out outside direction. In contrast, traditional work groups perform only the core production activities while support tasks are assigned to other individuals or groups. The distinction between traditional and self-managing teams is apparent at Pratt & Whitney's new plant near Halifax, described in Perspective 11–5.

Sociotechnically Designed Teams

Self-managing work teams evolved from the concept of **sociotechnical design,** which was introduced in the 1950s by Eric Trist and his colleagues at Britain's Tavistock Institute.[52] Sociotechnical design theory basically states that every work site consists of two interdependent parts, the technological system (machines, tools, production processes, etc.) and the social system (individual skills, needs, interpersonal relations, etc.). To maximize organizational effectiveness, both systems should be designed concurrently or at least be adapted to match each other. Management must therefore consider the potential effects of new technology on the social structure and redesign one or both elements to improve their compatibility. A balance must be struck between production demands and employee needs in order to maximize the operation's productivity.[53]

An important element in the sociotechnical design concept is that the optimal situation typically occurs when employees work in teams and have sufficient autonomy to manage the work process. In other words, technology should be designed or adapted to facilitate team dynamics, job enrichment, and employee well-being. Some self-managing work team interven-

sociotechnical design
A perspective stating that a work site's technological and social systems should become more compatible in order to increase organizational effectiveness and employee well-being.

tions are primarily changes in the social system to fit the existing technology, but Trist and other sociotechnical advocates claim that these situations will prove ineffective if the technological and social systems remain incompatible.[54]

Sociotechnically designed plants with self-managing work teams are not new, but their popularity has increased dramatically since the early 1980s. One of the earliest formal applications was reported in the early 1970s at Volvo's Kalmar plant in Sweden.[55] The automobile manufacturer replaced the traditional assembly line with fixed work stations at which teams of approximately 20 employees assemble and install components in an unfinished automobile chassis. Each team elects its own leader, divides the work tasks, and controls the speed of operation.

Volvo's Kalmar plant creates a strong team orientation, but recent evidence suggests that its productivity is among the lowest in the automobile industry and is not sufficiently flexible. In other words, in its attempt to accommodate the social system, Volvo may have compromised technological efficiency beyond an optimal level. Meanwhile, Japanese automobile manufacturers have adopted a team approach through a modified assembly line work process. This combination of production efficiency and team orientation partly explains why Toyota and other Japanese firms have the lowest production costs, highest product quality, lowest employee absenteeism, and lowest employee turnover in the industry.[56]

Self-Managing Work Teams and Sociotechnical Design at Shell Canada

One of the most successful sociotechnically designed plants in North America is Shell Canada's chemical plant in Sarnia, Ontario.[57] The $200 million facility, which employs about 200 people and produces 50 grades of polypropylene and 2 grades of isopropyl alcohol, is unique because it was one of the first to break away from the traditional departmentally designed facility and adopt a more holistic, team-based form of work organization.

The project began in 1973 when Shell decided to look at alternative work arrangements in the United States and Europe. The company realized that several problems existed with traditional chemical plants, including underutilization of human resources, excessive control of employees, inability to respond quickly to problems, poor communications, artificial status differences, job dissatisfaction, high turnover, and low employee commitment. In June 1975, a task force developed a seven-page philosophy statement for the new chemical plant. This statement was approved by top management and the group proceeded to design the facility. Union and technical staff were appointed to the task force in 1976 and Shell's new Sarnia plant began operation in 1979.

Shell Canada's Sarnia plant differs from a traditional plant in several ways (see Exhibit 11–9). In a traditional chemical operation, employees become specialists in a particular department, such as chemical reactions, polypro-

EXHIBIT 11–9	Work Organization at Shell Chemical's Sarnia Plant

Traditional Design	Shell Chemical's Sociotechnical Design
Individual tasks and responsibilities	Team tasks and responsibilities
Single-skilled employees	Multiskilled employees
Several departments	One department
Supervisors	Coordinators
Four or five management levels	Three management levels
Restricted access to information	Shared information
Overt status symbols	No overt status symbols
Several job classifications	One job classification
Pay-for-task system	Pay-for-knowledge system

Source: Adapted from T. Rankin and J. Mansell, "Integrating Collective Bargaining and New Forms of Work Organization," *National Productivity Review* 5, no. 4 (1986), pp. 338–47.

pylene extrusion, warehousing, maintenance, scheduling, or the quality-control laboratory. In contrast, the sociotechnically designed plant functions as a single department operated by a 20-person process team. There are six process teams working in rotating 12-hour shifts to keep the plant in continuous operation. These teams are largely self-managing as they assign work, provide or arrange for technical training, authorize overtime, schedule vacations, and help select new recruits.

All process team members are assigned to the same job classification, but a pay-for-knowledge reward system (see Chapter 4) awards different rates of pay based on the number of skills (called *job knowledge clusters*) employees have mastered. Employees are expected to become multiskilled—they are eventually trained in each area of the plant plus one support field—so that the team has the required skills and flexibility to fulfill its mandate. Status differences are minimized by providing one parking lot and lunchroom for both management and employees.

In addition to the process teams, Shell's Sarnia plant has one craft team whose members make complex repairs and train process team members to handle routine maintenance problems. Supervisors found in a traditional plant are replaced by coordinators who provide guidance and oversee the interests of management. A joint committee of union executive and senior managers at Shell's Sarnia plant oversee the various permanent committees and ad hoc task forces that exist within the plant. These committees decide how to organize the work, introduce new technology, define the team coordinator's role, maintain team autonomy, and help resolve conflicts. Every committee relies strongly on consensus building with employees and continually ensures that its decisions are consistent with the philosophy statement mentioned earlier.

The technical structure of the Shell plant is quite different from traditional chemical operations, particularly regarding the communications and information network. Traditional plants have two separate control centres for processing polypropylene and isopropyl alcohol, whereas a single control system operates both processes at Shell's Sarnia plant so that all team members can work together. The computer system directly provides process team members with all available information, including the financial implications of operating decisions such as the effects of temperature changes in the extrusion process on production efficiency.

Team norms and rules are explicitly structured and constantly evolving through a participative process. Before the plant opened in 1979, the company held a 28-hour structured exercise where team members identified areas for which explicit norms should be established. These lists were discussed among all teams, a consensus was reached, and the agreed-upon rules were documented in the *Good Work Practices Handbook* (GWPH). Any manager, union official, or team member can request a change in or interpretation of any rule in the GWPH. Typically, a task force is formed to investigate the request, consult with plant employees and management, and make recommendations.

Overall, Shell Canada's chemical plant in Sarnia has had an impressive record of success.[58] The plant was designed to produce 70,000 tonnes of polypropylene annually, but has recently been producing more than twice that amount. Product quality has been excellent and the process teams have a good record of getting the system back to full operation following production interruptions. Very few grievances have been processed, employee turnover is low, and the plant has maintained an average safety record.

The company has also had its setbacks. Absenteeism was initially very low, but is now marginally higher than other Shell production locations. Most process team members have reached the top rate in the pay-for-knowledge system, so there is some concern over the effects of "topping out." Perhaps the most significant problem occurred during the mid-1980s when middle and first-line managers stopped holding problem-solving meetings and began to shift power back into their own hands. Fortunately, a more participative philosophy was reestablished in 1988 when the union and management strengthened the GWPH, a new plant manager focussed attention back to team autonomy, and an organizational effectiveness advisor was hired to develop a teamwork renewal program.

Effectiveness of Self-Managing Work Teams

Shell Canada's favourable experience with a sociotechnically designed plant and self-managing work teams has prompted several other companies, including Canadian General Electric, Pratt & Whitney Canada, Northern Telecom, Dupont Canada, and Gulf Canada, to adopt similar work arrangements. Empirical research, in addition to the many anecdotal accounts, have found that most SMWTs improve team effectiveness.[59] Team members tend to be more satisfied and experience decreased turnover, absenteeism, and accident rates. Task performance decreases during the start-up phase because employees are learning new jobs and work environments, but performance eventually increases above that of traditional arrangements. Product quality increases and production costs often decrease through team members' innovations. Another advantage of SMWTs is their high degree of flexibility. This is particularly true for just-in-time production processes where the work unit must be able to quickly change product lines to complete incoming customer orders.

Canadian General Electric's jet engine plant in Bromont, Quebec, illustrates the extent to which SMWTs can improve productivity. One year after its 1983 startup, the Bromont plant produced engines at 27 percent lower costs than General Electric's operation in Vermont, which manufactures the same product using the same technology under a traditional management structure. Productivity at the Bromont operation has subsequently increased by more than 300 percent, mainly because it requires fewer people (no inspectors or middle managers) and has a more motivated work force.[60]

Self-managing work teams may provide an excellent opportunity for improved productivity as well as employee well-being, but companies must first address management concerns about losing power and control and adopting new facilitator roles.

Fear of Losing Power and Control.   Lower and middle managers are reluctant to pass power and control to lower levels in the organization. Many believe that the total amount of power within an organization is fixed and, consequently, when employees gain power through participation, managers necessarily lose power.[61] Some supervisors also worry that their staff will not be able to perform some of the additional activities previously done by management. For example, managers in one organization were very reluctant to let work teams call customers for feedback on orders because they were worried that workers might be vulgar or unable to handle irate customers. As one manager put it, the company should "keep the animals in the warehouse as far away from customers as possible!" After some debate, it was agreed that calling customers would be an important part of each self-managing team's duties.[62]

Adjusting to the Facilitator Role.   It is often difficult for supervisors to adapt to their new roles as work team facilitators. Many do not understand what facilitating involves, while others tend to slip back into their traditional supervisor styles. Facilitators maintain a difficult balancing act because they cannot get directly involved with team dynamics. It is also a potentially stressful position because facilitators have a vested interest in the team's success, but it is the team's responsibility to manage its internal conflicts. Consequently, they must learn to address team members differently, in particular, demonstrating their association with the group but without actual leadership or direct power. In one organization, role plays helped managers adjust to their new roles as facilitators.[63]

SUMMARY

• Employee involvement (or participation) occurs when employees take an active role in the process of making decisions that were not previously within their mandate. Employee involvement may be formal or informal, direct or indirect, and voluntary or legislated. The level of participation may range from an employee providing specific information to management without knowing the problem or issue, to complete employee involvement in all phases of the decision process.

• Employee involvement may lead to higher decision quality, decision commitment, employee job satisfaction, and employee development in decision-making skills.

• The Vroom–Yetton–Jago model helps managers decide how much employee involvement should occur under various conditions. The model considers several problem attributes to determine which of the five participation levels would be best in a particular situation.

• Team decision making is often beneficial for employees and the organization, but this process has a number of potential problems, including longer time requirements, conflict among team members, pressure toward conformity, groupthink, and polarized decisions.

• Team decision making may be improved by having a neutral team leader, maintaining optimal team size, trying to seek consensus, and encouraging constructive controversy when discussing a problem and its possible solutions. Other approaches to team decision making, such as brainstorming, nominal group technique, and Delphi method, should also be considered to improve decision effectiveness.

• Quality circles are small teams of employees who meet on a regular basis to identify quality-control and productivity problems, propose solutions to management, and monitor the implementation and consequences of these solutions in their work area. The basic logic behind QCs is that properly trained shop-floor and office employees are in the best position to discover unrecognized quality problems. While testimonial reports paint a glowing picture of QCs, recent evidence suggests that many are short-lived and barely recover their start-up costs.

• Self-managing work teams are groups of employees assigned almost total responsibility for managing a specific work process. They differ from traditional work units in that they control and decide their own work activities and are responsible for most support tasks. SMWTs are typically effective, but they often receive resistance from supervisors because of the supervisors' fear of losing power and inability to switch into a facilitator role.

• Sociotechnical design theory states that every work site consists of two interdependent systems—the technological system and the social system—and that both systems should be compatible to maximize organizational effectiveness. Self-managing work teams emerged from sociotechnical theory based on the idea that the optimal work setting typically occurs when employees work in teams and have sufficient autonomy to manage the work process. Shell Canada's chemical plant in Sarnia, Ontario, is one of the best-known examples of a sociotechnically designed plant with self-managing work teams.

DISCUSSION QUESTIONS

1. In what ways might employee involvement improve organizational decision making?

2. What is the main purpose of the Vroom–Yetton–Jago model? How can managers learn to use the recommendations from this model?

3. What are the conditions under which groupthink is most likely to occur?

4. What is constructive controversy? How can team leaders ensure that constructive controversy exists in their decision-making meetings?

5. Compare the advantages of brainstorming with the Delphi technique.

6. Under what conditions should organizations implement quality circles?

7. What are the critical elements of sociotechnically designed plants?

8. Describe the characteristics of a typical self-managing work team.

NOTES

1. M. Murphy, "Paring the Pyramid," *Small Business* 8, no. 6 (June 1989), pp. 81–84.

2. E. E. Lawler III, *High-Involvement Management* (San Francisco: Jossey-Bass, 1986), Chapter 1; and R. E. Miles, "Human Relations or Human Resources?" *Harvard Business Review,* July–August 1965, pp. 148–63.

3. K. W. Harrigan, "Making Quality Job One—A Cultural Revolution," *Business Quarterly,* Winter 1984, pp. 68–71.

4. V. H. Vroom and A. G. Jago, *The New Leadership: Managing Participation in Organizations* (Englewood Cliffs, N.J.: Prentice Hall, 1988), p. 15.

5. D. V. Nightingale, "The Formally Participative Organization," *Industrial Relations* 18 (1979), pp. 310–21; M. N. Lam, "Forms of Participation: A Comparison of Preferences between Chinese Americans and American Caucasians," *Canadian Journal of Administrative Sciences* 3 (June 1986), pp. 81–98; and E. A. Locke and D. M. Schweiger, "Participation in Decision-Making: One More Look," *Research in Organizational Behavior* 1 (1979), pp. 265–339.

6. H. C. Jain (ed.), *Worker Participation: Success and Problems* (New York: Praeger, 1980); R. Long, "Recent Patterns in Swedish Industrial Democracy," in R. N. Stern and S. McCarthy (eds.), *The Organizational Practice of Democracy* (New York: Wiley, 1986), pp. 375–85; and R. J. Adams and C. H. Rummel, "Workers' Participation in Management in West Germany: Impact on the Worker, the Enterprise and the Trade Union," *Industrial Relations Journal* 8 (1977), pp. 4–22.

7. B. A. Macy, M. F. Peterson, and L. W. Norton, "A Test of Participation Theory in a Work Re-Design Field Setting: Degree of Participation and Comparison Site Contrasts," *Human Relations* 42 (1989), pp. 1095–1165.

8. Lawler, *High-Involvement Management,* Chapters 11 and 12.

9. R. Likert, *New Patterns of Management* (New York: McGraw-Hill, 1961); D. McGregor, *The Human Side of Enterprise* (New York: McGraw-Hill, 1960); and Chris Argyris, *Personality and Organization* (New York: Harper & Row, 1957).

10. Vroom and Jago, *The New Leadership: Managing Participation in Organizations,* pp. 19–20, 55.

11. L. K. Michaelson, W. E. Watson, and R. H. Black, "A Realistic Test of Individual versus Group Consensus Decision Making," *Journal of Applied Psychology* 74 (1989), pp. 834–39; J. P. Wanous and M. A. Youtz, "Solution Diversity and the Quality of Group Decisions," *Academy of Management Journal* 29 (1986), pp. 149–59; and N. R. F. Maier, "Assets and Liabilities in Group Problem Solving: The Need for an Integrative Function," *Psychological Review* 74 (1967), pp. 239–49.

12. R. Dubin, "Union–Management Co-operation and Productivity," *Industrial and Labor Relations Review* 2 (1949), pp. 195–209.

13. J. Richards, G. Mauser, and R. Holmes, "What Do Workers Want? Attitudes towards Collective Bargaining and Participation in Management," *Relations Industrielles* 43 (1988), pp. 133–50.

14. J. R. Hollenbeck, C. R. Williams, and H. J. Klein, "An Empirical Examination of the Antecedents of Commitment to Difficult Goals," *Journal of Applied Psychology* 74 (1989), pp. 18–23; and L. Coch and J. R. P. French, Jr., "Overcoming Resistance to Change," *Human Relations* 1 (1948), pp. 512–32.

15. L. Gabinet, "The Human Side of Chemical Valley," *Canadian Petroleum,* June 1982, pp. 58–60.

16. M. Pollock and N. L. Colwill, "Participatory Decision Making in Review," *Leadership and Organization Development Journal* 8, no. 2 (1987), pp. 7–10; S. J. Havlovic, "Quality of Work Life and Human Resource Outcomes," *Industrial Relations,* 30 (Fall 1991), pp. 469–79; and K. I. Miller and P. R. Monje, "Participation, Satisfaction, and Productivity: A Meta-Analytic Review," *Academy of Management Journal* 29 (1986), pp. 727–53.

17. R. M. Kanter, *The Change Masters* (New York: Simon & Schuster, 1983); J. A. Conger and R. A. Kanungo, "The Empowerment Process: Integrating Theory and Practice," *Academy of Management Review* 13 (1988), pp. 471–82; and W. Bennis and B. Nanus, *Leaders* (New York: Harper & Row, 1985).

18. N. Bayloff and E. M. Doherty, "Potential Pitfalls in Employee Participation," *Organizational Dynamics* 17 (1989), pp. 51–62.

19. V. H. Vroom, *Some Personality Determinants of the Effects of Participation* (Englewood Cliffs, N.J.: Prentice Hall, 1960).

20. A. J. Marrow, "The Risk and Uncertainties of Action Research," *Journal of Social Issues* 20 (1964), pp. 5–20; and N. J. Adler, *International Dimensions of Organizational Behavior* (Boston: Kent, 1986), pp. 138–40.

21. Vroom and Jago, *The New Leadership: Managing Participation in Organizations,* pp. 151–52.

22. R. H. G. Field, "A Test of the Vroom–Yetton Normative Model of Leadership," *Journal of Applied Psychology* 67 (1982), pp. 523–32; R. H. G. Field, W. C. Wedley, and M. W. J. Hayward, "Criteria Used in Selecting Vroom–Yetton Decision Styles," *Canadian Journal of Administrative Sciences* 6 (June 1989), pp. 18–24; D. Tjosvold, W. C. Wedley, and R. H. G. Field, "Constructive Controversy, the Vroom–Yetton Model, and Managerial Decision Making," *Journal of Occupational Behaviour* 7 (1986), pp. 125–38; and W. W. Liddell et al., "A Modification of 'A Test of the Vroom–Yetton Normative Model of Leadership,'" *Proceedings of the Annual ASAC Conference, Organizational Behaviour Division,* 9, pt. 5 (1988), pp. 67–76.

23. D. V. Nightingale, *Workplace Democracy: An Enquiry into Employee Participation in Canadian Work Organizations* (Toronto: University of Toronto Press, 1982).

24. D. Tjosvold and R. H. G. Field, "Effects of Social Context on Consensus and Majority Vote Decision Making," *Academy of Management Journal* 26 (1983), pp. 500–06.

25. I. L. Janis, *Groupthink: Psychological Studies of Policy Decisions and Fiascoes,* 2nd ed. (Boston: Houghton Mifflin, 1982); and I. L. Janis, *Crucial Decisions* (New York: Free Press, 1989), pp. 56–63.

26. P. E. Tetlock, "Identifying Victims of Groupthink from Public Statements of Decision-Makers," *Journal of Personality and Social Psychology* 49 (1979), pp. 1565–585.

27. G. Whyte, "Groupthink Reconsidered," *Academy of Management Review* 14 (1989), pp. 40–56.

28. D. G. Myers and H. Lamm, "The Group Polarization Phenomenon," *Psychological Bulletin* 83 (1976), pp. 602–27; and D. Isenberg, "Group Polarization: A Critical Review and Meta-Analysis," *Journal of Personality and Social Psychology* 50 (1986), pp. 1141–151.

29. D. Kahneman and A. Tversky, "Prospect Theory: An Analysis of Decision Under Risk," *Econometrica* 47 (1979), pp. 263–91.

30. F. A. Schull, A. L. Delbecq, and L. L. Cummings, *Organizational Decision Making* (New York: McGraw-Hill, 1970), pp. 144–49.

31. Tjosvold and Field, "Effects of Social Context on Consensus and Majority Vote Decision Making."

32. D. Tjosvold, *Team Organization: An Enduring Competitive Edge* (Chichester, England: Wiley, 1991); and D. Tjosvold, "Participation: A Close Look at Its Dynamics," *Journal of Management* 13 (1987), pp. 739–50.

33. J. Schreiner, "How to Become a Great Canadian Company," *Financial Post 500,* Summer 1987, pp. 40–44.

34. D. M. Schweiger, W. R. Sandberg, and P. L. Rechner, "Experiential Effects of Dialectical Inquiry, Devil's Advocacy, and Consensus Approaches to Strategic Decision Making," *Academy of Management Journal* 32 (1989), pp. 745–72.

35. A. F. Osborn, *Applied Imagination* (New York: Scribner, 1957).

36. R. N. Taylor, *Behavioral Decision Making* (Glenview, Ill.: Scott, Foresman, 1984), pp. 44–47; and A. P. Hare, *Handbook of Small Group Research,* 2nd ed. (New York: Free Press, 1976), p. 319.

37. A. L. Delbecq, A. H. Van de Ven, and D. H. Gustafson, *Group Techniques for Program Planning: A Guide to Nominal Group and Delphi Processes* (Glenview, Ill.: Scott, Foresman, 1975).

38. W. C. Tate, "Measuring Our Productivity Improvements," *Business Quarterly,* Winter 1984, pp. 87–91.

39. D. M. Hegedus and R. Rasmussen, "Task Effectiveness and Interaction Process of a Modified Nominal Group Technique in Solving an Evaluation Problem," *Journal of Management* 12 (1986), pp. 545–60; and S. Frankel, "NGT + MDS: An Adaptation of the Nominal Group Technique for Ill-Structured Problems," *Journal of Applied Behavioral Science* 23 (1987), pp. 543–51.

40. Tjosvold and Field, "Effects of Social Context on Consensus and Majority Vote Decision Making"; and S. G. Green and T. D. Taber, "The Effects of Three Social Decision Schemes on Decision Group Process," *Organizational Behavior and Human Performance* 25 (1980), pp. 97–106.

41. N. Dalkey, *The Delphi Method: An Experimental Study of Group Decisions* (Santa Monica, Calif.: Rand Corporation, 1969); and H. A. Linstone and M. Turoff (eds.), *The Delphi Method: Techniques and Applications* (Reading, Mass.: Addison-Wesley, 1975).

42. R. D. Needham and R. C. de Loë, "The Policy Delphi: Purpose, Structure, and Application," *Canadian Geographer* 34 (1990), pp. 133–42; and W. G. Rieger, "Directions in Delphi Developments: Dissertations and Their Quality," *Technological Forecasting and Social Change* 29 (1986), pp. 195–204.

43. Taylor, *Behavioral Decision Making,* p. 182.

44. O. L. Crocker, J. S. L. Chiu, and C. Charney, *Quality Circles: A Guide to Participation and Productivity* (Toronto: Methuen, 1984); B. Portis, P. R. Ingram, and D. J. Fullerton, "Effective Use of Quality Circles," *Business Quarterly,* Fall 1985, pp. 44–47; and R. P. Steel and R. F. Lloyd, "Cognitive, Affective, and Behavioral Outcomes of Participation in Quality Circles: Conceptual and Empirical Findings," *Journal of Applied Behavioral Science* 24 (1988), pp. 1–17.

45. B. King, "Quality Circles Have Achieved Acceptance," *Financial Post,* January 18, 1986, p. 15; and R. Winters, "Sharing Decision-Making Boosts Profits: Consultant," *Montreal Gazette,* September 16, 1987, p. C1.

46. Steel and Lloyd, "Cognitive, Affective, and Behavioral Outcomes of Participation in Quality Circles: Conceptual and Empirical Findings"; and S. D. Saleh, Z. Guo, and T. Hull, "The Use of Quality Circles in the Automobile Parts Industry," *Proceedings of the Annual ASAC Conference, Organizational Behaviour Division* 9, pt. 5 (1988), pp. 95–104.

47. E. E. Lawler III and S. A. Mohrman, "Quality Circles after the Fad," *Harvard Business Review* 63, 1 (1985), pp. 64–71; and Lawler, *High-Involvement Management,* Chapter 4.

48. C. Stohl and K. Jennings, "Volunteerism and Voice in Quality Circles," *Western Journal of Speech Communication* 52 (Summer 1988), pp. 238–51.

49. Lawler and Mohrman, "Quality Circles after the Fad"; and H. P. Sims, Jr., and J. W. Dean, Jr., "Beyond Quality Circles: Self-Managing Teams," *Personnel* 62, no. 1 (January 1985), pp. 25–32.

50. P. S. Goodman, R. Devadas, and T. L. G. Hughson, "Groups and Productivity: Analyzing the Effectiveness of Self-Managing Teams," in J. P. Campbell, R. J. Campbell, and associates, *New Perspectives from Industrial and Organizational Psychology* (San Francisco: Jossey-Bass, 1988), pp. 295–327.

51. Goodman, Devadas, and Hughson, "Groups and Productivity: Analyzing the Effectiveness of Self-Managing Teams," pp. 296–97.

52. E. L. Trist, G. W. Higgin, H. Murray, and A. B. Pollock, *Organizational Choice* (London: Tavistock, 1963); and T. Cummings, "Self-Regulating Work Groups: A Socio-Technical Synthesis," *Academy of Management Review* 3 (1978), pp. 625–34.

53. H. F. Kolodny, C. P. Johnston, and W. Jeffrey, *Quality of Working Life: Job Design and Sociotechnical Systems,* revised ed. (Ottawa: Supply and Services Canada, 1985); J. B. Cunningham, "A Look at Four Approaches to Work Design," *Optimum* 20–21 (1989–90), pp. 39–55; J. E. Kelly, "A Reappraisal of Socio-Technical Systems Theory," *Human Relations* 31 (1978), pp. 1069–99; and W. Pasmore, C. Francis, J. Haldeman, and A. Shani, "Sociotechnical Systems: A North American Reflection on Empirical Studies of the Seventies," *Human Relations* 35 (1982), pp. 1179–1204.

54. Goodman, Devadas, and Hughson, "Groups and Productivity: Analyzing the Effectiveness of Self-Managing Teams," p. 314.

55. W. F. Dowling, "Job Design on the Assembly Line: Farewell to Blue-Collar Blues," *Organization Dynamics,* Autumn 1973, pp. 51–67; and P. G. Gyllenhammar, *People at Work* (Reading, Mass.: Addison-Wesley, 1977).

56. J. P. Womack, D. T. Jones, and D. Roos, *The Machine that Changed the World* (New York: Macmillan, 1990); O. Hammarström and R. Lansbury, "The Art of Building a Car: The Swedish Experience Re-examined," *New Technology, Work and Employment* 2 (Autumn 1991), pp. 85–90; J. F. Krafcik, "Triumph of the Lean Production System," *Sloan Management Review,* Fall 1988, pp. 41–52.

57. The material in this section is based on N. Halpern, "Sociotechnical System Design: The Shell Sarnia Experience," in J. B. Cunningham and T. H. White (eds.), *Quality of Working Life: Contemporary Cases* (Ottawa: Supply and Services Canada, 1984), pp. 31–75; D. A. Ondrack and M. G. Evans, "The Shell Chemical Plant at Sarnia (Canada): An Example of Union–Management Collaboration," in H. C. Jain (ed.), *Worker Participation: Success and Problems* (New York: Praeger, 1980), pp. 257–73; T. Rankin and J. Mansell, "Integrative Collective Bargaining and New Forms of Work Organization," *National Productivity Review* 5, no. 4 (1986), pp. 338–47; and N. Herrick, *Joint Management and Employee Participation* (San Francisco: Jossey-Bass, 1990).

58. B. Sheehy and G. Peckover, "You Get What You Pay For," *Industrial Management* 12, no. 7 (September 1988), pp. 24–26.

59. J. A. Pearce II and E. C. Ravlin, "The Design and Activation of Self-Regulating Work Groups," *Human Relations* 40 (1987), pp. 751–82; Goodman, Devadas, and Hughson, "Groups and Productivity: Analyzing the Effectiveness of Self-Managing Teams," pp. 307–14; and R. A. Guzzo, R. D. Jette, and R. A. Katzell, "The Effects of Psychologically Based Intervention Programs on Worker Productivity: A Meta-Analysis," *Personnel Psychology* 38 (1985), pp. 275–91.

60. "Work Innovations in Canada Multiplying," *Quality of Working Life: The Canadian Scene* 9, no. 1 (1986), pp. 10–11; and "Partners in Search of Perfection," *Canadian Business,* October 1990, suppl. p. 10.

61. Pollock and Colwill, "Participatory Decision Making in Review"; J. O'Toole, *Making America Work* (New York: Continuum, 1981), p. 115.

62. C. C. Manz, D. E. Keating, and A. Donnellon, "Preparing for an Organizational Change to Employee Self-Management: The Managerial Transition," *Organizational Dynamics* 19 (Autumn 1990), pp. 15–26.

63. Ibid., pp. 23–25.

CHAPTER CASE

EASTERN PROVINCE LIGHT AND POWER COMPANY

I work as a systems and procedures analyst for the Eastern Province Light and Power Company. The systems and procedures department analyzes corporate policies, procedures, forms, equipment, and methods to simplify and standardize operations. We apply "organized common sense" to develop new practices and to improve old ones.

Requests for analysis of organizational problems are submitted to the systems and procedures department by persons of department head or higher status. Our manager places projects in line for consideration and assigns them to an analyst on the basis of availability; projects are accepted and assigned on the FIFO (first in–first out) method. Projects must undergo analysis, design, and implementation before a change in procedure is realized. What follows is a description of a problem assigned to me. I am in the midst of investigating it right now.

The Problem

For some time, management had been concerned with the inventory carrying charges that accrue when material is stored in company warehouses. Not only is there a cost attached to carrying inventory for future use, but there are additional related costs such as labour to handle the inventory, warehouse usage in terms of square feet taken up in storage, and clerical time used to account for materials flowing into and out of inventory. One type of material stored is office supplies—pens, writing pads, forms, stationery, envelopes, and dozens of similar items. A desire to reduce the costs of storing these items prompted the head of the department of purchasing and material control to submit a request for study by systems and procedures.

The request came in the required written form. It described the current procedures, estimated their costs, and invited us to explore ways of changing the procedures to reduce costs. In brief, at the time the study request was submitted, purchases of office supplies were made through 11 vendors. The items were stored in a common warehouse area and disbursed to using departments as requested. As is customary, I convened a meeting of the requesting manager and others who seemed most directly involved in the problem.

The First Meeting

I opened the meeting by summarizing the present procedures for purchasing and storing office supplies and the estimated costs associated with these problems. I explained that we were meeting to explore ways of reducing these costs. I suggested we might try to generate as many ideas as we could without being too critical of them and then proceed to narrow the list by criticizing and eliminating the ideas with obvious weaknesses.

Just as soon as I finished my opening remarks, the head of purchasing and material control said that we should conduct a pilot study in which we would contract with one of the regular vendors to supply each involved department directly, eliminating company storage of any inventory. The vendor would continue to sell us whatever we usually purchased from it, but would sell and deliver the items to various departments instead of to our central purchasing group. A pilot study with one vendor would indicate how such a system would work with all vendors of office supplies. If it worked well we could handle all office supplies this way.

She went on to explain that she had already spoken to the vice-president to whom she (and, through intermediate levels, the rest of us) reported and that he recognized the potential savings that would result. She also said that she had gone over the idea with the supervisor of stores (who reported to her) and that he agreed. She wanted to know how long it would take me to carry out the pilot study. I looked at a few faces to see if anybody would say anything, but nobody did. I said I didn't know. She said, "Let's meet in a week when you've come up with a proposal." The meeting ended without anything else of any real substance being said.

I felt completely frustrated. She was the highest-ranking person in the meeting. She had said what she wanted and, if her stature wasn't enough, she had invoked the image of the vice-president being in agreement with her. Nobody, including me, had said anything. No idea other than hers was even mentioned, and no comments were made about it.

I decided that I would work as hard as I could to study the problem and her proposed pilot study before the next meeting and come prepared to give the whole thing a critical review.

Between Meetings

I talked to my boss about my feeling that it seemed as though I was expected to rubber-stamp the pilot study idea. I said that I wished he would come to the next meeting. I also said that I wanted to talk to some people close to the problem, some clerks in stores, some vendors, and some buyers in purchasing to see if I could come up with any good ideas or find any problems in the pilot study area. He told me to learn all I could and that he would come to the next meeting.

My experience with other studies had taught me that sometimes the people closest to the work had expertise to contribute, so I found one stores clerk, two buyers, and two vendor sales representatives to talk to. Nobody had spoken to any of them about the pilot study and the general plan it was meant to test. This surprised me a little. Each one of these people had some interesting things to say about the proposed new way of handling office supplies. A buyer, for example, thought it would be chaotic to have 17 different departments ordering the same items. She thought we might also lose out on some quantity discounts, and it would mean 17 times the paperwork. A vendor said he didn't think any vendor would like the idea because it would increase the number of contacts necessary to sell the amount that could be sold now through one contact—the buyer in the purchasing department. A stores clerk said it might be risky to depend upon a vendor to maintain inventories at adequate levels. He said, "What if a vendor failed to supply us with, say, enough mark-sensing tools for our meter readers one month, thereby causing them to be unable to complete their task and our company to be unable to get its monthly billings out on time?"

The Second Meeting

Armed with careful notes, I came to the next meeting prepared to discuss these and other criticisms. One of the stores clerks had even agreed to attend so that I could call upon him for comments. But when I looked around the conference room, everyone was there except the stores clerk. The head of purchasing and material control said she had talked to the clerk and could convey any of his ideas so she had told him it wasn't necessary for him to come.

I pointed out that the stores clerk had raised a question about the company's ability to control inventory. He had said that we now have physical control of inventory, but the proposal involved making ourselves dependent on the vendor's maintaining adequate inventory. The head of purchasing and material control said, "Not to worry. It will be in the vendor's own interest to keep us well-supplied." No one, including my boss, said anything.

I brought up the subject of selecting a vendor to participate in the pilot study. My boss mentioned that I had told him some vendors might object to the scheme because the additional contacts would increase their costs of sales. The head of purchasing and material control said, "Any vendor would be interested in doing business with a company as big as Eastern Province Light and Power." No further comments were made.

I mentioned that it was the practice of the systems and procedures staff to estimate independently the costs and benefits of any project before undertaking it, and also to have the internal auditing department review the proposal. I said we would need to go ahead with those steps. I asked the head of purchasing and material control to give me the name of somebody in her area I should contact to get the costs of the present system. She said that it really didn't seem necessary to go through all the usual steps in this case since she had already submitted an estimate. Besides, it was only going to be a pilot study. She said, "I think we can all agree on that and just move ahead now with the designation of a vendor." She looked around the table and nobody said anything. She said, "Fine. Let's use Moore Business Forms." Nobody said anything. She then said to me, "OK, let's get back together after you've lined things up."

Discussion Questions

1. What symptom(s) exist in this case to suggest that something has gone wrong?
2. What are the root causes that have led to these symptoms?
3. What actions should the organization take to correct these problems?

Source: D. R. Hampton, *Contemporary Management* (New York: McGraw-Hill, 1981). Used with permission.

EMPLOYEE INVOLVEMENT CASES

Case 1: New Machines Decision Problem

You are a manufacturing manager in a large electronics plant. The company's management is always searching for ways of increasing efficiency. The company has recently installed new machines and put in a new simplified work system, but to the surprise of everyone, including yourself, the expected increase in productivity was not realized. In fact, production has begun to drop, quality has fallen off, and the number of employee separations has risen.

You do not believe that there is anything wrong with the machines. You have had reports from other companies using them that confirm this opinion. You have also had representatives from the firm that built the machines go over them, and they report that the machines are operating at peak efficiency.

You suspect that some parts of the new work system may be responsible for the change, but this view is not widely shared among your immediate subordinates, who are four first-level supervisors, each in charge of a section, and your supply manager. The drop in production has been variously attributed to poor training of the operators, lack of an adequate system of financial incentives, and poor morale. Clearly, this is an issue about which there is considerable depth of feeling among individuals and potential disagreement among your subordinates.

This morning you received a phone call from your division manager. He had just received your production figures for the last six months and was calling to express his concern. He indicated that the problem was yours to solve in any way that you thought best, but that he would like to know within a week what steps you plan to take.

You share your division manager's concern over the falling productivity and know that your people are also disturbed. The problem is to decide what steps to take to rectify the situation.

Case 2: Coast Guard Cutter Decision Problem

You are the captain of a 72 metre Canadian Coast Guard cutter, with a crew of 16, including officers. Your mission is general at-sea search and rescue. At 2:00 A.M. this morning, while en route to your home port after a routine 28-day patrol, you received word from the nearest Canadian Coast Guard station that a small plane had crashed 100 kilometres offshore. You obtained all the available information concerning the location of the crash, informed your crew of the mission, and set a new course at maximum speed for the scene to commence a search for survivors and wreckage.

You have now been searching for 20 hours. Your search operation has been increasingly impaired by rough seas, and there is evidence of a severe storm building to the southwest. The atmospherics associated with the deteriorating weather have made communications with the Coast Guard station impossible. A decision must be made shortly about whether to abandon the search and place your vessel on a northeasterly course to ride out the storm (thereby protecting the vessel and your crew, but relegating any possible survivors to almost certain death from exposure) or to continue a potentially futile search and the risks it would entail.

Before losing communications, you received an update advisory from Atmospheric Environmental Services concerning the severity and duration of the storm. While your crew members are extremely conscientious about their responsibility, you believe that they would be divided on the decision of leaving or staying.

Discussion Questions (for both cases)

1. To what extent should your subordinates be involved in this decision? Choose from among the options AI, AII, CI, CII, or GII described in the text.
2. What factors led you to choose this alternative rather than the others?
3. What problems might occur if less or more involvement occurred in this case (where possible)?

Source: Adapted from V. H. Vroom and A. G. Jago, *The New Leadership: Managing Participation in Organizations* (Englewood Cliffs, N.J.: Prentice Hall, 1988). © 1987 V. H. Vroom and A. G. Jago. Used with permission of the authors.

EXPERIENTIAL EXERCISE

DESERT SURVIVAL EXERCISE

Purpose: This exercise is designed to help you understand the potential advantages of team decision making compared with individual decision making.

Situation

It is approximately 10:00 A.M. in mid-July and you have just crash landed in the Sonora Desert of the southwestern United States. The light twin-engine plane, containing the bodies of the pilot and the copilot, has completely burned. Only the air frame remains. No one else has been injured.

The pilot was unable to notify anyone of your position before the crash. However, ground sightings, taken before you crashed, indicated that you are 100 kilometres off the course that was filed in your VRF flight plan. The pilot had indicated before you crashed that you were approximately 110 kilometres south–southwest from a mining camp, which is the nearest known habitation.

The immediate area is quite flat and, except for occasional barrel and saguaros cacti, appears to be rather barren. The last weather report indicated that the temperature would reach 43° Celsius—which means that the temperature within 1 foot of the surface will hit 52°. You are dressed in lightweight clothing—short-sleeved shirts, pants, socks, and street shoes. Everyone has a handkerchief. Collectively, your pockets contain $2.83 in change, $85.00 in bills, a pack of cigarettes, and a ballpoint pen. Before the plane caught fire, your team was able to salvage the 15 items listed in the chart below.

Instructions

Your task is to rank these items according to their importance to your survival. In the "Your Individual Ranking" column, indicate the most important item with "1," going through to "15" as the least important. Next, the instructor will form teams of four or five members and each team will rank order the items in the second column. Team rankings should be based on consensus, not simply averaging the individual rankings.

When the teams have completed their rankings, the instructor will provide the expert's ranking, which can be entered in the third column. Next, compute the absolute difference between the individual ranking and the expert's ranking, record this information in column four, and sum the absolute values at the bottom of column four. In column five, record the absolute difference between the team's ranking and the expert's ranking, and sum these absolute numbers at the bottom. A class discussion of the relative merits of individual versus team decision making will follow.

Desert Survival Tally Sheet

Items	Step 1 Your Individual Ranking	Step 2 The Team's Ranking	Step 3 Survival Expert's Ranking	Step 4 Difference between Steps 1 and 3	Step 5 Difference between Steps 2 and 3
Mirror					
Sunglasses					
Flashlight					
Knife					
Compass					
Water					
Top coat					
Parachute					
Pistol					
Map					
Plastic raincoat					
Compress kit with gauze					
Edible desert animals					
2 quarts of vodka					
Bottle of salt tablets					
Total					
(The lower the score, the better)				Your score	Team score

Source: Reprinted by permission from pages 52–54 and 125 from the instructors manual to accompany *Organization and People: Readings, Exercises, and Cases in Organizational Behavior, 4th ed.* by J. B. Ritchie and P. Thompson. Prepared by Scott Howard, Robin Zenger Baker, and David Ulrich; Copyright © 1988 by West Publishing Company. All rights reserved.

12

Organizational Power and Politics

LEARNING OBJECTIVES

After reading this chapter, you should be able to:

Outline
The five bases of power in organizations.

Explain
How information can become a power base.

List
Five ways to increase potential power through nonsubstitutability.

Identify
Four strategies to increase potential power through visibility.

Outline
The types of political activity found in organizations.

Identify
Ways to control dysfunctional political behaviour in organizational settings.

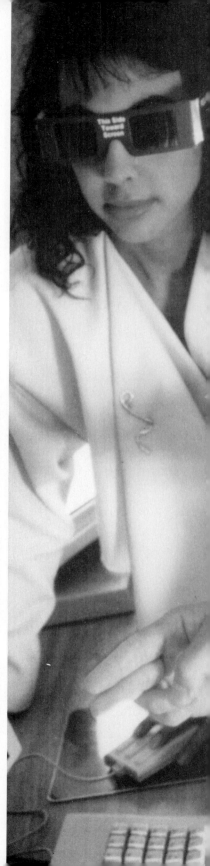

CHAPTER OUTLINE

CTV Network/Brooke Palmer

The CTV Television Network provides as much drama in its own boardroom as it does on prime time. CTV is controlled by seven shareholders, each of whom owns several local (i.e., affiliate) CTV television stations from St. John's to Victoria. These affiliates are ferociously protective of their regional turf and unwilling to surrender any more power than necessary to CTV network management. The CTV president has limited voting power and virtually no funds to start his own initiatives. Excess CTV revenues are siphoned off by the affiliates through an unorthodox revenue-sharing system that keeps the network in perpetual poverty. So the president has to go cap in hand to the affiliates to fund new programs and facilities.

Each shareholder, no matter how small or large, has a single vote on the board of directors. Thus, Newfoundland Broadcasting Co., with a tiny stake in the operation, has enough formal power to scuttle the plans of the heavyweights. But this has not prevented CTV's largest shareholder, Baton Broadcasting Inc., from wielding its substantial advertising power in other ways. Baton, which owns seven stations (including the network's flagship station CFTO in Toronto), has captured the lion's share of CTV's production work by refusing to purchase television programs proposed by other affiliates. This tactic has been effective because Baton's stations account for 35 percent of the network's advertising revenue and many CTV programs would be unprofitable if Baton's stations did not air them.

Baton Broadcasting has made no secret of its desire for CTV to have a single majority shareholder—preferably itself—and has been putting pressure on the other owners for a new voting structure that would bring this about. Rumours are flying that Baton will pull out of the CTV network if it does not get its way. Others disagree, saying that Baton is dependent on CTV for its production work. Moreover, if Baton goes independent, the Canadian government might approve a new CTV affiliate in the lucrative Toronto market. That risk alone would keep Baton in the CTV fold.

Baton's threats and the escalating power struggle have motivated CTV's shareholders to try to redistribute formal voting power more equitably. They tried to do this in the late 1980s, but failed. This time, the survival of the CTV Television Network may be at stake.[1]

CTV's predicament is somewhat unique, but power and politics exist in every organization. Some writers even suggest that power is the essence of organizations.[2] Power is necessary to coordinate organizational activities, but it might also serve personal objectives that threaten the organization's survival. As such, effective managers need to be aware of the dynamics of power and how to control political behaviour.

This chapter examines the themes of power and politics within organizational settings. We begin by defining power and presenting a basic model depicting its dynamics. Next, five bases of power are discussed, including a closer look at information as an important source of power in organizations, followed by the contingencies necessary to translate those sources into meaningful power. The latter part of this chapter looks at the sometimes troublesome (and always interesting) theme of organizational politics. We investigate the various types of political activity that are found in contemporary organizations, the conditions under which organizational politics thrives, and the ways that it can be controlled.

THE MEANING OF POWER

Power is the capacity of a person, team, or organization to influence others who are in a state of dependence.[3] Power is not the act of changing others' attitudes or behaviour; it is only the *potential* to do so. People frequently have power that they do not use or are even aware of. Using a physics analogy, power is similar to a large round rock resting at the top of a steep hill. It exerts no force and has no momentum, yet it has a tremendous capacity to change the landscape when it eventually rolls down the hill. Just like the dormant rock, power is neither good nor bad until its potential is activated. Thus, we should be concerned not only with how power is acquired, but with how it is applied in organizational settings.

power
The capacity of a person, team, or organization to influence others who are in a state of dependence.

Power and Dependence

Power exists when one party perceives that he or she is dependent on the other for something of value.[4] This relationship is shown in Exhibit 12–1, where Person A has power over Person B by controlling something that Person B needs to achieve his or her goal. You might have power over others by controlling a desired job assignment, useful information, or even the privilege of being associated with you! These dependency relationships are an inherent part of organizational life because work is divided into specialized tasks and the organization has limited resources with which to ac-

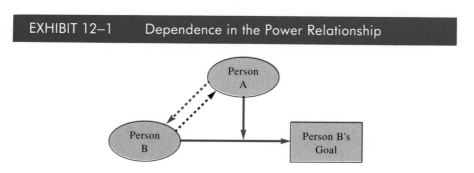

EXHIBIT 12–1   Dependence in the Power Relationship

PERSPECTIVE 12–1 Horse Power at a Canadian Racetrack

A Canadian racetrack faced a shortage of top-quality horses that the public would like to see race. The racetrack's managers did everything they could to attract and keep good horses around in order to draw more people to the track. This gave the horse suppliers (owners and agents) a great deal of power because they controlled the valued resource needed to help the racetrack managers achieve their personal and organizational objectives.

The horse suppliers' power is evident in at least two ways. First, racetrack managers consulted with the horse suppliers before any change was planned on or around the track, even though they had no obligation to do so. Second, when the provincial government threatened horse suppliers who did not pay the provincial sales tax on the horses they bought, the horse suppliers exercised their power by influencing the racetrack's vice-president to settle the matter with the government for them.

Source: C. Rinfret, P. Ross, M. Wolfe, and C. Sabourin in a paper submitted to H. Mintzberg. Cited in H. Mintzberg, *Power in and around Organizations* (Englewood Cliffs, N.J.: Prentice Hall, 1983), p. 39. Used with permission.

complish its goals. Power is activated in these situations when the power-holder threatens the dependent relationship, such as when a highly knowledgeable employee threatens to leave the organization.[5] Our point here is that power exists when you control resources that others want and they are aware of it.

In all relationships, the dependent person or work unit also holds some power over the dominant participant. Exhibit 12–1 illustrates this by the thin dotted line from Person B to A. This **counterpower,** as it is known, is strong enough to at least maintain A's participation in the exchange relationship.[6]

counterpower

The capacity of a person, team, or organization to keep a more powerful person or unit in the exchange relationship.

This interdependent relationship of power and counterpower is apparent in the opening vignette of this chapter. The CTV network and most of its affiliates are dependent on Baton Broadcasting because it controls a large advertising market and the revenues from this market are necessary to fund new programs. But, Baton is also dependent on CTV, at least enough to maintain its membership in the network. Baton's studios are making money producing CTV programs and its continued affiliation with CTV limits the probability that the Canadian government would open another television station in Baton's lucrative Toronto market. Thus, Baton has substantial power over CTV because it controls a large advertising market, but CTV has enough counterpower to keep Baton affiliated with the network.

Power and Scarce Resources

So far, we have explained that power is derived from controlling something that someone else wants.[7] Returning to the CTV story, the network wants Baton's lucrative Toronto market for advertising revenues and Baton wants

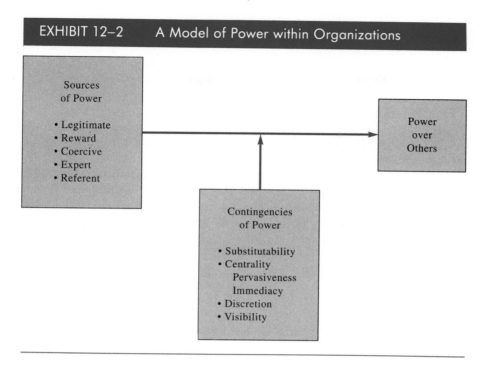

EXHIBIT 12-2   A Model of Power within Organizations

Sources
of Power

• Legitimate
• Reward
• Coercive
• Expert
• Referent

Power
over
Others

Contingencies
of Power

• Substitutability
• Centrality
   Pervasiveness
   Immediacy
• Discretion
• Visibility

CTV's television production work. Notice that both dependencies exist only because of scarce resources. CTV would not be dependent on Baton if the other affiliates provided enough advertising revenue to justify high-cost programs. Similarly, Baton would not be dependent on CTV if it could get enough television production business elsewhere.

Overall, we are saying that people are dependent on others when insufficient resources exist for everyone who desires them. In short, resource scarcity creates dependence which, in turn, creates power. The importance of scarce resources in power and dependence relations is illustrated in Perspective 12–1.[8]

A Model of Power in Organizations

We have said that power is the capacity to influence others and that it exists in social relationships involving dependence and scarce resources. But to more thoroughly understand and manage the dynamics of power within organizational settings, we must consider the sources from which power is derived and the related contingencies that determine whether or not these power bases will generate power.

The model shown in Exhibit 12–2 provides a useful overview upon which to build the discussion that follows. This model suggests that power is derived from five sources: legitimate, reward, coercive, expert, and referent.

But tapping into one or more of these power bases only leads to increased power under certain conditions. These conditions, or contingencies of power, include the person's or subunit's substitutability, discretion, visibility, and two forms of centrality: pervasiveness and immediacy.

SOURCES OF POWER IN ORGANIZATIONS

Some time ago, French and Raven listed five core bases of power within organizations (see Exhibit 12–3).[9] Without these power bases, employees would be unable to influence their coworkers and managers would be unable to coordinate their staff. French and Raven's list of power bases is not perfect; it has been justifiably criticized on a number of grounds. But it provides a useful starting point in our journey toward understanding and managing organizational power.

Legitimate Power

legitimate power

The capacity to influence others through formal authority, that is, the perceived right to direct certain behaviours of people in other positions.

Legitimate power refers to formal authority over others, that is, a person's or subunit's perceived right to influence certain behaviours of people in other positions. People holding higher positions in the organization usually have more legitimate power.[10] However, lower-level employees may also have legitimate power over their superiors. For example, they usually have a right to request information and assistance from the manager.[11]

You might think that legitimate power is a right given by the organization, but a more accurate perspective is that it exists only when agent *and the targets* agree to this authority relationship.[12] The right of someone to exer-

EXHIBIT 12–3	French and Raven's Five Bases of Power
Power Base	**Definition**
Legitimate power	The perceived right to influence certain behaviours of people in other positions.
Reward power	The ability to influence others by controlling the distribution of rewards valued by others and the removal of negative sanctions.
Coercive power	The ability to influence others by controlling the distribution of punishment and removal of rewards valued by others.
Expert power	The ability to influence others by possessing knowledge that is believed to help others accomplish their goals.
Referent power	The ability to influence others based on their identification with and respect for the referent's ideas and requests.

cise power over others must be *legitimized,* that is, it must be accepted and possibly internalized by all concerned. For example, managers have the right to ask employees to stay overtime only when employees accept the manager's right to make this request. This reflects the ever-present mutual dependence of employees and managers in their role relationships.

The degree of legitimate power varies from one situation to another. In the extreme, formal authority refers to the notion of suspending judgment and allowing the person with authority to guide your behaviour. Some organizations expect employees to abide unswervingly by supervisor's orders while other organizations expect employees to question and even refute management's directives if they do not appear to be in the organization's best interests. Legitimate power is also stronger in some societies than others. For instance, obedience to authority is strong in South Korea as a result of Confucian values and military training. In contrast, Canadian values emphasize individualism and self-determination, so managers in this country cannot rely on legitimate power alone to coordinate work force activities.[13]

Reward Power

Reward power exists for those who control the allocation of rewards valued by others and the removal of negative sanctions (i.e., negative reinforcement). Managers have power by virtue of their formal authority over the distribution of organizational rewards such as pay, promotions, time off, vacation schedules, and work assignments. Employees may have reward power by expressing praise and extending personal benefits within their discretion to other coworkers. As organizations delegate responsibility and authority, work teams gain reward power over their members. Employees may have reward power over their superiors through subordinate appraisals whereby subordinates evaluate the performance of their bosses. In each situation, the target values these outcomes and is motivated to comply with the powerholder's request if it increases the probability of receiving the desired rewards.

reward power
The capacity to influence others by controlling the allocation of rewards valued by them and the removal of negative sanctions.

Coercive Power

Coercive power, which is based on the ability to apply punishment and remove rewards (i.e., extinction), is one of the earliest recognized sources of power.[14] Managers have coercive power through their authority to reprimand, demote, and fire employees. Labour unions might use coercive power tactics, such as withholding services, to influence management in collective agreement negotiations. Team members sometimes apply sanctions, ranging from sarcasm to ostracism, to ensure that coworkers conform to team norms. Punishment may have undesirable consequences, as we mentioned in Chapter 4.[15] But when used appropriately, control over adverse outcomes can represent an important power base.

coercive power
The capacity to influence others through the ability to apply punishment and remove rewards affecting these people.

Expert Power

expert power
The capacity to influence others by possessing knowledge or skills that they want.

Expert power exists when an individual or subunit depends on another person or subunit for valued information. Employees with unique knowledge or skills may be very powerful if the organization is dependent on this expertise to achieve organizational objectives, such as operating complex equipment. Others acquire expert power by networking with coworkers to maintain a current knowledge of organizational events. These people are well-known for their "inside" information, which may be helpful to others.[16]

Expert power exists throughout the organizational hierarchy. Employees may depend on executives to professionally coordinate and manage the organization, but these executives also depend on employees to get the work done! A former CEO of Maple Leaf Mills acknowledges the expert power employees have over managers:

> I still couldn't run a flour mill if my life depended on it, or any of the other operations we have. I am helpless without people and I tell them that all the time. I tell them how important they are and how I couldn't do their job, but together we have a job to do.[17]

Referent Power

referent power
The capacity to influence others by virtue of the admiration for and identification with the powerholder.

charisma
A form of interpersonal attraction whereby others develop a respect for and trust in the charismatic individual.

People have **referent power** when others identify with them, like them, or otherwise respect them. This form of power usually develops slowly and is largely a function of the person's interpersonal skills.[18] Referent power is related to the concept of **charisma.** Charisma is a word with many meanings, but it is often viewed as a form of interpersonal attraction whereby followers develop a respect for and trust in the charismatic individual. (We will discuss charisma as a leadership characteristic in Chapter 14.) Referent power is usually associated with organizational leaders, but subordinates may also have referent power over their superiors. Managers admire productive employees and are more willing to accommodate their requests. Some employees also develop referent power over others through impression management strategies, including the ingratiation tactics described in Chapter 7.[19]

INFORMATION AS A POWER BASE

Information is a potentially important power base in two ways. First, people and subunits might control the flow and interpretation of information to others. By virtue of their organizational position and legitimate power, they receive information and are authorized to selectively distribute it to others. Second, as a variation of expert power, people may be able to help the organization cope with environmental uncertainties. Both power bases have received a lot of attention in the literature and are discussed here as an extension of French and Raven's previously described power bases.

Control over Information Flow

Closely related to legitimate power is the right to control the flow and interpretation of information to others. Information control is usually accorded to people in specific positions and corresponds to the formal communication network. For example, one manager effectively influenced the selection of a new computer by controlling the information that organizational decision makers received about alternate choices.[20] Through secrecy (withholding information) and selective dissemination of facts, the manager was able to construct the realities that he wanted others to perceive.[21]

Exhibit 12–4 shows how information control is strongest in highly centralized organizational structures, as shown by the wheel formation, because information flows through a central person or subunit. The individual or department in the middle of this configuration is the gatekeeper of information and can influence others through the amount and type of information they receive. This source of power is less likely to occur in the all-channel structure where information is freely exchanged among everyone. However, the all-channel network conflicts with the need for organizational efficiency and, except in small work teams and for specific types of information, the wheel pattern tends to emerge.[22] Consequently, power through the control of information is common in most organizations.

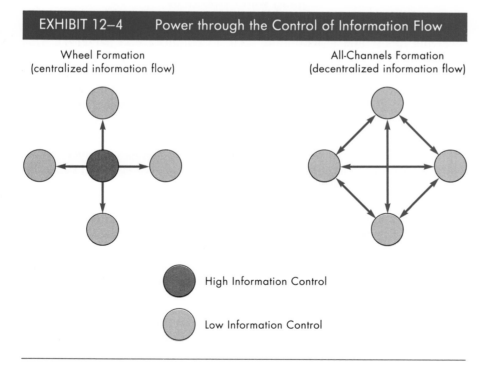

| EXHIBIT 12–4 | Power through the Control of Information Flow |

Wheel Formation
(centralized information flow)

All-Channels Formation
(decentralized information flow)

High Information Control

Low Information Control

PERSPECTIVE 12–2   How Jocelyne Côté-O'Hara Helps B.C. Tel Cope with Uncertainty

Senior executives at B.C. Tel consider themselves lucky to have Jocelyne Côté-O'Hara as vice-president of government relations. "Other companies are envious we have her," says Gord MacFarlane, B.C. Tel chairman. As a Canadian government employee during the 1970s and early 1980s, Côté-O'Hara worked her way through the Treasury Board and eventually into the Prime Minister's office as a policy advisor. With her unique background and government contacts, she has elevated B.C. Tel's profile in Ottawa and guided its subsidiaries to government officials they hardly knew existed.

Equally important is her role in forecasting and sometimes preventing government policy changes that may affect B.C. Tel. Her department tracks a myriad of policy areas and keeps in regular contact with the Canadian Radio–Television and Telecommunications Commission, which regulates B.C. Tel's business, for any hints of future policy changes. "I'm B.C. Tel's early warning system," she says.

Côté-O'Hara also serves an important role in occasionally trying to prevent shifts in government policy by asserting her company's point of view. However, one friend notes that the B.C. Tel vice-president uses persuasion and influence very carefully. "Jocelyne works in a more even-handed fashion than traditional lobbyists." Côté-O'Hara explains further: "Nowadays, you have to be sensitive to broader interests. I want to maximize return for B.C. Tel shareholders, but also ensure quality service for its subscribers."

Source: I. Allaby, "Jocelyne Côté-O'Hara," *Canadian Business*, August 1988, p. 43.

Coping with Uncertainty

Organizations are open systems that interact with their environments by receiving inputs and transforming them to outputs (see Chapter 1). This process involves varying degrees of uncertainty, that is, a lack of information about future events.[23] Uncertainty interferes with the organization's need to routinize human activities. Consider the troubles that Canadian steel producers would face if they did not know where to find tomorrow's supply of raw materials or how much demand will exist for their products next week. They could not plan production, arrange long-term contracts with suppliers, or adjust their product lines to satisfy future customer needs. Thus, to operate more efficiently and ensure continued survival, organizations need to cope with environmental uncertainties.[24]

strategic contingencies model
A model stating that a person's or subunit's power is a function of the ability to cope with critical organizational uncertainties, as well as the nonsubstitutability and centrality of the person or subunit.

Individuals and subunits gain power by being able to cope with organizational uncertainties. This is the basis of the **strategic contingencies model.** A strategic contingency is a critical activity for accomplishing organization goals, and coping involves any way to effectively deal with environmental uncertainties in that critical activity. In their study of Canadian breweries and container companies, Hinings and his colleagues identified three general strategies to help organizations cope with uncertainty:[25]

- *Prevention*—The most effective strategy is to prevent environmental changes and variations from occurring. For example, financial experts acquire power by preventing the organization from experiencing a cash shortage or defaulting on loans.

- *Forecasting*—The next-best strategy is to be able to predict environmental changes or variations. In this respect, marketing specialists gain power by predicting changes in consumer preferences.
- *Absorption*—People and subunits also gain power by absorbing or neutralizing the impact of environmental shifts as they occur. A classic example is the ability of maintenance crews to come to the rescue when machines break down and the production process grinds to a halt.

There is some evidence that people in specific occupations gain power due to increasing environmental uncertainties in their areas of expertise. For example, many top organizational positions have been filled by finance personnel in recent years as corporate taxation policies and equity market practises have become more turbulent and complex.[26] As Perspective 12–2 describes, some civil servants have also gained prominent positions in the private sector because of their ability to prevent, predict, and absorb the uncertainties of government activities.

THE CONTINGENCIES OF POWER

Power over others requires more than just tapping one or more power bases. Hinings and his colleagues identify three factors that determine whether coping with uncertainty (or access to any other power base) is translated into actual power. These include substitutability and two types of centrality: pervasiveness and immediacy.[27] Other writers have subsequently added discretion and visibility to the list.[28] Keep in mind that these are not sources of power; rather, they moderate the potential force of a power base.

Substitutability

Substitutability refers to the availability of alternatives. Power increases with the nonsubstitutability of a valued resource because this strengthens the dependence on those who control access to the resource. Power is strongest when someone has a monopoly over a valued resource. Conversely, power decreases as the number of alternative sources of the critical resource increases.

Numerous strategies, including those listed in Exhibit 12–5, have been used by individuals and subunits to increase their power through nonsubstitutability. While we certainly do not recommend that you use these actions if they undermine organizational effectiveness, you should at least be aware that they exist and have been applied by others. Labour unions attempt to organize as many people as possible within a particular trade so that employers have no other source of labour supply.[29] Many professional groups—including lawyers, accountants, and doctors—have gained bargaining power through legislation prohibiting people outside the profession from engaging in certain practises. They also use jargon and control educational programs to restrict access to their special knowledge base.

substitutability

The extent to which those dependent on a resource have alternative sources of supply of the resource or can use other resources that would provide a reasonable substitute.

EXHIBIT 12–5	Strategies for Enhancing Power through Nonsubstitutability

Strategy	Example
Acquire all other sources of the critical resource.	High "union density" of a trade or industry.
Become the exclusive authority over the critical resource through statute or organizational policy.	Exclusive statutory rights of medical and legal professionals to engage in certain activities.
Limit distribution of unique knowledge base.	Use of jargon and limited access to specialized educational programs.
Avoid written documentation of special procedures.	Verbal communication of special formulas.
Customize required activities originally designed by others.	Redesigning equipment outside of manufacturer's specifications.
Limit entry of alternative sources.	Refusing to hire someone else in your area of expertise.

One study reported that maintenance workers in the French tobacco processing industry had tremendous power both because they could cope with the industry's only major environmental uncertainty—machine breakdowns—and because they had taken several precautions to ensure that their maintenance skill was nonsubstitutable.[30] Only the dozen or so maintenance workers in each factory knew how to repair the machines because they avoided sharing their knowledge with others. They did not talk to production workers and ensured that maintenance procedures were not documented. Even the original manufacturer's knowledge of the machines could not weaken the maintenance workers' power because machine designs had been altered over the years and only the maintenance staff knew the details of these alterations.

Substitutability refers not only to other sources that offer the resource, but also to substitutions of the resource itself. For instance, trade unions are weakened when companies introduce technologies that replace the need for their union members. This occurred when automatic switching systems were introduced in the telecommunications industry a few years ago. At one time a strike by telephone employees would have shut down the system, but technological innovations now ensure that telephone operations continue during labour strikes and reduce the need for telephone operators during normal operations. These and other technological changes have had the effect of substituting employees and thereby reducing union power.[31]

Finally, we should point out that information-based resources become substitutable when they are documented and routinized through standard operating procedures.[32] As expertise becomes documented, the organization can more easily transfer this knowledge to others through training. This explains why the maintenance workers in the French tobacco industry trained each other verbally and deliberately avoided documenting their practises. As soon as the industry had this information in writing, it could train replacements and the maintenance crews would become substitutable.

Centrality

Another strategic contingency of power is **centrality,** namely, the extent and nature of interdependence with other parts of the organization. There are two dimensions of centrality: pervasiveness and immediacy.[33]

- *Pervasiveness*—**Pervasiveness** refers to the number of other people or units affected by the powerholder. According to the strategic contingencies model, power increases with the number of others dependent on the powerholder's activities. An organization's finance or accounting department, for instance, may have a high level of pervasiveness because its budgeting activities affect virtually everyone in the organization.

- *Immediacy*—**Immediacy** refers to the extent that an employee's or subunit's activities quickly and substantially affect the work activities of others in the organization. Basically, power increases with the speed and severity that other work activities are impeded by the subunit's actions.

A good way to think about centrality in the organization is to imagine how many people would be affected and to what degree their work would be hampered if a particular employee was suddenly absent or a work unit ceased to exist for an extended period of time. High pervasiveness would exist if most other employees in the organization were affected. High immediacy would exist if others were virtually unable to operate soon after the absence begins.

The concepts of pervasiveness and immediacy are well-known in labour–management relations. Labour unions try to increase pervasiveness by negotiating work rules that require the use of union members wherever possible. They apply the immediacy principle in negotiations by planning strike actions around critical times in the work process. Perspective 12–3 highlights a few recent examples of labour union strategies to increase negotiation power through immediacy.

Discretion

The freedom to exercise one's judgment—to make decisions without referring to a specific rule or receiving permission from someone else—is another important contingency of power in organizations. Even with expertise, charisma, or any other power base, it is extremely difficult for employees or work teams to become powerful in areas where their discretion is limited. Managers may have legitimate power over subordinates, but this power is

centrality
The extent and nature of interdependence that the individual or subunit has with other parts of the organization.

pervasiveness
A form of centrality referring to the number of other people or units affected by the powerholder.

immediacy
A form of centrality referring to the extent that an individual's or subunit's actions quickly and substantially affect the work activities of others in the organization.

PERSPECTIVE 12–3   The Power of Timing in Labour Disputes

The saying "timing is everything" could well be the theme of labour relations strategy in many recent disputes. Every year, thousands of collective agreements are renegotiated, most without overt conflict. But when labour union leaders believe that strike action is necessary, they want the disruption to have an immediate effect on the employer so that employees are off the job for as little time as possible. Here are three prominent examples where labour union leaders have used immediacy to leverage their power in a contract dispute.

- More than 120 tankers were stranded along the St. Lawrence Seaway and Great Lakes as Canadian Coast Guard crews went on strike. The Canadian government worked quickly to end the strike, which began in November, a month before the

shipping season ends. The timing was critical because ice had begun to form along the Seaway and Coast Guard ice-breakers were keeping a path open for the tankers to reach the ocean or the Montreal port. Without the ice-breakers, the Seaway would quickly ice over and the tankers would be stranded until the next spring. One government official explained the seriousness of the situation: "We're talking here about a question of hours, we're no longer talking about a question of days. . . . This is an emergency and it's important to get this thing resolved."

- A wave of illegal public sector strikes hit Quebec just weeks before the provincial election. More than a quarter of a million public servants closed schools and community colleges, paralyzed the

limited where formal procedures explicitly outline the managers' required activities. Even those with expert or referent power cannot exercise this power where their discretion is curtailed by organizational rules.

Consider the plight of first-line supervisors. They must administer programs developed from above and follow specific procedures in their implementation. They administer rewards and punishments, but often must abide by precise rules regarding their distribution. Indeed, supervisors are often judged not on their discretionary skills, but on their ability to follow prescribed rules and regulations. This lack of discretion makes supervisors largely powerless even though they may have access to some of the power bases described earlier in this chapter.[34]

Visibility

Power does not flow to unknown people in the organization.[35] Rather, it only exists when others are aware that they have something of value. Visibility is simply the idea that power is influenced by perceptions and that people gain power by being seen as possessing valued resources. If an employee has unique knowledge to help others do their job better, the employee's power base will yield power only when others are aware of this unique knowledge. Thus, one gains power not only by having valuable talents, but by making them known.

There are several ways to increase visibility, including the strategies summarized below:[36]

provincial civil service, and made the lives of hospital patients even more difficult. This put the incumbent government in a bad light as the strikes produced chaotic scenes of people scrambling to rearrange their lives. A senior labour union official candidly acknowledged that the protests were strategically timed: "If [the premier] is reelected with a big mandate, why would he be more conciliatory [after the election]?"

- About 1,000 announcers, stagehands, makeup artists, and clerical workers at the Canadian Broadcasting Corporation in Toronto went on a

two-day strike that threatened preparations for radio and television airing of the annual Juno awards. CBC had been given the contract to air the awards ceremony nationally. A CBC spokesperson said that the strike would make preparations "very difficult," but the most noticeable effect would be the presence of management staff both on air and behind the scenes to replace the striking workers. Union officials knew that CBC would use managers to replace strikers, but also believed that CBC management were scrambling to get the set-up work done on time.

Sources: M. Gooderham, "Seaway Strike May Strand More than 120 Tankers," *Globe and Mail,* December 12, 1989, p. A14; S. Delacourt, "Two-Day Walkout at CBC Will Put New Announcers on TV and Radio," *Globe and Mail,* November 8, 1986, pp. A1, A2; I. Peritz, "Labour Strife Looms Large as Election Nears," *Montreal Gazette,* September 9, 1989, pp. B1, B5; and "Quebec Public Service Paralyzed by Strikes," *Winnipeg Free Press,* September 15, 1989, p. 16.

- *People-oriented jobs*—Visibility increases with the number of people you normally interact with, so direct your career toward people-oriented jobs that require extensive contacts rather than isolated technical positions.
- *Face-to-face contact*—Visibility is more likely to occur through direct face-to-face contact. This suggests that you should present your own reports to management, rather than leave them to someone else. You should also introduce yourself when the appropriate opportunity exists.
- *Task forces*—You should welcome opportunities to participate in important task forces. In addition to the valuable learning experience, these committees give you the opportunity to work closely with—and get noticed by—senior people in the organization.
- *Mentoring*—Mentoring is the process of "learning the ropes" of organizational life from a senior person within the company. This learning experience assists your career, as we shall discuss in Chapter 16, but mentors also help to increase your exposure and visibility in the organization.[37]

THE CONSEQUENCES OF POWER

Before concluding our discussion of power in organizations, we should say something about what people *do* with power. Power is the capacity to influence people up, down, and across the organizational hierarchy.[38] A manager's power might be used to ensure that employees follow safety procedures. Coworkers influence each other to abide by the team's informal norms. Subordinates influence their superiors to change work assignments.

There are basically three different consequences of influence, depending on the type of power base used and how effectively it is activated.[39] The least effective outcome is *resistance,* whereby the targetted person opposes the request and actively tries to avoid carrying it out. Resistance and employee dissatisfaction are most common when the powerholder applies coercive power,[40] but similar results may occur when other power bases are used arrogantly or in a manipulative way. *Compliance* occurs when people are motivated to implement the powerholders' request for purely instrumental reasons. This outcome is most common when using reward and legitimate power. *Commitment* is the strongest consequence of influence, whereby people identify with the powerholder's request and are motivated to implement it whether or not there are any extrinsic benefits for doing so. Commitment is the most common consequence of expert and referent power.

Another consequence of power is its effect on the powerholder. As we learned in Chapter 2, some people have a strong need for power and are motivated to acquire it for personal or organizational purposes. These individuals are more satisfied and committed to their jobs when they have increased responsibility, authority, and discretion.[41]

Finally, we should warn you that people who acquire too much power often abuse their position to better their personal interests and to gain more power.[42] Employees who acquire more power than others around them have a tendency to use their influence more, devalue their less-powerful coworkers, and decrease their interpersonal associations with them. They also use their existing power to further strengthen their power base so that, if left unchecked, powerful employees eventually become even more powerful. In short, there appears to be some truth in Lord Acton's well-known statement that "power tends to corrupt; absolute power corrupts absolutely."[43]

ORGANIZATIONAL POLITICS

organizational politics
Attempts to influence others using discretionary behaviours for the purpose of promoting personal objectives; discretionary behaviours are neither explicitly prescribed nor prohibited by the organization and are linked to one or more power bases.

Organizational politics is a concept that everyone seems to understand until they are asked to define it. Many of us hold a "rational" view of organizations, in which political behaviour is a necessary evil. It is the shady side of organizational life in which people are manipulated without their consent and, sometimes, without their knowledge. Other people see organizational politics as an inherent and often necessary part of organizational life. For this reason, effective managers must be good politicians, particularly at higher levels in the corporation.[44]

We define **organizational politics** as attempts to influence others using discretionary behaviours for the purpose of promoting personal objectives.[45] Discretionary behaviours are neither explicitly prescribed nor prohibited by the organization and are linked to one or more power bases. Recall from the opening vignette that Baton Broadcasting captured most of CTV's production business by threatening to refuse any programs produced by other affiliates. This action is certainly not encouraged or sanctioned by the network, but neither is it prohibited. These threats are informal behaviours that fall somewhere between acceptable and unacceptable.

People engage in political activities to achieve personal objectives, including the acquisition of more power, usually at the expense of others. A manager who influences others to change a company policy or decision would be working against the interests of other managers who want the organization to follow another path. In this respect, political behaviours usually occur under conditions of organizational conflict, which we will discuss more fully in the next chapter.[46]

Organizational Politics: Good or Bad?

Political actions serve the individual's or team's self-interests, but this does not necessarily mean that the consequences are unfavourable for the organization. Exhibit 12–6 lists some of the positive and negative consequences of

EXHIBIT 12–6	Helpful and Harmful Consequences of Organizational Politics

	Percentage Mentioning Item
Helpful	
Achieves organizational goals, gets job done	26
Helps organizational survival, health, processes	26
Increases visibility of ideas, people, etc.	20
Improves coordination, communication	18
Develops teams, group functioning	12
Develops an esprit de corps and channels energy	10
Improves decision making	7
Harmful	
Distracts from organizational goals	45
Misuses resources	32
Creates divisiveness and infighting	22
Produces tension, frustration, poor organizational climate	20
Allows incompetent employees to get ahead	15
Reduces coordination, communication	10
Damages the organization's image, reputation	10

Source: D. L. Madison, R. W. Allen, L. W. Porter, P. A. Renwick, and B. T. Mayes, "Organizational Politics: An Exploration of Managers' Perceptions," *Human Relations* 33 (1980), Table 4.

PERSPECTIVE 12–4   Power and Politics at the Canadian Imperial Bank of Commerce

For the past three decades, the Canadian Imperial Bank of Commerce (CIBC) has been such a battlefield of politics that one writer has called it "the Beirut of Canadian business." The story begins with Neil McKinnon, top banker at CIBC from 1956 until 1973. McKinnon maintained an effective intelligence network across Canada and held power close to his chest. Within the bank, McKinnon restricted access to important documents and, when on overseas visits, would often lock his door so that no one else could see them. This left senior managers dependent on McKinnon for important information about the bank's operations.

The problem was that McKinnon was better at nurturing his personal power than at nurturing his staff. Rising stars in the bank were viewed more as threats than logical successors and many good people were brought up through the ranks only to be cut down by McKinnon. For example, Gordon Sharwood, CIBC's general manager during the late 1960s, wanted a troublesome account split with another bank, but McKinnon disagreed. One morning at breakfast, Sharwood read in the morning paper that McKinnon had appointed a colleague to Sharwood's position as general manager of the bank! McKinnon refused to talk about the executive reshuffling, so Sharwood cleared out his desk.

By the early 1970s, CIBC's board of directors were worried that McKinnon's politics were undermining the bank's public image and management succession plans. To deflect this concern, McKinnon established a committee on the bank's distribution of power. He had intended to shelve and forget the committee's report but, ironically, it was endorsed by the board of directors and effectively removed all of McKinnon's executive powers. The next year, McKinnon resigned rather than face the humiliation of being officially ousted.

The CIBC board later appointed Russell Harrison as chairman but, still sensitive to McKinnon's legacy, also gave substantial power to the new president, Donald Fullerton. Harrison initially appeared willing

organizational political activity, according to one survey of executives and managers. As you can see, there are several potentially favourable outcomes of organizational politics. For example, political tactics can help organizations achieve their objectives where traditional influence methods may fail. A manager might use politics to influence an important organizational strategy which, in the long run, may be good for the organization. Political actions are also used by individuals to acquire more power. This, again, may be good or bad for the organization, depending on the circumstances.

While political behaviour is sometimes beneficial, it is more often perceived as harmful to the organization. In companies where employees frequently use political maneuvers to get their way and these activities are accepted as normal behaviour, the long-term consequences can be quite damaging. Political behaviours reduce interpersonal trust, increase alienation and, in the long term, can threaten organizational effectiveness through lower profitability and the loss of valuable staff.[47] Such has been the case at the Canadian Imperial Bank of Commerce, described in Perspective 12–4, which has been called "the Beirut of Canadian business."

to share power but, in 1980, he demoted Fullerton on the grounds that it was too difficult making decisions with two people at the top. By 1983, Harrison was being criticized as too autocratic and secretive. Some claimed that he held onto power at the bank only because of support from a group of Western Canadian board members (known as the "Western Mafia") who were sympathetic to Harrison's Manitoba roots.

Several talented CIBC executives quit during Harrison's tenure, but Fullerton stayed and was eventually given new challenges, first in international banking and later in corporate strategy. Finally, in 1984, Harrison gave Fullerton the position of chief executive officer to manage internal affairs. Harrison planned to manage external relations as the bank's chairman for the next three years, but soon after taking power, Fullerton removed Harrison's name from certain circulation lists so that the chairman no longer received the information so vital to his position. The message was clear to all: Harrison had lost power. Harrison retired as chairman in 1985, two years before his expected departure.

It is too early to tell whether Fullerton will continue the ways of his predecessors or use power for the organization's benefit. Fullerton has been emphasizing the need for more teamwork and delegation, but others claim that he makes strong use of his power. According to a former Commerce executive: "Fullerton wants to keep everybody off-guard until he builds up his power base."

Sources: P. C. Newman, *The Canadian Establishment* (Toronto: McClelland & Stewart, 1975), Chapter 4; R. McQueen, *The Money Spinners* (Toronto: Macmillan, 1983), Chapter 4; A. Toulin, "Bank of Commerce Chairman Steps Down as Chief Executive," *Toronto Star,* January 20, 1984, pp. E1, E3; M. Mittelstaedt, "CIBC Again Beset by Rumours; This Time over New President," *Globe and Mail,* February 1, 1985, p. B3; S. Gittins, "Retirement No Life of Leisure for ex-CEOs," *Financial Post,* February 13, 1989, p. 17; and T. Tedesco, "Unrest on the CIBC's Flagship," *Financial Times,* November 26, 1990, pp. 1, 4.

TYPES OF POLITICAL ACTIVITY

Researchers are just beginning to understand the dynamics of corporate political behaviour, so we have only a sketchy idea of the tactics that are used. However, a few writers have at least developed a tentative list of political tactics used in organizational settings. Some of the more prominent tactics are described below (see Exhibit 12–7).[48]

Attacking or Blaming Others

Political actors attack or blame others either as a reaction to unfavourable situations or as a proactive strategy to neutralize rivals. As a reactive tactic, politicians try to minimize or avoid being associated with undesirable situations through scapegoating—attempting to transfer blame to others—or by physically and symbolically distancing themselves from the event. Proactive attacks attempt to make rivals look bad in the eyes of decision makers. For instance, a politically minded manager who is competing for a promotion might find ways to let senior management know about past mistakes made by other managers who are also in line for that promotion.

EXHIBIT 12–7	Types of Political Behaviours in Organizations

- **Attacking or blaming others**
- **Distributing information selectively**
- **Controlling channels of communication**
- **Forming coalitions**
- **Cultivating networks**
- **Creating obligations**
- **Managing public images**

Attacking and blaming others is almost always dysfunctional for the organization because it undermines innovation and directs everyone's energy toward defending their actions rather than seeking new opportunities. This is exactly what happened at Massey-Ferguson, once Canada's leading farm machinery manufacturer, a few years before it went bankrupt. One classic example occurred after a competitive bid was made to sell a shipment of tractors to the Egyptian government. Two departments of Massey were involved in the proposal and both had agreed on the price of each tractor. The company won the contract, but when it was discovered that they could have charged $300 or $400 more for each tractor, the senior managers in both departments gave their staff the job of producing detailed reports showing that it was the other department that had made the error.[49]

Distributing Information Selectively

Information is perhaps the most frequently used political tool, as we saw in the earlier story about politics at the Canadian Imperial Bank of Commerce. Outright lying and falsification are (hopefully!) rare in organizations, but several other strategies have been used to get one's way. These include:

- Withholding (filtering) information that may be damaging to one's position or would give power to others.
- Avoiding people and situations that might force the powerholder to reveal damaging information.
- Overwhelming people with so much information that they cannot interpret it all and, in fact, must depend on the politician for a summary interpretation or conclusion.
- Burying or obscuring damaging information in a dossier of otherwise neutral information.
- Bringing in outside "Experts" who support the powerholder's personal view of the contentious issue.

Controlling Channels of Communication

Closely related to the selective use of information is the selective control of interpersonal communication. Through legitimate authority, employees often have the power to inhibit or facilitate direct communication and interaction among other people. This privilege, when used outside of normal procedures to promote personal objectives, becomes a powerful political tool. Secretaries who manage their superior's agenda may be playing politics in this way by arranging appointments for some people more easily than for others. Managers engage in political behaviour by shaping meeting agendas around their personal interests. The timing or existence of certain issues on the agenda often affects the amount of attention the item receives. Thus, if the manager wants to avoid a decision on a particular item, he or she might place it near the bottom of the agenda so that the committee either doesn't get to it or is too fatigued to make a final judgment.[50]

Forming Coalitions

In Chapter 10, we explained that a coalition is a special kind of interest group in which people form an alliance around a specific issue to influence people outside the team with respect to that issue. Many organizational decisions result from the influence of several competing coalitions. A typical manager may be associated with two or more coalitions at a time to influence organizational decisions or secure more resources.

Why are coalitions politically effective? One explanation may be that a collection of people may create more legitimacy than several people working individually.[51] Coalitions create a sense that an issue has broad rather than isolated support. By banding together, coalition members reinforce and further mobilize support for their position.[52] They also hope to increase their power over individuals outside the coalition by demonstrating their strength in numbers. Coalitions are relatively short-lived alliances, disbanding when the issue is resolved or lost.

Cultivating Networks

Networking refers to cultivating social relationships with superiors, subordinates, peers, and people outside the organization for the purpose of accomplishing one's goals. As we mentioned earlier in this chapter, effective organizational leaders are usually highly skilled at networking because it keeps them in touch with important organizational activities. This knowledge builds their expert power base and prevents them from becoming too dependent on a few subordinates for this information.

Networking also makes it easier to enlist support from colleagues when needed because a mutual respect has already been established. Thus, networking develops a form of referent power through the friendships culti-

networking
The act of cultivating social relationships with others for the purpose of accomplishing one's goals.

vated. In some instances, these friendships may give well-connected employees a positive "halo," which leads to favourable decisions by others in the network. In other words, networking is sometimes a political tactic to take advantage of situations where "It's not *what* you know, but *who* you know, that counts."

Creating Obligations

The law of reciprocity plays an interesting role in some organizational political tactics.[53] You may recall from Chapter 10 that the obligation to help someone who has once helped you is an almost universal norm and is deeply embedded in Canadian society. Some political tacticians actively look for ways to serve others for the purpose of building up IOUs that can later be called in. For example, an employee who has helped someone else might later ask that person for support on a particular issue. The indebted coworker is more likely to agree to this than if there was no debt to repay. Some organizational politicians are able to leverage these debts for a far greater return than whatever was given in the first place.

Managing Public Images

Recall from Chapter 7 that people manage the identities that others assign to them. Many impression management activities are done routinely to satisfy the basic norms of social behaviour. But impression management becomes a form of organizational politics when used deliberately to get one's way in organizations. Political actors build favourable images through ingratiation (directly or indirectly flattering and agreeing with the target person), publicizing one's successes, carefully dressing and grooming to show alignment to a particular coalition, and creating the appearance of being part of the inner circle of organizational power.

CONDITIONS FOR ORGANIZATIONAL POLITICS

Organizational politics is more commonly found under certain conditions than others. These conditions, shown in Exhibit 12–8, include scarce critical resources, complex and ambiguous decisions, organizational change, political norms, and personal characteristics of the participants.[54]

Scarce Critical Resources

Political behaviour is more prevalent when resources are scarce and important to someone. For example, if the organization is flush with cash, you will probably get most of your requested operational budget through the legitimate process of submitting a proposal. But when budgets are slashed and

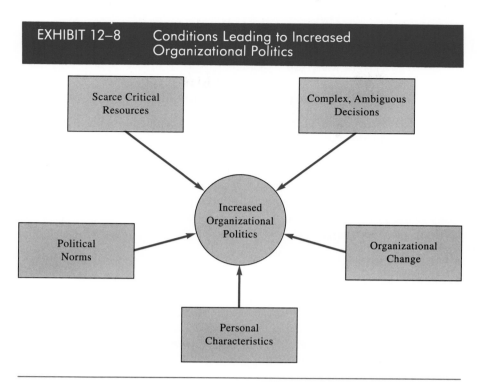

EXHIBIT 12–8   Conditions Leading to Increased Organizational Politics

few additional funds are available, political behaviours emerge to accompany the legitimate processes. Similarly, employees are more likely to engage in political behaviours when threatened with a loss of resources or benefits. These political actions are taken to safeguard and secure these resources and maintain the status quo.[55]

Complex and Ambiguous Decisions

Political behaviours are more common where decisions are nonprogrammed and the decision choice must be based on complex goals.[56] Recall from Chapter 9 that nonprogrammed decisions are those in which decision makers cannot rely on a clear set of criteria or principles to make choices among competing alternatives. Nonprogrammed decisions occur in unique, complex, or ill-defined situations requiring the decision maker's judgment, intuition, and creativity because standard operating procedures do not exist.

Organizational politics is more prevalent under these conditions of ambiguity and uncertainty because the decision maker is naturally given more discretion over decision criteria and alternatives. This discretion becomes the object of political behaviour to influence the factors that should be considered as well as their relative importance in determining the decision outcome. As you might expect, political behaviours are more common at higher levels in the organization where nonprogrammed decision making is more frequent.[57]

Organizational Change

Political tactics are more common during major organizational changes, particularly where there is a lot of uncertainty and risk of losing existing resources.[58] We will discuss resistance to organizational change in Chapter 15. At this point we will simply point out that much of this resistance involves political behaviours aimed at retaining the status quo. Those who want to *encourage* specific changes, such as guiding innovations to reality, are also likely to use political behaviours, particularly where formal power bases will be insufficient to overcome resistance by others.[59]

Political Norms

Political behaviours are neither formally accepted nor rejected by the organization, but every organization has norms governing the permissibility of these informal behaviours. In some organizations, political actions are discouraged and, indeed, severely curtailed by peer pressure. In other organizations, political behaviour is rampant, not only because of the conditions previously described, but because organizational norms support these behaviours. As with any dominant corporate value, a political culture is maintained by organizational rewards, the behaviours of its leaders, and other factors we will describe in Chapter 16 on organizational culture.

When organizational politics becomes so embedded that political behaviour continues to escalate, then the organization may become what Henry Mintzberg has called a **political arena**.[60] A political arena is a setting in which organizational politics is endemic and virtually out of control. The political arena is normally a temporary condition, particularly when organizations are in transition. But companies that are unable to stabilize out of the political arena will become paralyzed as the myriad of individual goals replace organizational objectives and human energies are directed toward protecting turf.

political arena
A setting in which organizational politics is endemic and virtually out of control.

Personal Characteristics

Some employees are more likely than others to engage in organizational politics by virtue of their personalities and personal values. Here we summarize three personal characteristics associated with political behaviours.[61]

Need for Power.   In Chapter 2 we introduced the need for power as a desire to control one's environment, including people and material resources. Effective managers have a relatively high socialized power need in which they seek and use power to fulfill organizational goals. Less-effective employees have a strong personal power need, whereby they seek power for the experience of power itself and to fulfill personal interests. In either form, need for power begets political behaviour to acquire the power and achieve objectives.

Machiavellianism. **Machiavellianism** is a personality trait in which people believe that deceit is a natural and acceptable way to influence others. Machiavellian employees seldom trust others and frequently use power to manipulate others toward their own personal goals, whether or not these goals are favourable to the organization.

Internal Locus of Control.   Individuals with a strong external locus of control tend to be passive because they believe that life's events are largely beyond their control (see Chapter 7). In contrast, people with a high internal locus of control feel that they are very much in charge of their own destiny. Consequently, internals are more likely then externals to engage in political behaviours to shape their lives and the world around them. This does not mean that internals are naturally political; rather, they have a greater tendency to turn to political action when political conditions are present.

CONTROLLING POLITICAL BEHAVIOUR

The conditions described above that fuel organizational politics also give us some clues regarding the ways to potentially minimize it. This is particularly useful where political behaviours are dysfunctional or are out of control. Here are some potentially effective strategies to control dysfunctional political behaviour in organizational settings:

- Ensure that a sufficient supply of critical resources exists at all times. This is not easy, but it is possible to ensure that sufficient inventory and cash flow exist in many cases.
- Where resources are necessarily scarce, introduce rules and regulations to specify the use of these resources.
- Wherever possible, establish clear selection criteria in important decisions.
- Establish a free flow of information so that the organization is less dependent on a few people at the centre of a communication wheel.
- Use effective organizational change management practises, particularly education and participation, to minimize uncertainty during the change process (see Chapter 15).
- Restructure team and organizational norms (as described in Chapter 10) to reject political tactics that appear to interfere with organizational effectiveness.
- Select managers with a moderately strong socialized need for power and weak Machiavellianism.

Machiavellianism
A personality trait in which people believe that deceit is a natural and acceptable way to influence others.

- Provide opportunities for open and candid dialogue to resolve conflicts among employees and work units.
- Forewarn coworkers about political tactics so that individuals are more likely to be exposed when trying to practice them.

SUMMARY

- Power is the capacity of a person, team, or organization to influence others who are in a state of dependence. Power exists when one party perceives that he or she is dependent on the other for something of value. People are dependent on others when insufficient resources exist for everyone who desires them.
- French and Raven have identified five power bases: legitimate (formal authority), reward (positive and negative reinforcement), coercive (punishment and extinction), expert (knowledge), and referent (charisma and attraction).
- Information is frequently used as a power base in organizations. Power is acquired by controlling the flow and interpretation of information to others who require that information. This information control is usually related to legitimate power. Coping with uncertainty through prevention, forecasting, or absorption is another information-based source of power. This type of power is associated with expert power.
- Power bases are leveraged into actual power only under certain conditions. Individuals and subunits are more powerful when they are nonsubstitutable, that is, they have exclusive control over valued resources. Power increases with centrality, both in terms of the number of people affected and how quickly others are affected. Power also increases with the amount of discretion accorded to the person or work unit and its visibility to others.
- Influence is the main result of power in action, but this may range from resistance (opposing the request where possible), to compliance (fulfilling the request for instrumental reasons) and commitment (fulfilling the request because the target identifies with it or the powerholder). Power also has effects on the powerholder. People with a high need for power feel more satisfied and committed to their jobs when they have power. However, many people tend to act abusively when given too much power.
- Organizational politics are attempts to influence others using discretionary behaviours for the purpose of promoting personal objectives. Discretionary behaviours are neither explicitly prescribed nor prohibited by the organization. Political activities may be beneficial to organizations in some situations, but people tend to have an unfavourable view of organizational politics.
- Organizational politics takes many forms, but the most common tactics include attacking or blaming others, distributing information selectively,

controlling channels of communication, forming coalitions, cultivating networks, creating obligations, and managing public images.

• Organizational politics is more likely to occur where there are scarce critical resources, complex and ambiguous decisions, organizational change, and team norms or organizational cultures that tolerate or promote political behaviours. Individuals are also more likely to engage in organizational politics when they have a high need for power (particularly personal power), a Machiavellian personality, and an internal locus of control.

DISCUSSION QUESTIONS

1. Of what relevance are dependence and scarce resources in organizational power?

2. Comment on the accuracy of this statement: "Legitimate power is assigned by the organization to jobholders."

3. What do we mean by "coping with uncertainty"? Describe three general strategies to help organizations cope with uncertainty.

4. Suppose you have formal authority to allocate performance bonuses to your employees. What conditions must exist before this power base is translated into actual power?

5. Describe one strategy to secure power for each of the contingencies of power in organizations.

6. How might employees use (and misuse) information as a political tactic?

7. Why are political behaviours more common at higher levels in the organization?

8. Describe one strategy to control politics for each of the conditions that encourage politics in organizations.

NOTES

1. J. Partridge, "CTV Tries to Break Impasse," *Globe and Mail,* November 21, 1990; Patricia Best, "Broadcast Blues," *Financial Times,* May 9, 1988, pp. 26–28; Renate Lerch, "CTV Power Struggle Darkening," *Financial Post,* November 16, 1987, p. 7; Edward Greenspon, "The Off-Camera Drama at CTV," *Report on Business Magazine,* June 1987, pp. 32–36; and Eric Reguly, "CTV under Siege," *Financial Post,* March 30, 1987, pp. 1–2.

2. R. M. Cyert and J. G. March, *A Behavioral Theory of the Firm* (Englewood Cliffs, N.J.: Prentice Hall, 1963).

3. G. Johns, *Organizational Behavior: Understanding Life at Work* (Glenview, Ill.: Scott, Foresman, 1988), p. 426; and H. Mintzberg, *Power in and around Organizations* (Englewood Cliffs, N.J.: Prentice Hall, 1983), Chapter 1.

4. D. Knights and J. Roberts, "The Power of Organization and the Organization of Power," *Organizational Studies* 3, no. 1 (1982), pp. 47–63; R. A. Dahl, "The Concept of Power," *Behavioral Science* 2 (1957), pp. 201–18; R. M. Emerson, "Power-Dependence Relations," *American*

Sociological Review 27 (1962), pp. 31–41; and A. M. Pettigrew, *The Politics of Organizational Decision-Making* (London: Tavistock, 1973).

5. J. P. Kotter, "Power, Dependence, and Effective Management," *Harvard Business Review,* July 1977, pp. 125–36; and K. M. Bartol and D. C. Martin, "When Politics Pays: Factors Influencing Managerial Compensation Decisions," *Personnel Psychology* 43 (1990), pp. 599–614.

6. T. R. Mitchell and J. R. Larson, Jr., *People in Organizations* (New York: McGraw-Hill, 1988), p. 406.

7. D. Mechanic, "Sources of Power of Lower Participants in Complex Organizations," *Administrative Science Quarterly* 7 (1962), pp. 349–64; and J. Pfeffer, *Power in Organizations* (Marshfield, Mass.: Pitman, 1981).

8. Mintzberg, *Power in and around Organizations,* p. 39.

9. J. R. P. French and B. Raven, "The Bases of Social Power," in D. Cartwright (ed.), *Studies in Social Power* (Ann Arbor: University of Michigan Press, 1959), pp. 150–67; and P. Podsakoff and C. Schreisheim, "Field Studies of French and Raven's Bases of Power: Critique, Analysis, and Suggestions for Future Research," *Psychological Bulletin* 97 (May 1985), pp. 387–411.

10. D. Tjosvold, "Power and Social Context in the Superior–Subordinate Interaction," *Organizational Behavior and Human Decision Processes,* June 1985, pp. 281–93.

11. G. A. Yukl, *Leadership in Organizations*, 2nd ed. (Englewood Cliffs, N.J.: Prentice Hall, 1989), p. 15.

12. W. E. Halal, "The Legitimacy Cycle: Long-Term Dynamics in the Use of Power," in A. Kakabadse and C. Parker (eds.), *Power, Politics, and Organizations* (Chichester, England: Wiley, 1984), pp. 47–64; and P. M. Blau, *The Dynamics of Bureaucracy* (Chicago: University of Chicago Press, 1955).

13. R. P. Kearny, *Warrior Worker* (New York: Henry Holt, 1991), pp. 69–74; and N. J. Adler, *International Dimensions of Organizational Behavior* (Boston: Kent, 1986), pp. 36–41.

14. M. Weber, *The Theory of Social and Economic Organization* (Glencoe, Ill.: Free Press, 1947).

15. R. J. Burke and D. S. Wilcox, "Bases of Supervisory Power and Subordinate Job Satisfaction," *Canadian Journal of Behavioural Sciences* 3 (1971), pp. 183–93.

16. J. A. Conger and J. P. Kotter, "General Managers," in J. W. Lorsch (ed.), *Handbook of Organizational Behavior* (Englewood Cliffs, N.J.: Prentice Hall, 1987), pp. 392–403; and R. E. Kaplan, "Trade Routes: The Manager's Network of Relationships," *Organizational Dynamics,* Spring 1984, pp. 37–52.

17. A. R. Aird, P. Nowack, and J. W. Westcott, *Road to the Top* (Toronto: Doubleday Canada, 1988), p. 77.

18. Yukl, *Leadership in Organizations,* 2nd ed., Chapter 2.

19. For a complete discussion of impression management tactics in various organizational situations, see Robert A. Giacalone and Paul Rosenfeld (eds.), *Impression Management in the Organization* (Hillsdale, N.J.: Lawrence Erlbaum Associates, 1989).

20. A. Pettigrew, "Information Control as a Power Source," *Sociology* 6 (1972), pp. 187–204.

21. L. E. Greiner and V. E. Schein, *Power and Organization Development* (Reading, Mass.: Addison-Wesley, 1988), Chapter 3; M. N. Wexler, "Conjectures on the Dynamics of Secrecy and the Secrets Business," *Journal of Business Ethics* 6 (1987), pp. 469–80; and S. P. Feldman, "Secrecy, Information, and Politics: An Essay on Organizational Decision Making," *Human Relations* 41 (1988), pp. 73–90.

22. N. M. Tichy, M. L. Tuchman, and C. Frombrun, "Social Network Analysis in Organizations," *Academy of Management Review* 4 (1979), pp. 507–19; and H. Guetzkow and H. Simon, "The Impact of Certain Communication Nets upon Organization and Performance in Task-Oriented Groups," *Management Science* 1 (1955), pp. 233–50.

23. D. J. Hickson, C. R. Hinings, C. A. Lee, R. E. Schneck, and J. M. Pennings, "A Strategic Contingencies Theory of Intraorganizational Power," *Administrative Science Quarterly* 16 (1971), pp. 216–27.

24. J. D. Thompson, *Organizations in Action* (New York: McGraw-Hill, 1967); and Cyert and March, *A Behavioral Theory of the Firm.*

25. C. R. Hinings, D. J. Hickson, J. M. Pennings, and R. E. Schneck, "Structural Conditions of Intraorganizational Power," *Administrative Science Quarterly* 19 (1974), pp. 22–44.

26. N. Fligstein, "The Intraorganizational Power Struggle: Rise of Finance Personnel to Top Leadership in Large Corporations, 1919–1979," *American Sociological Review* 52 (1987), pp. 44–58.

27. Hickson, Hinings, Lee, Schneck, and Pennings, "A Strategic Contingencies Theory of Intraorganizational Power"; and Hinings, Hickson, Pennings, and Schneck, "Structural Conditions of Intraorganizational Power."

28. R. M. Kanter, "Power Failure in Management Circuits," *Harvard Business Review,* July/August, 1979, pp. 65–75.

29. M. Gunderson, "Union Impact on Compensation, Productivity, and Management of the Organization," in J. C. Anderson, M. Gunderson, and A. Ponak (eds.), *Union–Management Relations in Canada,* 2nd ed. (Don Mills, Ont.: Addison-Wesley, 1989), pp. 347–70.

30. M. Crozier, *The Bureaucratic Phenomenon* (London: Tavistock, 1964).

31. E. Bernard, *The Long Distance Feeling* (Vancouver: New Star Books, 1982); E. Zureik, V. Mosco, and C. Lochhead, "Telephone Workers' Reaction to the New Technology," *Relations Industrielles* 44 (1989), pp. 507–31; and S. McGovern, "Strikes Don't Stop Employers Cold Any More," *Montreal Gazette,* September 24, 1988, p. C1.

32. D. J. Brass, "Being in the Right Place: A Structural Analysis of Individual Influence in an Organization," *Administrative Science Quarterly* 29 (1984), pp. 518–39.

33. Hickson et al., "A Strategic Contingencies Theory of Intraorganizational Power"; and J. D. Hackman, "Power and Centrality in the Allocation of Resources in Colleges and Universities," *Administrative Science Quarterly* 30 (1985), pp. 61–77.

34. Kanter, "Power Failure in Management Circuits"; B. E. Ashforth, "The Experience of Powerlessness in Organizations," *Organizational Behavior and Human Decision Processes* 43 (1989), pp. 207–42; and J. W. Medcof, "The Power Motive and Organizational Structure: A Micro–Macro Connection," *Canadian Journal of Administrative Sciences* 2, no. 1 (1985), pp. 95–113.

35. J. M. Kouzes and B. Z. Posner, *The Leadership Challenge* (San Francisco: Jossey-Bass, 1988), pp. 173–75.

36. D. A. Whetton and K. S. Cameron, *Developing Management Skills* (New York: HarperCollins, 1991), pp. 293–95.

37. K. Kram, *Mentoring at Work* (Glenview, Ill.: Scott, Foresman, 1985); C. A. McKeen and R. J. Burke, "Mentor Relationship in Organizations: Issues, Strategies, and Prospects for Women," *Journal of Management Development* 8 (1989), pp. 33–42; E. A. Fagenson, "The Power of a Mentor," *Group & Organization Studies* 13 (1988), pp. 182–94; and N. Colwill, *The New Partnership: Women and Men in Organizations* (Palo Alto, Calif.: Mayfield, 1982).

38. R. W. Allen and L. W. Porter, *Organizational Influence Processes* (Glenview, Ill.: Scott, Foresman, 1983).

39. Yukl, *Leadership in Organizations,* pp. 12, 44.

40. T. R. Hinkin and C. A. Schriesheim, "Development and Application of New Scales to Measure the French and Raven Bases of Social Power," *Journal of Applied Psychology* 74 (1989), pp. 561–67; French and Raven, "The Bases of Social Power"; and A. R. Elangovan, "Perceived Supervisor-Power Effects on Subordinate Work Attitudes and Behaviour," *Proceedings of the Annual ASAC Conference, Organizational Behaviour Division* 11, part 5 (1990), pp. 80–89.

41. J. W. Medcof, P. A. Hausdorf, and M. W. Piczak, "Opportunities to Satisfy the Need for Power in Managerial and Nonmanagerial Jobs," in N. Lam and R. J. Long (eds.), *Proceedings of the Annual ASAC Conference, Personnel and Human Resources Division* 12, pt. 8 (1991), pp. 80–87.

42. D. Kipnis, *The Powerholders* (Chicago: University of Chicago Press, 1976); and G. R. Salancik and J. Pfeffer, "The Bases and Use of Power in Organizational Decision Making: The Case of a University," *Administrative Science Quarterly* 19 (1974), pp. 453–73.

43. G. E. G. Catlin, *Systematic Politics* (Toronto: University of Toronto Press, 1962), p. 71.

44. C. Kirchmeyer, "Organizational Politics from the Manager's Point of View: An Exploration of Beliefs, Perceptions, and Actions," *Proceedings of the Annual ASAC Conference, Organizational Behaviour Division* 9, pt. 5 (1988), pp. 57–66.

45. L. W. Porter, R. W. Allen, and H. L. Angle, "The Politics of Upward Influence in Organizations," *Research in Organizational Behavior* 3 (1981), pp. 109–49; and P. J. Frost and D. C. Hayes, "An Exploration in Two Cultures of a Model of Political Behavior in Organizations," in R. W. Allen and

L. W. Porter (eds.), *Organizational Influence Processes* (Glenview, Ill.: Scott, Foresman, 1983), pp. 369–92.

46. A. Drory and T. Romm, "The Definition of Organizational Politics: A Review," *Human Relations* 43 (1990), pp. 1133–54; and P. J. Frost, "Power, Politics, and Influence," in F. M. Jablin, L. L. Putnam, K. H. Roberts, and L. W. Porter (eds.), *Handbook of Organizational Communication: An Interdisciplinary Perspective* (Newbury Park, Calif.: Sage, 1987), pp. 503–48.

47. P. Kumar and R. Ghadially, "Organizational Politics and Its Effects on Members of Organizations," *Human Relations* 42 (1989), pp. 305–14; and K. M. Eisenhardt and L. J. Bourgeois III, "Politics of Strategic Decision Making in High-Velocity Environments: Toward a Midrange Theory," *Academy of Management Journal* 31 (1988), pp. 737–70.

48. R. W. Allen, D. L. Madison, L. W. Porter, P. A. Renwick, and B. T. Mayes, "Organizational Politics: Tactics and Characteristics of Its Actors," *California Management Review* 22, no. 1 (Fall 1979), pp. 77–83; and V. Murray and J. Gandz, "Games Executives Play: Politics at Work," *Business Horizons,* December 1980, pp. 11–23.

49. P. Cook, *Massey at the Brink* (Toronto: Collins, 1981), pp. 207–08.

50. Frost, "Power, Politics, and Influence."

51. J. Dowling and J. Pfeffer, "Organizational Legitimacy: Social Values and Organizational Behavior," *Pacific Sociological Review* 18 (1975), pp. 122–36.

52. W. B. Stevenson, J. L. Pearce, and L. W. Porter, "The Concept of 'Coalition' in Organization Theory and Research," *Academy of Management Review* 10 (1985), pp. 256–68; and S. B. Bacharach and E. J. Lawler, *Power and Politics in Organizations* (San Francisco: Jossey-Bass, 1980).

53. A. R. Cohen and D. L. Bradford, "Influence without Authority: The Use of Alliances, Reciprocity, and Exchange to Accomplish Work," *Organizational Dynamics* 17, no. 3 (1989), pp. 5–17.

54. S. C. Goh and A. R. Doucet, "Antecedent Situational Conditions of Organizational Politics: An Empirical Investigation," *Proceedings of the Annual ASAC Conference, Organizational Behaviour Division* 7, pt. 5 (1986), pp. 77–86; and R. H. Miles, *Macro-Organizational Behavior* (Santa Monica, Calif.: Goodyear, 1980), Chapter 6.

55. T. D. Jick and V. V. Murray, "The Management of Hard Times: Budget Cutbacks in Public Sector Organizations," *Organization Studies* 3 (1982), pp. 141–69.

56. C. Hardy, *Strategies for Retrenchment and Turnaround: The Politics of Survival* (Berlin: Walter de Gruyter, 1990), Chapter 14.

57. J. Gandz and V. V. Murray, "The Experience of Workplace Politics," *Academy of Management Journal* 23 (1980), pp. 237–51.

58. Pettigrew, *The Politics of Organizational Decision-Making,* p. 169.

59. P. J. Frost and C. P. Egri, "Influence of Political Action on Innovation: I," *Leadership and Organizational Development Journal* 11 (1990), pp. 17–25; and V. E. Schein, "Organizational Realities: The Politics of Change," *Training and Development Journal* 39 (February 1985), pp. 37–41.

60. H. Mintzberg, "The Organization as Political Arena," *Journal of Management Studies* 22 (1985), pp. 133–54; and Mintzberg, *Power in and around Organizations,* Chapter 23.

61. Porter, Allen, and Angle, "The Politics of Upward Influence in Organizations," pp. 120–22; and R. J. House, "Power and Personality in Complex Organizations," *Research in Organizational Behavior* 10 (1988), pp. 305–57.

CHAPTER CASE

CANTRON LTD.

Cantron Ltd., a Canadian manufacturer of centralized vacuum systems, was facing severe cash flow problems in 1985 due to increasing demand for its products and rapid expansion of production facilities. Steve Heinrich, Cantron's founder and majority shareholder, flew to Germany to meet with management of Rohrtech Gmb to discuss the German company's willingness to become majority shareholder of Cantron in exchange for an infusion of much-needed cash. A deal was struck whereby Rohrtech would become majority shareholder while Heinrich would remain as Cantron's president and general manager. One of Rohrtech's senior executives would become the chairperson of Cantron's Board of Directors and Rohrtech would appoint two other Board members.

This relationship worked well until Rohrtech was acquired by a European conglomerate in 1987 and the new owner wanted more precise financial information and controls placed on its holdings, including Cantron. Heinrich resented this imposition and refused to provide the necessary information. By 1989, relations between Rohrtech and Cantron had soured to the point where Heinrich refused to let Rohrtech representatives into the Cantron plant. He also instituted legal proceedings to regain control of the company.

According to Canadian law, any party who possesses over two-thirds of a company's shares may force the others to sell their shares. Heinrich owned 29 percent of Cantron's shares whereas Rohrtech owned 56 percent. The remaining 15 percent of Cantron shares were held by Jean Parrot, Cantron's head of operations in Quebec. Parrot was a long-time manager at Cantron and remained on the sidelines throughout most of the legal battle between Rohrtech and Heinrich. However, in late September of 1990, Parrot finally agreed to sell his shares to Rohrtech, thereby legally forcing Heinrich to give up his shares. When Heinrich's bid for control failed, Rohrtech purchased all remaining shares and Cantron's Board of Directors (now dominated by Rohrtech) dismissed Heinrich as president and general manager in October 1990. The Board immediately appointed Parrot as Cantron's new president.

Searching for a New General Manager

In the spring of 1990, while Heinrich was still president and trying to regain control of his company, the chairman of Cantron's Board of Directors received instructions from Rohrtech to hire a management consulting firm in Toronto to identify possible outside candidates for the position of general manager at Cantron. The successful candidate would be hired after the conflict with Heinrich had ended (presumably with Heinrich's departure). The general manager would report to the president (the person eventually replacing Heinrich) and would be responsible for day-to-day management of the company. Rohrtech's management correctly believed that most of Cantron's current managers were loyal to Heinrich and, by hiring an outsider, the German firm would gain more inside control over its Canadian subsidiary.

Over 50 candidates applied for the general manager position and three candidates were interviewed by Cantron's chairman and another Rohrtech representative in August 1990. One of these candidates, Kurt Devine, was vice-president of sales at an industrial packaging firm in Toronto and, at 52 years old, was looking for one more career challenge before retirement. The Rohrtech representatives explained the current situation and said that they were offering stable employment after the problem with Heinrich was resolved so that the general manager could help settle Cantron's problems. When Devine expressed his concern about rivalry with internal candidates, the senior Rohrtech manager stated: "We have a bookkeeper, but he is not our choice. The sales manager is capable, but he is located in New York and doesn't want to move to Canada."

One week after Heinrich's dismissal and the appointment of Parrot as president, Cantron's chairman invited Devine to a meeting at a posh Toronto hotel attended by the chairman, another Rohrtech manager on Cantron's Board of Directors, and Parrot. The chairman explained the recent events at Cantron and formally invited Devine to accept the position of vice-president and general manager of the company. After discussing salary and details about job duties, Devine asked the others whether he had their support as well as the support of Cantron's employees. The two Rohrtech representatives said "Yes," while Parrot remained silent. When the chairman left the room to get a bottle of wine to toast the new general manager, Devine asked Parrot how long he had known about the decision to hire him. Parrot replied, "Just last week when I became president. I was surprised . . . I don't think I would have hired you."

Confrontation with Tom O'Grady

Devine began work at Cantron in early November and, within a few weeks, noticed that the president and two other Cantron managers were not giving him the support he needed to accomplish his work. For example, Parrot would call the salespeople almost daily, yet rarely speak with Devine unless the general manager approached him first. The vice-president of sales acted cautiously toward Devine. But it was Tom O'Grady, the vice-president of finance and administration, who seemed to resent Devine's presence the most. O'Grady had been promoted from the position of controller in October and now held the highest rank at Cantron below Devine. After Heinrich was dismissed, Cantron's board of directors had placed O'Grady in charge of day-to-day operations until Devine took over.

Devine depended on O'Grady for information because he had more knowledge than anyone else about many aspects of the business outside of Quebec. However, O'Grady provided incomplete information on many occasions and would completely refuse to educate the general manager on some matters. O'Grady was also quick to criticize many of Devine's decisions and made indirect statements to Devine about his inappropriateness as a general manager. He also mentioned how he and other Cantron managers didn't want the German company (Rohrtech) to interfere with their company.

Devine would later learn about other things O'Grady had said and done to undermine his position. For example, O'Grady actively spoke to office staff and other managers about the problems with Devine, and encouraged them to tell the president about their concerns. Devine overhead O'Grady telling another manager that Devine's memoranda were a "complete joke" and that "Devine didn't know what he was talking about." On one occasion, O'Grady let Devine send out incorrect information about the organization's structure even though O'Grady knew that it was incorrect "just to prove what an idiot Rohrtech had hired."

Just six weeks after joining Cantron, Devine confronted O'Grady with his concerns. O'Grady was quite candid with the general manager, saying that everyone felt that Devine was a "plant" by Rohrtech and was trying to turn Cantron into a branch office of the German company. He said that some employees would quit if Devine did not leave because they wanted Cantron to maintain its independence from Rohrtech. In a later meeting with Devine and Parrot, O'Grady repeated these points and added that Devine's management style was not appropriate for Cantron. Devine responded that he had not received any support from Cantron since the day he had arrived even though Rohrtech had sent explicit directions to Parrot and other Cantron managers that he was to have complete support in managing the company's daily operations. Parrot told the two men that they should work together and that, of course, Devine was the more senior person.

Decision by Cantron's Board of Directors

As a member of Cantron's Board of Directors, Parrot ensured that the matter of Devine was discussed at the January 1991 meeting and that the Board invite O'Grady to repeat his story. Based on this testimony, the Board decided to remove Devine from the general manager job and give him a special project instead. O'Grady was immediately named acting general manager. The chairman and other Rohrtech representatives on Cantron's Board were disappointed that events did not unfold as they had hoped, but they agreed to remove Devine rather than face the mass exodus of Cantron managers that Parrot and O'Grady had warned about.

In late April of 1991, Devine attended a morning meeting of Cantron's Board of Directors to present his interim report on the special project. The Board agreed to give Devine until mid-June to complete the project. However, the Board recalled Devine into the boardroom in the afternoon and Parrot bluntly asked Devine why he didn't turn in his resignation. Devine replied: "I can't think of a single reason why I should. I will not resign. I joined your company six months ago as a challenge. I have not been allowed to do my job. My decision to come here was based on support from Rohrtech and upon a great product." The next day, Parrot came to Devine's office with a letter of dismissal signed by the chairman of Cantron's board of directors.

Discussion Questions

1. What political tactics were used by O'Grady against Devine?
2. How does information play a role in organizational power and politics in this case?

3. What conditions existed that may have increased the level of organizational politics at Cantron Ltd.?

4. What, if anything, would you have done differently after Heinrich left the company?

EXPERIENTIAL EXERCISE

ORGANIZATIONAL POLITICS EXERCISE

Purpose: This exercise is designed to help you understand the situations in which organizational politics occurs by comparing your personal ranking for various situations against the rankings of others in the class and across Canada.

Instructions: Individually rank order the situations listed in the table according to the extent to which you think politics plays a part. In the first column, mark a 1 for the most political situation through to 11 for the least political. Next, the instructor will form teams of four or five members and each team will rank order the items in the second column. Team rankings should be based on consensus, not simply averaging the individual rankings.

When the teams have completed their rankings, the instructor will provide the rankings based on a survey of Canadian managers, which can be entered in the third column. Next, compute the absolute difference between the individual ranking and the managers' ranking, record this information in column four, and sum the absolute values at the bottom of column four. In column five, record the absolute difference between the team's ranking and the managers' ranking, and sum these absolute numbers at the bottom. A class discussion of the role of politics in organizational decisions will follow.

Sources: R. L. Daft, K. D. Skivington, and M. P. Sharfman, *Cases and Applications: Organizational Theory* (St. Paul, Minn.: West, 1987), pp. 303–05; idea originally suggested by Don Hellreigel. Scoring sheet is based on J. Gandz and V. V. Murray, "The Experience of Workplace Politics," *Academy of Management Journal* 23 (1980), pp. 237–51.

Scoring Sheet

Decisions	1 Individual Ranking	2 Team Ranking	3 Managers' Ranking	4 Absolute Difference between Columns 1 and 3	5 Absolute Difference between Columns 2 and 3
Management promotions and transfers					
Entry-level hiring					
Amount of pay					
Annual budgets					
Allocation of facilities, equipment, offices					
Delegation of authority among managers					
Interdepartmental coordination					
Specification of personnel policies					
Penalties for disciplinary infractions					
Performance appraisals					
Grievances and complaints					

	Team Number						
	1	2	3	4	5	6	7
Team scores							
Lowest individual score on each team							

13

Organizational Conflict, Negotiation, and Justice

LEARNING OBJECTIVES

After reading this chapter, you should be able to:

Describe
The conflict cycle.

Discuss
The beneficial and dysfunctional consequences of conflict.

Identify
The sources of conflict.

Outline
The five interpersonal styles of conflict management.

Summarize
The structural approaches to managing conflict.

Describe
The characteristics of an effective negotiator.

Identify
The elements of effective third-party conflict-resolution procedures.

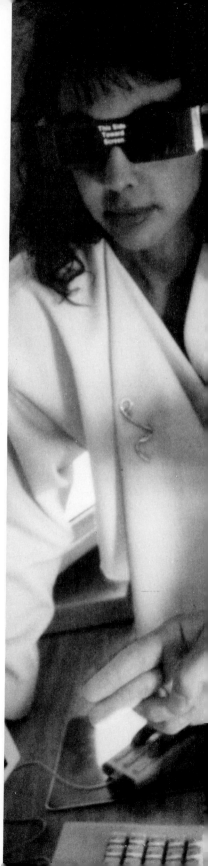

Cardinal River Coals Ltd.

Cardinal River Coals Ltd. was a hotbed of conflict in the early 1980s. The Hinton, Alberta, coal mine had lost 342 days to work stoppages over the previous eight years and was plagued by an exceptionally high number of grievances and injuries. At one time, both union and management officials considered this friction to be normal. "As managers we thought we were doing a good job," says assistant mine manager Ron Stard. "We were breaking production records everywhere—when we weren't on strike."

But the conflict continued to escalate. Local 1656 of the United Mine Workers of America, which represents Cardinal River's employees, began paying members $5 apiece for the grievances they filed. Supervisors frequently abused the four-step progressive discipline system by handing out the verbal and written warnings, suspension notice, and the pink slip all at one time! This hostility spilled over to the small community of Hinton, where everyone from the firm was labelled as either "company" or "union." There were incidents where foremen would cross the street just to avoid walking by a shop steward. A warehouse worker invited to attend a retirement party for a manager was asked to leave her shop steward husband at home.

In November 1982 the company fired two union stewards, so the union announced that its members would go on strike within 14 hours. Union and management officials used this time to resolve the dispute and were so successful that they agreed to settle several other long-standing grievances. Both parties enjoyed this rare cooperation, but how could they improve labour–management relations in the long term?

The solution came in the form of relations by objectives (RBO), a process of improving relations by identifying common objectives and then looking for ways to effectively implement those goals. Union and management officials at Cardinal River Coals agreed to introduce RBO with the assistance of John Poplar, an experienced RBO mediator. Poplar began the process in late 1983 by conducting a retreat attended by over 90 union and management representatives. Throughout the four-day meeting, participants were asked to discuss their perceptions of each other, analyze their conflict, and agree upon strategies to overcome these problems. "It was almost like a religious experience," recalls one union official.

The results of RBO surprised both union and management representatives. The number of grievances has fallen from 140 in 1982 to only a handful in 1991. The union membership has endorsed three collective agreements without a strike, the latest of which was signed two months before the previous one had expired. The worldwide demand for coal dropped substantially during the late 1980s, yet thanks to labour–management cooperation, Cardinal River coal is now highly rated by Japanese steel producers and the company operates at record capacity with one-half of the previous work force. These productive gains have extended the life of the mine and increased job security.[1]

The opening story is about relations between union and management, but conflict occurs every day between individuals, work units, and organizations of all types. As in the Cardinal River story, conflicting parties often feel an antagonism toward each other that can escalate into serious conflict episodes. The parties might develop negative stereotypes of each other, further reinforcing a competitive orientation toward resolving their differences. Cardinal River's experience has a happy ending because the participants applied a conflict-resolution strategy that was effective under those circumstances. We will describe relations by objectives and other conflict management practices later in this chapter.

This chapter begins by defining conflict, describing the conflict cycle, and discussing the consequences and sources of conflict in organizational settings. Five conflict-management styles are described next, followed by a discussion of the structural approaches to conflict management. The last two sections of this chapter introduce two important types of procedures for resolving conflict: negotiation and third-party resolution.

WHAT IS CONFLICT?

Conflict exists when people believe that others have deliberately blocked, or are about to block, their goals or activities.[2] Conflict may occur when one party obstructs another's efforts in some way, but it also exists when this intervention is anticipated. Thus, conflict may be an act or intention to block another party's goals. Conflict is ultimately based on perceptions, so it is also possible to have conflict whenever one party *believes* that another might obstruct its efforts, whether or not this situation actually exists.

Conflict can be found within people, between people, between work units, and between organizations. *Intra-role conflict* exists within the person, such as when employees have job duties that conflict with their personal values or they receive contradictory orders from different superiors. Intrapersonal conflict was discussed in Chapter 5 in the context of role-related stress, so this chapter will mainly examine conflict between individuals, work units, and organizations.

conflict
Any situation where someone believes that others have deliberately blocked, or are about to block, their goals or activities.

The Conflict Cycle

Conflict should be viewed as a dynamic, interactive cycle rather than as a static event. *Conflict episodes*—the interactions between employees with differing interests—only represent the observable tip of the proverbial iceberg.[3] Conflict episodes are preceded by perceptions and attitudes and, in turn, influence subsequent perceptions and attitudes between the parties. Thus, conflict is a cyclical process. Depending on the content and nature of this reciprocal communication, conflict may further escalate or defuse.[4]

Exhibit 13–1 illustrates the cyclical nature of conflict. Conflict begins only when one or more people involved perceive that a conflict exists.[5] Specifically, based on various information cues, they develop a belief that the other party has opposing interests and may interfere with their personal goal attainment. Conflict might exist even where the parties have no likelihood or intention of interfering with each other. Conversely, outsiders may see potential conflict between two parties, but conflict does not actually occur because the parties are unaware of their opposing interests.

The conflict cycle follows the attitude–behaviour model described in Chapter 8. Conflict perceptions are a set of beliefs that evoke an emotional response in the form of attitudes toward the opponent and his or her actions. These attitudes are transformed into behavioural intentions and ultimately into actions toward the other party. Attitudes toward the opponent and

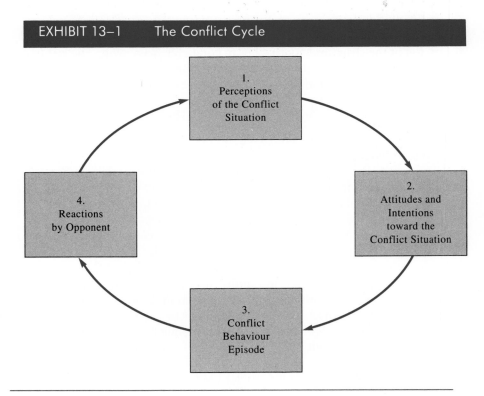

EXHIBIT 13–1   The Conflict Cycle

1. Perceptions of the Conflict Situation

2. Attitudes and Intentions toward the Conflict Situation

3. Conflict Behaviour Episode

4. Reactions by Opponent

Sources: Based on L. R. Pondy, ''Organizational Conflict: Concepts and Models,'' *Administrative Science Quarterly* 12 (1967), pp. 296–320; and K. W. Thomas, ''Conflict and Negotiation Processes in Organizations,'' in M. D. Dunnette (ed.), *Handbook of Industrial/Organizational Psychology,* 2nd ed. (Palo Alto, Calif.: Consulting Psychologists Press, in press).

conflict situation are therefore important because they influence the nature of the conflict episode and, in particular, the styles and strategies used by each participant to manage the conflict situation. The conflict episode influences each party's perceptions and attitudes toward the situation as well as their subsequent actions in the conflict situation. These actions, in turn, affect subsequent perceptions of the situation.

CONSEQUENCES OF ORGANIZATIONAL CONFLICT

Managers spend more than 20 percent of every working day in some form of conflict-management activity.[6] Most often, they try to *suppress* rather than effectively *manage* conflict. These actions reflect the traditional notion that conflict is inherently bad for organizations and should be avoided at all costs. A more appropriate perspective is that conflict has positive as well as negative outcomes and that managers must determine the best way to maximize its benefits and minimize the dysfunctional consequences.[7] Similarly, **conflict management** should be defined as interventions designed to alter the level and form of conflict such that organizational effectiveness is optimized. It is not simply a matter of suppressing, ignoring, or avoiding conflict, although these options are occasionally appropriate.[8]

conflict management
Any intervention that alters the level and form of conflict such that organizational effectiveness is optimized.

Potential Benefits of Conflict

As shown in Exhibit 13–2, conflict potentially improves decision making and team dynamics. Conflict improves many aspects of the decision-making process,[9] and conflict episodes are typically symptoms of underlying problems

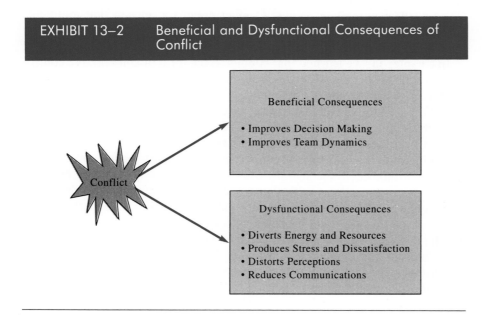

EXHIBIT 13–2   Beneficial and Dysfunctional Consequences of Conflict

Conflict

Beneficial Consequences
- Improves Decision Making
- Improves Team Dynamics

Dysfunctional Consequences
- Diverts Energy and Resources
- Produces Stress and Dissatisfaction
- Distorts Perceptions
- Reduces Communications

In the late 1970s, James O'Toole, a management professor at the University of Southern California, was invited to address 30 Federal Express managers on the topic of productivity. O'Toole had gotten no more than 10 minutes into his talk when a young manager interrupted by saying, "Professor O'Toole has made an interesting point about planning that runs counter to a major decision top management made a couple of weeks ago. I suggest we ought to reexamine that decision now in light of what we have just learned."

To O'Toole's amazement, the managers picked up the suggestion and turned directly to a no-holds-barred debate. What was surprising was that the lower-level managers made the top managers defend their decision. When it was clear they couldn't defend it, the younger managers asked the bosses to change it—which they did, then and there.

This rough-and-tumble exchange lasted for about an hour. At the end of that time, they all got up to lunch without a trace of hard feelings, or a sign that anyone had won or lost face, power, or status. O'Toole was sure that this openness and willingness to raise tough questions and challenge accepted wisdom was normal at Federal Express because he was the only one in the room who found the exchange unusual. In fact, O'Toole had never seen such a healthy debate in any organization. If Federal Express could retain this ability to learn and change, it was a good bet that they would continue to be a remarkable success.

The only bad news was that Professor O'Toole didn't get the opportunity to finish his speech . . . and they forgot to pay him!

Source: Based on J. O'Toole, *Vanguard Management* (New York: Berkley Books, 1985), pp. 290–91.

that must be addressed by the organization.[10] For example, employee complaints may suggest that a company policy needs to be changed to more closely reflect prevailing values. Conflict creates a tension that motivates decision makers to recognize the problem, search for solutions, and thereby relieve the tension.[11]

In Chapter 11, we learned that conflict in the form of constructive controversy energizes people to debate issues and evaluate alternatives more thoroughly.[12] As we can see in Perspective 13–1, constructive controversy challenges the team's dominant preferences and avoids the problem of groupthink by evaluating solution alternatives more critically. In this way, conflict becomes a catalyst for change and improved decision making.

Conflict between work units can strengthen team dynamics and task orientation within each social unit. Similarly, when conflict exists between organizations, employees within each firm tend to strengthen their linkages. Team cohesiveness increases when members experience conflict with an external source because this conflict is viewed as a threat or challenge, which rallies members around the team and its activities. The team becomes more important to individual members and they are more willing to abide by prescribed roles to overcome the threat. Conflict also increases the salience and importance of the team's goals. Under conditions of moderate conflict, this motivates team members to work more efficiently toward these goals, thereby increasing the team's productivity. As one writer explains, ''More organizations are dying from complacency and apathy than are dying from an overabundance of conflict.''[13]

Dysfunctional Consequences of Conflict

There is, of course, a darker side to conflict in organizations. When managed poorly, conflict draws attention away from the task and diverts energy and resources toward nonproductive activities (see Exhibit 13–2). It provokes organizational politics, as described in Chapter 12, by motivating people to attack or undermine the activities of their adversaries. These aggressive responses further escalate the conflict and make it more difficult to return to normal work patterns. The conflicting parties may even set aside their organizational responsibilities and focus on defeating the adversary.[14] This often results in frustration, job dissatisfaction, and stress. Unbridled conflict may cause employees to escape from the situation through turnover or absenteeism.

Another potential problem is that conflict episodes generate negative stereotypes and emotions toward the other party that further amplify differences while causing each side to overlook their similarities and common interests. This perceptual process reduces the motivation for the parties to communicate with each other, which makes it more difficult for them to discover common ground and ultimately resolve the conflict.[15]

Mismanaged conflict can be costly to organizations as well as the individuals involved. In their analysis of conflict episodes at a Canadian engineering firm, Janz and Tjosvold learned that conflict caused employees to ignore advice, avoid communicating with some coworkers, and let design flaws remain to make others look incompetent. Overall, the researchers estimated that dysfunctional conflict cost the company $12,000 a year per employee in time and materials, and $30,000 if project days lost are taken into account.[16]

SOURCES OF CONFLICT IN ORGANIZATIONS

What are the sources of conflict between people, work units, and organizations? We often hear people say that two people have personality conflicts, but this explains relatively few disputes.[17] Even where the personalities of two people are incompatible, specific situational conditions must exist before conflict is likely to occur. Exhibit 13–3 lists six conditions that increase the likelihood of conflict. Of these, only differentiation might be labelled a characteristic of the person; the others are conditions of the job or work environment.

Goal Incompatibility

The operative goals of an individual or work team may be in conflict with the goals emphasized by others in the organization. The production department strives for cost efficiency by scheduling long production runs, whereas the

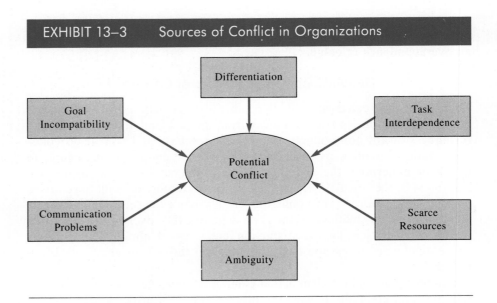

EXHIBIT 13–3   Sources of Conflict in Organizations

marketing team emphasizes customer service by delivering the client's product as quickly as possible. If the company runs out of a particular product line, the production team would prefer to have clients wait until the next production run. This infuriates sales representatives who would rather change production as quickly as possible to satisfy consumer demand.[18]

Incompatible goals are further reinforced by unique performance criteria and reward systems.[19] The production team might receive performance bonuses based on production efficiency, while the sales team's bonus might be determined from sales volume. This strengthens each unit's dedication to their own objectives and further entrenches the conflict between them.

Differentiation

Le Château, the Montreal-based clothing manufacturer and retailer, recently faced a period of rapid growth, so company president Herschel Segal decided to pump the upper echelons with new managers from larger corporations. Unfortunately, the new managers clashed with executives who had been with the company for some time. "We ended up with an old team and a new team and they weren't on the same wavelength," explains Segal.[20]

Le Château's experience represents a relatively common source of organizational conflict where people hold significantly different beliefs and attitudes due to their unique backgrounds, experiences, or training. Le Château experienced conflict because its newly hired managers had radically different experiences working in large firms and, consequently, held different beliefs than the long-term managers about how the company should expand its operations.

Similar problems occur between line and staff specialists because of their unique training and experiences. By remaining in narrow career paths, these people learn to see problems in a particular way and have difficulty understanding other perspectives. Organizations institutionalize this differentiation by hiring people for their technical knowledge and encouraging them to become even more specialized through narrow career paths. Task specialization, which results from the division of labour (see Chapter 5), may help the organization become more efficient, but it also increases potential conflict through differentiation.

Conflict and Cultural Diversity.   Racial, gender, and cultural diversity are now common in most Canadian companies. Organizations have much to gain from a multicultural work force, particularly in terms of creative decision making, but an increasingly diverse work force also requires more effort to manage potential conflict resulting from this type of differentiation. In particular, communication problems are more common in ethnically diverse work teams. Minorities are often excluded from key organizational information and are less willing to disclose their own ideas and opinions to others.[21] These conditions often cause employees from diverse backgrounds to become suspicious and create negative stereotypes of each other.

Task Interdependence

Task interdependence exists when employees and work teams share common inputs to their tasks or directly depend on others for materials, assistance, or information.[22] As a general rule, potential conflict increases with the level of task interdependence. This occurs because highly interdependent work units require better coordination, communication, and mutual adjustment to maintain work performance. As the level of task interdependence increases, there is a greater risk that one team will disrupt or interfere with the performance of another team.[23]

As depicted in Exhibit 13–4, there are three fundamental levels of task interdependence.[24] **Pooled interdependence** is the weakest form of interdependence (other than independence), whereby work units operate independently except for reliance on a common resource or authority. The division of Noma Industries Ltd. that manufactures Christmas tree lights has pooled interdependence with the electric lawn mower division because they share Noma's common financial resources.

Conflict is more likely to occur under conditions of **sequential interdependence,** where the output of one person or unit becomes the direct input for another person or unit. This interdependent linkage is found in manufacturing operations where the final assembly team is dependent on subassembly teams to maintain quality parts and sufficient inventory.

The highest level of interdependence is **reciprocal interdependence,** in which work output is exchanged back and forth among individuals or work units. This relationship exists between bus drivers and maintenance crews in

pooled interdependence
The lowest level of interdependence whereby individuals or work units operate independently except for reliance on a common resource or authority.

sequential interdependence
A moderate level of interdependence whereby the output of one person or unit becomes the direct input for another person or unit.

reciprocal interdependence
The highest level of interdependence whereby work output is exchanged back and forth among individuals or work units.

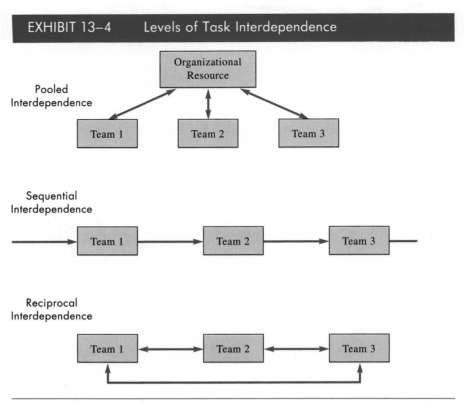

EXHIBIT 13–4   Levels of Task Interdependence

Pooled Interdependence

Organizational Resource

Team 1   Team 2   Team 3

Sequential Interdependence

Team 1 → Team 2 → Team 3

Reciprocal Interdependence

Team 1 ↔ Team 2 ↔ Team 3

Source: Based on J. D. Thompson, *Organizations in Action* (New York: McGraw-Hill, 1967), pp. 54–56.

virtually every Canadian transit authority. Drivers are dependent on the maintenance crews to keep the buses in good repair, while the maintenance crews are dependent on the drivers to operate the vehicles wisely so that their work is minimized.

Scarce Resources

We have explained that work units experience the lowest form of interdependence when their only linkage is sharing a common pool of resources, such as physical space, operating budgets, and centralized services. But even this situation might produce conflict when the shared resources are in short supply.[25] Basically, employees and work units tend to compete with each other when resources are insufficient for everyone to fulfill their objectives. This is particularly true when the resource pool is physically indivisible, such as when two departments must share one photocopier. It may be possible to divide up this precious resource through time sharing, but physically splitting the machine in half would not have the desired effect.

Ambiguity

Conflict is more likely to arise when roles, objectives, and jurisdictions are ambiguous. Under these conditions, work activities lack coordination and one team may end up doing things that are contrary to the goals and expectations of the other party. In contrast, the existence of clearly defined rules, procedures, and decision criteria prevent conflict (except over forming these rules) because resources are allocated through programmed decision making and the rules serve as a definitive source of legitimate power before disputes can begin.

Conflicts are particularly common in organizational settings where the boundaries of authority are unclear. Consider the situation where the business and economics departments at a university share responsibility for the same course offering. Disputes arise over who controls the curriculum, whose faculty should teach the course, and who controls the assignment of teaching assistants to this course. The departments have their own sets of goals and conflict is likely to occur over some of these issues until programmed decision rules can be agreed upon.

Communication Problems

The extent to which conflict escalates or is averted often depends on how well the parties communicate to each other. Task interdependence requires efficient and rich transmission of information to coordinate work activities with minimal disruption. When communication is limited, errors are more likely to occur and each party becomes a liability to the other in the quest to achieve team goals.

Communication problems are more common when employees have diverse backgrounds, training, and life experiences. These sources of differentiation tend to limit communication, so the parties resort to negative stereotypes to fill in missing information and reinforce their own distinct identities. This problem occurred at the Children's Television Workshop (CTW), producers of *Sesame Street*. When CTW decided to go into product licensing, management faced the difficult task of getting the creative production staff to work with the business types in the organization. When the business specialists talked about the "bottom line," the production staff interpreted this as "no quality," further reinforcing their negative stereotype of the people in the pinstriped suits. Similarly, the business types quickly concluded that the production people were "flaky artists." It required some intensive discussions and clarifications before the parties developed a better understanding and respect for each other.[26]

Finally, communication plays an important role in the conflict cycle. When one party communicates its disagreement in an arrogant way, opponents are more likely to heighten their perception of the conflict. Arrogant behaviour also sends a message that the party intends to be competitive rather than cooperative. This may lead the other to reciprocate with a similar conflict management style.[27] People with high authoritarianism and dogmatism are particularly likely to increase conflict by virtue of the way they behave toward others.

INTERPERSONAL APPROACHES TO CONFLICT MANAGEMENT

There are basically five interpersonal styles of approaching the other party in a conflict situation. As we see in Exhibit 13–5, each approach can be placed in a two-dimensional grid reflecting the person's motivation to satisfy his or her own interests (called *assertiveness*) and to satisfy the other party's interests (called *cooperativeness*).[28]

* *Avoiding*—Trying to smooth over or avoid conflict situations altogether.
* *Competing*—Trying to win the conflict at the other's expense based on the belief that one party's gain will necessarily be the other party's loss.
* *Accommodating*—Complete cooperation with little or no attention to one's own interests. At the extreme, accommodating means giving in completely to the other party's wishes.

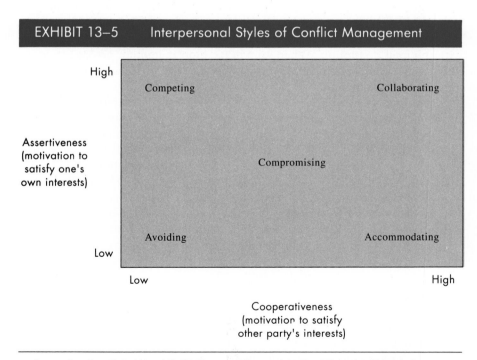

EXHIBIT 13–5   Interpersonal Styles of Conflict Management

Source: Based on T. Ruble and K. W. Thomas, "Support for a Two-Dimensional Model of Conflict Behavior," *Organizational Behavior and Human Performance* 16 (1976), p. 145.

- *Compromising*—Reaching a middle ground through bargaining in which one party is willing to give up something to get something else.
- *Collaborating*—Combines the maximum levels of assertiveness and cooperativeness and involves sincere efforts to resolve the conflict through problem solving.

Individuals tend to prefer one conflict management style over another because it is compatible with their personality or has been used successfully in the past. Cultural background is another important determinant of the style used to resolve conflict.[29] For example, Russians tend to adopt a competing orientation more than Canadians. However, the best interpersonal style depends on specific conditions.[30]

Avoiding may be appropriate where the issue is trivial to everyone affected, the problem will be resolved in the near future through structural changes, or any action style other than avoidance could trigger further escalation of the conflict. It is most effective as a temporary tactic to cool down heated disputes. However, avoiding persistent conflict situations for too long can frustrate others. Competing may be necessary where the person knows that he or she is correct, the dispute requires a quick solution, and the other party would likely take advantage of more cooperative strategies. However, organizational relationships are rarely in complete opposition, so a competing style is difficult to justify.

Accommodating may be appropriate when your original position is wrong, the other party has substantially more power, or the issue is not as important to you as to the other party. Compromise may be effective under win–lose conditions where both parties have equal power and are under time pressure to settle their differences. However, this style often results in an unsettling half-way resolution for both parties. Finally, collaborating offers the best possible outcomes when both sides have a high level of trust and openness and it is possible to find a mutually beneficial solution to the dispute.

Distributive and Integrative Orientations

The five conflict management styles reflect either a distributive or integrative orientation. Collaboration is the only style that represents a purely **integrative orientation** because the person or team believes that through cooperation the parties will find a mutually beneficial solution. This is also known as a *win–win orientation,* because it takes the view that the resources at stake are expandable rather than fixed if the parties work together to find a creative solution to their problem. Previous research has confirmed that collaboration is desirable in most organizational situations.[31] Collaboration is more likely than competition to result in higher productivity, especially for problem solving and related tasks.[32]

integrative orientation
The view that the resources at stake are expandable rather than fixed if the parties work together to find a creative solution to their problem; also known as a win-win orientation.

distributive orientation
The view that the parties are drawing from a fixed pie and the amount received by one is therefore inversely proportional to the amount received by the other; also known as a win-lose orientation.

The other four conflict management styles reflect a distributive orientation.[33] A **distributive orientation** is the view that the parties are drawing from a fixed pie and the amount received by one opponent is therefore inversely proportional to the amount received by the other.[34] This is also known as a *win–lose orientation,* because the dominant perception is that one party will lose if the other wins.

A distributive orientation may occasionally be appropriate, but most organizational relationships rarely involve completely opposing interests. Rather, the typical situation involves *mixed motives*—the parties have both distributive and integrative components. Even in relations between organizations, leaders are learning that collaboration is possible and desirable under some circumstances. Japanese manufacturers have known this for some time and have collaborated on the development of several new technologies in recent years. The competing style has the strongest distributive orientation and typically creates dysfunctional outcomes in contemporary organizations. There is a high motivation to win, so conflict episodes, misused energy, and reliance on political tactics are common. We will return to the topic of distributive and integrative orientations in our discussion of negotiation behaviour.

STRUCTURAL APPROACHES TO CONFLICT MANAGEMENT

The conflict-management styles described above focus on how to approach the other party in a conflict situation, but another perspective is to alter the conditions that produce potential conflict. The structural changes shown in Exhibit 13–6 operate on the fundamental causes of conflict and can be used either to increase or decrease the level of conflict or potential conflict. We will first discuss these strategies in terms of reducing conflict and later point out ways to stimulate conflict through structural changes.

Emphasizing Superordinate Goals

superordinate goals
Common goals—such as organizational objectives—held by conflicting parties that are more important than the subordinate goals over which the groups differ.

Employees may have incompatible departmental goals, but they invariably have common organizational interests, called **superordinate goals.** Examples of superordinate goals include warding off competing businesses or providing better customer service. In their daily activities, employees often lose sight of these common goals and focus instead on incompatible departmental and individual goals. By emphasizing superordinate goals, incompatible departmental goals become less important and conflict is reduced.[35] For example, one Canadian organization was able to end a long-standing feud between its production and engineering units by sending representatives from both teams to meet directly with clients. Through these visits, the superordinate goal of satisfying client needs was rekindled and both teams became more aware of how they needed to cooperate with each other to achieve this goal.

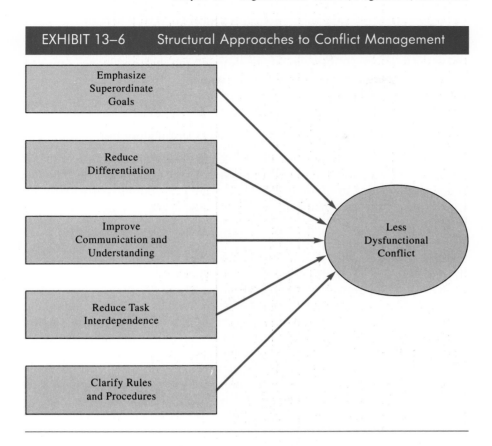

EXHIBIT 13–6   Structural Approaches to Conflict Management

A related method is to increase employee awareness of interorganizational conflicts, such as the threat of losing market share to new competitors. By communicating these organizational challenges, organizational survival and related superordinate goals overshadow narrower intergroup differences. Finally, superordinate goals can be emphasized through the reward system. By introducing rewards based on team rather than individual performance, employees are more likely to give superordinate goals a higher priority over individual task objectives, thereby increasing cooperation and resource sharing.

Reducing Differentiation

A logical strategy for minimizing differentiation is to encourage a generalist rather than specialist career orientation. This may be at odds with traditional concepts of work efficiency (e.g., division of labour), but Japanese firms often move employees around to different jobs, departments, and regions so that they acquire a broader knowledge to serve clients more holistically and learn to appreciate different perspectives of the business.[36] Along the same idea, IBM, 3M, and a few other North American firms rotate line personnel temporarily into staff departments (personnel, purchasing, finance, etc.) to ensure that line and staff people work cooperatively and develop a better understanding of each other's needs.[37]

Improving Communication and Understanding

Several strategies exist to help individuals and work teams develop or maintain more accurate perceptions of each other. These activities draw upon the concepts described in Chapter 7 on improving perceptions, particularly by empathizing with the other party and increasing the open area in the Johari Window.

Social Activities.   One way to reduce negative stereotypes and misconceptions of others is to create opportunities for interaction, particularly through sports and other nonwork activities. Canadian Hunter Explorations Ltd. has been able to minimize dysfunctional conflict among its geologists, petroleum engineers, and other specialists by increasing their interaction in various activities. John Masters, president of Canadian Hunter, explains this strategy: "We expand the horizons of our engineers and geologists by constant association, by osmosis. We have lunch meetings, management meetings, social occasions. We provide the environment for them to rub together, then let nature take its course. Suddenly an engineer starts to think like a geologist and vice versa."[38]

Special Meetings.   A more direct approach is to bring the conflicting parties together for the sole purpose of threshing out their differences. For example, the Children's Television Network (described earlier) was able to correct perceptions between its production and business managers by holding weekly show-and-tell sessions that resulted in a better understanding and empathy. Both sides soon realized that they had common interests and that their extreme stereotypes of each other were inappropriate. As we describe in Perspective 13–2, Ace Toyama, president of Nissan Canada Inc., recently followed a similar strategy to improve relations between his Canadian and Japanese staff members.

intergroup laboratory
A structured conflict management intervention in which the parties discuss their differences and decide ways to improve the relationship.

Intergroup Laboratories.   When relations between two or more work teams are openly hostile, it may be advisable to bring the parties together under controlled conditions with the assistance of a third-party facilitator.[39] Exhibit 13–7 outlines the basic elements of an **intergroup laboratory** (also called a *confrontational meeting*), which is conducted by trained consultants over two or three days at an off-site location. The basic objective is for the

PERSPECTIVE 13–2   Reducing Conflict through Dialogue

Soon after Ace Toyama became president of Nissan Canada Inc., he noticed that the employees were divided into two camps—the Canadians who distributed and sold vehicles, and the Japanese executives who received privileged information and devised new corporate strategy. The conflict was not obvious at first, but Toyama observed that the Canadians were reluctant to hand information over to the Japanese managers on what used to be their private fiefdom. Meanwhile, the Japanese managers kept to themselves and limited their communication with the Canadians. All around, there seemed to be a lack of trust between the two factions.

This was an unacceptable situation for Toyama because he needed to build the Canadians and Japanese into an integrated management team. His first step was to give the Canadians the same information that was formerly for Japanese eyes only, including profitability data and new product plans. This made the Canadians feel more like their Japanese counterparts. It wasn't long after that the Canadians volunteered more of their information to the Japanese strategists.

Toyama's next step was to unblock perceptual differences between the Canadian and Japanese managers by introducing free-for-alls where sacred cows were openly discussed. Members of either faction could throw out any questions they wanted to ask the others. The sessions have led to more harmony and interaction for everybody. For example, at one session a Canadian blurted out, "Why do you guys never eat lunch with us?" A Japanese director replied, "It is so hard for me to speak English all day. The only break I get is lunch." This revelation had not occurred to the Canadians. They had previously felt slighted by the fact that the Japanese managers ate together and never expressed an interest to join the Canadians for a meal. By opening the lines of communication, these misunderstandings were removed and the Canadians and Japanese managers developed a stronger working relationship.

Source: Based on W. Trueman, "CEO Isolation and How to Fight It," *Canadian Business*, July 1991, pp. 28–32.

conflicting groups to discuss their differences and decide ways to improve the relationship. However, this can only be accomplished by first restructuring each party's perceptions and attitudes toward each other. Therefore, a unique feature of this intervention is for both sides to share their images of themselves and each other to discover distortions and misunderstandings. Intergroup laboratories have been used to improve relations between union and management, headquarters and field employees, and line and staff employees.

Relations by Objectives.   **Relations by objectives (RBO)** is a form of intergroup laboratory that was first introduced in the 1970s by government mediation services in Canada and the United States to improve union–management relations. RBO has the added feature of emphasizing goal setting so that the parties are able to resolve their differences in a specific and timely fashion. For instance, the RBO sessions at Cardinal River Coals (described at the beginning of this chapter) resulted in 16 specific goals and action plans,

relations by objectives
A form of intergroup laboratory designed to improve labour-management relations.

EXHIBIT 13–7   Elements of an Intergroup Confrontational Meeting

Step	Description
1. List issues requiring joint problem solving.	Participants jointly identify and prioritize the issues and relationship problems that should be debated.
2. Prepare team self-images and images of the other team.	Each side meets separately to list on flip charts (1) its perceptions of itself, (2) how the other team perceives it, and (3) its perceptions of the other team. These images provide the existing perceptions, attitudes, and difficulties that need to be examined and overcome.
3. Exchange images.	The teams meet to discuss and compare these images of themselves. The participants jointly review the relationship problems listed in step 1 in light of these image presentations.
4. Discuss functional problems in light of image presentations.	Mixed teams are formed, preferably made up of people with similar duties on each side, to discuss their differences in light of the revealed images. This provides an opportunity to reevaluate previous misconceptions in work activities.
5. Review and plan.	Participants meet to prepare a unified list of the problems they had identified and defined. Specific actions required to bring about desired changes are discussed.
6. Follow up.	Teams agree upon ways to follow up the strategies discussed at the meeting. This typically includes a future meeting that reviews and evaluates progress.

Source: Based on R. Blake, H. A. Shepard, and J. S. Mouton, *Managing Intergroup Conflict in Industry* (Houston: Gulf Publishing, 1964), pp. 114–21.

which were monitored and refined at subsequent sessions. According to one recent study of 48 RBO interventions in Canada, most union–management relationships have benefited from this process.[40] However, intergroup laboratories and RBO are effective only when the parties have a long-term relationship, are motivated to improve their relationship, and focus on general relationships rather than specific issues.[41]

Reducing Task Interdependence

Conflict occurs when people are dependent on each other, so another way to minimize dysfunctional conflict is to reduce the level of interdependence between the parties.

Create Buffers.   Where task interdependencies are sequential or reciprocal, conflict can be reduced by introducing buffers to loosen the relationship. This is often accomplished by building up inventories so that one work unit is not immediately dependent on another for receiving its input. There is, of course, a cost to this because inventories represent idle capital and increase production costs. Still, building up inventories may be essential in some situations to create a buffer that reduces the risk of costly disputes between interdependent work units.

Use Integrators.   **Integrators** are employees who coordinate the activities of differentiated work units toward the completion of a common task.[42] For example, an individual might be responsible for coordinating the efforts of the research, production, advertising, and marketing departments in launching a new product line. In some respects, integrators are human buffers. They reduce the direct interaction among work units with diverse goals and perspectives. Integrators rarely have direct authority over the departments they integrate, so they must rely on referent power and persuasion to manage conflict and accomplish the work. Integrators need to work effectively with each unit, so they must possess sufficient knowledge of each area.

integrator
An employee who coordinates the activities of differentiated work units toward the completion of a common task.

Duplicate Resources.   A deceptively simple way to reduce task interdependence is to duplicate and divide the shared resource so that each unit has its own. Rather than increasing the size of the pool that two people or work units share, it may eventually be possible to divide the resource so that each unit has control of its own. We have to worry about cost effectiveness, but this strategy may be feasible where the organization needs to expand to meet increasing demand for its products or services.

Combine Jobs.   Combining jobs is both a form of job enrichment and a way to reduce task interdependence. Consider a toaster assembly system where one person inserts the heating element, another adds the sides, and so on. By combining these tasks so that each person assembles an entire toaster, the employees now have a pooled rather than sequential form of task interdependence and the likelihood of dysfunctional conflict is reduced.

Clarifying Rules and Procedures

Conflicts that are caused by scarce resources and ambiguous allocation of those resources may be solved directly by establishing rules and procedures. If two departments are fighting over the use of a new laboratory, a schedule might be established that allocates the lab exclusively to each team at certain times of the day or week. In some respects, the schedule reduces resource interdependence by dividing it up among those who need it to fulfill their goals. It also reduces the need for direct contact between the parties, thereby minimizing the likelihood of episodes that might further escalate the conflict.

STIMULATING CONFLICT

We previously explained that conflict management involves either decreasing or increasing the amount of conflict between the parties. Most of the strategies described in the previous section can be reversed to stimulate conflict.[43] Some specific conflict stimulation actions include the following:

- *Increase resource scarcity*—Limit the availability of resources that individuals and work teams must share.
- *Increase task interdependence*—Centralize resources so that they form a common pool shared by several people or work units; introduce just-in-time inventory systems and reciprocal work flows.
- *Increase ambiguity*—Use ambiguous criteria to allocate important organizational resources.
- *Introduce devil's advocacy*—As described in Chapter 11, forcing some members of a homogeneous team to take an opposing position on a decision can help everyone take a second look at the issue more critically, thereby encouraging constructive controversy.
- *Build heterogeneous teams*—Bringing together people with different backgrounds and experiences increases conflict in decision making, but when managed properly can also result in more creative decisions.
- *Emphasize and reward departmental goals*—Conflict tends to increase when employees concentrate on goals within their own work unit and are rewarded for doing so.

RESOLVING CONFLICT THROUGH NEGOTIATION

negotiations
Deliberate attempts by conflicting parties to directly resolve their differences by defining or redefining the terms of their interdependence.

Negotiations are deliberate attempts by conflicting parties to directly resolve their differences by defining or redefining the terms of their interdependence.[44] Formal and informal negotiations can be found in most organizational activities. Employees negotiate with their supervisors over next month's work assignments; suppliers negotiate with purchasing managers over the sale and delivery schedules of their product; union and management representatives negotiate over wages and other changes to the collective agreement.

Some writers suggest that negotiations are more successful when the parties adopt an integrative orientation, while others caution that a distributive frame of mind is appropriate in most cases.[45] The dilemma is that the parties tend to reach a mutually satisfactory solution when they understand each other's needs. Yet information is power, so information sharing gives the other party more power to leverage a better deal if the opportunity occurs. Skilled negotiators often adopt a *cautiously* integrative orientation at the outset by sharing information slowly and determining whether the other side will reciprocate. They adapt a more distributive orientation only when it becomes apparent that an integrative solution is not possible or the other party is unwilling to use a collaborative style.

Bargaining Zone Model of Negotiations

We can look at the negotiation process in terms of each party's movement within a bargaining zone.[46] Exhibit 13–8 displays one possible bargaining zone situation. This linear diagram illustrates a purely distributive relationship—what one party gains the other loses—whereas each party's bargaining range would be perpendicular in more integrative situations. As this model illustrates, the parties typically establish three key negotiating points:

- *Initial offer point*—The team's opening offer to the other party; this may be its best expectation or a pie-in-the-sky starting point.
- *Target point*—The team's realistic goal or expectation for a final agreement.
- *Resistance point*—The point beyond which the team will not make further concessions.

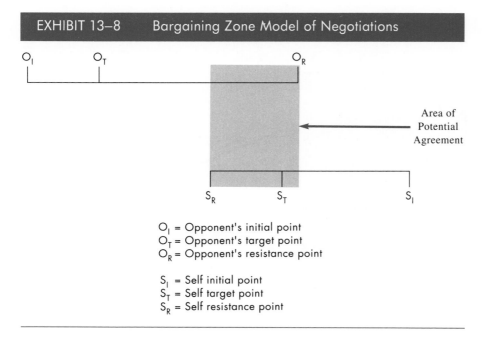

EXHIBIT 13–8	Bargaining Zone Model of Negotiations

O_I = Opponent's initial point
O_T = Opponent's target point
O_R = Opponent's resistance point

S_I = Self initial point
S_T = Self target point
S_R = Self resistance point

The parties begin negotiations by describing their initial offer point for each item on the bargaining agenda. In most cases this is recognized only as a starting point, and both sides will offer concessions. Neither the target nor resistance points are revealed to the other party in distributive situations. However, each side tries to discover the other's resistance point and, if possible, move it closer to its own initial offer point. In purely integrative settings, on the other hand, the objective is to find a creative solution that keeps both parties as close as possible to their initial offer points.

SITUATIONAL INFLUENCES ON NEGOTIATIONS

We cannot cover all of the detailed aspects of negotiations between individuals, teams, and organizations, but Exhibit 13–9 outlines the main features that influence the nature and outcomes of this process. As you can see, negotiations are strongly influenced by negotiator behaviours as well as characteristics of the situation in which the interactions occur. Four of the most important situational factors are location, physical setting, time, and audience.

Location

In sports, home teams usually have an advantage over their opponents. They have the benefit of audience support, a familiar rink or playing field, easier access to resources, and the ability to maintain comfortable routines. Opponents, on the other hand, are weary from travel-related stress and are

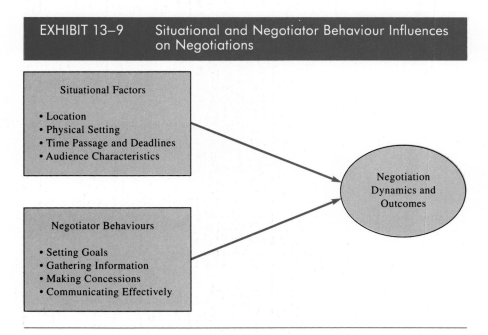

EXHIBIT 13–9   Situational and Negotiator Behaviour Influences on Negotiations

Situational Factors

• Location
• Physical Setting
• Time Passage and Deadlines
• Audience Characteristics

Negotiator Behaviours

• Setting Goals
• Gathering Information
• Making Concessions
• Communicating Effectively

Negotiation Dynamics and Outcomes

dependent on the host for facilities and information. The advantages of holding negotiations on your own turf are similar to being the home team in sports.[47]

Negotiating parties are often careful to choose a neutral site so that neither side is a home team. But skilled negotiators are not averse to using location to their advantage if this tactic does not threaten the level of trust between the parties. For instance, Edgar Kaiser, Jr., former head of the Bank of British Columbia, is known for his fishing trips on Vancouver Island, which are used to corner executives with whom Kaiser wants to negotiate. One executive familiar with Kaiser's tactics explains: "We always start out in two canoes with a guide each. Then halfway up the stream Edgar switches boats, sends the two guides off on their own, and we get down to business."[48] Opponents from Toronto or New York are certainly at a disadvantage negotiating with Kaiser somewhere along the Campbell River in the backwaters of British Columbia!

Physical Setting

In Chapter 6 we noted that the physical arrangement of tables and chairs can affect the nature and quality of communication.[49] These physical arrangements are so important in negotiations that talks between governments have been delayed because the parties could not agree on the shape of the table! In negotiations, people who sit face to face are more likely to develop a we–they perspective and, consequently, a distributive orientation toward the conflict situation. When an integrative or single-team approach is preferred, both parties are encouraged to disperse their representatives around a circular table and meet in an informal setting. Labatts Breweries tried this approach a number of years ago in an attempt to keep negotiations nonadversarial. At one point, they even tried to negotiate without a table to create a single-team perspective.[50] The physical distance between the parties and formality of the setting can also influence the parties' orientation toward each other and the disputed issues.

Time Passage and Deadlines

Time is an important factor in negotiations for two reasons. First, the more time people invest in negotiations, the more committed they are to reaching an agreement. This increases the parties' motivation to resolve the conflict, but it also makes them more vulnerable to unwarranted concessions in an attempt to save the negotiations. Second, time deadlines are an important part of goal setting in negotiations, but they may become a liability when exceeding deadlines is costly.[51] Negotiators make concessions and soften their demands more rapidly as the deadline approaches. This occurs because the deadline rather than the opposing party's strength or skill becomes the primary threat, so making concessions no longer conveys a sign of weakness.

Skilled negotiators use deadlines to their advantage by keeping their own time limits more flexible and less costly than the opponents'. For example, one Brazilian company invited a group of Americans to negotiate a contract the week before Christmas. The Brazilians knew that the Americans would want to return to the United States by Christmas, so they delayed agreement until the last minute to extract more concessions from their visitors. The final agreement definitely favoured the Brazilians.[52] Japanese negotiators have been known to use similar tactics, so visiting negotiators are advised to keep their deadlines flexible (e.g., keep the airline ticket's return date open) or avoid telling the Japanese hosts when the plane will leave![53]

Audience Characteristics

The nature and complexity of negotiations changes when the negotiators' audiences are present rather than absent from the proceedings. Audiences include constituents for whom the parties are negotiating or members of the general public who have a more indirect interest in the results. When an audience is present or has direct surveillance over the proceedings, negotiators are more likely to be competitive than collaborative in order to create a favourable image to their constituents. Under these conditions, the negotiators are less willing to make concessions and more willing to engage in overtly political tactics against the other party in order to save face.[54] Audiences may also be drawn into the negotiations by acting as a source of indirect appeals. The general public often takes on this role when groups negotiate with provincial or federal governments.[55]

NEGOTIATOR BEHAVIOURS

Several behaviours of the parties influence the dynamics and outcomes of the negotiations. Negotiators should, of course, be able to understand the negotiation content, use their judgment wisely, and think under pressure. Some of the other significant factors include setting goals, making concessions, gathering information, and communicating effectively.

Setting Goals

Before beginning deliberations, effective negotiators plan their strategy and establish a set of goals regarding their initial offer, target, and resistance points. The resistance point is particularly important because it becomes the threshold beyond which the parties reach an impasse. Planning and goal setting are so important that some writers refer to effective negotiation as "bargaining by objectives."[56] One survey of business negotiations with the Japanese reported that planning was the factor most responsible for success or failure of negotiations.[57]

Gathering Information

Information is power, so effective negotiators spend more time listening to the other party and asking questions to probe them for details of their position. An effective strategy for listening and understanding the opponent's position is to have several people represent the team at the bargaining table. Ideally, each team member develops an expertise on certain issues and is responsible for listening intently when the negotiators discuss them at the table. Most team members would remain silent except to discuss matters with other members of their own team. This division of labour reduces the chance that important information is overlooked and enables the negotiating team to maintain an expertise on every aspect of the negotiated issues.[58]

Making Concessions

Negotiation is a process of making offers and counteroffers and of making concessions in an attempt to reach a mutually agreeable settlement. Concessions are important in negotiations because they (1) enable the parties to move toward the area of potential agreement, (2) symbolize each party's motivation to bargain in good faith, and (3) tell the other party of the relative importance of the negotiating items.[59] These points suggest that effective negotiators should make concessions. But how many concessions should be offered to the other side? The answer partly depends on the other party's strategy, perceptions, and expectations.[60] For instance, Russian negotiators make few concessions and tend to view the opponent's concessions as a sign of weakness rather than good faith.[61]

Aside from cultural differences, it appears that the best strategy is to be moderately tough and give just enough concessions to communicate sincerity and motivation to resolve the conflict.[62] Being too tough can undermine relations between the parties, particularly when they will enter other negotiations in the future. Giving too many concessions, particularly early in the proceedings, implies weakness and encourages the other party to use power and resistance. Once again, we must emphasize that perceptions of toughness or weakness in concession making vary from one person to the next, particularly across cultures. Overall, negotiators need to carefully read the situation and know when another concession must be given to move the parties toward agreement.

Communicating Effectively

Some writers suggest that effective communication is the essence of good negotiations.[63] Studies on negotiator behaviour report that effective negotiators communicate in a way that maintains effective relationships between the parties. Specifically, they tend to (1) discuss issues rather than people, (2) avoid making irritating statements such as ''I think you'll agree that this

EXHIBIT 13–10   Results of Poor Negotiations

"Actually, no — the negotiations aren't going at all well."

Source: *Financial Times,* May 14, 1990, p. 30. Reprinted by permission of Nick Hobart.

is a generous offer,'' and (3) use effective persuasion tactics by managing the content of their messages. (See Chapter 8 for a discussion of persuasion.)[64] In general, they try to avoid escalating the conflict into the type of situation illustrated in Exhibit 13–10.

THIRD-PARTY CONFLICT RESOLUTION

In negotiations, the disputing parties usually meet directly to resolve the problem by themselves, but this is not always desirable or necessary. For example, negotiating would probably be ineffective where two employees are competing for the same promotion. One problem is that they might not resolve their differences in a timely and peaceful manner. Another concern is that their solution might not be in the organization's best interest. Therefore, formal third-party conflict-resolution systems exist in virtually all organizations. There are many types of third parties, but we will mainly discuss formal procedures where the decision is made by someone other than the disputants.[65]

Distributive versus Procedural Justice

The success of third-party procedures depends on the extent to which they are perceived as fair. One form of fairness, called *distributive justice,* refers to perceived equity in the distribution of resources. The concept of distribu-

| EXHIBIT 13–11 | Six Rules to Maximize Procedural Justice |

Procedural Rule	Description
Consistency rule	Procedure for making resource allocation decisions must be consistent across time and persons.
Bias suppression rule	Personal self-interest and blind allegiance to narrow preconceptions should be prevented.
Accuracy rule	Decisions must be based on as much good information and informed opinion as possible.
Correctability rule	Opportunities must exist to modify (i.e., appeal) decisions.
Representativeness rule	The process must represent the concerns of all important subgroups and individuals.
Ethicality rule	The process must be compatible with prevailing moral and ethical standards.

Source: G. S. Leventhal, "What Should Be Done with Equity Theory?" in K. J. Gergen, M. S. Greenberg, and R. H. Willis (eds.), *Social Exchange: Advances in Theory and Research* (New York: Plenum, 1980), pp. 27–55.

tive justice is closely linked to equity theory, which we introduced in Chapter 3. According to this perspective, third-party decisions must distribute resources in a manner proportional to each party's inputs. Thus, employees with the best performance or the longest seniority should be awarded the highest salary, the preferred vacation schedule, or the nicest office, depending on the resource in dispute.

In addition to being fair in its decision outcomes, a third-party system must be perceived as fair in the process used to arrive at the decision. This is known as **procedural justice**.[66] Exhibit 13–11 summarizes the six principles that lead employees to believe that the decision-making procedure is fair. These principles should be considered in any third-party system.

procedural justice
Perceptions of fairness regarding the process used to decide the exchange and distribution of resources.

Types of Formal Third-Party Complaint Systems

There are many types of third-party conflict-resolution systems for management and nonmanagement staff in Canadian organizations. Labour laws provide unionized employees with well-defined grievance and arbitration systems, but many companies have also introduced third-party procedures for nonunion staff.[67] Some of the more prominent complaint systems are described below.[68]

Hierarchical Process.   A formal hierarchical process of conflict resolution is a form of grievance procedure in which employees are advised to first take their concerns to their immediate supervisor, then to successively higher levels in the organization. The objective is to resolve employee complaints at the lowest possible level and to ensure that immediate supervisors are primarily responsible for staff relations. Other complaint systems tend to supplement rather than replace the hierarchical procedure.

Open-Door Policy.   A true open-door policy exists when employees may take their concerns to *any* level of management.[69] This approach is effective only when status differences are minimized and managers are sincerely willing to listen when someone does call on them.

Third-Party Arbitration.   In third-party arbitration, a neutral person outside the organization is hired to listen to the parties and make a final binding decision. Labour laws provide this conflict resolution system to unionized staff, but it is rarely available to nonunionized employees in Canada. Queen's University and Woodward's Department Stores are exceptions. The arbitrators selected to hear nonunion complaints are usually the same professionals who decide cases involving union employees.

Peer Tribunals.   Peer tribunals consist of a panel of coworkers who investigate or listen to a formal complaint. The tribunal's decision is either submitted as a recommendation to senior management or becomes the organization's binding decision. Queen's University's peer system for nonunion support staff is described in Perspective 13–3. Notice that this system also includes hierarchical and arbitration procedures.

Upward Communications Coordinators.   The Royal Bank, Royal Trust, Hong Kong Bank of Canada, Bank of Nova Scotia, and other large Canadian firms employ coordinators to help employees voice their complaints or opinions to senior management in confidence. Generally, an in-house coordinator receives employee complaints in writing or through a telephone hotline, usually a toll-free number. The questions are then sent anonymously to the manager best able to answer the question and the reply is mailed by the coordinator to the employee. The number of complaints received varies, but Royal Bank's RSVP program processes over 800 letters each year.

Ombuds Officer.   While most upward communication coordinators passively transmit questions and answers between employees and managers, *ombuds officers* are typically employee advocates who try to mediate problems between the parties. Ombuds officers must maintain a high degree of independence from management influence in order to maintain credibility and trust. They usually do not have the power of an arbitrator to present binding decisions, so persuasion and creative problem solving are applied to work out an acceptable resolution between the parties. Queen's University's staff liaison officer described in Perspective 13–3 is an ombudsperson for nonunion staff.

PERSPECTIVE 13–3   Queen's University's Complaint System for Nonunion Support Staff

Queen's University at Kingston, Ontario, has developed an innovative third-party complaint system for its nonunion support staff. Support staff are first encouraged to resolve their problems directly with their immediate supervisor and department head. However, if the problem remains unresolved, employees can request assistance from the staff liaison officer (an ombudsperson for employees), a senior member of the human resource department, or a grievance officer. Grievance officers are coworkers or administrators who have been specially trained in conflict resolution. They help employees determine whether there is cause for a formal complaint and describe the formal appeal board process.

If a complaint cannot be resolved informally, employees may approach the staff liaison officer to request an appeal board hearing. The appeal board is a panel of three nonmanagement employees who hear the complaint. One member of the board is selected by the employee, another by the head of the department to whom the complaint is directed, and the third by the first two appointees. The appeal board convenes the meeting within one week of its formation and listens to the presentations from both sides of the dispute. The procedure specifically emphasizes that the parties to the dispute shall personally present their viewpoint (i.e., no legal counsel) in order to maintain an atmosphere of constructive, informal inquiry. The board then prepares a report that is submitted to the staff liaison officer within one month.

The parties, as well as the Director of Personnel Services, are informed of the appeal board's decision. All original appeal board documents are sealed in the university's vaults. Within two weeks of the board's decision, either party may request a formal hearing before an independent external arbitrator. The person requesting the arbitration must deposit a fee of $250 with the staff liaison officer. The arbitrator's decision is final and binding on the griever and the university.

Source: S. L. McShane, "Conflict Resolution Practices for Nonunion Employees," *Human Resources Management in Canada,* January 1991, pp. 35,527–36.

Characteristics of Effective Conflict-Resolution Systems

There are several features of effective conflict-resolution systems. Perhaps the most important of these is that employees who use the system are protected from reprisal. In particular, management must change the often-prevailing view that an individual's career opportunities are limited if he or she presents a concern. The conflict-resolution process should be relatively easy to use by employees at all organizational levels. Where more complicated aspects of the process necessarily exist, a specially trained coworker or company representative should be available for assistance and support. Supervisors and others involved in the dispute-resolution process must receive training to handle employee concerns quickly and openly. They must also develop the philosophy that conflict resolution is an effective human relations strategy rather than evidence of management imperfections.

Effective conflict-resolution systems follow specific timetables so that the process is not delayed. For example, managers should respond to complaints received through the hierarchical process within a few days. Finally, third-party systems must be objective and neutral. Admittedly, it is difficult for supervisors to be completely neutral when their decisions and actions are being criticized. Third-party arbitration provides one of the few avenues for neutrality, but organizations may dislike the lack of control resulting from this process.

Third-party conflict-resolution mechanisms can be difficult to implement and maintain, yet they are an important part of an effective strategy to build a dedicated work force. Ultimately, the quality of management policies and practices will determine how often these conflict resolution systems are needed. But as long as employees disagree with supervisory and corporate decisions, mechanisms should be in place to resolve matters efficiently and effectively.

SUMMARY

- Conflict exists when people believe that others have deliberately blocked, or are about to block, their goals or activities. It is a dynamic, interactive cycle that begins when one or more people involved perceive that a conflict exists. These perceptions lead to attitudes toward the opponent and his or her actions which, in turn, may be transformed into behavioural intentions and a conflict episode involving the other party. The conflict episode influences each party's perceptions and attitudes toward the situation as well as their subsequent actions in the conflict situation.
- Conflict should be viewed as having both positive and negative consequences. Conflict management represents interventions designed to alter the level and form of conflict such that organizational effectiveness is optimized. The beneficial outcomes of conflict are found mainly in improved decision making and team dynamics. On the negative side, conflict diverts energy and resources toward nonproductive activities, creates feelings of frustration, increases perceptual distortion, and reduces communication effectiveness.
- The sources of conflict deal mainly with the situation, although personal characteristics also have an effect. Conflict potential increases under conditions of goal incompatibility, differentiation, task interdependence, scarce resources, ambiguity, and communication problems.
- There are basically five ways to approach the other party in a conflict situation: competing, avoiding, compromising, collaborating, and accommodating. Most of these styles adopt a distributive orientation in which someone believes that one party will lose if the other wins. The collaborative style represents an integrative orientation in which the person believes that the resources at stake are expandable rather than fixed if the parties work together to find a creative solution to their problem.
- Structural approaches to conflict management directly apply to the sources of conflict. They include emphasizing superordinate goals, reducing differentiation, improving communication and understanding, reducing task

interdependence, and clarifying rules and procedures. By altering these conditions, conflict may be reduced or stimulated, depending on the desired effect.

• Negotiations are deliberate attempts by conflicting parties to resolve their differences by defining or redefining the terms of their interdependence. Negotiators should adopt an integrative orientation wherever possible, although a distributive orientation may be necessary in situations where each party's interests are directly opposed.

• The dynamics and outcomes of negotiations are influenced by several situational factors, including location, physical setting, time, and audience. Some of the more important characteristics and behaviours of the parties include setting goals, making concessions, gathering information, and communicating effectively.

• Third-party conflict-resolution systems exist in virtually every organization. To be effective, these systems must consider the perceived fairness of the decision outcomes, called *distributive justice*. They must also consider *procedural justice*—fairness in the procedures used to make the decision.

• Some formal third-party complaint systems include the hierarchical process, open-door policy, third-party arbitration, peer tribunals, upward communications coordinators, and ombuds services. In addition to following procedural justice principles, third-party systems should be easy to use, offer protection from reprisal, offer timely settlement, ensure that supervisors are trained in dispute resolution, and provide objectivity and neutrality.

DISCUSSION QUESTIONS

1. Describe the conflict cycle. When does the cycle escalate rather than defuse?

2. How does conflict benefit the decision-making process?

3. What effect does differentiation of the work force have on conflict? What types of differentiation might influence conflict in organizations?

4. Identify three types of interdependence and give an organizational example for each.

5. What is the competing style of conflict management? Under what conditions is this style appropriate? What problems may occur when the competing style is used?

6. What is an intergroup laboratory? What effect does it have on conflict?

7. What effect does time have on negotiations?

8. What conditions increase the procedural justice of third-party conflict-resolution systems?

NOTES

1. Personal communication with Cardinal River Coals Ltd. September, 1991; quotations are from D. Burn, "They Had a Problem . . . But They Fixed It," *Canadian HR Reporter,* November 14, 1988, pp. 16–17.

2. D. Tjosvold, *Working Together to Get Things Done* (Lexington, Mass.; Lexington Books, 1986), pp. 114–15.

3. G. Wolf, "Conflict Episodes," in M. H. Bazerman and R. J. Lewicki (eds.), *Negotiating in Organizations* (Beverly Hills, Calif.: Sage, 1983), pp. 135–40.

4. M. Deutsch, *The Resolution of Conflict: Constructive and Destructive Processes* (New Haven, Conn.: Yale University Press, 1973); and J. P. Folger and M. S. Poole, *Working through Conflict* (Glenview, Ill.: Scott, Foresman, 1984).

5. This model and related discussion is based on L. R. Pondy, "Organizational Conflict: Concepts and Models," *Administrative Science Quarterly* 12 (1967), pp. 296–320; and K. W. Thomas, "Conflict and Negotiation Processes in Organizations," in M. D. Dunnette (ed.), *Handbook of Industrial/Organizational Psychology*, 2nd ed. (Palo Alto, Calif.: Consulting Psychologists Press, in press).

6. H. Mintzberg, *The Nature of Managerial Work* (New York: Harper & Row, 1973); and K. W. Thomas and W. H. Schmidt, "A Survey of Managerial Interests with Respect to Conflict," *Academy of Management Journal* 19 (1976), pp. 315–18.

7. D. Nightingale, "Conflict and Conflict Resolution," in G. Strauss, R. Miles, C. Snow, and A. Tannenbaum (eds.), *Organizational Behavior: Research and Issues* (Belmont, Calif.: Wadsworth, 1976), pp. 141–64; and M. P. Follett, "Constructive Conflict," in E. M. Fox and L. Ulwick (eds.), *Dynamic Administration: The Collected Papers of Mary Parker Follett* (New York: Hippocrene, 1982), pp. 1–20.

8. J. Kelly, "Making Conflict Work for You," *Harvard Business Review* 48 (July–August 1970), pp. 103–13.

9. D. Tjosvold, *The Conflict-Positive Organization* (Reading, Mass.: Addison-Wesley, 1991).

10. A. C. Filley, *Interpersonal Conflict Resolution* (Glenview, Ill.: Scott, Foresman, 1975), pp. 4–7.

11. Pondy, "Organizational Conflict: Concepts and Models."

12. D. Nadler, J. Hackman, and E. Lawler, *Managing Organizational Behavior* (Boston: Little, Brown, 1979), Chapter 12.

13. S. P. Robbins, *Managing Organizational Conflict: A Nontraditional Approach* (Englewood Cliffs, N.J.: Prentice Hall, 1974), p. 19.

14. R. R. Blake and J. S. Mouton, *Solving Costly Organizational Conflicts* (San Francisco: Jossey-Bass, 1984).

15. R. R. Blake and J. S. Mouton, "Union–Management Relations: From Conflict to Collaboration," *Personnel* 38, no. 6 (1961), pp. 38–51; and E. Van de Vliert, "Siding and Other Reactions to a Conflict: A Theory of Escalation toward Outsiders," *Journal of Conflict Resolution* 25 (1981), pp. 1554–60.

16. T. Janz and D. Tjosvold, "Costing Effective vs. Ineffective Work Relationships," *Canadian Journal of Administrative Sciences* 2 (1985), pp. 43–51.

17. J. A. Seiler, "Diagnosing Interdepartmental Conflict," *Harvard Business Review* 41 (September–October 1963), pp. 121–32.

18. J. M. Dutton and R. E. Walton, "Interdepartmental Conflict and Cooperation: Two Contrasting Studies," *Human Organization* 25 (1966), pp. 207–20.

19. R. E. Walton and J. M. Dutton, "The Management of Conflict: A Model and Review," *Administrative Science Quarterly* 14 (1969), pp. 73–84.

20. Adele Weder, "Le Château Cleans House, But Its U.S. Stores Are in a Mess," *Financial Times,* March 4, 1991, p. 6.

21. C. Kirchmeyer and J. McLellan, "Capitalizing on Ethnic Diversity: An Approach to Managing the Diverse Workgroups of the 1990s," *Canadian Journal of Administrative Sciences* 8 (June 1991), pp.

72–79; and E. J. Mighty, "Valuing Workforce Diversity: A Model of Organizational Change," *Canadian Journal of Administrative Sciences* 8 (June 1991), pp. 64–70.

22. M. N. Kiggundu, "Task Interdependence and the Theory of Job Design," *Academy of Management Review* 6 (1981), pp. 499–508; and M. N. Kiggundu, "Task Interdependence and Job Design: Test of a Theory," *Organizational Behavior and Human Performance* 31 (1983), pp. 145–72.

23. P. C. Earley and G. B. Northcraft, "Goal Setting, Resource Interdependence, and Conflict Management," in M. A. Rahim (ed.), *Managing Conflict: An Interdisciplinary Approach* (New York: Praeger, 1989), pp. 161–70.

24. J. D. Thompson, *Organizations in Action* (New York: McGraw-Hill, 1967), pp. 54–56.

25. W. W. Notz, F. A. Starke, and J. Atwell, "The Manager as Arbitrator: Conflicts over Scarce Resources," in Bazerman and Lewicki (eds.), *Negotiating in Organizations*, pp. 143–64; and E. H. Neilson, "Understanding and Managing Intergroup Conflict," in J. W. Lorsch and P. R. Lawrence (eds.), *Managing Group and Intergroup Relations* (Homewood, Ill.: Irwin Dorsey, 1972), pp. 329–43.

26. R. H. Waterman, *The Renewal Factor* (New York: Bantam, 1987), p. 126.

27. R. A. Baron, "Reducing Organizational Conflict: An Incompatible Response Approach," *Journal of Applied Psychology* 69 (1984), pp. 272–79.

28. K. Thomas, "Conflict and Conflict Management," in M. D. Dunnette (ed.), *Handbook of Industrial and Organizational Psychology* (Chicago: Rand McNally, 1976), pp. 889–935. For similar models, see R. R. Blake and J. S. Mouton, *The Managerial Grid* (Houston: Gulf Publications, 1964); and M. A. Rahim, "A Measure of Styles of Handling Interpersonal Conflict," *Academy of Management Journal* 26 (1983), pp. 368–76.

29. B. M. Hawrysh and J. L. Zaichkowsky, "Cultural Approaches to Negotiations: Understanding the Japanese," *International Marketing Review* 7, no. 2 (1990).

30. K. W. Thomas, "Toward Multi-Dimensional Values in Teaching: The Example of Conflict Behaviors," *Academy of Management Review* 2 (1977), pp. 484–90.

31. R. J. Burke, "Methods of Resolving Superior–Subordinate Conflict: The Constructive Use of Subordinate Differences and Disagreements," *Organizational Behavior and Human Performance* 5 (1970), pp. 393–41.

32. D. W. Johnson, G. Maruyama, R. T. Johnson, D. Nelson, and S. Skon, "Effects of Cooperative, Competitive, and Individualistic Goal Structures on Achievement: A Meta-Analysis," *Psychological Bulletin* 89 (1981), pp. 47–62.

33. R. J. Lewicki and J. A. Litterer, *Negotiation* (Homewood, Ill.: Irwin, 1985), pp. 102–6.

34. R. E. Walton and R. B. McKersie, *A Behavioral Theory of Labor Negotiations: An Analysis of a Social Interaction System* (New York: McGraw-Hill, 1965).

35. M. Sherif, "Superordinate Goals in the Reduction of Intergroup Conflict," *American Journal of Sociology* 68 (1958), pp. 349–58.

36. M. Zimmerman, *How to Do Business with the Japanese* (New York: Random House, 1985), pp. 170, 200; and W. G. Ouchi, *Theory Z* (New York: Avon, 1982), pp. 25–32.

37. T. J. Peters and R. H. Waterman, Jr., *In Search of Excellence* (New York: Harper & Row, 1982), pp. 312–13.

38. T. Peters and N. Austin, *A Passion for Excellence* (New York: Random House, 1985), p. 147.

39. Blake and Mouton, *Solving Costly Organizational Conflicts,* Chapter 6; R. R. Blake and J. S. Mouton, "Overcoming Group Warfare," *Harvard Business Review,* November–December 1984, pp. 98–108; and R. Beckhard, *Organization Development: Strategies and Models* (Reading, Mass.: Addison-Wesley, 1969).

40. P. D. Bergman, *Relations by Objectives: The Ontario Experience* (Kingston, Ont.: Industrial Relations Centre, 1988).

41. M. H. Bazerman and R. J. Lewicki, "Contemporary Research Directions in the Study of Negotiations in Organizations: A Selective Review," *Journal of Occupational Behaviour* 6 (1985), pp. 1–17.

42. P. R. Lawrence and J. W. Lorsch, *Organization and Environment* (Homewood, Ill.: Irwin, 1969).

43. E. Van de Vliert, "Escalative Intervention in Small Group Conflicts," *Journal of Applied Behavioural Science* 21 (Winter 1985), pp. 19–36.

44. Walton and McKersie, *A Behavioral Theory of Labor Negotiations: An Analysis of a Social Interaction System;* for a similar definition see S. B. Bacharach and E. J. Lawler, *Bargaining: Power Tactics and Outcomes* (San Francisco: Jossey-Bass, 1981).

45. For a critical view of collaboration in negotiation, see J. M. Brett, "Managing Organizational Conflict," *Professional Psychology: Research and Practice* 15 (1984), pp. 664–78.

46. R. Stagner and H. Rosen, *Psychology of Union–Management Relations* (Belmont, Calif.: Wadsworth, 1965), pp. 95–96, 108–10; and Walton and McKersie, *A Behavioral Theory of Labor Negotiations: An Analysis of a Social Interaction System,* pp. 41–46.

47. Lewicki and Litterer, *Negotiation,* pp. 144–46; and N. J. Adler, *International Dimensions of Organizational Behavior* (Boston: Kent, 1986), pp. 160–61.

48. P. C. Newman, *The Acquisitors* (Toronto: Seal, 1981), p. 85.

49. Lewicki and Litterer, *Negotiation,* pp. 146–51; and B. Kniveton, *The Psychology of Bargaining* (Aldershot, England: Avebury, 1989), pp. 76–79.

50. B. M. Downie, "Union–Management Co-operation in the 1980s and Beyond," in J. C. Anderson, M. Gunderson, and A. Ponak (eds.), *Union–Management Relations in Canada* (Don Mills, Ont.: Addison-Wesley, 1989), pp. 261–83.

51. Lewicki and Litterer, *Negotiation,* pp. 151–54; and D. G. Pruitt, *Negotiation Behavior* (New York: Academic Press, 1981), pp. 73–74.

52. Adler, *International Dimensions of Organizational Behavior,* p. 162.

53. Zimmerman, *How to Do Business with the Japanese,* p. 101; and H. Cohen, *You Can Negotiate Anything* (New York: Bantam, 1982), pp. 93–95.

54. Lewicki and Litterer, *Negotiation,* pp. 215–22; and Pruitt, *Negotiation Behavior,* pp. 44–45.

55. V. V. Murray, T. D. Jick, and P. Bradshaw, "To Bargain or Not to Bargain? The Case of Hospital Budget Cuts," in Bazerman and Lewicki (eds.), *Negotiating in Organizations,* pp. 272–95.

56. R. C. Richardson, *Collective Bargaining by Objectives: A Positive Approach,* 2nd ed. (Englewood Cliffs, N.J.: Prentice Hall, 1985).

57. R. Tung, *Business Negotiations with the Japanese* (Lexington, Mass.: Lexington Books, 1984).

58. Lewicki and Litterer, *Negotiation,* pp. 177–80; and Adler, *International Dimensions of Organizational Behavior,* p. 161.

59. Lewicki and Litterer, *Negotiation,* pp. 89–93.

60. N. J. Adler and J. L. Graham, "Business Negotiations: Canadians Are Not Just Like Americans," *Canadian Journal of Administrative Sciences* 4 (1987), pp. 211–38.

61. Adler, *International Dimensions of Organizational Behavior,* p. 149.

62. Kniveton, *The Psychology of Bargaining,* pp. 100–101; J. Z. Rubin and B. R. Brown, *The Social Psychology of Bargaining and Negotiation* (New York: Academic Press, 1976), Chapter 9; and Brett, "Managing Organizational Conflict," pp. 670–71.

63. L. L. Putnam and M. S. Poole, "Conflict and Negotiation," in F. M. Jablin, L. L. Putnam, K. H. Roberts, and L. W. Porter (eds.), *Handbook of Organizational Communication: An Interdisciplinary Perspective* (Beverly Hills, Calif.: Sage, 1987), pp. 549–99.

64. Adler, *International Dimensions of Organizational Behavior,* Chapter 7.

65. V. V. Murray, "Some Unanswered Questions on Organizational Conflict," *Organization and Administrative Sciences* 6 (1975), pp. 35–53.

66. J. W. Thibaut and L. Walker, *Procedural Justice: A Psychological Analysis* (Hillsdale, N.J.: Lawrence Erlbaum Associates, 1975); and R. Folger and J. Greenberg, "Procedural Justice: An Interpretive Analysis of Personnel Systems," *Research in Personnel and Human Resources Management* 3 (1985), pp. 141–83.

67. A. W. J. Thomson and V. V. Murray, *Grievance Procedures* (Lexington, Mass.: Lexington Books, 1976).

68. S. L. McShane, "Conflict Resolution Practices for Nonunion Employees," *Human Resources Management in Canada,* January 1991, pp. 35,527–36.

69. F. A. Schull, A. L. Delbecq, and L. L. Cummings, *Organizational Decision Making* (New York: McGraw-Hill, 1970), pp. 152–53.

CHAPTER CASE

MAELSTROM COMMUNICATIONS

Sales manager Roger Todd was fuming. Thanks to, as he put it, "those nearsighted addleheads in service," he had nearly lost one of his top accounts. When told of Todd's complaint, senior serviceperson Ned Rosen retorted, "That figures. Anytime Mr. Todd senses even the remotest possibility of a sale, he immediately promises the customer the world on a golden platter. We can't possibly provide the service they request under the time constraints they give us and do an acceptable job."

Feelings of this sort were common in the departments both Roger and Ned worked for in Maelstrom Communications. Sales and service, the two dominant functions in the company, never saw eye to eye on anything, it seemed. The problems dated well back in the history of the company, even before Roger or Ned were hired some years ago.

Maelstrom Communications is a franchised distributionship belonging to a nationwide network of communications companies that sell products such as intercom, paging, sound, and interconnect telephone systems. Maelstrom competes directly with the Bell System companies in the telephone hardware market. Equipment installation and maintenance service is an integral part of the total package Maelstrom offers.

Modern telephone system hardware is highly sophisticated, and few, if any, system users have the technological know-how to do their own equipment servicing. An excellent service record is crucial to the success of any company in the field. After the direct sale of a Maelstrom system, the sales force maintains contacts with customers. There is nothing the salespeople dislike so much as hearing that a customer hasn't received the type of service promised at the time of sale. On the other hand, service technicians complain of being hounded by the salespeople whenever a preferred customer needs a wire spliced. As Ned Rosen put it, "I can't remember the last time a service request came through that *wasn't* an emergency from a preferred customer."

Maelstrom's owner and president, Al Whitfield, has a strong sales background and views sales as the bread-and-butter department of the company. He is in on all major decisions and has final say on any matter brought to his attention. He spends most of his time working with sales and marketing personnel, and rarely concerns himself with the day-to-day activities of the service department unless a major problem of some sort crops up.

Next in line in Maelstrom's corporate hierarchy is the vice-president in charge of production, Lawrence Henderson. Henderson is responsible for the acquisition and distribution of all job-related equipment and materials and for the scheduling of all service department activities. His sympathies lie primarily with the service department.

Each week Whitfield, Henderson, and all members of the sales force hold a meeting in Maelstrom's conference room. The sales personnel present their needs to Henderson so that equipment can be ordered and jobs scheduled. Service requests reported to salespeople from customers are also relayed to Henderson at this point. Once orders for service have been placed with production, sales personnel receive no feedback on the disposition of them (unless a customer complains to them directly) other than at these weekly meetings. It is common for a salesperson to think all is well with his or her accounts when, in fact, they are receiving delayed service or none at all. When an irate customer phones the sales representative to complain, it sets in motion the machinery that leads to disputes such as the one between Roger Todd and Ned Rosen.

It has become an increasingly common occurrence at Maelstrom for sales personnel to go to Henderson to complain when their requests are not met by the service department. Henderson has exhibited an increasing tendency to side with the service department and to tell the salespeople that existing service department priorities must be adhered to and that any sales requests will have to wait for rescheduling. At this point, a salesperson's only recourse is to go to Whitfield, who invariably agrees with the salesperson and instructs Henderson to take appropriate action. All of this is time consuming and only serves to produce friction between the president and the vice-president in charge of production.

Discussion Questions

1. Use the conflict cycle to describe the events in this case.
2. What situational conditions have created the conflict in this case?
3. What actions should the organization take to manage the conflict?

Source: Written by Daniel Robey in collaboration with Todd Anthony.

EXPERIENTIAL EXERCISE

UGLI ORANGE ROLE PLAY

Purpose: This exercise is designed to help you understand the dynamics of interpersonal and intergroup conflict as well as the effectiveness of negotiation strategies under specific conditions.

Instructions: The instructor will divide the class into an even number of teams of three people each, with one participant left over for each team formed (e.g., six observers if there are six teams). One-half of the teams will take the role of Dr. Roland and the other half will be Dr. Jones. Teams will receive the appropriate materials from the instructor. Members within each team are given 10 minutes to learn their roles and decide negotiating strategy. After reading their roles and discussing strategy, each Dr. Jones team is matched with a Dr. Roland team to conduct negotiations.

Observers will receive observation forms from the instructor, and two observers will be assigned to watch the paired teams during prenegotiations and subsequent negotiations. At the end of the negotiations, the observers will describe the process and outcomes in their negotiating session. The instructor will then invite the negotiators to describe their experiences and the implications for conflict management.

Source: This exercise has been prepared by Robert J. House.

14

Leadership in Organizations

LEARNING OBJECTIVES

After reading this chapter, you should be able to:

Explain
Why the trait approach provides an inadequate
understanding of leadership.

Define
The two main leader behaviour clusters identified by the
Ohio State researchers.

Describe
The "hi-hi" leadership hypothesis.

Outline
The path-goal theory of leadership.

Identify
The four features of transformational leadership.

Explain
Why leaders are given too much credit or blame for
organizational events.

Edward Gajdel photographer ©
copyright

In three short decades Isadore Sharp has built Toronto-based Four Seasons Hotels Inc. into the largest and most successful luxury hotel chain in the world. Five of Four Seasons' hotels have been ranked among the top eight in North America, ten have received the American Automobile Association's coveted Five Diamond award (more than any other company), and Sharp has been named Hotelier of the World. Sharp credits his impeccable staff for the company's success, but friends and associates say that his leadership has made the difference. "From the beginning, Sharp knew what he wanted," recalls Four Seasons board member and investor Edmond Creed. "Other people would have skimped on amenities and staffing. But Issy wanted the best." Another director, Benjamin Swirsky, adds: "Sharp's personal stamp becomes corporate mythology."

Sharp's vision is that the Four Seasons name will be synonymous with carefully crafted elegance and service. This was apparent in his first hotel, built in Toronto in 1961. But the company vision became clear to Sharp in the early 1970s in a strained partnership with the Sheraton chain to build a hotel across from Toronto's city hall. The project grew to over 1,400 rooms and became the antithesis of Sharp's personal vision as a hotelier, so he quickly sold his stake. "Our involvement with the Sheraton crystallized what we wanted to build—medium-sized hotels which cater to the luxury market," says Sharp. As if energized by this experience, Sharp moved quickly to build small but elegant hotels across North America.

Sharp leads by example rather than by fiat, modelling his rigorous standards of quality and elegance to more than 9,000 employees at over 25 properties around the world. In spite of his penchant for details, the "Issy Sharp" style of leadership is more like a coach than a commander. "The way he pays attention to his people makes a tremendous difference," explains the general manager for Four Seasons' New York hotel. "If I have a problem he won't just tell me how to solve it, he will make me part of the solution. He'll ask me, how do you think we can make this better?"

Further evidence of Sharp's leadership is his persistence and optimism through the ups and downs of the hotel business, including a tragic fire at Toronto's Inn on the Park in 1981. Says Sharp: "You need that, you might call it, fanatical belief that it will work. You must at points in time overcome a lot of skepticism and the naysayers and disbelievers. And on the downside if you risk and lose, it doesn't stop you. You're able to pick up the pieces and start over again."

Isadore Sharp is quickly approaching his vision of the Four Seasons chain—to make it the standard by which hotel luxury is measured. This vision, formed over 30 years ago, has become Four Seasons' competitive edge.[1]

EXHIBIT 14–1   Perspectives of Leadership in Organizations

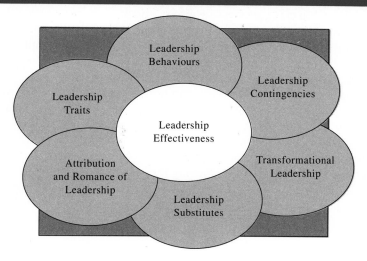

What makes Isadore Sharp an effective business leader? One factor is certainly the ability to create, communicate, and model his vision for a better hotel chain. Sharp is also known for his superb interpersonal skills. He is supportive and friendly toward his staff and has an uncanny knack of remembering their names. Yet he is quick to keep people focussed on the task and to provide clarity when employees need direction to accomplish their work.

As we describe the leadership of Isadore Sharp—or any other leader in the private or public sector—it becomes apparent that there are many ways to approach this concept. Exhibit 14–1 illustrates the major leadership perspectives that we will explore in this chapter. As you can see, some researchers have studied the traits of great leaders, others have looked at their behaviours, and still others have investigated external contingencies that might moderate leader effectiveness. At various points in time, experts have contrasted managers who improve employee effectiveness with those who transform the organization. A few have documented organizational strategies to substitute leaders in specific contexts. Finally, there is increasing interest in the romance of leadership, that is, attributing organizational events to leaders through perceptual biases. Before introducing you to these various perspectives, however, let's first tackle the complex meaning of leadership in organizational settings.

THE MEANING OF LEADERSHIP

Leadership has been contemplated and debated since the days of Greek philosophers. It has captivated the interest of political scientists and organizational theorists for most of this century. Yet, as James MacGregor Burns

leadership
The process of influencing other team members beyond routine compliance toward defined team or organizational objectives more than the team members influence the leader.

acknowledged, "Leadership is one of the most observed and least understood phenomenon on earth."[2] With this warning in mind, we will cautiously define **leadership** as a process whereby the leader influences other team members toward defined team or organizational objectives more than the team members influence the leader. Moreover, the leader's influence is incremental in the sense that influence is exerted over and above mechanical or routine compliance within normal role relations.[3]

An important element of this definition is that leaders direct followers toward a specific set of functional goals. Experts say that leaders are instruments of organizational action because they are able to maintain a tight fit between the organization and its environment.[4] Effective leaders help the work team to define (or redefine) its ultimate objectives, design an enterprise distinctively adapted toward achieving these objectives, and ensure that the structure and process serve that ultimate function.[5] Leaders keep the work unit on track, by focussing on the ultimate goal as well as the processes required to hold the team together.

Leadership and Influence

Leadership involves some combination of power and persuasion to redirect the attitudes and actions of others toward specified goals. This influence extends beyond normal role expectations to transform work activities. In other words, leadership is about change. It implies activity, movement, getting work done.[6] It energizes and mobilizes people by altering their motivation or competencies beyond normal job duties.

One problem with defining leadership, as we have mentioned, is that so many perspectives have emerged from several disciplines. Consequently, it is exceedingly difficult to discuss leadership as a cohesive body of knowledge. At this point in time, the best we can offer is a clear overview of the major schools of thought on the subject over the past century, beginning with the earliest: the trait approach.

TRAIT PERSPECTIVE OF LEADERSHIP

traits
Personal characteristics, such as appearance, personality, intelligence, and skills, that differentiate one person from the next.

Since the beginning of recorded civilization, people have been interested in the traits that distinguish great leaders from the rest of us. **Traits** include the numerous personal characteristics—appearance, personality, intelligence, and skills—that differentiate one person from the next. The ancient Egyptians demanded authority, discrimination, and justice from their leaders. The Greeks called for wisdom, justice, shrewdness, and valour. For the first half of the 20th century, researchers used scientific methods to determine whether these and other traits actually distinguish leaders from lesser souls. By identifying the traits that predict leadership effectiveness, experts could help select company presidents more scientifically.

In spite of the popular notion that great leaders possess unique characteristics, the quest for a universal set of leadership traits has been less than successful. In a decisive review of the results up to 1948, Ralph Stogdill concluded that while some personal attributes may be relevant to leadership in some situations, people do not generally become great leaders by virtue of their traits in all situations.[7] Thus, the characteristics of an effective military leader are different from those of a head of a research laboratory.

In a subsequent review of studies up to 1970, Stogdill acknowledged that a few leadership traits, including those listed in Exhibit 14–2, were somewhat consistent predictors of effective leadership across studies. However, he pointed to the importance of situational influences on the relevance of some traits and noted that skills rather than personality or physical features represented the most consistently reported traits. These conclusions were echoed by research on managerial selection that has found that skills are better predictors than personality traits of a manager's subsequent job performance.[8] Furthermore, Stogdill observed that traits have a generally weak association with effectiveness measures, suggesting that leadership involves a lot more than a set of personal attributes.

Based on these findings, we must be careful not to place too much emphasis on traits to explain why some people are effective leaders while others are not. In addition to the problems just mentioned, many traits, particularly personality constructs, are difficult to measure accurately. Another concern is that traits don't tell us what behaviours leaders use to be effective. Leadership training can impart skills and even alter some personality characteris-

---

EXHIBIT 14–2   Personality Traits and Skills of Successful Leaders

Personality Traits	Skills
Adaptable to situations	Conceptually skilled
Alert to social environment	Creative
Ambitious and achievement-oriented	Diplomatic and tactful
Assertive	Fluent in speaking
Cooperative	Intelligent
Decisive	Knowledgeable about team tasks
Dependable	Organized (possesses administrative ability)
Dominant (desires to influence others)	Persuasive
Energetic (high activity level)	Socially skilled
Persistent	
Self-confident	
Tolerant of stress	
Willing to assume responsibility	

Source: Adapted with permission from G. A. Yukl, *Leadership in Organizations,* 2nd ed. (Englewood Cliffs, N.J.: Prentice Hall, 1989), p. 176.

tics, but until we understand which leadership behaviours are important, our ability to develop future leaders will be limited. Finally, we must not forget Stogdill's warning that situational factors have a considerable influence on leader effectiveness. By investigating these contingencies more fully, we will be better able to understand, predict, and control leadership effectiveness.

Self-Monitoring and Leadership

Notwithstanding our reservations about trait theories, there may be one personality trait—self-monitoring—that is useful for people in leadership positions. You may recall from Chapter 7 that "high self-monitors" are people who are sensitive to situational cues, such as the behaviour of others, and can readily adapt their own behaviour appropriately. There is increasing evidence that high self-monitors are more likely to emerge as informal leaders in small groups.[9] They are adept at perceiving changes in team dynamics and adjusting their own behaviour to match the group's new requirements. For instance, they quickly sense when tension or conflict are impeding the team's performance and can shift to a more supportive style to correct the situation.

Self-monitoring is quite different from other personality traits because it directly considers the importance of leader behaviours. More important is the fact that most contemporary leadership theories (in particular, contingency theories) assume that leaders can quickly and accurately perceive a situation and adjust their behaviour accordingly. In other words, they *expect* leaders to be high self-monitors.[10]

BEHAVIOURAL PERSPECTIVE OF LEADERSHIP

The end of World War II marked a decisive shift toward a more behavioural perspective of leadership theory and research. The behavioural perspective attempts to answer the basic question of what leader behaviours are most effective. This new line of thought emerged from a disenchantment with the trait approach as well as a general trend in the social sciences during the 1940s and 1950s toward the study of human behaviours rather than attitudes and personality constructs.

Consideration and Initiating Structure

Two research teams that contributed most to the behavioural perspective were located at the University of Michigan and Ohio State University.[11] Working fairly independently, both teams wanted to identify the clusters of behaviour that distinguish effective from ineffective leaders. The Ohio State research program was the most comprehensive in this regard. A list of over 1,800 leadership behaviour items were statistically analyzed and eventually grouped into two categories called *consideration* and *initiating structure:*

- **Consideration** includes behaviours indicating mutual trust and respect for subordinates, a genuine concern for their needs, and a desire to look out for their welfare. For example, a leader who is high on consideration would being willing to accept employee suggestions, do personal favours for employees, support their interests when required, and treat employees as equals.

- **Initiating structure** includes behaviours in which the leader defines and structures work roles and relations among employees and with regard to the leader. These leaders assign employees to specific tasks, clarify their work duties and procedures, ensure that they follow company rules, and push them to reach their performance capacity. Kenneth Rowe, the hard-driving yet very successful founder and CEO of Halifax-based IMP Group, could be labelled a leader with high initiating structure, as we describe in Perspective 14–1.

consideration
A cluster of leadership behaviours indicating mutual trust and respect for subordinates, a genuine concern for their needs, and a desire to look out for their welfare.

initiating structure
A cluster of leadership behaviours that defines and structures work roles and relations among employees and with regard to the leader.

To this day, consideration and initiating structure are the two most widely measured dimensions of leader behaviour in the scholarly research. These categories are strikingly similar to the two dimensions developed at the University of Michigan (which they called *employee* and *job-centred behaviours*). Researchers initially thought that consideration and initiating structure were at opposite ends of a behaviour spectrum, but they eventually discovered that these behaviour groups are independent from each other.[12] This means that it is possible for one person to use both consideration and initiating structure when supervising employees. Some leaders may be high on both, low on both, or anywhere in between, as shown in Exhibit 14–3.

There has also been some speculation that male leaders are more likely to rely on initiating structure, whereas female leaders are more likely to use consideration.[13] These are widely held beliefs, but research has consistently found that male and female leaders do not differ in their amounts of consideration and initiating structure and have equally satisfied subordinates.[14]

The "Hi-Hi" Leadership Hypothesis

Another objective of leadership scholars was to determine which combination of leader behaviours was optimal. After some preliminary work, they hypothesized that both consideration and initiating structure behaviours were positively associated with leadership effectiveness. In other words, the most effective leader would exhibit high levels of both types of behaviour. This became known as the **"hi-hi" leadership hypothesis.**[15]

Most of the studies conducted during the 1940s and 1950s supported the hi-hi leadership hypothesis. Specifically, researchers found that subordinates have higher levels of satisfaction and lower absenteeism, grievances, and turnover when their supervisors exhibit high levels of consideration.[16] Subordinates have somewhat higher absenteeism and turnover when their supervisors exhibit high initiating structure, but this leadership style seems to increase productivity and team unity. Several Canadian educational lead-

hi-hi leadership hypothesis
A proposition stating that effective leaders exhibit high levels of both consideration and initiating structure.

Kenneth Rowe is the quintessential hard-driving business leader. Rowe founded Industrial Marine Products Ltd. (now called IMP Group Ltd.) in 1967 out of the ashes of two bankrupt Nova Scotia foundries. In 1970, he developed IMP's aerospace division by buying a failing Dartmouth aircraft parts maker. Since then he has purchased and turned around more than a dozen other companies. The IMP Group now boasts 1,500 employees and revenues of over $175 million.

In building IMP, Rowe has earned a reputation as a tough manager and calculating business leader. Some claim that he developed this strong task-orientation while serving in the British merchant marine. Whatever the reason, Rowe is a lone-wolf operator who runs his companies with a skeleton crew of managers and takes hands-on management to an extreme. Complains one former executive: "It's annoying to work for Rowe because he's involved in everything, he's always looking over your shoulder."

Rowe is particularly finicky about keeping costs down, no matter how small the expense. He goes around turning off office lights and begrudges the expense of a water cooler. Rowe prefers soup at his desk because he doesn't like spending money in restaurants. Getting expense reports approved by Rowe is nightmarish. "He'll challenge a vice-president over spending too much on a meal," recounts a former IMP executive.

Rowe has a sense of humour and is usually approachable, but he prefers confrontation to consultation and is apt to shout at people who do things wrong. Rowe concedes that he demands much of himself and others. "I work myself hard, and that's a good example to the rest," he says. He also admits to being blunt with employees. "But I don't lose my temper often, unless someone does something very stupid," he quickly adds. "Then I'm most likely to fire him." Indeed, Rowe is renowned for firing employees who aren't up to scratch. He once fired an entire management group of a newly acquired company in a single day.

Rowe defends his strong emphasis on initiating structure by pointing out the risk he takes in turning around failing companies. And as for low salaries among IMP Group staff, Rowe says: "In the Maritimes, you can't pay top dollar and survive. Compa-

nies have come down here and have attracted people away from us by offering more, but they usually fail anyway."

Some may criticize Rowe's lack of consideration for employees, but no one can disagree that his leadership style has contributed to an extremely well-run organization. "We need 10 more Ken Rowes down here," says a Dartmouth-based senior executive of Moosehead Breweries Ltd. "He starts things. He's a builder." In the difficult economy of Atlantic Canada, IMP Group's financial picture is impressive. Insiders say the company enjoys low debt and superb profits. "We do very nicely," Rowe agrees.

Sources: Based on M. Salter, "Canada's Toughest Bosses," *Report on Business Magazine*, December 1987, p. 79; R. Siklos, "The Black Knight That's Hunting Leigh," *Financial Times*, March 28, 1988, pp. 10–11; and A. Bruce, "Rowe Mirrors Maritime Spirit," *Globe and Mail*, March 9, 1987, p. B13.

ership studies also supported the hi-hi leadership hypothesis. Some of these investigations reported that student scores on provincial exams were higher in schools whose principals exhibited high consideration and high initiating structure. Other studies discovered that the level of teacher consideration and initiating structure was positively related to student academic achievement.[17]

More recent evidence in favour of this hypothesis has been reported by Dean Tjosvold, using students in a Canadian university.[18] He discovered that students working on a decision-making exercise performed best when their student "manager" demonstrated high levels of concern for production as well as personal warmth. Students with the lowest performance worked with managers demonstrating lots of personal warmth but no concern for production.

The hi-hi leadership hypothesis is intuitively appealing because many managers easily identify with the need to provide high levels of both sets of behaviours to their employees. The hypothesis helps us understand why managers such as Joan Dawe, described in Perspective 14–2, are effective leaders. The executive director of the St. John's Hospital council in Newfoundland uses high consideration to help associates work together more effectively and high initiating structure to keep them on track. Dawe's hi-hi leadership style has enabled her to achieve organizational objectives while satisfying the personal needs of her staff and colleagues.

PERSPECTIVE 14—2   Joan Dawe's "Hi-Hi" Leadership Style

Committed and caring. That's how people describe Joan Dawe, executive director of the St. John's Hospital Council in Newfoundland. Dawe is committed because she will see any task through to completion, and caring because she believes in the basic worth and integrity of others. She is flexible, people-oriented, and, above all, has the ability to communicate with groups.

Dawe's commitment is evident in her ability to pull together divergent and potentially competing interests in Newfoundland's financially strapped health-care industry. When Dawe accepted the executive director position, skeptical colleagues and cautious observers warned of the confrontations she could ex-

pect when challenging the traditional and deep-rooted philosophies of St. John's hospitals. Yet after only a few years in the job, her management style is beginning to pay off.

"We are only beginning," claims Dawe with contagious enthusiasm. "At one point there were over 175 people in 25 advisory committees talking about how they could improve and make services more efficient by sharing! Now, [the Newfoundland] government has endorsed our plan and we are beginning to work towards our preferred future."

Dawe's effective combination of consideration and initiating structure leadership styles has enabled her to improve collaboration and understanding

The Managerial Grid®

Managerial Grid

A behavioural model of leadership developed by Blake and Mouton that assesses an individual's leadership effectiveness in terms of his or her concern for people and concern for production.

In the early 1960s Robert Blake and Jane Mouton formulated the **Managerial Grid,** which adopts the idea that leaders are more effective if they have both a high concern for people and a high concern for production.[19] These dimensions form the Grid (republished as the Leadership Grid Figure in 1991 by Robert R. Blake and Anne A. McCanse) shown in Exhibit 14—4. Concern for people roughly corresponds to consideration while concern for production is similar to initiating structure.

Five leadership styles serve as benchmarks within the managerial grid. Blake and Mouton believe that *team management* is the ideal leadership style because it combines optimal levels of concern for people and production. This style is also known as "9,9" management because it represents the highest scores on the two dimensions. Early versions of this model adopted the hi-hi leadership hypothesis wholeheartedly by stating that effective leaders exhibit an integration of high concern for people and high concern for production. More recently, Blake and Mouton have redefined the concept. They now see the 9,9 leadership style as a "versatile" approach which may vary tactics depending upon the situation but continues to operate consistent with a strategy based on 9,9, principles.[20]

Team-management leaders rely on commitment, participation, and conflict resolution to seek results. In contrast, *authority-compliance managers* (9,1) try to maximize productivity through power and authority; *country club managers* (1,9) focus on developing good feelings among employees even when production suffers; *middle-of-the-road managers* (5,5) try to maintain the status quo by adopting a middle-of-the-road approach; and *impoverished managers* (1,1) do the minimum required to fulfill their leadership role and keep their job.

among the divergent organizational units under the St. John's Hospital Council umbrella. "The day is over when we can continue to act in isolation," she points out. "We will need to work with each other, and that means a real appreciation of each other's roles. There can't be dialogue without that appreciation. It also means being accountable, which is really no more than should be expected."

While Dawe's strong orientation toward people shines through, she is also focussed on the job that must be done. "Although I have faith in people," she says, "we must always remember the issues are complex and very important. We cannot ignore the facts of life. That means never losing sight of the task at hand."

Joan Dawe's leadership style has guided her career through a succession of increasingly responsible positions in Newfoundland's health-care field. As her mentor, Sister Mary Fabian Hennebury says: "Joan is one of the very few people who are actually born managers."

Source: Based on "Movers and Shakers," *Health Care*, February 1987, pp. 10–12.

Blake and Mouton designed the Managerial Grid as an organizational development intervention to improve leadership as well as relations between managers and employees within work units. The program has been implemented in hundreds of organizations throughout Canada and the United States. The first phase of the intervention consists of a one-week seminar in which managers learn about the grid philosophy as well as their own leadership style on the managerial grid. Participants are involved in numerous problem-solving situations intended to help them move toward a more team-management style. Later phases of the intervention include seminars to improve relations between the manager and his or her staff, relations between staff in different departments, and organizational goal setting. In other words, what begins as a program for improving an individual's leadership style is ultimately intended as an organizationwide change strategy. The entire program may require several years to complete.

Limitations of the Leadership Behaviour Perspective

The behavioural perspective of leadership produced a taxonomy of leadership behaviours that laid the foundation for more contemporary models and brought us closer to identifying ways to improve leadership in organizations. The hi-hi leadership hypothesis was also an appealing way to view effective leadership.

However, the leader behaviour research has a number of drawbacks. One problem is that more recent reviews have found less support for the idea that effective leaders are high on both consideration and initiating structure in all situations.[21] Another concern is that consideration and initiating structure

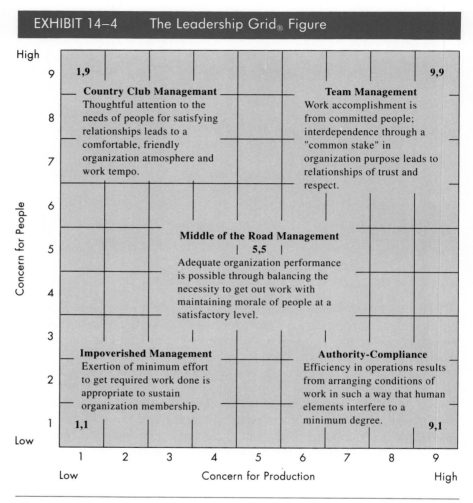

EXHIBIT 14–4   The Leadership Grid® Figure

1,9 Country Club Management
Thoughtful attention to the needs of people for satisfying relationships leads to a comfortable, friendly organization atmosphere and work tempo.

9,9 Team Management
Work accomplishment is from committed people; interdependence through a "common stake" in organization purpose leads to relationships of trust and respect.

Middle of the Road Management 5,5
Adequate organization performance is possible through balancing the necessity to get out work with maintaining morale of people at a satisfactory level.

1,1 Impoverished Management
Exertion of minimum effort to get required work done is appropriate to sustain organization membership.

9,1 Authority-Compliance
Efficiency in operations results from arranging conditions of work in such a way that human elements interfere to a minimum degree.

Concern for People (vertical axis, Low to High)

Concern for Production (horizontal axis, Low to High)

Source: The Leadership Grid® Figure from *Leadership Dilemmas—Grid Solutions,* by Robert R. Blake and Anne Adams McCanse. Houston: Gulf Publishing Company, p. 29. Copyright © 1991, by Scientific Methods, Inc. Reproduced by permission of the owners.

have been defined in many ways over the years, making it difficult to interpret results across studies.[22] Critics are also concerned that the use of employee questionnaires rather than direct observation to measure leader behaviours may have biased the results.

Finally, the behavioural and trait approaches share a common problem: they are both universal theories that explore the best predictors of leadership under all conditions. The potential influence of environmental factors, such as the nature of the task and characteristics of followers, is not recognized.[23] This severely limits the predictive value of these approaches and explains why they have been largely set aside in favour of contingency theories of leadership, which we describe next.

CONTINGENCY THEORIES OF LEADERSHIP

After several decades of research on leader traits and behaviours had produced mainly inconclusive results, behavioural scientists eventually came to the deceptively simple conclusion that the most appropriate leadership behaviour style depends on the situation.

During the 1960s and 1970s, several contingency theories of leadership emerged to address this new perspective of leadership research. Each of the models described in this section identifies a set of leader behaviours or styles as well as a set of situational conditions. These situational conditions—such as the tasks to be accomplished and the employee or work team characteristics—moderate the relationship between leader behaviours and individual or team outcomes. Thus, a manager's actions may be effective in one situation and quite ineffective in another. Effective leaders are those who accurately diagnose the situation and adapt their behaviours to fit those conditions. As we stated earlier, they must have a high self-monitor personality. They must be both insightful and flexible.[24]

Path-Goal Theory of Leadership

Path-goal leadership theory was developed and refined by Martin Evans, Bob House, and their associates and is arguably the most comprehensive contingency model of leadership. As shown in Exhibit 14–5, the model considers four distinct leader behaviours and several contingency factors leading to three indicators of leader effectiveness: employee motivation, employee satisfaction, and acceptance of the leader.[25]

Path-goal theory has its roots in the expectancy theory of motivation that we described in Chapter 3. Its fundamental proposition is that leader behaviour is effective if it increases employee motivation by strengthening the connection between employee performance and the satisfaction of employee needs. The model also suggests that leader behaviour is effective if it is an immediate source of employee satisfaction or increases the probability of future satisfaction.[26]

Leadership Styles.   Path-goal theory suggests that managers can accomplish their objectives using four basic leadership styles: directive, supportive, participative, and achievement-oriented. Each of these styles is described in Exhibit 14–6. The model contends that effective leaders are capable of selecting the behavioural style that best suits the situation. Moreover, it is possible to adopt more than one style at a time. For example, a leader might be both supportive and participative in a specific situation.

You might have noticed that each of these leadership behaviours has been discussed elsewhere in this book under different topics. Directive leadership echoes our discussion in Chapter 2 on the importance of clear task perceptions in employee performance. Participative leadership overlaps with the Vroom–Yetton–Jago model of employee involvement (see Chapter 11), par-

path-goal leadership theory
A contingency theory of leadership based on expectancy theory of motivation. Path goal suggests that effective leaders strengthen the employee's connection between their performance and need satisfaction.

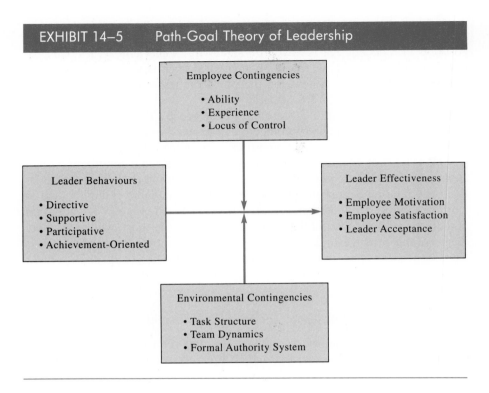

EXHIBIT 14–5   Path-Goal Theory of Leadership

Employee Contingencies

- Ability
- Experience
- Locus of Control

Leader Behaviours

- Directive
- Supportive
- Participative
- Achievement-Oriented

Leader Effectiveness

- Employee Motivation
- Employee Satisfaction
- Leader Acceptance

Environmental Contingencies

- Task Structure
- Team Dynamics
- Formal Authority System

ticularly in terms of the two consultative styles (CI and CII). Achievement-oriented leadership reflects the philosophy of goal setting (Chapter 2) as well as positive expectations in self-fulfilling prophecy (Chapter 7). Supportive leadership was introduced in Chapter 5 where we stated that social support tends to help employees in stressful situations.

Contingency Factors. As a contingency theory, the path-goal model states that each of these four leadership behaviour styles will be effective in some situations but not in others. The two sets of situational variables believed to moderate the relationship between a leader's style and effectiveness are (1) personal contingencies of subordinates and (2) environmental contingencies on subordinates (see Exhibit 14–5 above).[27]

According to the model, directive leadership should be applied where employees have an external locus of control, are inexperienced, the task is unstructured and complex, or there are few organizational rules to guide the work process. In other words, leaders should clarify duties where duties are unclear and provide structure where structure is lacking. The idea here is that leaders should minimize role ambiguity on the grounds that it undermines employee effectiveness.[28] However, directive leadership becomes a form of close supervision where employees are competent, have an internal

EXHIBIT 14–7	Hersey and Blanchard's Situational Leadership Theory

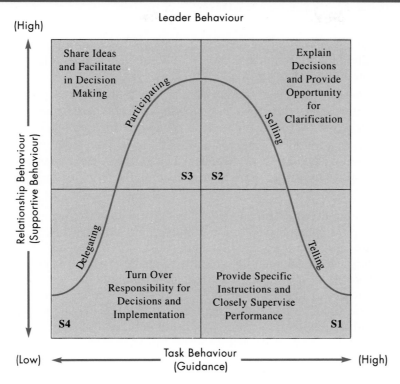

Source: P. Hersey and K. H. Blanchard, *Management of Organizational Behavior: Utilizing Human Resources,* 5th ed. (Englewood Cliffs, N.J.: Prentice Hall, 1988), p. 171.

- *Telling*—Involves describing what the employee should do and how to do it (similar to directive leadership in the path-goal theory). Telling is most appropriate where the person or team lacks ability and willingness to perform the task.
- *Selling*—Involves open dialogue and persuasion to help the employee become committed to the directive. Selling is most appropriate where the individual or group lacks ability to do the task but is at least motivated to give it a try.
- *Participating*—Involves supporting and facilitating without providing much guidance or direction. Participating is best where someone has just learned to do the task but lacks confidence and motivation.
- *Delegating*—Involves observing and monitoring the employee without providing much support or direction. Delegating is most appropriate where the employee or team is motivated and able to accomplish the task.

The situational leadership model is popular among practising managers as a leadership training intervention, but Hersey and Blanchard have provided little empirical evidence to directly support the model's validity. The model has recently been evaluated by others with mixed results.[36] It appears that the Hersey–Blanchard model is correct in presuming that new employees with limited ability require more direction and less support. However, the model is less successful at predicting the best leadership style for those with higher levels of readiness. Perhaps as a result of these problems, Hersey and Blanchard are working on revisions to the situational leadership model.[37]

Fiedler's Contingency Model

Fiedler's contingency theory

A contingency leadership theory based on the idea that leader effectiveness depends on whether the person's natural leadership style is appropriately matched to the situation.

One of the earliest and most widely researched contingency theories of leadership was developed by Fred Fiedler.[38] According to **Fiedler's contingency theory,** leader effectiveness depends on whether the person's natural leadership style is appropriately matched to the situation. The theory examines two leadership styles and three factors used to determine which style is most effective in a particular situation.

Leadership Style.   Fiedler refers to leadership style as "a relatively enduring set of behaviours which is characteristic of the individual regardless of the situation."[39] A person's leadership style is relatively stable over time because it is linked to his or her personality. In the short term, people can act differently in different situations, but they tend to maintain the same general leadership style over time. This is different from the other contingency theories, which assume that leaders can easily adapt their behaviour.

Fiedler developed the least-preferred coworker (LPC) scale to measure leadership style. Individuals are asked to think about their least-preferred coworker and to rate this person on an adjective checklist (tense/relaxed, nasty/nice, gloomy/cheerful, etc.). High-LPC leaders give more favourable ratings to their least-preferred coworker, whereas low-LPC leaders give relatively unfavourable ratings. Fiedler contends that high-LPC leaders have a relationship-oriented style, whereas low-LPC leaders are more task-oriented. LPC may be considered a measure of the leader's preferences for either maintaining relationships or accomplishing tasks.

Contingency Factors.   Fiedler contends that the preference for a high or low LPC style depends on the level of *situational control,* that is, the degree of power and influence that the leader possesses in a particular situation. Situational control is affected by three factors, in the following order of importance:[40]

* *Leader–member relations*—The most important factor is the degree to which employees trust and respect the leader and are willing to follow his or her guidance.
* *Task structure*—The second-most important factor is the degree of task structure. Highly structured tasks are those with a set of clear operating procedures to guide the work team, whereas unstructured tasks are vague and ambiguous.
* *Position power*—The third factor is the leader's position power, that is, the extent to which he or she possesses legitimate, reward, and coercive power over subordinates.

These three contingencies form the eight possible combinations shown in Exhibit 14–8 and create a continuum of *situation favourableness* from the leader's viewpoint. Good leader–member relations, high task structure, and strong position power create the most favourable situation for the leader because he or she has the most power and influence under these conditions. The least favourable situation for the leader exists where leader–member relations are poor, the task is unstructured, and the leader's position power is weak.

As the diagram in Exhibit 14–8 illustrates, low-LPC leaders are more effective where the situation is either very favourable or unfavourable. High-LPC leaders are more effective where the situation is moderately favourable or unfavourable. According to Fiedler, low-LPC leaders are better suited to highly favourable conditions because employees only require someone to give directions so that they can get on with the job. Low-LPC leaders are also more appropriate when conditions are very unfavourable because their strong will and task orientation are needed to counterbalance the team's power and guide it through an ambiguous task.[41]

Matching Situations with Leadership Styles.   As a contingency theory, Fiedler's model recognizes that one leadership style is not best in all situations. So what should be done to maximize leadership effectiveness? Fiedler says that while people can alter their behaviour with the situation, it is

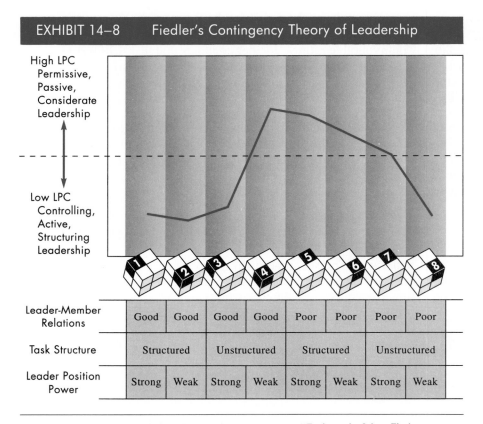

EXHIBIT 14–8   Fiedler's Contingency Theory of Leadership

High LPC
Permissive,
Passive,
Considerate
Leadership

Low LPC
Controlling,
Active,
Structuring
Leadership

	1	2	3	4	5	6	7	8
Leader-Member Relations	Good	Good	Good	Good	Poor	Poor	Poor	Poor
Task Structure	Structured		Unstructured		Structured		Unstructured	
Leader Position Power	Strong	Weak	Strong	Weak	Strong	Weak	Strong	Weak

Source: Reprinted by permission of *Harvard Business Review*. "Engineer the Job to Fit the Manager," by F. E. Fiedler, September–October, 1965, p. 118. Copyright 1965 by the President and Fellows of Harvard College; all rights reserved.

relatively difficult to maintain a particular leadership style that is incompatible with the individual's personality over an extended period of time. Consequently, the most effective strategy is to change the situation so that it matches the leader's style rather than vice versa.

Fiedler outlines several ways to alter the three situational control factors.[42] Leader–member relations may be improved (or weakened) by changing the team's membership. The team's work can become less structured by introducing new problems that do not easily fit into existing procedures. Task structure may be increased by creating more programmed decision rules or breaking complex work into smaller, more routine parts. Finally, leader power may be increased through several strategies described in Chapter 12, such as channelling all information through the leader or increasing the leader's visibility as the source of legitimate power.

Is Fiedler's Contingency Model Accurate?   Some reviews have concluded that Fiedler's contingency model is generally accurate, at least for some octants.[43] However, the theory has been severely criticized by others and its acceptance as a theory of leader effectiveness is quickly waning. In particular, the validity of the LPC scale is in doubt and there is no scientific justification for placing the three situational control factors in a hierarchy. Moreover, it seems that leader–member relations is actually an indicator of leader effectiveness (as in the path-goal theory) rather than as a situational factor. Finally, the theory considers only two leadership styles, whereas other models present a more complex and realistic array of behaviour options.[44]

In spite of these problems, Fiedler's contingency theory makes two important contributions. First, unlike other models, it emphasizes the importance of the leader's control over subordinates and includes the potential relevance of leader power as a contingency of leader effectiveness. Second, whereas other contingency models presume that leaders can alter their behaviour, Fiedler offers the unique advice that it may be easier to engineer the situation than to change the leader's style.

TRANSFORMATIONAL LEADERSHIP

The behavioural and contingency theories of leadership that we have just described are primarily rational models of the supervisor–subordinate exchange relationships that prescribe the most appropriate management behaviours to improve employee effectiveness. This aspect of leadership, called **transactional leadership,** involves the manager's use of legitimate, reward, and coercive power bases to facilitate and direct employees toward accomplishing task and organizational objectives.[45]

Transactional behaviours are important because they improve productivity and employee well-being by facilitating work arrangements and linking task accomplishment to valued rewards. However, they represent only one part of the total leadership concept. The other aspect of leadership, called **transformational leadership,** supplements transactional activities by communicating a vision and inspiring employees to strive for that vision.[46] Transformational leaders are agents of change. They broaden and elevate the interests of their followers and motivate them to transcend their own self-interests in favour of team or organizational interests.[47] Some leaders are charismatic revolutionaries; others use more subtle approaches to commit the team or organization toward new directions. Leadership theorists early in this century who searched for traits of great leaders were, in fact, mainly investigating the transformational element of leadership.

Transformational leaders such as Timothy Eaton, H. R. McMillan, and Elizabeth Arden dot the landscape of Canadian history. Samuel Cunard, founder of Cunard Steamship Lines, is arguably one of this country's most visionary business leaders. The unschooled son of a Halifax dockyard worker, Cunard was known for his far-sighted optimism and fervent imagination, which he used to literally transform ocean navigation during the 1800s. His vision of an "ocean railway" in which people could cross the Atlantic in safety and on schedule was unimaginable at the time, yet perseverance and commitment from his staff eventually brought his vision to life.

transactional leadership
Using legitimate, reward, and coercive power bases to help employees accomplish existing tasks and organizational objectives more effectively.

transformational leadership
Transforming organizations by creating, communicating, and modelling a vision of a desired state of affairs, and inspiring employees to strive for that vision.

Cunard's distinctly transformational leadership style is described by one writer: "And there is no doubt that [Cunard] could see an opportunity when it was no more than a dot on the horizon, seize it confidently, persuade others it was a good idea and transform it into a highly successful enterprise."[48]

Managers versus Leaders

The terms *transactional* and *transformational leadership* were coined in 1978 by James McGregor Burns, but leadership writers have been subtly aware of the difference for much longer. For example, Zaleznik's distinction between "managers" and "leaders" closely parallels transactional and transformational leaders.[49] Bennis and Nanus suggest that the difference between managers and leaders is much like the difference between productivity and organizational effectiveness: managers do things right, whereas leaders do the right things (see Chapter 1).[50]

There is currently a flurry of writing and research on the dynamics of transformational leadership. While it is too early to provide detailed and validated information about this process, we can identify four common elements of transformational leadership running throughout the recent batch of literature. As illustrated in Exhibit 14–9, these features include creating a strategic vision, communicating the vision, modelling the vision, and building commitment toward the vision.

Creating a Strategic Vision

Transformational leaders are the brokers of dreams.[51] They help shape a strategic vision that becomes an overarching focus of attention, the superordinate target that draws organizational members together. Visions articulate a unique view of a realistic and attractive future for the organization.[52]

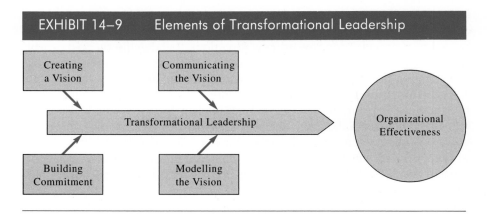

EXHIBIT 14–9   Elements of Transformational Leadership

Visions represent the *substance* of transformational leadership. They grab the attention of followers and provide a challenging goal toward which their commitment is directed. Isadore Sharp, described at the beginning of this chapter, transformed his vision of a luxury hotel chain into a competitive advantage for Four Seasons. Perspective 14–3 describes Moses Znaimer as another transformational leader whose vision of a television station for the ''new Toronto'' is equally impressive.

The leader's vision must reflect a future state of affairs that is ultimately accepted and valued by organizational members. This is accomplished partly by shaping the vision around goals that are already meaningful to employees and partly by communicating the vision in a way that is consistent with the employees' prevailing values.[53] Strategic visions might originate with the leader, but they are just as likely to emerge from employees, clients, suppliers, or other constituents. Effective leaders draw upon the images that are generated from these sources and push them toward reality. Visions typically begin as abstract ideas that become progressively clearer through critical events and discussions with staff about strategic and operational plans.[54] Returning again to Isadore Sharp's leadership, we see that his vision was crystallized following his experience with a project involving ITT's Sheraton Hotel chain.

Communicating the Vision

If vision is the substance of transformational leadership, then communicating that vision is the process. Effective leaders are able to communicate meaning and elevate the importance of the visionary goal to organizational members.[55] This involves two skills: framing the vision around a grand purpose and symbolizing the vision to amplify meaning.

Framing the Vision.   *Framing* refers to seeing issues from a particular perspective. Effective leaders frame their messages around a grand purpose with emotional appeal to the audience (employees, clients, suppliers, etc.). These emotional appeals typically represent social values, such as personal freedom, alternative choices, expanding knowledge, or creating happiness for the organization's constituents. George Cohen, the ebullient CEO of McDonald's Canada, has successfully realized his dream of McDonald's in Moscow by effectively framing this vision. Cohen views his mission not of selling hamburgers in foreign countries, but of ''making the world a better place'' through ''hamburger diplomacy.'' Cohen's dream of having McDonald's in the Soviet Union was formed at the 1976 Montreal Olympics where he met members of the Soviet delegation. Gaining McDonald's admittance into the Soviet Union became an obsession, which turned into reality in 1988. Through hamburger diplomacy, Cohen was able to dedicate his associates as well as Soviet officials to achieving this seemingly insurmountable challenge.[56]

As founder and CEO of Toronto's largest and quirkiest television station, CITY-TV, as well as rock video stations MusiquePlus and MuchMusic, Moses Znaimer has a right to fancy himself an outsider, even a revolutionary. Critics and fans alike agree that he is idiosyncratic, countercultural, and definitely antiestablishment. Znaimer has assumed the mantle of a lone rebel struggling to break new ground against menacing regulators and elephantine competitors.

Being studiously different has brought great success to Znaimer and the entertainment businesses he runs. CITY-TV, owned by CHUM Ltd. since 1977, consistently soars in the local TV ratings race. MuchMusic and MusiquePlus, seen on cable TV in millions of Canadian homes, have become cultural flagships for young people. And Znaimer hopes to carry this success on to his latest passion, Interactive Entertainment Inc., which, among other things, has produced a futuristic ride called Tour of the Universe, at the foot of Toronto's CN Tower.

Znaimer's transformational leadership is most apparent in the unique and highly successful character of CITY-TV. Founded in 1972 by Znaimer and three other investors on a shoestring budget, CITY-TV reflects Toronto's cultural diversity both on the air and in the boardroom, where Anglo-Saxons find themselves side by side with Italian developers and Jews in the needle trades. "I set about systematically to create a company that reflected what I could feel in my own life, which is a new Toronto," explains Znaimer. "We

Symbolizing the Vision.   Transformational leaders bring their visions to life through symbols, metaphors, stories, and other vehicles that transcend plain language.[57] Samuel Cunard effectively communicated his dream of a transcontinental steamship line using the "ocean railway" metaphor. This metaphor reflected the values of safety and reliability that were easily accepted by employees during an age when ocean travel was a risky business. Organizational stories represent another way to communicate meaning better than facts and figures. Music has also been used to communicate meaning in a way that can never be replicated with words. For instance, before shooting the movie *Ordinary People*, director Robert Redford asked his cinematographers to listen to Pachelbel's *Canon in D*. Redford said to them: "I want you to listen to this, and I want you to think about what a suburban scene would look like if it corresponded to the music."[58]

Modelling the Vision

Transformational leaders not only talk about a vision, they enact it. They step outside the executive suite and explicitly demonstrate that the vision is real and important. In effect, leaders are the embodiment of the vision and a guide for representative behaviour.[59] David Berlew calls this "walking the talk": behaving in ways both large and small that symbolize the values the leader is articulating.[60] In some respects, walking the talk distinguishes the transformational leader from the sly marketer. It demonstrates the leader's conviction toward achieving the goal.

said the point of this company is that it's urban, it's downtown."

As the son of Soviet emigrants, Znaimer grew up in the heart of Montreal's Jewish community. So when CITY-TV started, he easily identified with Toronto's large immigrant population and had no difficulty shaping the station into his multicultural image of the city.

Two decades after creating CITY-TV, Znaimer shows no signs of slowing down. Despite failures at two CRTC hearings (the Canadian government's communications watchdog), he is determined to gain approval to take the CITY-TV format to Ottawa. Znaimer also has visions of planting similar stations in Montreal and Vancouver and of transforming CITY-TV into a superstation by beaming its signal via satellite to all parts of the country.

People who have worked with Znaimer say he's relentless in the pursuit of his goals and will likely succeed in his endeavours. Peter Herrndorf, publisher of *Toronto Life* and former CBC executive, describes him as a passionate man. "He has tremendous energy, a lot of chutzpah, a lot of style. Moses is a man who bubbles over with ideas."

Source: Based on D. Hogarth, "TV Revolutionary with Hobnail Guccis," *Financial Post*, February 21, 1990, p. 12.

Walking the talk includes manipulating the mundane symbols, patterns, and settings that are the executive's tools. Meeting agendas, promotion criteria, executive work schedules, and physical settings within the organization should be consistent with the vision and its underlying values. Employees, clients, and other constituents are executive watchers who look for these signs and symbols as evidence that the leader's vision is sincere.[61]

To model the vision effectively, leaders must be reliable and persistent in their actions. Bennis and Nanus refer to this as "positioning," whereby leaders acquire and wear their vision like clothes. They stay on course, thereby legitimizing the vision and providing further evidence that they can be trusted.[62] We tend to trust leaders when we know where they stand on organizational issues and how those issues relate to the organizational environment.

Building Commitment toward the Vision

Transforming a vision into reality requires employee commitment. Effective leaders build this commitment in several ways. Through words, symbols, and stories, they transfer an emotion that inspires and energizes people to adopt the vision as their own. By enacting their vision and staying on course, leaders instill a "can do" attitude. Their persistence and consistency reflect an image of honesty, trust, and integrity. These features enable leaders to gain commitment and support from followers because they legitimize the leader's beliefs and values.[63]

Leaders also build commitment through their contagious enthusiasm and confidence in the future. They engage in a positive form of self-fulfilling prophecy (see Chapter 7) by demonstrating their optimism that the challenge can be overcome.[64] Recall from our opening vignette that Isadore Sharp called this a "fanatical belief that it will work." David McCamus, head of Xerox Canada, also recognizes the need for leaders to generate and maintain this positive attitude: "I have an approach I call 'success management,'" says McCamus. "Everybody comes to a company wanting to be successful. So, you've got to institutionalize success. You've got to make it the norm."[65]

Finally, employees become dedicated through their involvement in forming and shaping the organization's future vision. As mentioned before, many organizational visions originate from employees and are adopted and focussed by leaders. Involvement in the transformation process bonds employees to the vision and its operational ramifications.

Charisma and Transformational Leadership

Are transformational leaders charismatic? This question has been the source of much controversy and confusion among leadership experts. As we mentioned in Chapter 12, charisma has acquired several meanings in our society. It has been described by some writers as a personality trait that transformational leaders use to build commitment in followers toward their vision.[66] This power is similar to referent power that we described in Chapter 12. Other writers imply that charisma is another label for transformational leadership, that is, charismatic leaders are so called because they use the transformational activities described above to get results.[67]

In our opinion, charisma is an overused term that adds little value to the concept and process of transformational leadership. It is either a redundant label for transformational practices or represents a personality trait with unknown parameters. We must be careful not to view charisma as the "gee whiz" perspective of transformational leadership.[68] This merely creates a black box theory in which charisma is everything wonderful about leaders that we don't understand. This point is nicely phrased by David Morton, chairman and CEO of Alcan Aluminum Ltd.: "Beware of charismatic leaders," Morton warns. "Business is not a religion or a mystery; it's a part of life. Those who want to be leaders in business must see their own shortcomings and lead, not push."[69]

LEADERSHIP SUBSTITUTES

leadership substitutes
Characteristics of the employee, task, or organization that either limit the leader's influence or make it unnecessary.

Leadership substitutes include characteristics of the employee, task, or organization that either limit the leader's influence or make it unnecessary. When substitute conditions are present, employees are effective without the leader. Indeed, these conditions may neutralize any effect the leader's actions would otherwise have on employees.

EXHIBIT 14–10	Substitutes for Leadership	

	Will Tend to Neutralize	
Characteristic	**Relationship-Oriented**	**Task-Oriented**
Of the subordinate:		
1. Ability, experience, training, knowledge		X
2. Need for independence	X	X
3. "Professional" orientation	X	X
4. Indifference toward organizational rewards	X	X
Of the task:		
5. Unambiguous and routine		X
6. Methodologically invariant		X
7. Provides its own feedback concerning accomplishment		X
8. Intrinsically satisfying	X	
Of the organization:		
9. Formalization (explicit plans, goals, and areas of responsibility)		X
10. Inflexibility (rigid, unbending rules and procedures)		X
11. Highly specified and active advisory and staff functions		X
12. Close-knit, cohesive work groups	X	X
13. Organizational rewards not within the leader's control	X	X
14. Spatial distance between superior and subordinates	X	X

Source: Adapted from S. Kerr and J. M. Jermier, "Substitutes for Leadership: Their Meaning and Measurement," *Organizational Behavior and Human Performance* 22 (1978), p. 379.

Exhibit 14–10 lists several substitutes for leadership and indicates the type of leadership behaviour—relationship-oriented or task-oriented—that is replaced or neutralized. For example, inflexible work procedures keep employees directed toward organizational goals, so it would be redundant or impossible to provide task-oriented behaviours under these conditions. Similarly, cohesive work teams replace the need for both types of leader behaviour because these functions are provided by coworkers.

The leadership substitutes model is embedded in several contemporary organizational practices, including self-managing work teams (see Chapter 11) and individual self-management. In self-managing work teams, supervisors are largely replaced by cohesive work units and improved performance-feedback channels. The leadership substitutes concept also applies to individual self-management, whereby employees manage themselves through goal setting, self-assessment, and feedback. In both practices, supervision of employees has been replaced by several of the factors listed in Exhibit 14–10.[70]

Two important observations can be made when we examine the list of leader substitutes in the context of other leadership perspectives described in this chapter. First, these substitutes seem to replace or neutralize transactional rather than transformational leadership. Leadership substitutes help employees do their jobs more effectively, but they do not establish new directions for the organization or build employee commitment to the organization's strategic vision.

The second observation is that many of these substitutes are discussed in the contingency leadership theories presented earlier. As an example, path-goal theory states that directive leadership is unnecessary—and possibly dysfunctional—when employees are competent (high ability, experience, etc.), the task is structured, and work procedures are clearly defined. These three contingencies are identified in Exhibit 14–10 as substitutes for task-oriented leadership (roughly the equivalent of path-goal's directive leadership). Thus, the leadership substitutes perspective is compatible with the contingency perspective of leadership.

THE ATTRIBUTION AND ROMANCE OF LEADERSHIP

Our discussion of leadership substitutes introduces a somewhat skeptical view of the relevance of leaders in organizations, but it pales against recent suggestions that leaders might be given too much credit (or blame) for organizational outcomes. The trait, behaviour, contingency, and transformational leadership perspectives make the fundamental assumption that leaders "make the difference." Leaders do account for some variance in organizational effectiveness,[71] but as one writer has recently quipped, "It is easier to believe in leadership than to prove it."[72] Several cognitive psychologists now suggest that three perceptual processes cause people to inflate the importance of leadership in explaining organizational events. These processes, shown in Exhibit 14–11, include attribution errors, stereotyping, and the romance of leadership.

Attributing Leadership

Recall from Chapter 7 that people have a strong need to understand why events occur so that they can feel more confident about how to control them in the future. The attribution process involves attributing the cause of these events either to characteristics of the person (internal attributions), such as ability and motivation, or to characteristics of the situation (external attributions), such as resources and luck. In the context of leadership, people are more likely to attribute organizational outcomes to leaders than to environ-

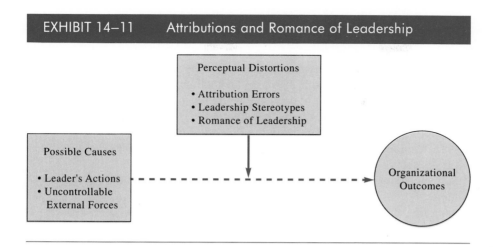

EXHIBIT 14–11   Attributions and Romance of Leadership

mental conditions because the effects of external forces are not as apparent.[73] Leaders are given credit or blame for many events that are primarily beyond their control because these external forces are not apparent to observers. Leaders reinforce this belief by taking credit for organizational successes.[74]

Stereotyping Leadership

Employees have a shared set of expectations and stereotypes regarding the notion of what constitutes an effective leader.[75] These preconceived ideas of how leaders should behave are used to decide who has leadership qualities and whether they are effective. By relying on these stereotypes, employees basically evaluate leadership effectiveness more on the actions of leaders than on their outcomes. This perceptual bias leads people to see organizational events as a result of leadership initiatives simply because the individual *looks like* an effective leader.

The Romance of Leadership

A third perceptual distortion of leadership, called the "romance of leadership," suggests that people want to believe leaders make a difference for two basic reasons.[76] First, leadership is a useful handle to simplify the causal meaning of organizational phenomena. Rather than trying to gain a detailed understanding of complex events, we prefer the more efficient explanation that they are the result of effective or ineffective leadership. Second, there is a strong tendency in Canada and other Western societies to believe that life events are generated more from people than from uncontrollable natural forces.[77] This illusion of control is satisfied by believing that events result from the rational actions of leaders. In short, employees feel better believing that leaders make a difference, so they actively look for evidence that this is so.

The attribution and romance of leadership perspective questions the importance of leadership, but it also provides valuable advice to improve leadership effectiveness. This approach highlights the fact that leadership is a perception of followers as much as the actual behaviours and characteristics of people calling themselves leaders. Potential leaders must be sensitive to this fact, understand what followers expect, and act accordingly. Individuals who do not make an effort to fit leadership prototypes will have more difficulty managing employees and bringing about necessary organizational change.[78]

SUMMARY

- Leadership is the process of having an incremental influence on other team members toward defined objectives more than they influence the leader. This involves some combination of power and persuasion to bring about change in others.

- The major approaches to understanding leadership in organizations include (1) leader traits, (2) leader behaviours, (3) contingencies on effective leader behaviours, (4) transformational leadership, and (5) leadership substitutes. Leadership experts have also recently introduced the idea that we may have overplayed the importance of leadership as a cause of organizational outcomes.

- For the first half of the 20th century, researchers attempted to identify the traits that predict leadership effectiveness. They eventually concluded that traits have a weak effect on leader effectiveness and that few traits have any importance across all situations.

- By the end of World War II, the focus had shifted toward a more behavioural perspective of leadership. Researchers classified leader behaviours into two categories—consideration and initiating structure—which they found were independent of one another. The behavioural approach developed the "hi-hi" leadership hypothesis, meaning that the most effective leaders exhibited high levels of both types of behaviours. This hypothesis has since been cast into doubt. The managerial grid, a popular management training intervention, was born out of the behavioural approach, although its authors now claim a more contingency approach.

- The contingency approach is based on the idea that the most appropriate leadership behaviour style depends on the situation. Effective leaders are those who accurately diagnose the situation and adapt their behaviours to fit those conditions. The prominent contingency models include path-goal theory, situational leadership, and Fiedler's contingency theory. Each of these models suggests that characteristics of the employee, task, and environment moderate the effectiveness of a particular leadership style.

• Transactional leadership includes rational models of the supervisor–subordinate exchange relationships that prescribe the most appropriate management behaviours to improve employee effectiveness. Transformational leadership supplements transactional activities by communicating a vision and inspiring employees to strive for that vision. The four basic elements of transformational leadership include creating a strategic vision, communicating the vision, modelling the vision, and building commitment toward the vision.

• Leadership substitutes include characteristics of the employee, task, or organization that either limit the leader's influence or make it unnecessary. Substitutes are used in self-managing work teams, individual self-management, and other contemporary organizational practices that empower employees.

• People engage in perceptual distortions that tend to give leaders too much credit or blame for organizational outcomes. Through attribution errors, leaders are given credit or blame for many events that are primarily beyond their control because these external forces are not apparent to observers. By relying on leadership stereotypes, people tend to evaluate leadership effectiveness more on the actions of leaders than on their outcomes. Finally, individuals want to believe in leadership because it simplifies the causal meaning of organizational phenomena and supports the need (at least in Western countries) to believe that life events are generated from people rather than uncontrollable natural forces.

DISCUSSION QUESTIONS

1. What conditions are necessary for leadership to exist?
2. Why should we be careful about using personal traits to explain why some people make effective leaders?
3. What is the "hi-hi" leadership hypothesis? How is this hypothesis adopted in the managerial grid? How have the authors of the managerial grid shifted toward a more contingency perspective in recent years?
4. What motivation theory is applied by path-goal theory? How?
5. Discuss the similarities of the path-goal and situational leadership theories.
6. Of what importance is communication in transformational leadership?
7. How do transformational leaders build commitment toward their vision?

8. Why do people tend to give leaders too much credit or blame for organizational outcomes?

NOTES

1. K. Foss, "Isadore Sharp," *Foodservice and Hospitality,* December 1989, pp. 20–30; J. DeMont, "Sharp's Luxury Empire," *Maclean's,* June 5, 1989, pp. 30–33; P. King, "Building a Team the Sharp Way," *Canadian Business,* November 1990, pp. 96–101; D. Chong, "Power Is Proprietorship," *Canadian Business,* December 1988, p. 54; and I. Sharp, "Quality for All Seasons," *Canadian Business Review* 17, no. 1 (Spring 1990), pp. 21–23.

2. J. M. Burns, *Leadership* (New York: Harper & Row, 1978), p. 2.

3. B. M. Bass, *Stogdill's Handbook of Leadership* (New York: Free Press, 1981), p. 16; and D. Katz and R. L. Kahn, *The Social Psychology of Organizations* (New York: Wiley, 1966), pp. 300–303.

4. D. Miller, M. F. R. Ket de Vries, and J. M. Toulouse, "Top Executive Locus of Control and Its Relationship to Strategy-Making, Structure, and Environment," *Academy of Management Journal* 25 (1982), pp. 237–53; and S. Withane, "Leadership Influence on Organizational Reorientations: A Strategic Choice Model," *Proceedings of the Annual ASAC Conference, Organizational Behaviour Division* 7, part 5 (1986), pp. 218–27.

5. P. Selznick, *Leadership in Administration* (Evanston, Ill.: Row, Peterson, 1957), p. 37.

6. R. M. Stogdill, *Handbook of Leadership* (New York: Free Press, 1974), p. 63.

7. Stogdill, *Handbook of Leadership,* Chapter 5.

8. N. Schmitt, R. Z. Gooding, R. A. Noe, and M. Kirsch, "Meta-Analyses of Validity Studies Published between 1964 and 1982 and the Investigation of Study Characteristics," *Personnel Psychology* 37 (1984), pp. 407–22.

9. R. J. Ellis and R. S. Adamson, "Antecedents of Leadership Emergence," *Proceedings of the Annual ASAC Conference, Organizational Behaviour Division* 7, part 5 (1986), pp. 49–57; and H. Garland and J. F. Beard, "Relationship between Self-Monitoring and Leader Emergence across Two Task Situations," *Journal of Applied Psychology* 64 (1979), pp. 72–76.

10. R. S. Adamson, R. J. Ellis, G. Deszca, and T. F. Cawsey, "Self-Monitoring and Leadership Emergence," *Proceedings of the Annual ASAC Conference, Organizational Behaviour Division* 5, part 5 (1984), pp. 9–15.

11. R. Likert, *New Patterns of Management* (New York: McGraw-Hill, 1961); E. A. Fleishman and E. F. Harris, "Patterns of Leadership Behavior Related to Employee Grievances and Turnover," *Personnel Psychology* 15 (1962), pp. 43–56; and G. A. Yukl, *Leadership in Organizations,* 2nd ed. (Englewood Cliffs, N.J.: Prentice Hall, 1989), pp. 74–80.

12. R. L. Kahn, "The Prediction of Productivity," *Journal of Social Issues* 12, no. 2 (1956), pp. 41–49; and P. Weissenberg and M. H. Kavanagh, "The Independence of Initiating Structure and Consideration: A Review of the Evidence," *Personnel Psychology* 25 (1972), pp. 119–30.

13. V. E. Schein, "Relationships between Sex Role Stereotypes and Requisite Management Characteristics among Female Managers," *Journal of Applied Psychology* 60 (1975), pp. 340–44.

14. K. K. Lush and M. J. Withey, "Gender as a Moderator in the Path-Goal Theory of Leadership," *Proceedings of the Annual ASAC Conference, Organizational Behaviour Divison* 11, part 5 (1990), pp. 140–49; and G. H. Dobbins and S. J. Platts, "Sex Differences in Leadership: How Real Are They?" *Academy of Management Review* 11 (1986), pp. 118–27.

15. Stogdill, *Handbook of Leadership,* Chapter 11.

16. A. K. Korman, "Consideration, Initiating Structure, and Organizational Criteria—A Review," *Personnel Psychology* 19 (1966), pp. 349–62; and E. A. Fleishman, "Twenty Years of Consideration and Structure," in E. A. Fleishman and J. C. Hunt (eds.), *Current Developments in the Study of Leadership* (Carbondale, Ill.: Southern Illinois University Press, 1973), pp. 1–40.

17. T. B. Greenfield, "Research on the Behaviour of Educational Teachers: Critique of a Tradition," *Alberta Journal of Educational Research* 14 (1968), pp. 55–76; and A. F. Brown, "Reactions to Leadership," *Educational Administration Quarterly* 3 (1967), pp. 62–73.

18. D. Tjosvold, "Effects of Leader Warmth and Directiveness on Subordinate Performance on a Subsequent Task," *Journal of Applied Psychology* 69 (1984), pp. 222–32.

19. R. R. Blake and J. S. Mouton, *The Managerial Grid III* (Houston, Texas: Gulf Publishing, 1985).

20. R. R. Blake and J. S. Mouton, "Management by Grid Principles or Situationalism: Which?" *Group and Organization Studies* 7 (1982), pp. 207–10.

21. L. L. Larson, J. G. Hunt, and R. N. Osborn, "The Great Hi-Hi Leader Behavior Myth: A Lesson from Occam's Razor," *Academy of Management Journal* 19 (1976), pp. 628–41; and A. K. Korman, "Consideration, Initiating Structure, and Organizational Criteria—A Review," *Personnel Psychology* 19 (1966), pp. 349–62.

22. G. Yukl, "Toward a Behavioral Theory of Leadership," *Administrative Science Quarterly* 6 (July 1971), pp. 414–40.

23. S. Kerr, C. A. Schriesheim, C. J. Murphy, and R. M. Stogdill, "Towards a Contingency Theory of Leadership Based upon the Consideration and Initiating Structure Literature," *Organizational Behavior and Human Performance* 12 (1974), pp. 62–82.

24. R. Tannenbaum and W. H. Schmidt, "How to Choose a Leadership Pattern," *Harvard Business Review,* May–June 1973, pp. 162–80.

25. M. G. Evans, "The Effects of Supervisory Behavior on the Path-Goal Relationship," *Organizational Behavior and Human Performance* 5 (1970), pp. 277–98; M. G. Evans, "Extensions of a Path-Goal Theory of Motivation," *Journal of Applied Psychology* 59 (1974), pp. 172–78; and R. J. House, "A Path-Goal Theory of Leader Effectiveness," *Administrative Science Quarterly* 16 (1971), pp. 321–38.

26. R. J. House and T. R. Mitchell, "Path-Goal Theory of Leadership," *Journal of Contemporary Business,* Autumn 1974, pp. 81–97.

27. Ibid.

28. R. T. Keller, "A Test of the Path-Goal Theory of Leadership with Need for Clarity as a Moderator in Research and Development Organizations," *Journal of Applied Psychology,* April 1989, pp. 208–12.

29. D. A. Ondrack, "Examination of the Generation Gap: Attitudes toward Authority," *Personnel Administration* 34 (May–June 1971), pp. 8–17.

30. Yukl, *Leadership in Organizations,* pp. 102–4; and J. Indvik, "Path-Goal Theory of Leadership: A Meta-Analysis," *Academy of Management Proceedings* 1986, pp. 189–92.

31. W. J. Reddin, "The 3-D Management Style Theory," *Training and Development Journal* 21 (April 1967), pp. 8–17; and W. J. Reddin, *Managerial Effectiveness* (New York: McGraw-Hill, 1970).

32. R. P. Vecchio, "Situational Leadership Theory: An Examination of a Prescriptive Theory," *Journal of Applied Psychology* 72 (1987), pp. 444–51.

33. W. J. Reddin, *The Output-Oriented Organization* (Aldershot, England: Gower Publishing, 1988), Chapter 7.

34. P. Hersey and K. H. Blanchard, *Management of Organizational Behavior: Utilizing Human Resources,* 5th ed. (Englewood Cliffs, N.J.: Prentice Hall, 1988).

35. Ibid., pp. 177–80.

36. W. Blank, J. R. Weitzel, and S. G. Green, "A Test of the Situational Leadership Theory," *Personnel Psychology* 43 (1990), pp. 579–97; and Vecchio, "Situational Leadership Theory: An Examination of a Prescriptive Theory."

37. For a somewhat different version of the model described here, see K. H. Blanchard, P. Zigami, and D. Zigami, *Leadership and the One Minute Manager* (New York: William Morrow and Co., 1985).

38. F. E. Fiedler, *A Theory of Leadership Effectiveness* (New York: McGraw-Hill, 1967); and F. E. Fiedler and M. M. Chemers, *Leadership and Effective Management* (Glenview, Ill.: Scott, Foresman, 1974).

39. Fiedler and Chemers, *Leadership and Effective Management,* p. 40.

40. F. E. Fiedler, "Engineer the Job to Fit the Manager," *Harvard Business Review* 43, no. 5 (1965), pp. 115–22.

41. Ibid.

42. F. E. Fiedler and J. E. Garcia, *New Approaches to Effective Leadership* (New York: Wiley, 1987).

43. L. H. Peters, D. D. Hartke, and J. T. Pohlman, "Fiedler's Contingency Theory of Leadership: An Application of the Meta-Analysis Procedures of Schmidt and Hunter," *Psychological Bulletin* 97 (1985), pp. 274–85.

44. For a summary of criticisms, see Yukl, *Leadership in Organizations,* pp. 197–98.

45. B. J. Avolio and B. M. Bass, "Transformational Leadership, Charisma, and Beyond," in J. G. Hunt, H. P. Dachler, B. R. Baliga, and C. A. Schriesheim (eds.), *Emerging Leadership Vistas* (Lexington, Mass.: Lexington Books, 1988), pp. 29–49.

46. J. Seltzer and B. M. Bass, "Transformational Leadership: Beyond Initiation and Consideration," *Journal of Management* 16 (1990), pp. 693–703.

47. J. M. Burns, *Leadership* (New York: Harper & Row, 1978).

48. S. Franklin, *The Heroes: A Saga of Canadian Inspiration* (Toronto: McClelland and Stewart, 1967), p. 53.

49. A. Zaleznik, "Managers and Leaders: Are They Different?" *Harvard Business Review* 55, no. 5 (1977), pp. 67–78; and A. Zaleznik, *The Managerial Mystique* (New York: Harper & Row, 1989).

50. W. Bennis and B. Nanus, *Leaders: The Strategies for Taking Charge* (New York: Harper & Row, 1985), p. 21.

51. L. Sooklal, "The Leader as a Broker of Dreams," Manchester Business School, Working Paper no. 108 (1985); and R. C. Hodgson, "Transformational Management," *Business Quarterly* 53, no. 2 (Autumn 1988), pp. 17–20.

52. Bennis and Nanus, *Leaders: The Strategies for Taking Charge,* pp. 27–33, 89; J. M. Kouzes and B. Z. Posner, *The Leadership Challenge* (San Francisco: Jossey-Bass, 1988), Chapter 5; and N. M. Tichy and M. A. Devanna, *The Transformational Leader* (New York: Wiley, 1986).

53. D. E. Berlew, "Leadership and Organizational Excitement," in D. A. Kolb, I. M. Rubin, and J. M. McIntyre (eds.), *Organizational Psychology: A Book of Readings* (Englewood Cliffs, N.J.: Prentice Hall, 1974).

54. T. J. Peters, "Symbols, Patterns, and Settings: An Optimistic Case for Getting Things Done," *Organizational Dynamics* 7, no. 2 (Autumn 1978), pp. 2–23.

55. J. A. Conger, "Inspiring Others: The Language of Leadership," *Academy of Management Executive* 5, no. 1 (February 1991), pp. 31–45.

56. L. Black, "Hamburger Diplomacy," *Report on Business Magazine* 5 (August 1988), pp. 30–36.

57. J. Pfeffer, "Management as Symbolic Action: The Creation and Maintenance of Organizational Paradigms," *Research in Organizational Behavior* 3 (1981), pp. 1–52; and Kouzes and Posner, *The Leadership Challenge,* pp. 118–21.

58. Bennis and Nanus, *Leaders: The Strategies for Taking Charge,* pp. 35–36.

59. P. Tommerup, "Stories about an Inspiring Leader," *American Behavioral Scientist* 33 (1990), pp. 374–85.

60. Berlew, "Leadership and Organizational Excitement."

61. Peters, "Symbols, Patterns, and Settings: The Language of Leadership."

62. Bennis and Nanus, *Leaders: The Strategies for Taking Charge,* pp. 43–55.

63. S. A. Kirkpatrick and E. A. Locke, "Leadership: Do Traits Matter?" *Academy of Management Executive* 5, no. 2 (May 1990), pp. 48–60.

64. R. H. G. Field, "The Self-Fulfilling Prophecy Leader: Achieving the Metharme Effect," *Journal of Management Studies* 26 (1989), pp. 151–75.

65. A. R. Aird, P. Nowak, and J. W. Westcott, *Road to the Top* (Toronto: Doubleday Canada, 1988), p. 73.

66. B. M. Bass, *Leadership and Performance beyond Expectations* (New York: Free Press, 1985).

67. J. A. Conger and R. N. Kanungo, "Toward a Behavioral Theory of Charismatic Leadership in Organizational Settings," *Academy of Management Review* 12 (1987), pp. 637–47; and R. J. House, "A 1976 Theory of Charismatic Leadership," in J. G. Hunt and L. L. Larson (eds.), *Leadership: The Cutting Edge* (Carbondale, Ill.: Southern Illinois University Press, 1977), pp. 189–207.

68. J. M. Burns, ''Forward,'' in B. Kellerman (ed.), *Leadership: Multidisciplinary Perspectives* (Englewood Cliffs, N.J.: Prentice Hall, 1984), p. vii.

69. D. Forrest, ''50 Ways to Run a Company,'' *Canadian Business,* July 1991, p. 59.

70. C. A. Frayne, ''Improving Employee Performance through Self-Management Training,'' *Business Quarterly* 54 (Summer 1989), pp. 46–50; and C. C. Manz and H. P. Sims, *Superleadership: Leading Others to Lead Themselves* (New York: Simon and Schuster, 1989).

71. N. Weiner and T. A. Mahoney, ''A Model of Corporate Performance as a Function of Environmental, Organizational, and Leadership Influences,'' *Academy of Management Journal* 24 (1981), pp. 453–70.

72. J. R. Meindl, ''On Leadership: An Alternative to the Conventional Wisdom,'' *Research in Organizational Behavior* 12 (1990), pp. 159–203.

73. J. M. Tolliver, ''Leadership and Attribution of Cause: A Modification and Extension of Current Theory,'' *Proceedings of the Annual ASAC Conference, Organizational Behaviour Division* 4, part 5 (1983), pp. 182–91.

74. G. R. Salancik and J. R. Meindl, ''Corporate Attributions as Strategic Illusions of Management Control,'' *Administrative Science Quarterly* 29 (1984), pp. 238–54.

75. S. F. Cronshaw and R. G. Lord, ''Effects of Categorization, Attribution, and Encoding Processes on Leadership Perceptions,'' *Journal of Applied Psychology* 72 (1987), pp. 97–106; J. W. Medcof and M. G. Evans, ''Heroic or Competent? A Second Look,'' *Organizational Behavior and Human Decision Processes* 38 (1986), pp. 295–304; and A. deCarufel and S. C. Goh, ''Implicit Theories of Leadership: Strategy, Outcome, and Precedent,'' *Proceedings of the Annual ASAC Conference, Organizational Behaviour Division* 8, part 5 (1987), pp. 47–55.

76. Meindl, ''On Leadership: An Alternative to the Conventional Wisdom.''

77. J. Pfeffer, ''The Ambiguity of Leadership,'' *Academy of Management Review* 2 (1977), pp. 102–12; and Yukl, *Leadership in Organizations,* pp. 265–67.

78. Cronshaw and Lord, ''Effects of Categorization, Attribution, and Encoding Processes on Leadership Perceptions,'' pp. 104–5.

CHAPTER CASE

A WINDOW ON LIFE

For Gilles LaCroix, there is nothing quite as beautiful as a handcrafted wood-framed window. LaCroix's passion for windows goes back to his youth in St. Jean, Quebec, where he was taught how to make residential windows by an elderly carpenter. He learned about the characteristics of good wood, the best tools to use, and how to choose the best glass from local suppliers. LaCroix apprenticed with the carpenter in his small workshop and, when the carpenter retired, was given the opportunity to operate the business himself.

LaCroix hired his own apprentice as he built up business in the local area. His small operation soon expanded as the quality of windows built by LaCroix Industries Ltd. became better known. Within eight years, the company employed nearly 25 people and the business had moved to larger facilities to accommodate the increased demand from southern Quebec. In these early years, LaCroix spent most of the time in the production shop, teaching new apprentices the unique skills that he had mastered and applauding the journeymen for their accomplishments. He would constantly repeat the point that LaCroix products had to be of the highest quality because they gave families a "window on life".

After 15 years, LaCroix Industries employed over 200 people. A profit-sharing program was introduced to give employees a financial reward for their contribution to the organization's success. Due to the company's expansion, headquarters had to be moved to another area of town, but the founder never lost touch with the work force. Although new apprentices were now taught entirely by the master carpenters and other craftspeople, LaCroix would still chat with plant and office employees several times each week.

When a second work shift was added, LaCroix would show up during the evening break with coffee and boxes of doughnuts and discuss how the business was doing and how it became so successful through quality workmanship. Production employees enjoyed the times when he would gather them together to announce new contracts with developers from Montreal and Toronto. After each announcement, LaCroix would thank everyone for making the business a success. They knew that LaCroix quality had become a standard of excellence in window-manufacturing across Canada.

It seemed that almost every time he visited, LaCroix would repeat the now well-known phrase that LaCroix products had to be of the highest quality because they provided a window on life to so many families. Employees never grew tired of hearing this from the company founder. However, it gained extra meaning when LaCroix began posting photos of families looking through LaCroix windows. At first, LaCroix would personally visit developers and homeowners with a camera in hand. Later, as the "window on life" photos became known by developers and customers, people would send in photos of their own families looking through elegant front windows made by LaCroix Industries. The company's marketing staff began using this idea, as well as LaCroix's famous phrase, in their advertising. After one such marketing campaign, hundreds of photos were sent in by satisfied customers. Production and office employees took time after work to write personal letters of thanks to those who had submitted photos.

As the company's age reached the quarter-century mark, LaCroix, now in his mid-fifties, realized that the organization's success and survival depended on expansion into the United States. After consulting with employees, LaCroix made the difficult decision to sell a majority share to Build-All Products, Inc., a conglomerate with international marketing expertise in building products. As part of the agreement, Build-All brought in a vice-president to oversee production operations while LaCroix spent more time meeting with developers around North America. LaCroix would return to the plant and office at every opportunity, but often this would be only once a month.

Rather than visiting the production plant, Jan Vlodoski, the new production vice-president, would rarely leave his office in the company's downtown headquarters. Instead, production orders were sent to supervisors by memorandum. While product quality had been a priority throughout the company's history, less attention had been paid to inventory controls. Vlodoski introduced strict inventory guidelines and outlined procedures on using supplies for each shift. Goals were established for supervisors to meet specific inventory targets. Whereas employees previously could have tossed out several pieces of warped wood, they would now have to justify this action, usually in writing.

Vlodoski also announced new procedures for purchasing production supplies. LaCroix Industries had highly trained purchasing staff who worked closely with senior craftspeople when selecting suppliers, but Vlodoski wanted to bring in Build-All's procedures. The new purchasing methods removed production leaders from the decision process and, in some cases, resulted in trade-offs that LaCroix's employees would not have made earlier. A few employees quit during this time, saying that they did not feel comfortable about producing a window on life that would not stand the test of time. However, unemployment was high in St. Jean, so most staff members remained with the company.

After one year, inventory expenses decreased by approximately 10 percent, but the number of defective windows returned by developers and wholesalers had increased markedly. Plant employees knew that the number of defective windows would increase as they used somewhat lower-quality materials to reduce inventory costs. However, they heard almost no news about the seriousness of the problem until Vlodoski sent a memo to all production staff saying that quality must be maintained. During the latter part of the first year under Vlodoski, a few employees had the opportunity to personally ask LaCroix about the changes and express their concerns. LaCroix apologized, saying due to his travels to new regions, he had not heard about the problems, and that he would look into the matter.

Exactly 18 months after Build-All had become majority shareholder of LaCroix Industries, LaCroix called together five of the original staff in the plant. The company founder looked pale and shaken as he said that Build-All's actions were inconsistent with his vision of the company and, for the first time in his career, he did not know what to do. Build-All was not pleased with the arrangement either. While LaCroix windows still enjoyed a healthy market share and were competitive for the value, the company did not quite provide the minimum 18 percent return on equity that the conglomerate expected. LaCroix asked his long-time companions for advice.

Discussion Questions

1. Explain why Gilles LaCroix is a transformational leader.
2. Use path-goal theory to diagnose the leadership effectiveness of LaCroix and Vlodoski.

Source: © 1991 Steven L. McShane.

EXPERIENTIAL EXERCISE

LEAST-PREFERRED COWORKER (LPC) SCALE

Purpose.   This exercise is designed to help you diagnose your leadership style (high- or low-LPC score) and which situations are most appropriate for you as a leader, based on Fiedler's contingency model.

Instructions.   Think of the person with whom you work least well. He or she may be someone you work with now, or may be someone you knew in the past. This is not necessarily someone you liked least well; rather it should be the person with whom you have had the most difficulty in getting the job done.

Describe this person on the following scale by placing an X in the appropriate space between each pair of adjectives. There are no right or wrong answers. Your first thoughts are usually best, so work quickly. Please do not omit any items or mark any item more than once.

	8	7	6	5	4	3	2	1	
Pleasant	8	7	6	5	4	3	2	1	Unpleasant
Friendly	8	7	6	5	4	3	2	1	Unfriendly
Rejecting	1	2	3	4	5	6	7	8	Accepting
Helpful	8	7	6	5	4	3	2	1	Frustrating
Unenthusiastic	1	2	3	4	5	6	7	8	Enthusiastic
Tense	1	2	3	4	5	6	7	8	Relaxed
Distant	1	2	3	4	5	6	7	8	Close
Cold	1	2	3	4	5	6	7	8	Warm
Cooperative	8	7	6	5	4	3	2	1	Uncooperative
Supportive	8	7	6	5	4	3	2	1	Hostile
Boring	1	2	3	4	5	6	7	8	Interesting
Quarrelsome	1	2	3	4	5	6	7	8	Harmonious
Self-assured	8	7	6	5	4	3	2	1	Hesitant
Efficient	8	7	6	5	4	3	2	1	Inefficient

Gloomy	__	__	__	__	__	__	__	__	Cheerful
	1	2	3	4	5	6	7	8	
Open	__	__	__	__	__	__	__	__	Guarded
	8	7	6	5	4	3	2	1	

Source: F. E. Fiedler and M. M. Chemers, *Leadership and Effective Management* (Glenview, Ill.: Scott, Foresman, 1974).

Scoring.   You can determine your LPC score and its implicit leadership style by adding the numbers below each X that you have marked. If your score is 64 or above, you are a high-LPC person, meaning that you are relationship-oriented. If you score 57 or below, you are a low-LPC person, someone who is task-oriented. If your score falls between 58 and 63, you'll need to determine for yourself in which category you belong.

ORGANIZATIONAL PROCESSES

Highly skilled staff at Canadian National, assisted by space-age information technology, plan and coordinate train movements across Canada from the Crown corporation's new operations management centre in Montreal. This centre, the most advanced of its kind in the world, enables CN to significantly improve the quality, reliability, and safety of its distribution services to Canadian shippers.

15

Organizational Change and Development

LEARNING OBJECTIVES

After reading this chapter, you should be able to:

Explain
Why people resist organizational change.

Diagram
Force field analysis.

Discuss
Several strategies for reducing resistance to change.

Describe
How to diffuse successful organizational change projects.

Define
Organization development.

List
Four methods of data collection in organizational diagnosis.

Compare
Incremental with quantum organizational change.

Xerox Canada

Xerox introduced the world's first plain paper copier in 1959, launching the office technology company into an era of unprecedented growth. But competitors eventually introduced higher-quality and lower-priced copiers. By the late 1970s, Xerox was no longer leading the industry it had created. "What we saw was frightening," recalls one Xerox manager. "[Competitors] were getting products into the market faster, their products were more reliable and were being produced at less than half the cost of our machines."

In 1979, Xerox began a journey toward continuous quality improvement that would dramatically transform the organization's worldwide operations. The first step was to introduce a diagnostic process known as "competitive benchmarking," whereby specific Xerox products, services, and practices would be continuously compared against the toughest competitors or companies recognized as leaders in other industries. Competitive benchmarking identified the areas where Xerox required improvement, but it also made employees aware of how desperately Xerox needed to change its ways.

Xerox focussed the change process in 1982 through an intensive program, "Leadership through Quality." In Canada, every employee attended a six-day course that communicated the need for change and trained them with the tools necessary to fulfill their new roles in the transformed organization. By 1990, Xerox Canada was annually pouring nearly $1,600 per employee into training so that the entire work force would receive continuous instruction on quality and customer service.

To institutionalize the new corporate culture, Xerox Canada literally turned the organization upside down by placing customers at the top, followed by front-line employees, 13 district councils, a customer service council, and a management committee at the bottom. The inverted pyramid emphasized the need to give employees responsibility and authority to meet customer needs. Customer-focussed reward and feedback systems were introduced to further reinforce the new philosophy. District councils were established across Canada to search out customer issues, remove bureaucratic barriers to customer service, and provide a vital communications link between district and head office staff. This revolutionary departure from the company's traditional hierarchy produced some employee anxiety and middle management resistance, but these barriers to change were eventually reduced through the communication and training programs.

In 1989, Xerox Canada received the country's first Gold Award for Quality—a testament to the company's dramatic transformation. David McCamus, chairman of Xerox Canada, acknowledges that organizational renewal is difficult, but it can be accomplished through careful diagnosis, employee involvement, training, and other organizational change tools. Says McCamus:

Generally, people are not unwilling to change. However, they're unwilling to change if they think they are the victims of change. People welcome change as long as they feel that they are playing a role. The secret to creating a change-oriented organization or society is to have everyone fully understand what they are trying to accomplish and why they are changing. Most important, everybody has to have a role in the change agenda.[1]

Organizations exist in a sea of change. Increasing competition and technological change forced Xerox Canada to transform its traditional structure, employee attitudes, management style, and reward system. Campbell Soup, Giant Yellowknife Mines, Cardinal River Coals Ltd., and many other organizations described earlier in this book have survived and prospered by changing in the face of new environmental conditions. Unfortunately, Leigh Instruments, Massey Ferguson, AES Electronics, Lavelin Industries, Nabu Manufacturing, and many other Canadian companies have not adapted in time.

This chapter examines the effective management of change in organizations. We begin by considering some of the more significant forces for organizational change and the forces resisting change. Next, a general model is presented that considers these opposing forces and proposes ways to effectively manage the change process. The latter part of this chapter introduces the field of organization development (OD). In particular, we review the OD process, specific OD interventions, and an assessment of OD effectiveness.

FORCES FOR CHANGE

As open systems, organizations need to remain compatible with the external environments on which they depend. But these environments are constantly changing, so organizations must recognize these shifts and respond accordingly in order to survive and remain effective. Successful organizations recognize these pressures and take appropriate steps to maintain a compatible fit with the new external conditions. These organizations have adopted a cultural norm that accepts and, indeed, embraces change as an integral part of organizational life.[2]

The pressures for organizational change are too numerous to discuss here, but we can briefly mention a few significant conditions that have had a profound influence on Canadian businesses over the past decade or will force them to change in the near future.

Population Changes

Canadians are significantly different today than in 1900.[3] As Canada entered this century, a third of its population was under 15 years of age and only 5 percent was over 65. Life expectancy ran to about 50 years. Today, people can expect to live for more than 75 years, on average. More than 12 percent of the population is 65 or more years old, and this will rise to between 25 and 30 percent by the year 2040.[4]

In 1900, most Canadians lived on farms and very few advanced beyond primary school. Today, over 80 percent of us live in cities and over 40 percent have received some post-secondary education. Canada is now a much more culturally diverse society. Whereas immigrants arriving in Canada up to the 1950s came mainly from Europe, those entering Canada in the 1990s originate from virtually every part of the world.

Another dramatic change is the percentage of women who have entered the work force. As depicted in Exhibit 15–1, only 23 percent of working age women participated in the labour force in 1950. This is approaching 60 percent in the 1990s. At the same time, the male participation rate has dropped from 84 percent in 1950 to 76 percent today.

There are several implications of these population and labour force changes on organizational behaviour. Earlier in this book we mentioned that a culturally diverse work force requires new management practices to improve communication and minimize dysfunctional conflict. Reward systems must be changed to fit the needs and expectations of ageing employees. Employee involvement has become more common in response to an increasingly educated work force. Team dynamics and perceptions of women in society have been altered as more women take on paid employment. Equally significant organizational changes have been required to adapt to the changing demography and needs of Canadian consumers.

Changing Legislation

Organizations must adapt to changing legislation introduced by the federal, provincial, or municipal governments. A decade ago, the energy industry was jolted by the Canadian government's National Energy Program. In the mid-1980s, the trucking industry had to adapt quickly to deregulation. In the 1990s, similar adjustments may be expected in other industries. For instance, Air Canada, Canadian Airlines International, and other air transportation firms are anticipating the Canadian government's movement toward an ''open skies'' policy. Bell Canada, B.C. Tel, and other telephone utilities are also preparing their employees for significant adjustments if long-distance telephone systems are deregulated.

The Canada–United States Free Trade Agreement (FTA) has perhaps had the most dramatic effect on Canadian businesses in recent years. Consider the experience of CCL Industries Inc. Before free trade, the Toronto-based company had a booming business producing labels and containers in Canada for large U.S. manufacturers of brand-name products such as Javex and Arrid. But under free trade, many of these firms are serving the Canadian market from their U.S. facilities, thereby threatening CCL's survival. Fortunately, CCL's management anticipated these environmental changes by acquiring competing firms and expanding operations worldwide. Says Wayne

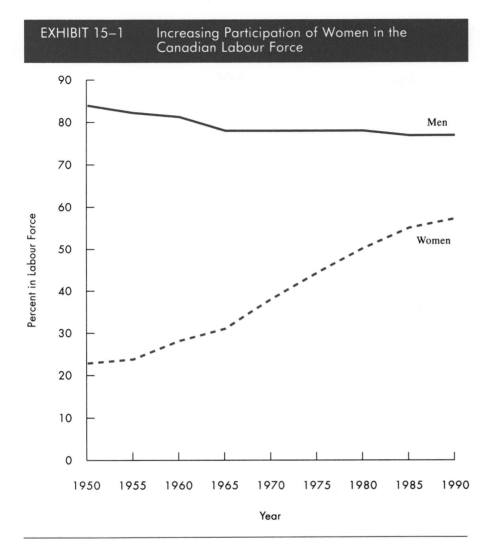

EXHIBIT 15–1   Increasing Participation of Women in the Canadian Labour Force

Source: Statistics Canada, *The Labour Force* (Ottawa: Minister of Supply and Services Canada, various years).

McLeod, CCL's president and chief executive officer, ''Free trade was the worst and best thing that ever happened to us. It forced us to become more focussed and much more aggressive to survive.''[5]

Increasing Competition

Partly as a result of new legislation, Canadian industry is experiencing higher levels of competition both at home and abroad. We are moving toward a global marketplace, so competitors are just as likely to be located in

Japan, Germany, Mexico, or the United States than somewhere else in Canada.[6] Add to this complexity the emergence of trading blocs in Europe, Asia, and other areas of the world. These blocs may create barriers to trade for some firms while increasing competition for others. They will certainly make life more complex for Canadian managers.[7]

Technological Changes

Technological changes in the workplace have occurred at a dizzying speed, and more than half of these advances in Canada over the past decade have been office related.[8] Clerical, professional, and management staff have experienced the introduction of microcomputers, electronic mail systems, facsimile (fax) machines, advanced telephone switching systems, and other electronic gadgetry.[9]

Meanwhile, computer-aided design/manufacturing systems have literally transformed many production processes. In doing so, they have significantly reduced employment levels and in most cases increased the skill requirements of remaining employees.[10] For example, Weston Bakeries has changed its Longueuil, Quebec, operation into the most technically advanced bakery in North America. As part of this transformation, 100 of the 350 existing employees have been trained in computerized manufacturing methods while the others have been transferred or laid off.[11] In effect, the new technology requires a relatively small team of highly skilled employees instead of a much larger number of low-skilled workers.

Many sociologists believe that technological changes reduce the skill levels of affected employees.[12] However, others have found either that job quality improves with technological change or that the effect depends on specific contingency factors.[13] In fact, one government report recently concluded that Canadian employees will require continuous skill renewal as they experience more frequent career changes resulting from future technological change and global competition.[14]

Mergers and Acquisitions

Dozens of mergers and acquisitions (M&As) have been consummated in Canada over the past few years—Molson Breweries with Carling O'Keefe, Manulife Financial with Dominion Life, Hostess Food with Frito-Lay Canada, Clarkson Gordon with Thorne Ernst & Whinney, and Imperial Oil with Texaco Canada, just to name a few.[15] Every M&A results in numerous changes to the organizations and employees affected. Organizational systems are altered, and employees may have to adjust to new management practices and corporate philosophies.

M&As also increase the threat of job loss or reduced power over organizational events. For instance, when Lloyds Bank Canada acquired Continental Bank, productivity in both organizations decreased as employees spent more time talking about what might happen to them. Some employees even admitted going out of their way to make things go wrong just to prove that the deal would not work![16] Overall, mergers and acquisitions are powerful organizational stressors requiring corrective actions to minimize employee resistance and health problems.[17]

RESISTANCE TO CHANGE

No matter how noble the cause, most organizational change efforts are resisted by employees, managers, clients, or other stakeholders affected.[18] Consider the experience of M&M Manufacturing Ltd., a Dartmouth, Nova Scotia-based firm that produces high-pressure pipes for offshore oil rigs. M&M recently introduced a quality assurance program with full management support. However, the company's 100 nonmanagement employees were less enthusiastic. Says one M&M manager, "Employees will, at times, give us silent resistance when we come out with a directive on new quality measures."[19]

At M&M, resistance to change took the form of silent procrastination from employees. In other situations, it may be manifested by complaints, higher employee absenteeism and turnover, or collective action (e.g., strikes, walkouts). Resistance is often an important symptom that problems exist, but this is even more reason to understand why resistance occurs and to prevent it wherever possible. Resistance is not typically an irrational act; instead, it stems from a logical motivation to maintain the status quo rather than comply with new behaviour patterns. The main reasons why people typically resist change are shown in Exhibit 15–2.[20]

Direct Costs

People resist change when they believe that the new state of affairs will have higher direct costs or lower benefits than the existing situation. This is most apparent where they face the threat of economic loss, such as lower wages, fewer perquisites, or reduced job security. Resistance also results when employees believe they will lose power. In our opening story, Xerox Canada had to deal with resistance from middle managers who believed that they would lose their power to nonmanagement employees. In Chapter 11, we mentioned a similar problem, which can occur when companies attempt to introduce self-managing work teams.

Saving Face

Unfortunately, some people resist change as a political strategy to "prove" that the decision is wrong or that the change agent is incompetent. For example, senior management in a mid-sized manufacturing firm purchased a computer other than the system recommended by the information systems department. Soon after the system was in place, several information systems

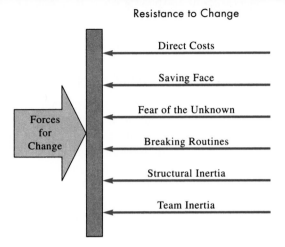

EXHIBIT 15–2   Forces Resisting Organizational Change

Resistance to Change

Direct Costs

Saving Face

Fear of the Unknown

Breaking Routines

Structural Inertia

Team Inertia

Forces for Change

---

employees allowed minor implementation problems to escalate in order to demonstrate that senior management had made a poor decision. This problem is most common in organizations where employees emphasize departmental rather than superordinate goals.

Fear of the Unknown

Change is resisted because it involves facing uncertainty. Employees might worry about lacking the necessary skills or losing valued work arrangements after the transition. Thus, change produces a psychological cost in the form of stress and the potential, but as yet unknown, loss of benefits in the new situation.

Breaking Routines

Change necessarily involves abandoning some habits and learning new ones. But human beings are creatures of habit; they invest time and effort forming comfortable role patterns to make their lives easier and more predictable. Resistance to change occurs simply because people must bear the cost of developing new routines while throwing away role patterns that they have mastered.

Structural Inertia

Organizations use selection, training, rewards, and other control systems to promote stability and predictability. But ensuring that employees perform specific tasks in a particular way creates a form of resistance, called **struc-**

tural inertia, that tries to maintain the status quo. Unless altered, these control systems conflict with the change effort and may undermine its success. Indeed, an important feature of effective change management is to reconfigure these control systems so that they maintain the desired behaviour patterns.

structural inertia
Organizational control systems that institutionalize and maintain the status quo.

Team Inertia

As we learned in Chapter 10, work teams evolve through several stages of development to create a set of norms and role expectations. This social structure enables team members to coordinate their activities while team cohesiveness produces the conformity necessary to ensure that members do not deviate from these predictable behaviour patterns. But this creates a **team inertia** that resists organizational changes that threaten existing role relations. This is particularly apparent where the team's norms are overtly antagonistic to the change itself.

team inertia
Team structures and processes that routinize behaviours, thereby maintaining the status quo.

MANAGING ORGANIZATIONAL CHANGE

Rather than letting the forces for change batter the organization and eventually dash it against the shoals, leaders must introduce changes to ensure continued organizational survival and effectiveness. But how should they manage this change process? Kurt Lewin, a leading behavioural scientist in the 1950s, introduced **force field analysis** to recognize the two sets of opposing forces that we have described above and to help us diagnose and manage these forces as part of an effective change management process.[21]

As shown in Exhibit 15–3, on one side of the force field model are the *driving forces,* which push organizations (or their subunits) toward a new state of affairs. On the other side are the *restraining forces,* which try to maintain the status quo. Stability occurs when the driving and restraining forces are roughly in equilibrium, that is, they are of approximately equal strength in opposite directions. Change occurs when the driving forces are stronger than the restraining forces. As you can see, this is a relatively simple, yet very useful, way of analyzing specific situations before beginning the change process.

To manage the change process effectively, Lewin suggested that it is first necessary to **unfreeze** the current situation by producing a disequilibrium between the two opposing forces. Unfreezing basically alters the four conditions for individual performance—ability, motivation, role perceptions, situational contingencies (see Chapter 2)—in favour of the change effort. This involves motivating people toward change by making them aware of the problems and providing the necessary skills, knowledge, and resources to execute the new behaviour patterns.

Unfreezing destabilizes the status quo and provides an opportunity to introduce new behaviours and attitudes. However, when the organization

force field analysis
A method of identifying and diagnosing the forces that drive and restrain proposed organizational change.

unfreezing
Part of the change process in which people are made aware of the need for change and are provided with the necessary skills, knowledge, and resources to execute new behaviour patterns.

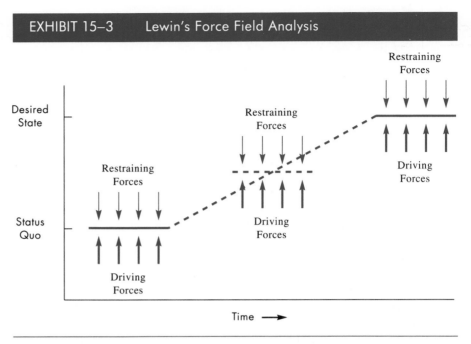

EXHIBIT 15–3   Lewin's Force Field Analysis

Source: Adapted from S. P. Robbins, *Organizational Behavior: Concepts, Controversies, and Applications,* 5th ed. (Englewood Cliffs, N.J.: Prentice Hall, 1991), p. 647.

refreezing

Part of the change process in which the desired behaviour patterns are restabilized and institutionalized so that previous patterns do not re-emerge.

has moved to the new equilibrium, it is necessary to **refreeze** the desired state of affairs. Refreezing restabilizes and institutionalizes the desired conditions. In other words, steps must be taken to ensure that the new attitudes and behaviour patterns are relatively secure against further change. Otherwise, the organization may slide back to its previous equilibrium.

UNFREEZING THE STATUS QUO

Based on force field analysis, we can see that disequilibrium occurs by increasing the strength of the driving forces and/or reducing the strength of the restraining forces. However, increasing the driving forces alone tends to be ineffective because the restraining forces often adjust to counterbalance the driving forces, rather like the coils of a mattress. The harder management pushes for new procedures without employee acceptance, the stronger employees tend to resist these changes. The result is a higher level of dysfunctional tension and conflict within the organization, which may threaten the change effort.

The preferred strategy for unfreezing is to reduce the sources of resistance to change described earlier. Kotter and Schlesinger describe six strate-

EXHIBIT 15–4	Methods for Dealing with Resistance to Change		

Approach	Situations Where Commonly Used	Advantages	Drawbacks
Education and communication	Where there is a lack of information or inaccurate information and analysis.	Once persuaded, people will often help with the implementation of the change.	Can be very time-consuming if lots of people are involved.
Participation and involvement	Where the initiators do not have all the information they need to design the change, and where others have considerable power to resist.	People who participate will be committed to implementing change, and any relevant information they have will be integrated into the change plan.	Can be very time-consuming if participators design an inappropriate change.
Facilitation and support	Where people are resisting because of adjustment problems.	No other approach works as well with adjustment problems.	Can be time-consuming, expensive, and still fail.
Negotiation and agreement	Where someone or some group will clearly lose out in a change, and where that group has considerable power to resist.	Sometimes it is a relatively easy way to avoid major resistance.	Can be too expensive in many cases if it alerts others to negotiate for compliance.
Manipulation and cooptation	Where other tactics will not work, or are too expensive.	It can be a relatively quick and inexpensive solution to resistance problems.	Can lead to future problems if people feel manipulated.
Explicit and implicit coercion	Where speed is essential, and the change initiators possess considerable power.	It is speedy, and can overcome any kind of resistance.	Can be risky if it leaves people mad at the initiators.

Source: Reprinted by permission of *Harvard Business Review*. "Choosing Strategies for Change," by J. P. Kotter and L. A. Schlesinger, March–April 1979, p. 111. Copyright 1979 by the President and Fellows of Harvard College; all rights reserved.

gies to deal with employee resistance. As we see in Exhibit 15–4, each strategy has certain advantages and drawbacks and the best approach depends on the situation.[22]

Education and Communication

Educating employees about the change effort and keeping them informed about its progress is typically the most important approach to minimizing resistance. This activity is time-consuming and costly, but an effective education and communication program will help people understand why change is needed, comprehend how the change will affect them personally, and provide them with the knowledge and skills to effectively adapt to the new conditions.

Xerox Canada used education and communication via its "Leadership through Quality" program to minimize resistance and increase employee motivation toward the desired conditions. Lumonics Inc. also used this approach when the Kanata, Ontario, laser technology firm was purchased by Sumitomo Heavy Industries Ltd. As soon as the purchase agreement was completed, managers at Lumonics offices around the world called their employees together to break the news and answer questions. Lumonics's managers had received briefings and fact sheets before the announcement to ensure that they would be able to address employee concerns accurately and frankly. The laser technology company quickly introduced a biweekly newsletter to keep employees informed and assure them that the purchase would not involve a corporate restructuring or a loss of economic benefits.[23]

Participation and Involvement

In Chapter 11, we explained that employee involvement tends to reduce resistance to change and increase employee motivation to implement decisions.[24] Although time-consuming, this approach is extremely valuable when employees possess information necessary to direct the change effort. Participation is also useful when employees would otherwise lack commitment to implementing the new conditions. Perspective 15–1 describes how employee involvement, along with retraining, represented two critical elements of effective change management at Labour Canada's Bureau of Labour Information.

Facilitation and Support

Organizational change is often stressful, so managers should use supportive leadership behaviours and introduce formal stress management programs to facilitate the change process. The first two strategies—education and participation—help in this regard, but employees may require counselling and assistance when the change occurs rapidly or is otherwise traumatic.[25] For instance, when C-I-L Inc. recently sold four of its divisions, it retained an outside consulting firm to help the 1,400 affected employees to cope with the stress of this event. This provided a support mechanism to help the employees adjust to the reality of losing C-I-L for another employer. In doing so, the company was able to preserve the human asset value of the divisions that would be sold.[26]

Negotiation and Agreement

Education, participation, and support are sometimes not enough to minimize resistance among those who will clearly lose out from the change activity. It may therefore be necessary to negotiate certain benefits to offset some of the

PERSPECTIVE 15—1   Participative Change at the Bureau of Labour Information

Until April 1987, services offered by Labour Canada's Bureau of Labour Information were provided by six different groups. This created much confusion as clients had difficulty knowing where to turn for which service. The existing system also stifled the development of valuable services while some activities continued to focus on information products that were no longer required by the Canadian public.

In 1985 and 1986, the Canadian government cut expenditures at Labour Canada as part of its effort to reduce the federal deficit. These cutbacks, along with increasing pressure to improve customer service, provided the impetus to change the bureau from a traditional industrial relations data-collection and publication activity to a highly productive client-oriented service centre within the Canadian federal government.

Employees were brought into the change process from the outset, beginning with a three-day "founding conference" that was attended by everyone in the organization. Teams were formed to redesign technology, equipment, and the processes for information collection and retrieval. Training and retraining were heavily emphasized. In fact, bureau staff received more training in two years than had been offered over the previous two decades combined! Bureau staff held "meet the client" sessions where they listened to their customers' priorities and needs regarding industrial relations information. These activities built commitment to the change effort because employees were part of the process and received the skills necessary to adapt.

Few people could imagine the incredible results of this change effort. The number of client requests doubled between 1986 and 1988 while the service operated with 39 percent fewer staff members. Letters began pouring into the government office praising staff members for their superb service. The Bureau of Labour Information has experienced a very low turnover rate and there is a long list of applicants who want to transfer to this revitalized organization.

Sources: Based on Auditor General of Canada, *Report to the House of Commons, Fiscal Year Ended 31 March 1988* (Ottawa: Supply and Service Canada, 1988), paragraphs 4.34–4.37 and Exhibit 4.6; and J. Clemmer, *Firing on All Cylinders* (Toronto: Macmillan of Canada, 1990), pp. 48–49.

cost of the change. Labour negotiations operate in this way. When management wants to ease work rules or introduce new technology on a large scale, it might negotiate with the union over job security or higher wages to offset the other losses from the change.

Manipulation and Cooptation

If the preceding strategies are ineffective, some change agents use subtle political tactics to reduce resistance to change. Information might be presented selectively so that employees are not aware of the problems they will face under the new conditions, or those who would potentially resist change might be coopted by having them endorse the change effort before they realize what is involved. While these and other political tactics are sometimes effective, we must warn you that they are just as likely to lead to future problems when employees discover they have been manipulated.

PERSPECTIVE 15–2   Organizational Renewal at Dana's Canadian Operation

Rene McPherson, the acclaimed American business leader who built Dana Corporation into a multi-billion dollar enterprise, has orchestrated numerous organizational transformations. Yet the former Dana CEO will always remember his earliest experience in organizational renewal, many years ago, when he was assigned the task of salvaging Dana's failing Canadian operation.

McPherson welcomed the challenge, but the Canadian operation's managing director interfered with McPherson's activities and made it impossible to change anything. After four months of frustration, McPherson called up his boss in the United States and said, "I'm leaving. As long as this guy is here, I can't get anything done." The top manager in Canada was soon transferred and McPherson was put in charge.

McPherson was now free to act, but he didn't. Instead, he spent several more months talking and listening to Canadian staff about the operations. Only then did he make changes. One day, McPherson called a meeting of the top people in the Canadian operation and said, "You know the old organization chart. Here's the new one." Except for McPherson and one other person, everyone at the meeting had been transferred to new assignments.

McPherson says he learned a valuable lesson from his experience in the Canadian operation. While participation, communication, and support are valuable tools in organizational renewal, change agents make the mistake of being too gentle with the people they see every day and who are most nearly their peers. But failing to force management colleagues to change ignores the damage being done to customers, employees further down the line, and other stakeholders. According to McPherson, managers sometimes have to get tough with their managerial peers to bring about effective renewal: "What you want to do is get everybody's attention. Mix things up at the top. Change everybody."

Source: From *The Renewal Factor* by Robert H. Waterman Jr., pp. 255–57. Copyright © 1987 by Robert H. Waterman Jr. Used by permission of Bantam Books, a division of Bantam Doubleday Dell Publishing Group, Inc.

Explicit and Implicit Coercion

Occasionally, managers must use coercion, such as threatening nonconformers with dismissal or denying pay increases, to overcome resistance to change. The problem with coercion, as we mentioned in Chapter 4, is that it may produce several adverse repercussions in employee relations. Consequently, it should be used only when speed is essential and other tactics are ineffective. A less punitive, yet equally effective strategy is to transfer those who resist change so that new initiatives can proceed. Perspective 15–2 describes how Rene McPherson, former CEO of Dana Corporation, used this approach several years ago to bring about organizational renewal at Dana's Canadian operation.

REFREEZING THE DESIRED CONDITIONS

Lewin's concept of refreezing suggests that certain actions need to be taken to institutionalize the desired state of affairs.[27] These are basically ways to establish structural and team inertia around the desired changes. Reward systems must be altered to reinforce the new behaviours and attitudes rather than previous practices. The previous behaviour patterns should no longer be rewarded and the new reward system must be equitable. Information and support must be continuously transmitted to reaffirm the new practices. Similarly, new feedback systems must be introduced and existing ones recalibrated to focus on the new priorities and performance goals. This process was very important at Xerox Canada, where competitive benchmarking, customer surveys, and other feedback mechanisms kept employees focussed on the company's new objectives. Finally, every successful change effort requires "champions" or "guardians" to remove obstacles and keep the process on track. These people also need to regularly communicate and model their vision of the new conditions.

Institutionalizing processes are more effective when the changes are congruent with other elements of the organizational system. For example, efforts to introduce employee involvement are likely to fail unless organizational structures and procedures are made more compatible with this intervention.[28] Institutionalization processes are also more effective when the goals of the change effort are clear and specific, the change process is easily understood in modules or stages, the external environment is relatively stable, and the change process has the support of top management or other powerful sponsors.

Diffusion of Change

Organizational change often begins with ideas from employees or the manager of one work unit, so the process naturally begins there before spreading to other areas of the firm. In fact, recent evidence suggests that most successful organizational transformations begin with pilot projects because these peripheral change activities offer greater flexibility and less risk than centralized organizationwide programs.[29] However, successful change depends not only on the institutionalization of these pilot projects, but also on their diffusion to other areas of the organization. **Diffusion** occurs when the new conditions are introduced and institutionalized elsewhere in the organization. In fact, unless organizational changes are diffused, the long-term survival of the pilot project itself is at risk.

Richard Walton has studied the diffusion of job enrichment and similar work restructuring programs at several organizations, including one of Alcan Aluminum's Canadian plants.[30] Walton discovered that work restructuring changes were more effectively diffused throughout the organization when the pilot study was successful within one or two years and received visibility through news media, oral presentations, and visits by interested parties. These conditions tended to increase top management support for the change program and convince other managers to introduce the change effort in their operations. Diffusion was also more likely to occur when labour union officials demonstrated their support and were actively involved in the diffusion process.

diffusion of change
The process of introducing and institutionalizing successful changes elsewhere in the organization.

Walton further observed that the diffusion strategy should not be stated too conceptually, otherwise it may be dismissed by others as too abstract or too difficult to put into action. Neither should it be stated too narrowly because the procedures might not translate easily to units operating under different conditions. Finally, without producing excessive turnover in the pilot group, managers and other staff who have worked under the new system should be moved to other areas of the organization. These people bring their knowledge and commitment of the change effort to work units that have not yet experienced it.

ORGANIZATION DEVELOPMENT

Lewin's force field analysis and the concepts of unfreezing and refreezing provide a useful starting point for understanding how to manage the change process. However, an entire field of study and practice has emerged that provides more detailed models and prescriptions for managing planned change in organizations.

organization development (OD)
A planned systemwide effort, managed from the top with the assistance of a change agent, that uses behavioural science knowledge to improve organizational effectiveness.

Organization development (OD) is a planned systemwide effort, managed from the top with the assistance of a change agent, that uses behavioural science knowledge to improve organizational effectiveness.[31] OD is a planned change effort because it generally follows systematic procedures. It takes a systems perspective by recognizing that organizations must remain compatible with their external environment and are complex entities with highly interdependent parts. Thus, OD experts try to ensure that all parts of the organization are compatible with the change effort.[32]

OD technologies have evolved from many of the organizational behaviour concepts described in this book. Indeed, several OD interventions relating to team dynamics, conflict management, and individual effectiveness have been introduced earlier. OD activities are aimed at improving organizational effectiveness. They help the organization to achieve its goals, survive and prosper within a changing environment, and address stakeholder needs (see Chapter 1). Finally, senior management and other powerholders in the organization must be committed to the goals and methods of the OD effort. Senior managers do not usually lead OD activities, but their commitment toward the program is essential.

action research
A data-based, problem-oriented process that focusses on organizational diagnosis and action planning, implementation, and evaluation of an intervention on the system involved.

OD as Action Research

Virtually all OD activities rely on **action research** as the primary blueprint for planned change. As depicted in Exhibit 15–5, action research is a data-based, problem-oriented process that focusses on organizational diagnosis and action planning, implementation, and evaluation of the intervention's effect on the system involved. This process may be repeated several times until the organization's objectives have been met.[33]

EXHIBIT 15–5   The OD Process: An Action Research Perspective

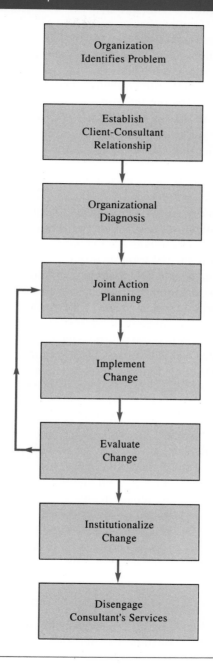

Action research is a highly participative process, involving the client throughout the various stages.[34] In fact, an important element of the process is to form and train an action research team consisting of people both affected by the organizational change and having the power to facilitate it.[35] Participation is a fundamental philosophy of OD, but it also increases commitment to the change process and provides valuable information to conduct organizational diagnosis and evaluation.

Since action research is an integral part of most OD programs, we will use this framework to describe the OD process on the following pages. Specifically, we will examine the important issues of forming a client–consultant relationship, conducting organizational diagnosis and planning, implementing change, and evaluating the results.

THE CLIENT–CONSULTANT RELATIONSHIP

change agent

A person who possesses enough knowledge and power to guide and facilitate the change effort. This may be a member of the organization or an external consultant.

Organizational change requires a **change agent,** such as a manager, consultant, labour union official, or anyone else who possesses enough knowledge and power to guide and facilitate the change effort. OD change agents are often consultants with special training and previous experience in applying the behavioural sciences and OD techniques.[36] Some large Canadian firms employ internal OD consultants in human resources departments to facilitate many organizational change efforts. External OD consultants are sometimes contracted to help management address specific organizational issues. During this phase, the client assesses the consultant's competence while the consultant fathoms the viability of the situation for introducing the OD process. Three important considerations are the client's readiness, the consultant's expected role, and the consultant's power base in the relationship.

Client Readiness

Consultants need to determine whether the client is motivated to participate in the process, is open to meaningful change, and possesses the ability and resources to complete the process. OD experts particularly watch out for "mafia contracts," in which senior management's real agenda is to hire a consultant to "fix" a department or dismiss a manager. These situations are incompatible with the OD process because the client is usually neither willing to change nor open to the OD process. It is also virtually impossible to develop a trusting relationship with everyone involved.[37]

Consultant's Expected Role

A critical decision when forming the relationship is the consultant's role in the change process. The consultant's role might range from providing technical expertise on a specific change activity to facilitating the change process. Many OD experts prefer the latter role, commonly known as **process**

consultation.[38] Process consultation involves helping the organization solve its own problems by making it aware of organizational processes, the consequences of those processes, and the means by which they can be changed. Rather than providing expertise about the content of the change, such as how to introduce quality circles, process consultants help participants learn how to solve their own problems by guiding them through the action research process.[39]

process consultation
A method of helping the organization solve its own problems by making it aware of organizational processes, the consequences of those processes, and the means by which they can be changed.

Several writers believe that OD consultants need to provide both process and technical expertise and must change their role with the client's needs. At one point they guide the process, while other times they provide new insights and information. But whatever their roles, OD consultants should occupy marginal positions in relation to the organization they are serving. This means that they must be sufficiently detached from the organization to maintain objectivity and avoid having the client becoming too dependent on them.[40]

Consultant's Power Base in the Relationship

The consultant's power base is seldom discussed overtly when forming the contract, but this is an important element in the relationship.[41] Effective consultants need to rely on expertise and perhaps referent power to have any influence on the participants. However, they *should not* use reward, legitimate, or coercive power because these bases may weaken trust and neutrality in the client–consultant relationship.

ORGANIZATIONAL DIAGNOSIS AND PLANNING

Action research is a problem-oriented activity that carefully diagnoses the problem (or opportunity) through systematic analysis of the situation. **Organizational diagnosis** involves collecting data about an ongoing system, organizing and interpreting these data (usually by the consultant), and feeding these data back to the client. This information is then used to conduct *joint action planning* (see Exhibit 15–6). The parties might cycle through this process several times until they agree on whether a problem exists, where the problem lies, and how the problem might be resolved. The main objective is that the problem and its context are properly diagnosed so that the correct OD intervention is selected. Bill Reddin, a well-known Canadian OD consultant, recalls two experiences involving poor or unsuccessful organizational diagnosis in Perspective 15–3.

organizational diagnosis
The systematic process of collecting data about an ongoing system, organizing and interpreting these data by the consultant, and feeding these data back to the client.

Data Collection and Feedback

A variety of data collection methods are available to conduct systematic organizational diagnosis.[42] Interviews are almost always used to collect diagnostic data because OD consultants can build rapport with the client, explore specific issues spontaneously, and cover a range of subjects. However,

PERSPECTIVE 15–3   Diagnosing the Need for Change: Confessions of an OD Consultant

Bill Reddin, one of Canada's best-known organization development consultants, has learned many lessons over the years about organization diagnosis. He specifically recalls two incidents in which the underlying problem did not call for a behavioural science solution or the OD consultant had plenty of solutions but could not find a problem:

*   I was once asked to plan a change program for a Montreal production subsidiary of a U.S. firm. Four of the subsidiary's general managers had been fired in six years for failure to show a profit. The trust level was low, and most managers had moved to a very low level of risk taking. After I had

started to unfreeze, team build, develop candor, etc., an independent study by the parent company uncovered major errors in the transfer-price system within the subsidiary and from the subsidiary to the parent company. When changes in these prices were introduced, profits started to appear, and the current general manager stayed with the company for eight years. The company had really needed a cost accountant rather than a change agent.

*   After some preliminary discussion, I met with the project team of a power utility. The utility was located in a poor section of a very poor area. From looking at the boots that some of the team members wore to the meeting I was convinced that they

---

EXHIBIT 15–6   Organizational Diagnosis and Joint Action Planning Cycle

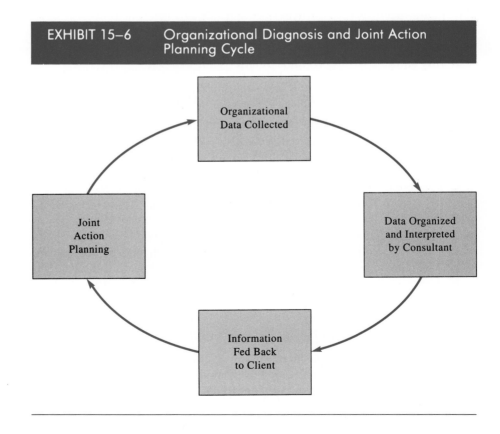

were not likely to be acquainted with recent developments in behavioural science. I was sure that these people needed something; the question was "What?" I suggested that we explore the concept of job enrichment and then heard explanations of what the four-man crew does and what the sole operator of a remote generator does. I gave my famous talk on "let's burn the job descriptions" and was told that they had no real job descriptions. I discussed employee participation as the wave of the future and then was told of the annual two-day meeting with the general manager at which anyone can question any issue and at which reorganization decisions arise from floor discussion. I suggested implementing MBO. They showed me detailed 10-year plans for the company. In desperation I asked how they selected pole linemen. I was told "They must not be overweight, must not be afraid of heights, and must not drink on the job." I left those people quietly, with as much grace as I could muster.

Source: W. J. Reddin, "Confessions of an Organizational Change Agent," *Group and Organization Studies* 2, no. 1 (March 1977), pp. 33–41.

they are susceptible to perceptual bias and are expensive in large client groups. Questionnaires allow the consultant to collect and quantify information from many people relatively easily and inexpensively, although they are more impersonal and inflexible than interviews. Direct observation can be used where small teams are involved, but this method is too time-consuming in large work units. Secondary data, such as monthly productivity records and union grievance reports, represent an unobtrusive source of diagnostic information, although they are sometimes too politically sensitive and expensive to retrieve.

The collected data are typically organized and interpreted by the consultant. The information is then presented to the client for the purpose of clarifying and reaching common agreement on the symptoms, problems, and possible solutions. Another purpose of the feedback is to energize participants to introduce any intervention that may be required. Just enough information should be presented to avoid information overload. The feedback should be neutral and descriptive to avoid perceptual defensiveness. The information should pertain to issues over which participants have control, so top management might receive data about the overall organization while department managers mainly receive information about their own units.[43]

Joint Action Planning

After data have been collected and fed back to the client, the consultant and client jointly discuss the findings and mutually agree on a course of action. You might recall from Chapter 4 that action planning outlines the means by

| PERSPECTIVE 15–4 | The·High-Speed Transformation of Richmond Savings Credit Union |

In 1983, Richmond Savings Credit Union was drowning in a sea of red ink, with loan losses exceeding the value of its capital base. The financial institution's new CEO, Don Tuline, moved quickly to change the situation by developing new services, introducing a new computer system to personalize client relations, and changing the service fee structure. Employees were slow to adapt to the new customer orientation, so special training and incentives were introduced to assist the change process. Tuline also fired the existing senior management team except for one lone survivor. "I had to have senior staff working with me who could work under pressure, who could see not just problems but solutions, and who had a strong marketing bent," explains Tuline.

Within just three years, Richmond Savings returned to profitability and a healthy balance sheet. Its computer system also won the top award from an American organization that monitors microcomputer applications in the financial industry. Still, the high-speed turnaround effort has taken its toll. As Tuline acknowledges: "We brought a number of changes in very rapidly and this added to the stress of our employees. They were nervous, always having to learn something new; there wasn't much fun in their jobs."

The change process also took its toll on Tuline. "I

which goals will be accomplished. In OD programs, the parties agree on specific prescriptions for action, including the appropriate change method and the schedule for these actions. This activity ensures that everyone knows what is expected of them and that standards are established to properly evaluate the process after the transition.[44]

IMPLEMENTATION AND EVALUATION

intervention
Any set of planned activities intended to improve the effectiveness of the client or relations between the client and consultant.

An **intervention** refers to any set of planned activities intended to improve the effectiveness of the client or relations between the client and consultant.[45] The OD process includes several interventions, including the consultant's entry into the relationship and the diagnostic process. Nevertheless, the focal intervention involves altering specific system variables identified in the organizational diagnosis and planning stage. These changes might alter tasks, strategic organizational goals, system controls (e.g., rewards), or interpersonal relationships. We will outline some specific OD interventions later in this chapter.

incremental change
An evolutionary approach to change in which existing organizational conditions are fine-tuned and small steps are taken towards the change effort's objectives.

Incremental versus Quantum Change

An important issue during implementation is the degree of change that should occur. **Incremental change** is an evolutionary strategy in which the organization fine tunes the existing organizational configuration and takes small steps towards the change effort's objectives. **Quantum change** (also called *strategic* or *frame-breaking change*) is a revolutionary approach in

quantum change
A revolutionary approach to change in which the organization breaks out of its existing strategies, structures, and behaviour patterns and moves toward a totally different configuration.

ended up with a heart attack," says the Richmond Savings CEO. "That forced me to realize I wasn't doing the organization any service by getting so stressed out. I've learned to pace myself better."

What would have eased this massive culture change? A slower pace, suggests Tuline—time for the organization to catch up to the changes. Rapid growth continues to be a potential Achilles heel for Richmond Savings as it opens new branches around Vancouver—it strains both employees and capital,

and there is never time to evaluate the previous transformation.

"But you can never stand still," adds Tuline, reflecting the prevailing philosophy at Richmond Savings. "To sustain our competitive advantages we have to continue to look ahead to how we can offer services to our members that they can't get elsewhere. And we have to ensure the technology is always upgraded to allow us to keep the initiative."

Sources: Based on C. Furlong, "Saving a Credit Union," *BC Business*, January 1989, pp. 40–49; and M. Zuehlke, "Bold Marketing Rescues Richmond Savings," *Small Business*, September 1990, pp. 14–17.

which the organization breaks out of its existing strategies, structures, and behaviour patterns and moves toward a totally different configuration.[46] Incremental change has typically been recommended by organizational change experts because it involves less risk to the organization and individual members, thereby reducing potential resistance. The organization has time to evaluate and alter the course of implementation in mid-stream. This allows for fine tuning in real time, rather than after the change has occurred. Finally, taking "one hop at a time" is less threatening and stressful to employees because they have time to adapt to the new conditions.[47]

In spite of the advantages of incremental change, quantum changes are sometimes necessary.[48] In order to maintain stability, organizational leaders usually delay making any changes until it is too late for incremental change. Moreover, some environmental shifts occur suddenly, so the company's survival may depend on quantum rather than incremental change. Quantum changes invariably include some type of reorganization, altering the company's structure, systems, and procedures. They tend to dramatically change core values, power relations, and patterns of interaction. This can be costly to employees and the organization, as Richmond Savings Credit Union discovered (see Perspective 15–4).

Some organizations have successfully developed a cultural norm of change, so that incremental change is continuous and quantum change is less traumatic. Such is the case at DMR Group Inc., a Montreal-based information system consulting firm, whose 2,000 employees maintain a sense of flexibility in job duties and work relationships. As one DMR employee explains: "We don't have job descriptions for the administrative staff because they would just go on forever. We're looking for people with flexibility there, as we are in our consulting staff.'' A DMR project manager adds: ''There is a structure of a kind, but it's a very loose structure. People work in a variety of fields despite where they may fit on the organization chart.''[49]

Evaluating OD Interventions

OD interventions cost time and money, so it makes sense to determine whether the intervention has actually occurred and whether it has produced the desired outcomes. It may seem rather obvious whether an intervention has taken place, but you should understand that behavioural science changes are not as definitive as, say, installing a computer or changing office furniture. For example, an OD intervention might try to enrich jobs by rearranging certain job duties, but until the process is evaluated, we can't be certain that this action actually has enriched those jobs.

The main thrust of OD evaluation is to receive feedback determining whether the intervention has had the desired effect. Evaluation is only possible, of course, if the client and consultant developed meaningful and specific program goals during the organizational diagnosis and action planning stage. But even with well-stated, relevant goals, OD interventions can be difficult to evaluate because their effect might not be apparent for several years. Another problem is the difficulty in deciding whether changes in market share, employee satisfaction, and other outcomes are caused by the OD intervention or extraneous factors such as economic changes, new personnel policies, and new technology. Evaluating OD interventions may be difficult at times, but the potential value of this information makes the challenge worthwhile.

ORGANIZATION DEVELOPMENT INTERVENTIONS

Organization development has expanded from its origins in the 1950s where it was primarily identified with interpersonal and small group dynamics. Today, OD covers virtually every area of organizational behaviour, as well as many aspects of strategic and human resource management. As such, it is virtually impossible to describe every intervention, but Exhibit 15–7 organizes the most prominent OD activities around the four kinds of organizational issues they are intended to resolve.[50]

Human Process Interventions

Human process interventions represent the oldest OD activities and address communication, problem solving, interpersonal relations, conflict management, leadership, and related issues. Team building, which we discussed in Chapter 10, is concerned with helping work teams become more effective. According to some writers, team building is currently the most popular OD

EXHIBIT 15–7   Types of OD Interventions

Human Process Interventions	Technostructural Interventions
• Team building • Laboratory training • Managerial Grid • Sensitivity training	• Job design • Quality circles • Self-managing work teams • Organization design • Parallel learning structures
Human Resource Management Interventions	Strategic Interventions
• Goal setting • Reward systems • Stress management • Career planning and development	• Open systems planning • Strategic planning • Corporate culture change

intervention and is applied indirectly in most OD activities.[51] Laboratory training was discussed in Chapter 13 and is a process of resolving dysfunctional conflict between groups. Grid organization development was described in Chapter 14 as a six-phase comprehensive intervention that begins with the Managerial Grid leadership theory. Bill Reddin's 3-Dimensional Managerial Effectiveness Seminar (3-D MES), which has been used at Falconbridge Nickel and other Canadian organizations, is another multifaceted human process intervention that relies on a grid-based leadership theory.[52]

Sensitivity Training. **Sensitivity training** (also called *T-group* or *encounter group*) is an unstructured and agendaless session in which a small group of people meet face to face, often for a few days, to learn more about themselves and their relations with others. The idea is for participants to becoming more sensitive to the effects of their own behaviour on others and the actions of others on them. In a typical sensitivity training meeting, the trainer explains his or her role as a resource person, then lapses into silence, leaving participants to grapple with establishing a purpose for their meeting. The trainer will intervene only to help participants understand the dynamics of their relations during the meeting, such as their own feelings and behaviours and the impact of their behaviour on themselves and others. In this respect, learning results from the "here-and-now" experiences of the participants through one's own disclosures and the immediate feedback from others during the session.[53]

sensitivity training
An unstructured, face-to-face session with no agenda, in which a small group of people learn through their interactions to become more sensitive to the effects of their own behaviour on others and the actions of others on them.

Technostructural Interventions

OD consultants have been increasingly involved in helping organizations change the structural elements of jobs and work relationships. Job design interventions, particularly those directed toward changing individual jobs, were discussed in Chapter 5 and are mostly aimed at increasing employee motivation through job enrichment. Quality circles and self-managing work teams were covered in Chapter 11 and involve increasing employee well-being, organizational problem solving, and productivity through employee involvement. OD experts have been interested in the sociotechnical design aspects of self-managing work teams since at least the early 1960s. Technostructural interventions also include redesigning entire organizations, which we will discuss in Chapter 17.

parallel learning structure

A social structure constructed alongside (i.e., parallel to) the formal organization with the purpose of increasing the organization's learning.

Parallel Learning Structures.   A **parallel learning structure** (also called a *collateral organization*) is a technostructural intervention in which a social structure is constructed alongside (i.e., parallel to) the formal hierarchy with the purpose of increasing the organization's learning.[54] Parallel learning structures are highly participative arrangements, comprised of people drawn from most levels of the larger organization who follow the action research model to produce meaningful organizational change. They are created to minimize the constraining features of the larger organization so that participants may communicate more freely and thereby solve organizational problems and opportunities more effectively.

All parallel learning structures include both a steering committee and one or more study teams. The steering committee creates a vision statement of the structure's objectives and designs the study teams. Study teams include a cross-section of organizational members who conduct organizational diagnoses, usually regarding specific issues outlined in the steering committee's vision statement. For instance, study teams might conduct surveys to discover barriers to the organization's quality improvement program. Eventually, the new attitudes, role patterns, and work behaviours recommended by these teams are transferred to the larger organization.

Human Resource Management Interventions

OD consultants have gained a greater appreciation of human resource management activities as behavioural science interventions. Goal setting was introduced in Chapter 2 as the process of establishing personal work objectives. Reward systems, which we described in Chapter 4, involve distributing money and other extrinsic benefits to motivate employees and fulfill organizational obligations. In Chapter 5 we discussed several types of stress management interventions to improve employee well-being and productivity by removing or helping people to cope with work-related stressors. Career planning and development practices, such as helping people adapt career anchors and choose career paths, are described in Chapter 16.

Strategic Interventions

The latest addition to the OD family are activities aimed at helping organizations improve their fit between corporate strategy, structure, culture, and the external environment.[55] Strategic planning interventions involve helping the organization shift strategic direction to become more compatible with existing environments. Open systems planning is a special type of strategic planning that involves developing a number of scenarios representing the present, future, and ideal environmental conditions for the organization. Participants compare the present conditions with the future and ideal scenario and develop strategic responses to these expected environmental changes. Finally, interventions that help organizations change and/or strengthen their corporate culture have been of particular interest to OD consultants and organizational leaders alike. We will discuss corporate culture in Chapter 16.

Organization Development in Canada

Organization development has had a colourful and well-documented history in the United States. There are many accounts of how Kurt Lewin's interracial training seminar in Connecticut during the summer of 1946 led to the birth of sensitivity training, intergroup laboratory, and other early OD techniques. Although Lewin died the next year, others who took up the challenge formed the National Training Laboratory (NTL) in 1947, providing a solid foundation for human process-based OD activities in that country as well as a place to train many OD consultants.[56]

Very little has been written about the early development of OD in Canada, although a few reports provide a sketchy outline of events.[57] Shortly after NTL started in 1947, a grass-roots group from Saskatchewan began attending NTL sessions and soon set up a comparable summer residential sensitivity training program in that province. By the mid-1950s, other Canadians had attended NTL and were introducing sensitivity training in human service settings. For example, the Canadian YMCA experimented with a residential laboratory training program, and in 1957 Sir George Williams (now Concordia) University began a human relations training program.

OD also captured the interest of educators, particularly in Ontario where Toronto's Forest Hill school system used NTL methods during the 1950s to help teachers and administrators work with alienated youth. Although OD interventions have occasionally been used to facilitate organizationwide change in Canadian educational systems,[58] most OD work in schools tends to focus on individual and professional development.[59]

Early OD Experiences in Canadian Business.   By the early 1960s, a few training professionals and general managers had introduced human process interventions in Canadian industry and invited American experts to facilitate OD interventions. Steinberg's Ltd., the Quebec-based supermarket chain, was perhaps one of the earliest businesses to practice OD in Canada.[60] In 1963, one of Steinberg's divisional general managers participated in a NTL sensitivity training session and soon after an American human relations scholar conducted a modified encounter group involving Steinberg's top management. By 1966, almost every member of Steinberg's senior management team had attended Blake and Mouton's Managerial Grid® seminars. Steinberg's management preferred Managerial Grid to sensitivity training because, as one manager explained: "The Grid is less threatening and more work oriented." By the end of the 1960s, nearly 2,000 of Steinberg's employees had completed the first phase of Grid OD and several hundred had participated in the team building (Phase 2) and intergroup building (Phase 3) parts of the program.

During the 1970s and 1980s, OD in Canada shifted from purely human process interventions to job design, quality circles, stress management, and other activities listed in the remaining three cells shown earlier in Exhibit 15–7.[61] This reflects a similar shift in the United States as part of OD's effort to become more relevant to business. Parallel learning structures have been sporadically applied in Canada over the years, such as in the federal government's transformation of Canada Employment Centres (then known as Canada Manpower Centres) during the early 1970s.[62] Several Canadian firms, including Xerox Canada described at the beginning of this chapter, have recently applied corporate culture change interventions.

EFFECTIVENESS OF ORGANIZATION DEVELOPMENT

Is organization development effective? Considering the incredibly broad spectrum of interventions within the rubric of organization development, answering this question is not easy. Nevertheless, a few studies have generally reported that organization development is effective much of the time. OD interventions seem to have a moderately positive effect on employee productivity and attitudes. According to some reviews, team building and laboratory training produce the most favourable results where a single intervention is applied.[63] Others report that self-managing work teams produce the best results.[64] One of the most consistent findings is that OD activities are most effective when they include two or more types of interventions. For instance, Blake and Mouton's Grid OD is effective because it includes team building, intergroup laboratory, and leadership development.

Researchers are just beginning to sort out the contingencies of OD effectiveness. For example, some writers have noted that many OD techniques originating from the United States do not work as well in other cultures.[65] Others have found that OD interventions applied to supervisors are more effective than those applied to nonmanagement employees.[66] Overall, organization development holds much promise, both as a process and a set of tools to improve organizational effectiveness, but the field will gain further momentum as it develops a more contingency-oriented perspective.

SUMMARY

• As open systems, organizations face numerous forces for change, such as changing population, changing legislation, increasing competition, technological changes, and mergers and acquisitions. Organizational change efforts are typically resisted, due to perceived higher direct costs, saving face, fear of the unknown, breaking existing routines, and structural and team inertia.

• Lewin's force field analysis identifies the forces for change and the forces resisting change. The model proposes that change occurs when the driving forces are stronger than the restraining forces. Lewin recommends unfreezing the status quo by reducing the resisting forces. This may be accomplished through education and communication, participation and involvement, facilitation and support, and negotiation and agreement. When absolutely necessary, manipulation, cooptation, and coercion may be effective.

• When change has occurred, several actions should be taken to refreeze or institutionalize the desired state so that the organization does not slip back into to its previous behaviour patterns. Pilot projects need to be diffused throughout the organization to ensure their success.

• Organization development (OD) is a planned systemwide effort, managed from the top with the assistance of a change agent, that uses behavioural science knowledge to improve organizational effectiveness. Planned change is based on the action research model, which calls for organizational diagnosis and action planning, implementation, and evaluation of the intervention's effect on the system involved.

• When beginning the OD process, the consultant must consider the client's readiness for change, the consultant's expected role in the process, and his or her power in the client–consultant relationship. Organizational diagnosis involves collecting data about an ongoing system, organizing and interpreting these data (usually by the consultant), and feeding these data back to the client. This is followed by action planning, in which a course of action is agreed on.

• The OD process actually includes several interventions, beginning with the consultant's entry into a relationship with the client. However, an important issue in the focal intervention is whether the change should be incremental or quantum, that is, whether the organization should fine tune the existing organizational configuration or move toward a totally different set of organizational systems.

- The earliest OD interventions addressed human processes such as inter-personal relations and conflict management. More recently, OD has shifted its emphasis toward technostructural, human resources, and strategic change interventions. In Canada, the earliest OD activities were directed toward helping alienated youth and related human service work in the non-business sector. Today, job design, quality circles, stress management, and other OD activities have been introduced in many Canadian businesses.

DISCUSSION QUESTIONS

1. Use Lewin's force field analysis to describe the dynamics of organizational change at Xerox Canada.

2. According to Lewin, what is the best strategy to move the status quo to a desired state?

3. Should managers first use manipulation, negotiation, or education to reduce resistance to change? Why?

4. Why should organizational leaders be interested in the diffusion of successful change efforts?

5. Outline the organization development process based on the action research model.

6. What roles might OD consultants adopt in the client–consultant relationship? What role characteristic is generally considered important for OD consultants?

7. What are parallel learning structures? Why are they used in some OD interventions?

8. Are OD interventions effective?

NOTES

1. C. R. Farquhar, "A Vision for Quality," *Canadian Business Review,* Summer 1991, pp. 7–15; D. R. McCamus, "Performance Measurement and the Quality Voyage," *CMA Magazine,* December/January 1991, pp. 8–12; M. Desjardins, "Managing for Quality," *Business Quarterly* 54 (Autumn 1989), pp. 103–7; K. Evans-Correia, "How Xerox Made Its Comeback," *Purchasing,* January 17, 1991, pp. 134–39; and B. Dumaine, "Can He Make Xerox Rock?" *Fortune,* June 17, 1991, p. 38.

2. P. E. Larson, *Winning Strategies* (Ottawa: Conference Board of Canada, January 1989) Report 36-89-E.

3. Economic Council of Canada, *Legacies* (26th Annual Review) (Ottawa: Supply and Services Canada, 1989), p. ix.

4. Ibid. Also see R. McKitrick, *The Current Industrial Relations Scene in Canada, 1989: The Economy and Labour Markets Reference Tables* (Kingston, Ont.: Industrial Relations Centre, Queen's University, 1989).

5. D. McMurdy, "Packaged for Growth," *Maclean's,* August 12, 1991, p. 31.

6. Economic Council of Canada, *Transitions for the 90s* (27th Annual Review) (Ottawa: Supply and Services Canada, 1990), Chapter 1.

7. N. Papadopoulos, "Trading Blocs: A Preliminary Typology and Implications," paper presented at the Annual ASAC Conference, Joint Panel with Policy and International Business Divisions, Whistler, B.C., June 1990. At the same session, see J. E. Denis, "A Canadian Perspective on the European Community."

8. Economic Council of Canada, *Innovation and Jobs in Canada* (Ottawa: Supply and Services Canada, 1987).

9. R. J. Long, *New Office Information Technology* (London: Croom Helm, 1987).

10. O. L. Crocker and R. Guelker, "The Effects of Robotics on the Workplace," *Personnel,* September 1988, pp. 26–36; S. D. Saleh and S. Pal, "Robotic Technology and Its Impact on Work Design and the Quality of Working Life," *Industrial Management,* May–June 1985, pp. 1–5; and S. D. Saleh and B. R. Hastings, "The Impact of Integrated Automation and Robotics on Plant Activities," *Canadian Journal of Administrative Sciences* 6 (March 1989), pp. 42–50.

11. R. Litchfield, "Solving an Education Crisis," *Canadian Business,* February 1991, pp. 57–64.

12. J. W. Rinehart, *The Tyranny of Work* (Toronto: Harcourt Brace Jovanovich, 1987); and H. Braverman, *Labor and Monopoly Capital* (New York: Monthly Review Press, 1974).

13. R. J. Long, "The Impact of New Office Information Technology on Job Quality in Canadian Firms," *Proceedings of the Annual ASAC Conference, Organizational Behaviour Division* 12, pt. 7 (1991), pp. 127–36; J. W. Medcof, "The Effect of Extent of Use of Information Technology and Job of the User upon Task Characteristics," *Human Relations* 42 (1989), pp. 23–41; and K. D. Hughes, "Office Automation: A Review of the Literature," *Relations Industrielles* 44 (1989), pp. 654–79.

14. Economic Council of Canada, *Legacies,* p. 1.

15. J. Lanthier, "People the Crucial Aspect of Mergers," *Financial Post,* July 24, 1989, p. 21.

16. P. McLaughlin, "Merger Doctors," *Vista* 2, no. 5 (May 1989), pp. 58–61.

17. J. H. Astrachan, *Mergers, Acquisitions, and Employee Anxiety* (New York: Praeger, 1990); G. A. Walter, "Culture Collisions in Mergers and Acquisitions," in P. Frost et al. (eds.), *Organizational Culture* (Beverly Hills, Calif.: Sage, 1985); and A. F. Buono and J. L. Bowditch, *The Human Side of Mergers and Acquisitions* (San Francisco: Jossey-Bass, 1989).

18. C. Hardy, *Strategies for Retrenchment and Turnaround: The Politics of Survival* (Berlin: Walter de Gruyter, 1990), Chapter 13.

19. J. Sims, "Quality Begins at Home," *Small Business* 8, no. 9 (September 1989), pp. 66–70.

20. D. A. Nadler, "The Effective Management of Organizational Change," in J. W. Lorsch (ed.), *Handbook of Organizational Behavior* (Englewood Cliffs, N.J.: Prentice Hall, 1987), pp. 358–69; and D. Katz and R. L. Kahn, *The Social Psychology of Organizations,* 2nd ed. (New York: Wiley, 1978).

21. K. Lewin, *Field Theory in Social Science* (New York: Harper & Row, 1951).

22. J. P. Kotter and L. A. Schlesinger, "Choosing Strategies for Change," *Harvard Business Review,* March–April 1979, pp. 106–14.

23. Lanthier, "People the Crucial Aspect of Mergers."

24. M. Pollock and N. L. Colwill, "Participatory Decision Making in Review," *Leadership and Organization Development Journal* 8, no. 2 (1987), pp. 7–10; and L. Coch and J. R. P. French, Jr., "Overcoming Resistance to Change," *Human Relations* 1 (1948), pp. 512–32.

25. R. J. Burke, "Managing the Human Side of Mergers and Acquisitions," *Business Quarterly,* Winter 1987, pp. 18–23.

26. H. Filman, "Everyone's Feeling Spooked? Call in the Stress-Busters," *Financial Times of Canada,* June 26, 1989, p. 5.

27. T. G. Cummings and E. F. Huse, *Organization Development and Change,* 4th ed. (St. Paul, Minn.: West, 1989), pp. 477–85; P. Goodman and J. Dean. "Creating Long-Term Organizational Change," in P. Goodman and associates (eds.), *Change in Organizations* (San Francisco: Jossey-Bass, 1982), pp. 226–79; and W. Warner Burke, *Organization Development: A Normative View* (Reading, Mass.: Addison-Wesley, 1987), pp. 124–25.

28. G. R. Bushe, "Quality Circles in Quality of Work Life Projects: Problems and Prospects for Increasing Employee Participation," *Canadian Journal of Community Mental Health* 3, no. 2 (Fall 1984), pp. 101–13.

29. M. Beer, R. A. Eisenstat, and B. Spector, *The Critical Path to Corporate Renewal* (Boston: Harvard Business School Press, 1990).

30. Ibid., Chapter 5; R. E. Walton, "The Diffusion of New Work Structures: Explaining Why Success Didn't Take," *Organizational Dynamics* 3, no. 2 (1975), pp. 3–22; and R. E. Walton, "Successful Strategies for Diffusing Work Innovations," *Journal of Contemporary Business,* Spring 1977, pp. 1–22.

31. R. Beckhard, *Organization Development: Strategies and Models* (Reading, Mass.: Addison-Wesley, 1969), Chapter 2. Also see Cummings and Huse, *Organization Development and Change,* pp. 1–3; and G. L. Lippitt, P. Langseth, and J. Mossop, *Implementing Organizational Change* (San Francisco: Jossey-Bass, 1985), Chapter 2.

32. Burke, *Organization Development: A Normative View,* pp. 12–14.

33. W. L. French and C. H. Bell, Jr., *Organization Development: Behavioral Science Interventions for Organization Improvement,* 4th ed. (Englewood Cliffs, N.J.: Prentice Hall, 1990), Chapter 8.

34. A. B. Shani and G. R. Bushe, "Visionary Action Research: A Consultation Process Perspective," *Consultation: An International Journal* 6, no. 1 (1987), pp. 3–19.

35. J. Cunningham, "The Action Research Approach to Organizational Change," *Optimum* 6, no. 2 (1975), pp. 33–55.

36. Beer, *Organizational Change and Development: A Systems View* (Glenview, Ill.: Scott Foresman, 1980), p. 9; and M. London, *Change Agents* (San Francisco: Jossey-Bass, 1988).

37. Beer, *Organizational Change and Development: A Systems View,* p. 79.

38. M. Beer and E. Walton, "Developing the Competitive Organization: Interventions and Strategies," *American Psychologist* 45 (February 1990), pp. 154–61.

39. E. H. Schein, *Process Consultation: Its Role in Organization Development* (Reading, Mass.: Addison-Wesley, 1969).

40. Burke, *Organization Development: A Normative View,* pp. 149–51; and Beer, *Organization Change and Development,* pp. 223–24.

41. L. E. Greiner and V. E. Schein, *Power and Organization Development: Mobilizing Power to Implement Change* (Reading, Mass.: Addison-Wesley, 1988); and Beer, *Organization Change and Development,* pp. 77–78.

42. D. Nadler, *Feedback and Organization Development: Using Data-Based Methods* (Reading, Mass.: Addison-Wesley, 1977); and J. A. Waters, P. F. Salipante, Jr., and W. W. Notz, "The Experimenting Organization: Using the Results of Behavioral Science Research," *Academy of Management Review* 3 (1978), pp. 483–92.

43. Beer, *Organization Change and Development,* pp. 97–99.

44. Ibid., pp. 101–2.

45. D. F. Harvey and D. R. Brown, *An Experiential Approach to Organization Development,* 3rd ed. (Englewood Cliffs, N.J.: Prentice Hall, 1988), pp. 93–94.

46. D. A. Nadler, "Organizational Frame Bending: Types of Change in the Complex Organization," in R. H. Kilmann, T. J. Covin, and associates, *Corporate Transformation: Revitalizing Organizations for a Competitive World* (San Francisco: Jossey-Bass, 1988), pp. 66–83; and London, *Change Agents,* Chapter 5.

47. J. M. Kouzes and B. Z. Posner, *The Leadership Challenge* (San Francisco: Jossey-Bass, 1988), Chapter 10; and C. Lindblom, "The Science of Muddling Through," *Public Administration Review* 19 (1959), pp. 79–88.

48. C. R. Hinings and R. Greenwood, *The Dynamics of Strategic Change* (Oxford, England: Basil Blackwell, 1988), Chapter 6; and D. Miller and P. H. Friesen, "Structural Change and Performance: Quantum versus Piecemeal-Incremental Approaches," *Academy of Management Journal* 25 (1982), pp. 867–92.

49. E. Innes, J. Lyon, and J. Harris, *The 100 Best Companies to Work For in Canada* (Toronto: HarperCollins, 1990), pp. 42–44.

50. Cummings and Huse, *Organization Development and Change,* pp. 127–33.

51. M. Sashkin and W. W. Burke, "Organization Development in the 1980s," *Journal of Management* 13 (1987), pp. 393–417.

52. W. J. Reddin, *The Output-Oriented Organization* (Aldershot, England: Gower Publishing, 1988), Chapter 7.

53. Cummings and Huse, *Organization Development and Change,* pp. 158–61.

54. G. R. Bushe and A. B. Shani, *Parallel Learning Structures* (Reading, Mass.: Addison-Wesley, 1991); and G. R. Bushe and A. B. Shani, "Parallel Learning Structure Interventions in Bureaucratic Organizations," *Research in Organizational Change and Development* 4 (1990), pp. 167–94.

55. Cummings and Huse, *Organization Development and Change,* p. 133; and French and Bell, *Organization Development,* pp. 165–69.

56. French and Bell, *Organization Development: Behavioral Science Interventions for Organization Improvement,* Chapter 3.

57. H. G. Dimock, "Thirty Years of Human Service Education and Training in Canada—One Perspective," *Canadian Journal of Community Mental Health* 3, no. 2 (1984), pp. 15–41; and H. G. Dimock, "Canada's Experience with Human Relations Training," *Annual Handbook for Group Facilitators* (San Diego, Calif.: University Associates, 1975), pp. 233–37.

58. L. B. Jones and K. A. Leithwood, "Draining the Swamp: A Case Study of School System Design," *Canadian Journal of Education* 14 (1989), pp. 242–60.

59. M. Fullan and M. Miles, "OD in Schools: The State of the Art," in W. L. French, C. H. Bell, Jr., and R. A. Zawacki (eds.), *Organization Development: Theory, Practice, and Research,* rev. ed. (Plano, Texas: Business Publications, 1983), pp. 493–500.

60. H. Rush, "Organization Development at Steinberg's Limited—A Case Study," in H. C. Jain, *Contemporary Issues in Canadian Personnel Administration* (Scarborough, Ont.: Prentice Hall of Canada, 1974), pp. 262–69.

61. N. J. Adler, "The Future of Organization Development in Canada," *Canadian Journal of Administrative Sciences* 1 (1984), pp. 122–32. Also see R. J. Long, "Patterns of Workplace Innovation in Canada," *Relations Industrielles* 44 (1989), pp. 805–24.

62. W. M. A. Brooker, "Integrating Social and Technical Change: A Pilot Project," *Optimum* 3, no. 2 (1972), pp. 55–65.

63. G. A. Neuman, J. E. Edwards, and N. S. Raju, "Organizational Development Interventions: A Meta-Analysis of Their Effects on Satisfaction and Other Attitudes," *Personnel Psychology* 42 (1989), pp. 461–89; and R. A. Guzzo, R. D. Jette, and R. A. Katzell, "The Effects of Psychologically Based Intervention Programs on Worker Productivity: A Meta-Analysis," *Personnel Psychology* 38 (1985), pp. 275–91.

64. R. J. Long, "The Effects of Various Workplace Innovations on Productivity: A Quasi-Experimental Study," *Proceedings of the Annual ASAC Conference, Personnel and Human Resources Division* 11, pt. 9 (1990), pp. 98–107.

65. A. M. Jaeger, "Organization Development and National Culture: Where's the Fit?" *Academy of Management Review* 11 (1986), pp. 178–90.

66. Neuman et al, "Organizational Development Interventions: A Meta-Analysis of Their Effects on Satisfaction and Other Attitudes."

CHAPTER CASE

REICHHOLD LIMITED

In October 1988, Mr. Chris Hill, fleet administrator of Reichhold Limited of Toronto, began to prepare a new Fleet Policy Manual to be used by the company in the selection of suppliers and cars for its fleet of 211 automobiles. At the time, the chemical company was leasing automobiles from 11 different leasing companies throughout Canada. The number of companies supplying automobiles had not resulted from any conscious effort to develop a diversified group of suppliers; rather, any executive with automobile acquisition responsibility had selected the leasing company he or she felt was most appropriate in the circumstances. Mr. Hill was aware that some benefits were realized from having more than one supplier. However, he was concerned about the resulting large variety of automobile models and lease conditions that made fleet management cumbersome and expensive.

The Company

Reichhold Limited was a medium-sized manufacturer of synthetic resins and other resin-based chemical products and printing inks, as well as a distributor of printing presses, paper cutting machines, specialty resins, adhesives, and decorative overlay. The company's operations were divided into the following five primary product groups:

1. *Surface coatings*—Reichhold was Canada's largest producer of resins for paint, surface coating, and textiles.

2. *Forest products*—The company supplied resins to the forest products industry for use as bonding agents in plywood, particle board, hardboard, and waferboard.

3. *Polyesters and plastics*—Reichhold produced polyester resin used in fiberglass reinforced plastics found in such products as snowmobiles and light boat hulls. Also, this division produced phenolic moulding compounds used in appliance handles and electrical switch boxes.

4. *Graphic arts*—A division, Canada Printing Ink, manufactured a full line of inks including letterpress, offset, lithographic, news, and specialty inks. Another division distributed equipment used in the printing industry, such as printing presses and paper-cutting machines.

5. *Other products*—Reichhold imported and distributed a wide variety of specialty resins and adhesives and marketed a full line of decorative overlay.

The Reichhold Automobile Fleet

Mr. Hill joined Reichhold Limited in August of 1988 as its first fleet administrator. At the time, Reichhold was leasing 211 automobiles from 11 different suppliers, but there was little or no coordination of the fleet with respect to type of automobile, type of lease, etc. The executive fleet of 12 automobiles was administered by the head office, but the 54 cars driven by division management personnel and the 145 cars driven by Reichhold division salespeople were administered on a part-time basis by various personnel in the divisions. Mr. Hill was hired by the corporate controller—to whom he reported—who believed that significant savings could be realized by centralizing all automobile fleet administration under one head office manager.

When Mr. Hill joined Reichhold Limited, three divisions were leasing their cars from national leasing companies. The Canada Printing Ink Division leased about 50 automobiles exclusively from Canadian Vehicle Leasing; Niagara Chemical leased 40 automobiles exclusively from Gelco; and another division leased its 15 company cars exclusively from Pattison. As a result, roughly half of Reichhold's total fleet was subject to open-ended finance leases. Two other divisions, on the other hand, leased their automobiles from eight local and regional leasing companies, usually for fixed terms of 36 to 48 months, subject to maximum odometer readings at the termination date. The most signifiant attempt to control fleet costs to date had been made by the purchasing manager of the Canada Printing Ink Division, who had set a maximum dollar retail value per car for each executive level within that subsidiary.

Most Reichhold divisions had a large number of automobile models, often ranging toward the upper end of the price range. Mr. Hill assumed that the variety was primarily a result of the lack of a selector list, which in turn suggested inadequate advice from the leasing companies. He did not expect unbiased advice from all suppliers, however, since some of them were "Big Three" dealers with a vested interest in leasing out specific models. In addition, it appears to Mr. Hill that some divisions had used automobiles to reward performance, particularly by sales representatives. For example, in one division, the top salesperson drove a top-of-the-line Oldsmobile equipped with most of the available options. While he conceded that such a strategy might be effective as a motivational tool, Mr. Hill was concerned that it would be inconsistent with developing a fleet that would be economical in terms of operating costs and lease payments and have a good resale value when the automobiles were retired.

As of mid-1988, the lowest monthly lease payment made by Reichhold was approximately $280, while the highest was about $400. Overall, the fleet was averaging 28,000 miles per car per year. However, with the fixed-term leases applicable to so many automobiles, a significant number were being retired with well over 100,000 miles on the odometer, and the company was being charged heavy excess mileage fees that would not have applied under open-end finance leases. It was not unusual for the company to be invoiced for more than $1,000 for excess mileage charges on a car upon termination of the lease.

Policy Objectives

Mr. Hill's primary mandate was to reduce Reichhold's total fleet costs to a minimum without impairing the effectiveness of the automobiles. This left him free to initiate any reasonable policy that did not attempt to reduce the number of miles driven by company cars.

Mr. Hill wanted to be certain that he looked at all reasonable alternatives before embarking on any changes. He also knew that any recommendations he did make would have to be fully justified.

Discussion Questions

1. Using the force field analysis technique discussed in the chapter, analyze this case. Be specific about the pressures for change and the resistances to change likely to be encountered in this situation. Identify which types of pressure and resistance are likely to be the strongest.

2. Who should be involved in designing changes to Reichhold's automobile policy—only Mr. Hill, or should Hill include others? From whom should input be sought? Justify your answers.

Source: Written by Professor M. Leenders. © 1985 Western Business School, The University of Western Ontario. Reprinted by permission.

EXPERIENTIAL EXERCISE

FORCE FIELD ANALYSIS

Purpose: This exercise is designed to help you diagnose organizational situations using force field analysis, as well as to identify strategies to unfreeze the status quo and refreeze the desired state.

Instructions: Participants should read the opening vignette in Chapter 12 (CTV Television). The class is then divided into teams of four to six people. Each team's first task is to diagnose the forces driving and constraining change at CTV Television using the diagram shown below. Next, each team identifies the changes it believes are necessary. Strategies to unfreeze the current situation and refreeze the desired conditions are then listed. The class reconvenes to hear each team's diagnosis and recommendations.

Force Field Analysis of CTV Television Network

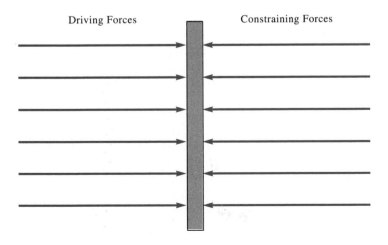

Driving Forces   Constraining Forces

16

Organizational Culture, Socialization, and Careers

LEARNING OBJECTIVES

After reading this chapter, you should be able to:

Distinguish
Between an organization's dominant culture and its subcultures.

List
Four type of artifacts through which organizational culture is communicated.

Explain
How to strengthen an organization's dominant culture.

Describe
The three stages of organizational socialization.

Explain
How socialization agents potentially assist new employees.

Outline
The stages that people pass through in their careers.

Discuss
The benefits of mentoring in organizations.

CHAPTER OUTLINE

What Is Organizational Culture?

Communicating Organizational Culture

Strengthening Organizational Culture

Organizational Socialization

Stages of Socialization

Managing the Socialization Process

Organizational Careers

Dynamics of Individual Careers

Organizational Career Management

Aitken-Wreglesworth Associates

When David Aitken and Peter Wreglesworth founded Aitken-Wreglesworth Associates (AWA) in 1981, they wanted to develop an architectural firm that would bring out everyone's creative talents. "Basically, our goal has been to build a co-creative enterprise," says David Aitken. "Our achitecture is born by tapping the strength of many people as they develop creativity. It is not divinely inspired by Peter and me—we don't believe in the heroic, maestro architectural model."

To achieve a co-creative enterprise, the founding partners have established an organizational culture around the notion of consensus reality. "Everyone holds a unique perception of reality," explains Peter Wreglesworth. "AWA people believe that these perceptions have value in their own right, so the expression of opinion is an important element of creativity in this firm." Many decisions ultimately rest with the partners and associates, but input from staff members is the norm rather than the exception. Indeed, AWA invests heavily in its employees through training programs on brainstorming, interpersonal skills, and personal development.

A related belief at AWA is personal accountability. Employees are expected to take ownership of their emotions and behaviour rather than assign blame elsewhere. Moreover, they should check out their perceptions rather than let them become reinforced and distorted. David Aitken gives an example: "If I don't think Peter approves of something I've done, I should check my perception with him rather than brood about it and find further evidence to support that perception." Peter Wreglesworth adds, "It requires personal courage and an environment of psychological safety to address interpersonal tensions. Creativity gets stuck when tensions exist and people are engaged in power struggles."

AWA's unique culture is apparent in the enthusiasm and sincere openness of its founding partners and employees. Clients appreciate the fact that consensus reality also applies to them as AWA staff members seek out their ideas, recognizing that the clients' opinions are important and valued. New employees experience AWA's culture through their treatment by colleagues. Observes one recently hired architect: "Every move is contemplated with every person's feelings included. 'How do you feel about it?' is an often-heard phrase around here."

Due to its talented staff and well-adapted organizational culture, Aitken-Wreglesworth Associates is now one of the largest architectural firms in Western Canada with nearly 100 staff. It has won major contracts with the Eaton's Centre in Burnaby, Simon Fraser University's Harbour Centre campus, and the redevelopment of Vancouver's downtown waterfront. In an industry that succeeds or dies by creative thinking, AWA's culture has become a catalyst for employee innovation and dedication. Says one AWA employee, "It's a little esoteric for some people, but it's not just lip service. I was wary of sloganism at first—I wasn't sure whether it was really true. But now, another traditional firm would have to pay me substantially more to get me to leave here."[1]

Few leaders have shaped their organizational culture as effectively as David Aitken and Peter Wreglesworth. This chapter begins by examining the complex meaning of organizational culture, followed by a discussion of how it is recognized and transmitted. Next, we consider specific strategies for maintaining a strong organizational culture. The second part of this chapter turns to the related topic of organizational socialization. Here, we examine how newcomers and other transitional employees adjust to the physical, social, and cultural dimensions of their work environment. The discussion also considers how to manage this process more effectively. The final part of this chapter looks at organizational careers, including career anchors, career stages, and several contemporary career management practises such as mentoring and alternative career paths.

WHAT IS ORGANIZATIONAL CULTURE?

Organizational culture is the basic pattern of shared assumptions, values, and beliefs considered to be the correct way of thinking about and acting on problems and opportunities facing the organization.[2] Culture operates unconsciously, serving as the automatic pilot of organizational behaviour as it provides direction and focusses attention on some events more than others. Organizational culture is therefore a deeply embedded form of social control whereby individuals abide by cultural prescriptions shared with others within the organization.

Organizational culture is a product of the collective experiences of employees as the organization adapts to its external environment. As such, it is shaped by critical events in the organization's history, by the organization's founder and subsequent leaders, and by the larger societal culture. People are motivated to adapt and internalize the organization's dominant culture because it fulfills their need for social identity, that is, it provides employees with personal meaning and connectedness with others. Organizational culture is part of the "social glue" that bonds people together and makes them feel part of the organizational experience.[3]

organizational culture
The basic pattern of shared assumptions, values, and beliefs governing the way employees within an organization think about and act upon problems and opportunities.

Artifacts of Organizational Culture

As illustrated in Exhibit 16–1, organizational culture lies beneath the surface of organizational behaviour. Assumptions represent the deepest part of organizational culture, whereas values and beliefs are somewhat closer to the surface. Although an organization's culture is not directly observable, it can be loosely interpreted through a constellation of visible artifacts. **Artifacts** represent the directly observable symbols and signs of an organization's culture, including its physical structures, ceremonies, language, and stories. Artifacts maintain and transmit shared meanings and perceptions of reality within the organization. While they are easy to see, artifacts are not always easy to decipher. To understand an organization's culture, you must examine its artifacts from several perspectives and search for common themes through diverse elements in the system.[4]

artifacts

The directly observable symbols and signs of an organization's culture, including its physical structures, ceremonies, language, and stories.

Organizational Culture Content and Strength

Organizations differ in terms of the content and strength of their cultures. The content of organizational culture refers to the relative ordering of beliefs and values.[5] For example, one firm might emphasize technological efficiency, while another focusses on customer service. Exhibit 16–2 lists the apparent content of dominant cultures in several Canadian organizations.

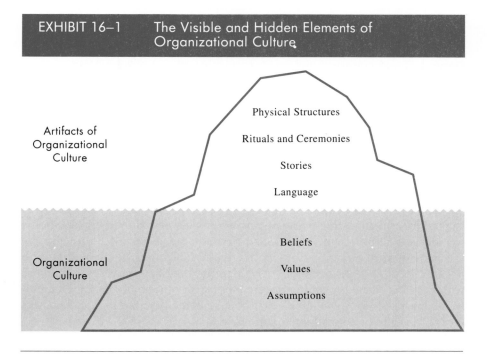

| EXHIBIT 16–1 | The Visible and Hidden Elements of Organizational Culture |

Artifacts of Organizational Culture

Physical Structures
Rituals and Ceremonies
Stories
Language

Organizational Culture

Beliefs
Values
Assumptions

EXHIBIT 16–2	Possible Cultural Values in Canadian Companies

Company	**Likely Dominant Cultural Values**
Eaton's (retailer)	"Goods satisfactory or money refunded"—respect for the customer.
Hees International (merchant bank)	Prudently use corporate expense accounts; avoid risky investments; take a major position in promising investments.
Du Pont Canada (chemicals)	Place highest priority on the physical safety and psychological well-being of employees; maintain high ethical standards to the public.
CAE Industries (flight and other simulators)	High technology research and manufacturing is the engine of corporate success.
London Life (insurance)	Rigorous organizational efficiency; measurable goal-oriented productivity improvements.
Sun Microsystems Canada (computers)	Aggressive, hard-driving, with minimal bureaucracy—like running a marathon—"Try for the impossible and settle for the absurd."
McDonald's Canada (fast food)	"Quality, service, cleanliness, and value"—e.g., don't try to squeeze too many milkshakes out of a gallon of mix.

Sources: L. Holstrom and A. Dugan, "The House That Jack Built," *Euromoney*, August 1990, pp. 20–29; F. G. Harmon and G. Jacobs, *The Vital Difference* (New York: AMA, 1985), pp. 59–60; S. Boyes, "DuPont Won't Tolerate Sexual Harassment," *Canadian HR Reporter*, June 13, 1988, p. 8; I. Allaby, "Landing Hard in the US," *Canadian Business*, February 1991, pp. 86–91; P. E. Larson, "Achieving Corporate Excellence," *Canadian Business Review*, Winter 1987, pp. 38–40; E. Innes, J. Lyon, and J. Harris, *100 Best Companies to Work For in Canada* (Toronto: HarperCollins, 1990), pp. 158–60; and C. Davies, "1990 Strategy Session," *Canadian Business*, January 1990, pp. 47–55.

This list should be viewed with some caution because it is extremely difficult to articulate an organization's dominant culture, let alone decipher its ambiguous artifacts. Nevertheless, this exhibit illustrates the diversity of cultures that likely exist in Canadian companies.

Cultural strength refers to the extent that the underlying assumptions, values, and beliefs are understood and widely shared throughout the organization, not just among top management. Strong cultures are long lasting, dispersed across subunits, deeply internalized by employees, and institutionalized through well-established artifacts.[6] Several writers claim that firms with strong cultures are better managed and have superior financial performance over the long term than those with weak cultures.[7] This makes a great deal of sense when we realize that culture guides both decisions and behaviour. It causes people to see the world in a certain way, and this interpretation may influence the organization's ability to adapt, ignore, or misunderstand environmental cues signalling the need for change. Strong cultures also create common bonds among employees, resulting in more efficient communication and higher levels of cooperation.

A strong organizational culture is valuable in many situations, but it may be a liability where the dominant beliefs and assumptions are incompatible with the external environment. For example, in his study of Canadian police forces, Gene Deszca concludes that many units need to change their centralized and authoritarian culture as police recruits become more educated and the public develops new expectations of law enforcement. Deszca warns: "The costs of maintaining a traditional police culture at the municipal level have simply become too high in both human and economic terms."[8] Whether the organization is a municipal police department or a leading high-technology manufacturer, the content of its culture must fit the external conditions.

Organizational Subcultures

When discussing organizational culture, we are actually referring to the dominant culture, that is, the themes shared most widely by the organization's members. However, organizations are also comprised of subcultures located throughout its various subunits.[9] Some writers suggest that the organization's dominant culture actually represents a "negotiated order" shaped by the subcultures. Put simply, the organization's dominant culture represents the common themes found in its subcultures.[10]

Some subcultures enhance the dominant culture by espousing parallel assumptions, values, and beliefs. Others are countercultures because they directly oppose the organization's core values. For example, when Shell Canada's senior management decided that the company should become more aggressive as well as move its headquarters from Toronto to Calgary, employees in the computer department formed a powerful counterculture, complete with its own underground newspaper, *Trash*, to voice their opposition to management's tactics. Interestingly, *Trash* became a popular vehicle for dissension—it was even read by senior management![11]

COMMUNICATING ORGANIZATIONAL CULTURE

Artifacts represent an important dimension of organizational culture because they are the means by which culture is communicated.[12] Artifacts come in many forms, but they may be generally classified into four broad categories: organizational stories, language, rituals and ceremonies, and physical structures and space.

PERSPECTIVE 16–1   Tales of Quality at Four Seasons Hotels

Quality service is a deeply held cultural belief among employees at Four Seasons Hotels. This is communicated through the many stories of extraordinary employee effort at this exceptional company:

- A bellman at the Four Seasons Yorkville hotel in Toronto wanted to return a briefcase that a visiting diplomat had left behind. Nothing unusual about this, except that the diplomat had left for Washington, D.C., so the bellman flew there at his own expense to personally ensure that the diplomat received the briefcase intact.

- Four Seasons staff received a call from visiting rock star Rod Stewart for someone to play the bagpipes in his suite. The employees were able to find a willing bagpipe player, even though Stewart phoned in the request around *midnight!*

- A guest at the Four Seasons hotel in San Francisco asked the concierge where he could buy a Canadian flag. He wanted to display the flag over his stadium box at the baseball game that night to show his support for the visiting Toronto Blue Jays. The concierge said "leave it to me" and soon arrived at the guest's room with a huge 10 by 12 foot Canadian flag! The hotel flies the Maple Leaf at its properties and the concierge lent the guest the hotel's spare flag.

- On a tour of the Four Seasons Montreal property, Isadore Sharp (the founder and CEO of Four Seasons) suggested that a certain credenza should be moved to another room. The general manager forgot about the request. During his next tour of the property some eight months later, Sharp paused to look at the piece of furniture, then asked politely, "Didn't we decide to move that credenza?" (Sharp's penchant for details and his keen memory are legendary.)

Sources: J. DeMont, "Sharp's Luxury Empire," *Maclean's*, June 5, 1989, pp. 30–33; and K. Foss, "Isadore Sharp," *Foodservice and Hospitality*, December 1989, pp. 20–30.

Organizational Stories

Organizational stories describe past organizational experiences, usually about the company founder or valiant employees, and serve as powerful social prescriptions of "the way things should (or should not) be done around here."[13] They provide human realism to individual performance standards and use role models to demonstrate that organizational objectives are attainable. As described in Perspective 16–1, Four Seasons Hotels has a strong "quality service" culture, partly because employees share stories about the company's past events and corporate heroes.

Organizational Language

As we mentioned in Chapter 6, language is an important element in transmitting and sustaining shared values. Specifically, people adopt metaphors and other special vocabularies that represent their perspective of reality.[14] At Federal Industries, CEO Jack Fraser has nurtured a unique culture through such phrases as "smell smoke," "no surprises," and "keeping trending right.'' These principles reflect Fraser's personal moral values and have formed the core criteria for decision making at the Winnipeg-based holding company and its many subsidiaries.[15] Subcultures also develop metaphors to symbolize their opposition to aspects of the dominant culture. For instance, employees at Merrill Lynch Canada refer to themselves as the ''Canadian colony'' and the company's world headquarters in New York as ''the palace.'' These metaphors communicate the tense relationship between Merrill Lynch and its Canadian subsidiary.[16]

Rituals and Ceremonies

rituals
The programmed routines of daily organizational life that dramatize the organization's culture.

ceremonies
Deliberate and usually dramatic displays of organizational culture, such as celebrations and special social gatherings.

Rituals are the programmed routines of daily organizational life that dramatize the organization's culture. They include such activities as how often senior managers visit subordinates, how meetings are conducted, how visitors are greeted, and how much time employees take for lunch. **Ceremonies** are planned activities conducted specifically for the benefit of an audience.[17] They are deliberate and usually dramatic displays of cultural assumptions, values, and beliefs. For instance, Domtar Forest Products proudly celebrates its safety record by distributing leather jackets to its employees at special presentation ceremonies. IBM, a master of celebration, appoints the top 10 percent of its sales staff to the Gold Circle Club, while others who surpass their basic quota become members of the One Hundred Percent Club.[18]

Physical Structures and Space

Physical structures and spaces often provide subtle images of the company's underlying values and beliefs.[19] The size, shape, location, and age of buildings might suggest the organization's emphasis on stability and strength or agility and creativity. For instance, the Royal Bank of Canada's relatively squat, yet solid-looking headquarters in Toronto conveys the undeniable image of financial security and strength. Indeed, the building literally glistens with 2,500 ounces of gold coating on its mirror-glass exterior, ostensibly for climate control within the building, but also conveying a deeper meaning.[20] (Some people half-jokingly suggest that if there was ever a run on the bank, Royal Bank could simply start melting its windows!)

Office design represents another relevant artifact. Organizational cultures that emphasize hierarchy tend to carefully measure offices so that higher officials have larger spaces and more expensive furniture. Procter & Gamble Canada, for instance, has a well-defined protocol for office size, furniture, and carpeting according to the person's position in the organization. In contrast, one Brazilian bank (Bradesco) has no private offices for its 137,000 employees, reflecting that organization's egalitarian and team-oriented culture. These values are further emphasized at the head office, where senior managers don't even have private desks; instead, they sit around two large tables in one room![21]

STRENGTHENING ORGANIZATIONAL CULTURE

We stated earlier that the strength of a culture improves the organization's effectiveness if the cultural content fits the external environment. Strengthening organizational culture therefore becomes an important objective. Exhibit 16–3 identifies the most important strategies used to perpetuate strong cultures.

Actions of Founders and Top Management

Founders have a major effect on organizational culture because, from the very beginning, they establish the organization's purpose and lay down its basic philosophy for interaction with the external environment.[22] We can certainly see the powerful influence of living founders such as Isadore Sharp at Four Seasons Hotels, Anita Roddick at The Body Shop, and Frank Stronach at Magna International. But there is evidence that the founder's

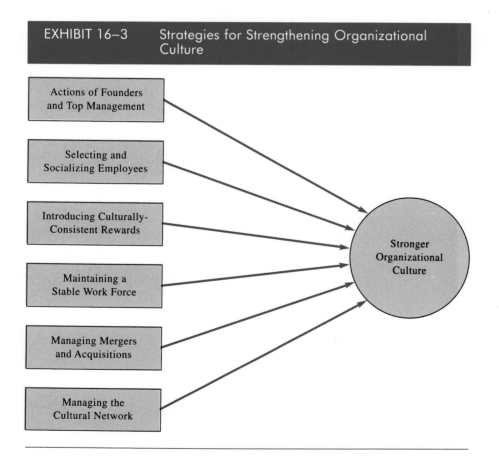

EXHIBIT 16–3   Strategies for Strengthening Organizational Culture

cultural imprint remains with the organization for many years after the reins are passed on. For example, Eaton's well-known credo of "goods satisfactory or money refunded" was established by Timothy Eaton soon after his first store opened in 1869.[23] To this day, service and value remain core values among Eaton's employees.

By communicating and enacting their vision of the future, transformational leaders are strengthening organizational culture.[24] Cultural values are particularly reinforced when leaders are consistent with the vision (i.e., "walking the talk"). Four Seasons founder and CEO Isadore Sharp maintains a strong quality-service culture by ensuring that managers are consistent with this cultural standard. "Employees watch their managers and take their cues from them, so our managers have to act as role models," says Sharp. "We made changes at the very top—head-office senior executives, hotel general managers—until those whom others would imitate were setting the proper standard. The message got through and superior service became our competitive edge."[25]

Selecting and Socializing Employees

Job candidates are typically hired on the basis of their skills and knowledge, but it is also useful to select applicants whose beliefs and values are consistent with the organizational culture so that this culture is strengthened.[26] For instance, Shell Canada Ltd. and Toyota Canada Ltd. carefully select people with a deeply ingrained team orientation to ensure that a team-based culture is perpetuated at their new plants.[27]

Organizations also maintain strong cultures by communicating the dominant values to job candidates and encouraging new hires to quickly internalize these values. This aspect of organizational socialization, discussed later in the chapter, allows newcomers to learn about the organization's culture through recruiting literature, orientation programs, and informal interactions with other employees. By describing "the way things are done around here" during recruitment, applicants can decide before being hired whether they identify with or reject the company's belief systems. This strategy also reduces employee turnover because selected employees are less likely to experience conflict with the organization's dominant values after they are hired.[28]

Introducing Culturally Consistent Rewards

Reward systems can strengthen an organization's culture when they reinforce behaviours that are consistent with cultural prescriptions.[29] Rewards also communicate dominant values through symbols and celebrations, such as awards for high achievers or community-spirited employees. Of course, conformity to team norms and other social reinforcements can weaken culture, even when financial rewards are aligned with the dominant values.

Still, by unblocking these countervalent forces, formal rewards can institutionalize new behaviour patterns and strengthen their underlying cultural beliefs.

Maintaining a Stable Work Force

An organization's culture and many of its artifacts are embedded in the minds of its employees. Organizational stories are rarely written down; rituals and celebrations do not usually exist in procedures manuals; and organizational metaphors are not found in corporate dictionaries. Thus, organizations depend on a stable work force to communicate and reinforce the dominant beliefs and values. The organization's culture can literally disintegrate during periods of high turnover or rapid expansion because employees have not sufficiently learned the ways to do things around the organization.[30] For this reason, some organizations try to keep their culture intact by moderating employment growth and correcting turnover problems.

Managing Mergers and Acquisitions

Until recently, mergers and acquisitions were decided almost entirely from a financial or marketing perspective; little consideration was given to differences in the organizational cultures of the companies involved. Yet attempting to merge two organizations with distinct values and beliefs could result in a cultural collision that would destabilize the dominant culture and threaten successful integration, even between organizations that were otherwise strategically compatible.[31] Various forms of intergroup conflict could develop, and the acquired employees would typically exhibit considerable resistance to change. The solution is to manage the change process as we described in Chapter 15 and reduce conflict through various strategies introduced in Chapter 13. As we see in Perspective 16–2, Bombardier Inc. has learned the importance of assessing a target firm's organizational culture.

Managing the Cultural Network

Organizational culture is learned, so an effective network of cultural transmission is necessary to strengthen the company's underlying assumptions, values, and beliefs. According to Max De Pree, the CEO of furniture manufacturer Herman Miller Inc., every organization needs "tribal storytellers" to keep the organization's history and culture alive.[32] The cultural network exists through the organizational grapevine, but it can be further supported by providing opportunities for frequent interaction among employees so that stories may be shared and rituals reenacted. Senior executives must tap into the cultural network, sharing their own stories and creating new ceremonies

Bombardier Inc., the Montreal-based transportation vehicle manufacturer, has acquired several companies over the years and developed a strict set of guidelines for deciding whether to proceed with new purchases. The targetted company must be in a niche of the transportation business, have sales of at least $300 million, and be in a sector where Bombardier can play a leadership role. But even if these conditions are met, Bombardier's management will walk away from the deal if the targeted company's cultural values are out of line.

An organization's values and beliefs aren't found at the bottom of a financial statement, so a management team conducts a personal diagnosis and evalu-

ation of the situation. "When we look at a possible acquisition, the first thing we look at in-house is whether or not we share the same values," says Bombardier president Raymond Royer. "What we are trying to do is to see if there is a common understanding of what we are trying to achieve as a company and what the firm we are looking at purchasing is trying to achieve."

Before purchasing Canadair from the Canadian government in 1987, Royer and other Bombardier managers interviewed Canadair's managers at all levels, asking them to assess their organization. Based on this process, Bombardier's management knew that a dramatic shakedown would be required

and other opportunities to demonstrate shared meaning. Company magazines and other media can also strengthen organizational culture by communicating cultural values and beliefs more efficiently.

ORGANIZATIONAL SOCIALIZATION

organizational socialization

The continuous process by which individuals learn the values, expected behaviours, and social knowledge necessary to assume their organizational roles.

Organizational socialization refers to the process by which individuals learn the values, expected behaviours, and social knowledge necessary to assume their roles in the organization.[33] It is a continuous process, beginning long before the first day of employment and continuing throughout one's career within the company.

Socialization is a process of both learning and change. As a learning process, newcomers try to develop a cognitive map of their new work environment. They want to make sense of the organization, including its physical arrangements, social relationships, and culture. To do this, they need to find reliable sources of information and discover what types of data are more important than others. While many facts may be easily available prior to joining an organization, newcomers are heavily dependent on coworkers for "soft" information, such as who has power, what is expected of newcomers, and how employees *really* get ahead in this organization or department.

Organizational socialization is a process of change as individuals adapt to the new work environment.[34] They develop new work roles based on a complex interaction of their self-identity and the expectations of others.

to transform the aircraft maker's sluggish bureaucracy into Bombardier's entrepreneurial and aggressive culture. "We are bringing Bombardier culture to Canadair and not the opposite," Bombardier CEO Laurent Beaudoin said confidently at the time. Canadair employees have since adopted a set of beliefs and values more closely aligned with those of Bombardier.

A similar cultural audit was conducted at Short Brothers PLC, Northern Ireland's largest employer, before Bombardier acquired it in 1989. "For Short, we went and did our investigation much more deeply," explains Royer. For example, besides meeting with all of Short's top executives and leaders of its seven labour unions, Bombardier invited employee representatives to visit their counterparts at Canadair. However, to remain neutral, Bombardier insisted that the Irish visitors make their own arrangements to meet the Canadair employees and their union representatives. Only after Bombardier's management was confident that a cultural connection could be made did it purchase Short Brothers from the British government.

Sources: D. Estok, "Putting a Bloom on Intangibles," *Financial Post 500,* Summer 1990, pp. 56–61; and A. Zerbisias, "How Do You Make a Turkey Soar?" *Report on Business Magazine,* October 1987, pp. 82–89.

They practice new behaviours and adopt norms to function more effectively as work team members. Finally, newcomers acquire and (to varying degrees) internalize organizational values and beliefs. While newcomers rarely conform completely to the forces of organizational socialization, few rebel entirely against these socialization attempts. Ideally, newcomers adopt a level of creative individualism in which they eventually accept the absolutely essential elements of the organization's culture and team norms, yet maintain a healthy individualism that challenges the allegedly dysfunctional elements of organizational life.

The Continuity of Organizational Socialization

Socialization is most intense when people first enter an organization, because they must learn about and adjust to an entirely new work context as well as learn role-specific behaviours. However, socialization is an ongoing process that is most intense immediately before and after any organizational transition. For instance, organizational socialization applies to employee transfers and repatriation from foreign assignments because people are moving to a new context in which they must learn and adopt new perspectives and behaviours.[35]

Exhibit 16–4 highlights the three main types of organizational transitions that people experience throughout their employment within an organization. *Vertical movement* includes moving up or down the organizational hierarchy, such as a promotion or demotion. *Lateral movement* involves moving

EXHIBIT 16–4   Three Types of Organizational Transitions

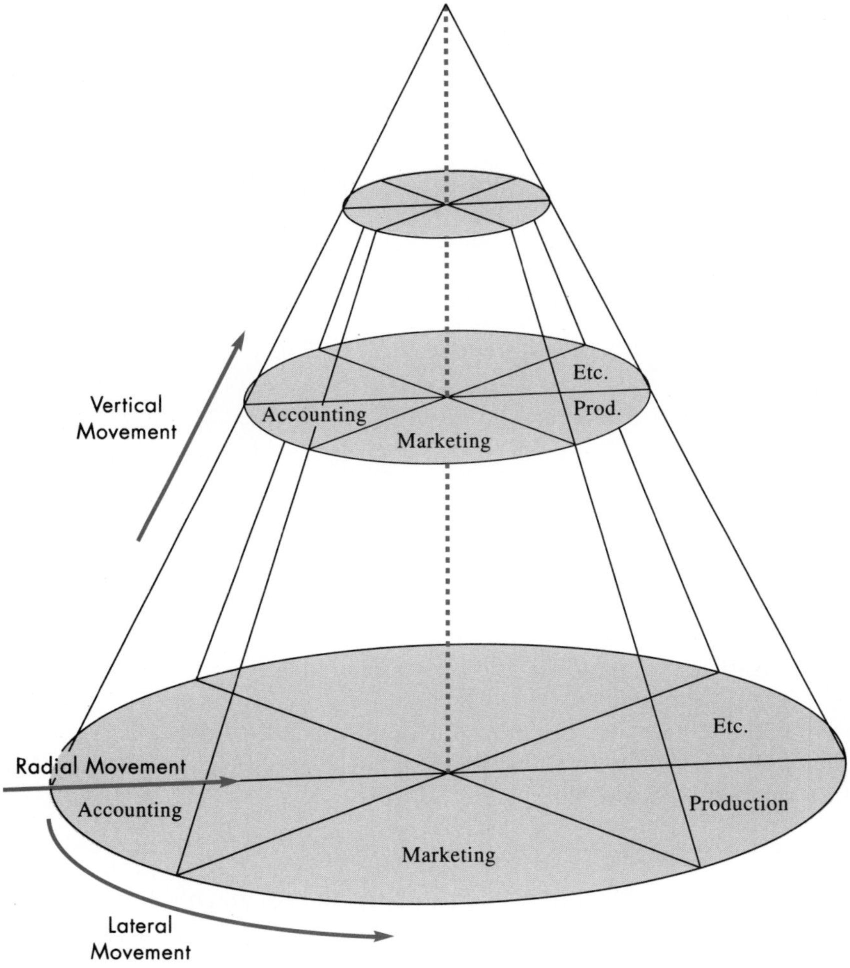

Source: Adapted from E. H. Schein, "The Individual, the Organization, and the Career: A Conceptual Scheme," *Journal of Applied Behavioral Science* 7 (1971), p. 404.

to another unit within the organization, such as to another department or region, without changing one's rank. *Radial movement* pertains to moving toward or away from a central role in the organization, such as the subtle transition from newcomer to insider. Overall, this model illustrates that the socialization process is ongoing, and throughout one's career is most intense during these transitions.

STAGES OF SOCIALIZATION

The organizational socialization process is typically described in terms of three stages as individuals move from outsiders to newcomers and then to insiders. As we see in Exhibit 16–5, these stages include anticipatory socialization, encounter, and metamorphosis.[36]

Stage 1: Anticipatory Socialization

The anticipatory socialization stage encompasses all of the learning and adjustment that occurs prior to the organizational transition, such as before the first day of employment. Individuals are outsiders, so they must rely on friends, employment interviews, recruiting literature, and other indirect information to form expectations about what it is like to work in the organization. The employer is also forming a set of expectations about the job applicant, such as the unique skills and vitality that he or she will provide the organization. The employer's and applicant's expectations about what each will contribute to and receive from each other form a **psychological contract.** Some expectations in the psychological contract might be explicitly stated, but many are implicit understandings or assumptions.

> **psychological contract**
> The employer's and applicant's expectations about what each will contribute to and receive from the other in the employment relationship.

The psychological contract represents a fundamental linkage between the organization and the employee, so effective anticipatory socialization requires an open exchange of accurate information. Unfortunately, as Exhibit 16–6 illustrates, four conflicts exist that potentially distort information sent and received by employers and job applicants.[37] Conflict A occurs between the employer's need to attract qualified applicants and the applicant's need for complete information to make accurate employment decisions. The psychological contract becomes distorted when employers provide only favourable information, causing applicants to accept job offers on the basis of incomplete or false expectations.

Conflict B occurs between the applicant's need to look attractive to employers and the organization's need for complete information to make accurate selection decisions. The problem is that applicants sometimes emphasize favourable employment experiences and leave out less favourable events in their careers. This provides employers with inaccurate data, thereby weakening the quality of organizational selection decisions.

Conflict C occurs when applicants avoid asking important career decision questions because they convey an unfavourable image. For instance, many applicants try to avoid enquiring about starting salaries and promotion opportunities because it makes them sound greedy or over-aggressive. Yet unless the employer presents this information, applicants might form incorrect expectations based on ambiguous information.

Finally, conflict D occurs when employers avoid asking certain questions or using potentially valuable selection devices because they might put the organization in a bad light. For instance, some employers refuse to use

EXHIBIT 16–5   Stages of Organizational Socialization

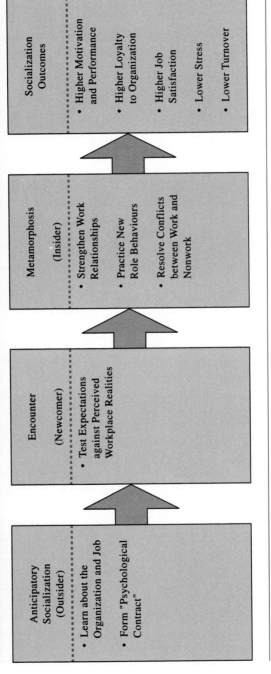

Anticipatory Socialization (Outsider)
- Learn about the Organization and Job
- Form "Psychological Contract"

Encounter (Newcomer)
- Test Expectations against Perceived Workplace Realities

Metamorphosis (Insider)
- Strengthen Work Relationships
- Practice New Role Behaviours
- Resolve Conflicts between Work and Nonwork

Socialization Outcomes
- Higher Motivation and Performance
- Higher Loyalty to Organization
- Higher Job Satisfaction
- Lower Stress
- Lower Turnover

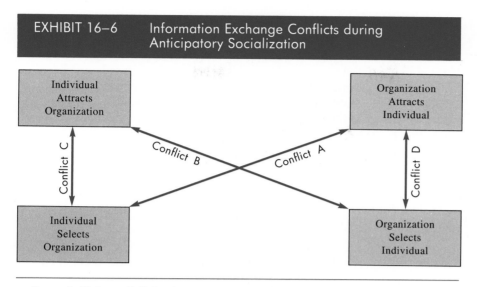

EXHIBIT 16–6   Information Exchange Conflicts during Anticipatory Socialization

Source: L. W. Porter, E. E. Lawler III, and J. R. Hackman, *Behavior in Organizations* (New York: McGraw-Hill, 1975), p. 134. Reprinted by permission.

aptitude or ability tests because they don't want to give the impression that the organization treats employees like mice running through a maze.

Postdecisional Justification.   Both employers and job applicants further distort their perceptions of the psychological contract through the process of postdecisional justification that we discussed in Chapter 9. After the decision to accept employment has been made, new hires subconsciously increase the importance of favourable elements of the job and justify or completely forget about some negative elements. At the same time, they reduce the quality of job offers that they turned down. Employers often distort their expectations of new hires in the same way. The result is that both parties develop higher expectations of each other than they will actually experience during the encounter stage.

Stage 2: Encounter

The first day of employment (or in the new situation) typically marks the beginning of the encounter stage of organizational socialization. During this stage, newcomers test their prior expectations with the perceived realities. The psychological contract is usually distorted by information exchange conflicts and postdecisional justification, so newcomers typically experience some degree of **reality shock**. Reality shock is the gap between what is and what ought to be. It is a form of discrepancy theory (described in Chapter 8) in which the perceived reality falls significantly short of the newcomer's

reality shock

The gap between preemployment expectations and the organizational reality employees experience as they begin work.

preemployment expectations. Some reality shocks are apparent as soon as the employee walks through the door, such as discovering that the promised office with a window will not be available until next year. Other shocks are more subtle, such as eventually realizing that the company's emphasis on profits over safety are at odds with the newcomer's own values.

High levels of reality shock are stressful for most newcomers, particularly where the discrepancy is unambiguous and a significant investment or sacrifice to join the organization has been made (such as moving to another city or turning down other potentially good jobs). Reality shock impedes the socialization process because the newcomer's energy is directed toward managing the stress rather than learning and accepting organizational knowledge and roles.[38]

Stage 3: Metamorphosis

The metamorphosis stage is also known as the ''change and acquisition'' or ''role management'' aspect of the socialization process. This is the stage where employees settle in as they make the transition from newcomers to insiders. During metamorphosis, employees strengthen relationships with coworkers and supervisors, practice new role behaviours, and adapt attitudes and values consistent with their new position and organization.

Metamorphosis also involves resolving the conflicts between work and nonwork activities. In particular, employees must redistribute their time and energy between work and family, reschedule recreational activities, and deal with changing perceptions and values in the context of other life roles. They must address any discrepancies between their existing values and those emphasized by the organizational culture. New self-identities are formed that are compatible with the new work environment.

MANAGING THE SOCIALIZATION PROCESS

Organizational socialization takes place whether or not it is managed by the organization. But since socialization can have a profound effect on organizational effectiveness and employee well-being, employers are encouraged to introduce several formal and informal strategies to facilitate this process. Some of the more important elements of effective socialization are described below.

Realistic Job Previews

realistic job previews (RJPs)
A realistic balance of positive and negative information from the employer about the nature of the job and work context.

Individuals are more effectively socialized into the organization when they receive a realistic balance of positive and negative information from the employer about the nature of the job and work context, called **realistic job previews (RJPs)**. RJPs address the information exchange conflict between the organization's need to attract job applicants and the applicants' need to

---

PERSPECTIVE 16–3   Giving a Realistic Job Preview of Raintown

A machinery distribution company had one of its operations on the north coast of British Columbia and, due to the limited pool of skilled people in the area, recruited most employees from the Lower Mainland and other areas of British Columbia. For some time the company had shown job applicants a film of the north coast operations, since it was too expensive to fly people up there for a visit. The film had been taken on one of the few sunny days in the northern Raintown community, so the new hires looked forward to the beautiful scenery, recreation, and work—all in sunny weather. However, after being hired and moved to Raintown, the chilling and unexpected realities of the dreary weather eventually became apparent. Turnover rates were very high, resulting in lower productivity and higher recruiting costs.

Company officials eventually discovered the cause of the high turnover and replaced the original Raintown film with a more realistic one taken on a rainy day. Within the next couple of years, managers reported a dramatic reduction in turnover with corresponding higher productivity. In fact, employees who have been shown the new film claim that the weather is not nearly so bad as they had originally expected because there is the occasional sunny day.

Source: S. L. McShane and T. Baal, *Employee Socialization Practices on Canada's West Coast: A Management Report* (Burnaby, B.C.: Simon Fraser University, December 1984), p. 38.

---

make informed decisions about job choices. The basic premise of RJPs is that rather than ''selling'' the job, organizations should provide all pertinent information, without distortion, to job applicants.[39]

RJPs improve organizational socialization by ensuring that applicants develop more accurate preemployment expectations. This reduces reality shock and increases job satisfaction, organizational commitment, and job tenure. RJPs represent a type of vaccination by preparing employees for the more challenging and troublesome aspects of work life. As we see in Perspective 16–3, RJPs may have a significant effect on the preemployment expectations and subsequent behaviours of new employees.

Employee Orientation

Employee orientation is the organization's systematic process of helping new employees make sense of and adapt to the work context.[40] It is a process of communicating work-related information, beginning with recruiting and continuing through the first few months of employment. Recent studies suggest that newcomers are more effectively socialized when they proceed through orientation and other formalized learning activities.[41] They also adjust more readily to the workplace when they receive positive social support from coworkers and supervisors.

Effective orientation programs ensure that realistic job previews are provided and that the organization maintains ties with successful job candidates before they begin work, such as through telephone calls or letters of wel-

employee orientation
The organization's systematic process of helping new employees make sense of and adapt to the work context.

come from their new supervisor and work team. Activities on the first day of work should symbolize the organization's commitment to its employees. Unfortunately, too many employees devote their first day of employment to filling out employee benefits forms or listening to an endless parade of managers describing their departments in numbing detail. Ideally, the opening orientation session should take only the first part of the day to convey a general welcome and provide high-priority information. Supervisors and coworkers should anticipate the new recruit's arrival by preparing the necessary facilities and symbols of membership (e.g., a desk with a name plate). To avoid information overload, several half-day orientation sessions should be presented over the first few weeks and months.

Socialization Agents

As a learning and adjustment process, organizational socialization is heavily influenced by coworkers, supervisors, and other socialization agents.[42] Socialization agents are potentially valuable sources of information for satisfying the newcomer's need for immediate knowledge. They further provide social support to help newcomers cope with the stress that typically accompanies encounter and metamorphosis. Finally, agents facilitate the socialization process by accepting and integrating newcomers into their work roles, particularly by being flexible and tolerant in their interactions with these new hires.

Coworkers.   Coworkers provide much of the information newcomers are seeking because they are easily accessible and can answer questions when problems arise. Coworkers also act as role models. By observing experienced employees, new recruits learn many of the behaviours that they believe are required for the job. To the extent that recruits are integrated into the work team, coworkers can provide a vital source of social support to minimize stress related to organizational socialization. Newcomers who are highly integrated into the work team also feel a stronger sense of loyalty to the organization and are less likely to quit their jobs within the first year of employment.[43]

Supervisors.   Supervisors are typically identified as the human face of the organization, so their attitudes, expectations, and behaviours have a significant influence on the organizational socialization of newcomers. Supervisors facilitate work role adjustment by giving newcomers challenging first assignments, providing constructive and timely feedback, buffering the newcomers from excessive demands, helping them to deal with work role conflicts, and facilitating their integration into the work team.[44]

Top Management.   Top management involvement in organizational socialization has received scant attention, yet recent evidence suggests that meeting with the CEO and other senior executives can have a lasting beneficial effect on new recruits. It humanizes corporate actions and increases the individual's identification with the company. The fact that senior managers would take time out from their busy schedules to meet new employees also symbolizes how much the organization values its people.[45]

ORGANIZATIONAL CAREERS

A **career** is a sequence of work-related experiences that people participate in over the span of their working lives.[46] The concept of a career has changed significantly over the past few decades. Everyone in the labour market has a career; it is not the exclusive domain of senior executives and professionals. We now appreciate the fact that a person's career might include lateral and even strategic downward moves, rather than just the traditional promotional climb through the organizational hierarchy. We also recognize that a career is not necessarily anchored in one occupation or organization; instead, it may cross several boundaries over the course of the person's working life. Finally, we now understand that both individuals and organizations benefit from well-managed careers and should therefore be mutually involved in career development.

career
A sequence of work-related experiences that people participate in over the span of their working lives.

Career Effectiveness

Career development has a powerful influence on organizational effectiveness and employee well-being.[47] Career activities affect the fulfillment of basic needs, so career effectiveness is related to employee motivation and satisfaction. In our society, career experiences shape individual self-worth because work is highly integrated with self-identity and the quality of life. Consequently, well-managed careers may boost self-esteem, minimize stress, and in the long term strengthen the employee's psychological and physical health.

Effectively managed careers benefit organizations as well as individuals. They enable employees to adapt to changing organizational needs which, in turn, help the organization to survive and prosper in a dynamic external environment. For example, IBM Canada's work force receives continuous training and career support so that the company can anticipate and respond to new technology and customer expectations without laying off people. IBM's well-developed career system minimizes obsolescence by ensuring that people are ready for new jobs when the old ones disappear. Finally, organizations tend to have a more dedicated work force by supporting career dynamics because employees feel a stronger relationship with their employer when their personal needs are satisfied through work.

DYNAMICS OF INDIVIDUAL CAREERS

For several decades, researchers in organizational behaviour and other disciplines have tried to understand the dynamics of individual careers. Some of the major themes specifically include career anchors, career stages, and career plateaus.

Career Anchors

career anchor
A person's self-image of his or her abilities, motivations, and attitudes relating to a particular career orientation.

As individuals gain experience in the world of work, they develop a self-image of their abilities, motivations, and attitudes relating to a particular career orientation, called a **career anchor**.[48] Career anchors represent personal career interests, perceptions of personal strengths and weaknesses, and beliefs about personal goals. Individuals adopt a particular anchor as a result of many life experiences, including their initial career activities as well as parental and educational influences. The word *anchor* is quite appropriate because career anchors stabilize the pattern of career decisions so that people maintain a particular career track rather than engage in a series of random career choices. As such, career anchors influence the selection of future job opportunities and help define each person's concept of career success.

Based on his investigations of MBA graduates, Edgar Schein has identified five career anchors, described in Exhibit 16–7. Schein has more recently suggested that other career anchors might exist. He has observed, for example, that some people have a strong service anchor, others thrive on pure challenge no matter what activity it is, and still others emphasize the need to integrate their career with other life activities. It is too early to tell whether these additional anchors are distinct from the original five. However, it is increasingly clear that the career anchor concept plays an important role in individual career activities.

Career Stages

According to several theorists, individuals pass through a series of career stages throughout their working lives, as we see in Exhibit 16–8. Each stage brings different challenges and personal transitions.[49] During the *exploration and trial stage,* young adults enter the work world, usually through part-time or summer employment. They investigate different career options, receive career-related training, possibly experience one or more false starts, and begin to develop a self-image in terms of new occupational and organizational roles.

During the *establishment and advancement stage,* employees experience feelings of career progress as they receive challenging assignments, promotions, and perhaps better opportunities with other organizations. Most people in this stage have developed career goals and a fairly well-defined career anchor. They are more motivated than in other stages to reach for career objectives and confirm their self-identities through career experiences.

The *midcareer transition stage* typically begins somewhere around age 40 and marks an important juncture toward future career progress. For some people, this stage is barely visible as their careers are characterized by

EXHIBIT 16–7	Five Career Anchors	

Career Anchor	Description	Example
Technical/functional competence	Motivated by the work itself; seeks technical competence in a functional speciality rather than in managerial processes.	Financial analyst
Managerial competence	Likes to analyze challenging problems and coordinate people to achieve results; seeks interpersonal competence and power.	Plant manager
Security and stability	Motivated by job security; expects to remain with one firm in the same geographic area over an entire career; conforms to organizational expectations.	Civil servant
Entrepreneurial creativity	Likes to launch new ventures, such as a new organization, product, or service that stands alone; desires a central role in new projects, although generally impatient.	Company founder
Autonomy and independence	Likes freedom from organizational constraints; motivated to practice technical skills with minimal limitations from others.	Professor

continued growth through further promotions and/or challenging assignments. However, most people begin a maintenance phase whereby they have established a satisfactory place in the work world and now try to hold on to it. They also tend to reassess their life priorities and begin to devote more attention to activities outside of the workplace. Rather than maintaining their career position, a few people in midcareer transition begin a long period of stagnation and decline. They become stuck in a dead-end job and typically engage in psychological withdrawal from organizational life.

The *career disengagement stage* is sometimes called the *decline* stage based on the idea that most people during these later years prepare for retirement and begin to psychologically remove themselves from the workplace. However, *disengagement* may be a more appropriate label because

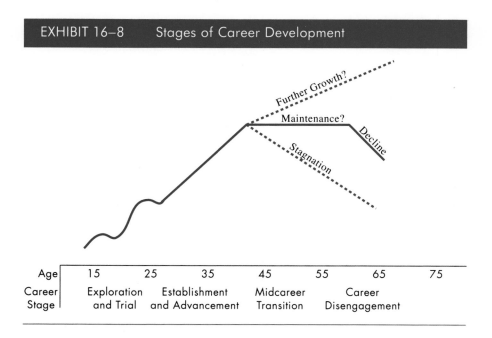

EXHIBIT 16–8   Stages of Career Development

Age	15	25	35	45	55	65	75
Career Stage	Exploration and Trial	Establishment and Advancement		Midcareer Transition	Career Disengagement		

many of those who retire embark on new life interests. They disengage from organizational life by taking on the role of observer and consultant rather than active participant in organizational activities. Of course, some people continue their organizational roles through the later years of life and begin disengagement only when their physical and mental powers decline.

The career stages model is far from perfect because every individual's experience is unique. Some individuals might pass through a particular stage more than once in their career. Some might pass through a particular stage quickly, others slowly. In spite of these individual differences, the career stages model represents a dynamic perspective of careers and, in particular, emphasizes the point that careers are integrated with other life activities.

Career Plateaus

career plateau

A point in a person's career beyond which the probability of further promotion through the hierarchy is very low.

As we saw in the career stages model, most people experience a career plateau at some time in their lives, typically in the midcareer transition stage. A **career plateau** is a point beyond which the probability of further promotion through the hierarchy is very low.[50] One reason why career plateaus are so common is that most companies are pyramidal, so the number of positions available for advancement decreases as people rise through the hierarchy. These organizational limitations are even more apparent in firms with a slow rate of growth or with a relatively young work force. Slow-growing companies do not create new positions as quickly, thereby limiting the number of promotional opportunities, and job vacancies are less frequent in companies with a young work force because of the lower rate of retirement.

People often experience career plateaus because they do not possess the knowledge and skills to progress beyond a certain level. For example, employees in technical jobs may experience limited career growth because they lack training to enter managerial positions. Career plateauing also occurs among those who have not kept abreast of technological changes in their field or industry. Some employees plateau early in their careers because they have no particular ambition to progress through the organizational hierarchy. Others plateau due to job burnout as they find it increasingly difficult to cope with the challenges of higher-level positions.

Depending on the individual's expectations and motivation, career plateauing may produce frustration and anger against the organization, eventually leading to deteriorated performance. However, career plateaus are readily accepted by many employees who want to avoid geographic relocation or the politics and stress of a position further up the organizational hierarchy.[51] As we shall discuss next, some of the causes of career plateauing may be avoided by redesigning organizational career paths and providing lifelong training, as is the case at Xerox Canada, Du Pont Canada, and IBM Canada. We must also redefine the traditional concept of career success from one of hierarchical progression to a deeper fulfillment of personal needs through challenging assignments and work experiences.

ORGANIZATIONAL CAREER MANAGEMENT

While individuals are largely responsible for their careers, organizations must also take an active role in career management. Some of the more important and innovative career management strategies include identifying and redesigning career paths, facilitating mentor relationships, supporting career development, and preparing employees for career disengagement.

Identifying and Redesigning Career Paths

A **career path** is the sequence of jobs that employees follow to achieve their career objectives. These routes are known as career paths because they represent a historical pattern of job promotions and transfers to reach a particular job and organizational level. For example, an Insurance Corporation of British Columbia adjuster who aspires to become a material damage supervisor would probably first receive training and experience as an estimator trainee, then as an estimator, and then as a material damage reviewer. Finally, the person would need to receive more training, this time in management skills, before being promoted to the material damage supervisor job.

Identifying historical career paths is valuable to employees because it helps them target interim positions for which they should train and compete.

career path
The sequence of job promotions and transfers that employees follow to achieve their career objectives.

Career path analyses also help organizations conduct human resource planning and assess training needs. However, while historical career paths may have prepared employees for specific jobs in the past, they might not be appropriate in the future. Therefore, when reviewing career paths you should determine whether the intervening jobs still provide the requisite knowledge, skills, and experience for the target job. If the duties and requirements of the target job or interim positions have changed, it may be necessary to search for a new sequence of organizational positions that provides the required experience and skills.[52]

parallel career ladders
Career paths within a technical or professional speciality, such as a series of engineering jobs, through which people are promoted.

Parallel Career Ladders.   One limitation with traditional career paths is that they encourage highly skilled professionals either to move into managerial positions in conflict with their dominant career anchor or to leave for better technical opportunities in other organizations. As an alternative, a few organizations have developed **parallel career ladders** within technical specialities that operate in tandem with the line management hierarchy. Parallel career ladders allow people to remain in a technical area while still receiving financial and self-actualizing rewards. Parallel ladders also maintain feelings of career progress, thereby reducing the frustration of career gridlock that is now so prevalent in the line management ladder.

Exhibit 16–9 illustrates a parallel career ladder similar to one found at IBM Canada. Notice that systems engineer trainees can maintain a technical career anchor for most of their working lives within the organization by aspiring to reach the position of a consultant systems engineer. This is a much-respected position that is equivalent in salary and status to a position in the top third of line management. Alternatively, systems engineers can shift over to line management at some point in their careers if they prefer this route.

Lateral Career Moves.   Most traditional career paths are directed toward moving up the organizational hierarchy. But promotional opportunities have become more scarce as the number of management layers is reduced and organizations become populated with young baby boomers. As a Du Pont Canada manager acknowledges: ''[Du Pont Canada employees] are suffering from the same problem every other company is: traditional movement up the corporate ladder isn't there. Downsizing and reducing layers of management have limited the opportunities. The crew ahead of me are all in their forties, and they are not going anywhere.''[53]

To avoid job stagnation, Du Pont and many companies are beginning to emphasize the value of lateral career moves. The idea behind lateral transfers is that employees can fulfill their personal needs in different jobs rather than moving through the management hierarchy. Lateral transfers also create a more flexible work force with a broader understanding of the entire organization. At General Motors of Canada, for example, company lawyers can be found in government relations and engineers can transfer to public

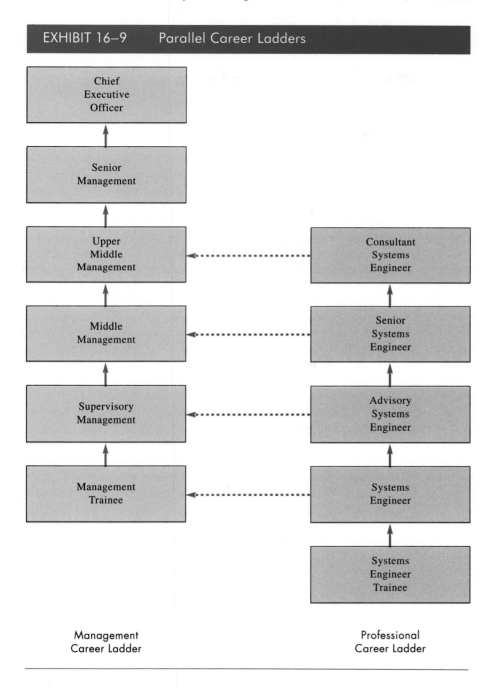

EXHIBIT 16–9   Parallel Career Ladders

Management
Career Ladder

Professional
Career Ladder

affairs because the company places few limits on lateral career mobility. Explains a General Motors manager: "We want everyone to have a broad range of experience—including those good, solid performers in the middle."[54]

Facilitating Mentor Relationships

One of the most recent interests in career management is the mentoring process. A **mentor** is a more senior person in the organizational hierarchy who counsels and helps a junior employee (called a *protégé*). Mentors facilitate the personal development and career advancement of their protégés by serving as role models, and by providing challenging assignments, guidance, counselling, and opportunities for visibility to top management. Mentors are important socialization agents, particularly as protégés move into management and professional career tracks. They communicate the organization's culture by describing how things are done around the organization. They help protégés navigate through the organizational politics jungle and serve as experienced sounding boards for the protégé's ideas and proposals.[55]

There is fairly strong evidence that employees with mentors are more likely to achieve career advancement, higher pay, and career satisfaction than those without mentors. Mentors benefit from this process as well. They are able to apply their organizational knowledge toward a meaningful purpose, learn new perspectives and ideas from their protégés, and fulfill personal needs for nurturing and supporting others. Indirectly, mentors are recognized for the successes of the protégés they have developed.[56]

Mentoring is traditionally an informal relationship between two people, but the Bank of Nova Scotia, Canadian Pacific Hotels (CP), and several other companies have recently developed formal mentoring programs. CP Hotels is experimenting with a program in which recently hired management trainees are matched with senior managers. Mentors and protégés join other pairs for dinner, participate in a joint training session, and then keep in touch with each other at least once monthly for the next year or longer. Senior managers have been eager to participate as mentors, and the program has helped attract talented new recruits to the organization. Another benefit of the mentoring program is that by keeping in touch with their protégés, senior managers are better informed about what is happening at CP's two dozen hotels across Canada.[57]

Directly assigning senior managers to junior staff, as at CP Hotels, sometimes has limited success because both parties must have common interests and values in order to form a meaningful social bond. An alternative method is to use sign-up lists and encourage junior employees to interview prospective mentors on the list. Other firms arrange opportunities for social interaction between potential mentors and protégés in the hope that natural relationships will form. Mentoring may also be encouraged through training programs and reward systems that increase a senior manager's ability and motivation to become a mentor.[58]

Supporting Career Development

One of the cornerstones of effective career management is for the organization to provide a supportive environment for employees to take greater control of their own career development. There are several strategic actions that firms should consider. Organizations must analyze, compile, and widely distribute information about jobs, career paths, and job vacancies so that employees have the information necessary to assist their career mobility and personal development. Career training sessions and self-assessment modules should be offered so that employees can make more effective career decisions.

Organizations also need to encourage supervisors to take a more active role in the career development of their employees. Career development should become part of the performance appraisal process whereby employees discuss their career aspirations with supervisors and develop specific action plans to achieve those objectives.[59] Finally, some companies might offer career counselling to help employees diagnose their career anchors and develop career development skills. As we see in Perspective 16–4, Ontario Hydro has become a leader in organizational career management by providing these and other career support systems.

Preparing Employees for Career Disengagement

Most organizations focus on ways to help employees entering the establishment and midcareer transition stages. Yet as the work force ages, more emphasis should be placed on helping individuals cope with the difficult disengagement stage of their careers. Preretirement planning seminars and counselling are offered by many Canadian firms, but most address only the financial planning aspect of retirement. Moreover, these sessions are typically offered to people just a few years before retirement—too late to make adequate preparation for financial security.

A more complete approach, which has been used by the Canadian Broadcasting Corporation, is to view disengagement as organizational entry in reverse.[60] From this perspective, employees should receive a complete orientation on what it will be like to live *without* being attached to an organizational role. Disengagement training and counselling sessions should help participants learn how to ease out of their organizational roles smoothly over a period of time and to enter other life activities. As in organizational socialization, they should learn about potential conflicts that may emerge with other family members and the change in self-image that must be formed in retirement. Just as organizations should offer realistic job previews to new recruits, innovative methods are required to provide realistic retirement previews. Finally, just as coworker integration is instrumental to effective organizational socialization, preretirement planning sessions should help disengaging employees form new attachments outside the organization, particularly in areas where they will be active in retirement.

PERSPECTIVE 16–4   Improving Career Management at Ontario Hydro

Ontario Hydro is changing the traditional view that career development is a luxury to the view that it is an essential tool for creating a committed and satisfied staff. The Crown corporation is overhauling its career management system because of several changes that, if left alone, would result in increased career anxiety and significantly lower job satisfaction for many employees. Ontario Hydro currently employs many well-educated midcareer people who expect promotions as a matter of course. At the same time, its employment equity program communicates to women and other designated groups that their promotional opportunities will increase in the future. Yet the company is flattening its organizational structure and lowering the number of people employed by the firm,

effectively reducing promotion opportunities by nearly 25 percent.

Ontario Hydro has launched several new programs and practises to deal with this dilemma. To overcome the reduced promotional opportunities, the company has reemphasized its promotion-from-within policy. It has also expanded efforts to define career in terms of lateral as well as upward moves. Increasingly, succession paths will require a broad base of experience as a prerequisite for promotion.

Another career management strategy has focussed on increasing career information and assistance to encourage employees to take control of their career development. A series of career self-assessment workbooks has been produced to help employ-

SUMMARY

• Organizational culture is the basic pattern of shared assumptions, values, and beliefs that govern behaviour within a particular organization. Organizational culture lies beneath the surface of organizational behaviour, but it can be loosely interpreted through visible artifacts. Artifacts are the primary means by which organizational culture is communicated. The four main types of artifacts that transmit culture are organizational stories, language, rituals and ceremonies, and physical structures and space.

• In addition to the dominant culture, organizations are comprised of subcultures located throughout various subunits. Some subcultures enhance the dominant culture by espousing parallel assumptions, values, and beliefs. Other units are countercultures because they adopt values that are in direct opposition to the organization's core values.

• Strengthening organizational culture is important if the cultural content fits the external environment. A strong culture is perpetuated through the actions of founders and top management. Culture is also strengthened by selecting and socializing employees, introducing culturally consistent rewards, maintaining a stable work force, managing mergers and acquisitions, and managing the cultural network.

• Organizational socialization refers to the process by which individuals learn the values, expected behaviours, and social knowledge necessary to assume their roles in the organization. It is a learning process in which newcomers try to make sense of their new work environment. It is also a

ees decide whether they want to pursue a particular career path and, if so, what types of skills and interests they should have to match them with various jobs in the organization. Ontario Hydro also set up a career centre that provides career planning workshops for all employees (on paid time) to help them see what new career opportunities might exist for them both inside and outside the organization. To complement these activities, an extensive job-posting program was introduced that advertises job vacancies throughout the 26,000-person organization every week.

Finally, Ontario Hydro has taken steps to improve the ability and motivation of supervisors to become effective career counsellors and mentors. Specifically, it has added career counselling and related skill development modules to the management training program. Career development has also been added as a performance appraisal dimension so that managers will be evaluated and rewarded for helping employees develop their careers. Overall, Ontario Hydro has moved quickly to fulfill its objective of providing a supportive and informative environment for employees to manage their careers more effectively.

Sources: D. Tyler, "Career Paths in the Face of Restraint," *Canadian Business Review,* Summer 1987, pp. 28–30; R. Harris, "Canadians Replace Layoffs with Voluntary Rightsizing," *Personnel* 68 (May 1991), pp. 15–16; and R. C. Franklin, "Promoting Equity at Hydro," *Canadian Business Review* 18 (Summer 1991), pp. 26–27.

process of change as newcomers practise new behaviours and adapt new perspectives in line with team norms and organizational culture.

• Organizational socialization is continuous, but it is most intense immediately before and after any organizational transition. Whether they are joining the organization or being transferred to another subunit, employees typically pass through three socialization stages: anticipatory socialization, encounter, and metamorphosis. To manage the socialization process, organizations should introduce realistic job previews and well-designed employee orientation programs. They must also recognize the value of coworkers, supervisors, top management, and other socialization agents.

• A career is a sequence of work-related experiences that people participate in over the span of their working lives. Career development is important to both employees and organizations. For example, effective careers fulfill the individual's basic needs while helping the organization maintain its flexibility in a dynamic environment.

• Career dynamics research has identified several basic career anchors around which people seem to orient their career decisions. There are also several career stages through which they pass in their lifetime. At some point around midcareer, many people experience a career plateau as their likelihood of further promotion dwindles.

• While individuals are largely responsible for their career development, organizations must also take an active role by redesigning career paths and helping employees identify the best path for their career development. Many companies provide information and training in support of career development. A few are finding ways to use mentoring as a way to facilitate career development. As the work force ages, firms must look at ways to prepare employees for career disengagement.

DISCUSSION QUESTIONS

1. Identify four types of artifacts used to communicate organizational culture. Why are artifacts used for this purpose?
2. What do we mean by the ''strength'' of organizational culture? Should organizations have strong cultures?
3. What is the role of transformational leadership in organizational culture?
4. Discuss what is meant by the statement, ''Organizational socialization is a process of learning and change.''
5. What is reality shock? Why do new employees typically experience reality shock when they enter organizations?
6. What functions do socialization agents provide in the socialization process?
7. What types of career changes possibly occur during the midcareer transition? Which transition is most common during this stage? Why?
8. Describe two strategies organizations are adopting as alternatives to the traditional career path up the management hierarchy.

NOTES

1. Based on an interview with David Aitken and Peter Wreglesworth, October 1991. Also see P. Schom-Moffatt, ''Architects of the New Age,'' *B.C. Business* 17, no. 3 (March 1989), pp. 29–33; and M. Murphy, ''Paring the Pyramid,'' *Small Business* 8, no. 6 (June 1989), pp. 81–84.

2. E. H. Schein, ''What Is Culture?'' in P. J. Frost, L. F. Moore, M. R. Louis, C. C. Lundberg, and J. Martin (eds.), *Reframing Organizational Culture* (Beverly Hills, Calif.: Sage, 1991), pp. 243–53; A. Williams, P. Dobson, and M. Walters, *Changing Culture: New Organizational Approaches* (London: Institute of Personnel Management, 1989); and A. L. Wilkins, ''The Culture Audit: A Tool for Understanding Organizations,'' *Organizational Dynamics,* Autumn 1983, pp. 24–38.

3. B. Ashforth and F. Mael, ''Social Identity Theory and the Organization,'' *Academy of Management Review* 14 (1989), pp. 20–39.

4. J. S. Ott, *The Organizational Culture Perspective* (Pacific Grove, Calif.: Brooks/Cole, 1989), Chapter 2.; W. J. Duncan, ''Organizational Culture: 'Getting a Fix' on an Elusive Concept,'' *Academy of Management Executive* 3, no. 3 (August 1989), pp. 229–36; and E. H. Schein, ''Organizational Culture,'' *American Psychologist,* February 1990, pp. 109–19.

5. A. deCarufel, ''Changing 'Corporate Culture' in the Public Sector: Lessons from Two Canadian Case Studies,'' *Proceedings of the Annual ASAC Conference, Organizational Behaviour Division* 8, pt. 5 (1987), pp. 37–46; and J. P. Siegel, ''Searching for Excellence: Company Communications as Reflections of Culture,'' *Proceedings of the Annual ASAC Conference, Organizational Behaviour Division* 5, pt. 5 (1984), pp. 1–8.

6. G. S. Saffold III, "Culture Traits, Strength, and Organizational Performance: Moving beyond 'Strong' Culture," *Academy of Management Review* 13 (1988), pp. 546–58; and Williams et al.. *Changing Culture: New Organizational Approaches*, pp. 24–27.

7. V. Sathe, *Culture and Related Corporate Realities* (Homewood, Ill.: Irwin, 1985), Chapter 2; J. B. Barney, "Organizational Culture: Can It Be a Source of Sustained Competitive Advantage?" *Academy of Management Review* 11 (1986), pp. 656–65; T. E. Deal and A. A. Kennedy, *Corporate Cultures* (Reading, Mass.: Addison-Wesley, 1982), Chapter 1; and C. Siehl and J. Martin, "Organizational Culture: A Key to Financial Performance?" in B. Schneider (ed.), *Organizational Climate and Culture* (San Francisco: Jossey-Bass, 1990), pp. 241–81.

8. G. Deszca, "The Communication of Ideology in Police Forces," *Canadian Police College Journal* 12 (1988), pp. 240–68.

9. J. Martin and C. Siehl, "Organizational Culture and Counterculture: An Uneasy Symbiosis," *Organizational Dynamics,* Autumn 1983, pp. 52–64; Ott, *The Organizational Culture Perspective,* pp. 45–47; and Deal and Kennedy, *Corporate Cultures,* pp. 138–39.

10. R. Lucas, "Political–Cultural Analysis of Organizations," *Academy of Management Review* 12 (1987), pp. 144–56.

11. C. Waddell, "Suffering from Shell Shock," *Report on Business Magazine,* March 1985, pp. 87–92.

12. J. S. Pederson and J. S. Sorensen, *Organizational Cultures in Theory and Practice* (Aldershot, England: Gower, 1989), pp. 27–29.

13. A. L. Wilkins, "Organizational Stories as Symbols Which Control the Organization," in L. R. Pondy, P. J. Frost, G. Morgan, and T. C. Dandridge (eds.), *Organizational Symbolism* (Greenwich, Conn.: JAI Press, 1984), pp. 81–92; and J. Martin and M. E. Powers, "Truth or Corporate Propaganda: The Value of a Good War Story," in Pondy et al., *Organizational Symbolism,* pp. 93–107.

14. L. A. Krefting and P. J. Frost, "Untangling Webs, Surfing Waves, and Wildcatting," in P. J. Frost, L. F. Moore, M. R. Louis, C. C. Lundberg, and J. Martin (eds.), *Organizational Culture* (Beverly Hills, Calif.: Sage, 1985), pp. 155–68.

15. J. F. Fraser, "Getting Back to Business Basics," *CMA Magazine,* February 1990, pp. 16–18; and E. Innes and L. Southwick-Trask, *Turning It Around* (Toronto: Fawcett Crest, 1989), pp. 26–28.

16. P. Best and J. Stackhouse, "The Palace Revolution," *Financial Times,* March 27, 1989, pp. 18, 20.

17. J. M. Beyer and H. M. Trice, "How an Organization's Rites Reveal its Culture," *Organizational Dynamics* 15 no. 4 (1987), pp. 5–24; and L. Smirchich, "Organizations as Shared Meanings," in Pondy et al., (eds.) *Organizational Symbolism,* pp. 55–65.

18. "Domtar Red Rock Sets Safety Record," *Canadian Forest Industries,* February 1989, p. 62; and W. S. Humphrey, *Managing for Innovation* (Englewood Cliffs, N.J.: Prentice Hall, 1987), pp. 129–30.

19. J. M. Kouzes and B. Z. Posner, *The Leadership Challenge* (San Francisco: Jossey-Bass, 1988), pp. 207–8.

20. P. Young, "Monuments to Money," *Maclean's,* November 26, 1990, pp. 72–73.

21. L. Schuster, "At a Bank in Brazil, Stress on Teamwork Pays Dividends," *The Wall Street Journal,* August 22, 1985.

22. E. H. Schein, "The Role of the Founder in Creating Organizational Culture," *Organizational Dynamics* 12, no. 1 (Summer 1983), pp. 13–28.

23. G. G. Nasmith, *Timothy Eaton* (Toronto: McClelland & Stewart, 1923); and M. E. Macpherson, *Shopkeepers to a Nation: The Eatons* (Toronto: McClelland & Stewart, 1963).

24. E. H. Schein, *Organizational Culture and Leadership* (San Francisco, Calif.: Jossey-Bass, 1985), Chapter 10; and T. J. Peters, "Symbols, Patterns, and Settings: An Optimistic Case for Getting Things Done," *Organizational Dynamics* 7, no. 2 (Autumn 1978), pp. 2–23.

25. I. Sharp, "Quality for All Seasons," *Canadian Business Review* 17, no. 1 (Spring 1990), p. 22.

26. Y. Wiener, "Forms of Value Systems: A Focus on Organizational Effectiveness and Cultural Change and Maintenance," *Academy of Management Review* 13 (1988), pp. 534–45.

27. J. Matthews, "Hiring: Nothing But Child's Play," *Canadian Business,* August 1991, p. 15; and K. Romain, "Teamwork at Toyota Raises Corolla Output," *Globe and Mail,* February 22, 1990, pp. B1, B4.

28. C. A. O'Reilly III, J. Chatman, and D. F. Caldwell, "People and Organizational Culture: A Profile Comparison Approach to Assessing Person–Organization Fit," *Academy of Management Journal* 34 (1991), pp. 487–516.

29. J. Kerr and J. W. Slocum, Jr., "Managing Corporate Culture through Reward Systems," *Academy of Management Executive* 1 (May 1987), pp. 99–197; Williams et al., *Changing Cultures: New Organizational Approaches,* pp. 120–24; and K. R. Thompson and F. Luthans, "Organizational Culture: A Behavioural Perspective," in Schneider (ed.), *Organizational Climate and Culture,* pp. 319–44.

30. W. G. Ouchi and A. M. Jaeger, "Type Z Organization: Stability in the Midst of Mobility," *Academy of Management Review* 3 (1978), pp. 305–14; and K. McNeil and J. D. Thompson, "The Regeneration of Social Organizations," *American Sociological Review* 36 (1971), pp. 624–37.

31. G. A. Walter, "Culture Collisions in Mergers and Acquisitions," in Frost et al., (eds.), *Organizational Culture,* pp. 301–14; A. F. Buono and J. L. Bowditch, *The Human Side of Mergers and Acquisitions* (San Francisco, Calif.: Jossey-Bass, 1989), Chapter 6; and Schein, *Organizational Culture and Leadership,* pp. 33–36.

32. M. De Pree, *Leadership Is an Art* (East Lansing, Mich.: Michigan State University Press, 1987).

33. J. Van Maanen, "Breaking In: Socialization to Work," in R. Dubin (ed.), *Handbook of Work, Organization, and Society* (Chicago: Rand McNally, 1976), p. 67.

34. C. D. Fisher, "Organizational Socialization: An Integrative View," *Research in Personnel and Human Resources Management* 4 (1986), pp. 101–45; and N. Nicholson, "A Theory of Work Role Transitions," *Administrative Science Quarterly* 29 (1984), pp. 172–91.

35. C. C. Pinder and K. G. Schroeder, "Time to Proficiency Following Job Transfers," *Academy of Management Journal* 30 (1987), pp. 336–53; and N. J. Adler, *International Dimensions of Organizational Behavior* (Boston: Kent, 1986), Chapter 8.

36. Van Maanen, "Breaking In: Socialization to Work," pp. 67–130; L. W. Porter, E. E. Lawler III, and J. R. Hackman, *Behavior in Organizations* (New York: McGraw-Hill, 1975), pp. 163–67; and D. C. Feldman, "The Multiple Socialization of Organization Members," *Academy of Management Review* 6 (1981), pp. 309–18.

37. Porter et al., *Behavior in Organizations,* Chapter 5.

38. M. R. Louis, "Surprise and Sensemaking: What Newcomers Experience in Entering Unfamiliar Organizational Settings," *Administrative Science Quarterly* 25 (1980), pp. 226–51; and D. L. Nelson, "Organizational Socialization: A Stress Perspective," *Journal of Occupational Behaviour* 8 (1987), pp. 311–24.

39. A. M. Saks and S. F. Cronshaw, "A Process Investigation of Realistic Job Previews: Mediating Variables and Channels of Communication," *Journal of Organizational Behavior* 11 (1990), pp. 221–36; J. P. Wanous and A. Colella, "Organizational Entry Research: Current Status and Future Directions," *Research in Personnel and Human Resources Management* 7 (1989), pp. 59–120; and J. P. Wanous, *Organizational Entry* (Reading, Mass.: Addison-Wesley, 1980), pp. 37–44.

40. S. L. McShane and T. Baal, "Rediscovering the Employee Orientation Process," *The Human Resource,* December–January 1988, pp. 11–14; B. Nota, "The Socialization Process at High-Commitment Organizations," *Personnel,* August 1988, pp. 20–23; and E. J. McGarrell, Jr., "An Orientation System That Builds Productivity," *Personnel* 60 (November–December 1983), pp. 32–41.

41. N. J. Allen and J. P. Meyer, "Organizational Socialization Tactics: A Longitudinal Analysis of Links to Newcomers' Commitment and Role Orientation," *Academy of Management Journal* 33 (1990), pp. 847–58; and G. R. Jones, "Socialization Tactics, Self-Efficacy, and Newcomers' Adjustments to Organizations," *Academy of Management Journal* 29 (1986), pp. 262–79.

42. Fisher, "Organizational Socialization: An Integrative View," pp. 132-37; R. Katz, "Time and Work: Toward an Integrative Perspective," *Research in Organizational Behavior* 2 (1980), pp. 81–127; and F. M. Jablin, "Organizational Entry, Assimilation, and Exit," in F. M. Jablin, L. L. Putnam, K. H. Roberts, and L. W. Porter, *Handbook of Organizational Communication* (Beverly Hills, Calif.: Sage, 1987), pp. 679–740.

43. S. L. McShane, "Effect of Socialization Agents on the Organizational Adjustment of New Employees," paper presented at the Annual Conference of the Western Academy of Management, Big Sky Montana, March 1988; and W. M. Evan, "Peer-Group Interaction and Organizational Socialization: A Study of Employee Turnover," *American Sociological Review* 28 (1963), pp. 436–40.

44. Fisher, "Organizational Socialization: An Integrative View," pp. 135–36; Porter et al., *Behavior in Organizations,* pp. 184–86.

45. S. L. McShane, "The Impact of Orientation Practices on the Socialization of New Employees: A Longitudinal Study," *Proceedings of the Annual ASAC Conference, Personnel and Human Resources Division* 9, pt. 9 (1988), pp. 52–61; and Jablin, "Organizational Entry, Assimilation, and Exit," pp. 698–701.

46. J. H. Greenhaus, *Career Management* (Chicago, Ill.: Dryden, 1987), p. 6; and D. T. Hall, *Careers in Organizations* (Glenview, Ill.: Scott, Foresman, 1976), p. 4.

47. Hall, *Careers in Organizations,* pp. 93–97; T. McAteer-Early, "Career Development and Health-Related Complaints: Development of a Measuring Instrument," *Proceedings of the Annual ASAC Conference, Personnel and Human Resources Division* 12, pt. 8 (1991), pp. 70–79; and R. J. Burke and E. R. Greenglass, "Career Orientations, Satisfaction and Health: A Longitudinal Study," *Canadian Journal of Administrative Sciences* 7 (September 1990), pp. 19–25.

48. E. H. Schein, "Individuals and Careers," in J. W. Lorsch (ed.), *Handbook of Organizational Behavior* (Englewood Cliffs, N.J.: Prentice Hall, 1987), pp. 155–71; and D. C. Feldman, *Managing Careers in Organizations,* (Glenview, Ill.: Scott Foresman, 1988), pp. 101–6. For research on a related set of career anchors or concepts, see R. P. Bourgeois and T. Wils, "Career Concepts, Personality and Values of Some Canadian Workers," *Relations Industrielles* 42 (1987), pp. 528–43.

49. Hall, *Careers in Organizations,* Chapter 3; Greenhaus, *Career Management,* Chapter 5; and J. Rush, A. Peacock, and G. Milkovich, "Career Stages: A Partial Test of Levinson's Model of Life/Career Stages," *Journal of Vocational Behavior* 16 (1980), pp. 347–59.

50. Greenhaus, *Career Management,* pp. 168–69; and Feldman, *Managing Careers in Organizations,* pp. 136–45.

51. M. G. Evans and E. Gilbert, "Plateaued Managers: Their Need Gratifications and Their Effort–Performance Expectations," *Journal of Management Studies* 21 (1984), pp. 99–108.

52. J. W. Walker, "Let's Get Realistic about Career Paths," *Human Resource Management,* Fall 1976, pp. 2–7.

53. E. Innes, J. Lyon, and J. Harris, *100 Best Companies to Work For in Canada* (Toronto: HarperCollins, 1990), p. 46.

54. D. T. Hall and J. Richter, "Career Gridlock: Baby Boomers Hit the Wall," *Academy of Management Executive* 4 (August 1990), pp. 7–22; and J. Sisto, "Onward and . . . Oops! What Happens When the Corporate Ladder Runs Out?" *Canadian Business,* July 1990, pp. 70–71.

55. R. J. Burke, "Mentors in Organizations," *Group and Organization Studies* 9 (1984), pp. 253–72; J. Godin and J. Y. Le Louarn, "Les Mentors Ont-il un Effet sur la Progression de la Carrière?" *Relations Industrielles* 41 (1986), pp. 505–18; and K. Kram, *Mentoring at Work* (Glenview, Ill.: Scott Foresman, 1985).

56. C. A. McKeen and R. J. Burke, "Mentor Relationship in Organizations: Issues, Strategies, and Prospects for Women," *Journal of Management Development* 8 (1989), pp. 33–42; and E. A. Fagenson, "The Mentor Advantage: Perceived Career/Job Experiences of Proteges versus Non-Proteges," *Journal of Organizational Behavior* 10 (1989), pp. 309–20.

57. M. Gibb-Clark, "Making Mentors," *Globe and Mail,* July 3, 1990, p. B4.

58. J. A. Wilson and N. S. Elman, "Organizational Benefits of Mentoring," *Academy of Management Executive* 4 (November 1990), pp. 88–94; R. A. Noe, "An Investigation of the Determinants of Successful Assigned Mentoring Relationships," *Personnel Psychology* 41 (1988), pp. 457–79; and Kram, *Mentoring at Work.*

59. J. B. Prince, "Designing Career-Sensitive Performance Appraisal Systems," *Proceedings of the Annual ASAC Conference, Organizational Behaviour Division* 4, pt. 5 (1983), pp. 164–72.

60. J. B. Shaw and L. L. Grubbs, "The Process of Retiring: Organizational Entry in Reverse," *Academy of Management Review* 6 (1981), pp. 41–47; A. L. Kamouri and J. C. Cavanaugh, "The

Impact of Pre-retirement Education Programmes on Workers' Pre-retirement Socialization," *Journal of Occupational Behavior* 7 (1986), pp. 245–56; and T. Reiman, "PRC at the CBC," *Benefits Canada,* September 1985, pp. 42–45.

CHAPTER CASE

THE CULTURAL COLLISION OF MANULIFE FINANCIAL AND DOMINION LIFE

In 1985, Manulife Financial was Canada's second-largest life insurance company, with assets of more than $16 billion and business dealings in 15 countries. Although the company was performing well internationally, it was losing market share within Canada, so senior management decided to decentralize Manulife's Canadian division and buy another insurance firm with a well-established Canadian base.

Dominion Life of Waterloo, Ontario, was put up for sale by its principal shareholder, an American insurance company, and seemed an ideal fit for Manulife, at least from a business perspective. It was an efficiently run, medium-sized operation with a healthy group life business, and its major shareholder was willing to sell. By purchasing Dominion and moving Manulife's Canadian operations from Toronto to Waterloo, Manulife would achieve its objective of separating its Canadian and international businesses. Recalls Manulife's chief actuary: "When Dominion Life came up as a possibility, I thought it was a 'saviour,' an instant, justifiable fix."

Announcing the Acquisition

The announcement that Manulife had purchased Dominion Life and would move its Canadian operations to Waterloo sent shock waves throughout the company's luxurious Bloor Street headquarters. Employees had become accustomed to Manulife's recently completed North Tower with its new fitness centre, beautiful gardens, and view of a park-like ravine in the heart of Toronto. The stress was not eased any when Manulife's CEO called employees to a meeting and bluntly announced that he was not concerned with moving people below the senior level to Waterloo! The company later backtracked on this ill-advised statement and eventually began to actively woo employees to Waterloo.

Dominion Life staff were equally stressed, but for somewhat different reasons. They had known for the past six months that Dominion was up for sale, but no other details of prospective buyers were provided. Consequently, unreliable rumours ran through the company with disturbing regularity. One story was that a construction group from Vancouver had purchased the company and intended to use it as a money-laundering front for the Mafia! News that Manulife had purchased the company finally reached Dominion's employees through the local newspaper, not through a company announcement. Morale was low and the uncertainties that lay ahead fueled more rumours.

Colliding Cultures

The merger process began when 10 entrepreneurial and aggressive Manulife managers moved their offices to Waterloo. They immediately began assessing duplications in personnel and set up task forces to deal with the logistics of the move. With the benefit of hindsight, one manager confided that the process was more difficult than they had anticipated. "We trivialized the whole thing," he says. "We underestimated the magnitude of just about the whole thing—the systems side, the administrative side, the new problems we had, and the culture change, too."

When a consulting firm was brought in to evaluate Dominion Life's management team, Manulife's team began to realize how much of a cultural chasm divided the two firms. Manulife's culture was aggressive, entrepreneurial, consultative, and sales-oriented. Dominion, by contrast, was more bureaucratic, formal, patriarchal, and focussed on financial controls. "Dominion was operationally driven, but hadn't been very successful in a marketing or sales sense," recalls a former Dominion executive. "It was a very expense-driven company." Moreover, Dominion's culture was "top-down driven and far less participative than Manulife's."

No one was prepared for the consequences of the culture shock of merging the two groups. Within six months of the merger, 70 of Dominion's 500 staff resigned, were given early retirement, or were fired. Only two of Dominion's senior management survived the merger; the others were fired or given early retirement because of their "poor fit" with Manulife's culture. Although Manulife handled the departures fairly, resentment and bitterness against the invading company ran high in Waterloo for some time afterwards.

Meanwhile, remaining Dominion employees experienced incredible stress as they tried to adjust to the cultural assumptions of their new employer. Recalls one survivor: "We saw Manulife's culture as a real opportunity, not a threat. But we also saw it as power without control or restraint. It was freedom, but we were frightened by it." Dominion employees also met arrogance on the part of some Manulife employees. Explains one manager: "People began to feel like secondhand goods—'I've been bought.'"

Other Problems Develop

As Manulife's business units moved to Waterloo, another problem emerged. Dominion Life was operated out of two different buildings and the increased pressure of added staff meant that another two office locations had to be rented. But even with four separate offices around Waterloo, conditions were cramped and uncomfortable. Some employees were squeezed into a basement originally built for storage, leaving some Manulife staff to wonder why they had agreed to transfer from their plush offices in Toronto.

One of the most serious crises during the merger occurred in the annuities business unit, where six of the seven key people at Manulife refused to move and the three annuities people at Dominion quit soon after the merger. As a result, every key person in that area had left the company within a span of two or three months. Annuity payments fell three months behind schedule before the problem was corrected.

These and other difficulties placed incredible pressure on the work force. Most employees had to work long overtime hours in cramped conditions to clear the backlog of work. New staff were hired to fill the gaps, resulting in lower productivity and a lot of unfamiliar faces. At the same time, employees from two very different organizational cultures had to learn to adjust to each other and operate as a single company.

Taking Action

Realizing that the merger process was in trouble, Manulife managers began to introduce better communication systems and think of ways for staff from the two companies to become better acquainted. For example, Manulife's employees were given bus tours of Waterloo and were put up in the homes of Dominion Life workers for orientation sessions. Focus groups and counselling were provided to help both Dominion and Manulife staff to cope with the stress.

Perhaps the single most effective action to strengthen the new organizational culture came in the form of a new building in 1988, two years after the merger began. Unlike the previous cramped quarters, the new structure has bright and comfortable offices looking onto landscaped gardens and parkland. This more closely represents Manulife's tradition of quality and concern for employees. Moving to the new Waterloo headquarters has "already done a lot to consolidate culture," agrees a senior manager, "making it possible to manage by walking around, function as a team, and much easier to communicate."

Discussion Questions

1. How are Manulife's and Dominion Life's cultures different? Explain how these cultural differences made the acquisition more difficult.
2. Discuss the relevance of organizational socialization in this case.
3. Discuss the relevance of physical structures in this case.
4. What could Manulife have done differently to improve the acquisition process?

Sources based on L. Welsh, "Manulife Plans Move to Waterloo," *Globe and Mail* (November 17, 1984), p. B3; and based on E. Innes and L. Southwick-Trask, *Turning It Around* (Toronto: Fawcett Crest, 1990), pp. 122–37.

EXPERIENTIAL EXERCISE

DEVELOPING AN ORIENTATION ACTION PLAN

Purpose.   This exercise is designed to help you to translate the concept and theory of organizational socialization into an action framework by designing an employee orientation process for a specific occupational group.

Instructions.   Participants should begin by reading the situation at Brandon Life and Casualty, described below. The class is then divided into teams of four to six people. Each team is asked to provide a set of action plans representing an effective employee orientation process for the people being hired at Brandon. Action plans should relate to organizational socialization issues and should apply to the following periods of time: (1) prehire, (2) posthire pre-employment, (3) first day, (4) remainder of first two weeks, and (5) after two weeks. When completed, each team will present its recommendations and the class will discuss the merits of each action plan.

Situation.   Brandon Life and Casualty Ltd. (BLC) is a major insurance company that intends to hire at least 10 actuaries this year. Actuaries do sophisticated calculations of premiums and annuities and must have completed a post-secondary education in mathematics as well as a special actuarial program. Consequently, BLC and other insurance companies must search throughout Canada to find qualified actuaries. BLC has not yet started its recruiting drive and has asked you to provide a set of action plans to improve the socialization of new actuaries into the organization. The cost of losing one actuary hired within the past two years is approximately $40,000, so BLC is willing to invest some money in an effective orientation process.

Employee Orientation Action Plans for Actuaries at Brandon Life and Casualty

Pre-Hire Action Plans

_____
_____
_____
_____

Post-Hire Preemployment Action Plans

_____
_____
_____
_____

First Day Action Plans

_____
_____
_____
_____

First Two Weeks Action Plans

_____
_____
_____
_____

Third Week Onward Action Plans

_____
_____
_____
_____

17

Organizational Structure and Design

LEARNING OBJECTIVES

After reading this chapter, you should be able to:

Describe
The five mechanisms used to coordinate work activities.

Explain
Why many companies are moving toward flatter structures.

Outline
The advantages and disadvantages of centralization.

Compare
The functional structure with the divisional structure.

Explain
Why multinational firms have difficulty selecting the best grouping.

Identify
Four contingencies of organizational design.

CHAPTER OUTLINE

Division of Labour and Coordination

Elements of Organizational Structure

Departmentation

Contingencies of Organizational Design

MacDonald Dettwiler & Associates

MacDonald Dettwiler & Associates Ltd. (MDA) of Richmond, B.C., is a world leader in customized computer-based systems development, with an impressive list of clients that includes NASA, the European Space Agency, the U.S. Air Force, and the Canadian government. As a contract-driven company, MDA depends on a unique organizational structure that makes the most efficient and effective use of its highly skilled work force. This structure primarily consists of four business units as well as several functional departments (engineering, finance, etc.) that report to the company president. The business units cover four specific product and/or client groups: meteorological systems, space and defense, geological information systems, and aviation. Each business unit has a permanent staff of marketing people as well as several temporary project teams that exist for the length of a specific contract (typically several months to a few years).

Most project team members are people deployed from MDA's engineering department rather than permanent staff from the business unit. In other words, the company uses a type of matrix structure in which engineers have a permanent manager within the engineering department as well as a temporary project manager for the duration of the contract. (A smaller sales department operates in a similar way, although engineering is the dominant skill requirement.) When MDA is awarded a new contract, the project manager submits to the engineering department descriptions of the personnel required and, where appropriate, the names of specific employees who would suit the project's needs. The project manager coordinates work activities and reviews the performance of the people assigned to him or her throughout the project.

The eight managers within the engineering department are responsible for resource assignment and assessment of the professionals under their command. Their primary goal is to ensure that their people are fully allocated to productive work activities and that these assignments provide the best possible results for the organization. They try to accommodate each project manager's request in light of competing demands for their employees. For example, when two project managers request the same employee, the engineering manager responsible for that person must use good judgment to ensure that the assignment decision is fair and ultimately in the organization's best interest. Engineering managers also make performance assessments and merit decisions regarding their employees based on the performance reviews submitted by project managers. Overall, both the project and engineering managers have a healthy balance of power in the matrix structure.[1]

This chapter introduces the different elements of organizational structure as well as the contingency factors that help determine which type of structure is best in a particular situation. You will learn, for example, why MacDonald Dettwiler & Associates uses a matrix structure to group its specialists around specific projects, whereas this approach is not appropriate for the core activities (making hamburgers) at McDonald's Restaurants of Canada. **Organizational structure** refers to the division of labour as well as the patterns of coordination, communication, work flow, and formal power that direct organizational activities. An organizational structure reflects the assumptions and values that are taken for granted by organizational leaders. They also reflect power relationships and ensure that certain behaviours and actions are carried out as expected.[2] Our knowledge of this subject provides the basic tools to engage in **organizational design,** that is, to create and modify organizational structures.

We begin our discussion by considering the two divergent processes in organizational structure: division of labour and coordination. This is followed by a detailed investigation of the four main elements of organizational structure: span of control, centralization, formalization, and departmentation. The latter part of this chapter examines the contingencies of organizational design, including organizational size, technology, external environment, and strategy.

organizational structure
The division of labour as well as the patterns of coordination, communication, workflow, and formal power that direct organizational activities.

organization design
The creation and modification of organizational structures.

DIVISION OF LABOUR AND COORDINATION

All organizational structures include two fundamental and opposing requirements: the division of labour into distinct tasks and the coordination of that labour so that employees are able to accomplish common goals.[3] Recall from our discussion in the opening chapter of this book that organizations are social entities in which two or more people work interdependently through deliberately structured patterns of interaction to accomplish a set of goals.[4] When people gather to collectively accomplish goals, they tend to divide the work into manageable chunks, particularly where there are a lot of different tasks to perform. They also ensure that everyone is working interdependently toward the same objectives as effectively as possible by introducing various mechanisms to coordinate work activities.

Division of Labour

We introduced the concept of division of labour in Chapter 5. Basically, it refers to the subdivision of work into separate jobs assigned to different people. Subdivided work leads to job specialization because each job now includes a narrow subset of the tasks necessary to complete the product or service.

Work may be divided horizontally and vertically, as we explained in Chapter 5. Horizontal job specialization involves distributing into different jobs the tasks required to provide a product or service. This is the predominant form of division of labour in almost all organized activity. Assembling a satellite at Spar Aerospace, for example, consists of thousands of specific tasks that are divided among hundreds of people. Vertical job specialization separates the performance of work from its administration. In other words, it divides the "thinking" job functions from the "doing" functions. For example, secretaries might perform word processing tasks whereas scheduling that work might be assigned to their immediate supervisor.

Organizations divide work into specialized jobs because it increases work efficiency.[5] Job incumbents can master their tasks quickly because work cycles are very short. Less time is wasted changing from one task to another. Training costs are reduced because employees require fewer physical and mental skills to accomplish the assigned work. Finally, job specialization makes it easier to match people with specific aptitudes or skills to the jobs for which they are best suited.

Coordination of Work Activities

While people working toward a common goal tend to divide tasks among themselves in order to reach their objective more effectively, they also require some means of coordinating these distinct jobs so that everyone is working in concert. Henry Mintzberg identifies five basic methods used to coordinate people and their work activities.[6] Mutual adjustment and direct supervision are "real time" coordinating mechanisms because work is coordinated while employees are in the process of doing it. This requires ongoing communication and feedback among participants to achieve their objectives. In contrast, standardization of work processes, outputs, and skills involves coordination by planning activities before the work begins. Participants have learned their roles before engaging in the work activity. The five coordinating mechanisms that follow represent the most basic elements of the organizational structure that hold the organization together:

mutual adjustment
The coordination of work activities among employees through informal communication.

- *Mutual adjustment*—**Mutual adjustment** achieves coordination by letting employees directly coordinate their efforts through informal communication. This is a highly flexible strategy, but it is also the most complicated when large groups of employees are involved in complex tasks.
- *Direct supervision*—Direct supervision centralizes coordination through one person who issues instructions and monitors work activities. This minimizes problems with informal communication among several people, but it becomes more difficult as the number of subordinates increase.
- *Standardization of work processes*—Work processes are standardized by specifying work content through procedures, instructions, and job descriptions. In effect, employee behaviour must abide by rules and regulations.

- *Standardization of outputs*—Standardization of outputs establishes the dimensions of the product or service to be delivered. For example, top management establishes objectives for its profit centres (e.g., return on investment) rather than specifying how to make the product or provide the service.
- *Standardization of skills*—Standardization of skills builds coordination into the person through intensive training. This occurs in a hospital operating room where the anesthesiologist, surgeon, and operating room nurses are able to complete many operations with little discussion because their training has taught them what to expect from the others and how to fulfill their own roles.

ELEMENTS OF ORGANIZATIONAL STRUCTURE

There are four basic elements of organizational structure. In this section, we introduce three of them: span of control, centralization, and formalization. In addition to describing the different types or degrees of these elements, we will indicate their relative advantages and disadvantages for organizational effectiveness and employee well-being. The fourth element of organizational structure—departmentation—is presented in the next section.

Span of Control

Span of control refers to the number of people directly reporting to a supervisor. Traditional management theorists prescribe a relatively narrow span of control, typically no more than 20 employees per supervisor and 6 supervisors per manager. These statements are based on the assumption that managers simply cannot monitor and control any more subordinates closely enough.

In spite of the universal prescriptions of the early writers, research suggests that the optimal span of control varies with specific circumstances.[7] We must keep in mind that span of control mainly considers coordination through direct supervision. However, other coordinating mechanisms, such as the three forms of standardization, might allow a much wider span of control. For example, there are reports of senior managers supervising more than 40 middle managers with no apparent difficulty.

A wider span of control may be possible where subordinates perform the same tasks because either work processes or outputs can be standardized. Where tasks are diverse, on the other hand, direct supervision becomes a more prominent coordinating mechanism. Managers simply cannot apply the same rules and practices to production staff as to marketing staff, for example. A wider span of control might also be possible when tasks are routine because work processes can be standardized and less time is required to discuss exceptional cases with subordinates. Finally, the optimal span of control depends on the supervisor's other duties. Someone whose

span of control
The number of people directly reporting to a supervisor. This element of organizational structure determines the number of hierarchical levels required in the organization.

main job is to supervise and coach employees may have a wider span of control than one who has many nonsupervisory tasks.

Tall and Flat Structures.   The average span of control within the organization determines the number of hierarchical levels required. As shown in Exhibit 17–1, a tall structure has many hierarchical levels that each have a relatively narrow span of control, whereas a flat structure has few levels that each have a wide span of control.[8] Ironically, while some writers were advocating a narrow span of control during the mid-1950s, Peter Drucker was calling for a maximum of seven hierarchical levels. More recently, Tom Peters has challenged management to cut the number of layers to three within a facility and to five within the entire organization.[9]

Air Canada, Domtar Inc., Labatt Breweries, and other companies have moved toward a flatter, or "delayered," organizational structure.[10] A flatter structure increases organizational productivity by cutting overhead costs. It is also consistent with the trend toward employee involvement and teamwork that we described in Chapters 10 and 11. The Toronto-Dominion Bank, for example, has moved toward a flatter organizational structure by cutting layers of middle management and dramatically widening the average span of control. Explains a T-D manager: "[We] have developed a very flat struc-

---

EXHIBIT 17–1   Span of Control and Tall/Flat Structures

**Tall Structure/
Narrow Span of Control**

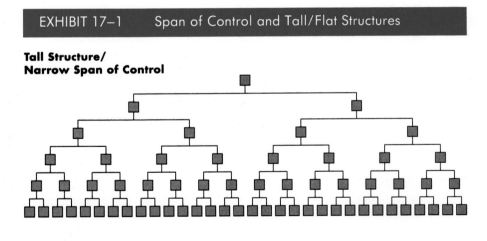

**Flat Structure/
Wide Span of Control**

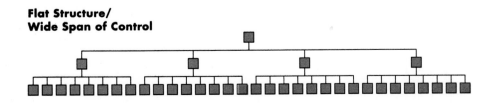

ture to accomplish [teamwork]. Branch managers report to divisional senior vice-presidents who report to the president. That's three layers and—believe me, for a bank—that's flat?''[11]

Centralization and Decentralization

Centralization means that formal decision authority is held by a small group of people, typically those at the top of the organizational hierarchy. **Decentralization** means that decision authority is dispersed throughout the organization. Centralization and decentralization refer to formal power and, as we have described throughout this book, there is a general trend toward decentralization as more decision-making power is given to people further down the organizational hierarchy.[12]

There are advantages of both centralization and decentralization. Centralized decision making increases uniformity and reduces the need for extensive reporting procedures. It also keeps top management more informed about organizational activities. However, many organizations have decentralized in order to increase their responsiveness to changing conditions and to satisfy increasing expectations among lower-level staff for involvement in organizational decisions.

Most organizations begin with centralized structures as the founder makes most of the decisions and tries to direct the business toward his or her vision. But as organizations grow, work activities are divided into more specialized functions, a broader range of products or services are introduced, and operations expand into different regions or countries. Under these conditions, decentralization occurs because neither the founder nor senior management have sufficient time or expertise to process all of the decisions that significantly influence the business.[13] Thus, structures become more decentralized when organizations grow and become more diverse.

While organizational size and diversity push for decentralization, other forces push for centralization.[14] Managers try to gain decision control during times of turbulence and organizational crisis. When the problems are over, decision-making power does not quickly return to the lower levels.

Another problem is that headquarters managers push for centralization to increase their organizational power and feelings of control over organizational activities. This happened at a company that operates the pharmacy departments of a large Canadian department store chain. At one time, local managers were allowed some control over the displays in their department, such as putting out umbrellas and cold remedies if the weather turned cold and wet in their area. Headquarters staff wanted and eventually received complete control of all displays, ostensibly because this would improve organizational efficiency and give customers a feeling of consistency among stores. But sales dropped because every store was required to display suntan lotion, even in places where the weather had been inclement for several weeks.

centralization
The degree that formal decision authority is held by a small group of people, typically those at the top of the organizational hierarchy.

decentralization
The degree that decision authority is dispersed throughout the organization.

PERSPECTIVE 17–1   Formalization at McDonald's Restaurants of Canada Ltd.

Formalization has been a way of life at McDonald's Restaurants of Canada Ltd. since 1968, when the company's first restaurant opened in this country. At the heart of McDonald's machine efficiency is the carefully guarded 658-page Operations and Training Manual. The book covers every activity in explicit detail, from making hamburgers in Chapter 1 to restaurant security and insurance in Chapter 26.

Every job is broken down into the smallest detail. Color photographs depict ingredients and individual products at every stage of preparation. These rules and procedures are further reinforced by videotapes to systematically train employees, three Canadian Institutes of Hamburgerology to develop McDonald's restaurant managers, and computerized machines to guide employee behaviour on the job. Says a Mc-Donald's of Canada vice-president: "I sometimes think we invented the word *system*."

With clearly detailed procedures and thorough training, McDonald's 600 Canadian restaurants operate as precisely as Swiss watches. Mustard is doled out in five perfect drops. A quarter ounce of onions and two pickles—three if they're small—are used per sandwich. Drink cups are filled with ice up to a point just below the arches on their sides. Take-out bags are folded exactly twice. French fries are stacked exactly six boxes high and one inch apart, with two inches between the stacks and walls of the freezer. Cooking and bagging fries are explained in 19 steps. The strict rules even prescribe what colour of nail polish to wear.

Formalization

formalization

The degree that organizations standardize behaviour through rules, procedures, formal training, and related mechanisms.

Formalization refers to the degree that organizations standardize behaviour through rules, procedures, formal training, and related mechanisms. Highly formalized organizations specify what employees should be doing and how they should be doing it. Job descriptions establish required work behaviours and performance goals. Instruction manuals describe the steps required to transform inputs to outputs. Communication patterns and interpersonal behaviours are regulated by detailed rules and procedures. Decisions are programmed and leave little room for individual initiative or discretion.[15]

Organizations formalize their structures to reduce the variability of employee behaviour so that clients receive reliable products and services. Canada Post uses almost militaristic work rules to provide reliable mail delivery. Air Canada formalizes work activities to maximize transportation safety and ensure that flight schedules are on time. As reported in Perspective 17–1, McDonald's Restaurants of Canada Ltd. has developed a highly formalized organizational structure to ensure that its hamburgers sold in St. John's, Newfoundland, look, taste, smell, and cost the same as those sold in Saanich, B.C.

Organizations tend to become more formalized as they age and grow in size. As firms age, roles and work activities become routinized, making them easier to document into standardized practices. Larger companies formalize as a coordinating mechanism because direct supervision and mutual adjust-

McDonald's standards ensure that supplies are used neither too generously nor too sparsely. A jar of Big Mac sauce should produce 170 to 180 servings. Between 111 and 135 pickle slicings should be expected per pound of pickles. A pound of lettuce should dress 24 to 28 sandwiches. A gallon of milkshake mix should yield anywhere from 15.2 to 15.6 milkshakes. If a home-office field consultant discovers that a licensee is squeezing 16 shakes out of a gallon, that licensee hears about it.

The operations manual also specifies how many people it will take to open in the morning, handle the lunchtime rush, and close up the restaurant at night. McDonald's licensees have some discretion, such as whether to add more people to the order counter than stated in the operations manual. But these decisions are the result of detailed management development at the company's training centres. Explains a McDonald's of Canada senior executive: "McDonald's is not a job. It's a way of life. You have to have hamburger in your brains and ketchup in your veins."

Sources: C. Davies, "1990 Strategy Session," *Canadian Business,* January 1990, pp. 49–50; G. Morgan, *Creative Organization Theory: A Resourcebook* (Newburg Park, Calif.: Sage, 1989), pp. 271–73; and K. Deveny, "Bag Those Fries, Squirt That Ketchup, Fry That Fish," *Business Week,* October 13, 1986, p. 86.

ment do not operate as easily. Formalization is also related to the extent that the organization's stakeholders have established specific standards and requirements. For instance, safety rules are introduced and strictly enforced to conform to government regulations. Specific accounting rules and procedures are followed so that the auditors will give the company a clean bill of financial health. Ethical standards of conduct are strengthened as the company faces increasing pressure from its shareholders.

Problems with Formalization.   Formalization sometimes decreases rather than increases organizational effectiveness. Rules and procedures reduce organizational flexibility, so employees follow prescribed behaviours even when the situation clearly calls for a customized response. Some work rules become so convoluted that organizational efficiency would decline if they were actually followed as prescribed. Indeed, many labour unions flex their power during negotiations by invoking a "work-to-rule" strike. During work-to-rule strikes, union members become less productive because they closely follow the formalized rules and procedures established by organization to allegedly increase work efficiency!

Another concern is that although employees with very strong security needs and a low tolerance for ambiguity like working in highly formalized organizations, others become alienated and feel powerless in these structures. Finally, rules and procedures have been known to take on a life of their own in some organizations. They become the focus of attention rather than the organization's ultimate objectives of producing a product or service and serving its dominant stakeholders.

Mechanistic versus Organic Structures

mechanistic structure
An organizational structure with a narrow span of control and high degrees of formalization and centralization.

organic structure
An organizational structure with a wide span of control, very little formalization, and highly decentralized decision making.

The three elements of organizational structure described so far—span of control, centralization, and formalization—are sometimes grouped into two distinct forms known as *mechanistic* and *organic structures*.[16] A **mechanistic structure** has a narrow span of control and high degrees of formalization and centralization. It is characterized by many rules and procedures, limited decision making at lower levels, large hierarchies of people in specialized roles, and vertical rather than horizontal communication flows. Tasks are rigidly defined, and are altered only when sanctioned by higher authorities. An **organic structure** is just the opposite. It usually has a wide span of control, very little formalization, and highly decentralized decision making. Communication flows in all directions with little concern for the formal hierarchy. Tasks are fluid, adjusting to new situations and organizational needs.

DEPARTMENTATION

departmentation
An element of organizational structure specifying how employees and their activities are grouped together, such as by function, product, geographic location, or some combination.

Span of control, centralization, and formalization are important elements of organizational structure, but most people think about organizational charts when the discussion of organizational structure arises. The organizational chart represents an important element in the structuring of an organization, called **departmentation.** Specifically, departmentation indicates how employees and their activities are grouped together. It is a fundamental strategy for coordinating organizational activities, as it influences organizational behaviour in the following ways:[17]

1. Departmentation forms command units, that is, a manager and his or her subordinates, as we described in Chapter 10. It therefore establishes a system of common supervision among positions and units within the organization.

2. Departmentation typically determines which positions and units must share resources. Thus, it establishes interdependencies among employees and subunits (see Chapter 13).

3. Departmentation usually creates common measures of performance. Members of the same command unit, for example, share the same departmental or team goals. Common budgets and other resources also provide a means by which the performance of subunits may be compared.

4. Departmentation encourages mutual adjustment among people and subunits. With common supervision and resources, members within

each configuration typically work in close proximity. This encourages frequent, informal communication among employees so that they may coordinate work activities.

There are almost as many organizational charts as there are businesses, but we can identify four pure types of departmentation: simple, functional, divisional, and matrix. Few companies fit exactly into any of these categories, but they represent a useful framework for discussing more complex hybrid forms of departmentation. In this section, we also introduce network and cluster structures as two emerging organizational forms.

Simple Structure

Simple structure refers to organizations that do not group employees into subunits, although a hierarchy may still exist.[18] Small businesses fall into this category, particularly when they employ only a few people, and offer only one distinct product or service. A small retail store, for example, would have an owner and several employees who share duties and may be assigned different tasks as the need arises. Employees are grouped in undifferentiated roles because there are insufficient economies of scale to assign them to specialized roles. Simple structures are flexible designs, yet they usually depend on the owner's direct supervision to coordinate work activities. Consequently, this structure is very difficult to operate under complex conditions.

Functional Structure

A **functional structure** organizes employees around specific skills or other resources. Employees with marketing expertise are grouped into a marketing unit, those with production skills are located in manufacturing, engineers are found in product development, and so on. Exhibit 17–2 illustrates a functional structure similar to one found at B.C. Hydro. While some departments report directly to the chief executive officer and others report to the president, all divide work activities into traditional functions. Organizations with functional structures are typically centralized in order to coordinate their activities effectively. Coordination through standardization of work processes is the most common form of coordination used in a functional structure. Most organizations use functional structures at some level or at some time in their development.

functional structure
A type of departmentation that organizes employees around specific skills or other resources.

Advantages and Disadvantages. An important advantage of functional structures is that they foster professional identity and clarify career paths. They permit greater specialization so that the organization has expertise in each area. Direct supervision is easier because managers have backgrounds in that functional area and employees approach them with common problems and issues. Finally, functional structures create common pools of talent

EXHIBIT 17–2   Functional Organizational Structure

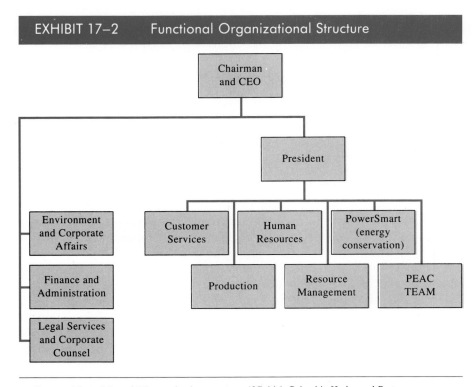

Source: Adapted from 1991 organization structure of British Columbia Hydro and Power Authority.

that typically serve everyone in the organization, thereby creating an economy of scale that would not exist if functional specialists were spread over different parts of the organization.[19]

Functional structures also have their limitations. Since people are grouped together with common interests and backgrounds, these designs promote differentiation among functions. Dysfunctional conflict is a potential problem for this reason, as well as the fact that functional units require high levels of interdependence (typically sequential or reciprocal, as we described in Chapter 13). A related concern is that functional structures tend to emphasize subunit goals over superordinate organizational goals. For instance, people who contribute to the same product or service are fragmented across functions and may contribute to several organizational outputs. Consequently, they tend to give lower priority to the product or service than to departmental goals. A third concern is that functional structures perpetuate specialization at the expense of more holistic management. Unless managers are transferred from one function to the next, they fail to develop a broader understanding of the business. Together, these problems require substantial formal controls and coordination when functional structures are used.

EXHIBIT 17–3   Three Types of Divisional Structure

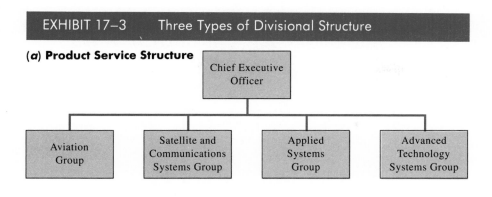

(a) Product Service Structure

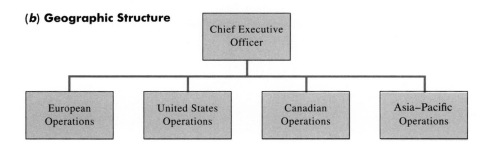

(b) Geographic Structure

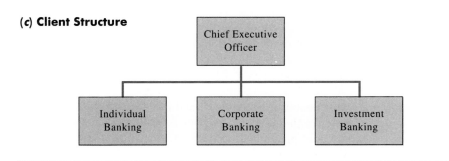

(c) Client Structure

Note: (a) is similar to Spar Aerospace Ltd.'s organizational structure; (b) is similar to the brewing businesses of Labatt Breweries; and (b) is similar to three divisions of the Canadian Imperial Bank of Commerce.

Divisional Structure

A **divisional structure** groups employees around outputs, clients, or geographic areas. Divisional structures are sometimes called *self-contained units* or *strategic business units (SBUs)* because they are normally more autonomous than functional structures and may be separate entities (e.g., subsidiaries) of the larger enterprise.

divisional structure
A type of departmentation that groups employees around outputs, clients, or geographic areas.

PERSPECTIVE 17–2   Bombardier's Divisional Structure

Bombardier Inc. is a diversified transportation equipment manufacturer with a strong allegiance to product-based organization design. The company's overall operation is divided into four product groups: mass transit, rail and diesel products, utility and recreational vehicles, and aerospace products.

The mass-transit group develops, produces, and markets subway cars, most recently to the cities of New York, Montreal, and the state of New Jersey. With recent acquisition of Pullman designs, Bombardier now holds a leadership position in rail passenger design and manufacturing. The mass-transit group has recently entered more unique markets, such as producing monorail cars for Walt Disney World in Florida. Perhaps the most exciting development will be the completion of single- and double-decker high-speed railway cars that will carry passengers through the English Channel Tunnel. The cars are fabricated at Bombardier's plant near Quebec City and assembled at its subsidiaries in Belgium and France.

Maintenance work represents the largest business activity in Bombardier's Rail and Diesel Products group, including repairing a fleet of buses near Montreal and overhauling commuter cars for the state of New Jersey. The group restarted production operations in the mid-1980s when it won a contract with Nigeria to build 50 diesel-electric locomotives and related parts. It is also in the process of developing a high-performance diesel engine for locomotive and marine products and is test marketing a natural gas-fuelled engine developed by the division.

The utility and recreational vehicles group consists of four product divisions. The snowmobile division is responsible for SKI-DOO snowmobiles. A recently formed marine products division develops, manufactures, and markets products for the water sports and leisure market, including the SEA-DOO personal watercraft that Bombardier launched in 1987. The industrial equipment division is mainly responsible for machinery used to groom ski hills, although it is poised to

Types of Divisional Structure.   As we see in Exhibit 17–3, there are several types of divisional structure. *Product/service structures* organize work activities around distinct outputs and, in doing so, tend to focus on specific client groups as well. Exhibit 17–3(*a*) displays a simplified variation of a product structure at Spar Aerospace Ltd. with its four distinct product groups.

Geographic structures establish organizational groupings around different locations. For example, both Labatt Breweries and Molson Breweries are generally organized around provincial operations, mainly because interprovincial trade barriers differentiate products, legislation, and distribution processes. Multinational organizations sometimes adapt a global geographic structure. For instance, Toronto-based Bata Ltd., the world's largest footwear company, is divided into Canada, Europe, Africa, South America, the Far East, and four other geographic divisions.[20] Exhibit 17–3(*b*) illustrates a design that is quite similar to Labatt's worldwide organizational structure.

Client structures organize work activities around specific customers. Canadian financial institutions have adopted a stronger market orientation during the 1980s and are now reorganizing their operations around specific client groups to reflect this new emphasis [see Exhibit 17–3(*c*)]. For example, the Canadian Imperial Bank of Commerce has reorganized its business into five strategic business units. Three of these—The Individual Bank, The

capture the increasing demand for urban snow-removal vehicles as existing municipal stock reaches the replacement stage. The logistics equipment division serves the market for military vehicles, including the delivery of four-wheel-drive utility vehicles to the Belgian army.

Bombardier's fourth product group—aerospace products—exists within the company's subsidiary, Canadair Ltd. This is perhaps the best example of Bombardier's dedication to product structures. Canadair had a highly centralized functional structure before it was acquired by Bombardier in 1987. Explains Bombardier CEO Laurent Beaudoin: "They had to report to three or four levels. In the end, nobody knew what he was responsible for." Bombardier quickly reorganized Canadair around two product groups, a client group, and the manufacturing function, thereby

allowing Canadair to decentralize authority and decision making. "You're responsible for not only your department, but also for your marketing, your development," Beaudoin told Canadair's management during the reorganization. "You're going to be responsible for your customer service and your costs. At the same time you have to make a profit."

Today, Canadair's two product divisions are responsible for the Challenger executive jet and a turboprop waterbomber, respectively. The military division develops and markets unmanned surveillance systems and does maintenance work for the Canadian Forces fleet of CF-18 fighter aircraft. In addition to doing work for the other divisions, Canadair's manufacturing division produces sections of the Boeing 767 airliner as well as components for other aircraft manufacturers.

Sources: Based on J. Daly, "A Ticket to Big Profits," *Maclean's,* June 3, 1991, p. 38; A. Zerbisias, "How Do You Make a Turkey Soar?" *Report on Business Magazine,* October 1987, pp. 82–90; and Bombardier Inc., *Annual Report,* January 31, 1988.

Corporate Bank, and The Investment Bank—are directed toward specific client groups. (Two other SBUs—The Administrative Bank and CIBC Development Corporation—provide administrative support services and manage the organization's real estate holdings, respectively.)

Advantages and Disadvantages.   The divisional form is a building block structure because it accommodates growth relatively easily. Related products or clients can be added to existing divisions with little need for additional learning, whereas increasing diversity may be accommodated by sprouting a new division. Organizations typically reorganize around divisional structures as they expand into distinct products, services, and domains of operation because coordinating functional units becomes too unwieldy with increasing diversity.[21]

Since divisional structures have self-contained resources, decision making may be delegated further down the hierarchy, thereby increasing flexibility at lower levels in the organization. Accountability increases because it is easier to identify more objective divisional goals and output measures against which to evaluate the unit's performance. They also tend to place more emphasis on clients and product quality since divisional goals and output measures are now directly related to these factors. As Perspective 17–2 describes, Bombardier Inc. makes extensive use of divisional structures, particularly around distinct product and client groups, because it provides autonomy and accountability to management and staff members within each division or strategic business unit.

In spite of their popularity, divisional structures increase the risk of duplication and underutilization of resources. Some firms, such as 3M Corporation, try to ensure that every division has a sufficiently large economy of scale by establishing a minimum sales volume for divisional status, but this is an imperfect rule to overcome the inefficiencies. Another concern is that while differentiation among functional specialities is reduced in divisional structures, differentiation among product groups may increase. Managers may be reluctant to share resources with other divisions even when sharing would improve organizational effectiveness, particularly where reward systems are based on the unit's rather than the organization's performance. Finally, while division autonomy is a potential advantage, it may reduce top management's control over the entire organization. Unless control mechanisms are introduced, the organization's senior management group might not be aware of a division's deviation from organizational standards or objectives until it is too late.

Matrix Structure

matrix structure

A type of departmentation that overlays a product-based structure (typically a project team) with a functional structure in an attempt to receive the benefits of both designs.

The **matrix structure** overlays a product-based structure (typically a project team) with a functional structure in an attempt to receive the benefits of both designs. In a matrix structure, employees are temporarily assigned to a specific project team, usually for no longer than a couple of years. They also have a permanent functional unit, typically known as a "home" department, to which they return when a project is completed. The result is that employees have two bosses—the project manager and the functional manager—within the matrix structure. The relative degree of supervisory authority of these two managers depends on the specific matrix configuration and duties of these managers.[22]

Exhibit 17–4 depicts a simplified matrix structure consisting of three functional departments that provide specialists to the three project teams. MacDonald Dettwiler's (MDA) matrix structure, described in the opening vignette, is a more complex variation of this because it consists of several project teams within each of the company's four business units. Most project employees at MDA are assigned from a single organizationwide engineering department, and each business unit employs a permanent team of marketing professionals.

Advantages and Disadvantages.   Matrix structures usually optimize the use of resources and expertise, making them ideal for project-based organizations with fluctuating workloads.[23] Specialists are housed within functional departments (e.g., engineering, marketing, etc.), yet the primary goal of functional managers is to see that these people are fully deployed in produc-

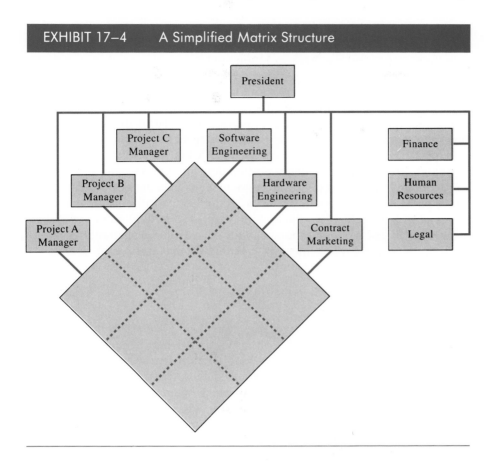

EXHIBIT 17–4   A Simplified Matrix Structure

tive work. Whenever a project requires specific skills, functional managers make the necessary assignments and, when the project is completed, they quickly assign these people to other projects requiring similar expertise.

By forming teams of people from different specialities who work in physical proximity to each other, matrix structures improve communication efficiency, project flexibility, and innovation compared to purely functional designs. They focus technical specialists on the goals of serving clients and creating marketable products. Yet by maintaining a link to their functional unit, employees are able to interact and coordinate with others in their technical speciality. For example, MacDonald Dettwiler's 20 engineers specializing in user interface technology are assigned to various project teams across the company's four business units, but their engineering manager ensures that they develop compatible interfaces so that the company's products all have the same look and feel.

Matrix structures have received considerable support, but they may generate conflict, power struggles, and stress if improperly managed.[24] Senior management must maintain a proper balance of power between project leaders and functional managers. Project managers must have a general management orientation and conflict-resolution skill to coordinate people with diverse backgrounds. Otherwise, dysfunctional conflict may arise among team members due to their diverse backgrounds and perspectives.

Functional managers must be effective at allocating human resources and maintaining fairness in the process and outcome of this distribution. This requires effective negotiation skills and a decision process based on the principles of procedural justice described in Chapter 13. It is not easy to coordinate 20 or 30 professionals, so functional managers require computer assistance to track each employee's assignment schedule, performance, and career paths. Finally, people who feel comfortable in structured bureaucracies tend to have difficulty adjusting to the relatively fluid nature of matrix structures. Stress is a common symptom of poorly managed matrix structures because employees must cope with two managers with potentially divergent needs and expectations.

Hybrid Structure

As organizations grow, they typically move from a simple to hybrid structure that combines two or more of the types of departmentation described above. Very few companies adopt a pure functional structure because work activities become too complex to coordinate activities across functions. Moreover, this design ignores the significance of product and geographical activities. The geographic divisionalized form enables firms in diverse markets to adopt local customs and preferences more readily. However, this tends to fragment product development and may isolate the international operations from each other. Product-based divisions are better at coordinating product development activities, but they may weaken the firm's ability to understand and adapt to unique client demands in different geographic markets. Finally, it is difficult to imagine a pure matrix structure since finance, human resources, and other functions typically apply across the entire company rather than within specific project teams.

Multinational Structures.   Selecting the best hybrid structure becomes increasingly important and difficult as organizations grow into multinational corporations (MNCs).[25] Recent research suggests that MNCs should develop structures and systems that maintain some balance of power and effectiveness across functional, product, and geographic groups.[26] In other words, they must ensure that functional managers do not dominate product managers, product managers do not dominate regional managers, and so forth.

Consider Northern Telecom, the Canadian-based multinational telecommunications manufacturer that recently reorganized around three global product groups representing public networks, private networks, and wireless systems. The company had previously emphasized its geographic subsidiaries as the primary organizing dimension, but this led to fragmented product development. Under the new structure, Northern Telecom's product groups are responsible for global product development, whereas its four geographically based subsidiaries—representing Canada, United States, Europe, and Asia–Pacific—are responsible for marketing and manufacturing in their territories.[27] The shift of power from geographic to product divisions illustrates only a small part of the complex structure of Northern Telecom because most units are further divided by function and a few have matrix structures.

Network Structure

Some organizational experts claim that organizations adopting any hierarchical structure will become dinosaurs within the next decade.[28] Functional and divisionalized forms are not sufficiently flexible, nor do they allow people to adapt quickly enough to increasing competition and changing conditions. These writers suggest that a **network structure** is better suited to increasing global competition. A network structure is an alliance of several organizations for the purpose of creating a product or serving a client.[29] In some cases, the original organization has spun off its functional departments into separate business units; in other cases, it may be a consortium of smaller firms beehived around a prime contractor in a major project.[30] Increasingly, the network structure is formed by an independent core firm that buys the services of independent companies to fulfill the functions normally provided by departments within the organization.

network structure
An alliance of several organizations for the purpose of creating a product or serving a client.

As illustrated in Exhibit 17–5, a network structure might have an entire product or service designed, manufactured, marketed, delivered, and sold by subcontracting firms located anywhere around the world. The core company's main function is to initiate the process and coordinate the activities of the subcontracting firms.

Advantages and Disadvantages.   Flexibility is the main advantage of network structures. If a product or service is no longer in demand, the core firm can wind down operations as contracts come to an end. If it wants to shift into a different type of product line, it forms new alliances with other firms offering the appropriate resources. Since network structures depend on markets rather than hierarchies to create products and services, they potentially make better use of skills and technology. The core firm becomes globally competitive as it shops worldwide for subcontractors with the best people and the best technology at the best price. It is not saddled with the same resources used for previous products or services.

A potential disadvantage of network structures is that they expose the core firm to the same market forces used to get the best resources. Other companies may bid up the price for subcontractors in any functional area,

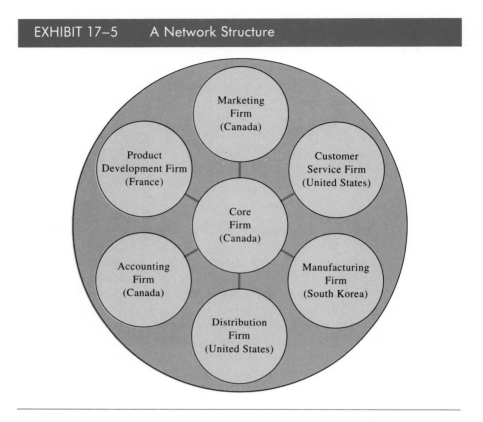

EXHIBIT 17–5   A Network Structure

whereas the short-term cost would be lower if the company hired its own employees to provide this function. Another problem is that while information technology makes worldwide communication much easier, it will never replace the degree of control organizations have when manufacturing, marketing, and other functions are in-house. The core firm can use arms-length incentives and contract provisions to maintain the subcontractor's quality, but these actions are relatively crude compared to those used to maintain performance of in-house employees.

Cluster (or Circle) Structure

cluster (or circle) structure
A type of departmentation consisting of self-contained units of people from different disciplines who work together on a semipermanent basis.

The **cluster (or circle) structure** is perhaps the most revolutionary type of unit grouping proposed in recent years. D. Quinn Mills (along with G. Bruce Fiesen) defines a cluster structure as a self-contained unit of people from different disciplines who work together on a semipermanent basis.[31] It is a highly decentralized design with very little formalization and a wide span of control.

EXHIBIT 17–6   The Cluster Structure

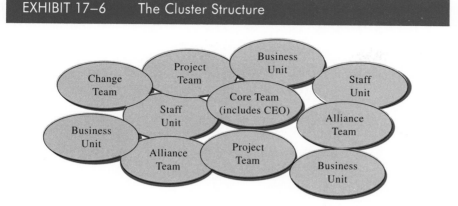

Source: Based on D. Quinn Mills, *Rebirth of the Corporation* (New York: John Wiley & Sons, 1991), p. 31.

A cluster organization has no hierarchy in the traditional sense of the word; rather, as we see in Exhibit 17–6, it consists of several circles, each focussed on a specific product, client, or activity. A cluster-based organization includes a core team comprised of top management, several business units (depending on the size of the firm) for specific external clients, staff units for internal clients, and project teams for specific projects. A change team is similar to the parallel learning structure introduced in Chapter 15 because it reviews and modifies broad aspects of the firm's activities. Finally, some organizations might have an alliance team consisting of people from other organizations working in a joint venture.

It is difficult to say whether any organization has wholeheartedly adopted the cluster structure, although Mills identifies Canadian General Electric, IBM Canada, and Royal Trustco as three firms that are at least moving toward this design.[32] Each has flattened the organizational hierarchy and has decentralized through the widespread use of self-managing work teams (not just for production staff). Self-managing work teams are somewhat akin to cluster structures, but clusters include more diverse skills and are not embedded in the traditional hierarchy in which self-managing work teams are found.

Asea-Brown Boveri (ABB), the Swiss-based industrial giant, has also moved toward the cluster design. Within the past few years, ABB has divided its 200,000 employees into 4,500 autonomous profit centres, averaging fewer than 50 people in each cluster.[33] But perhaps the best example of the cluster structure is found at Semco S/A, Brazil's largest marine and food-processing machinery manufacturer. As we describe in Perspective 17–3, Semco is organized into three circles and has delegated virtually complete responsibility to its employees.

Semco S/A is a fast-growing Brazilian company with 800 employees who manufacture marine pumps, digital scanners, and a variety of industrial equipment for the food-processing industry. Semco's management is based on three fundamental values: democracy, profit sharing, and information. Many aspects of the company reflect these values, but perhaps the most dramatic is its circular organizational structure.

Semco has four job titles—counsellors, partners, coordinators, and associates—and three management layers. Three concentric circles represent the three management layers. One tiny central circle consists of the five counsellors who integrate the company's activities. In traditional terms, this includes the president and top management team, although they prefer to be called counsellors. A second, larger circle contains the heads (called partners) of the eight divi-

sions. Finally, a huge third circle holds all of the other employees. Most of these people (called associates) perform the research, design, sales, and manufacturing work and have no one reporting to them on a regular basis. This circle also includes a few coordinators who serve as temporary or permanent team leaders.

The third circle consists of many small manufacturing cells. At the food-processing equipment plant, for example, one cell of employees makes only slicers, another makes scales, and so forth. Each cell is self-contained, so the work of people in that team is unaffected by other cells. Work teams are also formed without structure. Teams appoint their own coordinators rather than having this imposed from above by the partners or counsellors.

Status and money tend to reinforce organizational

CONTINGENCIES OF ORGANIZATIONAL DESIGN

Organizational theorists and practitioners are interested not only in the elements of organizational structure, but also the contingencies that determine or influence the optimal design. By understanding the best span of control, level of centralization and formalization, and type of departmentation in a particular situation, we can hopefully design a structure that will strengthen the organization's chances for survival. In this section, we introduce four contingencies of organizational design: size, technology, environment, and strategy.

Organizational Size

As you might expect, larger organizations have considerably different structures than smaller organizations.[34] Many studies have confirmed that organizational size—the number of people within the social entity—influences organizational structure. There is overwhelming evidence that larger organizations have greater job specialization due to a greater division of labour. The size of an organization reflects the breadth of its work activities, and it is virtually impossible for one person to comprehend everything to be done in a large business.

hierarchy in most companies, but not at Semco. It is not uncommon for an associate to make a higher salary than the coordinator who manages his or her unit. In fact, a few earn even more than the partners, so they can increase their status and compensation without entering the other circles.

Semco replaced the formalized rules and regulations that reinforce organizational hierarchy with the "rule of common sense," and made its employees responsible for using their own judgment. For example, the company scrapped complex rules about travel expenses, such as how much to spend on hotels and whether to charge the firm for a theatre ticket. Explains Semco president Ricardo Semler: "If we can't trust people with our money and their judgment, we

sure as hell shouldn't be sending them overseas to do business in our name."

The company is very, very rigorous about its financial controls—it wants the numbers ready for display by the 5th of each month. But these controls simply allow the coordinators and associates to have almost complete autonomy over the operations. They come in to work when they like, see all of the company's financial figures (including how much the partners earn), and make decisions about whether the company should acquire another business or move to new facilities. As Semler points out: "They can do whatever the hell they want. It's up to them to see the connection between productivity and profit and to act on it."

Source: Based on R. Semler, "Managing without Managers," *Harvard Business Review,* September–October 1989, pp. 76–84.

An increasing division of labour requires greater use of more elaborate coordinating mechanisms. Consequently, larger organizations are more likely to use standardization of work processes and outputs to coordinate work activities. These coordinating mechanisms create an administrative hierarchy and greater formalization. At the same time, mutual adjustment becomes less prevalent as a means of coordinating work activities. Finally, there is evidence that larger organizations are more decentralized. As we noted earlier in this chapter, neither the founder nor senior management have sufficient time or expertise to process all of the decisions that significantly influence the business as it grows. Therefore, decision-making authority is pushed down to lower levels, where incumbents are able to cope with the narrower range of issues under their control.[35]

Technology

In Chapter 1 we said that technology (such as equipment, work methods, and information) is used by organizational members to transform inputs into various outputs. Researchers interested in the effects of technology on organizational structure have classified technology in various ways and, in each case, have found that the best structure depends on the dominant type of technology used.

Woodward's Typology. During the 1950s, Joan Woodward studied 100 manufacturing firms in a region of England to test the hypothesis that technology determines the optimal structure.[36] She classified production systems used in the firms studied into three broad groupings: unit/small batch, mass production, and continuous process (see Exhibit 17–7). *Unit/small batch* firms design made-to-order products in small lots, such as specialty glass products, custom-made clothing, and satellites. *Mass production* operations manufacture standardized products in large volumes, typically using an assembly line system. Examples of mass production goods include automobiles, baked goods, and television sets. Finally, *continuous process* firms use continuous flow systems to refine homogeneous products, such as petroleum, gases, and pharmaceuticals.

Woodward's analyses found that each technology group seemed to have its own organizational structure and that the most successful firms within each group tended to have a structure most closely resembling the typical one for that group. Effective unit/small batch firms had organic structures with a product- or client-based departmentation. They generally lacked formalization and coordinated work activities through mutual adjustment. Direct supervision was also used where necessary, so these firms had a narrow span of control at the first level. Firms with mass production technology adopted a mechanistic structure with a high degree of formalization, standardization of work processes to coordinate work activities, and a wide span of control. Most had adopted a functional departmentation. Firms in the continuous process group were characterized by a somewhat organic structure, narrow span of control, a tall hierarchical structure, and standardization through skills and the technology itself. They tended to have a product-based form of departmentation.

Thompson's Typology. Recall from Chapter 13 that there are three fundamental levels of task interdependence: pooled, sequential, and reciprocal.

EXHIBIT 17–7   Woodward's Research on Technology and Structure

Type of Technology	Most Effective Structure	Coordination Required	Organizational Example
Unit/small batch production	Organic Narrow span of control Product grouping	Mutual adjustment Some direct supervision	Specialty glass
Mass production	Mechanistic Wide span of control Functional grouping	Standardization of work processes	Automobile assembly
Continuous process production	Organic Narrow span of control Product grouping	Standardization of skills Technology as a coordination tool	Oil refinery

With pooled interdependence, work units operate independently except for reliance on a common resource or authority. Sequential interdependence occurs when the output of one person or unit becomes the direct input for another person or unit. The highest level of interdependence is reciprocal interdependence, in which work output is exchanged back and forth among individuals or work units.

James Thompson has identified three types of technology, described in Exhibit 17–8, that correspond to the three levels of interdependence.[37] Thompson's main argument is that the higher the level of interdependence required by the technology, the more expensive the coordinating mechanism necessary to integrate the organization. In turn, the type of coordinating mechanism required determines the best organizational structure.

A *mediating technology* exists where constituents interact indirectly through the organization. For instance, banks mediate between depositors and borrowers. This type of technology relies on pooled interdependence and can easily adopt standardization as the most efficient coordinating mechanism. Consequently, it can adopt a formalized structure with more centralized decision making.

A *long-linked technology* involves processing work through a rigid sequential order, as in most assembly-line operations. Coordination is some-

---

EXHIBIT 17–8   Thompson's Typologies of Technology and Organizational Structure

Type of Technology	Level of Interdependence	Coordination Required	Organizational Example
Mediating	Pooled 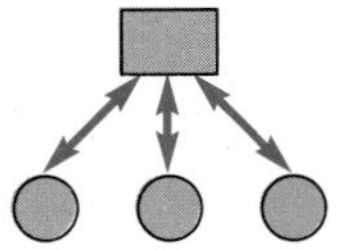	Standardization	Banks
Long-linked	Sequential 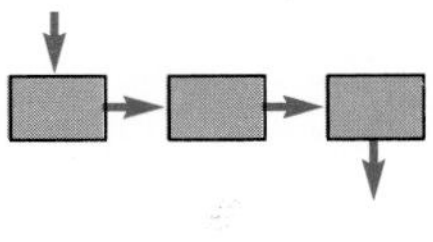	Planning, Meetings, Liaison Roles	Assembly Lines
Intensive	Reciprocal 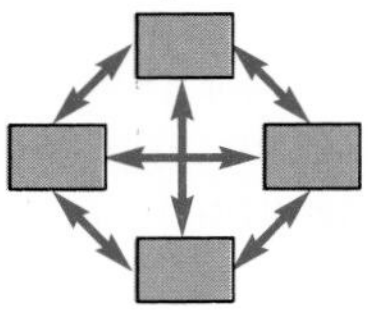	Mutual Adjustment	Customized Software Development

what more difficult with this type of technology because it requires careful planning and scheduling, some mutual adjustment, and liaison roles to oversee the operations (rather like direct supervision). Formalization is still possible with this type of technology, but the organizational structure must also consider some decentralization to accommodate short-term planning and mutual adjustment, where necessary.

Intensive technology involves pulling together people with special skills to solve unique problems or complete customized products and services. It creates reciprocal interdependence among the participants and requires mutual adjustment as the primary coordinating mechanism. The critical organizing principle here is that employees who need to interact with each other frequently (i.e., those involved in mutual adjustment) should be grouped into the same work unit. This calls for team-based designs, such as matrix and cluster structures. It also requires an organic structure (decentralization and low formalization).

External Environment

Throughout this book, we have emphasized the importance of the external environment as an influence on organizational behaviour. This influence extends to the best structure an organization should adopt. The external environment includes anything outside the organization, including its stakeholders (e.g., clients, suppliers, government), resources (e.g., raw materials, human resources, information, finances), and competitors. Mintzberg identifies four relatively distinct characteristics of external environments that influence the type of organizational structure best suited to a particular situation: dynamism, complexity, diversity, and hostility.[38]

Dynamic Environments. Dynamic environments have a high rate of change, leading to novel situations and a lack of identifiable patterns. In contrast, stable environments are characterized by regular cycles of activity and steady changes in supply and demand for inputs and outputs. For example, the women's fashion industry faces rapidly changing consumer tastes, whereas the market for drywall building materials is quite stable.

Research findings consistently support the conclusion that organic structures are better suited to dynamic environments.[39] Organic structures have low formalization, high decentralization, and a wide span of control, enabling employees to adjust their work activities and to coordinate new relationships through mutual adjustment. Network and cluster structures seem to be most effective in dynamic environments because they usually have these features. In stable environments, on the other hand, organizations introduce standardization as a more efficient approach to coordination. Events are more predictable, enabling the firm to apply rules and procedures.

Complex Environments.   Complex environments have more elements in the environment to consider than do simple environments. For instance, a multinational corporation has to take into account the interests of more stakeholders than does the corner grocery store. Decentralized structures seem to be better suited to complex environments because it is difficult for a central authority to comprehend all of the factors necessary to make effective decisions in all organizational contexts. By passing decision powers down the hierarchy, those closest to the environmental information are able to make more informed choices.

Diverse Environments.   Organizations located in diverse environments have a greater variety of products or services, clients, and/or jurisdictions. In contrast, an integrated environment is one in which the firm must understand only one client, product, and geographic area. The more diversified the organization's markets, the more it should adopt a divisionalized form aligned with that diversity. For example, if a company sells a single product around the world, it probably should organize around a geographic divisionalized form to reflect the diverse territories in which it operates. If it sells several different types of products or services in a single geographical area, then a product-based design may be preferred. As we explained earlier, multinational companies have difficult decisions to make because they are often diverse in terms of products, clients, and geographic markets. Typically, they create a hybrid structure around all three dimensions, giving priority to the divisional form that best fits its corporate strategy and culture.

Hostile Environments.   An organization's environment may range from munificent to hostile. Firms located in a hostile environment face greater scarcity of inputs and competition in the distribution of outputs. Hostile environments are typically dynamic ones because they reduce the predictability of access to resources and demand for outputs. As the availability of inputs decreases, the risk of shortages increases as suppliers gain power in the marketplace. Similarly, as competition for customers increases, the certainty that the organization's products or services will be purchased decreases.

To the extent that hostility is similar to dynamism, organic structures should be most appropriate for this environmental condition. However, Mintzberg suggests that extremely hostile environments drive organizations to temporarily centralize.[40] He explains that crises demand quick decisions, so organizations centralize because direct supervision is the tightest and fastest form of coordination. During organizational crises, such as the loss of a major client or supplier, the leader quickly steps in to make decisions. Ironically, as we mentioned in Chapter 9, centralization may result in lower-quality decisions during organizational crises because top management has less information, particularly where the environment is complex. If the hostile environment persists, the organization's survival may be at risk if centralized decision making continues.

Organizational Strategy

organizational strategy
The way the organization positions itself in its setting in relation to its stakeholders given the organization's resources, capabilities, and mission.

While size, technology, and environment influence the optimal organizational structure, these contingencies do not necessarily *determine* structure. Instead, there is increasing evidence that corporate leaders formulate and implement strategies that shape both the characteristics of these contingencies as well as the organization's resulting structure. **Organizational strategy** refers to the way the organization positions itself in its setting in relation to its stakeholders given the organization's resources, capabilities, and mission.[41] The idea that an organization interacts with its environment rather than being totally determined by it is known as **strategic choice**.[42] In other words, organizational leaders take steps to define and manipulate their environments, rather than let the organization's fate be entirely determined by external influences.

strategic choice
The idea that an organization interacts with its environment rather than being totally determined by it.

The notion of strategic choice can be traced back to the work of Alfred Chandler in the early 1960s.[43] Chandler's proposal was that structure follows strategy. He observed that organizational structures follow the growth strategy developed by the organization's decision makers. Moreover, he noted that organizational structures change only after decision makers decide to do so. This recognizes that the link between structure and the contingency factors described earlier is mediated by organizational strategy.

Chandler's thesis that structure follows strategy has become the dominant perspective of business policy and strategic management. An important aspect of this view is that organizations can choose the environments in which they want to operate. Some businesses adopt a **differentiation strategy** by bringing unique products to the market or attracting clients who want customized goods and services. They try to distinguish their outputs from those provided by other firms through marketing, providing special services, and innovation. Others adopt a **cost leadership strategy** in which they maximize productivity and are thereby able to offer popular products or services at a competitive price.[44]

differentiation strategy
The strategy of bringing unique products to the market or attracting clients who want customized goods and services.

cost leadership strategy
The strategy of maximizing productivity in order to offer popular products or services at a competitive price.

The type of organizational strategy selected leads to the best organizational structure to adopt.[45] Organizations with a cost leadership strategy should adopt a mechanistic, functional structure with high levels of job specialization and standardized work processes. This is similar to Woodward's category of mass production technology because assembly-line operations are typically the most efficient for single product/service outputs. A differentiation strategy, on the other hand, requires more of a batch technology and calls for greater use of mutual adjustment. MacDonald Dettwiler has adopted a differentiation strategy because it relies on unique contracts rather than mass market products. A matrix structure with less centralization and formalization is most appropriate here so that technical specialists are able to coordinate their work activities more closely with the client's needs. Overall, it is now apparent that organizational structure is influenced by size, technology, and environment, but the organization's strategy may reshape these elements and loosen their connection to organizational structure.

SUMMARY

- Organizational structure refers to the division of labour as well as the patterns of coordination, communication, work flow, and formal power that direct organizational activities. All organizational structures divide labour into distinct tasks and coordinate that labour to accomplish common goals. The primary means of coordination are mutual adjustment, direct supervision, and three forms of standardization (work processes, outputs, and skills).

- The four basic elements of organizational structure include span of control, centralization, formalization, and departmentation. Span of control—the number of people directly reporting to a supervisor—determines the number of hierarchical levels in the organization. The recent trend is toward flatter structures with a wide average span of control.

- Centralization refers to the extent that formal decision authority is held by a small group of people, typically those at the top of the organizational hierarchy. Organizational size and diversity push for decentralization, whereas centralization increases during crises and in response to management and staff needs for power. Formalization refers to the degree that organizations standardize behaviour through rules, procedures, formal training, and related mechanisms. Companies tend to become more formalized over time, but this can reduce organizational flexibility and employee satisfaction.

- Departmentation specifies how employees and their activities are grouped together. Organizations usually begin as simple structures, then develop into functional, divisionalized, matrix, or hybrid forms. A functional structure organizes employees around specific skills or other resources. A divisional structure groups employees around outputs, clients, or geographic areas. A matrix structure typically overlays a product-based divisional structure with a functional structure. Most larger organizations adopt a hybrid structure that includes some combination of functional, divisionalized, and/or matrix grouping.

- Two emerging organizational structures are networks and clusters (or circles). A network structure is an alliance of several organizations for the purpose of creating a product or serving a client. A cluster structure is a nonhierarchical design that consists of several circles, each focussed on a specific product, client, or activity.

• Four factors influence the best type of organizational structure to adopt. Larger organizations need greater job specialization and elaborate coordinating mechanisms than smaller firms. They also tend to be less centralized and more formalized. Several researchers have reported that the organization's dominant technology influences the best structure to adopt. For instance, small batch and continuous process operations are best suited with organic structures (low formalization and centralization), whereas those with mass production technology should adopt a mechanistic structure.

• Four environmental factors influence the optimal organizational structure. Organic structures are best suited to dynamic environments. Decentralized structures seem to be better suited to complex environments. Organizations in diversified environments should adopt a divisionalized form aligned with that diversity. Firms in moderately hostile environments should adopt organic structures to maintain flexibility. In extremely hostile conditions, firms tend to centralize, although this may be an ineffective strategy in the long term.

• While size, technology, and environment influence the optimal organizational structure, these contingencies do not necessarily determine structure; rather, organizational leaders formulate and implement strategies to define and manipulate their environments. These strategies, rather than the other contingencies, directly shape the organization's structure.

DISCUSSION QUESTIONS

1. How do mutual adjustment and direct supervision differ from the standardization of work processes, outputs, and skills?
2. Why are organizations moving toward flatter structures?
3. What are the advantages and disadvantages of formalization?
4. Why don't all organizations group people around product-based divisions?
5. What must top management, functional managers, and project managers do to make a matrix structure more effective?
6. What is a network structure? Why do some writers believe that a network structure is an effective design for global competition?
7. Explain how environmental dynamism, complexity, diversity, and hostility influence organizational structure.
8. What do we mean by "strategy follows structure?"

NOTES

1. Based on interviews with management at MacDonald Dettwiler & Associates, October 1991.
2. A. G. Bedeian and R. F. Zammuto, *Organizations: Theory and Design* (Hinsdale, Ill.: 1991), pp. 117–18. S. Ranson, R. Hinings, and R. Greenwood, "The Structuring of Organizational Structure," *Administrative Science Quarterly* 25 (1980), pp. 1–14.

3. H. Mintzberg, *The Structuring of Organizations* (Englewood Cliffs, N.J.: Prentice Hall 1979), pp. 2–3.

4. D. Katz and R. L. Kahn, *The Social Psychology of Organizations* (New York: John Wiley & Sons, 1966), Chapter 2.

5. H. Fayol, *General and Industrial Management,* translated by C. Storrs (London: Pitman, 1949); E. E. Lawler III, *Motivation in Work Organizations* (Monterey, Calif.: Brooks/Cole, 1973), Chapter 7; and M. A. Campion, "Ability Requirement Implications of Job Design: An Interdisciplinary Perspective," *Personnel Psychology* 42 (1989), pp. 1–24.

6. Material in this section is based on Mintzberg, *The Structuring of Organizations,* pp. 2–8.

7. D. D. Van Fleet and A. G. Bedeian, "A History of the Span of Management," *Academy of Management Review* 2 (1977), pp. 356–72; Mintzberg, *The Structuring of Organizations,* Chapter 8; and D. Robey, *Designing Organizations,* 3rd ed. (Homewood, Ill.: Irwin, 1991), pp. 255–59.

8. Mintzberg, *The Structuring of Organizations,* p. 136.

9. T. Peters, *Thriving on Chaos* (New York: Alfred A. Knopf, 1987), p. 359.

10. J. Lorinc, "Managing When There's No Middle," *Canadian Business,* June 1991, pp. 86–94.

11. L. Gutri, "Teamwork Puts Depth into Working," *Canadian HR Reporter,* April 18, 1988, p. 4.

12. J. Child, *Oganization: A Guide to Problems and Practice,* 2nd ed. (New York: Harper & Row, 1984); and Mintzberg, *The Structuring of Organizations,* Chapter 11.

13. A. Dastmalchian and M. Javidan, "Centralization and Organizational Context: An Analysis of Canadian Public Enterprises," *Canadian Journal of Administrative Sciences* 4 (1987), pp. 302–19.

14. Peters, *Thriving on Chaos,* p. 356–57.

15. Mintzberg, *The Structuring of Organizations,* Chapter 5.

16. T. Burns and G. Stalker, *The Management of Innovation* (London: Tavistock, 1961).

17. Mintzberg, *The Structuring of Organizations,* p. 106.

18. Ibid., Chapter 17.

19. Robey, *Designing Organizations,* pp. 186–89.

20. R. Collison, "How Bata Rules the World," *Canadian Business,* September 1990, pp. 28–34.

21. Robey, *Designing Organizations,* pp. 191–97; Bedeian and Zammuto, *Organizations: Theory and Design,* pp. 162–68.

22. S. M. Davis and P. R. Lawrence, *Matrix* (Reading, Mass.: Addison-Wesley, 1977); and H. F. Kolodny, "Managing in a Matrix," *Business Horizons,* March–April 1981, pp. 17–24.

23. K. Knight, "Matrix Organization: A Review," *Journal of Management Studies,* May 1976, pp. 111–30.

24. H. Denis, "Matrix Structures, Quality of Working Life, and Engineering Productivity," *IEEE Transactions on Engineering Management* EM-33 (August 1986), pp. 148–56; and J. L. Brown and N. McK. Agnew, "The Balance of Power in a Matrix Structure," *Business Horizons,* (November–December 1982), pp. 51–54.

25. A. M. Rugman, *Inside the Multinationals: The Economics of International Markets* (London: Croom Helm, 1981); and M. E. Porter, *Competitive Advantage* (New York: Free Press, 1985).

26. C. A. Bartlett and S. Ghoshal, "Managing across Borders: New Organizational Responses," *Sloan Management Review,* Fall 1987, pp. 43–53.

27. L. Surtees, "Power Shifts at Northern Telecom," *Globe and Mail,* February 14, 1991, pp. B1, B2.

28. T. Peters, "Prometheus Barely Unbound," *Academy of Management Executive* 4 (November 1990), pp. 70–84.

29. Ibid.; R. L. Daft, *Management,* 2nd ed. (Hinsdale, Ill.: Dryden, 1991), pp. 272–73; and R. Miles and C. Snow, "Organizations: New Concepts for New Forms," *California Management Review* 28, no. 3 (1986), pp. 62–73.

30. H. F. Kolodny, "Some Characteristics of Organizational Designs in New/High Technology Firms," in L. R. Gomez-Mejia and M. W. Lawless (eds.), *Organizational Issues in High Technology Management* (Greenwich, Conn.: JAI Press, 1990), pp. 165–76.

31. D. Quinn Mills (with G. Bruce Friesen), *Rebirth of the Corporation* (New York: John Wiley & Sons, 1991), pp. 29–30.

32. Mills, *Rebirth of the Corporation*, pp. 113–14, 195–96, and Chapter 16.

33. J. Arbose, "ABB: The New Energy Powerhouse," *International Management*, June 1988, pp. 24–30.

34. Mintzberg, *The Structuring of Organizations*, Chapter 13; and D. S. Pugh and C. R. Hinings (eds.), *Organizational Structure: Extensions and Replications* (Farnborough, U.K.: Lexington Books, 1976).

35. Robey, *Designing Organizations*, p. 102.

36. J. Woodward, *Industrial Organization: Theory and Practice* (London: Oxford University Press, 1965).

37. J. D. Thompson, *Organizations in Action* (New York: McGraw-Hill, 1967).

38. Mintzberg, *The Structuring of Organizations*, Chapter 15.

39. Burns and Stalker, *The Management of Innovation;* P. R. Lawrence and J. W. Lorsch, *Organization and Environment* (Homewood, Ill.: Irwin, 1967); and D. Miller and P. H. Friesen, *Organizations: A Quantum View* (Englewood Cliffs, N.J.: Prentice Hall, 1984), pp. 197–98.

40. Mintzberg, *The Structuring of Organizations*, p. 282.

41. R. H. Kilmann, *Beyond the Quick Fix* (San Francisco: Jossey-Bass, 1984), p. 38.

42. J. Child, "Organizational Structure, Environment, and Performance: The Role of Strategic Choice," *Sociology* 6 (1972), pp. 2–22.

43. A. D. Chandler, *Strategy and Structure* (Cambridge, Mass.: MIT Press, 1962).

44. M. E. Porter, *Competitive Strategy* (New York: Free Press, 1980).

45. D. Miller, "Configurations of Strategy and Structure," *Strategic Management Journal* 7 (1986), pp. 233–50.

CHAPTER CASE

STEER ELECTRONICS

Part One

Steer Electronics was founded in 1975 by Rudolph Steer, an electronics engineer with a Ph.D. Steel had worked for a larger firm for five years after receiving his doctorate, but decided to leave and start his own company with capital inherited from his grandfather's estate. Steer knew many top scientists and engineers at other companies, research labs, and universities. He was able to persuade four of them to join him in his new venture. With their help, Steer was able to hire a number of junior engineers and technicians to assist in the design, development, and production of the company's products.

Steer's first products were miniature servomechanisms designed for robotic assembly plants in the computer hardware industry. As computers became smaller and smaller, the tools used to assemble them had to become smaller as well. Steer's firm reached a modest breakthrough by adapting hydraulic machine principles to a small scale and integrating them with tiny electric motors controlled by microprocessors. The hydraulic features of Steer's servomechanisms enabled tiny robots to be powerful, while the electric motors improved accuracy. The company's customers were pleased with Steer's performance, as were Steer and his associates.

Steer Electronics was organized into four engineering areas: hydraulics, electronics, electrical, and electrochemical. The heads of these departments were, as Steer called them, "a first-class bunch of farmers—outstanding in their fields!" Their thinking and laboratory work continuously pressed forward to develop new technology to be applied to the company's products. Members in each department developed a close rapport with their head and enjoyed an excellent work climate.

Contact between departments was kept to a minimum by Steer's idea of how new concepts should be developed. Given a potential application, Steer would begin in hydraulics and then move sequentially through electrochemical, electrical, and electronics, in that order. Each project was handed off by one department to another as work progressed, and schedules were usually met with few problems. In fact, part of the genius of Rudolph Steer's design concept was the logical ease of developing new applications in stages.

Part Two

On January 3, 1985, Steer Electronics was awarded a contract to build a prototype for a high-speed robot being developed by a nearby firm. The robot manufacturer demanded greater speed in the robot's basic motions, because competition from Japanese companies threatened the loss of two computer manufacturers' business. The challenge was a novel one for Steer, who had always stressed accuracy above speed. To make matters worse, the contract called for working prototypes in four months, about half the time usually required for new projects.

Rudolph Steer decided that "Project Swifty," as it was dubbed, would be given to special project groups from each department. He instructed each department head to select the best engineer from his respective department. These project engineers, in turn, were directed to choose two engineers and two technicians to work exclusively on Swifty. Simultaneously, each team worked in its own department on aspects of the project that pertained to it. All groups became enthusiastic about the new challenge and worked vigorously for long hours trying to find ways to increase robotic speed.

Part Three

On February 13, 1985, the four project leaders met together for the first time since the project was started. The meeting was called to make sure that the future work of each team would be coordinated and that no group would be limited by progress made by another group. Very quickly, however, each project leader discovered that the work in the other groups already limited each's approach. Each project head then argued that his approach should be followed and that the other groups should change their designs accordingly. The meeting ended in discord as each leader refused to change his approach.

In the next two weeks, all four groups worked furiously to complete their designs before the other groups could finish theirs. Each thought that by being the first to finish, the others would have to conform to that department's approach.

The hydraulic and electronic groups finished first, with design concepts that appeared to be incompatible with one another. Then the head of the electrical project team, which was the slowest group, succeeded in proving that both of these designs were technologically impossible to build. Heated words were exchanged among the groups at this point, and frictions began to develop between other department members who were not assigned to Project Swifty. With six weeks of hard work down the drain, members of the project teams lost their former excitement about the project.

Part Four

On March 4, 1985, Rudolph Steer hired an experienced robotics engineer from a firm in Los Angeles. Her name was Kathy Harmon, a person with a master's degree who had worked with Rudolph Steer on a professor's research grant. Steer assigned Harmon as the leader for Project Swifty and directed the four project engineers to report to her. After examining the progress made so far, Harmon outlined a modified approach for the project and dismissed the previous technical arguments of the four groups. She gave each group a clear set of directions, set deadlines for completing the work on time, and required daily progress summaries on the work.

During the first week under her leadership, the project engineers tried desperately to find flaws in her modified design plan. They openly tried to discredit her and prove the value of their own approaches. However, her plan stood the test, and no one seemed able to prove her wrong. Given the tight schedules, the project engineers decided they'd better get on with the work. They met their deadlines and began to work more amicably with each other and with Harmon.

Kathy Harmon succeeded in getting the four project heads together several times to discuss their prior disagreements and to cooperate more with each other in solving current problems with Project Swifty. They quickly became impressed with her knowledge and skill in handling conflicts. Communication between the departments increased, and people throughout Steer Electronics renewed their enthusiasm for the project.

Discussion Questions

1. Why was the initial attempt to manage Project Swifty unsuccessful?
2. Was the design used in Part Two a team-based design? Why or why not?
3. What specific sources of conflict can be identified in Project Swifty? How was the appointment of Kathy Harmon as project leader instrumental in managing conflict?
4. After Project Swifty is completed, what role should Kathy Harmon be assigned at Steer Electronics?

Source: D. Robey, *Designing Organizations*, 3rd ed. (Homewood, Ill.: Irwin, 1991), pp. 237–39.

EXPERIENTIAL EXERCISE

DESCRIBING ORGANIZATIONAL STRUCTURES

Purpose.   This exercise is designed to help you to identify and describe the basic elements of organizational structure.

Instructions.   The instructor should form teams of four or five participants one week or more before this exercise is to be discussed. Each team will choose an organization and report its findings for discussion. Publicly traded companies should be selected because their annual reports are often the most informative sources about organizational structures. Team members should also search through *Canadian Business Index, Business Periodicals Index, Canadian Newspaper Index,* and other sources to find recent newspaper and magazine articles about the firm. Through these sources, team members should be able to answer many of the questions listed below.

Organizational Structure Questions

Departmentation

1.   Diagram the top levels of the organizational chart, based on the available information.
2.   Many large organizations are hybrids, but they still emphasize one pure type more than others. Does the organizational chart represent a predominantly functional, divisionalized, or matrix structure? If a divisionalized form is emphasized, does it focus on clients, products, or geography?
3.   If a matrix structure is used, which functional units are involved?
4.   Does the organization make much use of the network structure? If so, what aspects of the organization's activities are contracted out?

Span of Control

1.   Is this a tall or flat organization? How many hierarchical levels does it seem to have?
2.   Has the organization recently increased or decreased its span of control? If so, what reasons were given for this change?

Centralization

1.   In general, does this organization have centralized or decentralized decision making?
2.   To what extent do nonmanagement employees participate in organizational decisions?

Formalization

1. Does this organization make extensive use of rules and procedures to organize and coordinate work activities? If so, provide examples.
2. Do nonmanagement employees have much discretion over their work or do they act mainly on programmed decisions?

Glossary of Terms

Ability The learned capability and innate aptitude to engage in a task.

Action research A data-based, problem-oriented process that focusses on organizational diagnosis and action planning, implementation, and evaluation of an intervention on the system involved.

Actor–observer error A perceptual error whereby people tend to attribute their own actions more to external factors and the behaviour of others more to internal factors.

Aptitudes Natural talents that help people learn specific tasks more quickly and perform them better.

Artifacts The directly observable symbols and signs of an organization's culture, including its physical structures, ceremonies, language, and stories.

Assessment centres An employee selection procedure that uses group exercises, group discussions, and interviews with assessors to determine the best job candidate(s).

Attitudes An individual's feelings toward a person, group, event, idea, or any other attitude object.

Attribution process A perceptual process whereby we interpret the causes of behaviour in terms of the person (internal attributions) or the situation (external attributions).

Authoritarianism A personality trait referring to the belief that leaders have a right to expect blind acceptance and respect from subordinates by virtue of their position in the hierarchy.

Autonomy The degree to which a job gives employees the freedom, independence, and discretion to schedule their work and determine the procedures to be used to complete it.

Behavioural commitment A process of developing organizational commitment through cognitive dissonance.

Behavioural intentions An individual's intention (i.e., motivation) to perform a particular behaviour.

Behaviourally anchored rating scale A performance appraisal instrument, similar to graphic rating scales, with the performance levels anchored by job-related behaviours.

Behaviourism A perspective that focusses entirely on behaviour and observable events, in contrast to thoughts and other cognitions.

Beliefs An individual's perceptions of an attitude object's characteristics.

Bonus A reward system that provides lump-sum payments to reward employees for achieving specific objectives.

Bounded rationality decision model A model of decision making that assumes decision makers have limited information-processing capabilities and do not necessarily select the best possible alternative. It also recognizes that decisions will be based on incomplete knowledge and unclear problem definitions.

Brainstorming A freewheeling, face-to-face meeting in which team members generate as many alternative solutions to the problem as possible, and no one is allowed to evaluate any until all ideas have been presented.

Burnout The process of exhaustion, depersonalization, and reduced personal accomplishment resulting from prolonged exposure to stress.

Career A sequence of work-related experiences that people participate in over the span of their working lives.

Career anchor A person's self-image of his or her abilities, motivations, and attitudes relating to a particular career orientation.

Career path The sequence of job promotions and transfers that employees follow to achieve their career objectives.

Career plateau A point in a person's career beyond which the probability of further promotion through the hierarchy is very low.

Centrality The extent and nature of interdependence that the individual or subunit has with other parts of the organization.

Centralization The degree that formal decision authority is held by a small group of people, typically those at the top of the organizational hierarchy.

Ceremonies Deliberate and usually dramatic displays of organizational culture, such as celebrations and special social gatherings.

Change agent A person who possesses enough knowledge and power to guide and facilitate the change effort. This may be a member of the organization or an external consultant.

Charisma A form of interpersonal attraction whereby others develop a respect for and trust in the charismatic individual.

Cluster (or circle) structure A type of departmentation consisting of self-contained units of people from different disciplines who work together on a semipermanent basis.

Coalition A special interest group in which people form an alliance around a specific issue to influence people outside the team with respect to that issue.

Coercive power The capacity to influence others through the ability to apply punishment and remove rewards affecting these people.

Cognitive dissonance A state of anxiety that occurs when an individual's beliefs, attitudes, behavioural intentions, and behaviours are inconsistent with one another.

Cohesiveness The extent to which people are attracted to the team and are motivated to remain members.

Command unit A relatively permanent team consisting of a manager and his or her subordinates.

Commissions A reward system that ties earnings to the sales volume produced by the individual.

Communication The process by which information is transmitted and understood between two or more people.

Conflict Any situation where someone believes that others have deliberately blocked, or are about to block, his or her goals or activities.

Conflict management Any intervention that alters the level and form of conflict such that organizational effectiveness is optimized.

Consideration A cluster of leadership behaviours indicating mutual trust and respect for subordinates, a genuine concern for their needs, and a desire to look out for their welfare.

Constructive controversy Any situation where team members hold different opinions and assumptions and debate the issues through an open, healthy dialogue.

Content theories of motivation Theories that attempt to explain how people have different needs at different times.

Contingencies of reinforcement The four types of events following a behaviour that may increase (reinforce) or decrease the likelihood that the behaviour will be repeated.

Contingency (or situational) approach The idea that a solution may be effective in some situations but not others.

Continuance commitment An individual's willingness to remain with an organization for purely instrumental (e.g., financial) rather than emotional reasons.

Continuous reinforcement schedule A schedule that reinforces behaviour every time it occurs.

Corrective discipline The act of formally punishing employees who violate an organizational rule or procedure.

Cost leadership strategy The strategy of maximizing productivity in order to offer popular products or services at a competitive price.

Counterpower The capacity of a person, team, or organization to keep a more powerful person or unit in the exchange relationship.

Crisis Any unexpected situation that seriously threatens high-priority goals and requires a quick, nonprogrammed decision response.

Critical incidents Specific examples of effective or ineffective behaviour in a specific job, typically used to review employee performance or develop behaviourally anchored rating scales.

Decentralization The degree that decision authority is dispersed throughout the organization.

Decision making A conscious process of making choices among one or more alternatives with the intention of moving toward some desired state of affairs.

Decision risk The probability that a particular choice will lead to particular outcomes; sometimes also considers the potential cost of a bad decision.

Decision uncertainty The inability to predict future events with complete accuracy; specifically, the degree of inaccuracy of risk probabilities.

Delphi technique A structured team decision-making method that pools the collective knowledge of experts without face-to-face interaction, organizes and feeds the input back to the experts for further input, and repeats this cycle until a consensus or dissensus is reached.

Departmentation An element of organizational structure specifying how employees and their activities are grouped together, such as by function, product, geographic location, or some combination.

Devil's advocacy A form of structured debate to encourage constructive controversy, whereby one half of the team looks for faulty logic, questionable assumptions, and other problems with the team's preferred choice.

Differentiation strategy The strategy of bringing unique products to the market or attracting clients who want customized goods and services.

Diffusion of change The process of introducing and institutionalizing successful changes elsewhere in the organization.

Discipline without punishment A management practice that tries to avoid the use of punishment by counselling employees who have violated company rules and inviting them to participate in finding a solution to the problem.

Discrepancy theory A theory that partly explains job satisfaction and dissatisfaction in terms of the gap between what people expect to receive and what they actually receive.

Distributive justice Perceptions of fairness in the exchange and distribution of resources, such as employee effort for financial rewards.

Distributive orientation The view that the parties are drawing from a fixed pie and the amount received by one is therefore inversely proportional to the amount received by the other; also known as a win–lose orientation.

Division of labour The subdivision of work into separate jobs assigned to different people.

Divisional structure A type of departmentation that groups employees around outputs, clients, or geographic areas.

Dogmatism A personality trait referring to the extent that the person is open- or closed-minded about information contrary to his or her beliefs, and will tolerate others who deviate from organizational authority.

Downward communication The movement of information from upper to lower levels in the organizational hierarchy.

Effort The individual's actual exertion of energy.

Effort-to-performance expectancy An individual's perceived probability that a particular level of effort will result in a particular level of performance.

Employee assistance programs Special counselling services to help employees deal with stressful life experiences and overcome ineffective coping mechanisms such as alcoholism.

Employee involvement The active participation of employees in decision-making processes that were not previously within their mandate.

Employee loyalty A term commonly used to refer to organizational commitment.

Employee orientation The organization's systematic process of helping new employees make sense of and adapt to the work context.

Employee selection The process of deciding which applicants would best perform the job. This involves collecting information about the characteristics of job applicants and evaluating this information in light of the job duties and specifications identified through job analysis.

Employment discrimination A situation where people with equal qualifications have unequal employment opportunities due to their demographic characteristics.

Employment equity programs A set of comprehensive practices introduced to eliminate systemic discrimination.

Empowerment A feeling of control and self-confidence that emerges when people are given power in a previously powerless situation.

Equal pay for equal work Legislation prohibiting employers from paying women less than men performing the same job content.

Equity theory A process theory of motivation that explains how people develop perceptions of fairness in the distribution and exchange of resources.

ERG theory Alderfer's content theory of motivation, stating that there are three broad human needs: existence, relatedness, and growth.

Escalation of commitment The act of repeating an apparently bad decision or allocating more resources to a failing course of action.

Expectancy theory A process theory of motivation based on the idea that people will direct their effort toward those actions that are perceived to lead to desired outcomes.

Expert power The capacity to influence others by possessing knowledge or skills that they want.

Expert systems Computer programs that process complex decisions by adopting a series of decision rules used by human experts.

Extinction The removal or withholding of a desirable condition, the consequence of which is to decrease the frequency or probability of a behaviour in the future.

Feedback Information relating to the consequences of employee behaviour.

Fiedler's contingency theory A contingency leadership theory based on the idea that leader effectiveness depends on whether the person's natural leadership style is appropriately matched to the situation.

Figure/ground principle A principle of organizing information whereby our perceptions of objects (figures) depend on the contexts (ground) in which they are perceived.

Fixed interval schedule A schedule that reinforces behaviour after it has occurred for a fixed period of time.

Fixed ratio schedule A schedule that reinforces behaviour after it has occurred a fixed number of times.

Flexible benefits Employee benefits programs that allow employees to select benefits that match their particular needs.

Force-field analysis A method of identifying and diagnosing the forces that drive and restrain proposed organizational change.

Formalization The degree that organizations standardize behaviour through rules, procedures, formal training, and related mechanisms.

Friendship group An informal group bound together by common interests and the desire to affiliate with others having similar opinions.

Frustration–regression process A basic premise in ERG theory that people who are unable to satisfy a higher need become frustrated and regress back to the next lower need level.

Functional structure A type of departmentation that organizes employees around specific skills or other resources.

General adaptation syndrome A model of the stress process consisting of three stages: alarm reaction, resistance, and exhaustion.

Global job satisfaction A composition attitude representing a unique combination of a person's feelings toward the different job satisfaction facets.

Goal attainment approach Measuring effectiveness in terms of progress toward organizational goals.

Goals The immediate or ultimate objectives that employees are trying to accomplish from their work efforts.

Grapevine The organization's informal communication network that is formed and maintained by social relationships rather than the formal chain of command.

Graphic rating scale A type of performance appraisal instrument that presents raters with a list of subjective performance dimensions upon which employees are evaluated.

Group polarization The tendency for teams to make more extreme choices (either more risky or more risk averse) than the average team member would if making the decision alone.

Groupthink A situation in extremely cohesive teams where members are so motivated to maintain harmony and conform to majority opinion that they withhold their dissenting opinions.

Halo effect A perceptual error whereby our general impression of a person, usually based on one prominent characteristic, biases our perception of other characteristics of that person.

Heuristic A rule of thumb (decision rule) used repeatedly by people to help them evaluate alternatives under conditions of uncertainty.

Hi-hi leadership hypothesis A proposition stating that effective leaders exhibit high levels of both consideration and initiating structure.

Horizontal communication The exchange of information among people at the same level in the organizational hierarchy.

Immediacy A form of centrality referring to the extent that an individual's or subunit's actions quickly and substantially affect the work activities of others in the organization.

Impression management The process of attempting to manage the identities that others assign to us.

Incremental change An evolutionary approach to change in which existing organizational conditions are fine-tuned and small steps are taken toward the change effort's objectives.

Information overload A condition where messages are transmitted faster or in greater quantity than the employee can process effectively.

Ingratiation An impression management strategy whereby individuals deliberately try to create a more favourable impression of themselves to others.

Initiating structure A cluster of leadership behaviours that defines and structures work roles and relations among employees and with the leader.

Inoculation effect A persuasion strategy of warning listeners that others will try to influence them in the future and that they should be wary about the opponent's arguments.

Integrative orientation The view that the resources at stake are expandable rather than fixed if the parties work together to find a creative solution to their problem; also known as a win-win orientation.

Integrator   An employee who coordinates the activities of differentiated work units toward the completion of a common task.

Interest group   An informal group formed to accomplish an activity requiring some form of interaction.

Intergroup laboratory   A structured conflict management intervention in which the parties discuss their differences and decide ways to improve the relationship.

Intervention   Any set of planned activities intended to improve the effectiveness of the client or relations between the client and consultant.

Intuition   The phenomenon of knowing when a problem or opportunity exists and selecting the best course of action without the apparent use of reasoning or logic.

Jargon   Technical language understood by members of a particular occupational group, or recognized words with specialized meaning in specific organizations or social groups.

Job analysis   Systematic collection of information about jobs, including required tasks, equipment and other resources used, work context characteristics, and required employee attributes.

Job characteristics model   A job design model that relates five motivational properties of jobs to the individual's psychological states and several personal and organizational consequences.

Job design   The process of assigning tasks to a job and distributing work throughout the organization.

Job enlargement   A job design strategy to increase skill variety by broadening the range of tasks employees perform within their job.

Job enrichment   A job design strategy that assigns responsibility for scheduling, coordinating, and planning work to employees who actually make the product or provide the service.

Job evaluation   A procedure for systematically evaluating the worth of each job within the firm based on the duties performed and required employee characteristics.

Job feedback   The degree to which carrying out the required work activities provides employees with direct and clear information about their job performance.

Job rotation   The practice of moving employees from one job to another for the purposes of reducing monotony and increasing skill variety.

Job satisfaction   An individual's attitude toward the job and work context.

Job satisfaction facets   Attitudes regarding specific aspects (i.e., facets) of the job and work context.

Job specialization   The result of division of labour where each job now includes a narrow subset of the tasks required to complete the product or service.

Job specification   A description of the aptitudes, skills, and knowledge required to perform the job as well as preferred work-related interests.

Johari Window   A model of personal and interpersonal understanding that encourages disclosure and feedback to increase the open area and reduce the blind, hidden, and unknown areas of oneself.

Leadership   The process of influencing other team members beyond routine compliance toward defined team or organizational objectives more than the team members influence the leader.

Leadership substitutes   Characteristics of the employee, task, or organization that either limit the leader's influence or make it unnecessary.

Legitimate power   The capacity to influence others through formal authority, that is, the perceived right to direct certain behaviours of people in other positions.

Locus of control   A personality trait referring to the extent that people believe what happens to them is within their control; those who feel in control of their destiny have an internal locus, whereas those who believe that life events are due mainly to fate or luck have an external locus of control.

Machiavellianism   A personality trait by which people believe that deceit is a natural and acceptable way to influence others.

Management by objectives   A performance appraisal method whereby employee performance is evaluated against preestablished goals.

Management by wandering around   A management practice of having frequent face-to-face communication with employees so that managers are better informed about employee concerns and organizational activities.

Managerial Grid®   A behavioural model of leadership developed by Blake and Mouton that assesses an individual's leadership effectiveness in terms of his or her concern for people and for production.

Matrix structure   A type of departmentation that overlays a product-based structure (typically a project team) with a functional structure in an attempt to receive the benefits of both designs.

Mechanistic structure   A norganizational structure with a narrow span of control and high degrees of formalization and centralization.

Media richness   The capacity of a communication medium to transmit information.

Mentor   A more senior person in the organizational hierarchy who counsels and helps a junior employee (called a *protégé*).

Middle-range theories   Theories that attempt to explain specific aspects of organizational behaviour, rather than everything in the field.

Mixed consequence approach   A management practice that applies each of the four contingencies of reinforcement following various changes in employee performance.

Morale   The collective attitude of members of a work team toward the job, team, and organization.

Motivation   The internal forces that arouse, direct, and maintain a person's voluntary choice of behaviour.

Motivator–hygiene theory   A theory developed by Herzberg based on the idea that employees are motivated by characteristics of the work itself (called *motivators*) rather than the work context (called *hygienes*).

Mutual adjustment   The coordination of work activities among employees through informal communication.

Need hierarchy theory   Maslow's content theory of motivation, stating that people have a hierarchy of five basic needs—physiological, safety, belongingness, esteem, and self-actualization—and that as a lower need becomes gratified, individuals become motivated to fulfill the next higher need.

Needs   Deficiencies that energize or trigger behaviours to satisfy those needs.

Negative reinforcement   The removal or withholding of an undesirable condition, the consequence of which is to increase or maintain the frequency or probability of a particular behaviour in the future.

Negotiations   Deliberate attempts by conflicting parties to directly resolve their differences by defining or redefining the terms of their interdependence.

Networking   The act of cultivating social relationships with others for the purpose of accomplishing one's goals.

Network structure   An alliance of several organizations for the purpose of creating a product or serving a client.

Nominal group technique   A structured team decision-making technique whereby members independently write down ideas, present them in turn, clarify them, and then independently rank or vote on them.

Nonprogrammed decision   The decision process applied to unique, complex, or ill-defined situations whereby the full decision-making process is followed and judgment, intuition, and creativity are used.

Nonverbal communication   The transmission of meaning through any means other than words, such as actions, gestures, facial expressions, the sender's appearance, the timing of the message, and the context of the message.

Norms   The informal rules and standards that a team establishes to regulate and guide the behaviours of its members.

Occupational segregation   Barriers that prevent or inhibit women and other identifiable groups from entering higher-paying jobs in our society.

Open systems   Systems that interact and are interdependent with their external environment.

Organic structure   An organizational structure with a wide span of control, very little formalization, and highly decentralized decision making.

Organizational behaviour   The study of what people think, feel, and do in and around organizations.

Organizational citizenship behaviours   Employee behaviours that extend beyond the required job duties, such as helping others and facilitating a positive work environment.

Organizational commitment   A complex attitude pertaining to the strength of an individual's identification with and involvement in a particular organization; includes a strong acceptance of organizational goals, as well as a motivation to work for and remain with the organization.

Organizational comprehension   The extent to which employees understand the organization's physical, social, and cultural dimensions.

Organizational culture   The basic pattern of shared assumptions, values, and beliefs governing the way employees within an organization think about and act on problems and opportunities.

Organizational diagnosis   The systematic process of collecting data about an ongoing system, organizing and interpreting these data by the consultant, and feeding these data back to the client.

Organizational effectiveness   A multifaceted concept in which the organization "does the right things." This includes achieving organizational goals, adapting to the external environment as an open system, and addressing stakeholder needs.

Organizational goals   A desired state of affairs that organizations try to achieve.

Organizational politics   Attempts to influence others using discretionary behaviours for the purpose of promoting personal objectives; discretionary behaviours are neither explicitly prescribed nor prohibited by the organization and are linked to one or more power bases.

Organizational socialization   The continuous process by which individuals learn the values, expected behaviours, and social knowledge necessary to assume their organizational roles.

Organizational strategy   The way the organization positions itself in its setting in relation to its stakeholders given the organization's resources, capabilities, and mission.

Organizational structure   The division of labour as well as the patterns of coordination, communication, workflow, and formal power that direct organizational activities.

Organization design   The creation and modification of organizational structures.

Organization development (OD)   A planned systemwide effort, managed from the top with the assistance of a change agent, that uses behavioural science knowledge to improve organizational effectiveness.

Organizations   Social entities in which two or more people work interdependently through patterned behaviours to accomplish a set of goals.

Parallel career ladder   A career path within a technical or professional speciality, such as a series of engineering jobs through which people are promoted.

Parallel learning structure   A social structure constructed alongside (i.e., parallel to) the formal organization with the purpose of increasing the organization's learning.

Path-goal leadership theory   A contingency theory of leadership based on expectancy theory of motivation. Path-goal suggests that effective leaders strengthen the employee's connection between their performance and need satisfaction.

Pay equity   Legislation that requires pay levels assigned to female-dominated jobs to be comparable to those assigned to male-dominated jobs of similar value within the same establishment.

Pay-for-knowledge   A reward system in which employees within a job classification receive higher pay rates with the number of skill modules they have mastered.

Perception   The process of selecting, organizing, and interpreting information in order to make sense of the world around us.

Perceptual defense   A phenomenon whereby individuals perceptually ignore or misinterpret information so that it is less threatening and more acceptable to them.

Perceptual selection   The process of filtering (selecting and screening out) information received by our senses.

Performance appraisal   The systematic process of measuring and communicating how well employees are performing their jobs, as well as developing strategies to improve areas of poor performance.

Performance appraisal review   The process of communicating performance appraisal results to employees and discussing strategies for improving performance in the future.

Performance-related behaviours   Behaviours that directly or indirectly influence the achievement of organizational objectives.

Performance standard   A minimum acceptable level of job performance.

Performance-to-outcome expectancy   An individual's perceived probability that a specific behaviour or performance level will lead to various outcomes.

Personality   A set of relatively stable and consistent characteristics that help to explain a person's behaviour and distinguish him or her from other people.

Persuasion   A method of changing attitudes by directly communicating new information in a way that will increase the listener's probability of accepting what you are saying.

Pervasiveness   A form of centrality referring to the number of other people or units affected by the powerholder.

Piecework   A reward system that ties earnings to the number of units produced by the individual.

Political arena   A setting in which organizational politics is endemic and virtually out of control.

Pooled interdependence   The lowest level of interdependence, whereby individuals or work units operate independently except for reliance on a common resource or authority.

Positive reinforcement   The introduction of a desirable consequence that increases or maintains the frequency or probability of a particular behaviour in the future.

Postdecisional justification   A perceptual phenomenon whereby the preferred or selected option is made to appear more attractive and the discarded options less attractive.

Power   The capacity of a person, team, or organization to influence others who are in a state of dependence.

Predecision   Selecting a particular decision process, such as whether to involve others and how to collect information, after a problem or opportunity has been identified.

Prejudice   Negative attitudes, based on unfounded or blatantly incorrect beliefs, that are directed toward people belonging to an identifiable group.

Primacy effect   The tendency to quickly form an opinion of people or evaluate them based on the first information we receive about them.

Procedural justice   Perceptions of fairness regarding the process used to decide the exchange and distribution of resources.

Process consultation   A method of helping the organization solve its own problems by making it aware of organizational processes, the consequences of those processes, and the means by which they can be changed.

Process theories of motivation   Theories that describe the processes through which needs are translated into behaviour.

Productivity   The organization's efficiency in transforming inputs to outputs.

Productivity improvement (or gain-sharing) plan   A reward system usually applied to work teams that pays bonuses to employees based on cost reductions and increased labour efficiency.

Profit sharing   A reward system where the employer shares a portion of corporate profits with a designated group of employees.

Programmed decision   The decision process of relying on specific procedures to select the preferred solution without the need to identify or evaluate alternative choices.

Progressive discipline   An organizational discipline procedure where the severity of punishment increases with the frequency and severity of the infraction.

Projection   A perceptual error whereby people tend to ascribe their own characteristics to other people.

Psychological contract   The employer's and applicant's expectations about what each will contribute to and receive from each other in the employment relationship.

Psychological reactance   An emotional condition that forms when people feel pressured into accepting a particular point of view because they are not given the opportunity to consider other perspectives.

Punishment   The introduction of an undesirable consequence that decreases the frequency or probability of a behaviour in the future.

Quality circle   A small team of employees who meet on a regular basis to identify quality-control and productivity problems, propose solutions to management, and monitor the implementation and consequences of these solutions in their work area.

Quantum change   A revolutionary approach to change in which the organization breaks out of its existing strategies, structures, and behaviour patterns and moves toward a totally different configuration.

Rational economic decision model   A model of decision making that assumes managers consider all possible alternatives as well as all consequences to these alternatives and that the decision choice represents the highest possible payoff among the many options.

Realistic job preview   A realistic balance of positive and negative information from the employer about the nature of the job and work context.

Reality shock   The gap between preemployment expectations and the organizational reality employees experience as they begin work.

Recency effect   The tendency to give more weight to recent information when evaluating someone.

Reciprocal interdependence   The highest level of interdependence, whereby work output is exchanged back and forth among individuals or work units.

Re-earnable bonus   A reward system that typically includes a combination of salary increase and cash award for those who perform their jobs well.

Referent power   The capacity to influence others by virtue of the admiration for and identification with the powerholder.

Refreezing   Part of the change process in which the desired behaviour patterns are restabilized and institutionalized so that previous patterns do not reemerge.

Reinforcement   Anything following a behaviour that increases the likelihood of the behaviour being repeated.

Relations by objectives   A form of intergroup laboratory designed to improve labour–management relations.

Reward power The capacity to influence others by controlling the allocation of rewards valued by them and the removal of negative sanctions.

Reward system The activity of distributing money and other extrinsic benefits to motivate employees toward fulfilling organizational objectives.

Rituals The programmed routines of daily organizational life that dramatize the organization's culture.

Role ambiguity Any situation where employees are uncertain about their job duties, performance expectations, level of authority, and other job conditions.

Role conflict Any situation where individuals face competing demands, such as where obligations of the job are incompatible with the individual's personal values (person–role conflict) or where the individual receives contradictory messages from different people (intrarole conflict).

Role perception A person's beliefs about what is required to achieve the desired results, including the specific tasks that make up the job, their relative importance, and the preferred behaviours to accomplish those tasks.

Satisfaction-progression process A basic premise in need hierarchy theory that people become increasingly motivated to fulfill a higher need as a lower need is gratified.

Satisficing The process of looking for and selecting the course of action that is satisfactory or good enough rather than optimal or the best.

Scientific management The process of systematically determining how work should be partitioned into its smallest possible elements and how the process of completing each task should be standardized to achieve maximum efficiency.

Scientific method A set of principles and procedures to systematically understand previously unexplained phenomena.

Self-fulfilling prophecy A phenomenon whereby an observer's perception of someone causes the other person to actually behave in a manner consistent with the observer's expectation.

Self-managing work team A team of employees that completes a whole piece of work requiring several interdependent tasks and has substantial autonomy over the execution of these tasks.

Self-monitoring A personality trait referring to the extent that people are sensitive to situational cues and can readily adapt their own behaviour appropriately.

Self-serving bias A perceptual error whereby people tend to attribute their own success to internal factors and their own failures to external factors.

Sensitivity training An unstructured, face-to-face, and agendaless session in which a small group of people learn through their interactions to become more sensitive to the effects of their own behaviour on others and the actions of others on them.

Sequential interdependence A moderate level of interdependence whereby the output of one person or unit becomes the direct input for another person or unit.

Shaping The strategy of initially reinforcing crude approximations of the ideal behaviour, then increasing reinforcement standards until only the ideal behaviour is rewarded.

Situational contingencies Environmental conditions surrounding the job and beyond the employee's immediate control that constrain or facilitate employee behaviour and performance.

Situational leadership model A contingency leadership theory, developed by Hersey and Blanchard, stating that the best leadership style—telling, selling, participating, or delegating—depends on the individual's or team's readiness to accomplish a specific task.

Skill variety The extent that a job requires employees to use different skills and talents to complete a variety of work activities.

Skunkwork A team of employees "borrowed" from several functional areas of the organization that develops new products, services, or procedures, usually in isolation from the organization and without the normal restrictions.

Social facilitation A social phenomenon whereby people develop a heightened awareness or arousal in the presence of others that causes them to perform previously learned behaviours faster than when working in isolation.

Social loafing A social phenomenon whereby team members have lower work effort when their individual contribution to the team's performance is not easily distinguished.

Sociotechnical design A perspective stating that a work site's technological and social systems should become more compatible in order to increase organizational effectiveness and employee well-being.

Span of control The number of people directly reporting to a supervisor. This element of organizational structure determines the number of hierarchical levels required in the organization.

Stakeholder or multiple constituency model Measuring effectiveness in terms of addressing the preferences of the stakeholders—groups with a vested interest in the organization.

Standard hour plan A reward system that assigns a unit of time to each task and pays the employee for that time whether the job actually required more or less time to complete.

Stereotyping The process of using a few observable characteristics to assign someone to a preconceived social category and then assuming that the person also possesses other (usually less observable) characteristics of the group.

Strategic choice The idea that an organization interacts with its environment rather than being totally determined by it.

Strategic contingencies model A model stating that a person's or subunit's power is a function of the ability to cope with critical organizational uncertainties, as well as the nonsubstitutability and centrality of the person or subunit.

Stress An individual's adaptive response to a situation that is perceived as challenging or threatening to the person's well-being.

Stressor Any environmental condition that places a physical or emotional demand on the person.

Structural inertia Organizational control systems that institutionalize and maintain the status quo.

Substitutability The extent to which those dependent on a resource have alternative sources of supply of the resource or can use other resources that would provide a reasonable substitute.

Suggestion plan A reward system that encourages employees to submit ideas for improving product quality and work efficiency.

Superordinate goals Common goals—such as organizational objectives—held by conflicting parties that are more important than the subordinate goals over which the groups differ.

Symptom A deviation between what is and what ought to be, typically signalling the existence of an underlying problem or opportunity that should be dealt with to correct the symptom.

System An interdependent set of parts that functions as a whole to achieve a set of goals.

Systemic discrimination A type of employment discrimination whereby seemingly neutral corporate practices have a negative effect on the employment opportunities of qualified people belonging to certain demographic groups.

Task force (or project team) A team of people assigned to a short-term task or project.

Task identity The degree to which a job requires completion of a whole or identifiable piece of work.

Task significance The degree to which the job has a substantial impact on the organization and/or larger society.

Team building Any formal intervention directed toward improving the development and functioning of a work team.

Team effectiveness A multifaceted concept in which the team survives, successfully completes its objectives, and provides its members with satisfaction, well-being, and commitment.

Team inertia Team structures and processes that routinize behaviours, thereby maintaining the status quo.

Teams Two or more people who interact and mutually influence each other for the purpose of achieving common goals.

3-dimensional managerial model (3-D) A contingency leadership model developed by Reddin that expands Blake and Mouton's Managerial Grid to three dimensions.

Time and motion study The process of systematically observing, measuring, and timing the smallest physical movements to identify more efficient work behaviours.

Traits Personal characteristics, such as appearance, personality, intelligence, and skills, that differentiate one person from the next.

Transactional leadership Using legitimate, reward, and coercive power bases to help employees accomplish existing tasks and organizational objectives more effectively.

Transformational leadership Transforming organizations by creating, communicating, and modelling a vision of a desired state of affairs, and inspiring employees to strive for that vision.

Type A behaviour pattern A behaviour pattern associated with people having premature coronary heart disease; Type A's tend to be impatient, lose their temper, talk rapidly, and interrupt others.

Type B behaviour pattern   A behaviour pattern of people with low risk of coronary heart disease; Type B's tend to work steadily, take a relaxed approach to life, and are even-tempered.

Uncertainty absorption   A perceptual phenomenon whereby information loses some of the uncertainty on which it is based and develops an aura of precision as it moves away from its source.

Unfreezing   Part of the change process in which people are made aware of the need for change and are provided with the skills, knowledge, and resources necessary to execute the new behaviour patterns.

Upward communication   The movement of information from lower to upper levels in the organizational hierarchy.

Valence   The anticipated satisfaction or dissatisfaction that an individual places on an outcome.

Variable interval schedule   A schedule that reinforces behaviour after it has occurred for a variable period of time around some average.

Variable ratio schedule   A schedule that reinforces behaviour after it has occurred a varying number of times around some average.

Vroom–Yetton–Jago model   A model designed to help managers choose the optimal level of employee involvement in a particular situation.

Worker alienation   A psychological state whereby employees feel powerlessness and meaninglessness in their work lives, increasing removal from social norms, and a psychological separation of oneself from the activities being performed.

Work overload   Any situation where employees cannot keep up with deadlines or are given work that is beyond their skills or abilities.

Work underload   Any situation where employees receive too little work or are given tasks that do not make sufficient use of their skills or abilities.

Corporate Index

Name Index

Subject Index